Chris E. Fonvielle, Jr.

The

Wilmington Campaign

Last Rays of Departing Hope

The Wilmington Campaign: Last Rays of Departing Hope
by Chris E. Fonvielle, Jr.

Series: Battles & Campaigns of the Carolinas

10 9 8 7 6 5 4 3 2 1
First Hardcover Edition

ISBN 1-882810-09-0

Copyright © 1997 Chris E. Fonvielle, Jr.
Copyright © 1997 of maps Mark A. Moore

Includes bibliographic references and index

Savas Publishing Company
1475 S. Bascom Avenue, Suite 204,
Campbell, California 95008
(800) 848-6585

This book is printed on 50-lb. Glatfelter acid-free paper

The paper in this book meets or exceeds the guidelines for permanence and durability of the Committee on Production Guidelines for Book Longevity of the Council on Library Resources

To Nancy,
Mary Katherine and Anne Fletcher

A fanciful birdseye view of Fort Fisher, looking northward from the Mound Battery. On the Cape Fear River (left) are blockade runners and a Confederate ironclad. Wilmington is twenty miles upstream on the horizon. *Frank Leslie's Illustrated Newspaper*

Table of Contents

continued...

Table of Contents, continued...

Photos & Illustrations

(continued)

(continued from previous page)

Cartography

FOREWORD

I first met Chris Fonvielle in October 1993, at Jerry Russell's Civil War Round Table Congress in Wilmington, North Carolina. My initial impression was that he was an affable fellow, for within just a few minutes of introducing himself, he made my wife Nancy and I feel that he had been our friend for years.

The second thing that impressed me about Chris was his scholarly passion for Civil War history—particularly that of Wilmington and the Lower Cape Fear region. There was no overlooking his missionary zeal when the conversation turned to his doctoral dissertation, which at that time he was frantically trying to complete. The subject of his study was the Fort Fisher-Wilmington Campaign of 1864-1865, and he planned to write a book about it. Thus we found we had much in common for I, too, was writing a battle history on the three-day struggle at Bentonville. Chris, I also discovered, was born and raised in Wilmington, and his projected work would be the realization of a life's ambition. I remember thinking at the time that there was something fitting and right about his desire to tell the fascinating story of the campaign—an epic which had occurred so near his birthplace.

I also recall thinking that Chris had set himself a daunting task in attempting to tell a tale so ably told only a few years before by Rod Gragg. But as Rod would be the first to acknowledge—and as I would later discover—Chris' canvas proved to be far broader than Gragg's *Confederate Goliath*, encompassing not only the struggle for Fort Fisher but the entire campaign for Wilmington from its inception to conclusion, a detailed treatment from the high command down to the perspective of the enlisted man.

Chris and I parted as new friends and met again a few months later in February 1994, during the Civil War Fortification Study Group's traversal of eastern North Carolina's fort and battlefield sites. I regard that February weekend as pivotal for both of us. He had just finished his dissertation and was relieved that the writing was finally at an end. (Although the defense of his dissertation still loomed on the horizon, it was distant enough for Chris to ignore it for the moment and enjoy the weekend). He also said that he had been speaking with Theodore P. Savas of Savas Publishing Company, whom I knew as the publisher of the quarterly periodical *Civil War Regiments: A Journal of the American Civil War*. Chris had met Ted in Wilmington at the same October 1993 Round Table Congress. "Ted wants to publish groundbreaking studies on lesser-known campaigns," Chris excitedly related in his by-now-familiar earnest manner. For two unknown authors who feared the arbitrarily-imposed editorial and design restrictions of most publishing houses, Ted's *laissez faire* approach was an answer to our prayers. Chris suggested that since Ted was interested in his Wilmington study, he might also be interested in my own Bentonville manuscript. I acted on Chris' suggestion and my first book, *Last Stand in the Carolinas: The Battle of Bentonville*, appeared in January 1996. I owe Chris Fonvielle a debt of gratitude for putting me in touch with Savas Publishing Company. Moreover, Ted proved to be as good as his word in regard to the liberal use of excellent maps and explanatory notes.

By the time Chris and I met again in May 1994, he was *Dr.* Chris E. Fonvielle, Jr., and the occasion was a reception honoring the newly-christened academician. It was there I met the entire Fonvielle clan, including his mother, wife Nancy and two lovely daughters, discovering in the process just how fortunate a man Chris is. This marked an important occasion for me as well, because Chris advised me to contact David Roth of *Blue & Gray Magazine* about providing an article on the Battle of Bentonville. Chris had just completed his own monograph for the magazine on the Wilmington Campaign. Once again, thanks to Chris' recommendation, my own article appeared in the holiday 1995 issue—exactly one year after his.

It is no accident that Chris and I have followed the same path for the past several years. Both of us have been fortunate in finding publishers such as Ted Savas and Dave Roth, who were willing to take a chance on two previously unpublished authors. But it is more than that: Chris and I have undertaken to shed new light on the Civil War in North Carolina, a piece of the war that has been neglected for too long.

With the publication of *The Wilmington Campaign: "Last Rays of Departing Hope,"* the third book in the series "Battles & Campaigns of the Carolinas," this can no longer be said of the Fort Fisher-Wilmington battles. Chris has written the definitive study of this fascinating and complex campaign. He has also placed it within its proper strategic context with a blending of scholarly exactitude and enthusiasm for his subject that makes *Last Rays* such an informative and entertaining read. He demonstrates how the loss of Wilmington as a blockade running port hastened the downfall of the Confederacy by depriving it of its last supply link with the outside world. After imparting the importance of the city to the Southern war effort, Chris carries the reader into conferences of the Federal and Confederate high command, where he shows us how the campaign unfolded at the strategic, or operational, level. *Last Rays* offers compelling pen portraits of the campaign's major players, including the Confederacy's brilliant but erratic William Henry Chase Whiting; William Lamb, the gifted amateur engineer and defender of Fort Fisher; and the universally despised Braxton Bragg. Among the Federals we meet the mercurial, repugnant Ben Butler; the quietly competent Alfred Terry; and the arrogant old salt, David Dixon Porter.

Yet, much more than simply an operational study of an overlooked campaign, *Last Rays* also offers a briskly-paced, blow-by-blow account at the tactical level. Chris' narrative pulls readers into his drama and transports them from the smoking deck of a Union warship at the height of the naval bombardment of Fort Fisher, to the parapet along the fort's land face during the brutal hand-to-hand fighting for those vital square yards of sandy turf; from the open flatboat jammed with Federals in their attempt to cross Town Creek and surprise Johnson Hagood's outnumbered Southern defenders, to the side of a Confederate artilleryman pulling the lanyard on his piece one more time as his gun is overrun with bayonet-wielding Federal infantry.

A superb postscript weaves the final threads of Wilmington's Civil War history into place by detailing the fate of the fallen city from the perspective of soldier and civilian alike. Such a finale—a thorough understanding and appreciation of his hometown's history—could only have been written by Chris Fonvielle.

The deeply-researched narrative—complemented by previously unpublished photographs and helpful endnotes—is supported by almost three dozen excellent maps by the incomparable cartographer Mark A. Moore, whose maps also grace my study of Bentonville. I am confident Chris' important new book will take its rightful place as one of the classic campaign studies of the Civil War.

One last anecdote comes to mind. During Chris' tour of Wilmington during the Civil War Fortification Study Group's conference in February 1994, our intrepid guide led us into a particularly nasty thicket while uttering the battle cry, "follow a homeboy!" Everyone present found his enthusiasm irresistibly contagious—and plunged in right behind him. I heartily recommend every reader to do likewise with *The Wilmington Campaign: "Last Rays of Departing Hope."*

Mark L. Bradley
Raleigh, North Carolina
December 29, 1996

RECONCILIATION—AND APPRECIATION

The steamer *Wilmington* reached the landing at the Rocks about noon and disembarked the old veterans. It had been thirty-eight years since many of the former Confederate and Union soldiers and sailors had visited Fort Fisher. They walked through the deep sands of Federal Point to reach the fort a mile-and-a-half up the peninsula. For some time they wandered about its ruins, pointing to landmarks and recalling incidents of the battles fought there in 1864 and 1865. Most would never be back.

The reunion party was joined by several late-arriving and distinguished guests. Foremost among these were Col. William Lamb, Fort Fisher's Confederate commander, and Lt. Cmdr. James Parker, who led a division of U.S. sailors in the attack on the fort on January 15, 1865. Confederate veterans walking the sandy dunes recognized Lamb's thin, ramrod-straight carriage and rushed to touch, embrace and cheer their former commander. The Rebel yell of the aging warriors was not what it once was, but its meaning was as strong as ever.

The 67-year-old William Lamb, his head now covered in thick hair whitened by the passage of decades, slowly made his way down the fort's land face parapet. A throng of former warriors followed fitfully in his wake, listening to his words, reliving an earlier chapter of their lives. Eventually Lamb stopped and focused the attention of his curious entourage on the spot where his mentor and friend, Maj. Gen. William Henry Chase Whiting, had been severely wounded. The colonel also pointed to the area inside the fort where he himself had fallen with a broken hip after being shot during the 1865 battle.

While Lamb reminisced with his followers, James Parker descended the fort's immense sand walls to tour the now-silent parade ground, which had once held hundreds of fighting, wounded and dead soldiers. When he spotted Lamb on the fort's northeast salient near the ocean front, however, Parker walked over and rejoined his old foe. Side by side they stood silently on the imposing bastion, where Parker and his navy comrades had tried to breach the fort, only to be repulsed by Lamb and his equally determined riflemen. It had been a desperate and bloody fight. As the images and sounds of the great battle fought all those years ago came flooding back to these former enemies, Parker put his arms around William Lamb and exclaimed: "Thank God we stand here today as friends."

*   *   *

I do not remember a time when I was not interested in Cape Fear Civil War history. Having been born and raised in Wilmington, the war was a regular topic of conversation, as if it had only recently ended. Confederate leaders, including W. H. C. Whiting and William Lamb—were spoken of with great reverence. As a young child I recall being both fascinated and intrigued by such stories as the Lamb and Parker meeting on Fort Fisher's eroding northeast bastion.

My parents often took me and my siblings to the forts and battlefields around Wilmington, where these men, their comrades and their enemies had fought and died. My brother John and I would scramble over the huge Confederate sand forts playing war and searching for relics from the great battles. I still remember the time John, then about six years old, found an iron grapeshot along the muddy western shoreline of the Cape Fear River at Fort Anderson. To us the discovery was a treasure, and we could not have been more excited had we uncovered a cache of pirate gold.

With my curiosity piqued and my growing interest nurtured at every turn, I determined to learn as much as I could about Wilmington's role during the Civil War. What I discovered as I grew older was that very little had been written about the Confederacy's premier blockade running seaport. Local historians had documented only small portions of the story. Even

Civil War historians had neglected the subject until 1991, when Rod Gragg published *Confederate Goliath: The Battles for Fort Fisher.* Gragg's award-winning book gave Fort Fisher, the key to Wilmington's defensive system, the credibility it had so long deserved. But Fort Fisher—where the largest combined operations of the war were fought—was only part of the story of the Union effort to capture Wilmington, and the Confederacy's determination to hold the city in the war's last winter. *The Wilmington Campaign: Last Rays of Departing Hope* is the product of my lifelong ambition to tell the entire story.

Although my name alone adorns the dust jacket and title page of *Last Rays*, this book's publication was anything but a solo project. The team effort started with its publisher, Theodore P. Savas, of Campbell, California. I am indebted to Ted for honing the manuscript for publication, and for his willingness, indeed encouragement, to make this book both a visual as well as a reading experience. Thanks to Ted's "military historian's approach" to publishing, *Last Rays* is chock full of maps and illustrations to supplement the text.

To Mark and Nancy Bradley I owe a special thank you. Mark, in particular, spent many hours reading my manuscript (which meant having less time to spend with his beloved Nancy), and then offered valuable suggestions on how to improve it. His keen eye for detail and accuracy so well displayed in his own *The Battle of Bentonville: Last Stand in the Carolinas* (Savas Publishing Company, 1996), which ranks as one of the best campaign studies ever published, tightened and polished the narrative of *Last Rays*. Mark now also knows more about the Wilmington Campaign than he ever bargained for.

A campaign study needs a sufficient number of maps to assist the reader in understanding troop movements and dispositions, as well as to get a feel for the lay of the land. No cartographer working today produces finer visual presentations than Mark A. Moore. His incomparable maps grace the pages of most Savas publications, including *Last Rays*. I am indebted to his minute attention to detail, evident in each of his exceptional plates.

I am also indebted to Ed Bearss for reading the manuscript it its rough form and recommending changes and offering guidance. I first met Ed, a living legend in the Civil War community, in 1993 when he was leading a Wilmington Campaign tour for Jerry Russell's Congress of Civil War Round

Tables. Several things impressed me about Ed: his deep passion for Civil War history, his infectious enthusiasm and his animated performing style in conducting tours. I was honored when he agreed to review my work for publication.

No project dealing with Cape Fear history goes untouched by Beverly Tetterton, the historian at the New Hanover County Public Library in Wilmington. If she had lived during the Civil War, Beverly would probably have served as a blockade running pilot. For years she has guided me safely through the shoaled stacks of books and manuscripts at the library to safe passage among the "good stuff." She is the local historian's best friend.

A dedicated researcher always wants to hit one more town, one more state archive, one more historical society in the hope of finding that elusive and all-important tidbit of information. It is the thrill of the hunt! At some point, however, one must end the quest and write the story. I have spent twenty-five years accumulating material on the Wilmington Campaign, much of which I uncovered myself. Yet many of the scattered pieces of the giant puzzle were found and sent to me by other historians. Some of my best material was sent to me only in the last sixteen months, proving that old adage that you can never find it all, no matter how hard you try. The assistance of these dedicated historians enabled me to understand the Wilmington story more clearly.

Foremost among the best professional researchers is Steve L. Zerbe of Cherry Hill, New Jersey. Steve's skills and knowledge of depositories in the mid-Atlantic States (including many nooks and crannies I would have never located) enabled him to supply me with much valuable information.

The same is true of Henry Mintz of Shelby, North Carolina. On his many road trips in search of manuscript sources for his own projects, Henry never failed to check for Wilmington Campaign material. In the process he often found important information that made *Last Rays* a better book.

Despite the fact that he is a Chicago Bears fan and not a Green Bay Packers devotee (as I have been since 1962), Bruce Allardice kindly searched for Fort Fisher and Wilmington material for me in the "windy city." His efforts proved fruitful, if primarily from a blue-clad perspective. Bruce's penchant for thoroughness is apparent in his recent publication *More Confederate Generals In Gray.*

I also owe much to the fine people and institutions of St. Lawrence County; New York, who provided me with leads, manuscripts, and photos relating to Bvt. Brig. Gen. N. Martin Curtis, the unsung Union hero of Fort Fisher. The citizens of Ogdensburg in particular are proud of General Curtis' role in the battles of Fort Fisher, for which he was awarded the Medal of Honor. I would especially like to thank Persis Boyesen, Manley Nipe, Barbara Schaefer of the Rome Historical Society, Tim Wright of the St. Lawrence County Historical Association, and John M. Coski, of The Museum of the Confederacy, all of whom helped to make this book a reality.

Any Civil War historian worth his salt working on a naval-related topic must sooner or later turn in the direction of Charles V. Peery, M.D., of Charleston, South Carolina, one of the foremost collectors of naval documents and artifacts. I have been proud to call Charlie my friend for the past fifteen years, and thank him for his generosity in providing many of the previously unpublished images included herein.

My appreciation for additional manuscripts, photos and assistance also extends to Ralph Allen, Dan Barefoot, Charles Pattison Bolles IV, Mike Brake, Tom Broadfoot, Bob Browning, Robert Calder, Bruce B. Cameron, Eugene Canfield, Diane Cashman, Don Collins, Edwin L. Coombs III, Dan Deeks, Bob Duncan, Dave Ellis, Brett Favre, Lacy K. Ford, Rod Gragg, Dr. and Mrs. Charles P. Graham, Tom Greco, Agnes Guarrieri, Millie Hart, Louis Horne, Constance Knox, Paul Laird, William Lamb, James Legg, Don Lennon, Mr. & Mrs. Walter Lipke, Francis A. Lord, Hugh MacRae II, J.C. Maxwell, Steve McAllister, Jim McCallum, Jim McKee, Myrtle Meade, John Meadows, David Meagher (for handcrafting the exquisite Brooke cannon graphic), Laurine and Orville Mooberry, Bob Moore, Tom Morgan, Alvin J. Page, Martin Peebles, William M. Reaves, Timothy Reese, Dave Roth, Doug Shepard, Gary Slate, George Slaton, Barry Smith, Steve Solenfriend, Keats Sparrow, Ben Steelman, William N. Still, Jr., David Sullivan, John D. Taylor, Ethel and Walker Taylor III, John Tilley, Chris Truitt, Larry Walker, Richard Walling, Jerry Wildenhaus, Clyde Wilson, Stephen R. Wise, and Brian E. W. Wood.

Thanks also go to the following archivists, curators and their respective institutions: Jonathan Noffke of the Bellamy Mansion Museum; Jimmy Bartley, Tammy Bangert, Bert Felton, and Brenda Marshburn at the Brunswick Town State Historic Site; Tim Bottoms, Barbara Rowe, and Janet Seapker, at the Cape Fear Museum; Division of Archives and History, Raleigh, North Carolina; Richard Lawrence, Gehrig Spencer and Mark Wilde-Ramsing, Fort Fisher State Historic Site; The Lower Cape Fear Historical Society; Mae Stone of the New York Historical Society; Perkins Library, Duke University; Pat Hash and Alex Moore of the South Carolina Historical Society in Charleston; Southern Historical Collection, University of North Carolina; Randy Hackenburg and Michael J. Winey, United States Army Military History Institute; and Yale University Library.

To truly understand a battle or campaign, a historian has to know the land on which the engagements occurred. Many amateur archaeologists have willingly shared with me their vast knowledge of the Cape Fear forts, battlefields and encampment sites. I owe much to the following gentlemen for letting me "pick their brains," or tromp through the woods with them for the past umpteen years: Gerald Huffham, Ben Ingraham, Bennett Langley, Torrey McLean, John A. Robinson, Jay Taylor, R. E. Treadwell, and Dickie Wolfe.

The magnificent photographic reproduction work for *Last Rays of Departing Hope* was provided by the very talented Melva Calder of Melva Calder Photography of Wilmington, and by Jim Pleasants. My friend Jim also produced, some twenty years ago, the first extensive bibliography (now being revised) on Cape Fear Civil War history that led me to much useful material in writing *Last Rays.*

I would be remiss not to recognize the historians whose works on the Cape Fear's rich past inspired me to write my own study: James G. Burr, Diane Cashman, George Davis, William Lord DeRosset, Robert Fales, Crocket Hewlett, Andrew J. Howell, E. Lawrence Lee, Leora "Billie" McEachern, Elizabeth McKoy, Louis T. Moore, William M. Reaves, James Sprunt, Alan Watson, and Debbie Williams.

I offer this publication in memory of my former professor at the University of South Carolina, Thomas L. Connelly, as well as Robert Fales, E. Lawrence Lee, Leora "Billie" McEachern, Thomas V. Moseley, and especially my father, Chris Eugene Fonvielle (1921-1970).

None of my accomplishments, no success I have enjoyed or happiness with which I have been blessed, would have been possible without my wife Nancy. She has seen me through since 1982, and to her I dedicate this book.

She and our beautiful little girls, Mary Katherine and Anne Fletcher, have been patient and understanding while I hid myself away for weeks on end, tapping with an almost religious fervor on the keyboard to complete this project. I also extend thanks to my family for their encouragement, especially my mother Jane Fonvielle Strausser, my father-in-law Marvin E. Stokely, and my mother-in-law Connie E. Stokely (who had better rank me #1 son-in-law when this thing hits the shelves)!

Chris E. Fonvielle, Jr.
Wilmington, NC
January 25, 1997

The Federal Blockade
1861-1865

Blockading Squadrons

1. **North Atlantic:** Cape Charles, VA to Cape Fear, NC
2. **South Atlantic:** Cape Fear, NC to Key West, FL
3. **East Gulf:** West Florida Coast
4. **West Gulf:** Remaining Gulf Coast to the Mexican Border

Blockade Runners ran the Federal Blockade successfully from neutral ports in Bermuda, Cuba, and the Bahamas.

Bermuda

St. George

North Atlantic
674 Miles

570 Miles

Cape Fear

South Atlantic

N E S W

400 MILES

Atlantic Ocean

The Bahamas

Nassau

Caribbean Sea

Puerto Rico

San Jaun

Dominican Republic

Haiti

Port-au-Prince

Windward Channel

Cuba

Havana

Key West

Jamaica

Kingston

MD
WV
VA
Norfolk
KY
NC
New Bern
Beaufort
Wilmington
TN
SC
Charleston
GA
Savannah
AL
Fernandina
St. Augustine
FL
Pensacola
MS
Mobile
AR
LA
New Orleans
TX
Galveston
Corpus Christi
Matamoros

East Gulf Squadron

West Gulf Squadron

Gulf of Mexico

YUCATAN CHANNEL

Merida
Campeche
Chetumal

MEXICO

Mark A. Moore

Chapter 1

"There was not a more important place"

– Confederate Officer

THE PORT

The chase was on! The blockade runner *Advance* sliced through the white caps of the Atlantic Ocean as she raced desperately toward her destination, the port of Wilmington, North Carolina. In hot pursuit were three Union gunboats, firing a barrage of shells as they moved to intercept the *Advance* before she reached New Inlet, the northern-most entrance into the Cape Fear River and Wilmington's harbor. It was the classic and deadly cat and mouse game played on an almost daily basis at Cape Fear.

Captain Thomas Crossan of the *Advance* knew he was in trouble when he saw the sun rise that morning. As much as any sailor, he usually enjoyed dawn at sea as the sun magically appeared on the surface, changing the color of the water from inky black to a deep gray green. But sunrise was the last thing Crossan wanted to see on October 10, 1863. With it he would have to run past a cordon of Union gunboats in broad daylight, perhaps the greatest fear of a blockade running captain.

Like all blockade runners, Crossan preferred doing his business at night, the darker the better. Darkness increased the chances of eluding speedy enemy cruisers prowling shipping lanes along the Confederate coastline and "bar tenders" staking out harbor inlets. Avoiding blockading ships was risky any time. A daytime run against them was downright dangerous and foolish.

But Captain Crossan did not have much choice. He had made landfall too far north of his target, and now the *Advance* was low on coal and still more than thirty miles from the safety of Wilmington's docks. He knew it was only a matter of time before blockaders detected the *Advance* as she approached New Inlet, yet his only alternatives were to scuttle or surrender his vessel. He was unwilling to do either. But if Crossan could make it halfway to Wilmington, the *Advance* and her valuable cargo of supplies would be safe, protected by artillery in Fort Fisher at New Inlet. By October, 1863, Fort Fisher was the most powerful seacoast fortification in the South, and blockade runners depended on its big guns to keep pursuing blockaders at bay.

Crossan called the ship's officers together, explained the situation, and told them what he proposed to do. They understood, and calmly returned to their stations. The captain and pilot assumed their positions on the bridge, while firemen below stoked the boilers with the last bit of coal to raise a full head of steam. The remaining sailors assumed positions on the main deck to scan the horizon for the dreaded blockaders. As a former lieutenant in the Confederate Navy, Crossan did not fear battle. He had served as commander

Running the blockade into Wilmington, North Carolina. *Illustrated London News*

of the gunboat *Winslow* at the Battle of New Bern in the spring of 1862. As the *Winslow's* captain he could shoot back. The *Advance*, however, was an unarmed merchant vessel that relied on speed and stealth to slip past enemy ships.

Crossan pushed the *Advance* with all possible speed down the coast, running as close to the waves breaking on shore as the ship's pilot dared, hoping the lead colored steamer would be camouflaged against the backdrop of the sandy beaches. When the *Advance* was about eight miles from the river's entrance, Union gunboats came into view. The unsuspecting blockaders had retired for the day to their usual anchorage five miles east of New Inlet in the belief that a blockade runner would not challenge them after sunrise. The *Advance* slipped undetected to within five miles of New Inlet when the Union blockaders spotted her. The Federal ships slipped their cables and moved quickly to cut her off before she reached the bar. The faster *Advance*, with a solid head start, clipped along at about fifteen knots, racing for the safety of the inlet. The Union ships opened a heavy cannon fire, the projectiles whizzing around and over the *Advance*. Although several exploded nearby, none of them struck the fleeing ship. One Federal shot skimmed off the surface about half a mile from the *Advance*, and continued its unpredictable course, ricocheting in the direction of the runner. Although the crew and passengers thought the ship would be struck, the cannonball dropped harmlessly into the sea not ten yards away from her. "It was a scene of intense excitement," exclaimed the Reverend Moses D. Hoge, a passenger on board the *Advance*. "The shells were ploughing up the water and tearing up the sand on shore, bursting over and around us, and yet not one struck us. It was almost a miracle." The Federal gunboats continued their pursuit.[1]

Just when it seemed the blockaders might bag their quarry booming shots from Fort Fisher's cannon echoed across the water, warning them to back off. The Federal ships quickly abandoned the chase and retreated out of range of the Confederate artillery, but not before one of them was struck by a shell. Under the protection of Fort Fisher's batteries, the *Advance* steamed into New Inlet's channel. As they passed Fort Fisher, the crew cheered their defenders and hoisted the Confederate flag. The *Advance* was safe, but not quite home free. She suddenly ground to an agonizing halt on "the Rip," a bothersome shoal where the waters of New Inlet and the Cape Fear River met. Not until Sunday evening, October 11, did engineers secure the *Advance*'s release from the sand bar so she could steam on toward Wilmington.

Six miles north of New Inlet the *Advance* stopped again, this time under her own power at Fort Anderson on the west side of the river. There a Confederate officer checked the cargo manifest to make sure no illegal supplies were being smuggled into the Confederacy. Confederate law forbade trade with Northern states and importation of "Yankee goods," though such trade still occurred. As the cargo was examined a surgeon inspected for infectious diseases on board. Once the ship had received "proper clearance," she continued her journey to Wilmington, another fifteen miles upstream.[2]

When the *Advance* got within sight of Wilmington's skyline, her officers and crew hoisted a dram of rum to celebrate their successful run. It had been a ritual for sailors since colonial times to toast their safe arrival into Wilmington at the Dram Tree, an ancient cypress two miles south of the city on the east bank of the Cape Fear River. Soon thereafter the vessel docked along the Wilmington waterfront, a mile-long stretch of docks, piers, warehouses, and shipyards bustling with activity devoted primarily to blockade running. Black laborers loaded and unloaded ships and warehouses under the watchful eye of white overseers and commission merchants while Confederate soldiers stood guard nearby or marched in the streets. As foreign sailors roamed the waterfront, women and children gathered to take in the strange sights, sounds and smells of the seaport. Blockade running was king in Wilmington, and by the fall of 1863 the city was the South's principal blockade running seaport, one of the most important cities in the Confederacy. The *Advance*'s arrival explains why. Her valuable cargo of imported cloth, shoes, blankets, buckles, buttons, iron, steel, tools, and percussion caps and nipples for rifle-muskets would provide Southern soldiers with much-needed supplies.[3]

North Carolina and her sister Confederate states depended on this tenuous, often dangerous, yet beneficial waterborne trade to keep them alive. Blockade runners—the *Advance* and hundreds of ships like her—together with courageous and determined sailors like Thomas Crossan, brought vital supplies to both Southern armies and navies as well as to civilians. It was a commercial relationship the Confederacy desperately needed to maintain, and the Union desperately wanted to shut down.

From the start, President Abraham Lincoln knew the Confederacy would need logistical support from the outside world. Compared to the industrial might of the Northern states, the South's lack of manufacturing facilities placed it at a great disadvantage. Before the war Northern suppliers had provided the largely agrarian South with manufactured goods, while Southern planters had depended on Northern mercantile firms to ship their cotton to Europe. Secession and war ended that commercial relationship. The burgeoning Confederacy was forced to turn to European nations for material essential to waging war.

One of Lincoln's primary objectives was to prevent the Confederacy from establishing maritime trade relations with Europe. An effective blockade or the capture of strategic coastal cities would hinder the Confederacy's ability to procure badly-needed supplies and cripple the region's economy by restricting the export of its cash crops. The cannon that had subdued Fort Sumter were barely cool to the touch before President Lincoln, shortly after his call for 75,000 troops, announced a trade embargo against the states that had seceded from the Union—South Carolina, Georgia, Alabama, Florida, Mississippi, Louisiana, and Texas. The president proclaimed a naval blockade as of April 19, and eight days later extended the blockade to include North Carolina and Virginia, two states technically still in the Union. Angered by Lincoln's request for combat troops and naval interdiction, both North Carolina and Virginia passed ordinances of secession and joined the Confederacy.[4]

Lincoln's proclamation was a political gamble designed in part to solicit respect for the blockade by the world powers. Some of the president's advisers had encouraged him to close Southern ports to maritime commerce rather than attempt to blockade them. Such a course raised sticky legal issues, however, and European governments vowed to honor the blockade. Queen Victoria's neutrality proclamation of May 13, 1861, stated Great Britain's "determination to maintain a strict and impartial Neutrality in the contest," while warning British subjects against violating a lawfully established blockade. Following Great Britain's lead, France adopted a similar declaration three days later.[5]

In late June 1861, U.S. Secretary of the Navy Gideon Welles established the Blockade Strategy Board to draw up plans for sealing Southern ports by naval blockade or combined army-navy operations. Declaring a blockade and enforcing it, however, were entirely different matters, as Lincoln and Welles soon learned. For a host of reasons, the implementation of an effective blockade of the Southern coastline in the spring of 1861 was impossible. First and foremost there were not enough ships to do the job. At the war's outset the United States Navy comprised just ninety vessels, only forty-two of which were commissioned. More than half the fleet consisted of obsolescent sailing vessels used mostly for training sailors. Forty steam ships made up the balance of the fleet, but most of these were stationed in foreign waters or badly in need of repairs. Of the twelve vessels constituting the U.S. Navy's Home Squadron in the spring of 1861, only three steamers were ready for immediate blockade duty along the 3,549-mile-long Southern coastline, which was carved by some 189 inlets, harbors, bays, and coves.[6]

Other adversities plagued the Union blockade in addition to an insufficient fleet. Military strategists and politicians disagreed over the blockade's merit, denying unilateral support to the effort. The country's lack of sufficient shipbuilding yards and manufacturing shops for ships' engines and parts was compounded by labor disputes as well as by inadequate coal supplies and vessel repair facilities close to blockading stations. Inefficiency in the Navy Department and inexperience among sailors and officers in working along the American coastline was compounded by the loss of many U. S. Navy officers to Confederate service. But perhaps the biggest dilemma facing Lincoln's blockade was its general disregard by commercial interest groups. Many Europeans and some Northerners, lured by profits, evidenced little respect for the blockade. As the business of running the blockade became more and more lucrative and consequently stimulating to Europe's slumping economy, foreign heads of state ignored breaches of their official stances on the issue.[7]

European suppliers justified their own running of the blockade by questioning the blockade's legality, just as Lincoln's advisers feared. According to a treaty signed by the world's powers in Paris in 1856 (the United States was not a signatory but later complied with its provisions), a blockade was defined as a barricade of a belligerent nation's ports to prevent passage in wartime. President Lincoln, however, refused to recognize the Confederate States of America as a sovereign nation, insisting instead that secession was an unwarranted rebellion. Thus in some European circles Lincoln's declaration of a blockade contradicted international law: how could a nation blockade its own ports?

The 1856 Declaration of Paris also noted that "blockades to be binding must be effective, that is to say, maintained by a force sufficient to prevent access to the coast of the enemy." The U. S. Navy could not deploy a cordon of ships strong enough to stop blockade running. As a result Confederate commerce experienced little interruption early in the war, with ships entering and exiting Southern ports almost at will. The blockaders experienced utter frustration in trying to stop the contraband trade. "If the vessels were captured, even in entering principal ports, it was due rather to the stupidity of the persons attempting to run the blockade than to the effectiveness of the force employed to prevent it," observed a Union naval officer. "Our 'effective blockade' is a perfect farce," declared William Keeler, a paymaster on the blockader *Florida* off Wilmington. "I believe there is scarcely a night passes but what there are vessels of some kind run out or in."[8]

The blockade's ineffectiveness stimulated a booming business for blockade runners. Southern and British businessmen set up importing and exporting companies and developed strong trade alliances. Fraser, Trenholm & Co. of Charleston, South Carolina, and Crenshaw & Collie & Co. in London were two of the more prominent firms. Even the Confederate government and some Confederate states, North Carolina in particular, invested in blockade runners. Europe's desire for high-grade Southern cotton, the Confederacy's need for European supplies, and, most importantly, the potential for huge profits, attracted investors to run the risk of trading through the blockade.

The danger of capture increased as the Union navy grew and its dragnet of the South's coastal cities tightened, but greater risks also earned bigger dividends for blockade running investors. Cotton, the Confederacy's chief export and generally worth three to eight cents a pound, often brought ten times those prices in Europe. A steamer capable of transporting 1,000 bales of cotton could turn a profit of $250,000 for her shareholders in but a single trip. Thomas Taylor, who described himself as a "super cargo" of the Anglo-Confederate Trading company of Liverpool, claimed that the blockade runner *Banshee* paid a 700 percent profit for her investors in just eight runs. It was said if a blockade runner made two successful trips, and "afterwards was lost or captured, the investment in ship and cargo would be paid for."[9]

The ships' crews also could earn thousands of dollars in gold for each run through the blockade. Crenshaw & Collie paid $25,000 to the officers and crew of the *Venus* for each trip. The captain received $5,000, the pilot $3,500, and the chief engineer $2,500. Even the deckhands got $250 apiece, at a time when Confederate soldiers received less than $20 in inflated Confederate currency per month. James C. Stevenson, a teenaged purser's clerk on board the *Advance*, earned monthly wages of $50 in gold and received another $50 for each successful trip through the blockade. He sometimes earned an additional $150 to $200 by speculating in the cotton or turpentine he was permitted to carry on board the *Advance* and sell at ports-of-call. Stevenson estimated that as a boy of fifteen or sixteen years of age, he earned more than $25,000, the equivalent of the annual salary of the President of the Confederate States.[10]

Essentially, the trade was operated by Southern agents abroad—Caleb Huse and Edward C. Anderson—who purchased and stockpiled European-made war material for the Confederacy. Most of the products were manufactured in Great Britain, although significant quantities were produced in Austria, France and Prussia. Transatlantic merchantmen carried the goods to neutral ports, mainly in Bermuda, Nassau, and Cuba. Halifax, Nova Scotia, also saw limited use as a blockade running entrepot, but the Canadian port was too far from Confederate seaports to be of much advantage. Once these ports had been reached, the supplies were transferred to smaller vessels for the final run through the Federal blockade.

After arriving safely in Southern seaports, runners discharged their cargoes and reloaded for the return trip to the transshipment points. In exchange for its cash crops (predominantly cotton, naval stores, and lumber) the Confederacy imported rifle-muskets, revolvers, cannon, ammunition, swords, sabers, bayonets, knives, blankets, shoes, boots, cloth, leather, food, medicine, tools, lead, tin, copper, and iron. These military supplies, in turn, were shipped by rail throughout the South for distribution to the army and navy. Private investors brought in even larger quantities of personal articles, most of which were sold at public auction. The Confederate government did not prohibit civilian speculators from investing in and profiting from the trade.

Most blockade runners that brought in these supplies so crucial to the Confederacy's war effort were privately-owned vessels. Investors profited handsomely when popular items went on the auction block: English brandy, choice foreign wines, potted meats, jellies, loaf-sugar, coffee, and tea, as well as gloves, parasols, hoopskirts, corsets, flannels, bonnets, silk and calicoes for the ladies all added to the bank accounts of these investors. War demanded the steadfast support of the civilian population, and denying people on the homefront niceties and luxuries even in wartime might have undermined their morale and commitment to the war effort. Not until late in the conflict did the Confederate government more rigorously regulate the blockade running trade, in part by requiring companies to provide more space for government-owned property on board ships.

The excessive profits in and lack of restrictions on blockade running provoked many critics inside the Confederacy to define the business as corrupt, immoral and injurious to the cause. Most civilians and military personnel could not afford the exorbitant prices charged by import companies and as a result suffered from inflation. In the summer of 1861, Wilmingtonians paid 5¢ to 6¢ cents a pound for beef, 16¢ to 19¢ a pound for bacon, 12¢ to 15¢ cents per chicken, and 85¢ cents for a bushel of corn. Three years later they could expect to pay at least $2.50 a pound for beef, $5.50 to $6 a pound for bacon, $5.00 to $7.00 per chicken, and $18.00 to $20.00 for a bushel of corn. Citizens sarcastically remarked that they needed a wheelbarrow full of money to buy goods at the market you could take home in a basket. Some Southern military officers complained that profiteering in civilian goods tempted blockade running entrepreneurs to pay less attention to the needs of the government. "The public freight compared with the private freight was small," a Confederate soldier pointed out.[11]

That may have been true, but defenders of the trade maintained that blockade running was the Confederacy's best hope for supplying the necessities of its armies and citizens. The entire business benefited Southern producers of cotton and other commodities, employed thousands of people, and helped Southerners establish direct trade ties with European merchants. Although one observer described blockade running as "life preserving and death dealing," its advantages outweighed its disadvantages.[12]

Early in the war, when the Union blockade was inadequate, many types of vessels were employed as blockade runners—barques, schooners, tug boats and even "corn-crackers." But as the blockade tightened and captures of illicit vessels occurred more frequently, blockade runners succeeded in finding new ways to challenge the Union dragnet. As James R. Randall, a blockade running employee in Wilmington, pointed out, "the ingenuity of the blockade-breakers [was] fully equal to the blockade-keepers." Steamships that were faster and well-camouflaged were converted or constructed mainly in Great Britain especially for blockade running. These swift, sleek and light-draft ships traded regularly at Confederate ports after 1862.[13]

Captain Thomas Crossan's *Advance* was typical of the newer type of blockade running vessels. Caird & Co. of Greenock, Scotland, built the steamship in the summer of 1862. After several months of plying the Irish Sea as the packet steamer *Lord Clyde*, she was sold to the government of North Carolina and transformed into a blockade runner. Thomas Crossan was one of the ship's purchasing agents. The *Advance*, named for Zebulon B. Vance, North Carolina's popular wartime governor, was 236 feet long, weighed 431 registered tons, and was propelled by side wheel paddles capable of pushing her up to seventeen knots. She was owned solely by North Carolina until December 1863, when Power, Low & Co. of Wilmington was permitted to buy one-half interest in her. The sale allowed the state to expand its blockade running operations by investing in other steamers—the *Annie, Condor, Flamingo, Don* and *Hansa*, among others. The *Advance* made at least eight trips into Wilmington between spring 1863 and late summer 1864. On September 10, 1864, the *Santiago de Cuba* captured the *Advance* outward bound from Wilmington. In an ironic change of affairs, she was converted into a gunboat for use as a blockader. The *Advance* had performed well for more than a year before her capture, bringing much needed supplies into North Carolina and the Confederacy while turning a handsome profit for Power, Low & Co.[14]

Union reports attest to the prevalence of the blockade running trade. Secretary Gideon Welles claimed that by 1865, the U. S. Navy had captured 1,133 blockade runners and destroyed 335 others. Perhaps as many as 150 active blockade runners survived the war. Thus more than 1,600 vessels of all classes were engaged in blockade running. Of the total number of blockade runners, about 300 were steamships. These vessels attempted approximately 1,300 runs, of which 1,000—almost seventy-seven percent—were successful. The Carolina seaports, primarily Wilmington and Charleston, boasted an eighty-four percent success rate for sailing craft and steam runners. The average steamer broke the Union barricade four times before

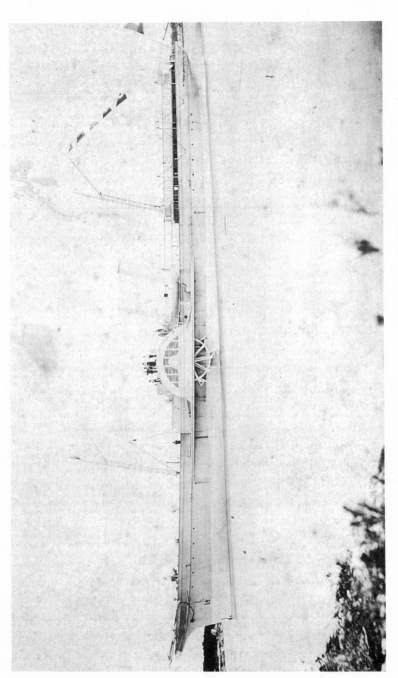

The blockade runner *Advance*, ca. 1863. Note the Confederate flag flying from the ship's stern. *Courtesy of Charles V. Peery*

being captured or destroyed. Four blockade runners, the *Ella*, *Annie*, *Alice* and *Fannie*, made a combined total of fifty-two trips through the blockade. The *Syren* proved to be the most fortunate blockade runner, making thirty-three successful trips.[15]

The U. S. Navy responded to this porous state of affairs by focusing its greatest number of ships along the sea lanes over which most blockade runners operated and at the entrances to the Confederacy's major seaports: Norfolk, Virginia; Beaufort, New Bern, and Wilmington, North Carolina; Charleston, South Carolina; Savannah, Georgia; Fernandina, Jacksonville and Pensacola, Florida; Mobile, Alabama; New Orleans, Louisiana, and Galveston, Texas. These cities' deep harbors and good interior lines of communication made them especially valuable to the Confederacy. Initially the Union blockade fleet comprised two commands—the Atlantic Blockading Squadron and the Gulf Blockading Squadron. In October 1861, these organizations were further divided into four groups: the North Atlantic Blockading Squadron, which patrolled the coast from Cape Charles, Virginia to Cape Fear, North Carolina; the South Atlantic Blockading Squadron, whose responsibilities extended southward to Key West, Florida; the East Gulf Blockading Squadron, which covered Florida's west coast; and the West Gulf Blockading Squadron, which was responsible for the remainder of the Gulf of Mexico shoreline to the Mexican border. Ships were assigned to a squadron as they were commissioned for service and directed to a blockading station where they were most needed. On April 30, 1861, just two weeks after the surrender of Fort Sumter, Norfolk became the first port to be blockaded. Charleston, Savannah, Mobile, and New Orleans were put under blockade the following month. Yet by mid-July, three months after Lincoln had declared the blockade, only four U. S. vessels were stationed along the North Carolina coast.[16]

The Federal navy eventually seized or put out of action most of the blockade runners. The Navy Department, led by the able Gideon Welles (whom President Lincoln endearingly called "Father Neptune") and his energetic Assistant Secretary Gustavus V. Fox, overcame many adversities to create a powerful and professional navy. Through the purchase and construction of warships and the conversion and chartering of merchant vessels, fire boats, ferries, and captured blockade runners, the fleet grew from a motley array of vessels in 1861 to a mighty force of 671 ships by war's end.

Some 471 of those vessels saw blockade duty. According to Welles' figures, the U. S. Navy eventually captured or destroyed ninety-two percent of vessels employed as blockade runners. Of the 300 steam blockade runners, 207 were seized and another seventy-nine were ruined.[17]

Despite its impressive record in eventually stopping most blockade runners, Welles' blockaders failed to halt the flow of supplies smuggled into the Confederacy by vessels that eluded capture. The influx continued until the last port was closed by a joint Union army-navy operation less than ninety days before the Confederacy surrendered. By that late date, private and public industrial achievements had made the South less dependent on imports.[18]

Still, blockade running augmented the Confederacy's fighting capability more than did its wartime industrial output. Between November 1, 1863, and October 25, 1864, blockade runners brought into the Confederacy 6,200,000 pounds of meat, 1,490,000 pounds of lead, 1,850,000 pounds of saltpeter (a key ingredient in gunpowder), 420,000 pairs of boots and shoes, 292,000 blankets, 408,000 pounds of coffee, 136,832 muskets, rifle-muskets, and carbines, and a large number of other articles. Most of this material entered through Wilmington, since blockade running at Charleston was uncertain by that point in the war. In a thirty-seven day stretch between October 31 and the first week of December 1864, nineteen steamers ran the blockade into Wilmington. They carried 328 cases of rifle-muskets, tons of ammunition, boots and shoes, blankets, buttons, buckles, cloth, tools, beef, pork, beans, coffee, saltpeter, zinc, iron, tin and other provisions for the government.[19]

A single shipment could arm and feed a regiment of troops (1,000 men) for a month. Even as the blockade tightened it was still too porous to completely stop the importation of European-manufactured goods. Although the Northern blockade of Southern ports became more effective as the war continued, it failed to achieve its avowed purpose. No Confederate army ever lost an important battle or campaign because it lacked guns, ammunition, supplies, or food.[20]

The favorite port-of-call for blockade runners was Wilmington, a beautiful, old town with a rich history. It started as New Liverpool, a small trading post on the east side of the Cape Fear River where it meets the

Northeast Cape Fear River, twenty-seven miles from where it empties into the Atlantic Ocean. In 1732 several enterprising merchants, traders, and artificers established businesses on land owned by John Maultsby. The next year John Watson and a group of developers laid off a town they called Newton on a grant adjoining New Liverpool, and began selling wooded lots. Royal Governor Gabriel Johnston moved to Newton in 1734 and immediately began transforming the township into a place of considerable importance. He instructed the colony's council to meet there, encouraged his friends to buy land, and, in 1740, incorporated it under the name of Wilmington, named for Spencer Compton, Earl of Wilmington and Governor Johnston's patron in England.

Over the years many well-known and colorful personalities made their home in the port city, including Cornelius Harnett, the leader of the colony's resistance to the Stamp Act in 1765 and considered the Samuel Adams of the South. William Hooper, signer of the Declaration of Independence, was also a native Wilmingtonian. In April 1781, Lord Cornwallis temporarily resided in Wilmington, establishing headquarters at the Burgwyn-Wright house as he planned his invasion of Virginia, an ill-fated campaign that resulted in the surrender of his British army and the end of the American Revolution. Earlier in 1781 the British had captured and occupied Wilmington, providing Cornwallis with a safe haven on the seacoast as he marched northward through the Carolinas, much as Maj. Gen. William T. Sherman would do eighty-four years later.

Even with its celebrated residents, Wilmington was best known as North Carolina's principal seaport. Engineering improvements in the Cape Fear River's navigability, the construction of railroads and the state's adoption of the plank road system stimulated Wilmington's growth in the antebellum era. The town grew by leaps and bounds, the population doubling between 1820 and 1840, and again from 1840 to 1860. Commerce also increased at an impressive rate, most of which centered on Wilmington's status as one of the largest naval stores markets in the world. Commission merchants exported huge amounts of turpentine, tar, rosin, pitch, and lumber to mostly northern cities—especially Baltimore and New York—as well as with the Caribbean islands. They also traded rice, peanuts, corn and an increasing amount of cotton for sugar, molasses, rum, and manufactured goods. Though hardly the most popular of the South's seaports, Wilmington enjoyed an ever-increasing prosperity during the antebellum era.[21]

On the eve of the Civil War Wilmington was the largest city in North Carolina. At least 9,552 people lived there in 1860, though there were probably more, missed by the census takers. Grand antebellum homes stood along broad avenues built on a sprawling sand ridge. One visitor remarked that Wilmington was a pleasant and pretty place and its citizens very refined and polite. The city market, constructed in the middle of Market and Front Streets, was at the center of the business district. Buyers ambled among the stalls filled with poultry, fish and produce. Slaves were also bought and sold here. Yet most of the city's commercial intercourse revolved around maritime trade, and the riverfront docks, piers, warehouses and the adjacent counting houses teemed with activity.

Wilmington also boasted an impressive industrial sector in a region largely devoid of industry. Two commercial shipbuilding yards prospered in Wilmington by 1861: James Cassidey's yard at the foot of Church Street on the banks of the Cape Fear River, and Benjamin W. and William L. Beery's shipyard on Eagles Island, just opposite the town. Both yards had been in operation since before the war, and both enjoyed additional prosperity when the Confederate government contracted with them to manufacture and repair vessels. Much of their machine work was provided by two metal fabric shops, Hart & Bailey's Iron and Copper Works on south Front Street, and Clarendon Iron Works on Queen Street between Surry and Water Streets. Clarendon's was started during the war to handle the South's increased demand for industrial output and to lessen the need for imports. An arsenal also operated in Wilmington early in the war. Until September 1862, Louis Froelich and B. Eastvan, under government contract, ran a munitions factory, where they manufactured swords, sabers, D-guard bowie knives or short swords, lances, bayonets, knapsacks and buttons.[22]

Three railroad lines and ample repair facilities served the city. The incomplete Wilmington, Charlotte & Rutherford Railroad traversed North Carolina's piedmont and served as the route along which were shipped naval stores, cotton and other commodities for exportation. During the war the WC&R was also a vital link between Wilmington and the Confederate Navy Yard in Charlotte, North Carolina. The Wilmington & Manchester Railroad indirectly connected Wilmington to Charleston, South Carolina, the most

View of antebellum Wilmington looking southeast across the Cape Fear River from Point Peter.
Gleason's Pictorial Drawing-Room Companion

important city on the south Atlantic seaboard, as well as other points further south. But Wilmington's most important rail line was the Wilmington & Weldon Railroad, which linked the city with Virginia by way of Goldsboro and Weldon, North Carolina. Upon its completion in 1840, the 162-mile-long railroad between Wilmington and Weldon was the longest in the world. By the Civil War the railroad had been extended another ninety miles to Petersburg, Virginia, and thus it took on even greater significance to the Confederacy when it became the main supply route for Robert E. Lee's Army of Northern Virginia.

The state ran a large and highly successful salt-making operation on Masonboro Sound ten miles east of Wilmington. By one official estimate the N. C. Salt Works and private salt enterprises along the nearby sounds produced 3,000 bushels of salt a day by evaporating sea water. A regular supply of salt, an important preservative for meat and fish, depended on Wilmington remaining in Confederate hands. The same was true for other commodities produced in the lower Cape Fear, such as naval stores, lumber, and rice—all of which the Confederacy badly needed. The town also possessed several turpentine distilleries, a cotton compress and three steam-powered sawmills.[23]

The war turned Wilmington "topsy-turvy," according to John Wilkinson, a famous blockade runner who frequently visited the city. Wilmington had always been an active seaport, but it became even busier once blockade running became big business. The Northern trade ended in the late spring of 1861 and Wilmington merchants postponed most coastal trade while they awaited the initial effects of Lincoln's highly publicized blockade. Even then Wilmington was not placed under surveillance until July 12, when the *Roanoke* assumed position off Cape Fear three months after the blockade had gone into effect. The *Daylight* relieved the *Roanoke* the following day, notifying Confederates onshore that Wilmington was officially under blockade. When a strong blockade failed to materialize, however, the blockade running business began and quickly flourished at Wilmington.[24]

Perhaps as many as 100 different steamers operated in and out of the city during the war. "We have a great many vessels to come in here," noted a Confederate officer, "as many as six in two nights and as many as nine in port at once." Another Confederate soldier claimed that Wilmington averaged an arrival and departure of a blockade runner every twenty-four hours.

The soldier's observation may have been a slight exaggeration, but it is true that in 1864 alone blockade running steamers made at least 166 runs into the city. Between May 25 and June 9 of that year, fifteen steamers broke through the Union barricade. "When you think of fifteen large and splendid steamers coming from abroad in as many days," an impressed observer noted, "it makes the blockade of Wilmington seem like a sham."[25]

No doubt the "sham" nature of the blockade prompted North Carolina to invest heavily in blockade running at Wilmington. According to Governor Vance the state imported 60,000 pairs of cotton handcards, leather for 250,000 shoes, 50,000 blankets, gray woolen cloth for 125,000 uniforms (the entire number of troops North Carolina sent into the war), 12,000 overcoats, 2,000 British Enfield rifle-muskets, 100,000 pounds of bacon, 500 sacks of coffee and $50,000 worth of medicine at gold prices. "Not only was the supply of shoes, blankets and clothing more than sufficient for the supply of the North Carolina troops," Vance claimed, "but large quantities were turned over to the Confederate government for the troops of other states." According to one estimate blockade running investments at Wilmington in 1864 alone amounted to $66,000,000 in gold and $65,000,000 in cotton exports. Little wonder that a Southern officer stated, "After the capital of the Confederacy there was not in the South a more important place than the little town of Wilmington, North Carolina."[26]

By July 1863, when Federal forces put Charleston under siege, Wilmington assumed the mantel as the most important seaport in the Confederacy. The city bustled with more commercial activity than ever before. Buyers, investors, and adventurers flocked to the port from all over the world. "Our town is full to overflowing with merchants and speculators, Jews and gentiles, men from the East, West, North and South who come to attend the advertised auction sale of goods," remarked a citizen. Wilmingtonians viewed these foreigners with curiosity, suspicion and humor. "At every turn you met up with young Englishmen dressed like grooms and jockeys, or with a peculiar coachman-like look," noted an astute observer. "These youngsters had money, made money, lived like fighting cocks, and astonished the natives by their pranks, and the way they flung the Confederate 'stuff' about. Of course they were deeply interested in the Confederate cause, and at the same time wanted cotton."[27]

To safeguard the Confederate cause at Wilmington the military moved in as well. The government stationed a large force of soldiers, sailors and marines there to protect its interests. The city soon became an armed camp as barracks, tents and earthwork fortifications cropped up. The blockade running trade also attracted thieves, rogues and prostitutes, and crime became rampant. "[Wilmington] is a perfect sink of iniquity," declared a Confederate soldier. A frightened resident reported that "[the city] was unsafe. There were frequent conflicts in the public streets between the crews of steamers in port and the soldiers stationed in town, in which knives and pistols were freely used. . . .The civil authorities were powerless to prevent crime." In fact, civil authorities were sometimes victims of crimes themselves. On the night of September 10, 1863, three policemen were severely beaten and stabbed by a group of drunk Texas soldiers in Paddy's Hollow, the town's "red light district." One soldier declared that he was "almost afraid to walk the streets from the passport office to quarters after 9 o'clock at night." Crime increased to such a state that military leaders prohibited blockade running seamen from leaving their ships after sundown, and civil authorities ordered all visitors to report to the mayor's office to register their names, business in town, and where they were staying.[28]

Blockade runners sometimes imported disease along with much needed supplies and social upheaval. On August 6, 1862, the steamer *Kate* brought yellow fever from Nassau, devastating Wilmington with a serious epidemic. Although several of the *Kate's* crew members died shortly after arriving in Wilmington, Lewis Swartzman, a thirty-six-year-old German-born wood and coal dealer, became the first confirmed yellow fever victim when he died on September 9. In the following three months deaths occurred so frequently that bodies could not be buried quickly enough. A mass grave was dug at Oakdale Cemetery in the city's eastern suburbs to accommodate the overflow. Business was suspended and stores closed their doors. Civilians, soldiers and sailors fled the city, the district commander temporarily moved his headquarters down river to Smithville, and blockade runners and visitors were banned from the city. "[Yellow fever] is raging in Wilmington to an alarming extent and I think you had better keep away from there," a soldier warned his family. "Poor Wilmington has been desolated with a fearful pestilence, the horrors of which are more easily imagined than described," claimed another.[29]

The only sounds in Wilmington's deserted streets were the clip-clop of horse-drawn "death wagons" and the footfalls of feet as doctors, ministers and the Sisters of Mercy scurried about attending to the ill. Residents who remained in the city were urged to wear a patch of cloth soaked in tar and peanut oil on their chests, believing that "gas tar" repelled the sickness. Burning rosin pots were also placed throughout the town to cleanse the air. Physicians of the time were unaware the Aedes mosquito was the disease's host. While most people blamed the *Kate* for bringing in the fever, some doctors reported that the disease struck Wilmington before the blockade runner's arrival. Before the epidemic ended in December with the onset of cool weather, 654 residents, or forty-three percent of the 1,500 reported cases, had died. Wilmington lost some of its most prominent citizens to the disease, including Dr. James H. Dickson, Reverend John L. Prichard of First Baptist Church, and the Reverend Dr. Robert B. Drane of St. James Episcopal Church, all of whom had succumbed to the fever while administering to its victims.[30]

Dismayed by the infiltration of foreigners, soldiers, sailors, criminals and disease, many of Wilmington's more affluent citizens left the city for havens inland or along nearby sounds. "Previous to the war Wilmington was very gay and social. But the war. . .sadly changed the place," lamented one resident. "No one familiar with this place prior to 1861 can fail to recognize the marked difference in Wilmington," observed the editor of the *Wilmington Daily Journal*. "It is indeed a changed town. . .some good, some bad, and some meddling." Ironically, Wilmington's decline into a bawdy, violent and unhealthy place paralleled its rise as the Confederacy's premier seaport.[31]

The city's popularity and longevity as a blockade runner haven was due mainly to five factors: geography, railroads, strong defenses, keen military leaders and Union inertia. Wilmington was ideally located for the business. The distance from Cape Fear southeast to Nassau in the Bahamas was only 570 miles, and to Bermuda, almost due east, but 674. Average travel time by ship was forty-eight hours to the former and seventy-two hours to the latter. The port city was safely situated twenty-seven miles up the Cape Fear River, far out of range of Union naval bombardment. During the Civil War the Cape Fear River had two navigable mouths: Old Inlet (also known as the

Western Bar), and New Inlet, a shallow strait to the northeast carved by a powerful hurricane in September 1761 through a sandy spit called the "Haul-over." A hundred years later, these two passageways gave blockade runners a choice of harbor entrances and exits. Old Inlet's channel reached a depth of some seventeen feet, and thus was considered the river's main bar. Only light-draft vessels could ply New Inlet, since its depth was only twelve feet at high tide and seven and a half feet at low tide.[32]

The task of maintaining an effective blockade of Old Inlet and New Inlet posed a demanding challenge to Federal ships. The Cape Fear estuary was extremely difficult to blockade, and blockade runners enjoyed continued success in that sector. Shoal waters and Confederate shore batteries guarding the inlets forced blockading vessels to stand out to sea, far from the narrow passageways blockade runners nimbly sneaked through. Smith's Island (or Bald Head Island as it is more commonly known, because of its bare, sandy beaches), and Frying Pan Shoals, a twenty-mile-long reef jutting out into the ocean, separated the inlets. Even though inside the harbor the distance between the inlets was only six miles, the expanse on the ocean side was eight times that distance, or almost fifty miles.

To cover both passageways, the Federal navy was compelled to divide its ships into two task forces. The First Division of the North Atlantic Blockading Squadron guarded the bar at New Inlet, watching for vessels coming in from Bermuda or Halifax. The Third Division ships barricaded the Western Bar and adjacent smaller inlets, or cruised on the so-called "Nassau track." Lighter draft blockaders moved in as close to the channels as the weather, time of day and Confederate shore batteries would allow. They pressed in even closer to shore at night. The "bar tenders" did not attempt to run down speedy blockade runners, leaving that task to faster steamers. As long as runners were in sight, blockaders gave chase. Federal cruisers supported the "bar tenders" and were a match for the swift blockade runners. These cruisers patrolled the shipping lanes further out to sea, watching for suspicious vessels approaching the Cape Fear.[33]

Still, blockade runners clearly had the advantage over Union ships at the Cape Fear. When they were ready for an outward-bound trip, blockade runners would drop down the Cape Fear River from Wilmington to Smithville (present-day Southport), a quaint village and popular summer resort on the west bank two miles from Old Inlet and four miles from New

Inlet. Smithville never became a significant blockade running port because it had no railroads or substantial highways. Yet the anchorage there gave blockade runners a good vantage point from which to view both blockading squadrons and to choose a time and spot to run the gauntlet. Inward-bound blockade runners determined their course according to wind, weather, tides, and blockaders. Those approaching Wilmington from Bermuda and Nova Scotia usually attempted to enter through New Inlet, while ships coming from Nassau generally used Old Inlet. They would make landfall well above New Inlet or below Old Inlet and creep along the coastline just outside the breakers before attempting the final dash through the Union web, preferably on dark, moonless nights. Blockade runners' low profile and light color made them difficult to detect against the backdrop of the wooded shoreline, and the roar of the ocean's waves muffled the hum of the ships' steam engines. More often than not runners eluded even the most vigilant blockaders. As one Union naval officer observed, "[blockading Wilmington] was very much like a parcel of cats watching a big rat hole; the rat often running in when they are expecting him to run out and visa versa."[34]

The "rat hole" was both the most important Confederate port then in operation and a principal distribution center. The superior river and rail lines of communication that enhanced Wilmington's antebellum maritime business cemented its preeminence as a Confederate seaport. Of the former, the Cape Fear River flowed far into the interior of the state and was navigable for small to moderate-size vessels as far inland as Fayetteville, 100 miles northwest of Wilmington. More importantly, three railroads connected Wilmington with other areas of the South. By 1864, the most important of these lines, the Wilmington & Weldon Railroad, had become the lifeline for Gen. Robert E. Lee's Army of Northern Virginia, then entrenched along the Richmond and Petersburg line of defenses.

That fact was not lost on the Federal high command.[35]

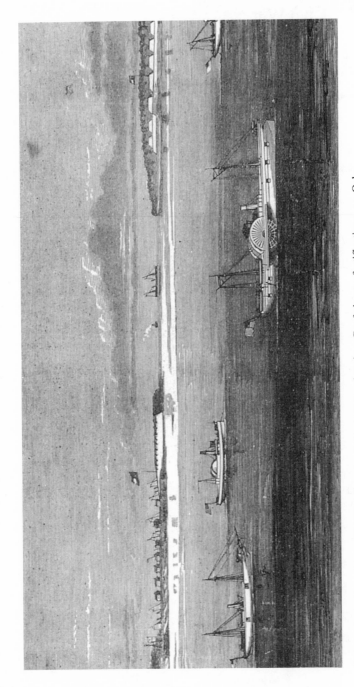

Union blockading ships off Old Inlet near Wilmington, showing Confederate fortifications on Oak Island (left), and Fort Holmes on Bald Head Island (right). *Harper's Pictorial History*

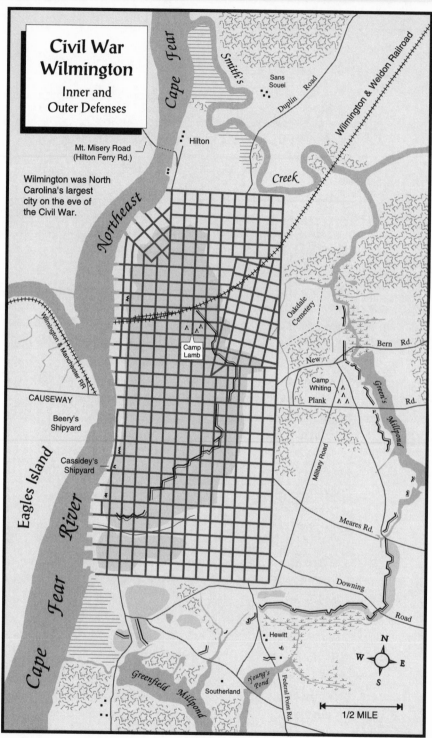

Civil War Wilmington

Inner and Outer Defenses

Mt. Misery Road
(Hilton Ferry Rd.)

Wilmington was North
Carolina's largest city on the eve of
the Civil War.

Cape Fear

Smith's

Sans Souei

Duplin Road

Wilmington & Weldon Railroad

Hilton

Creek

Northeast

Wilmington & Manchester RR

CAUSEWAY

Beery's Shipyard

Cassidey's Shipyard

Eagles Island

Cape Fear River

Camp Lamb

Oakdale Cemetery

Bern Rd.

New

Camp Whiting

Plank

Green's Millpond

Rd.

Military Road

Meares Rd.

Downing

Road

Hewitt

Cape Fear

Greenfield Millpond

Southerland

Young's Pond

Federal Point Rd.

N
W   E
S

1/2 MILE

Mark A. Moore

Chapter 2

"Not fortifications, but fiftyfications at least"

– Lt. Col. George Deas, chief of staff to Lt. Gen. Stephen D. Lee

THE FORTS

Confederate President Jefferson Davis visited Wilmington twice during the war. His first visit was in May 1861, while making his way from Montgomery, Alabama, to Richmond to assume his role as chief executive in the new Southern capital, and once again in early November 1863, on a return trip to Virginia from Tennessee. From the evening of November 5 to the morning of the 7th, the president visited with military officers, civilian dignitaries and prominent citizens. Although he spent considerable energy rubbing shoulders with these luminaries, Davis spent most of his time inspecting Wilmington's defenses—the number, appearance, and strength of which made a strong impression upon him. "He expressed himself much gratified," noted an observer, and pledged to do all in his power to safeguard the Confederacy's most important seaport.[1]

As Davis attested, a vast network of defenses protected the city of Wilmington. The fortifications also guarded the seaport's two inlets while shielding blockade runners and protecting the network of railroads feeding into and out of the city. Confederate engineers utilized abundant local resources—including sand and sod, slaves, Carolina heart pine, palmetto and live oak trees—to build a chain of earthen forts, batteries, and fieldworks stretching from Lockwood's Folly on the South Carolina line to Virginia Creek, twenty-five miles north of Wilmington. Next to Charleston, Wilmington was the most heavily fortified city on the Atlantic seaboard. "[The works are] not fortifications, but fiftyfications at least," exclaimed Lt. Col.

George Deas, a Confederate staff officer who inspected the Cape Fear forts in early 1864.[2]

While the city had more than its share of entrenchments, it lacked sufficient troops to man both the miles of fortified lines and the Cape Fear District's 100-mile-long coastline. Federal sailors occasionally exploited this weakness by launching shoreline excursions aimed at damaging salt-making facilities, confiscating supplies, terrorizing residents, and liberating slaves.

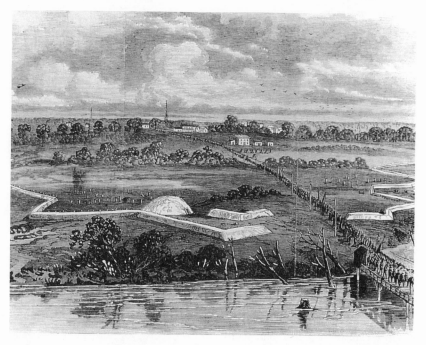

Wilmington's outer defenses at Green's Millpond (present day Burnt Mill Creek) on the Plank Road (Market Street). *Author's Collection*

On the night of April 21, 1864, a Federal landing party sabotaged the N. C. Salt Works near Whiskey Creek on Masonboro Sound and kidnapped about one-third of its work force. This vulnerability was ¸ot lost on the local Confederate high command. Wilmington and its main approaches, however, were heavily fortified, and until late in the war the Federals made no attempt to attack the city.

And for good reason. Brigadier General Joseph Reid Anderson and the district commanders who followed him planned and supervised the con-

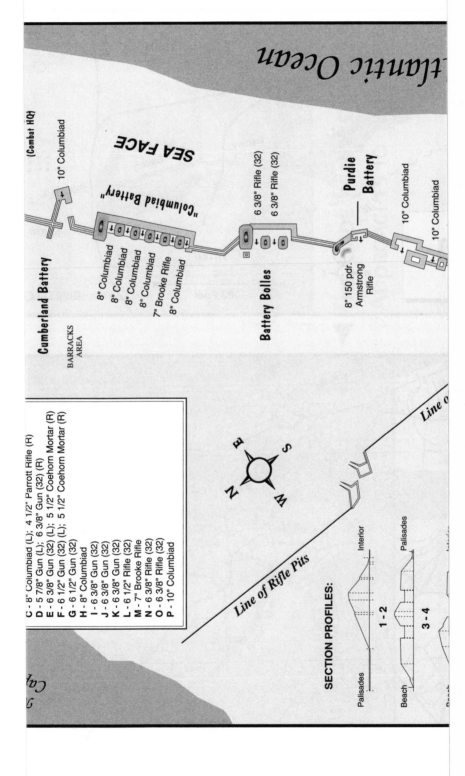

Atlantic Ocean

(Combat HQ)
10" Columbiad

SEA FACE

"Columbiad Battery"

Cumberland Battery

BARRACKS AREA

8" Columbiad
8" Columbiad
8" Columbiad
8" Columbiad
7" Brooke Rifle
8" Columbiad

6 3/8" Rifle (32)
6 3/8" Rifle (32)

Battery Bolles

Purdie Battery

8" 150 pdr. Armstrong Rifle

10" Columbiad

10" Columbiad

C - 8" Columbiad (L); 4 1/2" Parrott Rifle (R)
D - 5 7/8" Gun (L); 6 3/8" Gun (32) (R)
E - 6 3/8" Gun (32) (L); 5 1/2" Coehorn Mortar (R)
F - 6 1/2" Gun (32) (L); 5 1/2" Coehorn Mortar (R)
G - 6 1/2" Gun (32)
H - 8" Columbiad
I - 6 3/8" Gun (32)
J - 6 3/8" Gun (32)
K - 6 3/8" Gun (32)
L - 6 1/2" Rifle (32)
M - 7" Brooke Rifle
N - 6 3/8" Rifle (32)
O - 6 3/8" Rifle (32)
P - 10" Columbiad

Line of Rifle Pits

Line o

SECTION PROFILES:

Palisades
Interior
1 - 2
Beach

Palisades
3 - 4

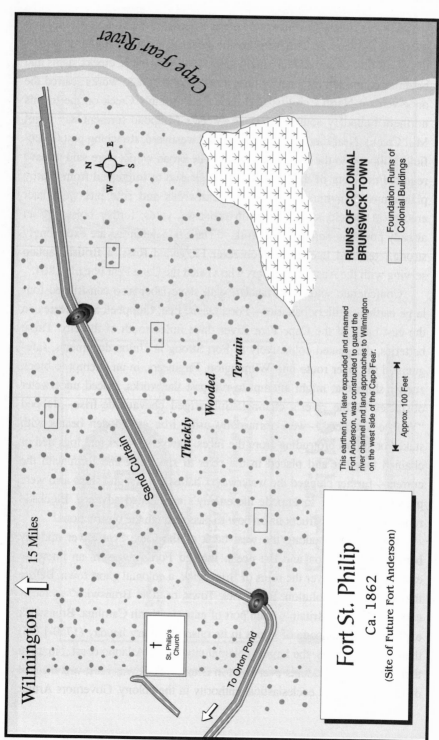

Wilmington ← 15 Miles

Cape Fear River

N
W E
S

Sand Curtain

Thickly Wooded Terrain

St. Philip's Church

To Orton Pond

RUINS OF COLONIAL BRUNSWICK TOWN

☐ Foundation Ruins of Colonial Buildings

This earthen fort, later expanded and renamed Fort Anderson, was constructed to guard the river channel and land approaches to Wilmington on the west side of the Cape Fear.

↔ Approx. 100 Feet

Fort St. Philip

Ca. 1862

(Site of Future Fort Anderson)

Mark A. Moore

Dobbs and William Tryon both lived at Brunswick Town for a time, and it was also the home of St. Philip's Church, one of two grand Episcopal houses of worship in the parish.

The emergence of Wilmington further upriver went hand-in-hand with Brunswick Town's decline. As one observer wryly noted, "Wilmington first became Brunswick's rival and then its gravedigger."[7] Brunswick found it difficult to compete with Wilmington, which was more conveniently located for commercial and population growth, and more safely tucked away from hurricanes that threatened the Carolina coast during the summer and autumn months. Wilmington absorbed the trade of planters along the upper branches of the Cape Fear River and flourished, resulting in a general exodus from Brunswick by 1775. It was the Revolutionary War, however, that doomed the struggling town. British troops sacked Brunswick when they raided the lower Cape Fear in the spring of 1776, and it lost all political leverage when the newly-created state legislature moved Brunswick County's seat of government to Lockwood's Folly, a place of relative safety from the Redcoats.[8]

Some former residents and squatters lived among the ruins of Old Brunswick until about 1840, but when Confederate engineers surveyed the site on March 22, 1862, thick vegetation had reclaimed the remnants of the old homes, the warehouses along the river front, and the governor's "palace" at Russellborough, a stone's throw north of town. Cedar trees of considerable size were also growing on top of the walls of St. Philip's Church. Brigadier General Samuel Gibbs French, Joseph Anderson's successor as of March 15, 1862, assigned Lt. Thomas W. Rowland, Cadet of Engineers, to "superintend the construction of a battery and line of intrenchments" at Brunswick. At that point the Cape Fear River was more than a mile wide, though the channel ran abreast of the west bank. French wanted a fort to guard both the channel and the land approaches to Wilmington from the west.[9]

Lieutenant Rowland set about his task by laying a straight line of earthworks through the middle of Brunswick Town, abutting the remains of the old courthouse, several homes and St. Philip's Church. Rowland intentionally covered many of the buildings' foundations and crumbled chimneys with his earthworks because he feared that the brick and ballast stones might become a hailstorm of life-threatening debris if hit by enemy artillery shells. Under Rowland (and subsequent engineers as the war progressed), laborers salvaged the stones and bricks to help build barracks for the soldiers. St. Philip's Church, whose ancient four-foot-thick brick walls are still standing, was left untouched. In fact, the earthwork fort was initially named for the old church. On May 11, 1862, Maj. William Lamb, the post commandant, christened the bastion Fort St. Philip, in tribute to the "silent witness to the successful struggle of our fathers for liberty and independence."[10]

On July 1, 1863, the earthwork was renamed Fort Anderson on behalf of Brig. Gen. George Burgwyn Anderson. Anderson, a native of Hillsborough, North Carolina, was a West Point graduate and lieutenant of dragoons in the U. S. Army before resigning his commission to become colonel of the 4th North Carolina Infantry. Described by one contemporary as a "furious fighter," Anderson received a battlefield promotion to brigadier general after impressing President Davis with his nerve and leadership at Williamsburg in the spring of 1862. He went on to lead his brigade in combat at Malvern Hill, South Mountain and Sharpsburg. While fighting in the latter battle near the Bloody Lane, a bullet found the general's right foot. Though not initially considered a life-threatening wound, infection set in and amputation of the limb became necessary. Anderson never recovered and died in Raleigh, North Carolina, on October 16, 1862.[11]

Work on the fort named in General Anderson's honor continued for almost three years. When completed, it was the area's strongest interior defensive work, mounting nine heavy cannon emplaced behind two massive twenty-four foot high earthen batteries along the river front. This powerful river-based artillery position was connected to a defensive sand curtain that extended west for almost one mile to Orton Pond. Buoyed mines (called "torpedoes") and pilings in the river complemented the fort's defenses. Fort Anderson also served as a clearing house and quarantine station where incoming blockade runners were checked for proper manifest papers, illegal cargoes ("Yankee goods"), and contagious diseases.[12]

Another considerable fortification, Fort Pender, built on the site of colonial Fort Johnston, protected Smithville's harbor. The original fort on the site was named for Royal Governor Gabriel Johnston, one of colonial Wilmington's biggest promoters. Fort Johnston was the Cape Fear's oldest existing defensive work. Commissioned in 1745, the fort was erected to guard the lower Cape Fear region against invasion by the Spanish, the French and pirates. Construction progressed slowly at first and had not been completed when two Spanish sloops sailed into the river in 1748 to attack Brunswick Town. After a brief battle, during which one of the Spanish vessels—the *Fortuna*—was blown up, the Spaniards retreated. The invasion prompted the British to increase their efforts to protect their interests along the Cape Fear, and the Crown supplied enough money to complete Fort Johnston by 1750. Unfortunately, it was a small, poorly constructed "tabby work" fort—a concretion of sand, lime, and oyster shells so weak that parts of it crumbled each time a cannon was fired from the parapet. The old fort was in a state of disrepair when the Cape Fear militiamen seized it from a U. S. Army fort keeper in 1861. Confederate engineers, who revamped and strengthened Fort Johnston by covering it with dirt and mounting seacoast guns, renamed it Fort Branch, for Brig. Gen. Lawrence O'Bryan Branch, who was shot through the head at Sharpsburg. It was later renamed Fort Pender, for Maj. Gen. William Dorsey Pender, who died from an infected wound suffered at Gettysburg. Both officers were prominent North Carolinians.[13]

The most important forts guarding Wilmington, however, were those located at the inlets to the Cape Fear River. The dual inlets offered blockade runners greater access to the harbor, but they also presented a series of defensive dilemmas for Confederate engineers. The distance from one another, separated as they were by Bald Head Island, was both a strength and a weakness, subjecting them to separate attacks by land and sea from the north or south. The defenses guarding each inlet were too far apart to assist one another in case of an attack; the fall of one inlet would probably result in the loss of the other. Thus a combination of strong mainland defenses, adequate transportation and communication between the inlets' fortifications, and ironclads to protect the harbor were essential to Wilmington's survival.[14]

Two substantial forts and a small battery on Oak Island guarded Old Inlet from the west. On the east end of the island stood Fort Caswell, an aging coastal installation built by U.S. Army engineers between 1826 and 1838. Named for North Carolina's first governor, Richard Caswell, Fort Caswell was designed and built as part of the U. S. coast defense after the War of 1812. It was an enclosed pentagonal casemated brick work with scarp walls loop-holed for musketry, flanked by caponniers and surrounded by a moat, or ditch. One of the fort's most famous early visitors was Robert E. Lee, a young lieutenant colonel of engineers making an inspection tour of

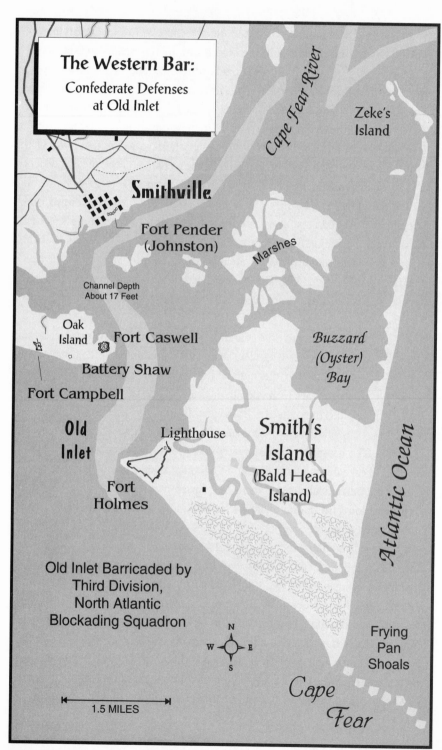

The Western Bar:
Confederate Defenses
at Old Inlet

Cape Fear River

Zeke's
Island

Smithville

Fort Pender
(Johnston)

Marshes

Channel Depth
About 17 Feet

Oak
Island
Fort Caswell

Battery Shaw

Buzzard
(Oyster)
Bay

Fort Campbell

Old
Inlet

Lighthouse

Smith's
Island
(Bald Head
Island)

Fort
Holmes

Atlantic Ocean

Old Inlet Barricaded by
Third Division,
North Atlantic
Blockading Squadron

N
W — E
S

Frying
Pan
Shoals

Cape
Fear

1.5 MILES

Mark A. Moore

coastal fortifications in the autumn of 1840.[15] Fort Caswell was also the site of one of the first overt actions against the United States during the secession crisis.

Concerned about a possible showdown at Wilmington between the Federal government and North Carolina similar to the potentially ruinous confrontation then developing at Charleston, a group of Southern nationalists calling themselves the Cape Fear Minute Men descended on Fort Caswell and Fort Johnston at Smithville on January 9, 1861. From information the militiamen deemed reliable, a revenue cutter—either the *Forward* or the *Harriet Lane*—was rushing U. S. troops to garrison Fort Caswell, much as Maj. Robert Anderson had done at Fort Sumter on December 26, 1860. Led by John J. Hedrick of Wilmington, the Cape Fear Minute Men quickly forced the surrender of Fort Johnston from Ord. Sgt. James Reilly. Hedrick and twenty others, accompanied by the Smithville Guards under Capt. Stephen D. Thurstin and a crowd of Smithville citizens, rowed across the harbor to take possession of Fort Caswell from its caretaker, Sgt. Frederick Dardingkiller. As soon as he received the news of the Cape Fear Minute Mens' action, Governor John W. Ellis ordered Hedrick and Thurstin to return the forts to U. S. authorities. North Carolina was still in the Union. With the existing relationship between the state and Federal governments, Ellis would not permit the unauthorized occupation of the forts.[16]

Only days after the firing on Fort Sumter, however, Governor Ellis instructed Col. John L. Cantwell, commander of the 30th North Carolina Militia, to take Forts Caswell and Johnston "without delay, and hold them until further orders against all comers." On April 16, Cantwell and 126 men from four local militia companies, the Wilmington Light Infantry, German Volunteers, Wilmington Rifle Guards and the Cape Fear Light Artillery, seized control of the forts. The captures took place five weeks before North Carolina passed its secession ordinance of May 20, 1861, but by then many North Carolinians believed it was only a matter of time before the state joined the Confederacy. The Southerners strengthened Fort Caswell by erecting a huge sand rampart around the old brick casemate walls and adding gun chambers and traverses. They also armed it with an imported British 8-inch 150-pounder Armstrong gun, five 6.4-inch 32-pounders, and two 8-inch, one 9-inch and six 10-inch columbiad smoothbore cannon. A mile to the west of Caswell stood Fort Campbell, a "well proportioned" sixteen-gun, two-mortar sand fortification. Between the two forts lay Battery Shaw, a small one-gun affair.[17]

To protect Old Inlet from the east and to defend the island against an amphibious assault, the Confederates built Fort Holmes on Bald Head Island. Bald Head was a semi-tropical paradise covered with thick groves of live oak and palmetto trees, exotic plants and numerous fresh water ponds and swamps full of snakes and alligators. The fort was named for Lt. Gen. Theophilus H. Holmes, organizer and early commander of the Southern Department of Coastal Defenses. Construction on the fort began in early September 1863, and though incomplete when abandoned sixteen months later, it contained one-and-a-half miles of earthworks interspersed with gun emplacements mounting eleven heavy seacoast cannon. The works extended from Bald Head Point, where the Cape Fear River met the ocean, up the south beach and then north across the island to Light House Creek. Despite its unfinished state, Fort Holmes discouraged the Federals from attempting to invade Bald Head Island. Its capture would have provided the Northerners with a base of operations and a siege line against Smithville and the forts guarding Old Inlet and New Inlet.[18]

Like Old Inlet, New Inlet was also protected by artillery emplacements and earthworks. Shore batteries guarded the beach strand on Federal Point and Masonboro Sound north of New Inlet. The most notable of these were Battery Anderson ("Flag Pond Battery" in Union accounts) and Battery Gatlin ("Half Moon Battery" to the Federals because of its crescent shape). Confederate artillerymen used batteries along the beach to duel with Union gunboats and safeguard stranded blockade runners that had been chased ashore—at least until their cargoes had been salvaged. Protecting the river on the east side was a gun battery on the summit of Sugar Loaf, a large fifty-foot-high sand dune on Federal Point peninsula directly opposite Fort Anderson. When Wilmington was seriously threatened by attack in 1864, Confederate engineers dug entrenchments from Sugar Loaf across the peninsula to Myrtle Sound, within sight of the ocean.[19]

Even with these impressive strategically placed forts and batteries, the key to Wilmington's defenses was Fort Fisher, the main guardian of New Inlet. Confederate authorities deemed the massive earthen fort impregnable, and with good reason. Colonel William Lamb, the fort's commander after the first year of the war, strengthened and expanded it from a patchwork of

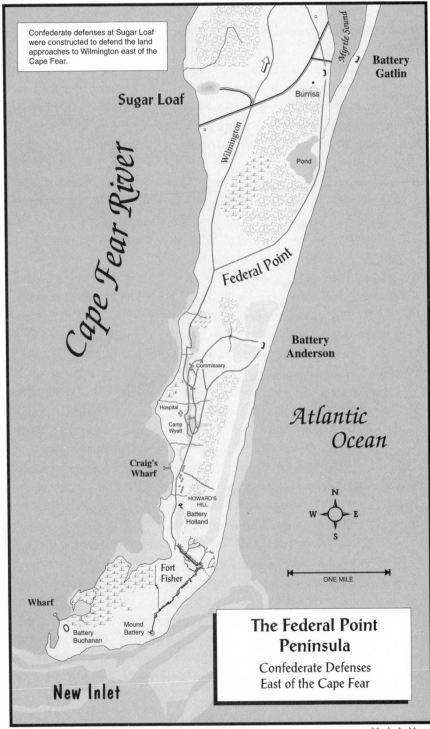

Confederate defenses at Sugar Loaf were constructed to defend the land approaches to Wilmington east of the Cape Fear.

Myrtle Sound

Battery Gatlin

Sugar Loaf

Burriss

Wilmington

Pond

Cape Fear River

Federal Point

Battery Anderson

Commissary

Hospital

Camp Wyatt

Atlantic Ocean

Craig's Wharf

HOWARD'S HILL

Battery Holland

N
W   E
S

Fort Fisher

ONE MILE

Wharf

Mound Battery

Battery Buchanan

The Federal Point Peninsula

Confederate Defenses
East of the Cape Fear

New Inlet

Mark A. Moore

sand batteries "one of the Federal frigates could have cleaned out with a few broadsides" into the most powerful seacoast fortification in the Confederacy.[20]

The earthworks comprising Fort Fisher stood on Federal Point, a narrow sand peninsula bounded by the Atlantic Ocean to the east and the Cape Fear River to the west. The sandy peninsula, aptly referred to as Confederate Point by its occupiers, tapered to a point at New Inlet. Federal Point was a desolate spot when Confederate engineers first surveyed it in the spring of 1861. Remnants of an ancient maritime forest of long leaf pine, live oaks, turkey oaks, scrub oaks, co-mingled with pocosins, thickets and small ponds coated the sand spit. Only a smattering of watermen and their families dared live so far from civilization. Yet Federal Point buzzed with activity when Confederate soldiers descended on the area to transform it into one of the South's most valuable forts.

On April 16, 1861, Col. John L. Cantwell was instructed to "make a sand battery" on Federal Point to guard New Inlet. But on or about April 24, it was Maj. Charles Pattison Bolles, not Cantwell, who began erecting artillery batteries about a mile from the tip of Federal Point. Bolles, a civil engineer intimately familiar with the area, had worked with John Newland Maffitt (who would become one of the Confederacy's most famous naval officers) on the Coast Geodetic Survey of Cape Fear in the 1850s. The design and location of Bolles' batteries were approved by Lt. Gen. Theophilus H. Holmes and then Maj. W. H. C. Whiting. Whiting, one of the Confederacy's top engineers and the inspector general of the defenses of North Carolina, was also Charles P. Bolles' brother-in-law. Under Whiting's supervision, Bolles erected his largest work close to the seashore with a direct line of fire on New Inlet, should Union warships try to squeeze into the harbor. A smaller battery was placed further up the beach.[21]

About two weeks later Bolles was transferred to Oak Island to oversee construction of a sand battery there. On May 7, Capt. William Lord DeRosset took over the defense of Federal Point at the head of the Wilmington Light Infantry, the first company of garrison troops to see duty at what would eventually become Fort Fisher. DeRosset stayed on the peninsula only ten days or so, but he was there long enough to strengthen Bolles' largest battery by adding one hundred yards of breastworks and mounting two 24-pounder smoothbore cannon en barbette, that is, elevated to fire over the parapet. DeRosset christened this redoubt "Battery Bolles," in honor of its architect. It was Fort Fisher's first armed redoubt.[22]

Construction on Federal Point continued in fits and starts throughout the summer and autumn of 1861. Progress on the batteries was haphazard at best as commanders came and went in "a babel of confusion," scoffed one officer. At least ten different officers directed work on the defenses in the first sixteen months of the war, largely because many of the best qualified to supervise the erection of defenses on Federal Point were transferred to other theaters of operations.[23] Major Whiting, for example, left for Virginia on May 15, 1861, to serve as chief engineer on Brig. Gen. Joseph E. Johnston's staff. Three days later, William Lord DeRosset, a member of one of Cape Fear's oldest and most prominent families, was promoted to major of the 3rd North Carolina Infantry and ordered to Virginia as well.[24] Construction on the batteries at New Inlet slowed during the summer as the Confederates concentrated on establishing Camp Wyatt, a camp of muster and instruction, one mile-and-a-half north of Battery Bolles. On August 31, 1861, Seawell (or Sewall) L. Fremont, colonel of the 1st Corps of North Carolina Volunteer Artillery and Engineers and a Wilmingtonian, was put in charge of the coast defense from the New River south to the South Carolina line. Fremont had been supervising fortification construction at the Cape Fear for most of the summer. Like Whiting, Fremont focused attention on developing batteries to guard the inlets at Wilmington in general, and particularly New Inlet.[25]

Seawell Fremont was a West point graduate and an assistant engineer in the pre-war U.S. Army. Fremont was also an old friend of William T. Sherman, although Sherman never forgave Fremont for rejecting his oath to the United States and joining the Confederate army. Assisted by John C. Winder and Richard K. Meade, both captains of North Carolina Engineers, Fremont planned and constructed extensive works on Federal Point. Fremont and Winder laid out a seashore casemate battery, Battery Meade, above Battery Bolles, started the two-gun Winder's Battery on Zeke's Island, a tidal marsh on the south side of New Inlet, built Batteries Anderson and Gatlin along the beach to the north, and fortified Camp Wyatt.[26] During his tenure as commander at the Cape Fear—probably in mid-September 1861—Fremont named the earthworks at the southern end of Federal Point "Fort Fisher." He did this to memorialize Charles Frederick Fisher, the popular colonel of the 6th North Carolina Infantry who was killed "while gallantly leading his men" in the Battle of Manassas on July 21, 1861. Before the war Fremont, then superintendent of the Wilmington & Weldon Railroad, had been a friend of Fisher, who was at that time president of the North Carolina Railroad.[27]

Lieutenant Samuel A. Ashe prepared Federal Point's ordnance for battle. Machinery for rifling cannon was brought in from Charleston, and old 6.4-inch 32-pounder smoothbore guns were modernized for greater shooting distance and accuracy. The timing on the ordnance improvements proved auspicious. Union blockaders often positioned themselves just two miles from shore to lob shells at Confederate work parties, driving them from their posts. Once emplaced, the newly rifled cannon kept the blockaders at a respectful distance and gave laborers and soldiers a greater sense of security as they labored to strengthen their defenses.[28]

In early September 1861, Brig. Gen. Joseph R. Anderson superseded Fremont as overall commander at Wilmington. Anderson was the first commander appointed by Richmond to head the District of the Cape Fear, North Carolina's Third Military District, established in December 1861. When Fremont decided to return to work as superintendent of the Wilmington & Weldon Railroad in January 1862, Anderson recommended John J. Hedrick, captain of the Cape Fear Light Artillery, to command Fort Fisher. Working first under Anderson's guidance and then under Brig. Gen. Samuel G. French, Anderson's successor, Hedrick remained in command on Federal Point until the summer of 1862. During that time construction and ordnance projects at Fort Fisher continued uninterrupted.[29]

Yet, few if any of these men would be as inextricably linked to the fate of the mammoth Federal Point bastion as Col. William Lamb, who in July 1862 was just another in a string of officers assigned to command Fort Fisher. The fort's new commandant had only just been elected colonel of the 36th North Carolina Regiment (2nd North Carolina Artillery). Lamb had been transferred across the river from his previous command post at Fort St. Philip, while his predecessor at Fort Fisher, Capt. John J. Hedrick, was sent as his replacement to the fort at Brunswick Town. When the young officer arrived at Fort Fisher about noon on July 4, he was probably appalled at what he found there, for its batteries were still scattered and poorly armed despite a year's worth of preparation. Lamb spent his first day on Federal

Point inspecting the battlements, and concluded that "as a defense of New Inlet against a Federal fleet, they amounted to nothing."[30]

Near the seashore, he found a quadrilateral work (Fort Fisher) mounting just six cannon, the largest of which were two 8-inch columbiads. The fort was flanked to the west and south by five detached batteries armed with eleven additional pieces of heavy artillery, four of them casemated in Battery Meade near the seashore. Yet Lamb considered only one of the seventeen cannon—a "long ranged rifle gun"—a piece of modern ordnance.[31]

Col. William Lamb of the 36th North Carolina Regiment (2nd North Carolina Artillery), gifted novice military engineer and commander of Fort Fisher. *Courtesy of William Lamb*

Lamb believed the Confederates had been fortunate Union gunboats had not pummeled both the work parties and the cluster of earthworks. He had personally witnessed the devastating effect of 11-inch Dahlgren shells and had read about the power of a 15-inch shell. "The frigate *Minnesota* could have destroyed the works and driven us out in a few hours," Lamb asserted.[32] The colonel determined at once to build a fortification of such size and strength that it could withstand the fury of the U.S. Navy's heaviest guns. But could he succeed where others had thus far faltered?

Nothing in William Lamb's past suggested he possessed innate talent as a military engineer. He was born on September 7, 1835, to a prominent and affluent family, residents of the Hampton Roads, Virginia area since before the American Revolution. Lamb's father, a noted lawyer, had served as mayor of Norfolk. The family's sprawling estate, Kenmure, occupied an entire city block near the port's waterfront, and Lamb enjoyed all the advantages of a young tidewater Virginia gentleman: good upbringing, attentive servants, and a fine education. As a teenager he attended the Rappahannock Military Academy, studying under William "Little Billy" Mahone, a future Confederate general and Lamb's post-war political ally. Lamb continued his education at William and Mary College in Williamsburg, Virginia, where he graduated Phi Beta Kappa in law. But at age twenty, Lamb was too young to take the state's bar exam, so his well-to-do father accommodated his son by purchasing half-interest in Norfolk's *Southern Daily Argus*, a Democratic newspaper that advocated secession. True to his heritage, Lamb also dabbled in local politics and commanded a militia company. Yet the extent of his military experiences when civil war broke out consisted of parading through the streets of Norfolk at the head of his infantry unit—the Woodis Rifles—and participating as an officer in the state guard at the execution of radical abolitionist John Brown in Charles Town, Virginia, on December 2, 1859.[33]

War came quickly to Hampton Roads, home of the Gosport Navy Yard and guardian of the James River and the lower Chesapeake Bay. Lamb and the Woodis Rifles manned a battery of artillery on Sewell's Point in a duel with the gunboat *Monticello* in May 1861. Although soon thereafter the Woodis Rifles became a company in the 6th Virginia Infantry, Lamb was not with his comrades when they traveled to the Virginia battlefront. Instead, he took an assignment as chief quartermaster in North Carolina, and in early

October 1861, was ordered to Wilmington. There he initially served on the staff of Brig. Gen. Joseph R. Anderson, a fellow Virginian most noted for being president of the Tredegar Irons Works in Richmond, the largest supplier of Confederate ordnance products. Lamb's devoted wife, Sarah Ann Chafee (whom he affectionately called "Daisy"), and two of their children joined him in Wilmington later that autumn.

Somehow (the circumstances remain unclear), Lamb made the transition from quartermaster to commandant of Fort St. Philip at Brunswick Town, where he was elected colonel of the 36th North Carolina Regiment, on May 14, 1862. His intelligence, dedication, and popularity secured his election as colonel. "I wish you could know him," wrote one of Lamb's admirers. "He is a Christian and a gentleman as well as a soldier."[34] "I don't believe we could have a better commander than Colonel Lamb," claimed another member of the 36th Regiment. "I like him splendid, and all the rest of the men likes him."[35] Lamb's organizational and command skills obviously impressed his then superior officer, Brig. Gen. Samuel G. French, who decided that Lamb's talents could best be utilized as commander of Fort Fisher. Daisy and the children followed him, to share "the dangers and privations" on the wild sandy beach of Federal Point. Soldiers built a small private cottage for the Lamb's one-half mile north of the fort.[36]

By then, however, Lamb was not satisfied merely to serve as post commandant. While at Fort Anderson Lamb had avidly studied the art of fortification construction, perhaps under the tutelage of his friend and adjutant Lt. Thomas W. Rowland. On a paymaster's trip to Charleston in December 1861, Lamb had purchased a book on the Crimean War, one that apparently detailed fort architecture. He became enthralled with the science of fortifications. As soon as he arrived on Federal Point, Lamb convinced General French to allow him to put to test his interest and acquired skills by completely redesigning Fort Fisher. French acquiesced, and for two-and-a-half years, under close supervision from his superiors—General French, Brig. Gen. Gabriel Rains, Brig. Gen. Louis Hébert, and Maj. Gen. W. H. C. Whiting—Lamb modified, expanded, and reinforced the fort. He built a series of elevated gun batteries which were protected by huge mounds of sand capable of absorbing the U.S. Navy's heaviest and most destructive metal projectiles. Fort Fisher's design was Lamb's own, though it was based on fortifications like the Malakoff, a Russian earthwork stronghold that had protected the city of Sevastopol in 1854, at the height of the Crimean War.

To save time and money, Lamb incorporated existing batteries into his new fort whenever possible. In some cases, Lamb had to rework or dismantle existing works because he deemed them inadequate or unsuitably positioned. Often the fort's garrison and as many as 500 slaves constructed bombproofs, barracks, magazines, gun emplacements, and mounted ordnance. When rumors of attack reached Federal Point, Lamb pushed his men harder, sometimes working them on Sundays and holidays. Though Lamb considered Fort Fisher far from complete when it was finally attacked, Confederate and Union experts alike hailed it as the largest and strongest seacoast fortification in the Confederacy, nicknaming it the "Gibraltar of the South," and the "Malakoff Tower of the South."

Shepherd's Battery from inside Fort Fisher, February 1865. The Wilmington Road entered the fort through the palisade gateway at the far left. *U.S. Army Military History Institute*

From a bird's eye view Fort Fisher looked like a giant number 7. The land face started about 100 yards from the Cape Fear River with a half bastion called Shepherd's Battery, and extended 480 yards toward the ocean, where it formed a full bastion with the sea face. The sand rampart, sodded with luxuriant marsh grass to prevent erosion, was twenty-three feet high and about twenty-five feet thick at the base. The parapet was interspersed with sixteen gun chambers mounting, en barbette (over the top) twenty-three heavy seacoast cannon: 8-inch and 10-inch columbiads; 6.4 inch 32-pounder smoothbore and rifle cannon; a 7-inch Brooke rifle; and two 24-pounder Coehorn mortars. The land face batteries were further supported by an 8-inch mortar mounted in their rear. Each artillery compartment was separated by a large traverse, an immense mound of sand nine to twelve feet higher than the parapet, to protect cannon and crews from enfilading fire. If a shell exploded in one gun chamber, soldiers and artillery in an adjacent chamber would be protected from flying shrapnel and debris. From ground level the seventeen land face traverses resembled, according to one observer, "a long row of immense haycocks."[37] Inside these traverses were hollowed-out bunkers, each containing an ordnance and powder magazine and a bombproof, where soldiers could seek refuge during a bombardment.

A minefield and a nine-foot high palisade consisting of sharpened pine logs loopholed for musketry were situated in front of the land face in the autumn of 1864. Engineers also cut a tunnel, called a postern or sally-port, through the middle of the land face so field artillery and sharpshooters could be deployed into an elevated demilune just outside of, but connected to, the fort's main walls. This position would allow the fort's defenders to fire into the flanks of attacking enemy troops. To provide an open field of fire for the defenders, the woods were cleared for half a mile north of the land face. The road to Wilmington ran along the river bank as it approached the fort at Shepherd's Battery.[38]

The land and sea fronts intersected at a full bastion, just 100 yards from the ocean's high water mark. This huge thirty-two-foot high battery in the northeast corner of the fort contained two large cannon: an 8-inch columbiad and an 8-inch Blakely rifle. From there the sea face defenses paralleled the shoreline for approximately 1,300 yards. A seventy-five yard four-gun emplacement, built in the same massive style as the land face batteries, connected with the northeast bastion. Joining this was a crescent shaped

Fort Fisher's most famous piece of ordnance: a British-made 8-inch 150-pounder Armstrong gun, mounted in Purdie Battery on the sea face. *U.S. Army Military History Institute*

earthwork—Battery Meade—originally built for casemated guns but converted by Colonel Lamb into a bombproofed hospital. Its protruding shape
reminded soldiers of a preacher's pulpit, so they referred to it as simply "the
Pulpit." The remainder of the sea front comprised eight self-contained batteries mounting an additional eighteen pieces of heavy ordnance, mostly
columbiads and Brooke rifles, all connected by a broad sand curtain.[39] The
pride of Fort Fisher's sea face ordnance collection, however, was a British-
made 8-inch 150-pounder Armstrong gun, imported as a gift for the Confederacy from Sir W. G. Armstrong & Co. of London in 1864. It came mounted
on a beautiful mahogany and rosewood carriage fitted with brass hardware
which, according to one soldier, made its appearance so ornamental that it
looked more like a piece of parlor furniture than a cannon. The gun crew
was so proud of it, so the story goes, that they worked diligently to keep it
bright and shiny.[40]

On the southern-most point of the sea face towered a forty-three-foot-
high conical shaped gun emplacement formally named Battery Lamb but
dubbed "the Mound." It was perhaps Colonel Lamb's most impressive engineering feat and, to be sure, Fort Fisher's most notable landmark. Laborers

constructed Battery Lamb during March-April of 1863 using a steam engine. The machine pulled cartloads of sand up an inclined railway to the top of scaffolding before dumping the sand over the side to create an enormous dune. When completed, the "Mound Battery's" massive profile could be seen for miles by blockade runners approaching New Inlet, and they came to depend on it for navigation and protection. Mounted on top of Battery Lamb were signal lights and two seacoast guns, a 10-inch columbiad and a 6.4-inch rifled 32-pounder, with a direct line of plunging fire into New Inlet's channel.[41]

New Inlet was further protected by Battery Buchanan, an elliptically-shaped earthwork constructed at the tip of Federal Point mounted with two 11-inch Brooke smoothbores and two 10-inch columbiads. Upon its completion in October 1864, Reddin Pittman, the talented young engineer who designed the battery, wanted to name it Augusta Battery on behalf of his girlfriend. The district commander overruled Pittman's sentimental request, however, and named it Battery Buchanan, in honor of Admiral Franklin Buchanan of the C. S. Navy. Battery Buchanan was also intended to be used as a citadel where Fort Fisher's garrison might retreat or reinforcements safely sent in under cover of darkness.[42]

The Cape Fear's massive earthwork defenses—Fort Fisher in particular—impressed everyone who viewed them, from President Jefferson Davis to the Union naval officers just offshore watching the forts and batteries being constructed. Rumor had it, wrote one Federal officer, that Fort Fisher "is a work of more labor than the pyramids." "The forts are superb works," exclaimed B. Lewis Blackford, a Confederate engineer assigned to Wilmington in the autumn of 1863. "I have seen no works anywhere in the Confederacy that would at all compare with them. [They are built] to withstand an indefinite hammering from any ordnance now known. General Whiting's great skill as an Engineer is shown at every step."[43]

The man most responsible for the Cape Fear's formidable defenses was Maj. Gen. William Henry Chase Whiting. Chase Whiting was regarded as one of the best engineers in the country, rivaling even his close friend P. G. T. Beauregard. Whiting's reputation was well-deserved, dating back to his school days at West Point and his work in the U. S. Army's pre-war Engineer Corps. Indeed, he seemed destined for greatness as a career army officer. His grandfather had fought in the American Revolution and his father, Levi Whiting, served in the U. S. Army for forty-one years, from the War of 1812 until his death in 1853 as a lieutenant colonel of the 1st Artillery.[44]

Whiting's parents came from Massachusetts, but he was born in the frontier town of Biloxi, Mississippi, on March 22, 1824. Though Southern-born, he was Northern-bred, his father having been reassigned to posts in the Northeast when Whiting was just a child. In 1833-1834, Levi Whiting served a stint at Fort Columbus on Governor's Island in New York harbor. Young Chase undoubtedly spent some of his time there exploring the fort's gun emplacements and casemates where, in a cruel twist of fate, he would return to die as a prisoner-of-war thirty-one years later.[45]

It soon became obvious that young Whiting was blessed with extraordinary intelligence and talent. At age twelve he enrolled in the Public High School of Boston, and later, when only fourteen years old, entered Georgetown College in Washington. Remarkably, Whiting completed the four-year college program in half that time, finishing second in his class. It was said that he could speak Latin fluently and not only surpassed most of his classmates intellectually, but could beat the majority of them in athletic competitions and games. He was especially good at shooting marbles.[46]

Because of his scholastic achievements and in part because of his father's high position in the army, Whiting received from President John Tyler an at-large appointment to the U.S. Military Academy in 1841. Four years later he graduated number one in his class with the highest grades ever attained by a cadet up to that time. He ranked first in nine of eleven subjects: Mathematics, Grammar, Philosophy, Drawing, Ethics, Chemistry and Mineralogy, Tactics, Artillery, and Engineering. He placed second in French and fourth in Conduct. Whiting's accomplishments were all the more impressive considering the graduating class of forty-one members included the likes of Louis Hébert, William F. "Baldy" Smith, Charles P. Stone, Fitz John Porter, and Barnard Bee—all of whom gained considerable distinction during the Civil War, although there is no record of how well they played marbles.[47]

Whiting's ranking at West Point elevated him into the U. S. Army's elite Engineer Corps. Commissioned a second lieutenant, Whiting's first assignment sent him to the Southwest, where he helped lay out a military road from San Antonio to El Paso, Texas, while fighting Comanches. Afterward, Whiting supervised river and harbor improvements and fortification

Maj. Gen. William Henry Chase Whiting. This magnificent image, the only known full standing portrait of the brilliant but broody commander of the District of the Cape Fear, was recently-discovered by Charles V. Peery. *South Carolina Historical Society, Charleston*

construction at Fort Pickens in Pensacola, Florida; Fort Carroll near Baltimore (then under the command of Lt. Col. Robert E. Lee); Fort Point in San Francisco; Fort Caswell near Wilmington; and Fort Pulaski in Savannah, Georgia. He was considered one of the best engineers in the country, "one of those engineers whom God, not West Point makes," noted the *Wilmington Daily North Carolinian*. He was promoted to first lieutenant on March 16, 1853, and captain December 13, 1858, a rank he held until he resigned his commission on February 20, 1861.[48]

When Georgia seceded from the Union, Whiting was stationed in Savannah, from which point he offered his services to the state. Governor Joseph Brown appointed Whiting major of state engineers, the same rank the Provisional Confederate Army offered to him on February 23, 1861. Despite his Northern heritage, Whiting surprised many by shunning his oath of allegiance to the United States and taking up a revolutionary cause against the country he had served illustriously for fifteen years. In defense of his decision, James R. Randall, a blockade running employee in Wilmington, explained that Whiting's "blood was all meridian." Whiting was not only Southern-born, but had spent most of his adult life in the South and had married a Southern lady, Katherine Davis Walker, described as "a pretty and agreeable" young belle from Wilmington. Over the years he had become deeply attached to the South, its people and culture—a way of life he intended to defend at all costs.[49]

As expected, Major Whiting's service in the Confederate army began with great promise. General P. G. T. Beauregard capitalized on Whiting's engineering talents in developing Charleston's defenses early in the war, where it was rumored that Whiting was the brains behind Beauregard's brawn. On April 21, 1861, Whiting accepted a position as inspector general of North Carolina's coastal defenses, headquartered in Wilmington. There he helped plan defenses for Cape Fear, his adopted home. But most of all Whiting craved a field command. When the opportunity arrived, he jumped at the chance to go to Harpers Ferry, Virginia, in mid-May 1861, to serve under his long-time friend, Gen. Joseph E. Johnston.

For his good work in transferring troops to Manassas in July of that year Whiting received a battlefield promotion to brigadier general from Jefferson Davis himself. Ironically, Whiting inherited the brigade of Barnard Bee, his popular West Point classmate who had been mortally wounded at Manassas.

In the spring and summer of 1862, Whiting commanded a division during the fighting against Maj. Gen. George B. McClellan's Army of the Potomac on the Peninsula. At Gaines' Mills, his division battled a force commanded by Fitz John Porter, Whiting's roommate at West Point. Impressed with Whiting, President Davis praised him as "heroic and highly gifted." Robert E. Lee called him a "good engineer and a hard laborer." Joe Johnston considered Whiting so wise that he called him "Solomon." Despite the noble endorsements, a dark side to Whiting's character emerged, personality traits that thrust him into disfavor with the Confederate high command, and led to his banishment from the war's main theater.[50]

Whiting's rapid advancement from major to brigadier general in just five months filled him with justifiable pride. His high position and his first rate intellect—of which he himself was thoroughly conscious—may have gone to his head. Whiting's critics described him as arrogant; his defenders, self-confident. Whichever it may have been, Whiting soon became critical of Davis' conduct of military affairs. It did not take long for his outspokenness and candor to alienate him from the Richmond authorities.

In the fall of 1861, President Davis directed General Johnston to reorganize his army so that regiments would be brigaded by state and led by general officers from those states. Whiting, then a brigadier in Johnston's army, did not want a purely Mississippi brigade and refused to obey what he believed was a foolish and suicidal policy. "[My troops] are used to me and I to them, and accustomed to act together," Whiting argued forcefully. "If [the authorities] in Richmond persist, they will be guilty of inconceivable folly." As far as Whiting was concerned, politicians had no business meddling in military affairs. His brash stance deeply offended Jefferson Davis, who had commanded a regiment of Mississippians in the Mexican War and who considered himself a military leader first and a politician second. Davis instructed General Johnston to rebuke Whiting for his "mutinous and disorganizing spirit." Unfortunately, the growing rancor between Whiting and his superiors did not end there. The following year Davis had to deal with a rumor that Whiting wanted Davis deposed and Joe Johnston elevated to military dictator of the Confederacy. And so it went.[51]

By the autumn of 1862, Davis had had enough of Whiting, believing him to be imperious, insolent, and insubordinate. Whiting complained to General Lee, but Lee thought that the clashes between Whiting and the

President were destructive. Besides, Lee too found Whiting annoying. However they may have regarded and disliked his personality, Davis and Lee were wise enough to not overlook Whiting's superior engineering skills. They may have wanted to remove the difficult general from the Virginia battlefront, but they still had need for his talents. As a result, when Lee restructured his army Whiting was quietly transferred to Wilmington. Whiting considered himself a victim of the army's reorganization but dutifully accepted his fate.[52]

In truth, Wilmington was the ideal spot for Whiting. It needed stronger defenses for protection from the enemy, and Whiting knew the area and its people well. He was assigned to command the District of the Cape Fear on November 8, 1862, and arrived in Wilmington nine days later, just as the yellow fever epidemic was fading. Local military men familiar with Whiting's ability lauded his arrival with great excitement. "We justly regarded the general as one of the few eminently fit appointments the War Department had made," stated one Whiting loyalist. "In Whiting, we had implicit faith." His troops affectionately called him "Little Billy"—he was short and slight of build—and they respected his boldness and defiant stand against authority. "The men in the Department of Wilmington loved, trusted, honored—yea, worshipped [General Whiting]," claimed Col. J. S. Fairly, one of Whiting's staff officers. "He is a good man and a brave General, and we will do our part to sustain him in his determination to defend the place to the last," stated another soldier. To keep Whiting and his supporters satisfied, Davis promoted him to major general on February 28, 1863.[53]

Not all Wilmingtonians viewed Whiting's return as a blessing. He did not endear himself to everyone, despite his marriage to a cherished young lady from a prominent Cape Fear family. "He was not popular with many of the citizens," remarked a Confederate officer, "as he was arbitrary and paid little attention to the suggestions of civilians." At the same time, he added, "[Whiting] was a gentleman at heart, incapable of anything mean or low, and of undaunted courage." Though Whiting hoped and ultimately expected to be restored to field command, he energetically and successfully bolstered Wilmington's defenses in the face of the Federal blockade and constant threats of amphibious assaults.[54]

Whiting had good reason to fear a Union offensive against Wilmington, for combined operations played an important role in Union naval strategy. In spite of its failure to establish and maintain a wholly efficient and effective blockade, the U. S. Navy worked reasonably well in tandem with the Union army to establish enclaves along the Confederacy's meandering coastline. These footholds strengthened the blockade and established bases from which the Federal army could threaten strategic points inside the Confederacy. At least that was the plan.

Early in the war the Atlantic coast had proved vulnerable to Union land and sea expeditions. Confederate access to and from Pamlico Sound, North Carolina, was slammed shut by the captures of Forts Hatteras and Clark on August 29, 1861. Nine weeks later a joint Union operation seized Port Royal, South Carolina. For the remainder of the war Port Royal served as a naval base for maintaining the South Atlantic Blockading Squadron.

These initial victories were preparations for attacks against more important Southern seaports. Galveston fell in October 1862. Although the Confederates eventually recaptured the Texas port, once the Federals gained control of the Mississippi River in July 1863, the gulf coast port was of practical use only to Southern armies operating in the Trans Mississippi theater. Charleston remained in Confederate hands until February 1865, though its usefulness as a blockade running port diminished once Union land forces occupied nearby sea islands in the spring of 1863 and began siege operations against the city that summer. By July of that year Wilmington was the last major seaport effectively open to maritime commerce on the Atlantic seaboard.[55]

The U. S. Navy had targeted Wilmington for capture almost since the beginning of the war. As early as September 1861, the Union Blockade Strategy Board had recommended attacking the seaport, but for a variety of reasons, the project remained low on the War Department's list of priorities for another three years. The Navy Department argued from the beginning that Wilmington could be captured only by a carefully planned and executed army-navy operation. The shoal waters and Confederate defenses at the Cape Fear, which prevented gunboats from getting close enough to shore to destroy the forts guarding the inlets, made a purely naval attack impractical. The army, with its own problems and priorities, remained indifferent to Wilmington's capture.[56]

The U. S. Navy had been especially intent on taking Wilmington in 1862. Federal arms had poked several serious holes in the shell of the

Confederacy by the second spring of the war, which witnessed the loss of seven of the Confederacy's principal seaports (Fernandina, Jacksonville and Pensacola, Florida; New Bern, North Carolina; Beaufort, South Carolina; New Orleans, Louisiana; and Norfolk, Virginia) between March and May. Savannah was sealed off to blockade running when Fort Pulaski fell that April. Most Union strategists believed that Wilmington would be a tough nut to crack, however, and throughout the war proposed a number of ideas for attacking the city.

On May 11, 1862, Secretary Welles instructed Flag-Officer Louis M. Goldsborough, the first commander of the North Atlantic Blockading Squadron, to prepare an immediate strike on Wilmington. Goldsborough was to attack Fort Caswell at Old Inlet with "all the force he could spare," including the famed ironclad *Monitor*, to be brought down from Hampton Roads, Virginia. The next day those plans were personally rescinded by President Lincoln, who preferred having Goldsborough move his gunboats up the James River and shell Richmond into surrender. Still, Goldsborough hoped to take ironclads to Cape Fear as soon as the work at Richmond was done. The flag officer never got his wish, as his flotilla remained in Virginia to assist Maj. Gen. George B. McClellan's Peninsula Campaign in the spring of 1862.[57]

The Navy Department continued to push for a joint operation against Wilmington, especially as Maj. Gen. Ambrose E. Burnside planned an assault against Fredericksburg in late autumn 1862. To draw attention—and perhaps enemy troops—away from Burnside's objective, Maj. Gen. John G. Foster proposed making a lightning raid into the interior of North Carolina from his base at New Bern. Once inland, the raiders would sever the Wilmington & Weldon Railroad connecting the Tarheel port to Virginia and then strike Wilmington from the north. At the same time, monitors could enter Old Inlet, while gunboats pounded the defenses at New Inlet. After finishing with Fort Caswell, the ironclads would advance upriver to attack Fort Fisher from the rear, thus sealing off both inlets.

Acting Rear Admiral Samuel Phillips Lee, who succeeded Goldsborough as commander of the North Atlantic Blockading Squadron, assembled a force of ironclads, including the *Monitor*, to cooperate with Foster, who believed that their support was critical to the success of his plan. Foster did not want to risk a solo attack for fear that a superior number of enemy troops would be drawn from Richmond or Charleston to challenge his army. A naval attack at Wilmington would force the Confederate high command to send troops to man the forts there. Foster advanced from New Bern on December 11 with 10,000 infantrymen, 640 cavalrymen, and 40 light artillery pieces. In less than a week he defeated enemy forces at Kinston, White Hall, and Goldsboro. Just as it began to look as though Foster's plan would bear fruit, the strike against Wilmington disintegrated when the *Monitor*, en route to Wilmington, sank in a storm off Cape Hatteras, North Carolina, on New Year's Eve 1862. The *Monitor* was the only ironclad Union naval authorities felt confident could float over the bar at Old Inlet.[58]

Variations of Foster's plan were discussed for some time to come, but the Navy Department's attention quickly shifted to Charleston, a more popular target. Although Secretary Welles considered Wilmington more important to the South logistically (it was the largest open seaport near the Virginia battlefront), he recognized that Northern public and political interest centered on Charleston, where the war had begun with the attack against Fort Sumter. As Gustavus Fox pointed out: "We should be inclined to skip Fort Caswell [and Wilmington], for the fall of Charleston is the fall of Satan's Kingdom."[59]

For most of the remainder of the war Admiral Lee continued to stress the necessity of closing Wilmington to blockade running. An increasing quantity of supplies was being funneled into the Confederacy through the port. But until late in the conflict the U. S. War Department showed no interest in providing troops necessary for a strike against the city. Combined operations on the Mississippi River—including the capture of New Orleans and Vicksburg—and against Charleston and Savannah took precedence, further postponing an attack on Wilmington. Perhaps the U. S. government underestimated the amount of supplies being run through the blockade at the North Carolina seaport. The army empathized with the navy's concern, but it placed little strategic value on a seaport in the "backwater" of the Confederacy. One high-ranking U. S. Navy officer believed the government's failure to move against Wilmington prolonged the war. "The works had been allowed to be built in the face of a heavy force of gunboats," he maintained. "When the works were first commenced they could easily have been knocked down and the gunboats could have gone up to Wilmington without difficulty. Had this been done the fate of the rebellion would have been decided a year sooner."[60]

In late summer 1864 the government's attitude finally changed. By then Wilmington was the only major Southern seaport open to blockade running. The Navy Department renewed its efforts to enlist the army's assistance in closing the Confederacy's last gateway. The decision was timely, as the administration was coming under heavy political pressure to go after Wilmington. In response President Lincoln personally sent envoys to U. S. Grant's headquarters in early September to discuss such an attack.[61]

An 1865 T. H. O'Sullivan photograph of the interior of Fort Fisher's northeast bastion (left) and the Pulpit Battery (right). *U.S. Army Military History Institute*

Gideon Welles, Secretary of the U.S. Navy. *U.S. Army Military History Institute*

Chapter 3

"To attack Wilmington is the most important
demonstration that can be made"

– U. S. Navy Secretary Gideon Welles

PREPARATIONS

For a while, at least, Lt. Gen. U. S. Grant listened politely to Assistant Secretary of the Navy Gustavus V. Fox and Maj. Gen. Quincy Gillmore as they made their pitch. After all, they had come with President Lincoln's blessing all the way from Washington to Grant's headquarters at City Point, Virginia, on a hot and muggy September 2, 1864. But their message did not particularly interest the commanding general. They wanted him to support a joint army-navy attack on Wilmington, the last major seaport open to blockade running, and Grant was not enthusiastic.[1]

That Wilmington remained open to Confederate commerce when all other important Southern ports along the Atlantic seaboard had been captured or closed had become an embarrassment to the U. S. Navy. Wilmington had been under a naval blockade for more than three years, yet Union ships could not stop the flow of supplies making their way in or out of the city. Throughout the spring and summer of 1864, Gideon Welles had been lobbying the Lincoln administration to support a combined operation against Wilmington. "Could we seize the forts at the entrance of Cape Fear and close the illicit traffic, it would be almost as important as the capture of Richmond on the fate of the Rebels, and an important step in that direction," the navy secretary argued.[2] While President Lincoln agreed with Welles' assessment of Wilmington's importance, he declined to press the War Department to move against a target it was reluctant to attack. By the time Fox and Gillmore visited Grant in early September, Grant's unrelenting campaign against Robert E. Lee's Army of Northern Virginia before Petersburg and Richmond occupied the Federal army's attention.

Rumors persisted in Washington that U. S. Navy officers had conspired with blockade running agents to keep the trade flourishing at Wilmington so that they, too, could profit from the trade, through bribes and payoffs. Welles disregarded the "newspaper gossip," staunchly defending his men against the accusations. He believed Admiral S. Phillips Lee, the commander of the North Atlantic Blockading Squadron, and his officers were loyal Union men. On the other hand, Welles considered Lee a cautious and timid man, and blamed him in part for "some defect in the blockade which [made] Wilmington appear an almost open port." Something had to be done to close Wilmington.[3]

But in order to do "something," the navy needed the army's assistance, for a naval task force alone could not possibly overcome the numerous obstacles posed by an attack at Cape Fear. Shallow waters, reefs, and strong Confederate defenses would prevent the warships from getting close enough to shore to be effective. Dangerous shoals had claimed ships for as long as seafarers had been plying local waters, and they were just as dangerous for Union blockaders as they had been for other vessels for hundreds of years. Indeed, Cape Fear was appropriately named. But with the aid of local pilots, blockading gunboats were able to move in closer to shore during the night, though Confederate artillery batteries kept them about five miles off shore during daylight hours.

The U. S. Army would have to play a principal role in attacking Wilmington. Yet the army balked at getting involved, frustrating Welles' efforts. "The importance of closing Wilmington and cutting off Rebel communication is paramount to all other questions. . .[but] it has been impossible," Welles lamented, "to get the War Department and military authorities to enter into the spirit of this work. They do not appreciate it."[4]

Circumstances finally turned in Welles' favor by mid-summer 1864. On August 5, Rear Admiral David G. Farragut led a squadron of monitors and warships past the forts guarding the entrance to Mobile Bay, Alabama, to capture the Confederate ironclad *Tennessee* and destroy three gunboats. The entire action took less than four hours from start to finish. Within the next two-and-a-half weeks, the forts defending Mobile Bay—Forts Gaines, Powell, and Morgan—were captured, sealing the last key Southern port in the Gulf of Mexico. The fall of Mobile left Wilmington as the only major seaport effectively open to maritime trade with the outside world, and provided the incentive Welles needed to bolster his case for a strike against the Carolina seaport.

By late August, the naval secretary was pushing hard to get President Lincoln to endorse his plan. Welles contended that the greatest assistance the government could offer General Grant would be to sever the lifeline through Wilmington that fed Lee's army. As long as blockade runners continued to bring in food, clothing, blankets, medicine, weapons, and ammunition, Lee could hold out indefinitely in the trenches around Petersburg and Richmond. That had been the main thrust of Welles' argument from the beginning.

Welles was not alone in his efforts to see Wilmington closed. Northern shippers were also pressing the administration to combat Wilmington-based commerce raiding ships, including the formidable *Tallahassee*. In a one week stint in August 1864, the *Tallahassee* destroyed twenty-five merchant and fishing vessels off the New England coast. According to intelligence reports, at least one other vessel—the blockade runner *Edith*—was being converted into a privateer at Wilmington. More lethal attacks by such ships could be devastating to Union commerce.[5]

In addition to stopping the feared Southern raiders, the capture of Wilmington might also offer some political advantages for President Lincoln. The chief executive needed more successes like Mobile Bay to bolster his faltering reelection campaign. Farragut's victory failed to convince war-weary Northerners that the Union was winning the war. Mobile was too remote and the naval battle there had been too brief to spark much interest among people in the North, who regarded the savage fighting in Virginia as crucial to the success of the Union. But the conflict in the Old Dominion had reached a stalemate. Federal casualties mounted frightfully during the spring and summer of 1864, as Grant relentlessly hammered away at Lee's army from the Wilderness to the outskirts of Petersburg. In a series of bloody assaults against Lee's strongly entrenched force at Cold Harbor on June 3, Grant lost 6,000 men in less than sixty minutes of fighting.[6]

Horrified by the slaughter, Grant's critics labeled him a butcher and began paying attention to the anti-war message of the Democratic party. The

Democrats argued that the North had already suffered too much in the fratricidal war, and campaigned for negotiating an end to the conflict. At their convention in August the Peace Democrats chose George B. McClellan, the former commander of the Army of the Potomac, as their nominee to oppose Lincoln in the November election. McClellan may have been unqualified to lead the army on the battlefield in 1862, at least in Lincoln's estimation, but the general still enjoyed immense popularity, especially among soldiers of his old command, and was regarded as a formidable adversary to the president in the upcoming political contest.

With all this in mind and more, Lincoln listened closely to Welles' latest proposal to attack Wilmington and ultimately gave it his blessing. He declined, however, to authorize Welles to proceed with his plans, instead deferring the issue to General Grant. Lincoln possessed great confidence in Grant's judgment about such military matters. Secretary of War Edwin M. Stanton concurred with the president, leaving the matter entirely up to the lieutenant general.[7]

Much to Welles' dismay, Grant expressed little enthusiasm for committing troops to strike Wilmington when he met with Fox and Gillmore on September 2. Grant did not see any real strategic advantage in attacking the seaport. In his view, he needed more soldiers, not fewer, to increase the pressure on Lee along the Petersburg-Richmond line, where the two armies had been slugging it out for three months. Already the Union lines were too long, stretching from Deep Bottom north of the James River, southward across the peninsula and the Appomattox River to the Weldon Railroad. Despite repeated frontal assaults against Lee's thinly defended works, the Army of the Potomac had been unable to break the deadlock.

Grant was hesitant to release any part of his command until his losses from the bloody fighting in Virginia had been replaced. Even then the commanding general believed that shifting a portion of his army further south might jeopardize the security of Washington, a risk that would concern many politicians—especially in this crucial election year. Grant needed only point to Lt. Gen. Jubal Early's bold raid to the gates of Washington in July 1864, to remind Northerners just how vulnerable the capital was to an attack, even that late in the war. With his army at full strength in Virginia, Grant could confidently rush troops to defend Washington in case of an emergency. That could not be as easily done if 10,000 soldiers—the estimated number of troops required to capture Wilmington—were involved in a major expedition 250 miles south of Petersburg.

Major General Henry W. Halleck, the U.S. Army chief of staff, stood with Grant on the Wilmington question. Halleck, who had never been an enthusiastic supporter of combined operations—especially after the costly failures to capture Charleston—believed that the War Department had "more irons now than we can keep from burning." He saw no reason to put another iron in the fire at Wilmington. Besides, Halleck resented the Navy Department for originating the idea to attack the seaport in the first place.[8]

Despite his misgivings, Grant recognized President Lincoln's political dilemma and agreed to consider the appeal delivered by Fox and Gillmore. Grant kept his promise. On September 5, Gideon Welles informed Admiral Farragut (the leading candidate to command the attack squadron at Cape Fear) that the commanding general had given the subject his prompt attention and had decided he could spare an army force at the appropriate time. The secretary understood Grant to say that troops might be ready to move by the first of October.[9]

Simply put, Grant signed on to the proposal because Lincoln liked it. The lieutenant general cared little for the politics of war, but he understood the political expediency of supporting Lincoln's reelection by capturing Wilmington. The political urgency for such a move, however, evaporated almost immediately. On September 2, the same day Grant met with Fox and Gillmore, Maj. Gen. William T. Sherman's 100,000-man "army group" captured Atlanta, one of the most important cities in the Confederacy. When news of the victory reached Washington two days later, Lincoln's reelection was all but assured by an exultant electorate satisfied that the tide had truly turned in the Union's favor. "[Sherman's success] will not be gratifying to zealous partisans who have just committed the mistake of sending out a peace platform, and declared the war a failure," gleefully noted a Lincoln confidante. Any doubts left as to the course of the upcoming election were erased by Maj. Gen. Phil Sheridan's decisive victories over Jubal Early's Confederate army in Virginia's Shenandoah Valley in late September and October 1864.[10]

In a letter of September 12, Grant congratulated Sherman on his "gigantic success" at Atlanta and requested his views on military matters and future operations. He informed Sherman of his plans to extend his army's position south of Petersburg while at the same time sending a large force against Wilmington. The latter part of the plan still worried him. Though he had agreed to support an attack against the city, he admitted to at least one high-ranking army officer that he really wanted "nothing to do with it." The astute Sherman tried to soothe Grant's anxiety. Take Wilmington, Sherman argued, and "[we] cut off all Foreign Trade to our Enemy. After you get Wilmington, you strike for Savannah & the [Savannah] River, [and] I [will] keep [Gen. John Bell] Hood employed & put my Army in fine order for a march on Augusta, Columbia, and Charleston. . . ." This was Sherman's first hint of his plan to invade South Carolina. It was a bold new strategy, the outline and potential of which Sherman might have seen more clearly than Grant. It certainly gave Grant something to consider that autumn as he plotted what he hoped would be an end to the Confederacy.[11]

Sherman's victory at Atlanta did not dampen the Navy Department's enthusiasm for launching an attack on Wilmington by early October, the date Grant had intimated an army force might be available for the mission. Naval officers suggested striking as soon as possible, before autumn and winter storms set in. Hurricanes usually hit the Carolina coast between August and October, but "nor'easters" and gales could be a problem through April. Heavy seas and strong winds could inflict more damage to a fleet of warships than Confederate shore batteries.

Matters could not progress without a sound plan, and thus one of Secretary Welles' first orders of business was to develop a methodology for capturing Wilmington. He consulted Maj. Gen. Quincy Gillmore, a veteran of combined operations along the Atlantic seaboard who had won recognition and praise for his actions in the early war captures of Port Royal, South Carolina and Fort Pulaski at Savannah, Georgia. As commander of the Department of the South in 1863-1864, Gillmore had planned and supervised assaults against Battery Wagner and Fort Sumter. On September 6, 1864, Gillmore presented two plans for taking Wilmington. Both were based largely on Admiral Lee's reconnaissances of the water approaches and defenses at Cape Fear, and on Lee's own recommendations for closing the Carolina seaport. The first plan called for 6,000 soldiers to capture Bald Head Island and Zeek's Island south of New Inlet. Once the army had established a beachhead, a naval fleet would bombard Fort Fisher, allowing light-draft monitors to push their way through New Inlet to seal the harbor.

Gillmore's second plan incorporated part of the first. A small number of soldiers would feint a landing on Bald Head and Zeek's Island while the larger contingent of a 12,000-man force would land on Federal Point to attack Fort Fisher. After reaching shore, the troops would construct an entrenched line across the peninsula as a fleet of gunboats supported the monitors' efforts to enter the Cape Fear River.[12]

Both Welles and Grant preferred the second plan. Federal Point would provide the army with more room to maneuver and establish, if necessary, a siege line against Fort Fisher similar to the one Gillmore had developed against Battery Wagner in the summer of 1863. Moreover, it would deposit an attack force closer to Wilmington, in position to move more quickly and easily against the city than if troops were landed on Bald Head Island or Oak Island.

Military experts also discussed an alternative attack against the defenses at Old Inlet instead of New Inlet, but decided against it. Fort Caswell, Fort Campbell, Battery Shaw and Fort Holmes guarded Old Inlet from two sides. Even if a navy fleet could silence those forts and push through Old Inlet, New Inlet would still be open to blockade runners. The Union warships and the army would have to move upriver to attack Fort Fisher from the rear, on the way attacking Fort Pender (Johnston) at Smithville and Fort Lamb on Reeves Point. The Federals were aware of these fortifications and believed there might be others. Wilmington was rumored to be as heavily defended as Charleston, still under Confederate control after fourteen months of siege warfare. Besides, Fort Fisher was a more politically inviting target, at least as far as Gideon Welles was concerned. The capture of the Confederacy's most powerful seacoast fortification would be a great victory for the Navy Department, which many considered was simply playing a supporting role to the army in the war—an impression that perturbed Welles.

Although the strike against Old Inlet was deemed too hazardous and thus not adopted, no one was acting under the assumption that an attack against the fortifications guarding New Inlet would prove to be an easy task. If the Federals could capture Fort Fisher, they would also gain control of the Cape Fear River directly behind the fort, thus isolating the fortifications south of that point. The initial debate among naval officers was whether monitors and large gunboats could even breach New Inlet. A sand bar and shoals closely guarded the shoreline at Fort Fisher, and the surrounding waters were littered with wrecked blockade runners. In addition, the inlet's narrow treacherous channel further complicated matters, for without the aid of pilots and guide buoys, the waterway was difficult to navigate—and undoubtedly filled with uncharted obstructions and torpedoes. Based on his observations, Admiral Lee doubted warships could push through New Inlet. Still, the navy hoped to try because Farragut had successfully employed a similar tactic at Mobile Bay.[13]

In addition to planning the Fort Fisher campaign, Secretary Welles moved promptly to select the right officer to command the attack flotilla. Above all else he wanted an aggressive commander. To many observers Admiral S. Phillips Lee was the logical choice. As the incumbent commander of the North Atlantic Blockading Squadron, his vast knowledge of Cape Fear's approaches and defenses appeared to qualify him to lead an armada. Lee had pushed hard during his two-year tenure with the squadron to organize a joint army-navy operation against Wilmington, but the army had repeatedly rejected his pleas for a supporting infantry force. In the autumn of 1864, at a time that should have been Admiral Lee's crowning moment, both the War Department and the Navy Department turned their backs on him. Grant had little faith in Lee's ability and informed Gustavus Fox that he would not be satisfied with him as naval commander at Wilmington. Gideon Welles agreed. "Lee is not the man for the job," he declared. "He has acquitted himself very well—has discharged his duties intelligently and firmly. But he can never be a great commander. Farragut would take the place three times while Lee was preparing, and hesitating, and looking behind for more aid." Welles personally liked Lee and knew he wanted the assignment, but he refused to offer it to him because, as he explained, "individual feelings, partialities, and friendships must not be in the way of public welfare." The secretary assigned a disappointed Lee to another command.[14]

With Lee out of the way Welles was free to offer the expedition to David Farragut, his first choice to command the assault flotilla. The admiral seemed to possess all the right qualifications, not the least of which was that he met with Grant's approval. Farragut's capture of New Orleans in April 1862, coupled with his recent success at Mobile Bay—where he had issued his famous "damn the torpedoes" order—made him the clear favorite to command at Wilmington. Moreover, Welles considered Farragut "earnest, unselfish [and] devoted to his country and service." But the hero of Mobile Bay had not always been the darling of Washington. Early in the war members of Congress had questioned the admiral's loyalty because he was Southern-born, a Southern resident and married to a Southern lady. His victories at New Orleans and Mobile Bay, however, besides giving the Union two great naval triumphs, squashed concerns about Farragut's devotion to his country.

Inasmuch as Welles wanted Farragut for the Wilmington expedition, he hesitated to ask him. Northerners undoubtedly expected Farragut to finish the job at Mobile by capturing the city itself, Welles reasoned. Of greater concern was the intelligence value to the Confederates that was sure to result by transferring Farragut from the West Gulf Blockading Squadron to the North Atlantic Blockading Squadron. Such a move would all but telegraph the planned strike on Wilmington and would stir the Southerners to prepare more rigorously for its defense. The navy secretary gave these concerns careful consideration and still decided that Farragut was the right man for the job. On September 5, he ordered Farragut north to assume command.[15]

Farragut surprised Welles by declining the assignment. The long and arduous campaigning in the Gulf and at Mobile Bay had left Farragut exhausted and in dire need of "rest and shore exercise." "I am anxious to do my best for the Country & ready to do what I can, and I am so unaccustomed to evade any order that I have been greatly pained at this inability to gratify the Dept.," Farragut explained. Welles understood, but was sorely disappointed nonetheless. "Just at this crisis Farragut unfortunately fails," Welles lamented. "It is unavoidable, a necessity. He would not ask relief if not compelled to. . .But who shall take his place?"[16]

The U. S. Navy boasted an array of talented officers—Louis Goldsborough, John Dahlgren, Samuel F. Du Pont, and Charles Henry Davis—among others. Yet Welles did not believe any of them equal to the hard duty the capture of Wilmington would demand. After Farragut bowed out, Gustavus Fox implored Welles to choose Rear Admiral David Dixon Porter, commander of the Mississippi Squadron and, ironically enough, Farragut's younger foster brother.

Admiral Porter was in Washington on navy business when he received word Secretary Welles and Assistant Secretary Fox wanted to see him about a pressing matter at the home of Postmaster General Montgomery Blair (who, in another irony, happened to be S. Phillips Lee's brother-in-law) on Saturday, September 17. Though out of town on business that day, Blair allowed the navy men to use his home for the top secret meeting. They spent much of the day together studying maps and charts of Cape Fear and discussing an attack on Wilmington. At the end of the meeting Welles offered Porter command of the naval task force. Porter balked at first, explaining that he preferred to remain with the Mississippi Squadron. Welles admitted that capturing the blockade runner haven would be a difficult task, one that would probably offer little thanks to Porter if he succeeded, and curses if he failed. With only minimal prodding from Welles and Fox, Porter reconsidered, admitting that if the navy "ordered him to go over Niagara Falls in an iron pot he should obey the order." There would be no such request, but the navy executives undoubtedly appreciated the sentiment. Porter was on board.[17]

The admiral knew the capture of Wilmington was an important assignment, one that would allow him the opportunity to redeem himself for his squadron's poor performance during the Red River Campaign in Louisiana in the spring of 1864, where he had come within a hair's breadth of losing his flotilla. His success at Wilmington might also elevate his standing in the navy even higher than Farragut's. After Farragut, Porter was probably the best known naval officer in the United States, and he enjoyed his celebrity status. Never one to shirk publicity, he was, in fact, a master of self-promotion.

David Dixon Porter was of "good old Massachusetts stock," and true to his heritage, might well have been born at sea. His great-grandfather, Alexander Porter, had been a merchant captain and had fought in the colonial wars. Porter's grandfather and namesake had commanded privateers and regular navy warships in the American Revolution while his father, also named David, had been a naval hero in the War of 1812. Since Porter's father was away at sea almost constantly, he did not even see his infant son for fifteen months after his birth on June 8, 1813, in Chester, Pennsylvania. With such a maritime background, it came as no surprise to those who knew him that young David Dixon Porter also wanted to become a sailor. Salt water ran in his veins, and he proved as worthy a seaman as any Porter who ever sailed. At age ten he took his first cruise in his father's ship-of-war, briefly served as a young teenager in the Mexican Navy, was a midshipman in the U.S. Navy by age fifteen, and fought valiantly in the Mexican War (against his former employer) as executive officer of the *Spitfire*.[18]

During the Civil War Porter won his first laurels fighting along the Mississippi River and quickly emerged as one of the navy's brightest and most successful executive officers. In April 1862, he commanded a mortar flotilla in his foster brother's capture of New Orleans. Six months later the Navy Department placed Porter at the head of the Mississippi Squadron. In that position he helped take Arkansas Post and Vicksburg in 1863. It was during the latter campaign that Porter established good professional and personal relationships with both U. S. Grant and William T. Sherman. In fact, Grant later wrote that "the Navy under Porter was all it could be during the entire campaign. Without its assistance the campaign could not have been successfully made." For his part in the capture of the stronghold, Porter was promoted to rear admiral and given the responsibility of maintaining control of the entire Mississippi River system.[19]

The sailor of "good old Massachusetts stock" was a man whom people either admired or despised, although in either case he demanded and received respect. Porter was acerbic, bombastic, authoritative and ambitious. For all his posturing, his officers were loyal to him, although his unabashed self-confidence and overbearing personality led many of his peers in the navy, as well as in the army, to view him with contempt. "I did not like Porter," commented an acquaintance. "He was very boastful [and] it was his delight to fill in the dinner hour with his theories on the right way to conquer the Confederacy. It was clear from his conversation that he believed but one person could accomplish it satisfactorily, and that was himself."[20]

If indeed one man could have conquered the Confederacy, it might well have been David Dixon Porter. He was smart, energetic and extremely capable. And he was tough—as tough as hide leather. Stocky and muscular, sporting a full beard and with piercing eyes, Porter looked every bit the part of the robust naval officer that he was. Even at age fifty-one, Porter was the sort of fighter any man would want by his side in a barroom brawl. The Wilmington expedition promised to be that—and much more.

Gustavus Fox held Porter in the highest esteem and valued his friendship, so it came as no surprise that he recommended his friend for the Wilmington assignment. Like Fox, David Farragut also endorsed Porter, despite the sibling rivalry that persisted between the two (though clearly more so on Porter's part than Farragut's). "Porter has had a long respite, is fresh & I feel will do as well as any man," Farragut maintained. While he respected Porter's ability, Gideon Welles expressed some concern about Porter's character. Simply put, he was not sure the admiral could be trusted. "[Porter could not always] be depended upon if he had an end to attain," Welles wrote, "and he had no hesitation in trampling down a brother officer if it would benefit him." Yet after considering all the other available candidates for the post, Welles decided "Porter is probably the best man for the service."[21]

The "best man" and his escort, Gustavus Fox, paid General Grant a courtesy call at City Point on September 20. The purpose of the visit was to present the commander of the Fort Fisher naval task force and sound out the lieutenant general on his choice for the ground forces commander. Having agreed to the joint operation, Grant now found himself having to select a capable officer to lead the expeditionary force. Secretary of War Stanton favored Maj. Gen. Quincy Gillmore, who wanted the assignment and had considerable experience in coastal campaigns. But Stanton backed down when Grant objected, arguing that Gillmore was too timid for such an important mission. Gillmore had failed to capture Charleston, and then in frustration had requested to be be reassigned. After traveling north to Virginia with his old corps, Gillmore ran afoul of Maj. Gen. Benjamin F. Butler, who blamed him for several military fiascoes in the spring of 1864 during the botched Bermuda Hundred campaign. Grant believed that Gillmore was not the sort of leader who could be relied upon to capture Wilmington. The high command attempted to spare Gillmore's feelings by telling him that they feared a recently-suffered horse riding injury had rendered him unfit for field duty. The record is unclear as to whether Gillmore believed them.[22]

What is clear, however, is that after Gillmore had been dealt with, Grant cast his gaze on another Butler subordinate, Bvt. Maj. Gen. Godfrey Weitzel, the relatively unknown chief engineer in the Army of the James. Why Grant chose Weitzel over other more high profile officers is not known, although he obviously believed Weitzel could do the job. The lieutenant general may have considered the appointment a simple matter of military protocol, since Wilmington fell within General Butler's sphere of command—the Department of Virginia and North Carolina. Whatever Grant's motivation, Weitzel appeared imminently qualified for the position.

The son of German immigrants, Godfrey Weitzel was born in Cincinnati, Ohio, on November 1, 1835. After attending local public schools, young Weitzel obtained a coveted appointment to West Point. He earned a commission as second lieutenant of engineers upon his graduation in 1855, second in a class of thirty-four. After leaving upstate New York, the young officer was assigned to work on fortifications at New Orleans. Additional knowledge on defensive works was obtained after the outbreak of the Civil War, when he constructed defenses in and around Washington and Cincinnati. Weitzel also gained valuable experience in combined operations, first while serving as Major General Butler's chief engineer in the 1862 operations at New Orleans, and subsequently with Maj. Gen. Nathaniel Banks at Port Hudson the following spring. As temporary commander of the XIX Army Corps' First Division, Weitzel led the failed attack on Sabine Pass, Texas, in September 1863, and later campaigned in western Louisiana. In the spring of 1864 he was transferred to Virginia, where he again served under Ben Butler, first as Second Division commander and then XVIII Corps commander in the Army of the James. Rumor had it that Weitzel's association with political generals like Butler and Banks stifled his professional army career. If General Grant heard the gossip he ignored it when he selected Weitzel to command the Wilmington expeditionary force.[23]

Having met with Porter and Fox on September 20, Grant called Weitzel to his headquarters at City Point to give him the news about his new assignment. When Weitzel arrived, Grant told him of his plans to secretly dispatch an army—in conjunction with the navy—to close the Cape Fear River to blockade runners and to make him commander of the land forces. The lieutenant general furnished Weitzel with maps of the Wilmington area, asked the chief engineer to study them carefully and to prepare for his new command. Weitzel called on Grant again the following day, requesting permission to travel to the Cape Fear to reconnoiter the enemy's defenses. Grant consented and Weitzel set sail at once, accompanied by Brig. Gen. Charles K. Graham, commander of the Army of the James' naval brigade.[24]

Weitzel and Graham spent three days (probably September 27-29) off New Inlet, closely examining the Confederate works on Federal Point. Weitzel also interviewed Admiral Lee (who was preparing to leave the squadron for his new command) and his naval officers, as well as North Carolinians serving as pilots on board Lee's blockaders. The boastful Tar-

Bvt. Maj. Gen. Godfrey Weitzel, the professional Union army engineer U. S. Grant believed possessed the skills necessary to conquer Fort Fisher. *Author's Collection*

heels claimed to know "every green pine tree between Wilmington and the mouth of the Cape Fear River." Weitzel even talked with a local spy, the president of the Loyal Union League of Wilmington. From them and from his own observations Weitzel formed a good idea of the enemy's strength—including a healthy respect for the powerful Fort Fisher, the key to Wilmington's defenses.

Immediately upon his return to Virginia and before he had a chance to report to Grant, Weitzel was placed in temporary command of the XVIII Army Corps by order of General Butler. Weitzel was replacing Maj. Gen. Edward O. C. Ord, who had been seriously wounded at Fort Harrison on September 29. The new corps commander worried that his position would interfere with Grant's instructions to him to make ready for an attack on Wilmington. While Grant suggested that Weitzel fulfill both roles, circumstances soon made the issue moot: Weitzel learned from Grant in mid-October that the Wilmington expedition was being postponed. The lieutenant general claimed that someone had been too free with information about the planned strike, and now the entire South was aware of it.[25]

As Grant noted, news of the proposed attack on Wilmington had leaked out. The commanding general would later blame the Navy Department for the blunder, but in truth, it would have been difficult for an enterprising reporter not to recognize that something was afoot. Since mid-September warships had been assembling at Hampton Roads, Virginia, headquarters of the North Atlantic Blockading Squadron. By late October, B. S. Osborn, a former correspondent with the *New York Herald* who now operated an independent news syndicate, offered to supply national newspapers (for a price, of course) with a "a full & accurate epitome of the grand movement against Wilmington." Osborn package included a list of the warships being fitted for the expedition, their armament, a map of the Confederate defenses at Cape Fear, and U. S. Navy orders.[26]

Grant's decision to postpone the attack would have been news to the navy had Grant taken the trouble to inform it of his decision. Secretary Welles continued to prepare for the expedition, carefully planning a method of attack and assigning warships to the task force. On September 22 Welles sent official instructions to Porter to assume command of the North Atlantic Blockading Squadron. Three weeks later, on October 12, the admiral arrived in Hampton Roads. The veteran naval commander hoisted the squadron's standard above his new flagship, the *Malvern*, and announced he was ready to attack Wilmington. "I have assumed command and am ready with a sufficient force to cover any landing that may be made by the Army," he boasted. "[But] from present appearances the Navy will be ready long before the Army." Much to Welles' and Porter's chagrin, the navy ended up waiting on the army much longer than they had expected.[27]

If and when an assault was launched against Wilmington, the major attempt would in all probability be against Fort Fisher, which guarded blockade runners' favorite approach to the harbor. Yet a battle at Fort Fisher seemed an unlikely threat to Confederate soldiers stationed there in the autumn of 1864. Alarms of an impending Union invasion were issued frequently, but the dreaded attacks never followed. "We are expecting an attack," an artillerymen wrote his wife, "or rather our Government and Genls are all the time." After a while the soldiers became immune to such warnings.[28]

While Wilmington's defenders may have grown complacent to external threats, their commander was more realistic about the likelihood of a Federal move against his district. General Whiting cautioned his troops that an attack at Cape Fear was inevitable as other Confederate seaports fell one-by-one into enemy hands. The soldiers paid little attention, instead taking solace in their strong defenses, good fortune, and the boldness of their leaders. "You will hear before many moons of the glorious battle on Confederate Point, in which Fort Fisher will cover herself with glory," Colonel Lamb boasted in a letter to his friend and former adjutant Thomas W. Rowland. To make the fort appear more warlike, Lamb festooned his headquarters with a Confederate flag and a British ensign, draped his sword, sash, and accouterments over the window, and hung a picture of Napoleon over the fireplace mantle. Lamb also told his men that the Federals would eventually besiege Fort Fisher and try to starve them out, but "we will eat up all our mules and horses and all the old cows before we give in."[29]

Lamb's defiant attitude proved infectious and instilled in his men a growing confidence. Even so, it was the not the sort of unshakable confidence veteran soldiers earn on a hard-fought battlefield. Thus far the only combat Fort Fisher's troops had encountered were regular artillery duels with Union gunboats, intermingled with occasional skirmishes with landing parties making forays along the shoreline—excursions the Confederates called "hen roosting raids." Fort Fisher's artillerymen had managed to drive off Federal gunboats that had run the blockade runner *Modern Greece* aground on June 27, 1862, and had moved in for the kill. In late August 1863, Capt. Daniel Munn and a detachment of cannoneers from Fort Fisher captured fourteen Union sailors trying to burn the blockade runner *Hebe* that had also been chased ashore while trying to enter New Inlet. There were similar fights over many more runners—the *Night Hawk*, *Phantom* and *Ella* among them.

The Southerners won most of the encounters, keeping the frustrated blockaders at bay. "We have had a number of duels with the blockaders, in all of which I have driven them off," Colonel Lamb bragged. "I keep the blockaders not less than six miles off."[30] Confederate soldiers joked that they kept the gunboats so far from shore that when the Federals fired their artillery they had to send a man along with the cannonball to show them where it hit. By the autumn of 1864, the Confederates at Fort Fisher had yet to be exposed to either small arms fire or heavy sustained fire from massed artillery. The untested garrison comprised mostly locals from the eight counties of southeastern North Carolina that comprised the District of the Cape Fear: New Hanover, Brunswick, Onslow, Bladen, Columbus, Sampson, Roberson, and Cumberland. Few of the soldiers had experienced front-line combat.

Dealing with the rigors of day-to-day life at Fort Fisher presented the Confederates with greater challenges than did sparring with Union sailors. Fort Fisher was a lonely, isolated post. It was five miles northeast of Smithville across the harbor, and more than nineteen miles south of Wilmington. Getting to Wilmington took more than two hours by steamer, three and a half hours by horseback, and nine hours by foot through the deep sands of the Federal Point Road. Soldiers seldomly saw family and friends, nor did they enjoy the social and cultural events either town had to offer. "[Fort Fisher] is the damndest place that it has ever been my misfortune to stop at," complained one disgruntled soldier. "We get but very little to eat and are cut off from all the world and the rest of mankind. The boats never come here and we never see any one except ourselves who we are very tired looking at." Another Southerner wrote: "We are in a very dreary and lonesome place, as lonesome and as hot as you ever saw."[31]

As the garrison soldiers attested, the weather at Fort Fisher was miserable at times. The sweltering heat of summer days made Federal Point almost desert-like, while the late fall and winter winds blew cold off the waters that all but surrounded the great sand bastion, chilling soldiers to the bone. Ironically, the substance of which the fort was primarily constructed—sand—also caused the troops serious discomfort. Above all else, sand was a soldier's constant companion and his main source of discontentment at Fort Fisher. Sand was everywhere—as far as the eye could see—and the granules had a nasty way of getting into everything a soldier owned: his uniform, brogans, blanket, rifle-musket and food. There was no refuge from it and it gave no mercy. "[Federal Point was] as desolate a sand bank as was ever seen," lamented a Confederate officer. "I get tired of the barren sand beds of Fort Fisher," complained another. Almost as annoying as the ever-present sand were the mosquitoes, deer flies and sand gnats (called no-see-ums because of their tiny size) that inundated Federal Point. These pesky insects made life miserable at Fort Fisher. "I call [this] a very pleasant place with one exception, the mosquitoes are worse here than I ever saw them," noted a soldier stationed at Camp Wyatt. "The King of mosquitoes had selected the locality for his Court," claimed B. Lewis Blackford, a Confederate engineer surveying Federal Point. "Those mosquitoes could sting through a double blanket without the least trouble."[32]

Despite their discomfort and deprivation, the garrison troops at Fort Fisher generally found it an acceptable place to be stationed. Life there was was certainly less dangerous and more bearable than it was for most troops in other theaters of the war. "We fare a grate deel bettor than the Soldiers in other parts of the Confederacy," admitted William A. Burgess of Company A, 40th North Carolina Regiment (3rd North Carolina Artillery). Soldiers occasionally escaped the monotony of post duty by going on furlough to Wilmington, though passes were harder to obtain after the yellow fever epidemic had wracked the town in 1862. They also spent off-duty hours swimming and fishing in the ocean or river, digging for clams and harvesting oysters along the shoreline. "We had good, comfortable quarters and a good deal of leisure time," recalled John M. Johnston of Company H, 36th North Carolina Regiment. "True guard duty was hard, especially in the winter on account of cold winds from the ocean, but in summer we had delightful times bathing in the surf." There was also little chance of being wounded or killed in action, which left disease as the only real danger faced by the soldiers. "I have left Fort Fisher at last," wrote David High, a private in the C. S. Signal Corps, "but I did not leave because I wanted to, for I had rather stay there than any place that I know while I have to stay in the war."[33]

While the weather and environment were at times challenging, so too was Colonel Lamb, who proved to be a stern taskmasker. Unlike many garrison commanders he made his soldiers—whom Lamb jokingly referred to as his inmates—work hard and drill regularly. The daily routine of fort building, which included shoveling sand, constructing barracks and mounting cannon—coupled with incessant drilling with light and heavy artillery and small arms—was exhausting and dull. Lamb insisted, however, that "no where in the Southern Army are soldiers treated with greater kindness & consideration by their officers than at Fort Fisher. Every thing is done for their comfort consistent with the Army regulations, and a better clothed, quartered & fed garrison is not to be found in the South." Though he worked his men hard, Lamb did everything he could to provide for their needs while preparing them for a Union attack, an event Lamb's superior, W. H. C. Whiting, predicted was coming soon.[34]

Although Lamb drilled his men and Whiting prepared his district for battle, the Richmond authorities downplayed the threat against the seaport. Indeed, the Confederate high command deemed Chase Whiting an alarmist. For years after assuming command of the Cape Fear District, Whiting had deluged the War Department in Richmond with requests for additional troops. "My first and last request will be for troops the instant they are available," Whiting matter-of-factly stated. "The Department is undoubtedly aware of the imminent need for them for the defense of Wilmington." This was the first of hundreds of letters and telegrams the persistent Whiting would pen requesting and sometimes demanding troops of President Davis, his high ranking generals, North Carolina's Governor Zebulon Vance, Secretary of War James A. Seddon, and nearly everyone else in the national and state high commands. Whiting's entreaties became so commonplace that in time the addressees paid scant attention to them. "Gen. Whiting writes that Wilmington is in imminent danger from a coup de main," recorded John B. Jones, a clerk in the War Department. Two days later, on August 28, 1863, Jones noted: "Another letter from Gen. Whiting, calls vehemently for reinforcements—or else the city and harbor are soon to be at the mercy of the enemy. He is importunate."[35]

"Importunate" or not, Whiting knew that officers in the War Department perceived him as both paranoid and bothersome, but he refused to back down in calling attention to what he described as Wilmington's "wants and difficulties." Perhaps better than anyone else, Whiting recognized the significance of the seaport to the Confederacy, maintaining that it was almost as important as the capital itself. "I do not know now that there is another place, excepting perhaps Richmond, we should not sooner see lost than this," he argued. The general clearly understood what the Union victory at Mobile Bay meant to the enemy, and he warned of the heightened threat to Wilmington to all in authority who would listen or at least feign doing so. "We are running very dangerous risks," Whiting told his mentor and superior officer General P. G. T. Beauregard. "I do not know that the enemy contemplate taking present advantage [of their success at Mobile Bay], but they are fools if they don't, and if they do I assure you that [we]. . . will not be able to make the resistance. . .The garrison of the forts is much too small."[36]

In early September, Secretary of War Seddon conceded that all indications based on intelligence sources and Northern newspaper reports suggested the Federals were preparing to attack Charleston again, or Wilmington. "You are aware of the great importance of continued trade from [Wilmington]," Seddon informed Whiting, as if the general needed reminding. "I need scarcely add any reason to stimulate your habitual vigilance to discover and guard against the approach of the enemy."[37]

Whiting had no doubt that Wilmington was the next target and he worried that his meager force would be insufficient to cover all possible points of attack. In late summer 1864, Little Billy commanded only 2,400 troops to guard both the city and about 100 miles of district shoreline—from Lockwood's Folly on the South Carolina border to Bogue Inlet in Onslow County—where Union troops could come ashore. "The enemy have too many lines of attack open to make self-sustaining forts of much avail," Whiting observed. The coast from New Inlet to the New River, about sixty miles distant, was defended by less than 1,200 men. Whiting maintained that "Fort Fisher alone ought never to be without a garrison of 2,200."[38]

It was these estimates that prompted Whiting to continue sending applications to Richmond for veteran infantrymen to augment his untested garrisons of artillerymen. He desperately wanted at least a division of

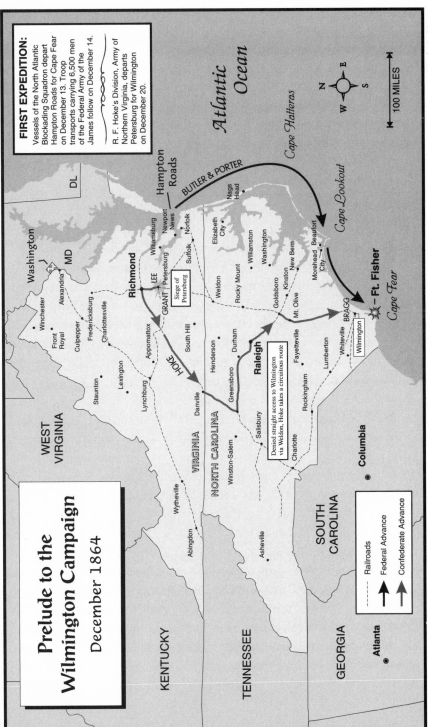

Prelude to the Wilmington Campaign
December 1864

FIRST EXPEDITION:
Vessels of the North Atlantic Blockading Squadron depart Hampton Roads for Cape Fear on December 13. Troop transports carrying 6,500 men of the Federal Army of the James follow on December 14.

R. F. Hoke's Division, Army of Northern Virginia, departs Petersburg for Wilmington on December 20.

Denied straight access to Wilmington via Weldon, Hoke takes a circuitous route

Railroads
Federal Advance
Confederate Advance

Atlantic Ocean

Cape Hatteras

Cape Lookout

Cape Fear

Ft. Fisher

BUTLER & PORTER

BRAGG

HOKE

GRANT

LEE

Siege of Petersburg

Hampton Roads

WEST VIRGINIA

VIRGINIA

NORTH CAROLINA

SOUTH CAROLINA

KENTUCKY

TENNESSEE

GEORGIA

MD

DL

Washington
Alexandria
Winchester
Front Royal
Culpepper
Fredericksburg
Charlottesville
Lexington
Staunton
Lynchburg
Appomattox
Richmond
Petersburg
Williamsburg
Newport News
Norfolk
Suffolk
Weldon
Rocky Mount
Williamston
Washington
Elizabeth City
Nags Head
Morehead City
Beaufort
New Bern
Kinston
Goldsboro
Mt. Olive
Henderson
Durham
Greensboro
Danville
South Hill
Salisbury
Winston-Salem
Charlotte
Rockingham
Fayetteville
Lumberton
Whiteville
Wilmington
Raleigh
Abingdon
Wytheville
Asheville
Columbia
Atlanta

100 MILES

N
W   E
S

Mark A. Moore

battle-hardened foot soldiers for a mobile strike force to challenge the enemy wherever they might attack at Cape Fear. In a letter to Maj. Gen. Jeremy F. Gilmer, one of the Confederacy's top engineers, Whiting explained his rationale for reinforcements. "The whole system of defense adopted [here] is predicated entirely on the presence of a movable force or army corps," he observed. "One veteran soldier will be worth a half dozen [militiamen]. The defenders here must go through an ordeal that only old soldiers can stand," he explained, "and it must be remembered that the garrisons here have never been in action."[39]

The Cape Fear District commander most feared a land assault against Wilmington from Union troops stationed at New Bern, North Carolina. Against such an attack, he believed, "the defenses of the city are useless [without a sufficient force of veteran troops]." If an attack at Wilmington succeeded, the enemy would gain control of the city, the harbor, the river, and most of Federal Point. Thus far, there had been no evidence the enemy contemplated an overland attack from New Bern. After all, the Federals had occupied the Craven County port since the spring of 1862, and for two-and-a-half years had never seriously threatened Wilmington, a mere ninety-three miles to the south. To counteract this potential imperilment, Whiting had constructed strong lines of auxillary earthworks just north of Wilmington at Virginia Creek, Holly Shelter Swamp and Scott's Hill.[40]

Whiting believed that even if the Federals did not attack by way of New Bern, they would attempt to land somewhere along the coast. He considered Masonboro Sound and Wrightsville Sound two potential landing spots. From there the Federals could bypass the main Confederate forts in their advance on the city. At the same time, those approaches would leave the Union troops without naval support once they moved inland. Judging from previous amphibious assaults, the most likely enemy landing sites would be on Oak Island, Bald Head Island or Federal Point. After establishing a beachhead, an invading army could operate against the forts guarding the passageways into the Cape Fear River, while Union warships blasted their way past the guns of the forts and into the harbor, much as they did at Mobile Bay. "The warning of Mobile is before us," Whiting predicted. Once the enemy "made good his foothold," the general claimed, "great disaster may occur."[41]

General Beauregard agreed with his friend Little Billy. At Whiting's and Robert E. Lee's request, Beauregard visited Cape Fear in early September 1864 to examine its defenses. After making his inspection, Beauregard reported to the War Department exactly as Whiting had time and again: infantry support was "most needed" at Wilmington. Despite Beauregard's assessment and Whiting's entreaties, only small numbers of state reserve troops arrived in Wilmington that autumn. Disgusted with Richmond's sloth-like behavior, Whiting directed an urgent appeal to Governor Vance for additional reinforcements and laborers. "At no time since the war began has the force to defend Wilmington been so small as it is now," Whiting complained, "[and] at no time has it been in greater danger."[42]

Despite his apparent unconcern, General Lee had never questioned Wilmington's importance as guardian of the Confederacy's principal supply route. As early as January 1863, Lee instructed the city to be defended "at all hazards." Nevertheless, he like many others believed Whiting was exaggerating the threat to Wilmington, and Lee chided the general for being so persistent in his demands for defensive troops. If and when the Federals moved to attack Wilmington, Lee promised Whiting, Confederate troops would be rushed to defend the city. Until that time came, however, troops were more needed in Virginia.[43]

The bold Federal capture of Mobile Bay forced Lee to reevaluate his position on Wilmington. Farragut's victory found the Army of Northern Virginia dug in along the Richmond-Petersburg line, and Lee was cognizant that his main artery of supplies ran through the Carolina seaport. Lee notified the military authorities at Cape Fear that the port must remain in Confederate hands, otherwise he "could not maintain his army." The general supposition in the Confederate War Department was that if Wilmington fell, Richmond was doomed.[44]

If the threat to Wilmington proved to be genuine, Lee wondered where he could find troops to meet the attack. Because of his predicament in Virginia he could ill-afford to detach his own beleaguered soldiers for the seaport's protection. The commanding general telegraphed General Beauregard asking him to exchange portions of his battle tested soldiers at Charleston for inexperienced troops at Wilmington, giving both places at least some veteran artillerymen. A yellow fever outbreak in Charleston combined with Beauregard's reassignment in October 1864 to command the Military

Division of the West, however, prevented Lee's request from being implemented. That meant North Carolina would have to provide the men and resources to defend Wilmington—at least until troops from Virginia should arrive. "I see no danger in using the garrisons of the forts to resist a landing or approach at other points to gain time for a concentration of troops," Lee wrote. He also asked Governor Vance to send troops deployed elsewhere in North Carolina to Cape Fear, noting that the enemy's recent success at Mobile might induce him to attack Wilmington, "and the importance of that is such that every effort should be made to defend it," Lee explained. Vance promised Lee he would do all he could and would send the state militia, poorly armed as it was, to help safeguard Wilmington. But echoing General Whiting, Vance suggested replacing the garrison troops at Wilmington with veterans from Lee's army who had the combat experience the artillerymen at Cape Fear lacked—well drilled and disciplined though they were.[45]

While the Confederate high command pondered which coastal city the Federals would strike next and where troops could be found to meet such an attack, Whiting continued strengthening Cape Fear's defenses and preparing his men for an assault he felt more certain than ever was coming soon. In addition to shoring up Wilmington's fortifications, Whiting called out the Home Guard, asked the navy to place additional obstructions and torpedoes in the Cape Fear River, and frequently visited Federal Point to confer with Colonel Lamb about the expected attack against Fort Fisher. He even pointed out to Lamb the area where the Federals would most likely come ashore if they targeted Federal Point for a beachhead. In obedience to Whiting's instructions, Capt. Francis Hawks of the Engineer Corps began constructing defenses between Sugar Loaf and Myrtle Sound in order to guard the head of the sound and the Federal Point Road, the main road to Wilmington. Light artillery units were dispatched to Sugar Loaf to contest an amphibious landing. Colonel Lamb, meanwhile, erected a palisade and planted torpedoes (mines) in front of Fort Fisher's land face to stymie an infantry assault launched against that sector. Perhaps as many as 500 black laborers were sent to Fort Fisher to assist Lamb and his men.[46]

While preparations ensued on Federal Point, Whiting petitioned the Navy Department to allow him to use the *Tallahassee* and the *Chickamauga* (the converted blockade runner *Edith*) to assist in defending the harbor. Those were the only two gunboats Whiting had at his disposal, and even they were of doubtful availability. Two ironclads, the *Raleigh* and the *North Carolina*, built in Wilmington for harbor defense, had both met an inglorious fate. The *Raleigh* ran aground and broke her keel on New Inlet's inner bar at low tide after a failed attempt to break the Union blockade in early May 1864. Four months later the *North Carolina*, used almost exclusively as a floating battery because she was so unwieldy, slipped under the river's murky waters after teredo worms ate through her hull at Battery Island off Smithville. Yet a third ironclad, the *Wilmington*, was under construction at Beery's Shipyard on Eagles Island, but it was questionable whether she would be completed in time to help turn back an attack.[47]

Whiting had already written to Richmond on several occasions protesting the government's authorization permitting the *Tallahassee* and the *Chickamauga* to operate as privateers in and out of Wilmington. Whiting believed the *Tallahassee's* success along the New England coast the previous August would only incite the United States government to move more quickly to shut down Wilmington by posting additional blockaders at its inlets or by attacking the place. Moreover, the recent destruction of the famed commerce raider *Alabama* off the coast of France would undoubtedly free additional U. S. warships to strengthen the blockade of Cape Fear. "One would think, to see the items copied from the Northern papers, that Wilmington was a perfect hornet's nest, swarming with cruisers to issue forth and sting the Yankee commerce to death," reported the *Wilmington Daily Journal*. That line of thinking—now commonplace in the Northern press—concerned General Whiting. Private grievances had a way of influencing public policy. Whiting argued that the *Tallahassee* and *Chickamauga* should be employed to protect Wilmington instead of engaging in adventures that would ultimately force him to defend the city.[48]

Not surprisingly, President Davis and Secretary of the Navy Stephen R. Mallory disagreed with Whiting. They believed the U. S. Navy would transfer some of its blockading ships at Cape Fear to chase down the *Tallahassee* and *Chickamauga*, which were then prowling the ocean's shipping lanes. Davis and Mallory insisted the two vessels were not warships, and could offer little protection for Wilmington against a determined naval attack. It would be more advantageous to use them to harass and weaken the enemy's commerce, they explained, and Wilmington was the only available base from which they could operate.[49]

Whiting was infuriated with the president's logic, and subsequent events proved the general right on both counts. The Federals not only strengthened the blockade of Wilmington but attacked the seaport as well. The *Tallahassee*, unable to procure enough coal for another long raiding voyage, was converted into a blockade runner and renamed *Chameleon*. In the end Whiting was successful in his efforts to secure the *Chickamauga* to help defend Wilmington, probably because General Lee intervened on his behalf.[50]

Despite Whiting's hard work and diligence, his days as commander of the Cape Fear District were numbered. When it became apparent the enemy would strike Wilmington, the Confederate high command disputed Whiting's ability to successfully defend the port. Whiting's superiors had long recognized and praised his skills as an engineer. Even Governor Vance, who had often clashed with the general over North Carolina's blockade running and salt production enterprises at Wilmington, respected Whiting's standing as an officer of "the highest order of talent." The problem was Whiting's reputed fondness for the "social glass." Rumor had it that the general drank too much liquor too often. "Whiting was an able & gallant officer," acknowledged a North Carolinian. "His greatest faults are unregulated thirst which he indulged at improper times." Though Whiting strongly denied the accusations, they caused Governor Vance and others considerable concern. "Only one thing has ever occurred to impair the universal confidence which you inspired by your diligence in fortifying the town," Vance wrote candidly to Whiting, "and that was a very general impression that you drank too much; that your nervous system had been injured by it."[51]

Whiting's reputation as a drunkard had dogged him for years, and only recently had the rumor once again reared its ugly head. In mid-May 1864, Beauregard arranged for his good friend from Wilmington to come to Virginia to help defend Petersburg, which was then threatened by the Army of the James under Maj. Gen. Benjamin F. Butler. Beauregard hoped Whiting might reclaim some credibility, tainted at it was by his alleged alcoholism. Beauregard entrusted Little Billy with a delicate tactical maneuver in an effort to surprise and capture Butler's main force at Drewry's Bluff. Whiting, however, failed to fulfill his assignment of striking the enemy's rear at Walthall's Station, thus enabling Butler's army to escape the trap so carefully planned to snare him.[52]

An angry subordinate, Brig. Gen. Henry A. Wise, charged Whiting with drunkenness on the battlefield. Whiting vehemently denied the accusation, asserting that he had been hampered by poor health and bad weather. Members of his staff publicly supported him, claiming that the general had consumed nothing but coffee and water since his arrival in Petersburg. Their words fell on deaf ears. The damage was done and Whiting's integrity suffered yet another hard blow. Nor did it help Whiting's cause that President Davis, no admirer of the general to start with, was visiting the battlefield at the time of the controversy and received a less than flattering account of Whiting's conduct. Even the sympathetic Beauregard had his doubts about his old friend. Saddened by the harsh indictments against him and his own poor performance on the battlefield, Whiting asked Beauregard to relieve him of the field command he had so desperately wanted. Beauregard consented, and a depressed Whiting returned to Wilmington.

News of Whiting's conduct at Petersburg spread like a brush fire into North Carolina. Most of the his soldiers remained undaunted by the rumors, because they liked and respected the general enormously. But Whiting's critics, Governor Vance in particular, held it against him. The governor suggested to the War Department that Whiting be replaced in Wilmington by General Beauregard. Vance believed the Creole general would be a great asset to the city, having prevented the Federals from capturing Charleston after fourteen months of siege warfare. "In case a real attack should be made upon Wilmington," Vance wrote General Lee, "I earnestly urge that General Beauregard should be sent there, and this not only because of the great confidence felt in him, but also because of the very little reposed in General Whiting. . .since the affair at Petersburg."[53]

Vance's logic did not result in any argument from Lee. "[Whiting] is a man of unquestionable knowledge suited to his position," Lee acknowledged, "but whether he would be able at the required time to apply these qualifications and to maintain the confidence of his command is with me questionable." Such faint praise from the commanding general was tantamount to a damning indictment. Lee had planned all along for Beauregard to be in command at whichever city was first attacked—Wilmington or Charleston. But President Davis, who disliked Beauregard even more than Whiting, overruled Lee. Davis had another officer in mind to command at Wilmington: General Braxton Bragg.[54]

Considering Wilmington's importance to the Confederacy, it was ironic, indeed foolish, that Davis would entrust the city's defense to Braxton Bragg, an officer whose resume was replete with battlefield indecisiveness and failure—as well as horrendous relations with his subordinates. It had not always been so. Bragg had been an exemplary cadet at West Point, where he graduated fifth out of fifty cadets in the class of 1837. He went on to serve with distinction in the Second Seminole War and in the War with Mexico, where in the latter conflict he was awarded three brevets. As a captain of artillery, Bragg earned significant distinction at the Battle of Buena Vista in February 1847, when future president Zachary Taylor ordered him to "double shot those guns and give 'em hell!" From that moment on Bragg's name became synonymous with double shotting artillery and giving the enemy hell.

Bragg rose to the rank of lieutenant colonel before resigning from the U. S. Army in 1856. According to an old army acquaintance, William T. Sherman, Bragg retired rather than obey a transfer order from the secretary of the war, Jefferson Davis, which would have sent Bragg into Indian territory. "Bragg hated Davis bitterly" after this, Sherman later claimed. Instead of returning to his hometown of Warrenton, North Carolina (where he had been born on March 22, 1817), Bragg moved to Louisiana to marry the wealthy Eliza Brooks Ellis. He found success in the Deep South with rewarding careers as both a sugar planter and state engineer. When Louisiana seceded from the Union the governor made Bragg a major general in command of state forces. Six weeks later, on March 7, 1861, Bragg was appointed brigadier general in the Confederate Army by his former adversary and the Confederacy's newly inaugurated president—Jefferson Davis. In an amazing ascent in rank, Bragg, in just thirteen months, rose from brigadier general to full general in the regular Confederate army, a position held by only seven other officers.

Bragg cut a striking figure in his double-breasted gray wool tunic with gold braid on the sleeves and stars on the collar denoting his rank as a general officer. He was tall, slender, sported a neatly trimmed salt-and-pepper beard, and had a head full of thick gray hair. Overall his appearance and demeanor gave Bragg an almost regal appearance. But comparisons to anything royal stopped at that juncture. Bragg's stooped posture and piercing eyes—deeply set beneath a thick brow and bushy eyebrows—combined with downturned thin lips to give him a foreboding countenance. Despite outward appearances, Bragg was a man of unquestioned intelligence and good breeding, and was highly regarded throughout the army as a strict disciplinarian, skillful organizer and efficient administrator.

By late June 1862, Bragg commanded the Army of the Mississippi (redesignated the Army of Tennessee in November 1862), a force he had

Gen. Braxton Bragg. By the time he was sent to take over command at Wilmington in October 1864, Bragg was one of the most vilified officers in the Confederate army. *U.S. Army Military History Institute*

helped assemble. In a bold strategic move later that summer, Bragg raided into Kentucky, penetrating further north than any other commander of the Confederacy's Western Department. Despite a promising start the campaign unraveled after an inconclusive engagement at Perryville, prompting Bragg to retreat back into Tennessee. The bloody draw at Perryville was followed by a series of stinging battlefield defeats for Bragg, each succeeded by vitriolic intra-army disputes. The field defeats merged with the command friction and culminated in a crushing loss of confidence in Bragg's leadership abilities. His failure to exploit an advantage gained by his army in the first day's fighting at Murfreesboro (Stones River) on December 31, 1862, led to his withdrawal three days later and the eventual abandonment of much of Tennessee the following summer. After reinforcements from Lt. Gen. James Longstreet's corps arrived from Virginia in September 1863, Bragg attacked Federal forces at Chickamauga, Georgia, but again blundered in not following-up what appeared to be a sweeping Confederate victory. Bragg instead settled for a siege of Chattanooga, southeastern Tennessee's principal railroad hub, a course his army was ill-equipped to follow. Bragg's inaction strained already fragile relationships with his senior officers, and several of them publicly criticized the general's strategy and called for his removal. The controversy became so heated that President Davis personally intervened, visiting Bragg and his generals to try and smooth things over. In the end Davis sustained Bragg and chastised his disaffected subordinate generals. It was only after his army was decisively beaten at Missionary Ridge on November 25 that Bragg resigned his command.[55]

In an attempt to ease the disappointment of a man he considered an old friend (Sherman's statement notwithstanding), Davis brought Bragg to Richmond to serve as general-in-chief and military adviser to the president. By then Bragg had apparently overcome his deep-seated hostility toward Davis. Despite the president's solid loyalty, Bragg was probably the most despised general officer in the Confederate army. His opponents caustically referred to him as the best general the Union army ever had.[56]

Much of the animosity that swirled about Bragg was generated by his own disposition, which Ulysses S. Grant, who had known Bragg in the old army, defined as "naturally disputatious. Bragg's own soldiers hated him so much that twice they tried to assassinate him in Mexico. In the prewar army Bragg's bad temper was legendary. He feuded with just about everyone he knew—including Braxton Bragg. One popular anecdote recounted how Bragg, while serving simultaneously as company commander and quartermaster, got into a dispute with himself and finally summoned the post commandant to resolve the problem. "My God, Mr. Bragg," the commander exclaimed, "you have quarrelled with every officer in the army, and now you are quarrelling with yourself!"[57]

Chronic ill health contributed to Bragg's acerbic temperament. He suffered from a legion of ailments, including migraine headaches, dyspepsia, dysentery, and stress. "This is a reason for certain eccentricities of temper now and then manifested by him," an observer pointed out. The war—both on the battlefield and against his contentious subordinates—had taken their toll on Bragg, who often appeared tired, pale, haggard and nervous. By the time he was ordered to Wilmington, Braxton Bragg was the most vilified and controversial officer in the Confederacy. The mere mention of his name evoked an emotional response, and by October 1864, his detractors far outnumbered his defenders. Thus it came as no surprise that Bragg's appointment to such an important post at a crucial hour drew swift and harsh criticism.[58]

If Richmond and North Carolina authorities were worried that Whiting did not instill confidence, certainly Bragg was no improvement. "General Bragg is going to Wilmington. Goodbye Wilmington," the *Richmond Enquirer* announced. The change in commanders was particularly distressing to Whiting loyalists, including the commander of Fort Fisher, William Lamb. "No one was so capable of defending the Cape Fear as the brilliant officer who had given so much of his time and ability for its defense," exclaimed the disappointed colonel. One of Lamb's lieutenants recalled that [Little Billy's] relief by Bragg brought gloom over the entire command."[59]

With good reason critics questioned Bragg's qualifications for his new command. Unlike Whiting, Bragg possessed no apparent emotional attachment to the region. He also had not labored for years in building defenses to protect the city, as had Whiting. As one Wilmingtonian pointed out: "Besides being a devoted Confederate, General Whiting has his home in the State, and in the town, and thus presents an additional guarantee. . .that nothing he can do will be wanting to contribute to a successful defence; yea, even though another man should be placed in the lead. . . ." Indeed, the new leader Bragg did not even seem to grasp the importance of the seaport to the

Confederacy, despite Lee's warning that if Wilmington fell, Richmond and the Army of Northern Virginia would soon fall with it. "Whether the importance of the harbor is such to justify the withdrawal of means from other points, also endangered," Bragg informed Lee, "your own judgment can best decide." In Bragg, Wilmington would find no enthusiastic advocate as it had in Whiting.[60]

General Lee could have stepped in to challenge Davis' appointment of Bragg to Wilmington, and at one point such an opportunity presented itself. When Governor Vance asked Jefferson Davis to appoint Maj. Gen. Daniel Harvey Hill commander of the eastern portion of the Department of North Carolina, in lieu of General Beauregard—Vance's and Lee's first choice—the president sought Lee's advice. While Lee considered D. H. Hill "brave, watchful, and patriotic," he also knew that Bragg and Hill did not get along and feared there would be a "want of harmony" between the two officers over Wilmington's defense. Lee counseled that as long as Bragg was at Wilmington, he should have control of the entire district. The commander of the Army of Northern Virginia apparently believed that even the unpopular Bragg would be better for Wilmington than the undependable Whiting.[61]

In public Whiting took the demotion in stride, though privately he admitted it both hurt and angered him. "I do not know what [Bragg] was sent to Wilmington for," Whiting lamented. "I had hoped that I was considered competent; I acquiesced with feelings of great mortification." Whiting's "feelings of great mortification" were not so much for himself as for the city. His main concern was Wilmington's protection. If the city could be saved, Whiting told Governor Vance, he was perfectly willing to serve under any officer—Beauregard, Lee, or even Napoleon, if he could be brought back from the dead—considered more capable or more acceptable than himself. Jefferson Davis considered Braxton Bragg more capable and more acceptable than Chase Whiting, and Davis' opinion was what counted.[62]

With little fanfare and much trepidation, Braxton Bragg arrived in Wilmington on October 22 to take command of the Cape Fear District. "Bragg the Unlucky is a Millstone which Mr. Davis persists in tying around our necks," one citizen complained. Three weeks later Bragg was assigned to head the newly-formed Department of North Carolina. This did not remove him from command at Wilmington, but enlarged his territorial responsibilities. So as not to wound General Whiting's pride too deeply, Bragg retained him as second in command, "in discharge of his former functions of administration and detail."[63]

In what must have been a pleasant change for Richmond, Bragg sent a favorable report to the War Department about conditions in Wilmington. He expressed some doubts about Whiting, whom he described as excited, anxious, and paranoid, but who was also industrious, zealous, and—above all—sober. Moreover, Whiting had seen to it that the defenses were well constructed and "prepared to oppose a . . .powerful naval attack." But Bragg feared that against a land attack, the troops would probably make only a "mere nominal resistance," because defensive earthworks were so scattered and the avenues of attack so wide open. Reserves had been slow coming in, but with good conduct on the part of the garrison troops and a little luck, Bragg expected a "successful defense against any naval attack which can be made."[64]

Like Whiting, Bragg was banking on the Federals to attack Wilmington as they had Mobile Bay, that is, by going against the forts guarding the river's entrances. If they did, Bragg believed the Confederates stood a solid chance of turning them back. The earthen forts were built to withstand a naval bombardment, but everything hinged on whether infantry troops could resist an enemy landing. Bragg considered a Union descent on Federal Point a dangerous prospect for Confederate defenders. If the Federals secured a foothold there, they would gain control of the Cape Fear River, rendering Wilmington worthless as a blockade running seaport. "If the harbor is lost," Bragg predicted, "[it] can only be recovered by means much greater than would suffice to hold it." As Whiting had already stated repeatedly and Bragg soon came to realize, a mobile force of veteran infantry troops was desperately needed at the Cape Fear.[65]

Whether Bragg could accomplish the job that Davis, Lee and Vance believed Whiting could not, would soon be decided. In late October, Confederate scouts reported that an armada of Union warships—including frigates and several armored vessels—was assembling at Hampton Roads, Virginia, for a strike on Wilmington. "What has been so long threatened and so much talked about seems to have come at last. The long deferred attack on Wilmington would appear to be at hand," reported the *Wilmington Daily*

Journal on October 22, 1864. "We have good reason to believe, from information received, that an attack is imminent, and may be looked for any day."[66]

The U.S. Government desperately wanted to close Wilmington on the Cape Fear River (shown here) to blockade running. *Author's Collection*

Admiral Porter's fleet assembling at Hampton Roads, Virginia, for the Wilmington expedition. *U. S. Army Military History Institute*

Rear Admiral David Dixon Porter, the caustic, conceited—and capable—commander of the Union naval task force assembled to capture Fort Fisher. *Courtesy of Charles V. Peery*

Chapter 4

"A Glare on the Horizon and a Dull Report."

– Capt. Thomas O. Selfridge, USS Huron

THE EXPERIMENT

Admiral Porter spent most of the autumn of 1864 organizing the huge fleet earmarked for the Wilmington expedition. By late October Porter's North Atlantic Blockading Squadron contained about 150 ships. One eyewitness noted that the numerous tall masts dominating Chesapeake Bay resembled a "dense forest." Remarked another, "Such a gathering of armed ships of war had never before been seen." Meanwhile, the gunboats' crews spent long hours in target practice and fitting their ships for battle. Amid all these preparations, Porter quietly sent two dozen ships south to tighten the blockade of the Cape Fear.[1]

At one point Porter had forty-five ships on the prowl for enemy commerce vessels attempting to enter or exit Wilmington's harbor—twice the normal complement of blockaders. By expertly positioning the additional "bar tenders" and patrol ships, Porter quickly increased the captures of blockade runners. Although he did not stop the trade, the business of apprehending blockade runners became so remunerative that Porter amassed a handsome sum of prize money. Since 1798 the Navy Department had offered monetary incentives for the capture of illicit vessels and contraband goods. The Prize Law of the Navy provided sailors and officers—often bored by the dull routine of serving "on the blockade"—with hefty rewards when captured cargo was sold through adjudication proceedings in Northern courts. Porter claimed that in a fifty-day stretch between mid-October and early December, his blockaders had captured or destroyed $5,500,000 worth of property at the Cape Fear that had been destined for the Confederacy. By law squadron commanders were entitled to one-twentieth of the prize money, meaning that Porter earned $275,000 during the seven-week stint. As the admiral himself admitted, "[he was getting] richer than it was desirable for a naval officer to be."[2]

With his bank account bulging and getting fatter by the day, Porter was no longer in a hurry to launch the attack on Fort Fisher. His only apprehension was that in postponing the operation his fleet might later fall prey to the late-autumn storms that often ravaged the North Carolina coast. But the newly-rich Porter "bottled-up his usual knack for impatience" and consoled himself by criticizing the army and capturing more blockade runners—and thereby becoming even richer. He realized the Navy Department would be unwilling, for political as well as strategic reasons, to maintain so many vessels on blockade duty at the Cape Fear, but he kept the additional ships there so long as the secretary of the navy did not protest.[3]

In reality, Secretary Welles' only complaint was that the army so far had failed to cooperate by supplying troops for the expedition. As October faded, Grant had yet to detach the promised units from the armies of the James and Potomac, both entrenched outside Petersburg and Richmond. The lieutenant general maintained he still did not have enough "disposable forces" for the Fort Fisher expeditionary force, and besides, the possibility of a surprise attack at the Cape Fear had been ruined by rumors of the expedition circulating in the Northern press.

Admiral Porter believed the commanding general had an ulterior motive for not providing the requisite troops. On October 18 Porter had traveled to City Point in order to, as he described it, "stir Grant up" and get things going. He came away from the meeting convinced that Grant simply was not interested in supporting the Fort Fisher campaign. "[Grant] wants to take Richmond (which can not be done) without outside aid. Take the forts [guarding the river approaches to Wilmington] and Richmond will fall," Porter argued. The veteran seaman was particularly displeased with Grant's lack of enthusiasm because Porter had closely cooperated with Grant two years before at Vicksburg. Personal feelings aside, the admiral maintained that Richmond would not fall until Wilmington was captured. "[Grant] can't

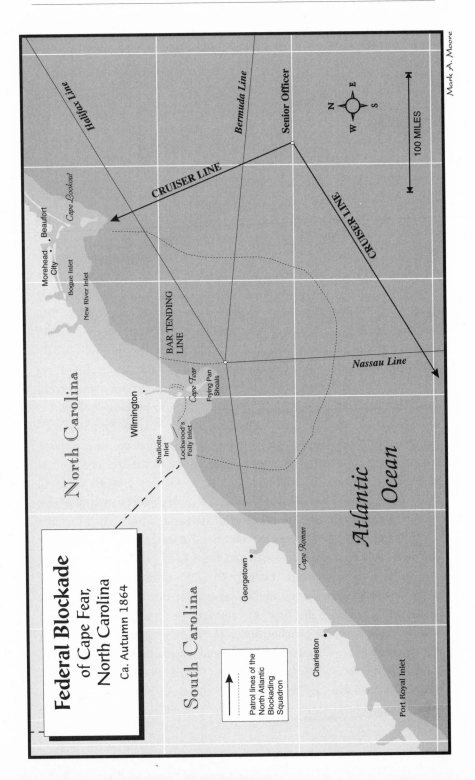

Mark A. Moore

move an inch & won't move an inch until Wilmington is taken," Porter predicted.[4]

In a final effort to light a fire under Grant, Porter appealed to Gideon Welles, who in turn sought the ear of President Lincoln. "[The] delay is becoming exceedingly embarrassing to [the Navy Department], and the importance of having the military authorities impressed with the necessity of speedy action has prompted the communication to you," Welles explained. "The public expect this attack, and the country will be distressed if it is not made. To procrastinate much longer will be to peril its success."[5]

Thanks to Welles' intervention, the political pressure to act was building on Grant. When Gustavus Fox paid the commanding general a visit in late October, Grant again agreed to provide troops for the expedition. The general accompanied Fox and Maj. Gen. Benjamin F. Butler (in whose department Fort Fisher lay) to see Admiral Porter at Hampton Roads to discuss the attack and smooth ruffled naval feathers. Porter, however, was more than just upset by Grant's attitude; he was also dissatisfied with Grant's choice of army commander. Porter was intimately familiar with Godfrey Weitzel, having fought with him at New Orleans and at Alexandria during the Red River Campaign. Although Porter acknowledged that Weitzel was a man of "considerable intelligence and engineering skills," he also believed Weitzel was timid and weak, and "the slave" of General Butler. "I knew from the first," Porter wrote, "that Weitzel was not the man to command an expedition requiring nerve." Once, while visiting Porter on board the *Malvern*, Weitzel inadvertently allowed a cabin door to slam in General Butler's face. An angry Butler cursed Weitzel, humiliating the subordinate in front of Porter and his staff. Porter turned to his chief of staff and whispered: "a [regular army] major general who has not the moral courage to knock down [a volunteer] major general who curses him, is not fit to assault Fort Fisher."[6]

Too bad, thought Porter, that Maj. Gen. Winfield Scott Hancock was unavailable, Maj. Gen. James McPherson dead, or that William T. Sherman "could not bring his brains here" to command the expeditionary force and deal forcefully with the haughty Butler. Porter even entertained the notion that Grant's choice of Weitzel may have been an unconscious expression of his disdain for the Wilmington Campaign. Despite Porter's disgust, Grant believed Weitzel was capable of performing the task. On paper, Weitzel was eminently qualified. At the very least Grant's selection displayed his political acumen, for Weitzel served under Benjamin F. Butler, the politically powerful commander of the Department of Virginia and North Carolina.[7]

Major General Benjamin Franklin Butler was widely regarded as a flamboyant, pompous, self-indulgent general who held sway in the military because of his high-powered connections in Washington. Not even President Lincoln dared challenge him—at least not until the 1864 elections were decided. Butler hailed from Massachusetts, where he had made his fortune and reputation as a successful, albeit controversial, businessman, lawyer and state politician. He was both brilliant and able. In 1861, Lincoln appointed Butler as the Union army's first major general of volunteers, a move the president later regretted, for Butler proved inept as a field commander and despotic as a military administrator. The Massachusetts general's debut as a field commander was less than impressive when a Confederate force soundly defeated him in the first notable land engagement of the war at Bethel, Virginia. Butler rebounded somewhat with a victory in the first Federal land and sea operation at Hatteras Island, North Carolina, in August, 1861.

Following Admiral Farragut's capture of New Orleans in 1862, Butler served a six-month stint as military governor of Louisiana. Headquartered in New Orleans, Butler came under fire for his controversial ruling policies, including a command to hang a Southern man for desecrating a U. S. flag, and the infamous "Woman's Order," an arrest warrant of New Orleans' women for prostitution if they showed disrespect toward Union officers. The dictatorial Butler once arrested a New Orleans lady for laughing as a Union funeral procession passed. He also allegedly stole money and silverware from local residents—hence his infamous moniker "Spoons" Butler. Southerners had another name for the hated general: "the Beast." Jefferson Davis branded him an outlaw, authorizing his capture as such and calling for his execution as a felon. "Benjamin F. Butler, cursed of God and abhorred of man," wrote a Confederate newspaper editor, "a man whose name is known from one end of Christendom to the other, and never recalled without its well-earned addition of 'the beast.'"

In a whirlwind of controversy, Butler was removed from command at New Orleans, only to be given command of the Department of Virginia and North Carolina, which included the Army of the James. In May 1864, Butler infuriated Grant when his bungling at Drewry's Bluff maneuvered his army

The Federal Department of Virginia and North Carolina was commanded by Maj. Gen. Benjamin F. Butler, the highly controversial officer whose soldiers called "Ol Cockeye," and Southerners dubbed "the Beast." *U.S. Army Military History Institute*

into a vise that almost led to its destruction at the hands of Generals Beauregard and Whiting. One observer noted the obvious when he stated that "[Butler] was a good lawyer, but a poor soldier." While the debacle at Drewry's Bluff further tarnished his already low military reputation, Butler's weighty political influence in the Democratic party enabled him to retain his position and escape the disciplinary action that might have befallen a less well-connected general. Lincoln could not afford to sack the man.[8]

In appearance, Benjamin Butler was at best odd-looking. The 46-year old rotund lawyer supported an oversized, square head, bald on top with hair growing only from the sides and back. His stooped shoulders propped up a fat, sagging face pierced with small beady eyes peeking through a pair of heavy eyelids upheld by twin puffy bags beneath. Butler initially sported a droopy mustache and, by the autumn of 1864, a scraggly chin beard. His wandering left eye gave him a cross-eyed countenance, and as might be expected, his soldiers sarcastically referred to him as "Ol' Cockeye." Despite his high rank, Butler held army regulations in contempt. He claimed he had never studied the army manual and never intended to. Even so, he loved the pomp and circumstance of military life, was often adorned in full regalia (double-breasted dress tunic, kepi, accouterments, and saber), and liked to parade around with his lackeys in tow. "[Butler] was all jingle and feathers and [had a] staff as large as all out doors," Admiral Porter observed.[9]

Yet for all his eccentricities, there was also an imaginative, curious, even daring side to Ben Butler. New technology enthralled him, and to his credit he experimented with it throughout the war. He employed hot-air balloons for reconnaissance missions, wire entanglements for defense, and tried—albeit unsuccessfully—to invent a rifle cannon. It therefore should have come as no surprise to anyone when Butler proposed to close Wilmington to blockade running by simply blowing up Fort Fisher or Fort Caswell with a gigantic floating bomb. As harebrained as that scheme may have sounded (or sounds today), Butler and quite a few others believed it had some merit.

The huge explosion of a Confederate bomb on board a Union ordnance barge docked at City Point, Virginia in mid-August 1864, and its resulting devastation of an adjacent supply depot, had caught Butler's attention. Grant certainly remembered that explosion, as it had almost cost him his life. Butler also took note of an accidental detonation of two powder barges between Erith and Woolwich, England, that had leveled nearby storehouses and buildings. Butler reasoned that the explosion of an enormous amount of gunpowder might also level the sand batteries of Fort Fisher and allow the Union army to march in uncontested and sweep up the stunned and demoralized Confederate survivors. "I believed that possibly," Butler later wrote, "by bringing within four or five hundred yards of Fort Fisher a large mass of explosives, and firing the whole in every part at the same moment—for it was the essence of the experiment to have the powder all exploded at the same instant—the garrison would at least be so far paralyzed as to enable, by a prompt landing of men, a seizure of the fort."[10]

Butler had suggested the idea to President Lincoln, Assistant Secretary Fox, and General Halleck while passing through Washington en route to New York in early November 1864. Lincoln was skeptical, but Fox latched onto the plan and ordered the U. S. Navy's Bureau of Ordnance to look into it. The bureau studied the matter and soon concluded that, under the right circumstances, it just might work. With that endorsement in hand, Fox assembled a host of ordnance experts in Washington to formulate a plan. Among them were Cmdr. Henry A. Wise, the U. S. Navy's Chief of Bureau of Ordnance (and in whose home the commission first met on November 23); Lt. Cmdr. William N. Jeffers, the navy's inspector of ordnance; and Brig. Gen. Alexander B. Dyer, the U. S. Army's Chief of Ordnance and inventor of the Dyer shell. After much discussion they reported that the explosion of a powder boat might so severely damage the Confederates' earthworks, artillery and morale that it could render them defenseless against a combined army-navy assault. The "experts" recommended stockpiling a large light-draft ship with 300 tons of gunpowder, one half to be supplied by the navy and the other half by the army, and then running her onto the beach as near to Fort Fisher as possible. Fort Fisher was the preferred target because it was constructed almost entirely of sand, unlike Fort Caswell, which was principally a masonry fort. If the powder vessel could be detonated close enough to the target, hurricane-force winds created by the explosion might demolish everything in their path for a quarter-of-a-mile or more.[11]

Dubious of the novel plan when he first learned of it, Porter studied it carefully, and sought the opinions of his own ordnance experts. In view of the stakes, the admiral decided it was a "risk worth the running." According to his calculations, such an explosion would "wind up Fort Fisher and the works along [Federal Point] beach." He concluded the powder boat experiment would either "prove that forts on the water are useless or that the rebels are proof against gunpowder." Above all else, Porter consented to the experiment because he was now anxious to get the expedition underway. "I am willing to take the powder-boat to get the [infantry] men," the admiral stated with no little honesty.[12]

The proposed powder boat experiment was not without its critics, foremost among them U. S. Grant and Gideon Welles. "I had no faith in the success of the scheme and so expressed myself," Grant later admitted. "It is at least foolish to think that the effect of the explosion could be transmitted to such a distance with enough force to weaken the fort. . .It will always be found in the end that the only way to whip an army is to go out and fight it." Welles evinced a similar lack of confidence in the project. Nor did Richard Delafield, the U. S. Army's Chief Engineer, believe in the powder boat scheme. According to his detailed study, a powder vessel would have to be grounded and exploded within 450 yards of the forts to have any chance of producing appreciable damage. Beyond that distance it would have about the same effect as "firing feathers from muskets would have on the enemy." Delafield argued that the explosive force of gunpowder alone, immense as it might be, could not injure the solid brick walls and sand ramparts of Fort Caswell. Although Fisher was made of sand, a ship could not safely approach any closer than 950 yards of the bastion's powerful batteries, more than double the safe approach distance of Fort Caswell. According to Delefield, the powder boat "could produce no useful result toward the reduction of those works" because the water approaches were too shallow to get a powder vessel near enough to do the job. Lieutenant Colonel Cyrus B. Comstock, General Grant's astute chief engineer, was more candid in his opinion of the proposal: "[Butler and Porter] are full of it!"[13]

Grant's innate skepticism and Delafield's critical report caused sufficient trepidation in the War Department to prompt Secretary Stanton to withhold his allotment of gunpowder. Nevertheless, Fox and Butler prevailed in the end. The two men, friends since their early days in Massachusetts, helped one another whenever a political boost was needed. Certainly political promotion was needed in this instance, and both men flexed their respective political muscles in an attempt to push the powder boat project along. Oddly, neither Grant nor Welles attempted to block their efforts. For his part, Welles doubted the Wilmington expedition could move forward without Butler's cooperation. Grant agreed to the experiment when his friend David D. Porter "seemed to fall in with the idea," and because he did not see that any "serious harm could come [of it]." President Lincoln concurred. "We might as well explode the notion with powder as with anything else," the chief executive jested.[14]

Now that the project had official backing, Admiral Porter offered to supply the sacrificial vessel: the *Louisiana*, a 295-ton, 143-foot long iron hulled screw steamer. She was a relatively new ship when Porter offered her up for destruction, having been constructed in 1860 by Harlan & Hollingsworth Co. of Wilmington, Delaware. In addition to capturing three blockade runners, she had also taken part in the conquests of Elizabeth City and New Bern, North Carolina in early 1862. For most of the war, however, the *Louisiana* had been used as a patrol boat in North Carolina's Albemarle Sound. Porter's ordnance experts liked her because she drew a light-draft (eight to eight and one-half feet of water when fully loaded), and they believed she could hold the requisite 300 tons of gunpowder to blow up Fort Fisher. Porter immediately ordered her sent to Norfolk, Virginia for refitting.[15]

Work on the *Louisiana* began as soon as she reached the Gosport Navy Yard on November 30. She was stripped of everything but her boiler and machinery, and workmen began the process of converting her into a floating bomb. A team of artisans disguised her to look like a blockade runner so she could slip under the guns of Fort Fisher without causing alarm. Laborers added a turtle back to cover the bow section, a false second smokestack, and a good coat of whitewash on the hull. Like most major projects, this one ran into some difficulties, first when the shipyard commandant refused to authorize round-the-clock work on her, and next because the army's portion of powder had not yet arrived. Porter complained that the delays threatened to sabotage the campaign, and once again Gustavus Fox intervened and soon had everyone concerned working apace.[16]

By this time Grant was growing impatient with the whole affair. On the same day the *Louisiana* steamed into Norfolk for her conversion, Grant had expressed his desire to see the expedition move "without a moment's delay" toward Wilmington. After months of seeming apathy, his sudden about face caught Porter, Weitzel and Butler by surprise. As it turned out, Grant had read newspapers from Savannah and Augusta that reported Braxton Bragg's arrival in Georgia with troops from Wilmington. The reinforcements were slated to aid Lt. Gen. William J. Hardee's efforts to block Sherman's March to the Sea. Bragg had left Wilmington on November 22 with about half of the soldiers stationed at Fort Fisher, Camp Jackson near Sugar Loaf, and Fort Holmes on Bald Head Island. With the principal forts protecting Wilmington depleted of troops (2,700 according to Major General Whiting), Grant believed that the Cape Fear estuary was ripe for the taking.[17]

Grant grew uneasy when December 4 passed without any sign of movement from either Weitzel or Porter. "I feel great anxiety to see the Wilmington expedition off both on account of the present fine weather, which we can expect no continuance of, and because Sherman may now be expected to strike the Sea Coast any day now leaving Bragg free to return," Grant informed General Butler. "I think it advisable for you to notify Admiral Porter and get off without any delay with or without your powder boat."[18]

Butler wired Porter immediately, asking when the navy might be ready to get underway for "Savannah" (The word "Savannah" was used in place of Wilmington, just in case the telegram fell into enemy hands). Porter, however, was still busy outfitting the *Louisiana* and making final preparations for the expected naval battle. Many of the ships' yards, top-masts and spars had been taken down, and everything that might be splintered—including launches and lifeboats—were removed from the decks. Sailors had covered the main decks with sand bags to prevent high-arcing, "plunging shots" from penetrating. They had also lashed chain cables to the sides of many of the warships to deflect Confederate artillery shells, so as to protect boilers and machinery. Arrangements were also made for the care of wounded sailors, with extra bandages, blankets, cots, and surgeons brought on board the vessels. All that now remained was to load additional ammunition for the gunboats and the army's portion of the gunpowder for the powder boat experiment.

Once the *Louisiana's* appearance had been changed to resemble a blockade runner, she was sent down to Craney Island at the mouth of the Elizabeth River to receive the gunpowder that would blow her into history. The army's powder did not arrive until the evening of December 5 or early the following morning. Navy Ordnance Bureau personnel carefully stacked the remaining bags and barrels of powder on the *Louisiana's* berth-deck, in the coal bunker, and in the deckhouse.[19]

When he learned Porter and Weitzel still had not advanced by December 6, Grant again pressed his subordinates to act. He ordered Butler to send an expedition up the Roanoke River to sabotage the Weldon Railroad and thus hamper the transfer of Confederate reinforcements from Virginia to Wilmington. The lieutenant general also issued detailed orders to General Weitzel for his campaign to capture Wilmington. These written instructions informed Weitzel that the primary objective was to close the seaport to blockade running by capturing Fort Fisher. A quick and successful strike at the Cape Fear would also provide the Federals with a staging area close enough to Georgia to quickly reinforce General Sherman if he needed additional troops. Grant's directive specifically instructed Weitzel to land his force on Federal Point and be ready to take advantage of the navy's effort to gain possession of Wilmington's harbor. The lieutenant general was counting on Porter to run his gunboats past Fort Fisher's batteries just as Farragut had done so successfully against the Confederate gun emplacements at Mobile Bay. "This is to be another Mobile affair," Grant told Weitzel. Should that strategy fail, and the Confederates stubbornly hold their works, Grant advised Weitzel to entrench and "co-operate with the navy [to] effect the reduction and capture of [the fort and batteries guarding New Inlet]." If Fort Fisher fell quickly, Weitzel might advance on Wilmington. That movement would be left to circumstances and Weitzel's discretion, but was secondary to severing the Confederacy's blockade running lifeline. In the event Weitzel failed to get his troops ashore, Grant wanted them returned to Virginia "without delay."[20]

Though Weitzel had met with Grant on at least three occasions to discuss the Fort Fisher expedition, he never saw the commanding general's written orders of December 6. Although Grant had given the orders to Butler to pass on to Weitzel, somewhere along the line a link in the chain of command broke. Weitzel apparently never saw any of Grant's written instructions and throughout the campaign operated under the assumption that he would command only the land forces, while Butler, as department head, would direct the expedition. This misunderstanding had disastrous implications for the Federals.[21]

To add to the confusion, it was Butler—not Weitzel—who conferred with Grant and Porter on important matters relating to the campaign, though Weitzel occasionally tagged along for the meetings. Much to Grant's and Porter's chagrin, Butler managed to finagle his way into leading the expedition. It began innocently enough, with Butler asking Grant if he could "make any suggestion that may occur to him in aid of the expedition."

Butler then requested to chaperone the army so he could supervise the powder vessel experiment and keep an eye on Weitzel, whom he considered inexperienced and not quite up to handling such an important mission. According to Butler, Grant consented. "I was to go in command," Butler claimed, "for a reason which was agreed upon between [the lieutenant general and me] in consultation. The reason was this, that General Weitzel, while a very able general, was quite a young man [he was twenty-nine], and I was very anxious to see this powder expedition go on and succeed, for it was a very grave one."[22]

Admiral Porter was furious when he heard the news, though he had suspected all along that Butler had ulterior motives. He had tried to be cordial with Butler during the campaign planning sessions, but did not "fancy the General." In fact, there had been bad blood between Porter and Butler since the Battle of New Orleans in 1862. After Porter's capture of the two bastions guarding the river approach to the city, Forts Jackson and St. Philip, Butler criticized the navy's performance as foolish and useless. The Massachusetts general claimed the navy's relentless bombardment had not damaged the masonry forts in the least. Porter understandably resented the criticism. The dispute festered between the two men, and by the time Porter and Butler were thrown together for the Wilmington expedition, they despised each other. Porter "hates me as the devil hates holy water," Butler candidly admitted.[23]

For his part, Porter claimed he wanted to "bury the hatchet" and establish a "courteous relationship" with Butler. They met on several occasions, usually on board the *Malvern*, and were cordial if not warm to one another, a courtesy expected of two high ranking military officers. Yet, their attempts to build a good working relationship were ill-fated, "for when men have once had an encounter of sharp words," Admiral Porter explained, "they are not likely ever again to be in complete accord with each other." In truth, their animosity went deeper than the exchange of "sharp words." Porter was convinced Butler was involved in illegal activities in the Department of Virginia and North Carolina, issuing unauthorized cotton and tobacco permits, furnishing the enemy with clothing and supplies, and accepting bribes and payoffs. The admiral even accused Butler of trying to enlist him in an insidious scheme to run cotton through his own blockade. In short, Porter did not trust the general and believed him to be a crook. He thought of

Butler merely as a politician and not a soldier—and certainly "not a man who should be intrusted with the lives of other men." Still, Porter was willing to ignore Butler's treachery and incompetence because he thought he had Grant's assurances that Butler "should not have any connections with the [Fort Fisher] expedition."[24]

The rancor between Porter and Butler did little to instill hope for the operation's success among the troops as well as the Union high command. Butler's own soldiers had little faith in their commander's ability, and complained about him before the expedition sailed. "Old Butler is here and perhaps will command the expedition in order to insure its failure," wrote Sgt. Maj. Edward K. Wightman of the 3rd New York Infantry. Well aware of the controversy between Porter and Butler, William T. Sherman made an ominous prediction about their mutual involvement in the Fort Fisher operation: "[Together they] will fail in their present undertaking," he warned Grant. "I take it for granted. . . ."[25]

Grant never intended for Butler to command the Fort Fisher expeditionary force. He later claimed he only learned of it when Butler stopped by headquarters at City Point on December 8 as he made his way down the James River to link-up with Porter at Hampton Roads. Despite persistent rumors to the contrary, Grant believed that Butler planned to remain in Virginia with the largest portion of his army, or accompany the expedition only as far as Beaufort, North Carolina, where he would direct final preparations for the powder boat experiment.[26]

That is not how Butler remembered it. After his final meeting with Grant before sailing, Butler understood "[he] was to stay [with the expedition] until General Weitzel successfully effected a landing." Nor did Admiral Porter accept Grant's explanation. "[Grant] could not help but know that General Butler was going in command of this expedition," the admiral contended. "The matter was constantly discussed with him. . .and everybody spoke of [Butler] as commander of the troops."[27]

General Weitzel claimed that from the outset Grant knew of Butler's plans to accompany the expedition, but declined to intervene, deeming it Butler's prerogative to go anywhere within the boundaries of his command. The lieutenant general later admitted as much. "The operations taking place within the Geographical limits of his Dept. I did not like to order him back," Grant explained. Admiral Porter privately blamed Grant for not standing up to Butler, but expressed no surprise when he did not. According to Porter, Butler used his considerable intellect, personal charm, and persuasive power to manipulate Grant. "Butler appeared to affect [Grant] like some hideous nightmare and took away all his spirit," Porter observed. Gideon Welles also noticed Butler's apparent intimidation of the lieutenant general. "It is unfortunate that Butler is associated with Grant," Welles lamented, "for he has great mental power which gives him undue ascendancy over his official superior." Whatever the reason, Butler accompanied the expedition and Porter had to make the best of it. The success of the operation depended on perfect harmony between the army and navy, but with Butler and Porter as co-commanders, the campaign was off to a bad start.[28]

Grant's eagerness to attack Wilmington right away made Butler fidgety and anxious to proceed as well. The Massachusetts general ordered his troops to break camp at Chaffin's Farm on December 7, and march to Bermuda Hundred on the James River where, on the following day, they embarked onto army transports. The men were supplied with the standard forty rounds of ammunition and seven days' rations of hardtack. They were instructed to carry few personal belongings with them: an overcoat, shelter tent or a rubber blanket, and one change of underclothes. On the night of December 8 they started downriver to join Admiral Porter's fleet at Hampton Roads, which they reached early the following morning.[29]

The navy was not ready to sail on December 9, for Porter was still loading the powder boat. Butler and Weitzel grew concerned that the postponement would enable enemy spies to discover the expedition's target. Porter promised to hurry, but just when the the Federals' advance appeared imminent, the weather turned against them. A "big blow" winter storm swept into Hampton Roads on December 10. Porter advised Butler to disembark his troops from the transports and get them to solid ground. The general stubbornly refused to heed the veteran seaman's warning, and kept his men and supplies loaded-up and ready to go. Packed away in the ships "like a lot of sheep in a pen," the troops waited for the storm to pass.[30]

The gale raged for three days, causing untold discomfort for Butler's soldiers in the dark, dank holds of the transport vessels tottering on the Chesapeake Bay. The cold was perhaps more brutal to the men than the swaying ships. Brigadier General Charles J. Paine, commander of two brigades of United States Colored Troops assigned to the expeditionary force,

reported that the thermometer on board the *Herman Livingstone* registered
2° below zero on December 12. Sergeant Major Edward K. Wightman said
it was so cold that his hair froze stiff while he was on the deck of the
Weybossett.[31]

When the winds finally subsided on December 13, Porter's armada
quickly put to sea. The admiral did not want to chance another delay by
remaining in port. As the sixty-four warships sailed away, a solitary cannon
at Fort Monroe fired a parting salute while ladies fluttered white handkerchiefs as they waved bon voyage. Before shoving off, Porter had asked
Butler to allow the navy at least twelve hours lead time, primarily because
his heavily-armed warships were weighty and slow, and the unseaworthy
monitors and the *Louisiana* would have to be towed. He also needed to stop
at Beaufort to take on more fuel and ammunition for the monitors, as well as
the last tonnage of gunpowder for the *Louisiana*. Butler agreed.[32]

At 3:00 a.m. on the day the armada sailed southward, Butler sent his
transports up Chesapeake Bay and the Potomac River to Mathias Point,
about 200 miles round trip from Hampton Roads. It was a move designed to
deceive Confederate spies of the real destination, as well as to relieve his
troops' discomfort. After sunset the ships turned around and came back with
lights extinguished, sailing in total darkness. Before sunrise on December 14
they rendezvoused at the mouth of Chesapeake Bay near Cape Henry.[33]

While Porter's ships sailed and Butler attempted to hoodwink the enemy, Grant was losing hope for the operation's success. He believed the
mission should have been launched ten or twelve days earlier. "What is the
prospect of getting your expedition started?" Grant telegraphed Butler at
Fort Monroe early on December 14. "I am just starting," Butler replied at
10:35 a.m. "The weather for the last six days, has been such that it would be
useless to be on the coast. Every thing is off in the best time possible." A
steamer that had been plying the waters off the Carolinas reported that the
seas were ideal for sailing. That was encouragement enough, and Butler and
his staff quickly boarded the army vessel *Ben De Ford* and departed Fort
Monroe to join the transports.[34]

Up to that point none of the enlisted men and few of the officers knew
their destination, although Wilmington was frequently mentioned around the
campfires. At Cape Henry the soldiers finally learned that Fort Fisher was

indeed their objective. About 4:00 p. m. December 14 the ships rushed toward the Cape Fear, at full steam with sails set to maximize their speed.[35]

The Federal transports carried 6,500 troops from the Army of the James, comprising the XXIV Army Corps' Second Division, commanded by Brig. Gen. Adelbert Ames, and two brigades of the Third Division of the XXV Army Corps, consisting of U. S. Colored Troops led by Brig. Gen. Charles J. Paine. Both of these units were new organizations formed just eleven days earlier. White troops of the X and XVIII Army Corps had been consolidated into the XXIV Army Corps, while black troops of those old units now comprised the XXV Army Corps. Ames' division contained about 3,400 troops, and Paine's brigades about 3,000. Lieutenant John Myrick's 6-gun Battery E, 3rd U. S. Army Artillery, accompanied the infantry units. Rounding out the expeditionary force were fifty hand-picked men from companies I and L of the 1st Connecticut Heavy Artillery, serving as orderlies and couriers, together with fifty cavalrymen. At General Weitzel's request, Lt. Col. Cyrus B. Comstock—Grant's chief engineer—accompanied the army.[36]

On Friday, December 15, Butler was surprised when his transports overtook and passed several navy vessels, including the *Vanderbilt, Brooklyn,* and *Powhatan.* After giving Porter a day's head start, Butler assumed all of the navy vessels would reach the Cape Fear about the same time as the army transports, which were set to rendezvous twenty-five miles off New Inlet. Butler, mindful of keeping his vessels secluded so as not to alert the Confederates, anchored his transport flotilla east of Masonboro Inlet after sunset on December 15 to allow any slower navy ships to catch up. Once anchored, Butler turned his attention to locating Porter and the remaining naval squadron. He steamed that evening in the *Ben De Ford* to the blockading station at New Inlet eighteen miles to the south, but no one on board the blockaders had seen Porter or his ships. Butler then sailed out to the rendezvous point, where he found the *Minnesota* and a few other ships, but Porter and the rest of his fleet were nowhere in sight. He finally learned from Commodore Joseph Lanman of the *Minnesota,* however, that Porter was still in Beaufort with most of the fleet. Communications between Butler and Porter had once again gone awry.[37]

With but little choice Butler and Weitzel remained with the blockading squadron at New Inlet and waited—and waited. For three days the two generals sat idly by awaiting Porter's arrival. Their soldiers, still on board the transports off Masonboro Inlet, made the best of a trying situation by playing cards, dominoes and checkers, or fishing, writing letters, reading, drinking, carousing, or just sleeping.

The troops certainly could not have asked for more perfect weather during their long wait. The weather was beautiful, with spring-like temperatures and calm seas. The mercury rose to 75° one afternoon—quite a difference from the sub-zero temperatures the soldiers had had to endure in Virginia just days before. "The [weather] has been very fine," declared an officer, "warm as May in New York." A pilot on board the *Ben De Ford* familiar with the Carolina coast said he had not seen prettier weather in twenty years. General Butler took advantage of the Indian Summer by having a gig lowered from his flagship and being rowed about for pleasure.[38]

Pleasurable hardly would have described the experience of many of Butler's infantrymen, despite the balmy weather. They had been on the seagoing transports for more than a week, some for the first time in their lives. For many of them it was a confusing, exhausting and sickening experience. "I know not ware we was, all we knowed, we knowed we was on the watter in the boat," wrote Simon Bennage, a recent conscript in the 76th Pennsylvania Infantry. "Still imprisoned board Stmr," complained Sgt. Maj. Christian Fleetwood of the 4th U. S. Colored Troops. "Oh when will this tiresome floating about end." Boredom quickly set in and the soldiers grew impatient for an end to their confinement. "Here we are kept without one thing to relieve the monotony and sameness," Fleetwood wrote. "We are rocked in the cradle of the deep." Many soldiers became seasick. As if that were not bad enough, the ships' water, food and fuel supplies were dwindling. The situation became so desperate that on some vessels the men were soon limited to half rations, while the transports' coal stocks were down to four days' worth. "Either we are not to land here or the expedition is commanded by a lunatic," raged a soldier in the 5th U. S. Colored Troops.[39]

Butler finally heard from the missing commanding naval officer on Sunday morning, December 18. A letter arrived from the admiral saying the fleet would be down from Beaufort some time during the day. Porter appeared that evening, five days after he had left Hampton Roads and three days after he was supposed to meet with the army. Supplying and fueling Porter's warships had taken much more time than the admiral had anticipated. Butler was still with the blockaders at New Inlet when word of Porter's arrival reached him. The general wasted little time in steaming out to join him at the rendezvous point.[40]

Sgt. Maj. Christian Fleetwood, 4th United States Colored Troops. *U.S. Army Military History Institute*

By the time Butler reached the fleet at 8:00 p.m., the wind had freshened and a light mist was falling. The change in the weather was a bad sign for the expeditionaries. Soon after his arrival Butler received a piece of shocking news. Fleet Captain K. Randolph Breese, who represented Admiral Porter on an official visit to the *Ben De Ford*, informed Butler that Porter had decided to explode the *Louisiana* at ten o'clock that night. In fact, the *Louisiana* was already steaming toward Fort Fisher. Breese handed the perplexed Butler a note from Porter, explaining that since the weather appeared to be taking a turn for the worse, it was best to start the attack immediately. At the same time, Porter recommended that if a storm did hit, the transports should head for shelter beneath Cape Lookout, ninety miles northeast of New Inlet.[41]

Butler was flabbergasted. Detonating the powder vessel before the army was prepared to go ashore would allow the Confederates time to repair damages and regain their composure to meet an assault. The army might not be able to land at all if the weather continued to deteriorate. Butler immediately sent General Weitzel and Lieutenant Colonel Comstock to confer with Porter on board the *Malvern*. Angry and frustrated by Porter's unilateral action, Butler refused to go himself, further widening the communication gap between he and Porter.[42]

Porter was unfazed by Butler's absence, as the discussion quickly focused on the powder boat. Weitzel and Comstock implored the admiral to delay the mission for at least eight hours so that the army would be in a position to land at daylight. The delay would also give the weather time to improve. After all, they reasoned, the army could not go ashore in darkness and heavy seas. Porter reluctantly agreed, shifting the target date to the morning of December 20. The admiral sent his fastest steamer, the recently captured blockade runner *Advance*, to intercept the *Louisiana*, but the mission proved unnecessary. Alexander C. Rhind, the powder boat commander, had already aborted the mission because of the worsening weather and was steaming back to the fleet's anchorage when the *Advance* intercepted him.[43]

The Federals hoped to attack as early as Monday afternoon December 19, when they awoke to pleasant weather and smooth seas. But by noon dark clouds were seen gathering in the west, the wind had flipped around to the northeast, and the ocean had begun to swell. Despite the threatening weather, Admiral Porter prepared for the expected attack by putting his fleet's divisions into lines of battle and familiarizing his commanders with their battle stations. For the lack of something better to do, General Butler followed Porter's flagship all day, "sailing about the neighborhood," and within sight of Fort Fisher. Porter's maneuvers cost the element of surprise the army had so jealously guarded until this time. Butler could clearly see the famous Mound Battery, and correctly assumed that the Confederates could see them as well.

Late Monday evening Porter's fleet put out to sea and braced itself for the impending storm. Butler, meanwhile, instructed his transports to make for Beaufort if they got dispersed, which occurred soon after the storm struck. Huge waves broke over the decks of the transports and the soldiers were tossed about below deck like toys in an overturned chest. The vessels had trouble maintaining formation and the danger of collisions in the raging sea was a constant threat. By midnight Butler was compelled to order his vessels to head for the safety of Beaufort. Most of his transports' coal and water supplies were nearly gone and his foot soldiers were too shaken to bear another squall. The landlubbers wanted desperately to set foot on dry ground again. Ultimately, Butler remained at Beaufort for four days—as long as Porter had the previous week.[44]

While the army and navy attempted to coordinate, the weather refused to cooperate. By Tuesday December 20, a heavy gale was blowing out of the southwest. Porter was determined to ride it out. Of Butler's troop transports, only the *Baltic* remained at sea with the navy vessels. Although many of Porter's warships were scattered by the storm, other than losing a few anchors the warships fared well—including the ironclads—though according to one eyewitness, "the [monitors] were frequently so submerged that only the turrets and smokestacks were visible." Even the *Louisiana*, weighted down as she was by hundreds of thousands of pounds of gunpowder, survived the storm intact.[45]

Bad climatological conditions are often an ally in wartime, and so it was for the Confederates at Federal Point. The sudden violent turn in the weather allowed them more time to prepare for the battle they had long anticipated but whose arrival they dreaded. As "Beast" Butler had suspected, Colonel Lamb's men spotted the Union armada rehearsing for the attack on Monday, December 19. The Confederates had been arduously scanning the horizon for enemy warships since the previous day. An exaggerated but generally accurate intelligence report reached Wilmington on December 18 with information that an enormous Federal fleet of eighty-five ships under Admiral Porter, together with 20,000 soldiers under General Butler, was en route to attack the city. Having received reports of the serious threat to Wilmington, General Bragg returned from Georgia to the "city by the sea" to resume command of the Department of North Carolina on December 17. As soon as the enemy vessels appeared off New Inlet, Lamb telegraphed the news to headquarters in Wilmington. The Federal invasion—so long feared and talked about—had finally come to the Cape Fear.[46]

Lamb acted immediately, requesting that supplies and troops be transferred forthwith to Fort Fisher. He also sent away the slave laborers and evacuated his wife Daisy and their children to the much safer west side of the Cape Fear River, at Orton Plantation a mile north of Fort Anderson. General Whiting made last-minute pleas to Richmond and Raleigh for reinforcements to aid in Wilmington's defense. "Information seems reliable of formidable attack here," Whiting wrote Secretary of War Seddon. "The troops ordered away [to Georgia in November] cannot return; if not helped, the forts may be turned and the city goes. The reduced garrisons are not able to hold [Wilmington] without support."[47]

Whiting rushed to Fort Fisher early on December 20 to "observe the enemy off New Inlet" and consult with Colonel Lamb. He and Lamb counted twenty-eight vessels within sight of the fort, many more than the regular complement of blockaders stationed there. The increase seemed to corroborate reports coming in of an impending attack. "Putting all the information I have together," Whiting explained to Brig. Gen. Louis Hébert in Smithville, "I am satisfied Fort Fisher is the point threatened. . .in its present condition I am exceedingly uneasy about it."[48]

As soon as he received the news from Whiting, Governor Vance issued a state-wide proclamation appealing to every man "who may be able to stand behind breastworks and fire a musket. . .[and] who has the spirit of a freeman in his bosom," to rally and meet him in Wilmington to turn back the Northern invaders. The governor must not have considered himself physically able to fight, because he never took his place among the defenders of Wilmington.[49]

General Lee still believed the threat to Wilmington was overstated and an attack improbable. But he also knew he could not afford to be wrong. With no little reluctance he detached Maj. Gen. Robert Frederick Hoke's Division of veteran soldiers from the Army of Northern Virginia for the city's defense. Hoke quietly evacuated his soldiers from their entrenchments at Petersburg and embarked them onto trains at Richmond for the journey south. Lee had no way of knowing whether Hoke's infantry would reach Wilmington in time to save it, but Lee had no viable option other than sending reinforcements as quickly as possible. The ultimate fate of the Confederacy might depend on their timely arrival.

Brigadier General William W. Kirkland's Brigade led the division's march toward Richmond early on December 21, followed shortly thereafter by Hoke's remaining three brigades: Brig. Gen. Johnson Hagood's, Brig. Gen. Thomas L. Clingman's (temporarily commanded by Col. William S.

Devane of the 61st North Carolina Infantry), and Brig. Gen. Alfred H. Colquitt's. Lee's selection of Hoke's Division was not a random one. Some of the regiments—the 8th, 31st, 51st, and 61st North Carolina Infantry of Clingman's Brigade, as well as the 7th Battalion and the 11th, 21st, 25th, 27th South Carolina Infantry of Hagood's Brigade—had experience in coastal warfare, including the defense of Battery Wagner on Morris Island and service on other sea islands near Charleston in 1863. Moreover, all of Hoke's regiments were familiar with Butler's Army of the James, having faced them as part of General Beauregard's force at Drewry's Bluff the previous May, and more recently, in mid-October, on the Darbytown Road near Richmond. Lieutenant General James Longstreet, one of Lee's corps commanders, commented that there were "no better troops" in the Army of Northern Virginia than those in Hoke's Division.[50]

Lee considered Hoke a talented general officer, one of the best in the army. From the war's first land battle in Virginia at Bethel, and in many subsequent engagements thereafter, Hoke had distinguished himself as a cool, courageous and capable combatant. Yet he was not a soldier by profession, and before the war had run his family's cotton mill and iron works in Lincolnton, North Carolina. Hoke's rapid ascension through the ranks of command reflected both his ability and the confidence his superiors had in him.

After enlisting as a private in the spring of 1861, Hoke was promoted to second lieutenant (and later major) of the 1st North Carolina Infantry. His meteoric rise continued with his elevation to lieutenant colonel of the 33rd North Carolina Infantry, and finally colonel of the 21st North Carolina Infantry, all in the space of just fifteen months. Hoke led his North Carolinians at the Battle of New Bern and in the Virginia Peninsula Campaign. His solid showing at Fredericksburg in December 1862 earned him a brigadier generals' commission the following month. His first battle as a general was almost his last when he suffered a serious wound while leading his brigade at Salem Church, during the Chancellorsville Campaign, on May 4, 1863. Forced home to Lincolnton to recuperate, Hoke missed the Gettysburg Campaign and was unable to return to the army until that autumn.

Hoke's crowning glory came on April 17, 1864, when he recaptured Plymouth on the Roanoke River in northeastern North Carolina, along with the town's 3,000 Union garrison troops. The Federals had occupied Plymouth—a hinge on Richmond's back door—for more than two years. For his success, Hoke received the thanks of the Confederate Congress, a major generalship, and a transfer back to the Virginia battlefront. Hoke, a thor-

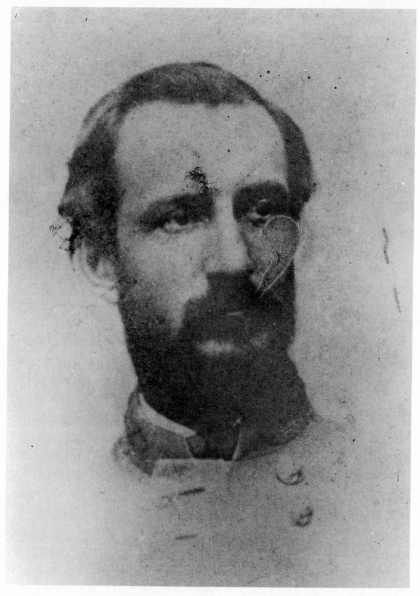

A previously unpublished alternate view of Maj. Gen. Robert F. Hoke, whom Robert E. Lee considered to be one of the most talented general officers in the Army of Northern Virginia. *Courtesy of Charles V. Peery*

oughly competent brigadier, proved a disappointment as a division commander. His Virginia tenure gained him little other than a reputation for being uncooperative and too cautious. At Fort Harrison south of Richmond on September 30, Hoke had implored General Lee not to counterattack in an attempt to recapture the worthless fort. Hoke's request was denied and his division was dreadfully bloodied in the ensuing battle, with Clingman's Brigade alone suffering fifty-eight percent casualties. Afterward Hoke was criticized for his hesitancy to support Lee's plans. In sending Hoke to Wilmington, Lee hoped the general would repeat his earlier home state success at Plymouth.[51]

But first Hoke had to get his troops to the Tarheel State. By the winter of 1864, most Southern railroads and rolling stock were in such bad shape that transferring troops and provisions from one point to another was risky and unpredictable. Machinery and materials for repairs had become increasingly difficult to procure, and skilled railroad workers had been conscripted into the armed services. Few locomotives still ran the tracks, which were often rickety and of varying gauges. Direct access to and from Wilmington via Weldon and Goldsboro was blocked by Federal forces, further hindering the movement of supplies and soldiers. Even so, Lee still relied almost exclusively on the railroads to receive the supplies he needed to sustain his army, and now Hoke would have to rely on those same dilapidated railroads to transfer his division to Wilmington. The troops were detoured along a circuitous route through Burke Station, Danville, Greensboro, Raleigh, and Goldsboro, a journey both long and arduous.[52]

Because the railroads were in such disrepair, the reinforcements had to be moved piecemeal. Snow, sleet and freezing rain further delayed the division's movement through Virginia. To make matters worse, conditions on board the trains were deplorable. The troops were packed tightly into the boxcars and onto flatcars like cattle going to market. Many soldiers were forced to stand on their feet in the overcrowded, slow-moving cars for much of the trip, or to run alongside them to keep their blood circulating. Temperatures plummeted to near zero at times, compelling some of the soldiers to build fires in the cars to keep warm—but at the risk of suffocating from the thick smoke. "The men suffered very much," recalled a North Carolina soldier. It took three days for one brigade to advance just forty-eight miles. The only bright spots of the trip were the receptions the soldiers enjoyed at stops along the way. Men of the 66th North Carolina Infantry consumed a barrel of "corn juice" in Raleigh that allegedly had been sent to the depot by Governor Vance himself, making the next leg of their journey somewhat happier. Then, at Goldsboro, Magnolia, Mt. Olive, and Wilmington, ladies greeted them with such food and provisions as could be spared.[53]

As Hoke's Division traveled toward Wilmington, Chase Whiting was in a frenzy preparing for the enemy invasion. He telegraphed General Hébert, his old West Point classmate and now overall commander of the fortifications guarding the Cape Fear's inlets, to send troops from the works at Old Inlet to bolster Colonel Lamb's skeletal force of artillerymen at Fort Fisher. Lamb had but 563 soldiers to man a mile of heavy artillery batteries—about half the fort's normal complement of artillerymen and 6,000 less than the number of enemy soldiers on board Butler's transports waiting to attack.

The remainder of Fort Fisher's garrison, led by Maj. James Martin Stevenson, Lamb's second-in-

Major James Reilly, 10th North Carolina Regiment (1st N.C. Artillery), shown here in a previously unpublished oil portrait. *Cape Fear Museum, Wilmington*

command, was still in Georgia with Bragg's expeditionary force. Whiting's pleas for additional reinforcements yielded a disappointingly small number of troops.

General Hébert visited Fort Fisher to inform Lamb that he had but few men to spare. He consented to dispatch 110 men of the 40th North Carolina Regiment (3rd North Carolina Artillery), 115 soldiers of the 13th Battalion North Carolina Light Artillery, and 140 boys of the North Carolina Junior Reserves. Hébert also sent to Fort Fisher two companies of the 10th North Carolina Regiment (1st North Carolina Artillery) commanded by Maj.

James Reilly—the same James Reilly who, as a former U. S. Army ordnance officer, had surrendered Fort Johnston at Smithville to the Cape Fear Minute Men in January 1861. When the war broke out, Reilly joined the Confederate army and landed in command of one of the most proficient front line artillery batteries in the Army of Northern Virginia. "Old Tarantula" Reilly, as he was known to his men, was gruff, temperamental and demanding. To General Whiting, Reilly was one of the most capable artillery officers in the army, and he was pleased to see him transferred from Virginia to Fort Fisher.[54]

Hébert's reinforcements, including Reilly's command, gave Colonel Lamb a total of 928 men and boys by December 23. An additional 443 reinforcements trickled into Fort Fisher during the battle, but Lamb never commanded more than 1,371 combatants, a third of whom were Junior Reservists, mere boys sixteen to eighteen years of age.[55]

In addition to these reinforcements, Whiting asked Flag Officer Robert F. Pinckney, Wilmington's naval commandant, to detach troops to help man the guns at Battery Buchanan, which was garrisoned by only a small force of sailors and marines under Lt. Robert T. Chapman. Whiting also pressed Capt. William James of the Engineer Corps to place additional torpedoes and sink obstructions—a disabled blockade runner or the gunboat *Chickamauga*—in New Inlet. Though technically Bragg's approval was required to implement these measures, it was Whiting who made most of the necessary arrangements for Wilmington's defense. Yet, the temperamental general was pessimistic about the port's survival. "Stripped as we are of forces," he told Bragg, "we shall have little time before the enemy will be upon the city."[56]

Strong, cold winds prevailed and the seas ran high through Thursday, December 22. When the weather finally improved by the following afternoon, Admiral Porter decided to detonate the *Louisiana*, with or without Butler, who had not yet returned from Beaufort with his army. Porter no longer cared if the general returned in time to witness the explosion, though he knew Butler was due back on Christmas Eve night. Butler had sent Capt.

H. C. Clarke of his staff down to New Inlet to inform the admiral that the attack could commence Christmas morning.[57]

Porter believed he had waited long enough. In his estimation, he had nothing to lose by beginning the attack early. If the powder boat explosion proved a success, the navy alone would be in a position to reap the laurels of victory. And why not? A deeply resentful Porter believed the navy's role in the Union war effort had been vastly underrated and unappreciated by both the army and the press, and he blamed General Grant in large part for it. "[Grant] wants magnanimity, like most officers of the army, and is so avaricious as regards fame that he will never, if he can help it, do justice to our department." Gideon Welles agreed. "The army is extolled, the Navy is ignored," he complained. "I do not recollect a single instance of generous award to the Navy by Stanton or Halleck." Porter hoped that a purely naval victory at Fort Fisher would humble the army's arrogant attitude.[58]

Porter, like Butler, was confident the "Monster Torpedo" would prove disastrous to Fort Fisher and its defenders. "The effect of the explosion will be simply very severe," Porter maintained,

> stunning men at a distance of three or four hundred yards, demoralizing them completely, and making them unable to stand for any length of time a fire from the ships [note that Porter makes no mention of the role of army in the assault]. I think that the concussion will tumble magazines that are built on framework, and that the famous Mound Battery will be among the things that were, and the guns buried beneath the ruins. I think that houses in Wilmington and Smithville will tumble to the ground and much demoralize the people, and I think if the rebels fight after the explosion they have more in them than I gave them credit for.[59]

If, on the other hand, the powder boat experiment failed, Porter could blame Butler for suggesting such a far-fetched scheme, one that had cost the country too much time and money. Porter claimed that the *Louisiana's* gunpowder alone exceeded $250,000, resources that could have been better utilized reducing the Confederate stronghold.

Porter gave Commander A. C. Rhind, the "cool and daring" officer in charge of the powder boat, the go-ahead to blow it up. It was a dangerous assignment, and Porter had warned Rhind that he and his men might be killed in the attempt. There was fame, glory and promotion to be won, Porter promised—if the experiment succeeded and Rhind survived. Though he did not divulge his true feelings, Porter did not expect to see Rhind or his men alive again. Rhind accepted the risk and carefully selected fourteen volunteers from his vessel, the *Agawam*, to assist him. Accompanying him as second-in-command was Lt. Samuel W. Preston, one of the most popular young officers in the fleet and a favorite of Admiral Porter.[60]

The plan had called for packing the *Louisiana* with 300 tons of gunpowder, but the ordnance workers had only enough time to place 215 tons on board (185 tons at Norfolk and another 30 tons at Beaufort), before General Grant pressed the expedition to go forward. To ensure the gunpowder—all 430,000 pounds of it—blew up instantaneously, the ordnance team installed an elaborate system of detonation devices, including a clock-work, candles with fuses and a slow-match. In the event these mechanisms failed, however, and to dissuade Confederate pickets from boarding, the officers consented to light a fire on the *Louisiana*. The fire would be ignited suffi-

Butler's powder boat, *Louisiana*. Jammed with 430,000 pounds of gunpowder, this floating bomb was expected by some Union ordnance experts to blow down the sand walls of Fort Fisher. *Harper's Weekly*

ciently distant from the gunpowder so that the flames would not reach the explosives unless the fuses failed.[61]

Rhind moved the *Louisiana* toward Federal Point at 10:30 Friday night, December 23. Because she was so heavily-laden and riding low in the water, the demolition ship had to be pulled into shallow waters by the *Wilderness*, guided in the darkness by the lights of the *Kansas*. At six fathoms the *Wilderness* cast off the *Louisiana*, which under her own steam began the last leg of her final voyage. As the powder ship eased away, the *Wilderness* anchored to wait for Rhind and his party to do their work and hopefully, somehow, make their getaway.

The plan went awry almost immediately. Rhind and his men soon discovered that it would be difficult and perhaps impossible to put the *Louisiana* on the beach near Fort Fisher. The extremely dark night prevented them from seeing the fort's silhouette and also complicated their task of avoiding the protruding hulks of sunken blockade runners in the shallows. They managed to make it through the deadly obstacle course by, ironically, following in the wake of a blockade runner (*Little Hattie*), which was making a dash for New Inlet. Porter had withdrawn all his vessels far offshore to protect them from the effects of the powder boat, a move that left New Inlet unguarded. The increasingly nervous Rhind was left to rely on his instincts to tell him when to detonate the *Louisiana*. When he heard the sound of crashing waves, Rhind estimated that he was about 300 yards from the fort's northeast bastion. He and his cohorts dropped anchor about 11:45 p.m., set the clocks and fuses, and lit the candles which would ignite the gunpowder one hour and thirty minutes later.

Unfortunately for the Federals, an undertow coupled with an offshore breeze pulled and pushed the *Louisiana* away from the beach, despite an incoming tide. Rhind dropped a second anchor to stabilize the ship. In order to ensure there would be an explosion, he lit a fire in the propeller shaft alley, which was already loaded with pine wood and kindling. Their hazardous duty complete, Rhind and his men abandoned the doomed ship and made their way in a small launch back to the *Wilderness*. It was twenty minutes after midnight. What no one realized until it was too late was that the *Louisiana* was anchored at least 500 yards away from the beach, 200 yards or more farther out to sea than Rhind believed. The strong undertow further compounded this error and slowly sucked the ship into deeper water.

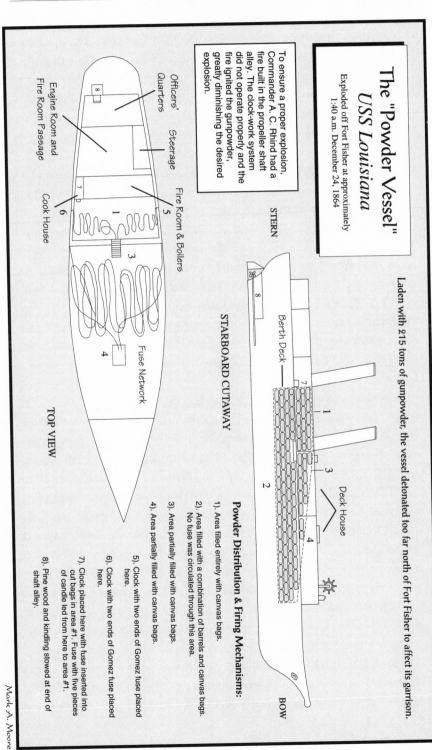

The "Powder Vessel"
USS Louisiana

Exploded off Fort Fisher at approximately
1:40 a.m. December 24, 1864

Laden with 215 tons of gunpowder, the vessel detonated too far north of Fort Fisher to affect its garrison.

To ensure a proper explosion, Commander A. C. Rhind had a fire built in the propeller shaft alley. The clock-work system did not operate properly and the fire ignited the gunpowder, greatly diminishing the desired explosion.

STERN

Officers' Quarters

Steerage

Engine Room and Fire Room Passage

Cook House

Fire Room & Boilers

Fuse Network

TOP VIEW

STARBOARD CUTAWAY

Berth Deck

Deck House

BOW

Powder Distribution & Firing Mechanisms:

1). Area filled entirely with canvas bags.

2). Area filled with a combination of barrels and canvas bags. No fuse was circulated through this area.

3). Area partially filled with canvas bags.

4). Area partially filled with canvas bags.

5). Clock with two ends of Gomez fuse placed here.

6). Clock with two ends of Gomez fuse placed here.

7). Clock placed here with fuse inserted into cut bags in area #1. Fuse with five pieces of candle led from here to area #1.

8). Pine wood and kindling stowed at end of shaft alley.

Mark A. Moore

As Rhind and his men performed their arduous task, Admiral Porter held his fleet in readiness about twelve miles off the coast. Despite the late hour and the prospect of an early morning battle, Union sailors and marines lined the gunwales of their vessels to await the giant explosion. Shortly after midnight they spotted several rockets in the western sky—Rhind's signal that the powder boat was set to detonate. Tension mounted as they stood by waiting for the detonation. For more than an hour they waited, while nothing happened. Finally, at 1:40 on Christmas Eve morning, the naval tars saw a quick, bright flame on the horizon that rose and then fanned out like a miniature fireworks display. Commander Daniel Ammen commented that from his vantage point on board the *Mohican*, the explosion resembled distant lightning. About thirty seconds after glimpsing the flash, the sailors heard several deep rumbles that sounded like an approaching thunderstorm, and felt a slight tremor on board the ships. Commander Rhind turned to the men and officers on the *Wilderness* and quipped, "There's a fizzle!" and then went below deck. "A glare on the horizon and a dull report were the indications that the floating mine had been sprung," noted Thomas O. Selfridge, captain of the *Huron*. "The powderboat prov[ed] an ignominious failure."[62]

As it turned out, the timing devices had failed to ignite the gunpowder, which was eventually detonated by the fire left behind by Rhind and his men. Although they were set to explode at 1:18 a.m., the timings mechanisms did not function as intended, perhaps because they had been improperly laid. The fuses had been run only into the bags in the deckhouse. Holes had been bored through the deck with candles placed in them, under which additional fuses were placed. In theory, the fuses would be lit when the candles burned down. But a failure to run fuses through every layer of gunpowder may have been the fatal error. Had the fuses been well-planted and operational, the explosion probably would have occurred at the prearranged time. The detonation, however, did not take place until twenty-two minutes later, and when it did, only a small portion of the powder ignited as the fire spread to the various storage compartments. The balance was either blown overboard or sank with the smoking wreck.

By the time the powder finally detonated, the opportunity to wreak destruction upon Fort Fisher—assuming there was merit in the original plan—had passed. When the explosion finally occurred, the *Louisiana* was half a mile or more away from the fort. In addition, she was not resting on the ocean bottom, a circumstance deemed crucial in producing the shock waves thought necessary to impact the defenders. All in all, it was an abysmal failure.[63]

The explosion was barely noticed inside Fort Fisher. Shortly after midnight the officer-of-the-day had reported a ship on fire up the beach. Colonel Lamb scurried to the parapet to have a look. Captain Lebby, who had just reported on shore after passing safely through New Inlet in the *Little Hattie*, suggested the vessel might be the *Agnes Frye*, a steamer that had sailed with him from Nassau two days before. Lamb watched the burning ship for about half an hour, and then turned in for the night. Soon afterward he was awakened by a sensation he likened to vertigo. A loud explosion, one that sounded similar to the report of a 10-inch columbiad being fired, followed. Within minutes, Lamb received a telegram from General Whiting in Wilmington, where the explosion had been plainly heard and felt, asking what had happened. Lamb replied that "a blockader got aground near the fort, set fire to herself and blew up."[64]

The explosion was the main topic of conversation among Fort Fisher's garrison the next morning, though many soldiers had not even been aroused from their sleep by the commotion. Confederate soldiers near Sugar Loaf, however, seemed to have received quite a jolt from the detonation. One officer stationed there noted that the explosion "jumped he and his men who were lying on the ground about like pop-corn in a popper." G. G. Young, on picket duty with the 2nd South Carolina Cavalry at Masonboro Sound, said that he and his comrades had watched the flames for nearly an hour, when suddenly there was a "tremendous blaze and high starry light then an awful report." An hour later one of Young's comrades reported another vessel on fire in the ocean, and Young mentioned to his fellow horsemen that the Federals must be burning wrecked blockade runners. The "fire," however, proved to be nothing more than a bright moon on the rise, a fact that created "quite a laughter" among the South Carolinians at Young's expense.[65]

In the end, the explosion of the *Louisiana* had no real effect other than "affording the Confederates upon the parapet a beautiful display of fireworks, gratis," a local reporter noted. Only later did Colonel Lamb and his soldiers learn that they had been the target of a floating bomb experiment.[66]

It was ironic that the *Louisiana* was constructed at one Wilmington (Delaware) and destroyed at another. For weeks afterward critics ridiculed the test explosion, referring to it as "Butler's Folly," "Butler's Toy," and the "*U.S.S. Volcano.*" Others, however, thought it was a fitting end for the *Louisiana.* After all, she had not suffered the ignominy of being decommissioned and put into mothballs like most unwanted warships, or worse, sold to a junk dealer for scrap metal. Instead, she had gone out in one magnificent flash on the front line—acquiring in the process greater fame upon her destruction than she ever would have gained as a patrol boat plying the sounds of North Carolina. Moreover, had the experiment succeeded, it might have revolutionized naval warfare against harbor defenses.

Even Admiral Porter conceded that it had been well worth trying. If the *Louisiana's* destruction accomplished nothing else, it started the Battle of Fort Fisher.[67]

Cmdr. A. C. Rhind, the "cool and daring" U.S. Navy officer who was placed in charge of the powder boat *Louisiana.*

Author's Collection

Wartime engraving of the Confederacy's premier blockade running seaport—Wilmington, N.C. This view looks northward up Front Street. The Cape Fear River is at left. *Frank Leslie's Illustrated Newspaper*

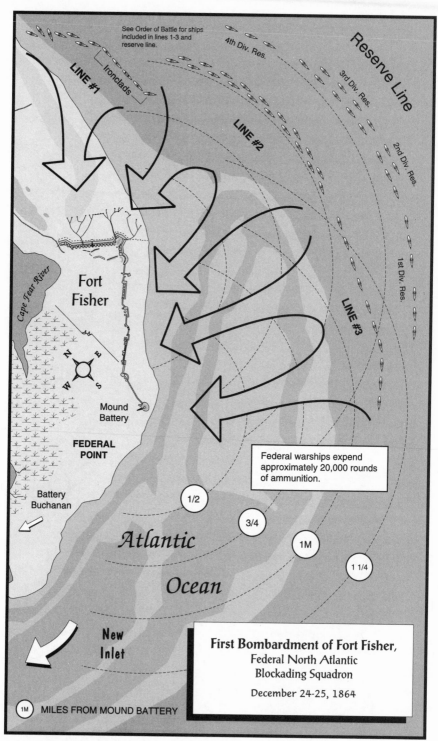

See Order of Battle for ships included in lines 1-3 and reserve line.

Reserve Line

LINE #1

Ironclads

4th Div. Res.

3rd Div. Res.

LINE #2

2nd Div. Res.

1st Div. Res.

LINE #3

Cape Fear River

Fort Fisher

N
E
W
S

Mound Battery

FEDERAL POINT

Battery Buchanan

1/2

3/4

1M

1 1/4

Federal warships expend approximately 20,000 rounds of ammunition.

Atlantic

Ocean

New Inlet

First Bombardment of Fort Fisher,
Federal North Atlantic Blockading Squadron

December 24-25, 1864

1M MILES FROM MOUND BATTERY

Mark A. Moore

Chapter 5

"Go ahead, boys, this is only the fortune of war"

– Coxswain William Shipman, USS Ticonderoga

FIRST STRIKE

From out of a dark gray mist that blanketed the ocean's surface on Christmas Eve morning the warships appeared one-by-one, steaming slowly westward to take up their battle stations. Colonel Lamb observed the Federal fleet's advance as he stood silently atop the parapet of the Pulpit Battery. "A grander sight than the approach of Porter's formidable armada toward the fort was never witnessed on our coast," Lamb marveled. As he and his meager garrison of artillerymen and teenaged soldiers manned their posts and watched in awe as the magnificent enemy fleet spread out before them, the colonel pondered General Lee's recent plea: Wilmington must be held.

At noon Lamb telegraphed headquarters in Wilmington that the Federal fleet was moving into position to attack. By then the winds had subsided and the sun had burned off the fog. The conditions for battle were ideal.[1]

It was "the most formidable armada ever assembled for concentration upon one given point," wrote General Grant of the U.S. Navy's impressive fleet of warships. The squadron comprised sixty-four vessels, including the navy's largest frigates: the *Minnesota*, *Colorado*, *Wabash*, *Susquehanna*, and *Powhatan*. Complementing these powerful, well-armed ships was a vast array of sloops, screw gunboats and sidewheel gunboats (called double-enders). Even converted blockade runners, such as the *Advance*, populated the task force. Porter's fleet also contained five armored vessels: the four monitors *Canonicus*, *Mahopac*, *Monadnock*, and *Saugus*, and the *New Ironsides*, the most powerful ship in the U.S. Navy. The *New Ironsides* was a massive, tortoise-shaped vessel covered with strips of thick iron plating. Although she was difficult to maneuver, she was considered invincible. Her battery consisted of twenty large cannon, fourteen of which were 11-inch Dahlgren guns.

Yet the *New Ironsides'* artillery comprised only a fraction of the 630 total cannon in the fleet. Just how outgunned the Cape Fear defenders were is evident when one considers that a single warship, the fifty-gun frigate *Colorado*, mounted more ordnance than Fort Fisher's forty-seven emplaced cannon. Moreover, both the *Wabash*'s forty-four guns and the *Minnesota*'s forty-six pieces virtually matched the Confederate artillery in number. The Federals believed their overwhelming firepower was necessary to assure Fort Fisher's reduction.[2]

Porter had his warships underway by 5:30 a.m., advancing side-by-side in a long column of twos. As they steamed slowly westward through the early morning sea mist and a gentle offshore breeze, chunks of charred wood from the destroyed powder boat bumped and scraped the ships' hulls. As the warships drew closer to the shore, the sailors and marines that manned them strained to glimpse whatever damage the *Louisiana* might have inflicted on the fort. Much to their disappointment, Fisher's ramparts still stood sharp and high, its stout stockade fence erect and intact. Though dissatisfied with the result, the Federals were not surprised. "It seems strange that Butler, who was ingenious, should have counted so much on the powder boat," remarked one of his soldiers, "but to expect to jar down an earthwork with its parapet twenty-five feet wide, with slopes well revetted with marsh turf and strengthened by traverses, was like expecting a strong wind to blow Bunker Hill into the Charles River." Before long the Federals would receive ample evidence that the fort's garrison had also survived the blast.[3]

At 12:40 p.m. the *New Ironsides* "opened the ball" by firing one of her huge 11-inch shells as she approached her assigned battle station off the northeast bastion. The iron round fell far short of its target, splashing into the surf and raising a huge column of water as the *New Ironsides* continued on

New Ironsides, considered the U.S. Navy's most powerful warship in the task force that attacked Fort Fisher. *Courtesy of Charles V. Peery*

her course. She was followed closely by the monitor *Canonicus*, which added to the dying thunder by sending a 15-inch cannonball toward the fort. But, like the preceding projectile, it too dropped shy of the fort's battlements. The double-turreted monitor *Monadnock* was next in line, also firing as she advanced. The ironclads hurled six rounds before one of their shells founds its mark, striking the exterior slope of the northeast bastion and showering its defenders with a geyser of sand. Colonel Lamb answered with his 10-inch gun in the Pulpit Battery on the sea face, its spherical shell ricocheting off the ocean's surface and bouncing through the smokestack of the approaching *Susquehanna*. This rather harmless exchange opened the most intensive naval bombardment of the war up to that time.[4]

The Federal ships initially experienced some delay in deploying into their assigned battle stations for want of coordination. Many of the commanders had never served together under any conditions, let alone the chaotic environment created by combat. As the ships reached their positions they joined in the bombardment. The gunboats deployed into three adjacent lines of battle forming an arc running north to south with lines of fire directed at both faces of Fort Fisher. The armored vessels and seven light-draft gunboats anchored about three-quarters of a mile northeast of the land front. The larger warships, spread out from one mile to a mile-and-a-quarter opposite the fort's sea face, added the weight of their metal while about twenty "small fry" gunboats were held in reserve a short distance beyond.[5]

Once they reached their positions, the warships unleashed continuous broadsides for almost five hours. The heavily-armed vessels fired salvos from their starboard sides, blasting Fort Fisher with nearly every type of projectile in the U.S. Navy's arsenal, from 3-inch rifle bolts to 15-inch cannonballs weighing more than 300 pounds. The deafening peals of heavy ordnance reverberated across the ocean's surface with such stunning violence "that the ocean fairly trembled," exclaimed an observer. "Bang, bang, bang, whiz, whiz, whiz, clash, clash, clash, all the time," wrote a reporter groping for words to describe the bombardment's sounds. The roar was "like the rattling of a thousand railways trains," recalled one sailor. The air was filled with shrieking projectiles, poofs of white smoke from exploding shells, and the pungent odor of sulphur. The sea was soon littered with discarded ammunition boxes, plumes of sand erupted as shells exploded on the fort's ramparts, and massive columns of water shot skyward as Confederate projectiles—fired in reply to the fleet—plunged into the ocean. "It was a splendid yet wicked sight," remarked B. F. Blair, a sailor on board the *Mohican*.[6]

On that memorable Christmas Eve the fleet fired about 10,000 rounds at Fort Fisher. The *Powhatan* hurled 236 9-inch shells, fifty-four 11-inch Dahlgren shells, and eighty-two 100-pounder Parrott shells toward the fort. The *Mohican* fired a comparable number of projectiles: 217 9-inch cannon-balls, 59 100-pounder shells, and 89 30-pounder Parrott shells. The *Colorado* delivered an astounding 1,569 projectiles into the fort, an average of one every twelve seconds for the duration of the day's bombardment. The barrage awed all who witnessed it. Daniel Ammen, the veteran commander of the *Mohican*, claimed that he had never seen a more terrific bombardment. "It has not been my lot to witness any operation comparable in force or in effect to the bombardment of Fort Fisher," he exclaimed.[7]

Manning the large naval guns was nasty work. "The roar of the cannon was something terrible," asserted one badly shaken sailor. "Every particle of flesh upon one's bones seemed to be slipping off, eyes stinging, and we were almost blinded by powder, smoke, and refuse; the guns and our clothing were almost white from saltpeter. . .and several men at my gun bled at the nose [from the concussion of incessant cannon fire]." "You know I ain't much of a hand to brag and praise myself," wrote Asa Beetham of the *Pontoosuc*, "but some of those shells I landed in those rebel batteries made the Capt. [W. G. Temple] fairly dance (he was on the paddle house all the time)." The *Pontoosuc*, Asa Beetham claimed, took up a station closer to the fort than any of the other wooden gunboats and "kept up a pretty heavy bombardment from the time the first shot was fired until dark."[8]

Surprisingly, the guns of the warships created more noise than damage to the fort. Some gunboats were positioned beyond their effective firing range, and many of their shells fell short of the fort. Gunpowder smoke hovered around the ships, obscuring the sight of the gunners. "[The] smoke [was] so thick at times [as] to completely hide the sun," observed a sailor. Lacking a clear view of the fort, gunners often missed their targets. Nevertheless, by 2:30 p.m. bursting shells had demolished Colonel Lamb's brick headquarters and had set ablaze most of the wooden barracks, destroying the soldiers' beds, blankets, overcoats and personal belongings. Sailors on board the warships could clearly see flames and columns of dense black smoke

billowing from the fort, and believed they had blown up a powder magazine.[9]

The cannonade, which was intended to break apart the fort and drive the
defenders from their positions, was an utter failure. Despite the tons of iron
and expended powder, only minor damage to the earthworks and seacoast
guns—and the soldiers that manned them—resulted. "Never since the in-
vention of gunpowder was there so much harmlessly expended as in the first
day's attack on Fort Fisher," a relieved Colonel Lamb commented. The
shelling disabled only four Confederate seacoast gun carriages and destroyed one light artillery caisson and its ammunition.[10]

Moreover, the day-long bombardment at no time threatened to drive the
Confederate artillerymen from their cannon on the sea face. In fact, the
poorly-delivered shells inflicted only twenty-three casualties on Lamb's garrison, and only four suffered mortal or serious wounds. Two in the latter
category were Privates Benjamin R. Merritt and Charles C. Cherry of Company F, 36th North Carolina Regiment. Both privates were injured when a
navy projectile exploded in their gun compartment. Their grave wounds
required the amputation of Merritt's left arm and Cherry's right leg. The
casualties might have been greater had it not been for the courage of two
privates from Company H of the same regiment, John Turner and Joseph
Brisson. When one of the enemy's mammoth shells dropped into their gun
chamber on the land face, Turner had the presence of mind to douse the fuse
with water from a sponge tub while his companion Brisson shoved the
projectile off the platform.[11]

During the height of the bombardment Colonel Lamb noticed that the
warships seemed to concentrate their fire on the fort's flags. The main
flagstaff on the parade ground was so shattered by bursting shells that the
garrison standard could not be raised. Lamb sent word to Capt. Daniel Munn
at the Mound Battery to hoist a battle flag there, sixty feet or more above the
beach and plainly visible to the Federals. Since the flagpole was not
equipped with halyards to secure the flag, Pvt. Christopher C. Bland of
Company K, 36th North Carolina, volunteered to shinny up the staff to
attach the silk standard. The daring flag-bearing private quickly drew a
heavy fire from the Union gunboats. Bland miraculously escaped unhurt and
even repeated his daring act amid the cheers of his comrades when the lower

Fort Fisher's most notable landmark, the Mound Battery, and her commander, Capt. Daniel Munn, 3rd Co. B, 36th North Carolina Regiment (2nd North Carolina Artillery). *U.S. Army Military History Institute*

end of the flag was cut loose by enemy projectiles. The flag flew throughout the remainder of the battle.

Convinced that the Federal vessels would concentrate their fire on any visible flag, Lamb determined to "put a [flag] where it would do the most good by causing the least harm." The daring colonel personally raised one on Shepherd's Battery at the far western end of the land face. Predictably, the warships lobbed numerous shells in that direction, though many over-shot the fort, harmlessly landing in the Cape Fear River. Although these elevated shots lobbed primarily by the *Alabama* and *Keystone State* did not harm the fort or its occupants, they did succeed in driving off the *Chickamauga*, a blockade runner-turned-gunboat that had come down river about mid-afternoon to support Fort Fisher.[12]

Unlike the Federals, the Confederates could not afford to carelessly waste any of their gunpowder or 3,600 projectiles. Lamb ordered his can-noneers to take careful aim at their targets and to fire slowly—once every thirty minutes—in order to conserve their precious ammunition. The 8-inch Armstrong gun of the sea face's Purdie Battery possessed only a dozen shells and about the same number of solid iron bolts. Fisher's commander also instructed his men to resist the temptation to concentrate their fire on a single vessel. Many of the enemy ships were out of range or regularly readjusting their positions, and thus presented difficult targets for the Con-federate defenders. Lingering smoke from both cannon fire and burning buildings inside the fort also made it difficult for the cannoneers to pinpoint their quarry. More importantly, the batteries on the sea face would need cool cannon muzzles and sufficient ammunition should the enemy gunboats at-tempt to push through New Inlet. In the first day's fight, Lamb's careful gunners expended only 672 projectiles.[13]

Throughout the bombardment the Southern defenders calmly went about their work, loading and firing as if engaged in target practice. The concussion from the artillery fire forced the soldiers to find unique ways to protect themselves from the shock to their bodies. Private George Washing-ton Benson claimed that he and his comrades stood on their tiptoes with their mouths wide open whenever the lanyard to their land face gun was being pulled. "If you didn't," Washington explained, "it would knock you silly and jar your teeth out."[14]

Despite their measured response, the Confederates succeeded in hitting many of their targets. About mid-afternoon, a 6.4-inch rifle projectile struck the starboard paddlebox of the *Pontoosuc*, passing through the engine room and bursting in the paymaster's storeroom. The explosion ignited the vessel, but her crew quickly smothered the flames. A similar shell pierced the port boiler of the *Mackinaw*, scalding ten men and almost extinguishing the fires in the furnace. The *Osceola* nearly sank after a 10-inch solid shot penetrated her hull below the waterline. Yet the gunboats suffered greater damage and more casualties from their own guns than from enemy fire. Defective 100-pounder Parrott rifles—cast iron guns strengthened with wrought iron bands at the breech—cracked or burst upon firing. As a result, five vessels, the *Ticonderoga*, *Yantic*, *Juanita*, *Mackinaw*, and *Quaker City*, lost both Parrott guns and gunners. Two sailors were mortally wounded when the *Yantic's* 100-pounder Parrott rifle burst, damaging the vessel so severely that her commander temporarily pulled her out of the battle.[15]

The most deadly self-inflicted damage occurred on board the *Ticonderoga* when a Parrott rifle exploded, killing eight crew members and

Bursting of a 100-pounder Parrott rifle and wounding of sailors on board the *Juanita*, December 24, 1864. *Harper's Weekly*

wounding eleven others. Acting Lieutenant Louis G. Vassallo was one of the more fortunate casualties. Vassallo was standing at the breech sighting the gun when without warning it erupted in hot smoke and flying iron. One metal fragment blew out his left eye, iron slivers peppered his skin, and hot gunpowder scorched his face. Asked if he was in much pain, Vassallo replied: "Oh, yes. I have an intense headache, but I will get well in fifteen days. I have been wounded twice before," he stated, "I don't believe this wound is much." The wounded lieutenant's prediction proved to be correct; although severely injured, he managed to survive.[16]

Many of Vassallo's mates were not so fortunate. The deck of the *Ticonderoga* had to be covered with sand to absorb the blood of the dead and wounded sailors. Noting the demoralizing effect the explosion of the Parrott rifle and the sight of the bloody, mangled bodies had on his men, Coxswain William Shipman, commander of the No. 2 gun nearby, encouraged his gunners to do their duty. "Go ahead, boys," Shipman ordered, "this is only the fortune of war." Shipman would later receive the Medal of Honor for his coolness under fire. Ultimately, Admiral Porter lost about forty-five sailors killed and wounded by the bursting of Parrott rifles, almost double the number of men Colonel Lamb lost during the Christmas Eve bombardment.[17]

Despite the rash of casualties from his own guns, an overconfident Admiral Porter believed that his warships had demolished the fort and nearly everyone inside. "I attacked the [batteries]. . .and silenced them in about an hour and a half," Porter boasted. "There being no troops here to take possession, I am merely firing at [the fort] now to keep up practice." Near sunset the bombardment reached its climax of beauty and terror. All of the larger vessels were engaged with the fort's batteries, both sides thundering away with their powerful guns. It was just dark enough to see the blazing cannon and quick flashes of bursting shells. Thick smoke from smoldering fires inside the fort spewed upwards, as the sun's fading light peeked through to dimly illuminate the fort's ramparts and cannon muzzles protruding from the parapet. "The battle was a magnificent scene," exclaimed an eyewitness. "It cannot be described, it must be seen."[18]

In Admiral Porter's opinion, his bombardment had been so devastating that the army need only to go ashore and take possession of the fort. When

Butler's troops had not returned from Beaufort by dusk, however, Porter called off the attack and ordered his ships to withdraw.[19]

Ben Butler's transports remained in Beaufort taking on coal and water, while workmen disposed of horses which had died on board the vessels during the recent gale. The relatively relaxed atmosphere disintegrated when Captain Clarke returned early on December 24 with the message that Admiral Porter planned to detonate the powder boat that same morning. An angry and confused Butler immediately set out on the ninety mile trip to New Inlet. The general hoped Porter would come to his senses in the meantime and postpone the battle until the army reached Fort Fisher.

As the *Ben De Ford* neared Federal Point, however, Butler and his men realized Porter had begun the attack without them. They glimpsed thick clouds of sulfurous smoke and ammunition cases floating on the water, and heard the distant rumbling of artillery pounding across the water like an approaching thunderstorm. Butler reached New Inlet about 5:30 p.m., just in time to witness the end of the bombardment and the withdrawal of Porter's fleet. The transports trailed Butler southward and reached the fort later that night.

Butler was convinced Admiral Porter had exploded the powder boat in the hope of destroying Fort Fisher before the army returned from Beaufort. Angry and distraught because Porter had bungled his pet project, Butler all but decided to abort the campaign and return immediately to Virginia. Why stay? Butler must have asked himself. The Confederates now had ample warning the Union army would soon assault the fort and would surely be prepared to contest the landing. General Weitzel agreed with Butler. If Porter thought he could take the fort without the army, Weitzel reasoned, let him try. But the prudent Cyrus Comstock asked Butler and Weitzel to reconsider. If Porter succeeded in capturing the fort alone, it would be a huge embarrassment to the War Department and might ruin Butler's and Weitzel's military careers. Having come this far, Comstock argued, the army commanders' reputations would best be served by cooperating with Porter and landing the troops.

A fuming Butler finally yielded to Comstock's persuasion. He would put ashore a strong reconnaissance force to inspect the enemy's defenses and then make his decision. Yet, Butler again declined to meet with Porter to prepare the next day's battle plan. Instead, he sent a messenger to the *Mal-*

vern to ask when Porter could see Weitzel to arrange the landing of the troops. Nor was Porter anxious to meet with Butler. The admiral informed the Massachusetts general that he was too lame from an accidental fall the day before to meet with Weitzel. The business of war would have to wait until morning, after Porter had gotten a good night's rest. Weitzel considered Porter's refusal to meet with the army commanders on board the *Ben De Ford* an affront to Butler, the expedition's senior officer. At Butler's request, however, Weitzel agreed to meet with Porter on board the *Malvern* at 6:30 Christmas morning to arrange the landing of the troops on Federal Point.[20]

The inter-service turmoil was not a good omen for the Federal soldiers about to take their turn at the Cape Fear's defenders.

General Whiting anticipated a warm reception for the Federal troops when they tried to come ashore. Late on Christmas Eve afternoon Whiting arrived at Fort Fisher with some of his aides: Maj. James H. Hill, the general's chief of staff and brother-in-law; Col. Robert Tansill, the district's inspector general; and Maj. W. C. Strong. Whiting had received Lamb's message regarding the impending attack about 1:00 p.m., and then had boarded the steamer *Cape Fear* bound for Fort Fisher. He entered the fort just as Porter's fleet was winding down its fierce bombardment. Bragg had approved Whiting's transfer to the fort and instructed him to take command of the defenses at the inlets, superseding General Hébert. Lamb offered to relinquish command of Fort Fisher to Whiting, but the general declined. He had confidence in Lamb's ability, and wanted merely to be at his side as an observer and adviser during the battle.[21]

While Fort Fisher and its occupants had suffered little during the lengthy bombardment, Whiting knew the cannonade was but a preliminary action preceding the real threat to the bastion: the Federal land force. He was counting on Robert F. Hoke's Division of veteran infantrymen to turn back Butler's troops when they came ashore. At about the same time Whiting arrived at the fort the vanguard of his hopes, regiments of Brig. Gen. William W. Kirkland's Brigade, arrived at Sugar Loaf, four-and-a-half miles north of Fort Fisher. Kirkland's troops had pulled into Wilmington about midnight on December 23, and took up a line of march for Sugar Loaf shortly after sunrise. Kirkland rode ahead of his command on horseback, reaching Sugar Loaf at 1:00 p.m. His troops, exhausted after the difficult train trip from Virginia and the fifteen-mile forced march from Wilmington, did not reach Sugar Loaf until three and a half hours later.[22]

Greeting the veterans upon their arrival was a ragtag force of state militia. These reinforcements consisted of about 800 teenaged boys from North Carolina Junior Reserves (the 4th, 7th, and 8th battalions), plus 400 men aged forty-five to sixty of the 8th Regiment North Carolina Senior Reserves, all brigaded together under the command of Col. John K. Connally. In a desperate bid to fill its depleted ranks, the Confederacy conscripted nearly everyone from sixteen to sixty who could shoulder a rifle. Veteran soldiers doubted the boy soldiers could even handle their firearms. "Some of the [Junior Reserves] can't hold their guns off hand to save their life," declared one veteran, "neither can they pull the hammer back to fire without putting the breech of the gun on the ground and put their foot on the hammer to cock it." They should never have been conscripted for service, Colonel Lamb complained, "it was robbing the cradle." Notable among the Senior Reserves at Sugar Loaf was William Pettigrew, brother of James Johnston Pettigrew, the renowned North Carolina brigadier general who had been mortally wounded at Falling Waters during Robert E. Lee's retreat from Gettysburg in mid-July 1863. Regardless of their military ability, the recruits and civilian volunteers were armed and present at Sugar Loaf. And they were ready to fight.[23]

Supporting Connally's reserves was a detachment of the 2nd South Carolina Cavalry, an artillery battery commanded by Lt. Col. John P. W. Read (a regular army officer), and Capt. Thomas J. Southerland's 2nd Co. I, 10th North Carolina Regiment (1st North Carolina Artillery). Two Whitworth artillery pieces, a 6-pounder rifle of Capt. Andrew Paris' Staunton Hill (Virginia) Artillery, together with a larger 12-pounder from Southerland's Battery (also known as the Wilmington Horse Artillery) were available. Ordnance experts considered the British-made Whitworth rifles among the best field pieces in the world, capable of firing with deadly accuracy up to five miles.[24]

General Kirkland inspected the Sugar Loaf defenses that faced the immense fleet of Union warships fanned out for several miles offshore. Connally had entrenched a company of his militia in newly-constructed earthworks on the mainland near Myrtle Sound, immediately in rear of Battery Gatlin on the beach. Lieutenant Colonel Read had detached a gun crew to man the 6.4-inch 32-pounder gun in Battery Gatlin, but hesitated sending a larger force. Read considered Battery Gatlin a deathtrap, exposed as it was on the narrow strip of beach on the east side of Myrtle Sound. Earlier he had requested permission to remove the cannon, well aware that if the Federals came ashore at Gatlin, his men would be unable to save the heavy gun. They would be lucky to even save themselves, because their only viable means of escape was to ford the sound. To protect the Confederates' avenue of retreat and to impede a nearby enemy landing, Read had also deployed a section of Southerland's Battery, commanded by Lt. Thomas C. Moore, near Connally's reserves just north of the home of James Burriss. The remainder of Connally's force was stationed at Sugar Loaf, a mile to the west.[25]

As soon as troops from his brigade reached Sugar Loaf, Kirkland deployed them to contest the expected Federal landing. One hundred soldiers of the 66th North Carolina Infantry, commanded by Maj. David S. Davis, replaced Connally's inexperienced Senior Reserves, who had been pulled off the line during the night of December 23. Kirkland placed Col. John E. Brown's 42nd North Carolina Infantry along the sound from Davis' position stretching southward toward Battery Anderson. Company A of the 42nd, consisting of about eighty men commanded by Capt. Jacob Koonts, was sent down to Battery Anderson halfway between Battery Gatlin and Fort Fisher. At General Whiting's request, Kirkland sent Lt. Col. Thomas Sharp's 17th North Carolina Infantry to reinforce Fort Fisher, but early Christmas morning the regiment marched to Koonts' support at Battery Anderson. Having positioned his command and with darkness fast approaching on Christmas Eve, Kirkland could only wait to see what the morning would bring.[26]

David W. Hodgekins, a surgeon on board the *Ben De Ford*, was up before sunrise on Christmas morning. A stillness had descended over the vast Union fleet lying just off Fort Fisher. But the calm of Christmas morning would soon be broken by the thunder of war, an irony that did not escape Dr. Hodgekins. "How sadly have we fallen that the anniversary of the day of the birth of Jesus Christ, who came to declare peace on earth and good will to men, should be spent in endeavors to take the lives of our fellow creatures in war," Hodgekins lamented. "The Sabbath we are commanded to keep holy [is] desecrated to gratify man's wild ambitions. [That we wage war on] this Sabbath. . .seems more than desecration." Though many servicemen, Confederate and Union alike, shared the doctor's feelings, war took precedence over Christmas sentiments.[27]

After Porter and Weitzel made arrangements to put the troops ashore, many of Porter's warships spent a dreary Christmas morning laying down a heavy cover fire near the army's landing site three miles north of Fort Fisher. The *Santiago de Cuba, Britannia, Tristram Shandy, Howquah, Fort Jackson* and at least twelve other ships pounded Battery Anderson and Battery Gatlin, as well as the woods behind and between them. Thinking these small gunboats were positioned too far from the beach for their shelling to be effective, Admiral Porter sent in the *Brooklyn* to show them how it was done. The *Brooklyn*, the fourth-largest ship-of-the-line in the armada, was a powerful 2,500-ton screw sloop with twenty-six big guns (mostly 9-inch and 11-inch Dahlgrens). Porter respected the fighting spirit of the *Brooklyn*'s commander, Capt. James Alden. Together they had assisted Farragut in the capture of New Orleans in 1862, and had repeatedly passed the Vicksburg gauntlet early the following summer. Alden knew how to bombard fortifications. He snuggled the *Brooklyn* close to Federal Point beach and opened fire with her huge guns to help clear out any enemy soldiers lurking in the area.[28]

The intense shelling by the *Brooklyn* and the other gunboats killed and wounded twenty soldiers of Kirkland's Brigade and an undetermined number of Connally's reserves on the Sugar Loaf line. "It was pitiful to see some of those gray-haired patriots [of the Senior Reserves] dead in the woods, killed by shells from the fleet," lamented one of General Kirkland's staff officers. The gunboats also drove Lieutenant Colonel Read's cannoneers out of Battery Gatlin. The fugitive gunners quickly crossed the sound to the mainland without having fired a shot from their cannon. Read responded to the Federal bombardment as best he could with his long-range field pieces, but he was soon grievously wounded and had to leave the field. Captain Southerland assumed command but in the confusion that followed was compelled to withdraw his artillery because of the fleet's heavy shell-

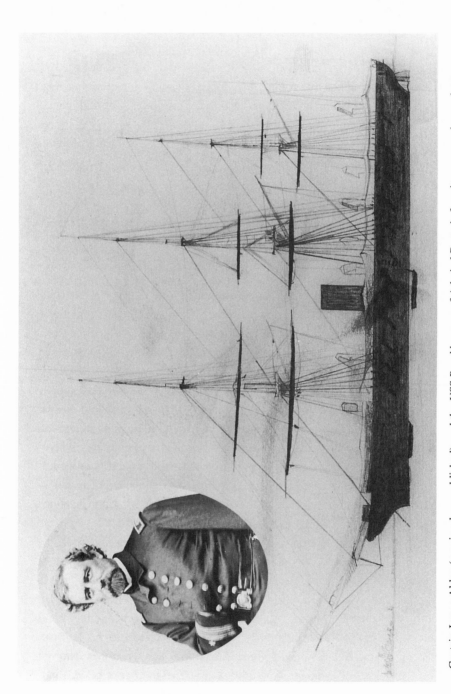

Captain James James Alden (previously unpublished) and the *USS Brooklyn*, one of Admiral Porter's favorite commanders and strongest warships. *Courtesy of Charles V. Peery and the U.S. Army Military History Institute*

ing. Soldiers of the 42nd North Carolina posted in the woods parallel to the beach wisely dug in and laid low.[29]

As the Confederates scrambled for cover, the first Union troops came ashore. Captain Alden made available all of the *Brooklyn*'s launches to ferry the troops to the beachhead, while Capt. Oliver S. Glisson of the *Santiago de Cuba* superintended the landing with forty-one gigs donated by the navy, along with a comparable number of army boats. The first launches shoved off for the sandy shore shortly before two o'clock on Christmas afternoon. The long line of boats resembled a huge sea serpent as it slowly wound its way toward the beach. The boats fanned out just before they reached the shoreline. "It was a beautiful sight," remarked a soldier in the 112th New York Infantry.[30]

Earlier, division commander Brig. Gen. Adelbert Ames had selected Col. Louis Bell and his troops of the Third Brigade to carve out the initial beachhead. Without consulting Ames, however, General Weitzel had personally instructed Bvt. Brig. Gen. N. Martin Curtis to hit the beach first with his First Brigade. The feisty Ames was furious when he learned Weitzel had preempted his orders. His anger only grew as the day wore on.

General Curtis was the first Union soldier to set foot on Federal Point. At 2:10 p.m. he rushed to the top of the nearest sand dune and planted a naval standard loaned to him by Captain Glisson, marking the spot where the troops should land. Even from a distance Curtis' hulking figure would have been easy to spot. At 6'7" and 225 pounds, the barrel-chested, heavily-bearded Curtis was one of the biggest men in Ames' division. Upon meeting Curtis before the war, Abraham Lincoln, who rarely encountered anyone taller than he at 6'4", reportedly asked, "Mr. Curtis, how do you know when your feet are cold?" Curtis' family, friends and comrades worried that the towering officer would eventually be felled by enemy bullets.

Though he looked the part, Newton Martin Curtis was not a soldier by profession. Before the war he had been a teacher, law student and postmaster in his hometown of DePeyster, New York, before managing his father's "scientific farm." When war broke out, Curtis entered the volunteer army as captain of Company G, 16th New York Infantry. A year later he was se-

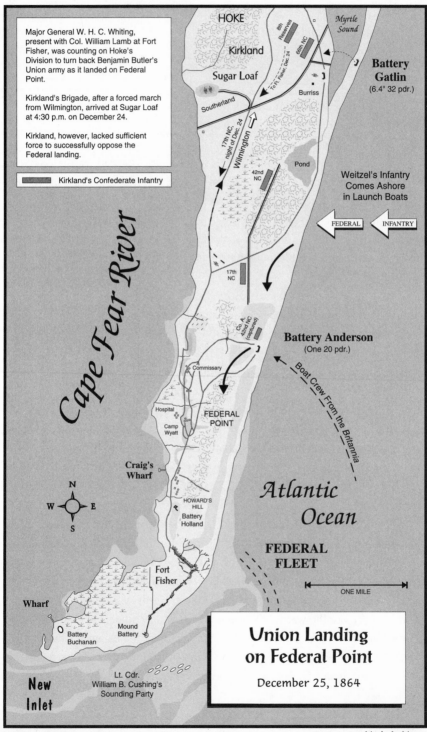

Major General W. H. C. Whiting, present with Col. William Lamb at Fort Fisher, was counting on Hoke's Division to turn back Benjamin Butler's Union army as it landed on Federal Point.

Kirkland's Brigade, after a forced march from Wilmington, arrived at Sugar Loaf at 4:30 p.m. on December 24.

Kirkland, however, lacked sufficient force to successfully oppose the Federal landing.

Kirkland's Confederate Infantry

HOKE

Myrtle Sound

Kirkland

Sugar Loaf

8th Reserves

66th NC

Battery Gatlin
(6.4" 32 pdr.)

To Ft. Fisher, Dec. 24

Burriss

Southerland

17th NC, night of Dec. 24

Wilmington

Pond

42nd NC

Weitzel's Infantry Comes Ashore in Launch Boats

FEDERAL   INFANTRY

17th NC

Co. A 42nd NC (captured)

Battery Anderson
(One 20 pdr.)

Boat Crew From the Britannia

Cape Fear River

Commissary

Hospital

Camp Wyatt

FEDERAL POINT

Craig's Wharf

N
W — E
S

HOWARD'S HILL

Battery Holland

Atlantic

Ocean

FEDERAL FLEET

ONE MILE

Fort Fisher

Wharf

Battery Buchanan

Mound Battery

Lt. Cdr. William B. Cushing's Sounding Party

New

Inlet

Union Landing on Federal Point

December 25, 1864

Mark A. Moore

Bvt. Brig. Gen. N. Martin Curtis, the unsung Union hero of Fort Fisher, in a previously unpublished photograph. *Ogdensburg (N.Y.) Public Library*

verely wounded in a small action at West Point, Virginia during the Peninsula Campaign. Upon recovery, Curtis spent the next two years performing mundane departmental duty before finally returning to front-line duty with a commission as colonel of the 142nd New York Infantry. With the 142nd

Curtis served General Butler's Army of the James at Cold Harbor and Petersburg in the spring and summer of 1864, earning valuable experience in the process. By early November, the 29-year-old New Yorker had been breveted a brigadier general and given command of the First Brigade of Adelbert Ames' division. Having sat out much of the war, Curtis was anxious to prove his mettle at Fort Fisher.[31]

That Christmas morning on Federal Point Curtis led a reconnaissance force of 500 infantrymen from his brigade, 450 from his old regiment, the 142nd New York, and 50 others from the 112th New York. Landing immediately after Curtis, General Weitzel ordered the brigade commander to push down the beach "as far as he could go," deploying flankers as he went in case the enemy was lurking on the peninsula. Curtis formed his men into line of battle, and accompanied by Weitzel, moved out to find the Rebels.[32]

On the beach about half a mile south of the landing area stood Battery Anderson (called Flag Pond Battery by the Federals), a small sand redoubt mounting a "Long Tom" 20-pounder rifle. The cannon was useless now, having burst into seven large pieces when firing at a Union blockader on the night of December 16. Hammered by naval fire all Christmas morning, Confederate soldiers manning the battery took shelter behind the work as Curtis' New Yorkers approached. Too far away to be reinforced by their besieged comrades at Fort Fisher or Sugar Loaf, and too outnumbered to offer much of a fight, the Confederates decided to give up. When a white flag was seen atop the battery, Union soldiers raced down the beach, hoping to be the first to receive the enemy's surrender.

Sailors on board nearby ships also saw the flag and quickly lowered gigs to row ashore and capture the Southerners. A boat crew from the *Britannia* won the contest, splashing ashore just ahead of Curtis' disappointed soldiers, bagging 70 privates and two officers in the process. A loud cheer went up from the fleet when the navy took the honors of capturing the first Confederates of the campaign. The prisoners turned out to be members of Capt. Jacob Koonts' Company A, 42nd North Carolina, Kirkland's Brigade, Hoke's Division. Three weeks earlier they had been battling General Butler's Army of the James near Richmond, but had since traveled 250 miles to the southeastern coast of North Carolina. The presence of veteran soldiers from the Army of Northern Virginia deployed on sand dunes in

North Carolina was irrefutable evidence that Chase Whiting and his defenders had been reinforced. The news troubled Ben Butler greatly.[33]

General Kirkland was likewise concerned after he heard a "deafening cheer" erupt offshore that he later learned was the U. S. Navy celebrating its capture of Koonts' command. Kirkland had been approaching Battery Anderson to "see how matters were going there" when the capture occurred. With his small force already thinly stretched along the beach, Kirkland could ill-afford to lose an entire company of soldiers. The combative North Carolinian decided to attack the Union-occupied battery with the remainder of the 17th North Carolina Infantry in an effort to free his captured men.

Lieutenant Colonel Sharp's North Carolinians, with Capt. Thomas J. Norman's men of Company G deployed as skirmishers, fired several volleys as they charged the battery, easily driving back the enemy's pickets. The main body of Federals managed to hold their ground against Lee's detached veterans, however, killing three, wounding 20 and capturing another officer and 10 Southerners. Kirkland quickly surmised that any further advance would be sheer madness since he lacked both the manpower and ammunition to contest the overwhelming Union force gathering on the beach. By this time at least a mile separated the 17th North Carolina and the 42nd North Carolina, and both flanks of the 17th were already being overlapped by Curtis' reconnaissance force. Kirkland observed numerous additional Union troops heading ashore under the protection of the Federal fleet. Should the enemy suddenly turn north to attack Battery Gatlin, only Connally's Southern reserves and 100 soldiers of the 66th North Carolina would be in position to meet them. If this small force was overrun, the road to Wilmington would be open. Kirkland wisely withdrew his entire force to Sugar Loaf, leaving only one gun of Captain Southerland's artillery on the Wilmington Road behind Battery Anderson to cover the retreat.[34]

While Curtis and Kirkland were sparring on the sand dunes, Admiral Porter had resumed his bombardment of Fort Fisher. The *New Ironsides*

opened fire just before 11:00 a.m., followed shortly afterward by the monitors. The monitor *Saugus* arrived in time to participate in the second day's fight, having undergone some last-minute adjustments in Beaufort. "Every time the monitors or the *New Ironsides* have fired, the shell passing through the air has sounded exactly like a train of cars starting from a depot and gradually going out of hearing," remarked a naval officer, "then comes the bang and we see a cloud of dirt thrown into the air from the side of the Fort." The other warships followed suit, throwing roaring projectiles at Fort Fisher for more than seven hours. "The fire farely licked out from their guns," commented Pvt. G. G. Young of the 2nd South Carolina Cavalry, "such a continued roar of artillery I never heard before, it sounded more like thunder than any thing of the kind I heard before." A Union sailor agreed with the assessment of his land foe. "The noise was like thunder," he noted, "heavy and deep, mingled with screaming bolts." Porter's ships eventually slackened their thunderous fire to conserve their rapidly shrinking ammunition stockpiles and to prevent their guns from overheating and bursting, as some had done the day before with such disastrous consequences. Even so, the ships fired almost 10,000 rounds at the fort—nearly as many as the day before, but with more deadly effect.

Among the casualties inside the fort were several teenaged soldiers of the Junior Reserves.[35]

During the night of December 24, Chase Whiting had ordered General Kirkland to send the contingent of Junior Reserves and 500 regular troops to Fort Fisher. Kirkland obeyed by dispatching the 4th, 7th, and 8th battalions of the North Carolina Junior Reserves, together with the veteran 17th North Carolina. The Junior Reserves were marched from Sugar Loaf through Fort Fisher to Battery Buchanan, from which point they were to be transferred by steamer to Bald Head Island. Once there they were to relieve Col. John J. Hedrick's veteran artillerymen of the 40th North Carolina Regiment, who were being brought over to reinforce Fort Fisher. The Junior Reserves reached Battery Buchanan before dawn on Christmas morning, but were prevented from boarding the transport because of low tide. Even when the tide became more favorable for boarding, fire from the Union gunboats kept the transport from docking.[36]

Anxious for additional reinforcements, Colonel Lamb requested that the Junior Reserves be brought back up to Fort Fisher. By then Federal Point was again under a heavy bombardment from Porter's warships. The young boys were pummeled by shells as they sprinted across the open sand plain between Battery Buchanan and Fort Fisher, "upon which a partridge could not hide himself," noted one soldier. Several of the neophyte soldiers were killed or wounded, including 17-year-old Pvt. Elias Davis of Company C, 7th Battalion, who was gruesomely cut in two by a large shell. By the time the survivors reached the fort, they were frightened and exhausted.[37]

While Union cannonballs tore into the boy soldiers near Battery Buchanan, boys and girls were tearing into paper-wrapped presents found underneath Christmas trees in Wilmington. Above the joyful noise of Christmas morning, the distant thunder of artillery was plainly audible in the city. Morning church goers at St. James Episcopal Church sang Christmas hymns to the accompaniment of rumbling cannon. "From battle and murder, and from sudden death," began the minister, "Good Lord, deliver us," responded the congregation—their prayer punctuated by the 'boom—boom—boom,' of heavy guns."[38]

Much of the Union warships' Christmas Day bombardment was concentrated on the southern end of Fort Fisher's sea face, especially against the Mound Battery. Admiral Porter hoped to soften up the batteries guarding New Inlet's channel before attempting to run his light-draft gunboats into the Cape Fear River. About noon Porter instructed Cmdr. John Guest, of the *Iosco* on the southern end of the navy's battle line to attempt to maneuver his ship into the channel. But the channel was improperly marked on the sounding charts and Guest had difficulty locating the entrance. This troubling development led Porter to assume that the wreckage of the blockade runners lying at the mouth of the inlet had changed the bar's formation. About 2:30 p.m. the admiral dispatched a party of small boats to find the channel and take soundings. This potentially hazardous expedition was led by Lt. Cmdr. William Barker Cushing, who had made several daring raids into the river in the past year. It did not take long for the Confederates to guess what Cushing was attempting, and they opened a blistering crossfire on his boats from batteries on the lower end of the sea face and at Battery Buchanan. A few accurate shots from the latter battery cut one of the launches in two and drove the rest back to their ships. Ordinary Seaman Henry Sands of the *Tacony* did not survive the misadventure. A well-aimed Confederate shell severed both of his legs at the knees and he quickly bled to death.[39]

Among the guns firing on Cushing's sounding party and Porter's gunboats of Line Three were two naval pattern 7-inch Brooke rifles taken off the sunken ironclad *Raleigh* and mounted en barbette along Fort Fisher's lower sea face. The Brooke rifles were manned by twenty-four sailors under Lt. Francis M. Roby, who had been sent ashore from the converted blockade runner *Chickamauga*. Roby and his men had been careful to swab the cannons' tubes with wet sponges to keep them cool and to scrape them out to prevent fouling. During the hottest part of the fight Christmas afternoon, however, both of the rifles burst. When the first gun exploded on only its third discharge about 2:30 p.m., every man in the compartment was knocked down by jagged and steaming iron pieces, and Lt. Thomas L. Dornin and five or six sailors were wounded. Miraculously, no one was killed. "It is truly wonderful that any of us escaped from the gun pit alive," remarked Midshipman Clarence Cary, the burst gun's commander. About an hour-and-a-half later, the other Brooke rifle, commanded by Passed Midshipman Thomas L. Berrien, exploded on its eighth discharge, but once again, no one was killed. "How the men escaped, God only knows," commented a thankful sailor. These were the only two cannon in Fort Fisher to burst during the battle, perhaps because they were inferior castings from the Confederate Naval Ordnance Works in Selma, Alabama. It is equally plausible that the sailors had been overloading the cannon with too much army gunpowder, which was stronger than the navy powder they were accustomed to using. The more powerful powder caused the guns to overheat—with predictable results.[40]

Braving the sea face guns that had repulsed Cushing's party, Admiral Porter personally inspected the inlet. As the *Malvern* steamed closer toward shore, however, Fort Fisher's 8-inch Armstrong gun sent an iron bolt through the ship's boiler, forcing the admiral to beat a hasty retreat. Still, Porter had learned much from his reconnaissance. New Inlet, it appeared, was too shallow and too torpedo-filled to maneuver without a pilot or buoys. In addition, the batteries he had boasted of silencing in an hour-and-a-half on the previous day were very much alive and ready to contest any attempt by the fleet to run past them. A reluctant Porter decided against any further attempts to enter the dangerous channel.

Although Porter and the navy had made little progress, the situation appeared more promising for Weitzel and the army up the beach. Shortly before three o'clock Christmas afternoon, Weitzel, Curtis and about 250 men from Curtis' old regiment, the 142nd New York advanced to within a mile-and-a-quarter of Fort Fisher's northeast bastion. Curtis had deployed the remainder of his reconnaissance force in skirmish formation as it moved southward from the landing zone. Weitzel was wisely wary of approaching too close to Fort Fisher for fear of drawing fire from the fort's artillery or taking casualties from friendly ships just offshore.

From his new position, a "slight elevation" near the beach, Weitzel had a good, if distant, view of Fort Fisher. The ground to the south and southwest toward the Cape Fear River had been stripped of trees and foliage, giving Confederate cannoneers a clear field of fire, but also enabling Weitzel to examine the fort's defenses. The general hoped to "ascertain the true condition" of Fort Fisher before deciding whether to launch a ground attack.[41]

It did not take long before Weitzel decided he did not like what he saw. Fort Fisher was the strongest fort he had ever encountered. From what he remembered of his reconnaissance of the fort with General Graham back in September—together with information he had received from naval officers on the blockade, spies, and other "reliable sources"—Weitzel believed Fort Fisher was a square-bastioned fortification with high earthen walls surrounded by a deep ditch. His view through his field glasses did not alter this belief.

Reality, however, was an entirely different matter. Instead of four walls, Fort Fisher had exactly half that. The mammoth fortress was just a two-sided earthwork with a half bastion, Shepherd's Battery, on the western end of the land face, a full bastion where the land and sea faces intersected, and no ditch at all. The maps and charts that both the Union army and navy officers were using depicting Fort Fisher as a four-sided work were wrong.

Weitzel, staring through his glasses at the fort, believed that Fisher was completely enclosed and thus far he had seen nothing to persuade him otherwise. Despite the intensive naval bombardment still in progress, Weitzel counted no fewer than seventeen big guns still atop the land face parapet and commanding the open ground across which his soldiers would have to charge. The palisade also appeared intact, and would pose a major obstacle to attacking infantry. Even the grassy slopes of the parapet and traverses appeared untouched. In short, Weitzel saw no evidence that Admiral Porter's massive two-day bombardment had damaged the fort in the slightest.

The general had a "distinct and vivid recollection" of similar battle situations. He had led three assaults against fortified positions—though none had been so daunting as Fort Fisher—and had been repulsed each time, losing many good men. Weitzel knew the tragic consequences of sending troops to attack forts that had not been sufficiently damaged by artillery fire. On Morris Island outside Charleston, South Carolina, Union soldiers had been slaughtered in repeated attacks against Battery Wagner in July 1863. Fort Fisher was much stronger than Battery Wagner, leading Weitzel to conclude that an assault upon the fort it in its present condition would be suicidal.[42]

As a result of his reconnaissance, Weitzel decided to return immediately to General Butler and report his findings. He ordered General Curtis to hold his advanced position and to assume command of the troops as they arrived from the landing area. Curtis was to report any changes in the situation. Anxious to get a closer look at the fort, Curtis requested permission to push his skirmishers forward. Weitzel agreed with some reluctance but insisted that Curtis not bring on an engagement with the enemy. Weitzel turned and trudged back up the beach to board a waiting transport.

No sooner had Weitzel departed than Curtis prepared to move toward Fort Fisher. The towering New Yorker assigned a reserve force to Lt. Col. Albert M. Barney, commander of the 142nd New York, with orders for him to collect the balance of the First Brigade as it arrived from the landing zone. He sent Capt. William A. Jones west with a party of soldiers to set up a picket post near the Cape Fear River. With his rear thus protected by troops near the beach and the river, Curtis felt more at ease in advancing against the fort, which he did with his remaining fifty troops, who picked their way southwestward across the peninsula toward Fort Fisher's western flank. Curtis' route was no accident, for it led his command away from the fire of the ships and to the shelter of the river bank.

About 900 yards north of Fort Fisher on a knoll known as Howard's Hill, Curtis and his small force stumbled onto Battery Holland, an abandoned Confederate redoubt. Holland's lone cannon had been spiked because the crew had been unable to move the heavy gun out of harm's way. Curtis surveyed Fort Fisher from the abandoned elevation, and though he saw numerous cannon muzzles protruding from the parapet, there was no sign of enemy soldiers. The curious and aggressive Curtis, pushing his orders to the limit, felt few qualms about pushing his troops even closer to the fort.[43]

Encountering no enemy resistance, forty skirmishers of the 142nd New York moved to within seventy-five yards of Shepherd's Battery, the huge earthen western salient. The Union skirmishers approached so close to the fort that ten men were wounded by friendly fire from Porter's vessels. Ironically, it was Porter's bombardment—not enemy fire—that stalled Curtis' advance. To the amazement of Curtis' men, no Confederates appeared on the parapet to open fire on them. Several of Curtis' more daring men even moved up to the vacant works to obtain trophies marking their advance.[44]

Soldiers of the 142nd New York's Company G were extending their skirmish line and digging in when a loud explosion on the fort's parapet caught their attention. When the dust settled they saw that a naval shell had knocked over a flagstaff on Shepherd's Battery opposite their position. The Confederate flag—the same one Colonel Lamb had placed on Shepherd's Battery the day before to draw the gunboats' fire—was hanging over the edge of the parapet. Private James Spring jumped up and started toward it, but was ordered back into line. Company G's commander, Lt. William Henry Walling, took Spring's place, telling his men to cover him as he made his way to the fort.

Walling's plucky act almost ended before it had begun. A stray shell from one of Porter's monitors exploded nearby, momentarily stunning him. Walling quickly recovered and dashed on. He managed to enter the fort by slipping through a break in the log palisade made by a projectile. Once

Lt. William Henry Walling, Co. G, 142 New York Infantry, in a previously unpublished view, and Shepherd's Battery, where Walling pilfered a Confederate flag in the December 1864 battle. *U.S. Army Military History Institute*

inside he moved to the right toward the Cape Fear River, as far beyond range of Porter's gunboats as he could get, before scaling the exterior slope of the fort and grabbing the flag. The garrison standard, according to Walling's estimate, was "six or seven feet on the pole and ten to twelve feet on the fly." Worried about being shot or captured by the Confederates or, alternatively, blown-up by the navy's missiles, Walling did not bother to remove the flag from the downed flagstaff. The brave (some might say reckless) lieutenant, dragged the twelve-foot section of flagstaff out of the fort the same way he had come in. "The pole was quite long and heavy," Walling recalled, "and rather hard to manage in getting through the gap in the palisade." Somehow he managed to yank it through and transport it safely to the skirmish line. Walling removed the flag from the staff, and—perhaps feeling a little guilty for having performed what Private Spring had first attempted—gave it to Spring to present to General Curtis. It was about 3:20 p.m. when Walling acquired his bunting trophy, a deed which his commanding officer called "one of the most gallant exploits of the war." It also earned Walling the Medal of Honor.[45]

Another enterprising New Yorker, Pvt. Henry Blair, a sharpshooter in the 142nd New York's Company F, sneaked to within forty-five feet of the gate on the west side of Shepherd's Battery, where the Wilmington Road entered the fort. Blair peeked into the fort and saw Confederate soldiers milling about at the entrance to a bombproof. He shot at them, and then ducked for cover along the edge of the road. When no one in the fort returned fire, Blair decided to remain where he was and make "further observations."[46]

While luck blessed Curtis' Federals that evening, it most certainly overlooked Confederate Pvt. Amos H. Jones, of Faison's Scouts. The 19-year-old mounted courier emerged from the fort at Shepherd's Battery, unaware that Curtis' skirmishers were lurking just beyond the fort's walls. Henry Blair, still hiding near the west gate, shot and killed the unfortunate youth, after which Blair and a comrade pilfered the young Confederate's belongings. Among other things, they found a dispatch from Maj. William Saunders, General Hébert's chief of artillery, ordering a battery of light artillery to be brought into the fort. After dumping Jones' body, Private Blair proudly mounted his captured horse and rode it back into Union lines.[47]

Yet a third daredevil, Lt. George Simpson of Company G, 142nd New York, an acting aide-de-camp on General Curtis' staff, also stole up to the fort's sally-port at Shepherd's Battery. When he had approached within fifteen or twenty paces, Simpson found a pair of mules—one killed by shell fire, and the other still harnessed to its dead mate. Simpson freed the surviving mule and rode it back to the skirmish line amid the cheers of his comrades.

Soon after, about 4:00 p.m., Simpson noticed a telegraph line running out of Fort Fisher (which linked the fort with Sugar Loaf and Wilmington). After unsuccessfully calling for a volunteer to climb one of the poles and cut the wire, Simpson himself shinnied up and hacked the copper wire in two with a hatchet. From Simpson's crow's nest position atop the telegraph pole, the interior of Fort Fisher was plainly visible. The fort was not, as the Union high command believed, an enclosed work. Simpson noted two mammoth earthen walls which converged at the ocean's edge. Both a tall log stockade fence and a wide but shallow depression fronted the land face. Simpson called it a ditch, though it would have been an inconsequential one, marking where the Confederates had excavated dirt to form the ramparts. A swampy morass skirted the outer edge of Shepherd's Battery, but a wooden bridge crossed the bog and approached the fort on the western end. The entrance was a mere opening in the palisade barricaded with a chest-high wall of sandbags. The rear of the fort, however, was entirely open. As for defenders, Lieutenant Simpson saw Confederates working two guns on the sea face, but the land face appeared unmanned.

Simpson slid down the telegraph pole, remounted his captured mule, and rode off to report his observations to General Curtis, who was investigating a report that a battery of Confederate artillery—probably Southerland's Artillery that General Kirkland had deployed to cover his withdrawal to Sugar Loaf—was escaping toward Wilmington. Curtis, en route to the fort when Lieutenant Simpson met him, was delighted to hear the good news. When Curtis and Simpson arrived at the front, the general was presented with the flag Lieutenant Walling had seized and informed about what the skirmishers had done and seen. Walling, Blair, Spring, Simpson and others described Fort Fisher's layout. Their accounts differed somewhat as to details, but all agreed that the fort was only a two-sided work. More importantly, it appeared to be virtually undefended. Their eyewitness testimony—coupled with his own quick appraisal of the defenses—convinced Curtis that Fort Fisher could be captured. Curtis concluded that if he could hurry the remainder of his brigade to the front, he would storm the fort.[49]

The New York general wasted no time, dispatching a message to Lieutenant Colonel Barney to bring forward the reserves of the First Brigade. Curtis also ordered Lieutenant Walling to maintain his skirmish line confronting Shepherd's Battery and to keep a close watch on the fort. Then the general took Walling's flag and accompanied by two of his aides, marched across the peninsula to the beach about 500 yards from their starting point. It was a dangerous trek. Shells from the gunboats shrieked overhead and exploded, raising plumes of sand on the ramparts nearby. At least two rifle-musket shots were fired from the fort at Curtis' party as it moved parallel to the land face. Curtis saw the bullets zip into the sand several yards away, and concluded that Confederate marksmen "had taken some observation of the altitude of the person they were shooting at, and aimed too high." The failure of the Confederate riflemen to hit their slow moving targets from a range of 100 yards only strengthened Curtis' belief that the work could be easily captured.[50]

Standing on the beach just 150 yards from Fort Fisher's northeast bastion, Curtis began waving Walling's captured flag in what can only be described as a crude effort to signal the fleet. Lacking a trained signalman, Curtis hoped that by waving the flag he could make the fleet understand that he intended to assault the fort and that the vessels should shift their fire so as not to endanger his soldiers. The sailors on board the ships may not have grasped the meaning of Curtis' pantomime, but they could admire a Union general who was brave enough to stand before the muzzles of enemy guns and dare them to open fire. The tars rushed to the ships' gunwales and cheered Curtis. Their ovations were so loud that they could be heard above the roar of the bombardment by those onshore.[51]

To Curtis, the navy now appeared more enthusiastic about capturing the fort than the army. As he looked up the beach in the direction of Lieutenant Colonel Barney's position, Curtis saw no evidence that the rest of his troops were advancing as he had instructed. Rather, they appeared to be milling about the beach. Greatly annoyed, Curtis stormed up the shoreline to learn the cause of the delay. On his arrival, Barney told the general that about the time he had received his message to advance, an order came in from General

Butler to withdraw and reembark. Barney had relayed the order to the front, but it obviously had failed to reach its destination.

Curtis was dumbstruck. Surely Butler had issued his order on the basis of faulty or incomplete information. The flag-holding general sensed that the opportunity to seize Fort Fisher was slipping from his grasp.[52]

Ben Butler had remained at sea throughout the day. While awaiting word from Weitzel, Butler had observed with great interest the landing of his troops, as directed by Brig. Gen. Charles K. Graham of the Army of the James' naval brigade. The Massachusetts politician-turned-general had just joined Graham on board the *Chamberlain* when Admiral Porter drew alongside in the *Malvern*. Porter hailed Butler through a speaking trumpet—the first personal contact the two commanders had had since leaving Hampton Roads almost two weeks earlier:

"How do you do, General?"

"Very well, I thank you," Butler responded cordially.

"How many troops are you going to land?" Porter inquired.

"All I can," Butler answered.

"There is not a rebel within five miles of the fort," Porter boasted. "You have nothing to do but to land and take possession of it."

"I think there is a man by the name of Weitzel who will find out if that is so," replied a skeptical Butler.[53]

The man who was to "find out if that is so" reported to Butler shortly thereafter, about 4:00 p.m. Butler welcomed Weitzel aboard the *Chamberlain*, and listened carefully as he described what he had seen. Unlike Porter, Weitzel voiced his opposition to an army attack against the largely uninjured and still powerful fort. He bluntly stated that "it would be butchery to order an assault on that work under the circumstances," and advised against launching it.[54]

Butler decided to steam in for a closer look at Fort Fisher and ordered the *Chamberlain* to move within a half-mile of the northeast bastion. From his new vantage point the defenses did indeed appear to Butler to be as strong as ever. Still, he was reluctant to abandon the attack, and ordered Lieutenant Colonel Comstock to go ashore with Weitzel and make a final assessment. Haunting Butler was the reasonable fear that his failure to capture Fort Fisher might result in his disgrace.

In compliance with Butler's instructions, Comstock, Weitzel and Lt. Col. Richard H. Jackson of Weitzel's staff went immediately ashore. Their ride was both wet and bumpy, for the wind was blowing and the sea had become choppy. As the three officers went ashore, Charles K. Graham confronted Butler with an ultimatum. "General, you have got to either provide for those troops to-night on shore some way, or get them off; because it is getting so rough that we cannot land much longer." Butler now saw that the odds were stacked against him. So far only 2,300 of his 6,500 troops had been put ashore. The hour was getting late and the ocean was becoming too choppy to land the remainder of Ames' and Paine's divisions, much less supplies. The regiments already at the landing area appeared vulnerable to an attack by an approaching enemy division estimated to be four times their number. Upon interrogating Confederate prisoners and deserters, Butler learned that Hoke's Division was being rushed to Federal Point to oppose the Union landing. Even if he could put more soldiers ashore, Butler doubted that Porter's warships could protect them after nightfall. The naval gun crews could not shoot accurately in the darkness and would run the risk of hitting their own men. Given these circumstances, Butler decided an assault against Fort Fisher was impracticable, and leaving his men on Federal Point was tantamount to courting disaster. He ordered the troops to reembark immediately.[55]

Back on the beach, General Curtis scribbled a reply to Butler's instructions: "Your order is held in abeyance that you may know the true condition of the fort: the garrison has offered no resistance; the flagstaff of the fort was cut by a naval shot and one of my officers brought from the rampart the garrison flag; another cut the telegraph wire connecting the fort with Wilmington; my skirmishers are now at the parapet." Curtis thrust the note into the hands of a courier who rushed up the beach to deliver it.[56]

Despite the confident tone of Curtis' note, the general knew he needed additional troops to capture Fort Fisher. So far only a fraction of his brigade had reached Barney's forward position, prompting a frustrated Curtis to send an officer up the beach to bring the remainder forward. Curtis marched with the soldiers he had on hand—less than 300—back to Battery Holland near the river. When he arrived, Curtis sent reinforcements to Lieutenant Walling on the skirmish line confronting Fort Fisher and deployed about forty soldiers of the 117th New York, commanded by Col. Rufus Daggett, to scout northward along the Wilmington Road. When Daggett's command passed Craig's Landing, a wharf on the Cape Fear River a half-mile above Battery Holland, Daggett was to extend his line eastward across the peninsula to the beach, linking-up with the pickets who had been thrown out earlier in the afternoon.[57]

No sooner had Curtis made these dispositions than an officer from General Butler approached and handed Curtis a second order to retreat. It had been only a short time since Curtis had responded to Butler's first order to withdraw, which led him to presume that Butler had not yet received his message. Curtis later discovered that that had indeed been the case. At any rate, Curtis dashed off another note to Butler, reiterating that he and his men were at the front and prepared to assault the poorly defended fort.[58]

By then daylight was giving way to a thick blanket of leaden clouds. As the sky darkened and the wind picked up, Curtis began to worry about his men. They were scattered all over the lower end of Federal Point, from Fort Fisher to the landing zone three miles away. The darkness would only compound their problems, for the warships would surely end their bombardment, leaving the skirmishers in front of Fort Fisher without artillery support. Left with few viable options, Curtis sent word to Lieutenant Walling to withdraw his men to Battery Holland, where Curtis had established his headquarters. He believed that concentrating his scattered forces was the best way to protect them until he had received authorization to attack the fort.[59]

At dusk, Comstock and Jackson appeared at Battery Holland, closely followed by General Ames and reinforcements from Curtis' First Brigade. Ames had also advanced Colonel Bell's Third Brigade, deploying it in line of battle about a mile to the rear. Unfortunately for Curtis, General Weitzel had returned to the ships. Curtis quickly briefed the officers on the situation and proposed to assault Fort Fisher in the wake of the naval bombardment. He was certain he could capture the fort with his brigade alone.[60]

For his part, General Ames was surprised to hear that Butler had ordered a withdrawal. He had received no such instructions from Butler and resented being bypassed. Ames' anger had been mounting since Weitzel had overridden his orders that morning by sending Curtis' brigade ashore ahead of Bell's brigade. The punctilious Ames regarded Weitzel's move as a blatant disregard of military protocol. By the time Ames had landed, both Curtis and Weitzel were already well down the beach on their way to Fort Fisher, leaving Ames little more to do the rest of the afternoon than oversee the landing of troops from the Second and Third brigades. It was not until Lieutenant Simpson appeared with a request from Curtis to meet him at the front that Ames discovered that Curtis had been communicating directly with General Butler—once again in defiance of the proper chain of command. Ames was incensed about these lapses in military etiquette and it was all he could do to control his temper.

By the time Ames joined Curtis near the front it was too dark for him to see much of Fort Fisher except its bumpy silhouette rising above the sandy peninsula. Still, he was willing to allow Curtis to assault the fort if it could be done that evening. "Go ahead and make it," Ames told Curtis in reference to the attack. Comstock agreed with Ames' decision. Curtis immediately redeployed his skirmishers, now supported by detachments of the 3rd, 117th and 142nd New York regiments.

Their confidence was high as the New Yorkers approached Fort Fisher in the twilight—at least until a withering fire of musketry and artillery opened upon them from inside the fort.[61]

Colonel Lamb knew it was coming. At 5:30 p.m. the Union warships had intensified their bombardment of the land face and palisade line. Surely a ground assault could not be far behind. The young colonel, charged with the responsibility of defending one of the most important posts in the Confederacy, issued orders for his soldiers to man the ramparts as soon as the enemy's naval bombardment ceased. He counted 130 incoming shells per minute, more than two every second exploding on or near the fort. This barrage had to be a prelude to an infantry assault.

The shelling ended at dark, just as Lamb expected. Acting on his instructions, artillerymen and riflemen rushed up from the bombproofs and into the fort's gun chambers atop the battlements. Many of the teenaged Junior Reserves, however, frightened by the horrific bombardment and the prospect of doing battle, were reluctant to vacate their shelters. Midshipman Clarence Cary, who served temporarily as an artilleryman and a courier for

General Whiting, attempted to bully the boy soldiers out of the bombproofs, "where they were huddled together like so many sheep." Cary used all the "Boatswains' Mate talk [he] had ever heard," to no avail. On the other hand, Col. Robert Tansill of Whiting's staff tried to coax the boys out with gentle persuasion. When gentleness failed to work, Tansill resorted to threats and imprecations. Colonel Lamb eventually appeared and greeted them with, "Don't be cowards, boys." One of the Reserves' young officers shouted in reply, "We are no cowards, Colonel," and then led his troops out of the bombproofs. Cheering as they went, the Junior Reserves poured over the parapet and through the center sally-port, manning the palisade line alongside their veteran comrades just as Curtis' line of skirmishers approached the fort.[62]

Lamb deployed 800 of his men and boys at the palisade in front of the land face rather than on the ramparts. By now it was after 6:00 p.m. and too dark to see the enemy's advance from the parapet, so Lamb prepared to meet the Federal attack from ground level. His plan was to fire grape and canister at the head of the assaulting column as it neared the timber fence, using both his heavy cannon and his light artillery emplaced at the center sally-port and at the gate on the west end of Shepherd's Battery. Lamb also had technicians ready to explode the electric torpedoes buried underground 200 yards in front of the land face. He also hoped that General Hoke's Division, which he assumed by this time was operating in the vicinity of Sugar Loaf, would strike the Federal rear. Confident of repulsing the enemy assault, Lamb stood defiantly on the parapet and peered into the darkness. Union sharpshooters fired blindly at the fort, but the bullets flew harmlessly over the heads of their targets. Lamb ordered his men to reply in kind and the Confederates poured rifle-musket volleys and artillery canister into Curtis' skirmishers. The fort's defenders quickly demonstrated that they were present and ready to fight.[63]

As the din of battle drifted back toward Battery Holland, General Ames grew uneasy. General Curtis had argued that the fort, virtually without defenders, was theirs for the taking. The sound of gunfire suggested otherwise, and Ames began to doubt the attack would be successful. For all his earlier aggressiveness, Curtis also had second thoughts about launching a nighttime assault. As fire began erupting from Fort Fisher, he proposed to hold his force in readiness for an attack after sunrise, when the navy could again provide supporting fire.

Neither Ames nor Comstock would authorize Curtis such a lengthy delay, as the hot fire emanating from the fort appeared to give both a case of cold feet. When Curtis pressed the point, the discussion degenerated into a dispute about the structure of the fort. Ames opened the debate by questioning Curtis "as to what the fort was." When Curtis replied it was merely a two-sided work, Ames insisted he was "entirely mistaken." Ames argued that Curtis lacked "sufficient knowledge of the fort" to make such claims, and therefore, his information concerning the garrison must be unreliable as well. On the other hand, Ames continued, Butler and Weitzel had good maps and reliable information from prisoners and deserters they had been interrogating all evening. Surely Butler was justified in issuing his orders to withdraw. Cyrus Comstock reluctantly agreed. At first he believed Ames should have allowed Curtis to attack the fort, but like Ames, changed his mind when it became apparent the Confederates would contest the attempt. Comstock thought an attack had no more than an even chance of succeeding. "[Comstock] could not encourage me in my action, and that I would have to take the responsibility, which he thought was a very grave one," Curtis later recalled.[64]

Another bone of contention arose between Ames and Curtis as to who would be held accountable in the event of an attack (and especially a repulse). Ames insisted that "responsibility would rest with the officer in immediate command." Ames later claimed that this statement meant that he had accepted responsibility for the attack. Curtis believed that he was on his own if he chose to override Butler's orders by remaining at the front. "[In the end, Ames and Comstock] did not regard the attack as feasible, and moreover did not wish to assume any responsibility for my disobedience of orders," Curtis maintained.[65]

Concluding that remaining at the front was both pointless and in disobedience to Butler's orders, Ames, Comstock and Jackson returned to the landing site, leaving Curtis and his men behind. Curtis held his position long after dark. The brazen general even went so far as to send back yet another plea to General Butler to allow his troops to attack the fort. "A brigade of battle-scarred veterans stood [at the gates of Fort Fisher] panting like leashed hounds eager for the dash," descriptively penned a Union soldier. Panting or not, Curtis' battle-scarred veterans would remain leashed before the walls of the fort.[66]

About 8:00 p.m. a third order arrived for Curtis to call off his attack. The bearer of these bad tidings was Capt. Birney B. Keeler, a former comrade of Curtis' in the 142nd New York, now serving as an adjutant on General Ames' staff. "Let me tell you," Birney confided to Curtis, "all the troops which have been landed, including the larger part of your brigade, Pennypacker's brigade, and Bell's brigade, have been taken on board the ships, and there is no one on land but your force and the flankers and pickets you have left out, and it will be entirely useless for you to expect any assistance." Curtis had suspected as much but he was bitterly disappointed all the same. After a two-day naval bombardment followed by an advance to the very walls of the fort, Curtis found it difficult to believe that his brigade had not been allowed to attempt an attack. At the same time, he realized there was nothing to be gained by delaying at the front any longer. A dejected Curtis called in his skirmishers and led them back up the beach in the darkness.[67]

On the way back they met Colonel Daggett and his squad of pickets from the 117th New York, who were returning from their reconnaissance of the Wilmington Road. To Curtis' surprise, Daggett's unit comprised a much larger group of soldiers than had been deployed earlier that evening, most of whom had now donned, oddly enough, gray uniforms. Indeed, Daggett and his troops were escorting 224 Confederate prisoners-of-war, boy soldiers of the 4th and 8th battalions of the North Carolina Junior Reserves and six officers, including Maj. John M. Reece, the units' commander.[68]

Major Reece and his boys had been part of Col. John K. Connally's Brigade of North Carolina Reserves, sent by General Kirkland from Sugar Loaf to Fort Fisher on Christmas Eve, and thence to Battery Buchanan. The following morning they came under severe enemy artillery fire as they marched back to Fort Fisher. According to Major Reece, his command could not squeeze into the overcrowded bombproofs during the naval bombardment, and thus were forced to seek shelter elsewhere. Acting without orders, Reece took his boys to the breastworks at Camp Wyatt, the abandoned camp of instruction a mile north of Fort Fisher. When the Union warships started shelling that area preparatory to the landing of Weitzel's troops, Reece shifted his force to a point beneath the river bank adjacent to the old camp.[69]

When the naval shelling finally ceased after sunset, Reece decided to march his command back to Fort Fisher, which he believed was under attack by Union infantry. He had heard the steady pop–pop–pop of small arms fire coming from the fort and thought his force could be of some assistance to Colonel Lamb. The reformed battalion marched down the river bank toward the fort. When Reece's column reached Craig's Landing, a black man informed Reece that Federal soldiers lurked close by. The major turned and looked at the young boys under his command and concluded that, armed and eager though they were, they would be no match for battle-hardened Union infantry. He preferred to surrender rather than see them slaughtered as some had been during the march from Battery Buchanan earlier that morning.

Reece wandered out into the darkness hoping to find an enemy soldier who would accept his capitulation. After walking only a few hundred yards he encountered Capt. John T. Thomas of Company F, 117th New York, and offered to surrender his command. Startled by Reece's sudden appearance and suspicious of his intentions—up to that time the Federals had no idea the Junior Reserves were even in the area—Thomas escorted Reece to the rear and presented him to Colonel Daggett. Daggett was also suspicious, but Major Reece succeeded in conveying his sincerity to a fellow Freemason, Capt. Almond R. Stevens of Company H, 117th New York. Stevens agreed to follow Reece to where his boys were resting and accept their surrender.

Unaware of their commander's actions, the Junior Reserves became anxious as time passed and their commander failed to return. When they heard men approaching their position along the river bank, they crouched down and cocked the hammers of their Enfield rifle-muskets. "Don't fire boys!" cried a familiar voice in the darkness. The youths recognized it as the voice of their commander, Major Reece. "No, major, we won't," came the reply. They were surprised when Reece appeared moments later with a lone Union officer in tow. Their surprise turned to shock when Reece announced that he had surrendered them. "Not by a damn sight," retorted Lt. F. M. Hamlin, who was standing near Reece. "Yes! Yes! I have," the major insisted. "We are surrounded and can't get away." "Yes," Captain Stevens added, "we have got you boys, you may as well give up." Stevens broke his

Captain John T. Thomas, Co. F, 117th New York Infantry. *Rome (N.Y.) Historical Society*

silence when it appeared that Reece was losing control of the situation. The Federal captain assured the Junior Reserves they would be better off as prisoners than as conscripts in their own beleaguered army. "We can't be any worse off, any how," stated a young soldier. "We have never received a cent of pay, nor scarcely anything to eat, except what we have picked up."[70]

Lieutenant Hamlin was appalled by what he perceived as a cowardly act. Refusing to surrender, he assembled eight of his comrades and simply melted into the darkness. No attempt was made to stop them, or perhaps no one noticed them as they marched up the river bank to Sugar Loaf, where Hamlin informed General Kirkland of Reece's surrender. When General Whiting learned of the incident, he became livid and called it an act of "shameful cowardice."[71]

As Hamlin and his group of associates walked their way to freedom, Captain Stevens rounded up his armed teenaged prisoners—each still carried a rifle-musket in hand—and marched them back to Daggett's position on the Wilmington Road. Stevens risked allowing the boys to keep their weapons because he did not want to leave them at Craig's Landing where they could be recovered by the enemy. He accepted Reece's promise that neither he nor his soldiers would attempt to escape or betray him. Colonel Daggett and his men were stunned when Stevens returned, single-handedly escorting more than 200 armed prisoners-of-war. Judging from the comments of the Union captors, the boys were not only unfed but malnourished. "I never saw such a lot of spindle shanks as they were," observed one of Daggett's soldiers. The New Yorkers quickly surrounded the boys, and then marched them over to the beach. By now Daggett had received Butler's order to withdraw to the landing zone for reembarkation on the transports. The colonel was leading his small force and his large contingent of gray clad prisoners when he met General Curtis heading in the same direction.[72]

When Curtis' command reached the reembarkation site near Battery Anderson sometime after 9:00 p.m., the tedious process of ferrying the troops back to the transports was well under way. Most of the troops had already reembarked, including Col. Louis Bell's and Col. Galusha Pennypacker's brigades of Ames' division, and General Paine's contingent of U.S. Colored Troops (the 5th USCT, and three companies of the 4th USCT). Some of Curtis' reserves had also resumed their places on board the ships. Curtis only managed to reembark a few more of his men as well as the captured Confederate officers, including Major Reece, before choppy seas forced him to abandon the effort.

The wind had been increasing all evening, and by 10:00 p.m. had whipped the ocean into a frothy frenzy. The waves were running so high that lifeboats approaching the beach faced the dangerous prospect of being swamped. Indeed, the massive breakers had already wrecked half a dozen or more launches along the shore. The *Sassacus* lost three of her boats in this manner during the operation. No man was rescued without first undergoing a thorough drenching in the pounding surf. One Union soldier (and perhaps one Confederate prisoner) drowned while attempting to get off the beach. At midnight General Ames reluctantly suspended the reembarkation. With boats no longer able to reach shore, Curtis and more than 600 of his men, together with about 200 Confederate prisoners, found themselves stranded on the beach.[73]

The deteriorating weather only made matters worse for the trapped soldiers. A light rain that had recently begun to fall turned into sleet as a cold front pushed into the area. The troops spent a miserably cold and wet night on the open beach without tents, blankets, rations or fresh water. "The cold December rains pelted us unmercifully, and we were thinly clad," recalled Lt. George Simpson. "We had come ashore in light marching order, without overcoats or blankets. The tempest raged so fearfully, that it was impossible for small boats to reach us, and here, without hardtack, whiskey, water or shelter, we were obliged to remain." To shield themselves from the howling wind and freezing rain, and to conceal themselves from the enemy, Curtis' men took refuge in and around Battery Anderson by digging holes in the sand and crawling inside. Curtis established his headquarters beneath a wrecked boat, probably the only dry spot on the beach. "I thought I had seen hard times," Lieutenant Simpson wrote, "but this night seemed almost too uncomfortable to endure. Every man experienced the most intense misery."[74]

Though it would have given Curtis' men scant consolation, Colonel Lamb and his garrison inside Fort Fisher were also suffering from the bad weather. Fearing a surprise attack on the fort, Lamb kept his soldiers at their posts all night in the driving wind and freezing rain. Both Curtis' and Lamb's troops would have agreed that this was a terrible way to spend Christmas. While their families and friends enjoyed the festivities of the holiday amid the comforts of home, Confederate and Union soldiers on Federal Point suffered terribly from hunger, exposure and loneliness. No bullets whizzed overhead, but this too was war. "The rain fell in torrents, wetting the troops and their arms," Lamb reported, stretching the truth a bit by declaring that the foul weather "did not dampen their spirits nor interfere with their efficiency."[75]

General Whiting spent much of the night strolling up and down the line speaking words of comfort and inspiration to the men and boys in an effort to alleviate some of their misery. "[Whiting's] presence was encouraging to the officers and men, who were devoted to him," remarked Lamb. Despite the inclement weather, both Lamb and Whiting feared a coup de main that night—especially an attack by U. S. marines in the open space beyond the southern flank of the fort's sea face, between the Mound Battery and Battery Buchanan. "Our case is very critical," Whiting warned General Bragg in a dispatch requesting both reinforcements for Fort Fisher and an attack on the enemy's rear by Hoke's troops at Sugar Loaf. Whiting was insulted by Bragg's answer. Should it become necessary to evacuate Fort Fisher, a despondent Bragg replied, the forts at Old Inlet would also have to be abandoned. A defiant Whiting informed Bragg that he would not "evacuate or give up [Fort Fisher] so long as a man is left to stand by his gun."[76]

About 3:00 a.m. on December 26, Confederate sentries reported sighting an enemy flotilla approaching the Mound Battery. The channel batteries immediately opened fire with grape and canister. Lamb sent Maj. James Reilly with two companies of soldiers from the land front to oppose the raiders, and soon thereafter followed in person with an additional battalion of reinforcements. When the supposed attack failed to materialize, General Whiting decided it was a false alarm.[77]

Admiral Porter had not even considered sending a marine raiding party against the fort that night. In his opinion there was no need for one. Porter believed his gunboats had silenced the fort, and at six o'clock Christmas evening sat down to enjoy a turkey dinner "as securely as if [he] were at home." Since Porter would be dining on a bird generously supplied by Capt. James Alden of the *Brooklyn*, the admiral invited Alden to join him.

"Well," said Alden as he entered the admiral's cabin on the *Malvern*, "you are taking the world quietly. Do you know what is going on?" he asked.

"No," replied Porter, "what's in the wind?"

"Why that man Butler is reembarking all his troops and is going away," Alden claimed. "He says the fort cannot be taken."

"Does he?" Porter replied. "Well let him go. We will take the place without him. What part of the turkey will you have?"[78]

The obviously unconcerned Porter may have assumed—or at least hoped—that Butler would remain in the area and resume the offensive at a more favorable time. In the meantime, the admiral planned to send his vessels to Beaufort to replenish their ammunition stockpiles, then return to the Cape Fear and renew the bombardment. The rumors of Butler's withdrawal were soon confirmed when Weitzel came on board the *Malvern* and acknowledged Butler's decision to abort the mission.[79]

The Massachusetts general followed up Weitzel's firsthand report later that night with a more detailed letter of explanation, stating that he and Weitzel were "fully of the opinion that [Fort Fisher] could not be carried by assault, as it was left substantially uninjured as a defensive work by the navy fire." In Butler's opinion, only a regular siege operation could reduce the fort, which, the major general added, "did not come within my instructions" from General Grant. Since the inclement weather had made it impossible to land more troops and supplies, there was no reason for the army to remain at the Cape Fear. "I shall therefore," Butler announced, "sail for Hampton Roads as soon as the transport fleet can be got in order."

Once he decided on his course of action Butler moved swiftly, setting sail for Hampton Roads early the following morning, December 26, leaving behind most of his transports—as well as General Curtis and his men, who were still marooned on Federal Point.[80]

An early war image of the 6' 7" N. Martin Curtis and New York comrades. On meeting the towering Knickerbocker, Abraham Lincoln reportedly asked: "Mr. Curtis, how do you know when your feet are cold?" *St. Lawrence County (N.Y.) Historical Association*

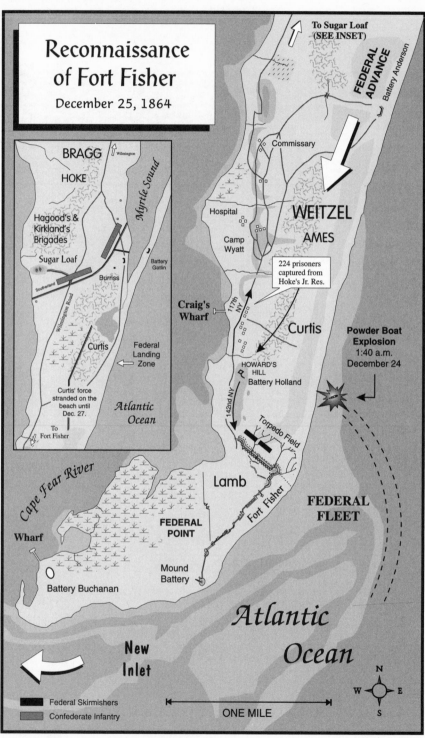

Reconnaissance of Fort Fisher

December 25, 1864

To Sugar Loaf (SEE INSET)

FEDERAL ADVANCE

Battery Anderson

Commissary

BRAGG   Wilmington

HOKE

Myrtle Sound

Hagood's & Kirkland's Brigades

Sugar Loaf

Burriss

Battery Gatlin

Southerland

Wilmington Road

Curtis

Federal Landing Zone

Curtis' force stranded on the beach until Dec. 27.

Atlantic Ocean

To Fort Fisher

Hospital

Camp Wyatt

WEITZEL

AMES

224 prisoners captured from Hoke's Jr. Res.

Craig's Wharf

117th NY

Curtis

Powder Boat Explosion
1:40 a.m.
December 24

HOWARD'S HILL
Battery Holland

142nd NY

Torpedo Field

Lamb

FEDERAL FLEET

Fort Fisher

FEDERAL POINT

Cape Fear River

Wharf

Battery Buchanan

Mound Battery

Atlantic Ocean

New Inlet

Federal Skirmishers

Confederate Infantry

ONE MILE

N
W   E
S

Mark A. Moore

Chapter 6

"The war continues and with such leaders
it will to the crack of doom"

– Joseph C. Canning, USN

RECRIMINATIONS

Monday, December 26 was yet another gray day at the Cape Fear. Although the rain had ceased, strong winds out of the northeast and rough surf made it impossible for the fleet to rescue General Curtis and his troops, stranded around Battery Anderson. Despite being ill with fever and chills, Curtis tried to boost the flagging spirits of his men with encouraging words. Morale among the soldiers of the 3rd New York Infantry improved slightly when they managed to acquire Lieutenant Walling's captured Rebel flag. The New Yorkers tore the banner into small pieces and passed the bits of cloth out as battle souvenirs. Such diversions were few and far between, however, as the soldiers spent most of their time improving their rifle pits between the high water line and the sand dunes and trying to keep warm with plank-fed fires from the wrecked boats along the beach. Some of the men also dug for fresh water, though what little they found was unfit for drinking.[1]

Curtis' men also scavenged for food, because it was not until late on the afternoon of the 26th that they were finally resupplied. About 3:00 p.m. an unidentified officer risked his life coming ashore with orders for Curtis to march his men to Masonboro Inlet the next morning, where the navy would again attempt to ferry them to the transports safe from the threat of a Confederate attack. Before the officer made his way back to a waiting lifeboat, Curtis requested that provisions be sent ashore for the men. Soon casks of pork, hardtack and even whiskey were heaved overboard from the ships. The precious cargo washed up on the beach north of Curtis' position, where squads of eager soldiers retrieved them. The hungry men rolled the casks down to camp, smashed them open and gorged themselves. Even the Confederate prisoners shared in the bounty—except for the whiskey. "In view of the youth of the prisoners, and the fact that they were not performing military duty," Curtis explained, "the whiskey was distributed exclusively to the officers and men of the brigade."[2]

The semi-trapped Federals dared not venture too far from their entrenched camp for fear of being shot or taken prisoner. Several of Curtis' men had already been captured, including Lt. Charles Smith, who had wandered behind enemy lines while recalling his pickets on Christmas night. It was another piece of startling intelligence, however, that gave Curtis even greater cause for concern. About noon on December 26, a deserter from the 2nd South Carolina Cavalry entered Curtis' camp and informed the general that Hoke's Division was assembling at Sugar Loaf to attack the stranded Union troops that very night. An alarmed Curtis immediately signaled the information to the fleet, prompting Admiral Porter to move fourteen gunboats into position to protect the troops on shore. "We knew there were some brave hearts in the gunboats in our rear, and that they would make desperate efforts. . .in repelling any attack the enemy might make upon us," stated one of Curtis' soldiers, "so we kept our courage up and our powder dry." As a precaution against such an assault, the warships vigorously shelled the woods to drive away any prowling Confederates.[3]

Despite the heavy fire from the gunboats, General Whiting and Colonel Lamb expected Braxton Bragg to attempt to capture the stranded Federal troops and free the Confederate prisoners-of-war. The much-maligned former commander of the Army of Tennessee had finally arrived at Sugar Loaf shortly before noon on the 26th, and Hoke reached that point several hours later, bringing with him Brig. Gen. Johnson Hagood's South Carolina brigade and the remainder of General Kirkland's regiments. Together with John Connally's militia and Southerland's and Paris' artillerymen, Bragg's force totaled 3,398 men—five times the number of enemy soldiers on the beach. Hoke's remaining two brigades were still en route to Wilmington. Despite this advantageous ratio, Bragg declined to attack the stranded Union troops, claiming that they were too well protected by the gunboats. Bragg's inaction dumbfounded Whiting. "It was a matter of grave charge against [Bragg] that the whole [Federal] force was not captured," Whiting later contended. "He had the force and the position." Colonel Lamb agreed, calling Bragg's behavior "incomprehensible."[4]

As both Whiting and Lamb foresaw, Bragg's excessive caution allowed the Federals the time they needed to extricate themselves from their dangerously exposed position. On the morning of December 27, the U.S. Navy overcame the rough weather and succeeded in rescuing Curtis and his men, who had remained at Battery Anderson and not marched north to Masonboro. Lifeboats had to make numerous perilous trips to shore through the choppy surf, which at times was so turbulent that some of the lifeboats had to be hooked to hawsers running back to the ships. As soon as the last group of soldiers had reembarked, Curtis cut the line tying his boat to the beach and was dragged through the surf to the waiting gig. N. Martin Curtis was the first Union soldier to land on Federal Point; at precisely 11:37 a.m., he was the last to leave.[5]

Still furious about how the affair ended, Curtis informed sailors from the *Nereus* who had picked him up that had he been "properly supported and timely reinforced" on Christmas evening, he would have captured Fort Fisher. Curtis' staff officers were no less angry than their chief. "One of the grandest and most expensive expeditions ever organized in our country has been terminated in a complete farce," commented Lt. George Simpson. Many of the enlisted men agreed with Simpson's assessment. "Probably a more mismanaged expedition never left our ports," claimed Sgt. Maj. Edward K. Wightman of the 3rd New York Infantry. By the early afternoon of December 27, Curtis and his men were on a transport heading back to their home base at Hampton Roads—and cursing Benjamin Butler for having deserted them.[6]

Whiting and Lamb could not believe what they were seeing. The two officers stood atop the battlements at Fort Fisher on the morning of December 27 and watched in disbelief (and no little disgust) as the Union soldiers safely withdrew from their beachhead. When Bragg arrived at the fort about noon, he appeared more interested in the effect of the bombardment than in the fate of the escaping Union soldiers and their youthful prisoners. Accompanying Bragg were General Hoke and the 21st South Carolina Infantry of Hagood's Brigade, whose presence merely underscored the opportunity squandered by Bragg. But Lamb and Whiting had little time to dwell on Bragg's inexplicable conduct, for they had to warn General Hébert at Smithville to watch for the enemy fleet, which might at that very moment be rounding the cape to attack the forts at Old Inlet.

As the Union transports and most of the warships sailed away, Confederate soldiers realized that the Battle of Fort Fisher was over, at least for the moment, and that they had won. The celebration began before the Federal ships were even out of sight. Amid all the cheering and backslapping, Lamb ordered a cannon crew to fire a parting shot at the warships. The fleet was far beyond range and the expenditure of powder and iron purely symbolic, but Lamb wanted the enemy to know that the fort had survived the terrible onslaught of metal and that its garrison was still defiant. As a final farewell, the post band mounted the parapet at the northeast bastion and played "Dixie."[7]

Fort Fisher had withstood the greatest naval bombardment in history. Those who had witnessed it would never forget it, and would insist that those who had not could never truly appreciate the ferocity, grandeur and excitement of the event. "It was, no doubt. . .the most terrific fire of any war yet known," General Whiting wrote. The Federal fleet had unleashed 20,271 projectiles against the fort—one shell every two seconds, or fifteen shells per defender—during the twelve hours of shelling on December 24-25. More than 1,275,000 pounds of iron rained down on the sand bastion. Yet, despite this overwhelming barrage, only three Confederate soldiers had been killed, two mortally wounded, eleven severely wounded, and forty-five slightly injured. Although portions of the earthworks were battered, the barracks destroyed, and areas inside and surrounding the fort were littered with unexploded projectiles and iron fragments, the bombardment had disabled only three of the fort's cannon. Moreover, the garrison had expended in response only 1,272 rounds, or slightly more than one third of the total number of projectiles in the fort's arsenal, excluding the grape, canister and light artillery shells fired at the Union ground forces on Christmas night. "A few guns, a few carriages, a patching up of sods," noted General Hébert, "and Fort Fisher will not show signs that it was attacked."[8]

More importantly, Wilmington remained open to the outside world. On the night of December 27, the *Wild Rover* ran the blockade into New Inlet, followed closely by the *Banshee* early the next morning, both carrying supplies vital to Lee's Army of Northern Virginia. The *Banshee* also brought in two 12-pounder Whitworth rifle cannon and four gun carriages, all of which ended up inside Fort Fisher. Soon after the *Banshee's* arrival, the *Little Hattie* ran out of New Inlet and headed for Nassau. Wilmington's blockade running traffic continued as if there had been no Battle of Fort Fisher.[9]

General Whiting considered the victory a miracle, a case of divine intervention with perhaps some assistance from the Federals. Whiting respected Fort Fisher's resilience as much as anyone. "The experience of that tremendous bombardment," he would write, "satisfies me as to the great powers of resistance of [earthen] forts to a stationary sea attack." All the same, he believed the storm that had raged from December 19 to the 23rd had been the Confederates' true salvation. "That great and irreparable disaster did not overtake us we owe to God," a relieved Whiting confessed. The delay in the enemy's attack caused by foul weather had allowed Confederate reinforcements to reach the fort. Their number—wildly exaggerated by Major Reece's story the night he surrendered his force of Junior Reserves—and the approach of Hoke's Division from Virginia had intimidated the Union army enough into withdrawing. Nor did the enemy gunboats attempt to cross the bar, a capability possessed by "even ordinary steamers," Whiting remarked, "to say nothing of those possessing great power of resistance to shot." Had the Federals landed on December 24 instead of the 25th, before Kirkland's Brigade was in position near the beach, they might have succeeded, in Whiting's words, "with any kind of energy and pluck."[10]

After the Almighty, Whiting regarded Colonel Lamb as most responsible for the defeat of the enemy. "This gallant and successful resistance, humanly speaking," Whiting informed the War Department, "is due to the untiring energy, the dauntless resolution, and brilliant courage of Colonel William Lamb, of the 36th North Carolina, devotedly supported by men that know him and will fight for him anywhere." High praise, indeed, for the

29-year-old journalist/lawyer-turned-soldier from the pen of one of the most respected military minds in the country. Whiting also recommended that Lamb be promoted to brigadier general of artillery—but only so long as he could be kept at Fort Fisher. "He cannot be spared from the important command he has graced." Whiting declared. General Bragg was also generous in his praise, sending his official congratulations to Lamb, Whiting, Kirkland, and the "brave garrison of Fort Fisher" for their "successful termination. . .of the arrogant invader."[11]

When news of the victory reached Wilmington, the citizens rejoiced. "When the glad news came in that the Fort was still ours, the reaction was great," observed one resident, "joy and happiness arose upon the Christmas air." Colonel Lamb's bravery and skill was praised as much in Wilmington as at Fisher. The editor of Wilmington's *Daily North Carolinian* exclaimed that the Federals, "having tried our Lamb and found him a lion," would not soon forget the punishment they had received.[12]

Success inevitably generates an abundance of gratitude, and other officers and soldiers besides Lamb received their share of adulation, including Maj. James Reilly and the Junior Reserves—endearingly tagged "Whiting's Pets." Much of the credit also went to General Whiting, whose "magnificent engineering skills," one admirer noted, had really saved Wilmington. "Now that Whiting has again shown himself a great master in the the the art of war, we suggest [those] who clamored so loudly against him will come down to Wilmington and exercise their marvelous talents by aiding General Whiting and the country [instead] of throwing dirt." That particularly sharp verbal barb was aimed directly at Governor Vance, who had called so eloquently for civilian defenders to meet him in Wilmington, but who had failed to appear as promised. Nevertheless, Vance received a trophy in token of his moral support: the battle flag that Private Bland had affixed to the staff above the Mound Battery during the height of the naval bombardment on Christmas Eve.[13]

Many Wilmingtonians believed Braxton Bragg was most responsible for spoiling the Federal attack—perhaps because Bragg and his boosters were saying as much—and they showered the general with praise. "General Bragg is about the best abused man in the country, or rather he has been," a Wilmingtonian reminded his fellow citizens, "and yet this abused man is a brave soldier, a pure patriot, and a skillful general. We remember the sneer of some Virginia papers when General Bragg was sent to this point and yet when the attack came. . .his conduct and bearing justified the confidence of the whole community." As a token of their appreciation, a group of admirers presented Bragg with a new gray wool uniform adorned with fancy gold braid. They also asked the department commander to escort them to Fort Fisher, to surprise the defenders with a party and a New Year's dinner. Four days into the new year, Bragg led a "goodly number" of the Ladies of the Soldiers Aid Society down river on board the steamer *Flora MacDonald*. The well-wishers docked north of Fisher at Craig's Landing and walked the remaining mile, stopping long enough to say a prayer over the grave of Pvt. Amos H. Jones, the young courier killed on Christmas afternoon. The ladies entered the fort and were immediately met by Colonel Lamb, who told them that they had just accomplished what the enemy had failed to do: taken the fort by storm. For several days Lamb played host to curious visitors and distinguished guests, including Governor Vance and Frank Vizetelly of the *Illustrated London News*. Although Lamb enjoyed being feted and flattered, the cruel business of war demanded his attention.[14]

The task of restoring Fort Fisher began almost immediately after the cessation of the bombardment. After burying his dead and sending the more seriously wounded to Wilmington for convalescence, Lamb put his men to work repairing gun carriages, remounting or replacing damaged cannon tubes, filling in shell holes on the earthworks and cleaning up the debris and numerous artillery shells scattered about the fort. It was during this process that Ordnance Sgt. Montgomery Long was killed by the explosion of a shell he was trying to remove. Lamb grieved for his friend, "the most useful officer he had," was how he described the fallen soldier. The landing of the Federals made apparent certain deficiencies that Lamb sought to correct, chief among them being the construction of a line of rifle pits from the lower sea face batteries to the river, with two redans for light artillery in the middle of the line to cover the fort's rear.

Lamb also repaired the telegraph wire between the fort and Sugar Loaf, laid a "submarine telegraph line" over to Battery Lamb on Reeve's Point, and requested a work force composed of black laborers. Additional ammunition, especially hand grenades, was requisitioned to resupply the fort, and Lamb sought to have torpedoes (mines) sown in the sea where the Union ironclads had been anchored. Fort Fisher's commandant also applied for blankets and uniforms to replace those destroyed by fire during the battle. All the while Lamb kept a constant vigil on the ocean's horizon, fully expecting the reappearance of the enemy fleet at any time. Both Lamb and Whiting, who remained at the fort until December 29, realized that they had been fortunate to survive the first battle. Yet neither harbored illusions about having seen the last of the Federals. "It can scarcely be possible that after such extraordinary preparations the enemy has altogether abandoned, or even long postponed, his designs upon this port," Whiting penned Secretary of War Seddon.[15]

Most of Wilmington's citizens also realized that they had been granted only a temporary reprieve. "The nest of pirates is safe," a citizen jested, "but our enemy is persevering, and although signally failing this time, will hardly be willing to give up the design so fondly entertained without making some further demonstration." That sentiment was echoed by others. "Of course, we take it for granted that after all the expenditure of money and munitions of war involved in the expedition with the great display of force made, the Yankee government will not likely feel satisfied with one repulse from a few sand hills at the mouth of the Cape Fear River," commented one resident. "We may expect an early visit from our friend Butler."[16]

General Bragg, however, did not share the anxiety felt by Lamb and Whiting and most Wilmingtonians. Having received several reports that the enemy fleet had reassembled at Beaufort before sailing northward, Bragg believed the Federals had abandoned their plans for taking the city. He was so convinced that he transferred the Junior Reserves to Goldsboro, dispersed the Home Guard, suspended the *Chickamauga's* patrols of the river, allowed Brig. Gen. Johnson Hagood a furlough, and secretly discussed a plan to recapture New Bern. Nor did he expedite Colonel Lamb's applications for ordnance and supplies for Fort Fisher. In fact Lamb complained that "it was impossible to obtain what was needed." What was needed even more than supplies, General Whiting argued, was a strong support force in the vicinity of Fort Fisher. The presence of General Hoke's troops had compelled the enemy to abort the first campaign and would do much to deter another effort. Hoke agreed, suggesting to Bragg that at least one brigade be kept at Sugar Loaf. Bragg, however, disagreed with his subordinates. On December 31, the "brave soldier, pure patriot, and skillful general," as one Wilmingtonian referred to Bragg, withdrew Kirkland's and Hagood's brigades from Sugar Loaf and sent them to rejoin the brigades of Clingman and Colquitt, bivouacked at Camp Whiting near Wilmington. With colors flying and bands playing, the returning troops marched into the city and were enthusiastically received by the people as "their victorious defenders."[17]

Bragg's wholesale abandonment of Sugar Loaf would prove to be a fatal mistake.

General Butler reached Hampton Roads on the evening of December 27, and immediately telegraphed General Grant announcing his return. He took the opportunity to explain his reasons for calling off the attack against Fort Fisher. Butler also used the telegram as a springboard for launching a complaint about Admiral Porter's decision to explode the *Louisiana* without waiting for the army to return from Beaufort, where it had been compelled to go after the navy had failed to rendezvous with the army off New Inlet at the prearranged time. Although surprised to see Butler back in Virginia, Grant was also relieved. He had just sent his aide-de-camp, Lt. Col. Horace Porter, with dispatches for Butler to return at once with his troops if they had not effected a landing on Federal Point. Grant had since received copies of Richmond newspapers reporting the repulse of Butler's army at Fort Fisher. If Butler's infantry wasn't going to assist in the reduction of Wilmington, Grant believed, then the troops should resume their positions in front of Richmond where their presence was sorely needed.[18]

Butler initially escaped criticism from Grant for both his handling of the fiasco and decision to abort the campaign. Grant even seemed to accept Butler's explanation that the navy was at fault. "The Wilmington expedition has proven a gross and culpable failure," Grant telegraphed President Lincoln. "After the expedition sailed from Fort Monroe three days of fine weather was squandered, during which the enemy was without a force to protect himself. Who is to blame I hope will be known." Before long nearly everyone involved, including Grant, would be blamed for the failure of the expedition.[19]

One of those about to be blamed for the mission's failure was Gen. N. Martin Curtis, who arrived with his men in Virginia late on December 28. Curtis barely had time to step off the ship before he heard a chorus of fresh insults against Butler, mostly from Butler's own troops, complaining that only "Ol Cockeye" had stood in the way of capturing Fort Fisher. "We returned. . .very much disgusted with our expedition," wrote Col. Alonzo Alden of the 169th New York Infantry. "It might have been a perfect success I am sure if there had been proper management." General Butler, grumbled another officer, "from his remote and safe position on the transports, saw a 'lion in the way,' and paddled us back to Fortress Monroe." "Curses enough have been heaped on Butler's head to sink him in the deepest hole of the bottomless pit," exclaimed Sergeant Major Wightman. "Had we been so roughly treated by the rebels there would be no end of cries of 'shame' and the accusations of 'barbarity' from the enlightened press."[20]

Early the next morning Curtis and two staff officers went ashore to eat breakfast at the Kimball Brothers Restaurant. While there they met Lt. Col. Orville E. Babcock of General Grant's staff. After exchanging pleasantries, Babcock mentioned the unsuccessful expedition and asked Curtis if he intended to see General Grant about it. "I will not," Curtis answered emphatically. "I am surprised at that," Babcock replied. Curtis had no intention of initiating a meeting with Grant, in light of the gossip then circulating about Fort Monroe. Rumor had it that Butler had lodged a protest with Grant over Curtis' disobedience of orders at Fort Fisher, and that a court martial was imminent. Curtis reasoned that if he was to be made a scapegoat, he was not going to deliver himself up to the lions. Babcock left the restaurant, but soon returned with Grant's compliments and a request that Curtis meet him on board his ship, the *River Queen*, which had docked at Fort Monroe that morning. Left with little choice in the matter, Curtis acquiesced.

Having spoken only briefly with Grant in the past, the meeting marked Curtis' first extended interview with the commanding general. He answered fully all of Grant's questions, emphasizing in particular that Fort Fisher was merely a two-sided earthwork, vulnerable to attack from the rear. When Grant questioned Curtis' description of the fort, saying that it was contrary to all intelligence reports, Curtis bluntly stated: "General Grant, you asked me to explain what was there. I do not propose to explain what other people have seen." Curtis also reiterated his belief that the fort should have been captured. The meeting came to an abrupt end when a staff officer brought in important dispatches from General Sherman in Georgia. As Curtis turned to leave, General Grant confided in him: "I agree with you, that the expedition had no business to be a failure." Although Grant's words relieved Curtis' anxiety concerning a court martial, he would soon find himself embroiled in a dispute with another superior officer.[21]

The same evening of his meeting with Grant, Curtis and some friends traveled to Norfolk for a "night on the town." He had just taken his seat at a downtown theater when an officer handed him a dispatch from General Weitzel, ordering him to report immediately to army headquarters at City Point. When Curtis arrived at the dock, a boat was waiting to take him upriver. Weitzel summoned Curtis in response to a telegram from Grant requesting more detailed information about Fort Fisher from the New York general. Weitzel inferred from Grant's message that a renewal of the campaign would depend largely on Curtis' testimony. In response to questioning from Weitzel, Curtis informed him that "after the navy had pounded the enemy to their bombproofs, with a continued fire, that [his] brigade alone would have captured the work; that it could still be done, but never so easily again, with proper management." Curtis' response annoyed Weitzel because it implied that the expedition's failure was the result of mismanagement. A heated debate ensued with neither general yielding ground on the subject.

On New Year's Day 1865, Weitzel heard statements from six of Curtis' soldiers of the 142nd New York—Lts. George W. Ross, George Simpson, William H. Walling, and Pvts. James Spring, Henry Blair and John White. All of these men had been in action on the front line at Fort Fisher, and each supported Curtis' claims. Lieutenant Simpson later claimed that Weitzel tried to persuade him to change his testimony. "[Weitzel] wished me to give a different statement, saying that if my [contradictory] statement obtained credence, another expedition would be ordered," Simpson reported. "This contingency seemed to trouble him." Indeed, the eyewitness testimony was an embarrassing—and potentially threatening—indictment against both Butler and Weitzel.[22]

Grant's investigation did nothing to faze Butler's belief in the correctness of his decision. The Massachusetts general continued to believe that he had acted correctly in response to Weitzel's judgment that an infantry assault against Fort Fisher would have been suicidal because the navy had not done enough to weaken Fort Fisher's defenses. "After a thorough reconnaissance of the work, finding it utterly impracticable for a land assault. . .I deemed it much better for the country to withdraw," Butler stated. "No so strong a work as Fort Fisher had been taken by assault during this war." General

Ames and Lieutenant Colonel Comstock supported Butler's assessment, noting that Curtis' advance would most likely have been halted by the strong force of Confederates that appeared on Fort Fisher's walls after the navy had ended its ineffective bombardment on Christmas night. Brigadier General Charles J. Paine maintained that "[Butler] was right, *entirely*" to have called off the attack. "The Fort could not by any possibility have been taken," Paine insisted. Among all the leading officers, only Curtis broke ranks to criticize Butler and Weitzel for not being more aggressive and for recalling their troops too soon—before they had received a full and accurate report from the front line. Curtis argued that it had taken more time to reembark his troops from the beach than it would have to land the 4,200 men still on board the transports.[23]

Not about to sit by and let the army affix blame, Admiral Porter joined the debate. Up to that point, Porter had been both conciliatory toward, and critical of, the army. Playing both ends against the middle, he realized that he needed the army's support to capture Fort Fisher and therefore sought to placate the War Department. "I do not pretend to place my opinion in opposition to General Weitzel, whom I know to be an accomplished soldier and engineer, and whose opinion has great weight with me," the admiral slyly informed Butler. His dispatches to the Navy Department, however, lambasted the army for giving up so easily. "I can't conceive what the army expected when they came here," Porter wrote Secretary Welles. "[Fort Fisher] was so blown up, burst up, and torn up that the people inside had no intention of fighting any longer. Had the army made a show of surrounding it, it would have been ours, but nothing of the kind was done."[24]

Privately Admiral Porter boasted that his fleet's bombardment had rendered Fort Fisher vulnerable to attack and that the army commanders had lacked the nerve to capture it. "The laurels [of victory were] thrown away by General Butler after they were laid at his feet by the Navy, and which neither he nor those with him had the courage to gather up," the admiral informed Sherman in Georgia. Angry at Grant for not upholding his promise to keep Butler away, Porter did not even bother requesting the lieutenant general renew the Fort Fisher expedition. He instead wrote directly to General Sherman, begging him to come to Wilmington and take the "crème de la crème of the rebellion. . . .Let our people see the folly of employing such generals as Butler," the admiral pleaded.[25]

Newspapers were quick to exploit the growing controversy. "Splendid Firing of the Fleet, But Little Damage Done," and "The Powder-Boat Exploded and Nobody Hurt," read the headlines of the *New York World* on December 30. The next day the paper reported: "Actions of General Butler's Force, What It Did and What It Did Not Do." Two weeks later, the *New York Herald's* lead story was "Admiral Porter's Criticism on Gen. Butler's Report. The Failure Placed on the Shoulders of the Army Commander." The expedition's failure sparked a political firestorm in the North. Both Butler and Weitzel were compelled to account more fully for their roles, and even Porter felt constrained to explain his actions. Butler and Weitzel were quick to defend themselves, placing full blame for the expedition's failure on the navy's delay in rendezvousing with the army and attacking when the weather was favorable and the defenses undermanned. Their subordinates agreed. "The Delay was Navy," exclaimed General Paine. "In my opinion the cause of the failure was the delay in making the attack," Comstock added. "Three good days of weather ensued, on any of which the army could have landed." General Grant held his chief engineer's judgment in the highest regard, and in light of Comstock's statement reported that "the failure before was the result of delays by the navy," though the lieutenant general noted that these delays may have been unavoidable.[26]

Admiral Porter responded forcefully to the criticism leveled at the navy, charging that it had been the army that had constantly postponed the expedition by refusing to donate troops or proceed without the powder boat, whereas the navy had been ready to sail since mid-October. Moreover, after the warships' massive shelling had silenced Fort Fisher, the army had declined to exploit the situation by assailing the fort. Butler and Weitzel countered that there was a big difference between a silenced fort and a silent one. They argued that Fisher was quiet because the garrison had been under strict orders to conserve its scarce ammunition, but the defenses and the armament were just as strong after two days of massive naval bombardment as they had been before it. Having failed to silence the fort's batteries by direct fire, the navy should have run past those guns into the Cape Fear River and attacked from the rear.

Porter, on the other hand, claimed that such a maneuver was impossible because New Inlet's channel was too difficult to navigate. The admiral insisted that running the sea face gauntlet was unnecessary because the gun tubes on the land front had been filled with sand, thus rendering them useless against a Union ground assault. The admiral further exaggerated that by Christmas night the Confederates had completely abandoned the fort, and that a determined force of 500 men could have taken the place. Weitzel countered Porter's wild claim by replying that naval officers such as Porter knew as little about a fort as army officers knew about a ship. The naval officers did not know the vulnerable points of a fort or how to regulate their fire in order to damage a fort. "That has been the trouble," Weitzel explained, "the utter ignorance of a regularly educated naval officer of the nature, character, weaknesses, and strong points of a fort."[27]

The back and forth "reasoning" between the competing branches finally caused Porter to lose his temper. Butler and Porter's own 100-pounder Parrott rifles were similar, retorted the admiral, in that the giant rifle "bursted for the same reason Butler did, they went off too fast!" But it was "all right" that Butler had failed to capture Fort Fisher, Porter asserted. Had he succeeded it would have made him the next president of the United States, an even greater calamity for the country than the failed Fort Fisher expedition.

Porter did not confine his criticism to Butler. He privately denounced Grant for having allowed Butler to accompany the expedition and for reporting that the navy did not attack the fort when it should have. "General Grant is always ready to take the credit when anything is done, and equally ready to lay the blame of the failure on the navy," Porter declared. "I think it was unhandsome in him to listen for a moment to the idle talk of Butler's staff, and his timid, calculating engineer, Comstock, who wanted some excuse for not doing their duty." The incensed naval officer also claimed that Grant exercised poor judgment in selecting Godfrey Weitzel as the army commander. He described Weitzel as a "dead failure. . .[who] had no more say than one of his negro sergeants. . . ." Porter blamed Weitzel even more than Butler for the Fort Fisher fiasco, because he believed that the former, a professional soldier, should have insisted on remaining until the fort fell into Union hands.[28]

Butler, on the other hand, claimed that Porter had never intended to demolish the fort, but had merely fired at it to amuse the enemy and embarrass the army when it went in for the attack. Porter's aim, declared Butler, was not to capture Fort Fisher, but to send "General Butler into private life." Naval officers responded to Butler's accusations with equal venom. "[Butler] is either a black-hearted traitor or an arrant coward," a war correspondent quoted one naval officer 'whose name is known in every household.' "He forced himself into the expedition and I believe he came down [to Wilmington] with the deliberate purpose of defeating the enterprise. He was determined to have his own way, and, seeing that he could not, was bent on thwarting everything." The highly publicized feud between Porter and Butler became an embarrassment to both the army and the navy.[29]

Grant eventually sided with his old friend Porter. The commanding general was infuriated with both Butler and Weitzel for disobeying his instructions. He had ordered them to entrench after landing on Federal Point if the Confederates still held the fortifications guarding New Inlet. They failed to do so. Grant also ordered them to cooperate with the navy in reducing the works, which was also not done.

Weitzel was utterly dumbfounded. He insisted he had never seen General Grant's instructions, and that if he had, the army would still be at the Cape Fear. Although Weitzel had advised against attacking Fort Fisher on Christmas evening, it was General Butler who had ordered the retreat. Butler acknowledged that he "was by no means unmindful of the instructions of the lieutenant general," but they did not contain an explicit directive to attack the fort. In addition, he was unable to bring about what he called an "effective landing." He would have dug in on Federal Point if his entire force of 6,500 troops had been able to get ashore, he maintained, but in his judgment, with only one third of the army able to land, and without supplies, he had little choice but to follow the course he eventually took.[30]

The controversy incited a Congressional investigation of the Fort Fisher affair. The Congressional Committee on the Conduct of the War convened from mid-January to mid-March 1865, interviewing many of the campaign's key participants. There was speculation that Butler had used his political influence to exploit the committee hearings as his private forum. After eight weeks of testimony the committee concluded that "the determination of General Butler not to attack Fort Fisher seems to have been fully justified by all the facts and circumstances then known or afterward ascertained." While that ruling may have salvaged Butler's credibility, it came too late to save his military career. At General Grant's request President Lincoln relieved Benjamin F. Butler of command of the Department of Virginia and North Carolina on January 7, 1865. Grant argued that Butler's dismissal was necessary because he had demonstrated his inability to command an army or a military department.[31]

The scrappy politico did not take his sacking lightly. Butler called himself a victim of "malicious enemies at headquarters," and only when the Committee on the Conduct of the War issued its ruling did he feel vindicated. In his farewell address the righteously indignant Butler proclaimed his innocence: "I have refused to order the sacrifice of such soldiers, and I am relieved from your command. The wasted blood of my men does not stain my garments. For my actions I am responsible to God and my country."[32] Butler also saw to it that his official campaign report was printed in the major newspapers throughout the North. Even so, Butler's military career was over. On January 11, 1865, Butler went home to Lowell, Massachusetts, where he awaited further orders that never came. Butler's subordinate, Godfrey Weitzel, was more fortunate. Grant let Weitzel off the hook since Butler had not disclosed his instructions for conducting the Fort Fisher mission. In late December 1864, Weitzel assumed command of the XXV Army Corps in Virginia, but Grant never regained full confidence in Weitzel's ability as a leader.

Admiral Porter escaped the Fort Fisher controversy with his reputation intact. Although he never admitted it, Porter must have known that his fleet had not performed up to his or the army's expectations—however unrealistic—to destroy Fort Fisher. Everyone involved had relied too much on the navy's firepower to bear the brunt of the dirty work, and Porter was as much to blame as anyone. He was arrogant, brazen and naive enough to believe that the navy's direct fire could demolish a sand fortification, enabling the army to simply march in and mop up. Porter even claimed to have bombarded the fort into submission in less than two hours on the first day of the battle. The admiral realized, albeit too late, that naval firepower alone could not drive the Confederates off Federal Point. Still, Porter considered the army's role as secondary to that of the navy and Butler apparently agreed with Porter. The failure of the powder boat experiment and of the naval bombardment placed a greater burden on the army—a role Butler had been unprepared for—especially after his powder boat had proved to be nothing more than a floating dud.

The Fort Fisher expedition had failed because there had been a lack of communication and cooperation between the army and navy commanders.

Porter complained that the planning sessions had been little more than social calls, with Butler asking a host of questions but offering few answers and remaining secretive about his designs. Butler had even declined to reveal to Weitzel Grant's tactical instructions or Butler's own intention to accompany the expedition. Worse yet, Porter and Butler did not meet again until they spoke through hailing trumpets on Christmas Day. This utter lack of cooperation and communication between the branches led to the poorly-timed detonation of the *Louisiana* and uncoordinated naval bombardment. The acrimonious relationship between Porter and Butler ensured their failure to capture the Malakoff Tower of the South. "The two great potentates of this fight—Porter and Butler—[became] entangled in controversy of rank or jealousy," lamented one naval officer. "I do not wonder that the war continues, and with such leaders it will to the crack of Doom."[33]

Gideon Welles and Gustavus Fox went to see President Lincoln at the White House on the afternoon of December 29, where the three men read Admiral Porter's dispatches concerning the ill-fated Battle of Fort Fisher. The disheartened president had already received Grant's telegram reporting the attack's failure. Like nearly everyone else, Lincoln was not surprised by Butler's behavior but wondered whether Admiral Porter had acted any better. A frustrated Welles asked the president what was to be done about the matter, but Lincoln had few ideas. The chief executive hoped that the blockading squadron now had enough vessels to at least close Wilmington to blockade runners, but he offered no advice on how to capture the port town. "I must refer you to General Grant," a dejected Lincoln replied.[34]

The Navy Department executives were both anxious to renew the attack, although Fox was apprehensive about the outcome. "The country will not forgive us for another failure at Wilmington," the assistant secretary remarked. Though Welles agreed, he immediately urged Grant to revive the operation. Welles told Grant that warships could approach nearer to Fort Fisher than had been expected, enabling the navy's firepower to keep the enemy away from their artillery. Welles conceded that the naval bombardment had been less than a complete success, but noted that Weitzel's infantry had landed easily enough on Federal Point. "Under all these circumstances," Welles told Grant, "I invite you to such a military cooperation as will insure the fall of Fort Fisher, the importance of which has already received your careful consideration." Then, with an air of finality, Welles informed Grant that if a second expedition could not be undertaken, Porter's grand armada would have to be dispersed and the chance to close the Confederacy's last gateway would be forever lost. Never again during the war would a fleet of this size and strength be assembled on the Atlantic coast.[35]

This time around, however, it required but little prodding to push Grant into launching the expedition. By the end of December Wilmington had assumed a new significance to the commanding general. The bungled campaign to capture Fort Fisher was partially offset by a concurrent Union triumph when William T. Sherman captured Savannah, Georgia. After his occupation of Atlanta, Sherman led a 60,000-man army across Georgia and into Savannah on December 22, 1864. It was a daring raid that Grant later admitted he would not have entrusted to any other commander in the army. The lieutenant general was relieved to see Sherman safe on the Atlantic coast and was anxious to transfer Sherman's powerful veteran legions by sea to Virginia to help him defeat the Army of Northern Virginia. Sherman had other plans, however, and Wilmington would ultimately prove important to their accomplishment.

Harkening back to his off-the-cuff remark to Grant following the capture of Atlanta, Sherman proposed to march his army toward Virginia by way of the Carolinas. While en route Sherman would "smash things generally," destroying the Confederates' South Carolina supply depots at Branchville, Columbia and Camden, and then either attack Charleston from the north or Wilmington from the southwest. Sherman favored a strike on Wilmington because he believed that Charleston was a "desolated wreck" hardly worth the time or effort it would take to "starve it out," especially once its railroads had been broken. Based on his experiences, Sherman believed Porter's fleet alone could not destroy the Cape Fear's defenses. After capturing Wilmington, Sherman proposed to "make a bee-line" for Raleigh or Weldon, and in so doing would place his powerful force in a position to attack Lee's beleaguered army. "Then the game is up with Lee," Sherman predicted, and the Army of Northern Virginia would be forced to evacuate its defenses at Petersburg and Richmond, enabling the Federals to crush it on open ground. Even if Lee somehow managed to endanger Sherman after abandoning Richmond, he reasoned, Sherman could always withdraw to the safety of the North Carolina coast.[36]

Both Sherman's plan and his confidence in it pleased Grant. The crowning benefit of such a campaign could well be the end of the Confederacy. At the very least Grant believed its success would "disorganize the South and prevent the organization of new Armies from their broken fragments." Grant's only apprehension about Sherman's proposed march was that the remnants of John Bell Hood's Confederate Army of Tennessee, badly bloodied at Franklin in November and almost annihilated on the hills outside of Nashville in December, might combine with other scattered armies to attack Sherman. If Lee detached troops from Petersburg to link up with Hood or Bragg, or if Lee himself abandoned the Petersburg-Richmond line to strike Sherman where his army could not easily be reinforced, the results could be disastrous. Ultimately Grant concluded that Lee was "averse to going out of Virginia," and surrendering Richmond, and decided that he and Sherman would defeat Lee by capturing the rest of the Confederacy. "Without waiting further directions then," Grant wrote Sherman, "you may make preparation to start on your Northern expedition without delay. Break up the rail-roads in South & North Carolina and join the Armies operating against Richmond as soon as you can."[37]

Having agreed to Sherman's bold plan, Grant was determined to guarantee its success. That meant providing Sherman with reinforcements, supplies and a safe haven on the coast should he need them. Although a Federal army had occupied New Bern, North Carolina since 1862, the railroads from that place had been damaged or blocked by the Confederates, and the Neuse River above the town was too narrow and shallow to be safely navigable. The Cape Fear River, on the other hand, was navigable all the way to Fayetteville 100 miles northwest of Wilmington, and three major railroads converged at the latter city from points south, west and north. Both the Cape Fear River and the railroads could be used to funnel soldiers and provisions to Sherman. Grant also wanted to insure Sherman's safe arrival in Virginia as quickly as possible. With Wilmington in Union hands, Sherman could advance toward Virginia without having to detour to the coast to capture the Carolina port town, or to hunt for provisions. Wilmington therefore assumed great importance to Grant. Located as it was halfway between Savannah and Richmond, it looked to be the best point from which to assist Sherman's army. Grant decided to attack the city with renewed vigor and promised

Welles, Fox and Porter he would resume the Fort Fisher campaign as soon as possible.[38]

Grant's decision was communicated to Admiral Porter on December 30. Hold on for a few days, he advised, and he would send down an increased army force "without the former Commander." Meanwhile, the army transports were being refueled at Hampton's Roads, which caused a slight delay in reembarking the troops. Grant urged Porter to occupy the Confederates at the Cape Fear so that Hoke's Division would not be returned to Virginia or sent after Sherman.[39]

Porter was elated at Grant's suddenly heightened interest in Wilmington. "Thank you for so promptly trying to rectify the blunder so lately committed," he wrote Grant. "I knew you would do it [and] I shall be all ready." Porter's elation notwithstanding, his old mistrust of the army washed over him like a cold rising ocean tide. Was Grant sincere? "I don't believe in Grant's troops coming. . . with another commander," was how he responded to Grant's message in a letter penned to Gustavus Fox. Porter's skepticism revealed his disgust over Grant's handling of the first Fort Fisher expedition, which the admiral believed had never interested the lieutenant general. "I do not feel kindly toward General Grant for the indifference in this matter," an indignant Porter wrote. He also felt betrayed when Grant originally sided with Butler and Weitzel in placing blame for the campaign's failure on the navy. But, if the second expedition came to fruition, at least Porter would have a chance to vindicate himself.[40]

While the admiral prepared his fleet for another battle, members of Grant's inner circle encouraged the general to reconsider Quincy Gillmore's original plan of attacking Wilmington by storming Bald Head Island or Oak Island, since Fort Fisher had proved too formidable to capture by direct assault. After considering the testimony of General Curtis and his soldiers, however, Grant decided to attack Wilmington by assaulting the works at New Inlet once again. Weitzel's command had landed easily on Federal Point and a portion of this force had remained unharmed on the beach for two days. Grant saw no reason why another successful landing at Federal Point could not be accomplished. A secure lodgment there would put the army in a more advantageous position from which to advance on Wilmington, which was the main objective of the second expedition. To gain control of the Cape Fear River, Grant hoped Porter would attempt to run light-draft vessels past Fort Fisher's sea face batteries, while the fire of the ocean-bound gunboats and the army troops kept the Confederates ducking for cover or down in their bombproofs.[41]

As for the army, Grant wanted it to play a more prominent, aggressive and harmonious role in the campaign, and he chose a commander he believed would now accomplish that: Bvt. Maj. Gen. Alfred Howe Terry. Grant had seldom come into contact with Terry, although he was familiar with his present command and its movements north of the James River in Virginia. In truth, Grant's aide-de-camp, Lt. Col. Horace Porter, had recommended Terry to command the army's Fort Fisher expeditionary force. Horace Porter and Terry had served together in the Port Royal Campaign in the autumn of 1861. Acting on his trusted aide's endorsement, Grant requested Terry to appear at headquarters on the afternoon of January 2, 1865. The meeting went well, and Grant was impressed by the general's character and quiet confidence.[42]

Born in Hartford, Connecticut, on November 10, 1827, Terry was the second of eleven children and a direct descendant of the founders of both Hartford and Yale University. When he was still a child his family moved to New Haven, where he attended local schools and, briefly, Yale Law School. He left Yale in 1849 without graduating to practice law in New Haven, and until the war served as Clerk of the Superior Court, and later as Clerk of the Supreme Court, of New Haven County. A towering 6'2", Terry was of slender build, fair-skinned and sported a neatly trimmed beard. He was also a musician, and he spent much of his free time—he remained a life-long bachelor—playing the flute and singing bass, often performing in concerts about New Haven.

When war came in 1861 and President Lincoln issued his call for troops, Terry recruited the 2nd Connecticut Infantry and was commissioned its colonel. After two months of drilling and training, Terry led his ninety-day regiment in the Battle of Manassas. Despite his inexperience and the Union army's defeat, Terry was commended for his "gallantry and excellent conduct." When the regiment's enlistments expired in August, Terry helped organize the 7th Connecticut Infantry, recruiting many of his former officers and soldiers for three years or the duration of the war. With Terry as its colonel, the 7th Connecticut participated in army-navy operations at Port Royal, South Carolina, in November 1861, and again at Fort Pulaski outside

The affable, modest and capable Bvt. Maj. Gen. Alfred H. Terry, commander of the Fort Fisher expeditionary force, January 1865. *Author's Collection*

Savannah the following April. Two weeks after the fall of Pulaski, Terry was promoted to brigadier general and led Union forces in actions on James and Morris islands outside Charleston in 1863. As commander of the Federal forces on Morris Island, he was scheduled to lead an assault against Battery Wagner, but the Confederates evacuated it several days beforehand. He went on to assume temporary command of the X Army Corps in the Northern District of the Department of the South.

In the spring of 1864, Terry's X Army Corps was transferred to Virginia, where Terry served as both division and corps commander in the Army of the James. The corps fought well around Petersburg and Richmond in the summer and autumn of 1864, and Terry had contributed more than his share to its field record. The 37-year-old Terry also garnered experience in command of the XXIV Army Corps, Army of the James. Given his solid record the modest general may have been one of the army's best kept secrets. When Lincoln met Terry for the first time, the president, who had certainly seen his fair share of generals, asked: "Why have we not seen you before?" Terry replied that his duties had kept him at the front. "As a commander [General Terry] won the confidence [of his men] by his coolness in action and by his clearness of perception in taking in the situation under which he was placed at any given time," observed General Grant.[43]

While respected as an excellent combat officer and strict disciplinarian, he also had something in common with his superior, Benjamin F. Butler: Terry was not a soldier by profession. He had not attended West Point or any other military academy. Yet before the conflict he had been an avid student of European military history and had briefly commanded a Connecticut militia company known as the New Haven Grays. The Connecticut native possessed innate military talents that, coupled with his ability to get along with superiors and subordinates alike, had thus far served him well during the war.

Grant assigned Terry command of almost 10,000 men that ostensibly were being sent to reinforce Sherman in Savannah. Grant himself spread the word that he was outfitting an expedition for Savannah rather than Wilmington because he was convinced that leaks to newspaper reporters had been largely responsible for the first campaign's failure. On December 19, 1864, five days before the first Battle of Fort Fisher, both the *Boston Daily Advertiser* and the *Philadelphia Press* had published articles detailing the U.S.

Navy's attack plans based on information sold to them by B. S. Osborn of New York. Three days later Richmond newspapers ran the same articles, alerting military authorities in Wilmington to the planned Union assault. The Navy Department was understandably embarrassed and angry. Gustavus Fox used his influence to have Osborn arrested and confined for six months in the Old Capital Prison in Washington. Grant was determined that the mistake of leaking information to the press would not be repeated.[44]

General Terry's force—officially designated Terry's Provisional Corps—comprised the same units from Butler's aborted expedition: Brig. Gen. Adelbert Ames' Second Division, XXIV Army Corps, supported by Capt. Richard H. Lee's four 3-inch Parrott rifles of the 16th New York Independent Artillery; and Brig. Gen. Charles J. Paine's Second and Third Brigades, Third Division, XXV Army Corps, with Lt. John Myrick's Battery E, 3rd U.S. Regular Army, four bronze 12-pounder Napoleon cannon. The 27th U.S. Colored Troops, however, replaced the 107th U.S. Colored Troops in the Third Brigade. General Terry also brought along his old unit, the Second Brigade, First Division, XXIV Army Corps, now commanded by Col. Joseph C. Abbott. This veteran brigade was experienced in joint operations, having fought under Terry on the Sea Islands near Charleston.

Should it be necessary to besiege Fort Fisher, the Provisional Corps also employed a siege train of sixteen 30-pounder Parrott rifles and twenty Coehorn mortars (with 500 rounds of ammunition for each gun). The siege guns would be manned by Companies B, G, and L of the 1st Connecticut Heavy Artillery, Capt. William G. Pride commanding, but would be supervised by Bvt. Brig. Gen. Henry L. Abbot , who was attached to Paine's Division, and seven companies of the 16th New York Heavy Artillery, which were temporarily attached to Abbott's Brigade. Lieutenant K. Samuel O'Keefe's two companies of the 15th New York Engineers, as well as Signal Corps, Ambulance Corps detachments and support personnel, rounded out the increased force of 9,632 officers and men. Once again Grant's chief engineer, Lt. Col. Cyrus Comstock, would accompany the expedition. He did so reluctantly, doubting the success of another attack so soon after the first attempt. But Terry, like Weitzel before him, had asked Grant for the talented Comstock's services and Grant readily complied.[45]

In case Terry needed reinforcements Grant instructed Maj. Gen. Philip Sheridan, who was still battling Jubal Early's decimated army in the

Shenandoah Valley, to send a division of troops to Baltimore, where it could embark if called upon. If these troops were needed Grant fully intended to send the combative "Little Phil" south with them, a fact that evidenced his serious desire to capture Wilmington. Grant considered early on accompanying the army to the Cape Fear himself but thought better of it since his absence would have left Ben Butler in command in southeastern Virginia. That grim prospect was one reason Grant requested the War Department to relieve Butler from duty. To further bolster Terry's force, Grant transferred Maj. Gen. John McAllister Schofield's XXIII Army Corps from Tennessee, where it had helped crush the Army of Tennessee, to Annapolis, Maryland, in mid-January 1865.[46]

The stage was set for the campaign to capture Wilmington.

During the last two days of 1864, soldiers of the XXIV and XXV Army Corps returned to their old camps north of the James River, the white troops marching to the vicinity of Fort Burnham to the New Market Road and the black troops to Chaffin's Farm. They had been gone for nearly a month, and had spent most of that time at sea. Many of the infantrymen had been confined to their ships since their departure from Bermuda Hundred on December 8. Much to their disgust, the tired, disheartened and dirty soldiers returned to discover that their huts and personal belongings had been robbed. No sooner had they shaken off the weariness of the sea, scoured the salty rust from their rifle-muskets and begun to settle in, then new marching orders arrived. On January 3-4, 1865, the troops returned to Bermuda Hundred, where they spent a miserable day in new-fallen snow with little or no shelter while they waited their turn to board the transports. "It is difficult to imagine a more uncomfortable bivouac," commented a Connecticut soldier.[47]

During the night of January 4 and the morning of the 5th, the army once again boarded the ships at Bermuda Hundred and sailed to Hampton Roads. General Grant personally accompanied General Terry and Lieutenant Colonel Comstock downriver to see the expedition off and issue last minute instructions. En route the lieutenant general divulged the real target to Terry. "The expedition intrusted to your command," Grant informed his subordinate, "has been fitted out to renew the capture of Fort Fisher and Wilmington ultimately." The news did not surprise Terry, who suspected all along he was going to the Cape Fear.[48]

Grant recommended that Terry's first objective should be to gain a foothold on Federal Point, from which place he could operate against Fort Fisher. Once a strong beachhead was established, Grant admonished, Terry

Brig. Gen. Adelbert Ames, the stout-hearted, temperamental commander whose division of the XXIV Army Corps was sent in to capture Fort Fisher. *Author's Collection*

was not to abandon his plans "until [the fort's] reduction is accomplished," or until he had received other orders from headquarters in Virginia. Grant handed the Connecticut general a sealed envelope containing full instructions in writing which were not to be opened until he was at sea.

Grant knew that cooperation between Terry and the mercurial David D. Porter was essential to the expedition's success. "It is exceedingly desirable that the most complete understanding should exist between yourself and the naval commander," he told Terry, no doubt remembering with considerable indignation the Butler-Porter communication fiasco. "I suggest, therefore, that you consult with Admiral Porter freely, and get from him the part to be performed by each branch of the public service, so that there may be a unity of action." Grant need not have worried. By all accounts Alfred H. Terry was modest, easygoing and reliable—a kind, compassionate man who made friends easily.[49]

The army flotilla sailed at 4:00 a.m. on January 6, with Terry's ship, the *McClellan*, taking the lead. Thanks in large part to Grant's enthusiastic cooperation, most of those involved in the Wilmington expedition were confident of success. One event, however, spelled trouble for the Federals. Conspicuously absent from the army flotilla as it sailed southward was Brig. Gen. Adelbert Ames. When Ames' designated ship *Atlantic* departed with the rest of the transports, Ames was not on board. Left with no other choice, the general was forced to sail from Hampton Roads on the hospital tender *Blackstone*, a situation that did not sit well with Ames. It took Ames two days to finally overtake the flotilla. According to one witness, a livid Ames slung "bitter and insulting words" at General Curtis, who was on the *Atlantic* with his brigade, accusing his subordinate of playing a "shabby trick" in purposely sailing without him.

Adelbert Ames was a scrapper. Though five months younger and almost a foot shorter than N. Martin Curtis, Ames outranked and probably believed he could physically outmatch his subordinate. He had always been that way. Since his boyhood days when he had battled street toughs in his hometown of Rockland, Maine, where he was born on October 31, 1835, Ames had earned a reputation as a formidable combatant despite his small stature. "Del" Ames, as his family and friends called him, seemed more destined for a maritime occupation than an army career. Many of his Puritan ancestors had been seafaring men, including his father, Capt. Jesse Ames, who made at least eight voyages around the world in his trading schooner. Young Del accompanied his father on at least one of those trips. But his real interest was in military history, and Ames had his heart set on attending the U.S. Military Academy at West Point. His family finally secured an appointment for him there in 1855. Curious, intelligent and ambitious, Ames graduated fifth in the class of 1861 and was commissioned a lieutenant of artillery.

Two months later Lieutenant Ames was severely wounded in the Battle of Manassas while commanding a section of guns in the 5th U.S. Artillery. Despite being weakened by loss of blood, Ames refused to leave the field, staying with his soldiers until the army retreated. For his courage he received a brevet promotion to major in the Regular Army and was eventually awarded the Medal of Honor. When he recovered from his wounds Ames served in the defenses around Washington, commanded a battery of artillery in the Peninsula Campaign, and led a regiment of infantry, the 20th Maine, in the battles of Sharpsburg and Fredericksburg. Although Ames would not be with them, the men of the 20th would later win everlasting fame for their spirited defense of Little Round Top at the Battle of Gettysburg. Ames also fought at Gettysburg, but by that time he was a division commander in O.O. Howard's XI Army Corps.

Ames temporarily left the fields of the Eastern Theater in 1864 for a brief stint with the X Army Corps in coastal operations around Charleston before returning to command a division in the XVIII Army Corps at Cold Harbor and Petersburg. That autumn he temporarily commanded the X Corps before assuming command of the Second Division of the newly-formed XXIV Army Corps in early December. Ames was already having problems with his new command, and most of these stemmed from a personality conflict with his First Brigade commander, N. Martin Curtis.[50]

The trouble between Ames and Curtis began in earnest when Ames accused his subordinate of deliberately leaving him behind in Virginia. General Curtis—as well as the members of Ames' staff—thought that the division commander was on board the *Atlantic* resting in his quarters hours before the ship departed Hampton Roads on January 6. Obviously he was not, but to Curtis the mistake was an honest one and he resented Ames' accusation that he had intentionally sailed without him. "Perhaps in all my years I never had anything to so thoroughly arouse my righteous indignation," Curtis later wrote. Although Curtis demanded an immediate apology from his superior, Ames—in a petty display of temper—turned on his heels and stormed off to his cabin. Only later did he attempt to apologize for his behavior, but to Curtis' way of thinking, the apology was offered too late and he refused to accept it. A chagrined Ames fanned the flames further by insisting that all further contact between the two men be limited to the "strictest official requirements." Curtis readily agreed. This type of falling out was exactly the sort of communication breakdown that Grant wished to avoid. On the first trip to Fort Fisher Curtis and Ames had played cards together; on the return voyage they would not even speak to each other.[51]

General Terry was unaware of his generals' bickering as he sailed into Beaufort on the morning of January 8. His ship was the first to arrive, with most of the transports reaching Beaufort later that evening. The Union effort was further hampered by a familiar adversary: bad weather. A violent storm slowed the army flotilla's advance, which could barely make headway against gale force winds and twenty-foot seas, and a number of ships foundered off Cape Hatteras. The men suffered terribly from seasickness. One unfortunate soul, Pvt. Charles Brown of Company D, 3rd New Hampshire Infantry, was washed overboard from the *General Lyon*. Although the army transports were instructed to remain twenty miles from Beaufort to prevent their discovery by Confederate spies, heavy seas so severely damaged four of the vessels that they had to be towed into the harbor for repairs. By that time Porter's fleet was ready to sail, but the inclement weather postponed its departure.[52]

The delay at Beaufort was not entirely lost time, for it enabled Porter and Terry to confer and hammer out a plan of battle. They had never personally met, and Porter in particular was apprehensive about the encounter. Porter had expressed his usual skepticism when he received Grant's telegram announcing that he had selected a volunteer general—and another of Butler's subordinates to boot—to command the Fort Fisher expeditionary force. "I hold it to be a good rule never to send a boy on a man's errand," the admiral replied to Grant. Porter hoped Grant would transfer Sherman's army from Savannah to the Cape Fear, or that his friend Sherman would march directly on Wilmington from the rear. "Grant is going to send here one of

Butler's men, who will likely white-wash Butler by doing just as he did," Porter complained to Gustavus Fox. "Don't be surprised if I send him home with a flea in his ear. . . ."[53]

Porter's first meeting with Terry did little to soothe the admiral's anxiety. He thought the general was "rather cold and formal in his manner. . . [without] the frankness of a true soldier." In truth, Terry may have been cautious about having to deal with the temperamental Porter, who impressed the general at first as being rather grim. But the more time Porter and Terry spent together, the more they liked each other. The ice soon melted and they got along well. "Here was a different sort of man from [Butler]," the admiral at last conceded. "I found General Terry a genial, clever officer. . . .He had no staff, wore no spurs and I don't think he wore a sword. He had a good head full of sense. . .and we soon understood each other." Indeed, the two commanders shared a common and intense determination to capture Wilmington—starting with Fort Fisher.[54]

With the exception of the blockaders Porter had withdrawn his fleet from the vicinity of Fort Fisher, hoping to lull the enemy into thinking the navy had abandoned the attack. In the two weeks since the battle, the warships had been undergoing repairs and had taken on an abundance of coal, water, provisions and ammunition at Beaufort. Porter intended his gunboats to finish the job without having to return to Beaufort for additional supplies. The seas finally subsided on January 12, allowing the fleet to sail, and by about 10:00 p.m. most of the fifty-eight warships and twenty-two army vessels had rendezvoused off New Inlet. Arrangements had been made to land the troops that night, but the fleet reached Fort Fisher so late that Terry and Porter decided to rest the men and put them ashore in the morning.[55]

On the night of January 12, Pvt. George Washington Benson of Company H, 36th North Carolina Regiment, was on guard duty at Fort Fisher. As he scouted along the beach, Benson peered into the darkness and glimpsed an increasing number of lights on the ocean. At first Benson saw only a few, but soon "there was a multitude of lights out there." Colonel Lamb also saw them. From his vantage point on the Pulpit he watched the twinkling lights of the "great armada," and by 10:00 p.m. had counted thirty enemy vessels.

The dreaded Union fleet was back and Lamb had not been warned of its approach by headquarters in Wilmington.

Cavalrymen and coast guards posted along the sounds and beaches as far north as Topsail, twenty-five miles above Wilmington, were supposed to be keeping a sharp lookout for enemy ships moving southward. As soon as the ships were spotted, couriers were to relay the news to General Bragg in Wilmington, who was to immediately telegraph that information to Colonel Lamb at Fort Fisher. Instead, Lamb received first warning of the Federal fleet's approach from his own mounted pickets. Now it fell to Lamb to notify the commanding general that the enemy was back, and Lamb was furious with Bragg for failing to warn him.[56]

It would not be the last time Bragg would fail him.

Rear Admiral David D. Porter (center) and executive officers on board the flagship *Malvern*: Lt. Cmdr. William B. Cushing (far left); Cmdr. A. C. Rhind (fifth from left); Lt. Cmdr. Thomas O. Selfridge (behind Porter's right shoulder); and Flag Lt. Samuel W. Preston (second from right). *U.S. Army Military History Institute*

Chapter 7

"Attack! Attack! It is all I can say and all you can do."

– Maj. Gen. W. H. C. Whiting to Gen. Braxton Bragg, January 15, 1865

REAPPEARANCE

On the day the Union armada sailed southward from Beaufort to renew the attack on Fort Fisher, Robert Hoke's Division staged a grand review for General Bragg and a large number of civilian dignitaries at Camp Whiting, near Green's Mill Pond one mile east of Wilmington. After a full day of spit and polish inspections, manual-of-arms drills and awe-inspiring marches, many tired soldiers turned in for the night. Other officers and enlisted men spent the night on the town, while a division band serenaded a group of local citizens. The soldiers' slumber and socializing were rudely interrupted when, just after midnight, a drummer beat the long roll, summoning the troops to assemble. Word had just come into camp that the Union fleet had again been spotted off Fort Fisher. The Federals would probably attack at first light, and Hoke's command was needed to defend Federal Point.[1]

Transferring Hoke's men to Federal Point in time to ward off an enemy attack was a difficult proposition. The division was encamped fifteen miles north of the fortified position at Sugar Loaf—a good seven hours' march away. While the river route was faster, there were not enough steamers to transport all 6,424 soldiers to Sugar Loaf. The high command in Richmond had cautioned Bragg as early as January 9 that a Union deserter of "considerable intelligence" had reported General Alfred H. Terry's corps sailing toward Wilmington. Bragg disregarded the message, as well as the advice of his subordinates to keep a brigade of Hoke's infantrymen at Sugar Loaf in the event of the enemy's reappearance. His decision to ignore these wise counsels was now coming back to haunt him.[2]

In obedience to Bragg's instructions, General Hoke rushed Kirkland's Brigade to Wilmington's downtown docks, where it boarded steamers bound for Gander Hall, a landing two miles north of Sugar Loaf. From there, the infantrymen would march to the sand dune defenses. Hoke's other three brigades were en route to Sugar Loaf via the Federal Point Road by 1:00 a. m., January 13. A contingent of 650 Senior Reserves bivouacked at Camp Lamb, in Wilmington's northern suburbs, was also sent to Sugar Loaf as reinforcements. Bragg, obviously concerned about the reappearance of the enemy, wired Governor Vance asking for "all his assistance."[3]

As Hoke's Division hustled southward, Colonel Lamb prepared for action at the fort. His immediate concern was for his family, asleep at their cottage near Howard's Hill north of the fort. Lamb quickly dispatched a message for Daisy to make ready to evacuate across the river with the children and their nurse as soon as he could come to say goodbye. Lamb also telegraphed General Hébert in Smithville, pleading for reinforcements from the other fortifications in the estuary. Fort Fisher's garrison numbered but 800 artillerymen of the 36th North Carolina Regiment, many of whom had only recently returned from fighting in Georgia. To Lamb's dismay, at least 100 of them were physically unfit for duty.

As soon as he had made the necessary arrangements for the coming battle, Lamb jumped on his horse and galloped to his home to see his family off. As he rode into the yard, the cottage appeared dark and silent. Although she had received his note, Daisy had dozed off and was not prepared to leave. Knowing that the enemy fleet would soon be shelling the beach and that he would be needed inside the fort, Lamb hurried his wife and children into a boat waiting to ferry them across the river. He allowed them only enough time to dress and grab a few keepsakes, leaving behind clothes, toys, household articles and many personal items. After a tearful farewell, Daisy and the children were pulled away from shore by the boatmen. As the enveloping darkness swallowed them from view, it suddenly occurred to Lamb that he might never see his wife or little ones again. Saddened, he remounted his horse and trotted back to the fort.[4]

Captain Solon A. Carter, assistant adjutant general on Brig. Gen. Charles J. Paine's staff, sat down in his stateroom on board the army transport *Champion* to pen a letter to his "own precious" wife, Emily, just hours before Terry's Provisional Corps was to hit Federal Point Beach. "Perhaps this may be my last letter to you," he wrote.

> Tomorrow we expect to be called upon to take the rebel fort Fisher. . . .I will leave the letter with the Capt. of the *Champion*. . .and if anything happens to me you will get the letter sometime. I never started in any enterprise in which I felt so little heart as the present. I can't account for my feelings, but I feel tonight as though there was a dark shadow hanging over me. I trust that it is all superstition, and that the same power that has protected me through dangers past will protect me tomorrow, and restore me err long to my wifey and darling baby.

The moon was still shining in a star-filled sky when the boom of a signal gun on board the *Malvern* aroused the Federals from their quarters at 4:00 a.m., January 13. By dawn the entire armada of fifty-eight warships—led by the *Malvern* and the frigates *Wabash*, *Minnesota*, and *Colorado*—and the twenty-two

Capt. Solon A. Carter, assistant adjutant general on Gen. Charles J. Paine's staff, in a previously unpublished image.

Author's Collection

army transports were in motion for Fort Fisher. As they approached Federal Point, a division of gunboats fanned out from the fleet to cover the landing of General Terry's Provisional Corps. The *Brooklyn* opened fire on Federal Point at 7:20 a.m., with the division's remaining dozen ships mounting a total of 109 cannon following her lead. For the next two-and-a-half hours, shells (sarcastically referred to as "rotten shots") rained into the woods skirting the area selected for landing the army four miles north of Fort Fisher. The army ships anchored just outside the navy vessels, and the soldiers began disembarking at 8:00 a.m. Porter donated two hundred boats, varying in size from "six oars" to "thirty oars," to carry the infantrymen to shore. The soldiers hit the beach above the head of Myrtle Sound, about one mile north of where Ben Butler's troops had landed three weeks earlier. It was General Terry's belief that going ashore in that area—a long, slender sand spit separated from the mainland by the sound—would allow his army, artillery, and supplies to land relatively unmolested by the Confederates.[5]

A light southwesterly breeze fanned a calm sea, but the surf was still rough because of the recent gale. Great swells broke hard and fast on the beach. Given the difficult circumstances, the landing operation ran as smooth as could have been expected. As the cutters pushed in close to shore, soldiers jumped overboard and splashed up to the beach amid the cheers of sailors on board the gunboats. The white soldiers of the XXIV Corps landed first with Col. Louis Bell's Third Brigade in the lead. Ferocious breakers capsized some of their boats, spilling the infantrymen into the frigid water. Even those soldiers lucky enough to step out of the launches usually received an unwelcome dunking thanks to the pounding, churning surf. "Loaded down as they were with ammunition, provisions, blankets, etc.," one Union soldier wryly observed, "there was some tall scrambling done on all-fours before they extricated themselves from their involuntary salt-water bath." Another eyewitness to the landing claimed that not one in ten men "got ashore dry shod."[6]

The whole episode was "an exciting and amusing sport" to both the sailors assisting the hapless landlubbers and those soldiers fortunate enough to have already reached dry ground. Men from both branches laughed and joked as the soaking infantrymen, chilled to the bone and shivering cold, emerged from the unmerciful sea. The laughter "grew into a roar that rivaled the noise of the breaking waves," noted one thoroughly entertained Union soldier. Some soldiers likened the landing to a frolic in the park, and for some, it may as well have been. Once ashore, the men basked in the balmy sunshine, built crackling fires to dry out their uniforms, boil coffee and roast newly-gathered oysters. They also listened to brass bands playing martial airs and watched their comrades come ashore. As one Federal put it, "[It

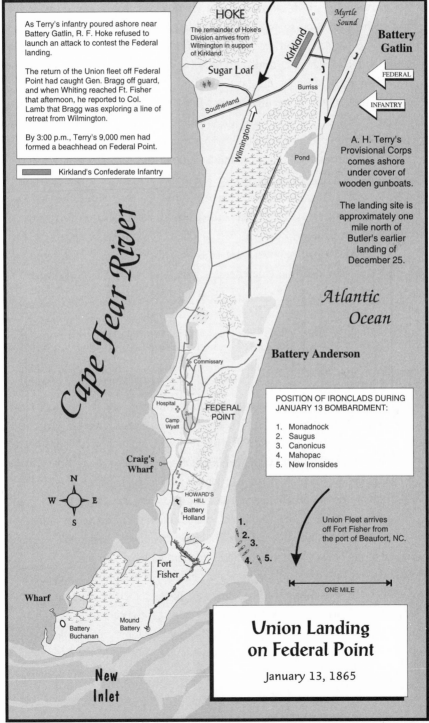

As Terry's infantry poured ashore near Battery Gatlin, R. F. Hoke refused to launch an attack to contest the Federal landing.

The return of the Union fleet off Federal Point had caught Gen. Bragg off guard, and when Whiting reached Ft. Fisher that afternoon, he reported to Col. Lamb that Bragg was exploring a line of retreat from Wilmington.

By 3:00 p.m., Terry's 9,000 men had formed a beachhead on Federal Point.

Kirkland's Confederate Infantry

HOKE

The remainder of Hoke's Division arrives from Wilmington in support of Kirkland.

Sugar Loaf

Southerland

Myrtle Sound

Kirkland

Battery Gatlin

FEDERAL

INFANTRY

Burriss

A. H. Terry's Provisional Corps comes ashore under cover of wooden gunboats.

The landing site is approximately one mile north of Butler's earlier landing of December 25.

Wilmington

Pond

Cape Fear River

Atlantic Ocean

Battery Anderson

Commissary

Hospital

Camp Wyatt

FEDERAL POINT

POSITION OF IRONCLADS DURING JANUARY 13 BOMBARDMENT:

1. Monadnock
2. Saugus
3. Canonicus
4. Mahopac
5. New Ironsides

Craig's Wharf

N
W — E
S

HOWARD'S HILL

Battery Holland

1.
2.
3.
4. 5.

Union Fleet arrives off Fort Fisher from the port of Beaufort, NC.

Fort Fisher

ONE MILE

Wharf

Battery Buchanan

Mound Battery

New Inlet

Union Landing on Federal Point

January 13, 1865

Mark A. Moore

was] a scene of much merriment that would do discredit to the jolliest of picnics." In addition to wet soldiers, a large amount of ammunition also soaked up the salt water and had to be dumped and replaced with a fresh supply brought ashore at midday by the U. S. Colored Troops. By then, the heavy surf had subsided and far fewer black soldiers involuntarily felt the chill of the Atlantic water than their white comrades. Still, Bvt. Brig. Gen. Albert M. Blackman and some of his men from the 27th U. S. Colored Troops experienced a baptismal disembarkment.[7]

Although many of his men made light of the landing, General Terry believed it was fraught with danger. He suspected that Confederate troops were nearby and wondered why they had not attacked him while he was most vulnerable. Anxious to learn the enemy's whereabouts, Terry sent a reconnaissance force from Col. Joseph C. Abbott's brigade across Myrtle Sound about 10:00 a.m. It did not take long for Abbott's men to confirm Terry's suspicion, for the Confederates were dug in on the western side of the sound. Rifle-musket shots rang out in the chilly morning air.[8]

Robert Hoke reached Sugar Loaf just as Terry's first Federal soldiers waded ashore on Federal Point. Only Kirkland's Brigade, which had been transported downriver on steamers, together with mounted pickets from Col. Thomas J. Lipscomb's 2nd South Carolina Cavalry, were there to greet him. Lead elements of Clingman's, Colquitt's, and Hagood's brigades were marching from Wilmington and just beginning to arrive at Sugar Loaf. Hoke immediately deployed some of Kirkland's men as skirmishers to check the Federals hitting the beach, and instructed Lipscomb's horsemen to scout the ground toward Fort Fisher. Hoke entrenched the bulk of his division on the Sugar Loaf line, and watched the Federal army land.[9] Kirkland's pickets settled in on the west side of Myrtle Sound and let loose a ragged volley into Abbott's skirmishers advancing from the east. Even as Kirkland checked the enemy, General Hoke refused to launch an all-out attack on the Union army beachhead, believing the Federals were too well-protected by the gunboats just offshore to warrant such a frontal assault. Moreover, Myrtle Sound prevented his force from engaging the Federals. "Owing to the intervening swamp and sound, it was impossible for us to attack the enemy at their

General Alfred H. Terry's Union troops landing on Federal Point, January 13, 1865. *Frank Leslie's Illustrated Newspaper*

landing point, even if the heavy metal of the fleet had not securely covered them," General Bragg later explained.[10]

Hoke's inaction bewildered many of his soldiers, who were confident they could push the Federals back into the sea if only their commander would authorize the attack. "We did nothing," complained a disgusted Asa King of the 66th North Carolina Infantry, "just lay quiet. . .and let the enemy land. We could have repulsed them if we had fired on them as they landed, which we were anxious to do. We received no orders from our officers, just let the Federals assemble a force together, then they commenced firing on us." It is difficult to fathom what Hoke was thinking as he withheld his troops. Perhaps the terrible beating his division had suffered at Fort Harrison the previous September preyed on his mind, making him wary of attacking across an open beach where his troops stood to be pummeled by both the U. S. Navy's heavy guns and the Federal infantrymen's rifled-muskets.[11]

Since the Federals were landing near Battery Gatlin and demonstrating in his front, Hoke mistakenly believed they intended to march directly on Wilmington, bypassing Fort Fisher altogether. "The enemy, apparently, is preparing to attack me," he anxiously telegraphed Bragg in Wilmington. As a result, Hoke maintained his defensive posture at Sugar Loaf in order to safeguard the main route to the city and observe the Federals' movements.[12]

Colonel Lamb watched the Union troops landing on the beach north of Fort Fisher with growing trepidation. General Whiting had predicted that if the Federals were allowed to establish a foothold on Federal Point, the fort's fall would be just a matter of time. With Whiting's ominous words in mind, Lamb wondered why the Federals were not attacked and why General Hoke had not sent reinforcements into the fort. "Where is Hoke?" Lamb inquired of headquarters in Wilmington. "The Yankees are landing a heavy force."[13]

While waiting impatiently for Hoke to come to his aid, Lamb battled the vast Union armada. Every man in the fort had assumed his post early that morning. An ominous silence enveloped the fort as its occupants watched the enemy warships approach. "All nature seemed to be resting," recalled Buckner L. Blackmore, a musician in 2nd Company A, 36th North Carolina. "You could hardly see a ripple on the ocean." The solitude was broken at 8:30 a.m. by Lamb's shrill but firm order for the fort to open the battle. "Cumberland Battery, fire!" he yelled. A moment later a columbiad belched forth a huge 10-inch solid iron ball. The projectile arched across the ocean's surface and struck broadside the *New Ironside's* iron-plated case-mate, bounced off, and dropped harmlessly into the sea. The fort's remaining guns quickly answered in support, and the battle was joined.[14]

While the wooden gunboats covered the U.S. troops going ashore, the armored vessels—again led by the *New Ironsides*—renewed the bombardment of Fort Fisher. The ironclads quietly took up their battle stations off the fort by 8:30 a. m. As if daring the Confederates to "open the ball," the monitors *Canonicus, Mahopac, Monadnock,* and *Saugus,* and the *New Ironsides,* anchored between 700-1,000 yards off the northeast bastion, somewhat closer than in the December attack. Admiral Porter deployed his ironclads at close range to learn the precise number and location of the fort's seacoast guns. He determined to rectify the mistake he had made in the first attack of permitting his gunboats to concentrate their fire on the enemy's flags. This time the admiral instructed his gunboat commanders to focus their efforts on destroying the fort's artillery—especially on the land front where the army might attack.[15]

The ironclad division engaged the fort until that evening, receiving in return the brunt of the fort's amazingly accurate fire in what Admiral Porter described as "quite a spirited engagement." The *Canonicus* was struck thirty-six times, the *New Ironsides* took twenty-five hits, and the *Saugus* eleven direct shots. Despite the Confederate's excellent shooting, the solid shot merely dented iron plates and broke some bolts, but inflicted no serious damage upon the embattled monitors. The greatest harm was caused by a 15-inch gun that burst on board the *Saugus,* severely wounding Seaman James Casey. The *Mahopac* also lost a 15-inch gun that burst on its second discharge. As a result of the ineffective Southern fire, the ironclads were able to maintain their positions off the northeast bastion throughout the day, hurling about 100 shots each at the earthen fort. "We aimed almost wholly at their guns, watching the effect of each shot, and waiting for the smoke to clear before firing another," reported Cmdr. Enoch G. Parrott of the *Monadnock.*[16]

Quartermaster Daniel D. Stevens was assigned the hazardous duty of watching the effects of the *Canonicus'* shots—from outside the vessel. He was also stationed on deck to take regular soundings so the monitor would not run aground. Confederate artillery projectiles roared and whizzed overhead as Stevens peeked from his hideaway behind the monitor's turret. The Confederate fire was both lively and accurate, and twice shot away the *Canonicus'* flag. Both times Quartermaster Stevens replaced it by climbing the flagstaff amid the enemy's screaming cannonballs, much as his Confederate counterpart, Pvt. Christopher C. Bland, had done on the Mound Battery during First Fort Fisher. Daniel D. Stevens was later awarded the Medal of Honor for his bravery under enemy fire.[17]

The Confederates concentrated their fire on the ironclads because they alone bombarded the fort for most of the 13th of January. By mid-afternoon, however, the successful landing of Terry's corps enabled the wooden gunboats to join the ironclads shelling Fort Fisher. The *Colorado* guided the vessels of Lines One and Two into position, generally the same stations they had occupied in the December attack, and by 4:40 p.m. another heavy bombardment was underway. Armed with a total of 396 cannon, this time around the warships (including the ironclads) delivered a steady, sometimes rapid, and much more accurate fire against the fort. Meanwhile, the vessels of the Third Division and the reserves, with an additional 198 guns, were kept outside. An eyewitness estimated that the number of shots fired while the "great bombardment" lasted could not have been less than four per second, with broadside

John S. Maxwell, sailor on board the *USS Advance*, from a previously unpublished image.

Courtesy of
Mr. & Mrs. Walter H. Lipke

after broadside unleashed without pause, punctuated by the deep bass reports of the ironclads' 15-inch guns. The intense shelling continued until 6:10 p.m. The afternoon sky was filled with so many projectiles, remarked B. F. Sands of the *Gettysburg*, that it seemed to be raining shells. A war correspondent who watched the bombardment from the deck from the hospital tender *Blackstone* agreed, remarking that "the continuous flash and roar from single guns and whole broadsides, with the shrieking and bursting of missiles, was more like the incessant roll of the loudest thunder than anything else." Another eyewitness likened the sound of the massive bombardment to the endless roar of Niagara Falls. "The fleet kept up a terrible shelling," observed John S. Maxwell, a sailor on board the *Advance*. "I don't see how the rebs stood it."[18]

The fact is, they did not stand it very well. The tremendous hail of iron projectiles crashing on the fort soon drove the Confederate defenders into their underground bombproofs. "It was the most terrible storm of iron and lead that I have ever seen during this war, [with] shells exploding so fast that it would seem to be one roaring sound," exclaimed an artilleryman. "The bombardment was too terrible to describe," another soldier observed, "it was a rain of shot and shell over us." "[We] were knocked down with sand bags [and] nearly buried in sand several times," complained Seaman Robert Watson of the C. S. Navy, who was serving on detached duty inside the fort. "Whenever [a shell] would strike near us in the sand it would throw the sand over us by the cart load."[19]

Within twenty minutes of the opening of the bombardment artillery projectiles severed the fort's telegraph line to Sugar Loaf as well as the "submarine cable" to Battery Lamb at Reeves Point, situated on the west side of the Cape Fear River. Thick smoke and swirling dust and sand prevented signal flags from being seen at Battery Lamb, compelling signal corps operators to sail to Smithville to communicate by telegraph with headquarters in Wilmington and at Sugar Loaf. The Fort Fisher garrison suffered most of all. Incoming navy shells began landing with pinpoint accuracy in the gun chambers, wounding whole detachments of gunners with a single blast. Nevertheless, the Confederate cannoneers tried to remain at their posts and return the fire of the warships. "The fort kept up as steady a fire as possible," asserted one gunner. "Our men behaved nobly and braved the hot waves of fire and smoke and deadly showers of cast iron."

Before long the fierce shelling had killed one artilleryman and a black servant, wounded forty-one others, and drove most of the balance of the garrison into the bombproofs.[20]

In the midst of the violent artillery duel, desperately needed reinforcements arrived at Fort Fisher. Six hundred and forty artillerymen, by way of the fortifications in the lower Cape Fear estuary, streamed into the besieged bastion, coming ashore at Battery Buchanan, together with another sixty sailors and marines. Even with these reinforcements, Colonel Lamb now had but 1,500 men to defend the mile of earthworks that composed Fort Fisher.

Late in the afternoon General Whiting and his staff also appeared, walking up from Battery Buchanan through the storm of shells that peppered the open terrain behind the walls. Lamb greeted his mentor with an offer to turn over command of Fort Fisher's defense. Whiting declined, stating that he had come as he had in the first battle, in a strictly advisory capacity. The deposed district commander also entered Fort Fisher bearing a dire message. "Lamb, my boy," Whiting sighed, "I have come to share your fate. You and your garrison are to be sacrificed."

Stunned by Whiting's pessimistic prediction, Lamb expressed the optimistic opinion that they would surely defeat the enemy again. Whiting's news, however, was less than encouraging. The return of the Federal fleet had caught Bragg off guard and he was showing signs of panic. Whiting claimed that when he left Wilmington at 1:00 p.m., Bragg was transferring government stores out of town and exploring a line of retreat. Lamb was dumbfounded. He and Whiting had harbored serious doubts about Bragg's ability and even his willingness to defend Wilmington—especially given his questionable conduct in the December battle, when he refused to assault the Union troops stranded on the beach and retain a brigade of infantrymen at Sugar Loaf in case the Federals returned. Now, those doubts gave way to grave concerns about Fort Fisher's fate. With enemy troops pouring ashore, Bragg and Hoke were doing nothing to stop them.[21]

By 3:00 p.m. on January 13, all of the Federal foot soldiers had landed on Federal Point virtually unopposed. General Terry could not have imagined a more satisfactory landing operation. Reportedly, Terry's only casualty thus far was Pvt. Charles A. Norton of Company K, 7th New Hampshire Infantry, who accidentally shot himself through the right hand while disembarking from a transport early that morning. Even so, Confederate prisoners captured during the day's skirmishing at Myrtle Sound claimed that Hoke's veteran division was entrenched at Sugar Loaf, and not battling William T. Sherman in Georgia, as intelligence sources had reported. The 66th North Carolina's Asa King was among the captives personally interrogated by General Terry. King and a number of his comrades had been captured by skirmishers from Abbott's brigade. The North Carolinian, who was furious that Hoke had not launched an attack against the enemy, refused to cooperate with his captors. His stoney silence elicited a surprising response from the commanding Union general. "Johnnie, I admire a man true to his country," said a respectful Terry.[22]

With his 9,600 men now massed on shore, Terry felt more confident of securing a position from which to operate against Fort Fisher. His first order of business was to construct a defensive line across Federal Point to protect the rear of the force that would advance on the fort. After studying maps of the area, Terry planned to anchor his army's right flank on the south end of Myrtle Sound. By commanding the headwaters of the sound and the adjacent beach, Terry believed supplies and reinforcements, if needed, could be landed more safely.[23]

Shortly before 5:00 p.m., Terry marched southward with Charles Paine's and Adelbert Ames' divisions. Terry left Abbott's brigade entrenched in the area where the troops had come ashore to protect the so-called "pyramid of hardtack" and other supplies, and to give the impression that the Federals remained at their beachhead. Terry instructed Colonel Abbott to burn numerous bonfires throughout the night to deceive the Confederates into thinking all of the Union troops were encamped along the shoreline.[24]

When he reached the head of Myrtle Sound, Terry turned most of his brigades westward to march toward the Cape Fear River. General N. Martin Curtis' brigade was held on the beach, while General Paine's two brigades of U. S. Colored Troops, followed by Galusha Pennypacker's and Louis Bell's brigades, struggled through the darkness and a mile of thick woods and swamps before the vanguard emerged on the bank of the Cape Fear

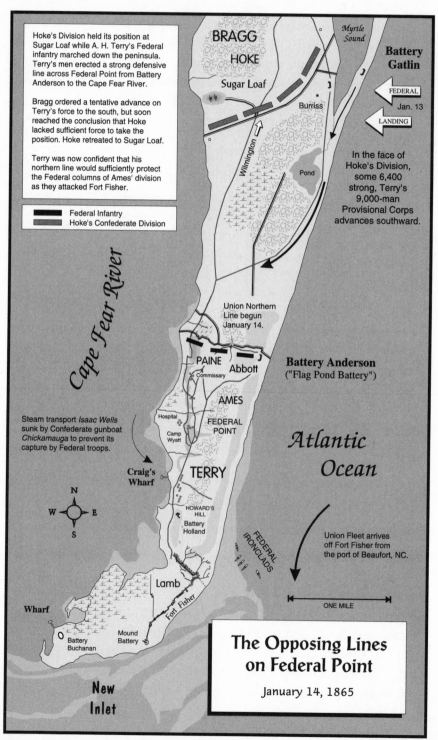

Hoke's Division held its position at Sugar Loaf while A. H. Terry's Federal infantry marched down the peninsula. Terry's men erected a strong defensive line across Federal Point from Battery Anderson to the Cape Fear River.

Bragg ordered a tentative advance on Terry's force to the south, but soon reached the conclusion that Hoke lacked sufficient force to take the position. Hoke retreated to Sugar Loaf.

Terry was now confident that his northern line would sufficiently protect the Federal columns of Ames' division as they attacked Fort Fisher.

■■■ Federal Infantry
■■■ Hoke's Confederate Division

BRAGG
HOKE
Sugar Loaf

Myrtle Sound

Battery Gatlin

Burriss

FEDERAL
LANDING

Jan. 13

In the face of Hoke's Division, some 6,400 strong, Terry's 9,000-man Provisional Corps advances southward.

Wilmington

Pond

Cape Fear River

Union Northern Line begun January 14.

PAINE Abbott
Commissary

AMES

Hospital

FEDERAL POINT

Camp Wyatt

Steam transport *Isaac Wells* sunk by Confederate gunboat *Chickamauga* to prevent its capture by Federal troops.

Craig's Wharf

TERRY

Battery Anderson
("Flag Pond Battery")

Atlantic Ocean

N
W — E
S

HOWARD'S HILL
Battery Holland

FEDERAL IRONCLADS

Union Fleet arrives off Fort Fisher from the port of Beaufort, NC.

Wharf

Lamb

Fort Fisher

ONE MILE

O
Battery Buchanan

Mound Battery

New Inlet

The Opposing Lines on Federal Point

January 14, 1865

Mark A. Moore

River about 9:00 p.m. Terry was not pleased with what he discovered. Despite what his maps indicated, an inspection of the area quickly determined it to be too swampy for constructing sufficient earthworks and too wide to be adequately defended. Moreover, the southern end of the sound was too shallow to prevent an enemy force from crossing to the beach and attempting to turn Terry's right flank. These circumstances prompted Terry to seek out higher ground further to the south, where Federal Point was narrower. After an intense search during the night of January 13 and into the early hours of the following morning, Terry selected the area west of Battery Anderson for his defensive line. The position was two miles north of Fort Fisher.[25]

By 2:00 a.m. Terry's men were erecting breastworks, using 800 shovels brought ashore for the job. They passed the tools back and forth for hours while the men "labored most vigourously," recalled one participant. Digging in the sand was comparatively easy work, made even easier by the lack of protest from enemy rifle-muskets. In just six hours the soldiers had dug a line trench, partially covered with abatis (sharpened stakes), three-quarters of a mile long from the ocean to the river. "By 1864, picks and shovels were as much a part of our. . .equipment as were muskets, and though we never liked them," admitted a soldier, "we had become experts in their use." Although the defenses—which incorporated Battery Anderson—were later improved, strengthened and expanded, by 8:00 a.m. on January 14—just twenty-four hours after coming ashore—Terry's corps had managed to establish a crude but formidable line of works on Federal Point. General Paine's two brigades were deployed to man the earthworks, while Terry rested Ames' division before moving toward Fort Fisher.[26]

While Terry's men moved sand, Lamb and Whiting prepared for the infantry attack they believed would be launched that night (January 13). Refusing to give up on Bragg, Whiting sent repeated messages via Smithville urging the general to oppose the Federals' advance on Fort Fisher. Whiting noted that the fort's garrison was too weak to withstand a determined assault, and that much-needed relief troops were slow coming in. "The enemy have landed in large force," Whiting informed Bragg. "You must attack them at once." When Bragg's assault did not materialize, Whiting reiterated his plea to the department commander: "They will assault me tonight. . .You must attack at once." By 8:00 p.m. Whiting was frantic. "Enemy are on the beach where they have been all day," the general exclaimed. "Why are they not attacked?" The artillerymen and officers at Fort Fisher passed a cold and sleepless night, keeping a constant vigil on the fort's battlements. In an attempt to dissuade the Federals from attacking, Confederate gunners fired rounds of canister up the beach every quarter hour.[27]

It would have shocked Chase Whiting to learn that Braxton Bragg did not share his concern about an imminent Union assault on Fort Fisher. Nor did the commanding general intend to attack the Federals massing on the beach. After reaching Sugar Loaf late on the afternoon of January 13, Bragg approved Hoke's disposition of the veterans and reserves along the Sugar Loaf line, and the deployment of the 2nd South Carolina Cavalry between the entrenched camp and Fort Fisher. There was nothing else to do but watch and wait, thought Bragg, for the enemy was still on the beach. "The command could not have been divided with any safety and to have placed it between the enemy and Fort Fisher would have enabled them to besiege our intrenched camp, and securely confine our entire force on the southern end of the peninsula," Bragg maintained. Both he and Hoke were depending on Colonel Lipscomb's cavalry to keep an eye on the Federals and to inform them if and when they advanced toward Fort Fisher.[28]

Despite Whiting fears, Bragg was convinced that the numerous swamps and heavy underbrush between Sugar Loaf and Fort Fisher would prevent the Federals from maneuvering into position to attack the fort that night. Bragg planned to stay close by the enemy, but to attack only if he "moved from under his shipping." In truth, given the warships' range of fire, the only way the Union army could have "moved from under his shipping" was if it transferred to the west side of the Cape Fear River—an unlikely scenario. So long as they remained on Federal Point, Union troops were covered by the gunboats. Bragg and Hoke overlooked or ignored that important fact and remained at Sugar Loaf all night "under the heavy shelling of the enemy's fleet."[29]

Bragg and Hoke rode out from camp early Saturday morning, January 14, to reconnoiter in the direction of Fort Fisher. The former scouted toward the beach while the latter rode southward along the river road. No word from the 2nd South Carolina Cavalry had come in during the night, leading Bragg to assume the Federals were still encamped within their beachhead. As expected, the department commander found the enemy in "strong force" at the landing site, but was shocked to learn from Hoke shortly before noon that Union troops were also entrenched on the bank of the Cape Fear River more than two miles southwest of where they had come ashore. Hoke and his party had been fired upon as they unwittingly approached the enemy's new position. Colonel Lipscomb's cavalrymen had failed to detect or report the enemy's nocturnal operation, apparently having withdrawn from their assigned posts.

The discovery seemed to spur Bragg to action. He considered the breaking of the Union line as "the highest importance," and ordered Hoke to dislodge the Federals at once, "if practicable." Hoke promptly formed his division into line of battle and advanced southward from Sugar Loaf. A closer inspection, however, showed the Federals were more strongly entrenched across the breadth of Federal Point than Hoke had at first determined. The division commander and his brigadiers quickly concluded that their soldiers were "unequal to the task" of overrunning the enemy's new position. Bragg went forward with his subordinates for a further examination and concurred with their assessment. By Bragg's estimate the Federals outnumbered Hoke's Division two-to-one (in truth the odds were three-to-two), and were well protected by their breastworks and the tremendous firepower of the U. S. Navy positioned just off shore.30

The former commander of the Army of Tennessee sat squarely on the horns of a serious dilemma. Should he attack or remain on the defensive? If an assault by Hoke failed, the way to Wilmington—and, indeed, all of North Carolina—would be open. If, on the other hand, he held the defensive, would Fort Fisher be captured? Having failed to capture the fort in December, Bragg was confident the Federals would again fail in their attempt if the fort was, as he later described it, stoutly defended by a "vigilant garrison." If the enemy could be held in check, the first change in the weather would disperse their fleet, leaving the Union army unsupported, cut off from its supplies, and in a "precarious position." It did not take long for Bragg to make a final decision.

Hoke's Division was withdrawn to Sugar Loaf, where it dug in and strengthened the position. That night, Bragg telegraphed General Lee in Richmond, reporting that the Federals had extended their line across Federal Point. After making a thorough examination of the enemy's strong defenses, he informed Lee, Hoke had decided not to attack. "[Hoke] considers it too hazardous to assault with such an inferior force," Bragg explained. The implication of the message was clear: Bragg was placing the responsibility for the decision not to assault the Federals squarely on Hoke's shoulders. The telegram also revealed Bragg's lack of faith in both in himself and Hoke's command.[31]

Captain Adrian Terry boasted that his brother, Gen. Alfred H. Terry (on whose staff Adrian served as assistant adjutant general), had "completely out-generaled" Bragg with both his night march and by establishing a defensive line across Federal Point. Terry's maneuver cut land-based communications between Sugar Loaf and Fort Fisher, thereby making the fort far less tenable. Throughout the morning of January 14, Terry's infantrymen-turned-excavators strengthened the breastworks they had constructed during the night, packing additional sand and emplacing abatis in front of the trenches. They also dug a series of "gopher holes," as the men referred to rifle pits, for pickets in front of the main line. Light artillery was also brought ashore and mounted behind the earthworks, making them even more impregnable. By noon the defenses were so impressive that Terry believed he could repel an attacking enemy force double his own number. With the situation well in hand, the general allowed his men to relax.[32]

Terry, however, allowed himself little time for rest. First he had to resolve the potentially demoralizing conflict between two of his subordinate officers—Generals Ames and Curtis. As his troops prepared for the impending battle, an angry Adelbert Ames approached Terry with his grievances concerning N. Martin Curtis. Terry was not pleased with what he heard. Ames stated that Curtis had ignored military protocol in communicating directly with Generals Butler and Weitzel during the December expedition, and had purposely sailed without him from Hampton Roads when the army flotilla had embarked on the second expedition. In short, Ames neither trusted nor respected Curtis. Terry, distressed by the extent of Ames' rancor, surprised his division commander by relieving him of all official duties relating to Curtis. Ames had hoped Terry would take some disciplinary action against Curtis, but did not expect Terry to relieve Curtis from his supervision. Later that morning, Terry instructed Curtis to report directly to him. Terry's first direct order to Curtis was for him to support a reconnaissance mission with his brigade. Although he had not slept for thirty-two hours, Terry knew that time was of the essence, and thus insisted on examining Fort Fisher that afternoon. Curtis' brigade advanced southward about 2:00 p.m. Leaving Ames in charge of the northern line, Terry and Lt. Col. Cyrus B. Comstock, followed Curtis soon thereafter.[33]

Chase Whiting was just returning to Fort Fisher when Curtis' brigade approached it late on the afternoon of January 14. Whiting had left the bastion to sail to Smithville earlier that morning to telegraph General Bragg at Sugar Loaf. When he arrived at Smithville, Whiting was surprised (and disappointed) to learn that Bragg's orders had changed. He was now requesting General Hébert to send reinforcements—that earlier had been sent to Fort Fisher—to the Sugar Loaf position by way of Gander Hall. Lamb and Whiting desperately needed these additional troops at Fort Fisher, and both officers believed they had Bragg's assurance that reinforcements would be sent. They were indeed fortunate the under strength fort had not been attacked the night before. While Hébert had dispatched a contingent of artillerymen to Fort Fisher during the night, no regular troops from Hoke's Division had yet arrived. "I must have a regiment to do duty," Whiting implored Bragg. "Men that fought their guns as mine did yesterday and will have to do to-day require some rest at night. . .Hoke promised me a regiment." Bragg replied that 1,000 veterans would reinforce Fort Fisher that night, but before that could take place, the companies that Hébert had earlier sent to the fort should be forwarded to Sugar Loaf.[34]

Bragg's instructions made no sense to Whiting. Why remove essential troops from the threatened point? he wondered. Fort Fisher was the Federals' target, not Sugar Loaf. Whiting felt compelled to explain the enemy's plans to Bragg. "The game of the enemy is very plain to me," lectured Whiting. "They are now furiously bombarding my land front; they will continue to do that, in order, if possible, to silence my guns until they are satisfied that their land force has securely established itself across the neck on the river." Whiting continued his explanation of the likely course of events, as he foresaw them unfolding:

> then Porter will attempt to force a passage by [the batteries] to cooperate with the force that takes the riverbank. I have received dispatches from you stating that the enemy had extended to the river-bank. This they never should have been allowed to do; and if they are permitted to remain there the reduction of Fort Fisher is but a question of time. This has been notified heretofore frequently both to you and to the Department. I will hold this place till the last extremities; but unless you drive that land force from its position I cannot answer for the security of this harbor. The fire has been and continues to be heavy, surpassing not so much in its volume as in its extraordinary condition even the fire of Christmas.[35]

Bragg tried to calm Whiting's anxiety by reassuring him that reinforcements from both Hébert and Hoke would render Fort Fisher impregnable against assault. Moreover, should the enemy advance on the fort, Bragg would attack his rear. Despite his superior's encouraging tone, Whiting was less than confident that Bragg would come to his support.[36]

The Union fleet remained silent until mid-morning on January 14, another bright and balmy winter day. The monitors and the *New Ironsides* had maintained a rotation fire every ten minutes during the night, but had discontinued their intermittent shelling before sunrise. Until 10:40 a.m. the ironclads lay quiet under the guns of the fort, resting and waiting for the other warships to return to their battle stations. Admiral Porter instructed the small wooden ships of Line One, which were posted nearest the land face, to support the ironclads' efforts to destroy the cannon on that front. The gunboats fired slowly and deliberately in their effort to weaken that side of the fort. "I could see that our fire had damaged some of their guns," the admiral later reported, "and I determined before the army went to the assault there should be no guns (within our reach) to arrest their progress." For more than seven hours the ships pounded Fort Fisher with a fury of metal projectiles, "blacksmiths' hops" one soldier called them. "The shower of shell. . .was terrible in the extreme," recalled one Confederate soldier on the receiving end of the artillery barrage. "One could no longer hear anything but one continuous roar that seemed louder than thunder."[37]

The horrific cannonade produced severe damage and numerous casualties inside the fort. In the December battle the fire of the fleet had been diffused, with at least one third of the missiles falling in the river beyond Fisher. When the gunboats finally found their range in the January attack, the results were vastly different. By the end of the second day's naval bombardment Lamb had lost all but three or four of his land face guns and at least 200 men killed and wounded, about thirteen percent of the garrison. The shelling was so intense that the fort's defenders found it virtually impossible to man their guns. The ironclads continued to "bowl their 11-inch and 15-inch shells along the parapet" after nightfall, making it difficult for the Confederates to repair damage, bury their dead or even cook meals outside without suffering additional casualties. The garrison was being worn down by sleeplessness, hunger and the emotional strain brought on by the incessant rumble and roar of artillery and exploding shells. To make matters worse, the Confederates lost a valuable shipload of supplies destined for Lamb's besieged garrison.[38]

On the afternoon of January 14, the steam transport *Issac Wells*, loaded with ammunition and cornmeal, approached Craig's Landing a mile north of Fort Fisher. Unbeknownst to the vessel's captain, soldiers from Curtis' brigade now occupied the area. Colonel Lamb, however, was aware of their presence. He had spotted the Federals as they passed his house, pushing his sentinels into the fort as they advanced. Lamb ordered his artillerymen to open fire on the approaching Union column, but the decision proved costly to the Southerners. Within a short time his cannoneers drew the wrath of the Union gunboats, which smothered Lamb's artillery crews with exploding shells, wounding several. Running out of options to save the transport, Lamb fired an artillery projectile across the bow of the *Issac Wells* in what proved to be a vain attempt to warn her crew of the impending disaster. Unable to grasp the meaning of Southern iron whizzing across her bow, the *Issac Wells* sailed obliviously on—right into the hands of Curtis' troops waiting on the river bank. The crew of the Confederate gunboat *Chickamauga*, which was stationed on the river and observed the "stupid surrender," had the presence of mind to send an iron bolt into the *Issac*

Wells' hull and sink her. If she wasn't going to sail under the Confederate banner, she was certain to be of no use to the enemy.

Lamb was livid. He could not fathom why the *Issac Wells* had not advanced to the safety of Battery Buchanan unless General Bragg had instructed the captain to put in at Craig's Landing—or had failed to warn him otherwise. Either way, the blunder deprived Fort Fisher's beleaguered garrison of much-needed supplies, and in Lamb's mind clearly reflected Bragg's ignorance of, or indifference to, what was happening on the southern end of Federal Point. Bragg could easily have gone by steamer from Sugar Loaf to Battery Lamb on Reeves Point where, with a pair of field glasses, he could have observed the enemy's every move in front of Fort Fisher. Yet thirty hours after the Federals had come ashore and subsequently taken possession of Craig's Landing, Bragg sent a steamer loaded with valuable provisions directly into enemy territory. To William Lamb it was yet another in a growing string of foreboding signs.[39]

Unlike Braxton Bragg, Alfred Terry was fully aware of what was going on at Fort Fisher. Supported by Curtis' brigade, Terry, Cyrus Comstock, and two of Terry's staff officers had advanced to Battery Holland, 900 yards north of Fort Fisher, by about 4:00 p.m. Curtis threw out skirmishers who then pressed even closer to the fort. Their movement was intended to clear the area of Confederate troops between the northern line and Fort Fisher, see what effect the naval bombardment was having on the mammoth earthen stronghold, and determine whether an infantry assault against the fort was feasible. It was Curtis' men who had enjoyed the extraordinarily good fortune of capturing the *Issac Wells*. The seizure of the supply ship prompted Terry to consider the possibility of converting her into a gunboat. He even went so far as to signal Admiral Porter to request cannon to mount on the captured steamer, but the unexpected shot from the *Chickamauga* sank her before Porter's reply was received. Terry wished he had artillery to rid himself of the bothersome Southern gunboat, which had been annoying his reconnaissance party since it had left the relative safety of the entrenched northern line. Exploding shells from the *Chickamauga* had wounded six

New York soldiers, including Capt. James H. Reeve of Company H, 3rd New York Infantry, whose right leg was blown off just below the knee.[40]

Despite the Confederates' harassing artillery fire and his mounting casualties, Terry was determined to get a good look at his objective. He studied the work for a considerable time from the summit of Battery Holland before advancing with Cyrus Comstock to within 400 yards of Shepherd's Battery, hiding in the marsh grass and bulrush along the river's edge. Although the reconnaissance was cut short by the *Chickamauga*, which had spotted the enemy officers and showered them with shells, Terry concluded that conditions appeared favorable for an infantry assault. From what he could determine, the naval bombardment had shattered the palisade, dismounted most of the land face artillery, and prevented the Confederates from manning their guns in force.[41]

Terry and Comstock withdrew to Battery Holland and conferred with Curtis. "Do you still believe the fort can be carried by an assault with such force as I can spare from the line established last night?" Terry asked the New Yorker. Curtis replied that he thought his brigade, bolstered by Ames' remaining two brigades, could capture the fort if troop dispositions were "properly made" and the navy vigorously supported the army's efforts. "In case an assault is ordered you will make it," Terry informed Curtis. "I will see Admiral Porter this evening and we will determine what course to pursue."[42]

Leaving Curtis and his brigade at the front, Terry and Comstock returned to headquarters near Battery Anderson on the northern line. That evening Terry called his executive officers together to discuss the proposed ground assault against the fort. Most of his subordinates were not of like mind and many expressed disapproval of the plan. The massive stronghold, they contended, could not be taken by frontal assault. Instead, they recommended a siege operation. Cyrus Comstock vigorously disagreed and proceeded to explain some of the difficulties endemic to seacoast siege operations. Getting the heavy artillery and equipment on shore was not going to be easy, Comstock pointed out. Up to that time, only three 30-pounder Parrott rifles of Gen. Henry L. Abbot's siege train had been landed. It was a slow and dangerous process, even with a smooth sea. Each gun had to be slung and hoisted overboard from the ships and then carefully lowered and placed on a launch, which could carry only one gun per trip. The boat then had to be pulled along a warp to the edge of the surf, and the gun rolled overboard into the ocean. The massive rifle-cannon were then literally dragged onto the beach by a team of 200 men pulling on ropes. Gun carriages were landed the same way. If the ocean became rougher, or if the enemy attacked, Comstock explained, the operation would have to be halted. Even if engineers succeeded in getting all the guns and equipment ashore and establishing a siege line, Fort Fisher would be still be difficult to capture so long as the Confederates controlled the Cape Fear River, by which they could be reinforced and resupplied. Terry weighed the opinions of his subordinates and sided with Comstock. A ground attack was decided upon, and Ames' division would deliver the punch.[43]

While the monitors maintained their incessant barrage of Fort Fisher on the evening of January 14, Terry, accompanied by Comstock, rowed out to meet with Admiral Porter on board the *Malvern* to discuss the plan of battle. Inside the admiral's cabin Terry informed the veteran seaman of the telling effects his massive two-day bombardment was having on Fisher. Realizing that the odds would never be better, the general proposed an infantry attack the following day. The troops were well rested and dried out after the soggy landing operation, Terry insisted, and prepared to do battle. An assault delivered in the late afternoon would enable the navy to spend most of the day further damaging the palisade, disabling the fort's remaining armament, and fatiguing the enemy's already exhausted garrison. The attack should be launched early enough, however, to allow the army time to capture the bastion during daylight, or give the commanders sufficient time to familiarize themselves with the fort's interior to continue operations after nightfall. There was an additional consideration. The assault would have to be carefully timed so that the Confederates would have as little opportunity as possible to bring up Hoke's Division to assault the Federal northern line or to reinforce the fort via the Cape Fear River.[44]

An enthusiastic Admiral Porter wholeheartedly endorsed Terry's battle plan. While General Grant had originally urged Porter to push his gunboats past the sea face batteries and into the harbor, the admiral reiterated his concern to Terry that New Inlet was too narrow and shallow to navigate under enemy artillery fire. Nevertheless, Porter wanted what he described as a "share in the assault," and determined to detach a sizable contingent of sailors and marines to help capture the fort. Armed with revolvers and "well-sharpened" cutlasses, they would "board the fort" in a seaman-like manner, as if boarding an enemy vessel. Porter had already mentioned the idea to Terry when they met in Beaufort, and, in his usual manner, the admiral had bragged to Secretary Welles that if the army failed again, the navy would "show the soldiers how to do it. I can do anything with. . .my own good officers and men," Porter boasted, "and you need not be surprised to hear that the webfooters have gone into the forts."[45]

Despite what General Terry may have thought of Porter's unorthodox strategy, he remained silent on the issue. Terry remembered Grant's insistence that there be a "unity of action" between he and Porter, and that he was to "rely on the admiral's judgment and his nerve to undertake what he proposes." At the very least, the commanders agreed that at the appropriate time, Terry would signal Porter to change his gunboats' direction of fire from Fort Fisher's land face to the sea face. Once the fire had been redirected, the army would advance against the western half of the land front while the naval column attacked the northeast bastion, where the land and sea faces intersected. There was, however, miscommunication about the exact time the ground assault should begin. Terry thought they had agreed on 3:00 p.m., while Porter believed the attack was to take place an hour earlier. As it turned out, this confusion would prove costly.[46]

Amid the booms of the ironclads' big guns Terry and Comstock departed the *Malvern* and returned to their camp on shore. Terry spent the rest of the night working out details of the planned assault, discussing them with no one except Comstock and his brother, Adrian Terry. Despite their commander's tight-lipped reticence, Terry's veterans knew an attack was inevitable. "We had been pretty certain all along that there was bloody work ahead of us," explained a Union infantryman. "I knew that desperate work was in store, [and] that many brave boys must fall," lamented Lt. Frank H. Lay of the 117th New York. The night was clear and bitterly cold—too cold for the soldiers to get much sleep. Orders restricted them from building camp fires because the *Chickamauga* was still within firing range, and occasionally lobbed a shell among the resting troops. So the men shivered in the darkness, mostly in silence, for each one knew that it might well be his last night. "A silence such as I never before witnessed seemed to rest on all, but it was not fear," acknowledged Lieutenant Lay. "Men are thinking of their loved ones far away."[47]

Many of General Curtis' men had little time to think about their families at home. Instead, they were kept busy digging in the Carolina sand. After dark Curtis deployed a fatigue party to construct four successive lines of rifle pits to within 175 yards of the fort's walls, with the distance between the lines decreasing as they neared the fort. The breastworks would allow soldiers to hopscotch their way toward the fort, taking shelter from Confederate artillery and sharpshooters before launching their final attack against the fort's shell-pocked but still imposing walls. Curtis placed forty sharpshooters in the largest entrenchment close to the fort's western salient, with instructions to pick off any Confederates who might appear on the ramparts. If and when an attack was made against the fort, the marksmen were to rejoin their command for the main battle.[48]

In the meantime, his men kept digging.

Colonel Lamb, who proved to be as indefatigable as General Terry, knew Curtis' soldiers were still in his front. He had watched the Federals mass at Battery Holland until it was too dark to see them. Concerned about their presence so near the fort, the audacious Lamb determined to attack them before they could mount their own assault. The colonel calculated that his garrison of 1,300 effectives and Hoke's Division of more than 6,400—plus Hoke's reserves—almost matched the enemy in numbers. Given the Confederates' superior knowledge of the lay of the land, a determined night assault might succeed in capturing or driving off the landed enemy, largely because the Federal navy could not adequately support them. General Whiting agreed, and sent a telegram with the proposal to General Bragg at Sugar Loaf.

As he awaited the department commander's reply, Lamb took Capt. Daniel Patterson's Company H, 36th North Carolina Regiment, outside the fort about 9:00 p.m. to determine the enemy's position and strength. The Tarheels clashed with Curtis' pickets, with both sides taking a few casualties and prisoners. Nine other companies waited just inside the fort walls for Lamb's command to attack Curtis' brigade. Lamb planned to launch his assault as soon as he heard Bragg's gunfire to the north.

The colonel and his eager soldiers waited in vain. Bragg did not attack or acknowledge Whiting's proposal, apparently deciding instead that the Federals were too strongly entrenched and a night attack over difficult terrain would prove too daunting. Bragg's silence did not bode well for the defenders of Fort Fisher. Moments before daylight, a thoroughly disgusted Colonel Lamb withdrew his skirmishers into the fort.[49]

Indeed Whiting must be right, Lamb pondered. He and his garrison were going to be sacrificed.

Sunday, January 15, dawned bright and chilly. The Federal ironclads—which had again rotated a continuous cannonade during the

Fort Fisher's northeast bastion under attack, January 15, 1865. *Illustrated London News*

night—increased their fire on the land face after sunrise. Porter signaled the remainder of the fleet to join the battle, and by 11:00 a. m. they had dropped their anchors and had begun firing. The gunboats took advantage of a smooth sea and sufficient practice to punish the fort and its beleaguered garrison. "On Sunday, the fire on the fort reached a pitch of fury which no language can describe," exclaimed General Whiting. By noon, every cannon on the land front had been dismounted or destroyed except an 8-inch columbiad at the northeast bastion and another at Shepherd's Battery. The palisade was so splintered that Colonel Lamb deemed it useless for defense. Although Lamb did not know it at the time, the bombardment had also severed the wires from the fort's electric batteries to the torpedoes planted 200 yards in front of the land face. Inside the fort, casualties continued to mount, as the warships dropped shells into the compartments where Lamb's artillerymen were desperately trying to man their remaining cannon, which soon proved to be impossible. Shells were bursting at a rate of about two every second, forcing the Confederates to again seek the safety of their bombproofs. "[The shells] were falling and bursting faster than the ticking of a watch," asserted one eyewitness.[50]

During the height of the bombardment, Lamb and Whiting finally heard from General Bragg. Reinforcements from Brig. Gen. Johnson Hagood's Brigade, which was led by Col. Robert F. Graham while Hagood continued his furlough in South Carolina, appeared inside Fort Fisher. The men had made a mad dash from Battery Buchanan through the storm of exploding shells to reach Lamb's position. Late on the night of January 14, Bragg had dispatched 1,000 South Carolinians from Hagood's Brigade by the steam transports *Sampson*, *Petteway* and *Harlee* from Gander Hall to Battery Buchanan. The *Sampson* reached Battery Buchanan during the early morning hours of January 15, disembarking Capt. D. G. DuBose's 21st South Carolina. In a comedy of errors, however, the vast majority of the South Carolinians, including Colonel Graham, never reached Fort Fisher.

After unloading DuBose's regiment, the *Sampson* was compelled to rescue Graham's other three regiments, which sat stranded on the *Petteway* and *Harlee*. Both ships had grounded near the docks at Gander Hall. The tedious transfer of troops to the *Sampson* occupied the rest of the night, so that it was mid-morning before she returned to Battery Buchanan. By then, Federal warships had resumed their bombardment of Fort Fisher. Gunboats

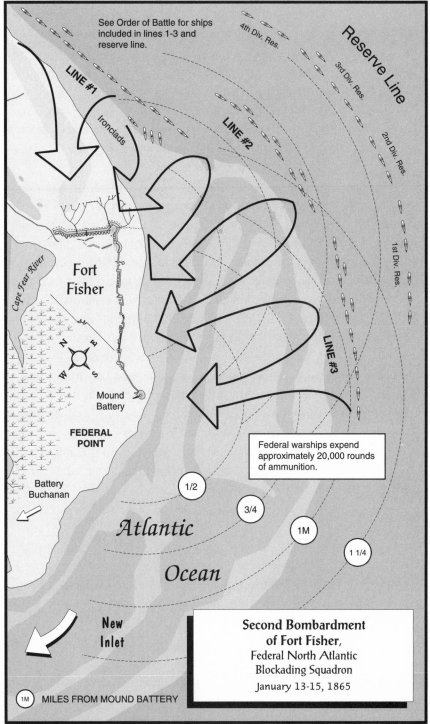

See Order of Battle for ships included in lines 1-3 and reserve line.

Reserve Line

4th Div. Res.

3rd Div. Res.

2nd Div. Res.

1st Div. Res.

LINE #1

Ironclads

LINE #2

LINE #3

Cape Fear River

Fort Fisher

Mound Battery

FEDERAL POINT

Battery Buchanan

Federal warships expend approximately 20,000 rounds of ammunition.

1/2

3/4

1M

1 1/4

Atlantic

Ocean

New Inlet

Second Bombardment of Fort Fisher,
Federal North Atlantic Blockading Squadron
January 13-15, 1865

1M MILES FROM MOUND BATTERY

Mark A. Moore

shelling the fort's lower sea face batteries spotted the *Sampson* across the open sand plain and directed a large part of their fire at her. Only portions of the 25th and 11th South Carolina regiments had been put ashore when the severe fire of the gunboats forced the *Sampson* to retreat to the relative safety of the Cape Fear River. Eventually she put in on the other side of the harbor at Battery Lamb. As the vessel sought safer waters, the South Carolinians who had landed at Battery Buchanan rested for a short while before moving up to the Mound Battery, and then to the main fort. Only 350 of the 1,000 South Carolina soldiers had actually landed.[51]

Regardless of their number, Lamb desperately needed the additional men. After two days of "ceaseless and terrific bombardment," Fort Fisher's garrison had dwindled to less then 1,200 effectives. The pathetically small number of reinforcements sent by Bragg—which increased the garrison to only 1,550 men—infuriated an already maddened Lamb, who cursed Bragg for not delivering the reinforcements sooner and under cover of darkness. "Never was there a more stupid blunder committed by a commanding general," the colonel ranted. "If [Hagood's] fresh brigade had been sent up to this point the night before they could have reached the fort unobserved, could have been protected until needed. . . ." As it was, the South Carolinians had to double-quick a mile across the fire-swept sand plain from Battery Buchanan to the Mound Battery, and then make the three-quarter-mile trek up the line of sea face batteries before reaching Fort Fisher's land front. They arrived shaken, exhausted—and fewer in number—at 2:30 p.m., only a short time before the Union ground forces struck the fort. Lamb herded them into an old commissary bombproof behind the center sally-port to allow them to catch their breath.

About the time South Carolinians reached the main fort, one of Lamb's lookouts yelled: "Colonel, the enemy are about to charge!" With the Federals set to launch their attack, Lamb asked General Whiting to send one last desperate plea to Bragg for help. "The enemy are about to assault; they outnumber us heavily," Whiting informed him. "Fleet have extended down the sea-front outside and are firing very heavily. . .Nearly all land guns disabled. Attack! Attack! It is all I can say and all you can do."[52]

As Whiting wired his last desperate plea to Bragg, the U. S. Navy's shore contingent, which the Confederates could plainly see on the beach, was poised to attack Fort Fisher. A force of 2,261 sailors and marines—volunteers from twenty-nine warships, including Admiral Porter's flagship—had landed about mid-day one and one-half miles north of the fort. They were a diverse group of combatants. For weeks these men had been confined aboard their respective vessels. Not only had they never drilled together; for the most part, they were unacquainted with one another. Many of them viewed the landing as a lark—an adventure that freed them from the confines of their ships, and offered them an opportunity to win fame and glory onshore. Few could have envisioned their ultimate fate before the mammoth walls of Fort Fisher.

Entrusted to command this heterogeneous group of tars and leathernecks was Fleet Capt. K. Randolph Breese, a nineteen-year navy veteran who had served with Admiral Porter throughout the war. Acting on Porter's instructions, Breese split his unique shore command into four divisions (according to the divisions of the fleet), with each unit commanded by that division's senior officer. Lieutenant Commander Charles H. Cushman, of the frigate *Wabash,* was assigned to command the First Division. Cushman's division would have the honor of leading the naval column in the assault on Fort Fisher's northeast bastion. Command of the Second Division belonged to the frigate *Minnesota's* Lt. Cmdr. James Parker, while the Third Division was led by Lt. Cmdr. Thomas O. Selfridge of the *Huron.* Four hundred marines, led by Capt. Lucien L. Dawson of the *Colorado*, formed the Fourth Division. Armed with Sharps & Hankins and Springfield rifles, the marines were designated as sharpshooters and given the responsibility for providing cover fire for the balance of the assaulting naval column.[53]

As the sailors and marines came ashore, Commander Breese dispatched a small contingent of tars to prepare breastworks for the marines as near to the fort as possible. Led by Flag Lt. Samuel W. Preston, the sailors dug three successive lines of trenches. The forward-most line of works scarred the sandy soil only 175 yards shy of Fort Fisher's shattered palisade and adjoined the rifle pits of General Curtis' skirmishers to the west. The sailors came under sporadic artillery and small arms fire from the fort as they labored on their defenses, and several men were wounded. Ensign S. H. Maunder of the *Huron* recalled that a shell burst directly over his work party

A never-before published image of Fleet Captain Kidder Randolph Breese, commander of the Union naval column that stormed Fort Fisher. *Author's Collection*

Lt. Louis Fagan,
U. S. Marine Corps

U. S. Army
Military History Institute

and scalped a sailor "as clean as if done by a Comanche Indian." The hairless sailor headed for the rear. Working on the beach outside Fort Fisher on January 15, 1865, was a risky occupation, as Acting Ensign Joseph Simms of the *Minnesota* attested. "Together with musketry, canister and grape fired by the enemy in front of us, and fragments of bursting shell fired by our ships at the rear and left of us," he later wrote in a classic bit of understatement, "intrenching near the face of Fort Fisher was not a very pleasant job."

As his navy sappers came under enemy fire, Breese sent a company of fifty marines under Lt. Louis E. Fagan to support them. Fagan's command also encountered heavy artillery fire as it advanced toward the front line of works about 11:00 a. m.. The defending fire compelled Fagan to deploy his men into a scattered skirmish line in order to minimize casualties. Even then, the men frequently plunged into the sand to avoid volleys of case balls zinging toward them. Not all of the Federals were quick enough in the act to prevent serious injury—or worse. Privates William Daley and Esek P. Bailey of the *Wabash* were severely wounded, with Daley's wound proving mortal. Fagan's men finally took shelter in Preston's entrenchments after crossing the deadly field of sand. The marines spent the next couple of hours taking pot shots at the Confederate artillerymen in an attempt to provide at least some cover for the entrenching sailors.[55]

As soon as Captain Dawson came ashore, Breese moved him up to occupy the freshly dug breastworks near the fort with the remaining 350 marines of his command. Breese instructed Dawson to keep up a "full fire" until the naval column advanced past his position, and then to join the sailors in the attack on the fort. In the event of a repulse, the marines should resume their position in the trenches to cover the sailors' retreat. Captain Dawson double-quicked his marines to the second line of breastworks about 600 yards from the fort, where he and his men anxiously waited while the sailors completed their work on the advance line.[56]

While the sappers dug and the marines engaged Lamb's gunners in an uneven exchange of lead for iron, the sailors—separated into three divisions of roughly 600 men each—moved down the peninsula to await the army's advance. Indeed, that was to be the naval column's cue to attack. Breese and his officers were laboring under the mistaken impression (caused by Admiral Porter's miscommunication with General Terry) that the assault was set to begin at 2:00 p.m. In anticipation of the impending attack, Breese pushed his large column of men within one-half mile of the fort's walls, far too close to the fort for them to remain there long. Confederate sharpshooters, while still too far away to be effective, fired menacingly at the prone sailors. Moreover, Confederate artillery opened on them with canister from the northeast bastion's surviving columbiad, the guns on the Mound Battery, and the two Napoleon cannon at the center

Capt. Lucien L. Dawson, U. S. Marine Corps commander at Fort Fisher, from a previously unpublished image.

Courtesy of Chris Truitt

sally-port. Armed with only Remington and Whitney revolvers, the Union sailors were too far out of range to return fire. Admiral Porter's own gunboats added to the deadly confusion surrounding the affair. The direction of fire from the Line One warships sent heavy iron shells screaming over the heads of the naval column. Unfortunately, a few projectiles failed to clear the prone tars at all and fell short or exploded prematurely, spraying the closely packed seamen with iron fragments. This was a type of warfare that few of them had experienced, and none were enjoying. The column grew restless as the shot and shells continued to rent the air above them and shake the ground into which they pressed themselves.

Fearing that his force might crumble under the mounting pressure, Commander Breese set out to find someone in the army who could tell him why the attack had been delayed. When he returned with the information that the assault would not begin until 3:00 p.m., Breese allowed his sailors to seek refuge from the incoming projectiles below the beach shelf near the waterline. As time passed the sailors milled about, complaining about the delay and their hunger. Most of them had not eaten since dawn, and many were weary and edgy from lack of nourishment as well as constant exposure to the incessant enemy and friendly fire. "We were getting hungry," admitted Lt. John Bartlett of the *Susquehanna*. "I was anxious to get into the fort to try some rebel provisions."[58]

At 3:00 p.m., Breese advanced his poorly formed divisions to within 600 yards of Fort Fisher. As his men took their positions, Breese sent word to Captain Dawson to move his marines from the trenches to the beach for shelter. Dawson was surprised by the order and asked the messenger, Lt. Benjamin H. Porter, if there was not some mistake. When Porter replied in the negative, Dawson did as he was instructed. By the time his force reached the shoreline, however, the first division of sailors had passed the marines. Although he attempted to keep his command separated from the sailors, Dawson found the task virtually impossible. The beach was simply too narrow to accommodate so many men, and the units were soon inextricably mixed together. The mass of marines and sailors waited under a continual menacing fire with still no sign of the U.S. Army's attack. The sailors were so anxious to attack that Breese began pondering whether he should strike the fort without waiting for the infantry.[59]

The Union army had spent the entire day preparing rigorously for the impending battle. The 15th New York Engineers erected batteries on the river's edge at old Camp Wyatt for Brig. Gen. Abbot's 30-pounder Parrott rifles to keep the *Chickamauga* at bay, while Cyrus Comstock spent the morning strengthening the northern line in anticipation of an attack by Hoke's Division. Manning the earthworks to contest an enemy onslaught were Colonel Abbott's brigade of 1,320 enlisted men and 65 officers, which Terry had finally brought down from its beachhead, and General Paine's 3,149 U. S. Colored Troops and their 160 white officers.

With Paine's and Abbott's brigades manning the defensive line, Penny-packer's and Bell's brigades of Ames' division, about 3,200 officers and foot soldiers, advanced toward Fort Fisher, halting near Craig's Landing about noon. With the exception of the skirmishers, Curtis' thousand-man-brigade, exhausted but ready for action, had maintained its position near Battery Holland since the previous evening. General Terry came down from the northern line about mid-morning to join Curtis, establishing his battle headquarters on top of Battery Holland. From this position the commanding general could communicate by signal flag with the navy and at the same time have a good view of the fort. In accordance with Terry's battle plan, Ames' brigades would attack in echelon, with Curtis' brigade—the 3rd, 112th, 117th, and 142nd New York infantry regiments—leading the charge. Like U. S. Grant, Terry respected Curtis' confidence, audacity and candor. In Curtis, the strong emotional mix had produced a capable and aggressive combat officer. "With your brigade on the parapet I shall feel certain of success," Terry told his subordinate a short time before the assault was scheduled to begin.[60]

In conference with Terry about mid-morning on the 15th, Curtis suggested making the attack with his brigade formed in line of battle, rather than in column of fours. Curtis believed that a two-rank formation would suffer fewer casualties than a dense column during the approach to the fort. Moreover, by using the rifle pits Curtis' men had constructed during the night, the brigades could advance on the fort in relative safety before charging across the open ground. The final rush would be made when the Southerners showed their intention to remain on the parapet to fight it out, and when Terry gave the signal to advance.[61]

After consulting with Cyrus Comstock Terry approved Curtis' plan. The change in deployment was passed along to the remaining general officers during a noon time council of war. Terry had a potentially larger problem than the deployment of his attacking legion: the still-feuding Curtis and Ames. Terry's selection of Curtis' command as the "forlorn hope" irritated Adelbert Ames, who sulked and kept his distance from the commanding general much of the afternoon. Terry, who paid little mind to Ames' petty behavior, was more concerned about Confederate reinforcements he had observed entering Fort Fisher. Terry and Comstock had watched from the summit of Battery Holland as the troops—Hagood's South Carolinians—landed at Battery Buchanan and moved toward the main fort. Though neither officer admitted it at the time, both later confessed they harbored serious reservations about launching an attack.[62]

Reinforcements in the fort or not, the assault was going to be dangerous work for the Union army. The sandy expanse in front of the land face was open for a greater distance than a rifle-musket could shoot. Most of the big seacoast guns on the parapet had been knocked out of action (at least so far as the Federals could judge), but four light artillery pieces swept the land approaches. Lamb had positioned two bronze 12-pounder Napoleons in the demilune at the center sally-port, from which point they could unleash enfilading fire left or right. Two additional pieces, a Napoleon and a 3.2-inch Parrott rifle posted between Shepherd's Battery and the river covered the Wilmington Road. Even if the Federals were able to penetrate the artillery screen, a muddy ditch or slough fronting the western salient blocked their direct approach in that sector. Although a wooden bridge that spanned the bog was left in position, the Confederates had removed the span's planks and left only the stringers. Despite these difficulties, Terry weighed two factors in his favor and decided to concentrate the army's efforts to enter the fort at that point. The first was that the fort's sally-port on the west end of Shepherd's Battery was not gated, but was enclosed by only a chest-high wall of sandbags. Second, a slight rise in the ground north of Shepherd's Battery would enable the brigades to advance closer to the fort comparatively unmolested than if they attacked at the center of the land front.

At 2:00 p.m. Terry began moving his troops into position for the assault. Acting on Terry's orders, Ames deployed sixty sharpshooters from Lt. Col. Samuel M. Zent's 13th Indiana Infantry, Louis Bell's brigade, to support

Curtis' skirmishers of the 142nd New York, who were posted in the forward breastworks within 175 yards of Fort Fisher. Armed with Spencer repeating rifles, these Hoosier crack shots protected Curtis' sappers, who continued to strengthen and expand the front line of rifle pits. Shortly afterward Curtis' remaining regiments advanced from their position at Howard's Hill to within 300 yards of the fort and laid down in the sand. As Curtis' men advanced, Ames supervised the movements of his remaining two brigades, advancing Col. Galusha Pennypacker's Second Brigade to Curtis' former position, and Colonel Bell's Third Brigade to the rear of Pennypacker's new line, maintaining about 200 yards distance between them. The navy eased its fire on that sector to allow the army to advance unscathed.[64]

As the bombardment slackened on the fort's western salient, however, Confederate sharpshooters appeared on the parapet to fire on the approaching Federal troops. The marksmen hit their targets with deadly accuracy. The gunfire was hard for the Federals to endure because they had no place to hide except in the shallow trenches. "We would dig a spell then grab our guns and bang at the rebs a spell, then go to digging again," remarked

A composite view Fort Fisher's land face, taken after the fall of the fort by T. H. O'Sullivan. Union ground forces observed this massive wall, fronted by the palisade, as

Newell Richardson of the 112th New York. Curtis' men used their tin plates and cups, knives, swords, bayonets and hands to dig deeper into the sand, but Confederate bullets continually found them. Private Charles Meeker, a three-year veteran of Company I, 117th New York, was struck in the head and killed instantly. "The number of stricken men, increasing from moment to moment, showed how well the veterans on the ramparts could aim," noted an impressed Union soldier. "Caps and clothing were pierced, swords and scabbards were hit, belts and canteens were cut." To make matters worse, the field artillery inside the fort fired canister and the *Chickamauga* on the river lobbed shells into the exposed Federal positions. "Death was busy in our ranks," reported a survivor.[65]

Three o'clock came and went before the army was in position to attack, and the exposed sailors and marines on the beach grew more anxious as the minutes crawled by. General Terry, however, was unwilling to advance until his troops were properly deployed. Finally, at 3:20 p.m., Ames informed Terry at Battery Holland that all was ready. Terry gave his division commander the go ahead to launch the assault and at the same time signaled

they deployed for their assault against the Confederacy's most powerful seacoast fortification. *Courtesy of Jim Pleasants*

The U.S. Navy's massive bombardment of Fort Fisher on January 13-15, 1865, destroyed or dismantled most of the bastion's seacoast artillery, including this 6.4-inch 32-pounder gun on the land face. The navy's effectiveness allowed U.S. Ground forces to attack Fort Fisher under less threat of being decimated by Confederate cannon fire. *USAMHI*

Admiral Porter to halt his bombardment of the land face batteries. By that time Porter's warships had unleashed most of the 19,682 shells they would fire on the battlements. No fort in history, in the veteran seaman's opinion, was more battered and ripe for the taking than Fort Fisher. At precisely 3:25 p.m., the warships blew their steam whistles in one great "soul stirring" blast. The attack on Fort Fisher was about to begin.[66]

For two and a half days, January 13-15, 1865, the U.S. Navy unleashed 19,682 shot and shell on Fort Fisher in an effort to soften the Confederate defenses for the impending Union ground assault. *Currier & Ives*

Chapter 8

"It was all too much for even demons..."
– *Hermit, a private in the 203rd Pennsylvania Infantry*

SECOND STRIKE

or the better part of an hour after his lookout reported that the enemy was preparing to storm the fort, Colonel Lamb dashed up and down the land face and through the bomb-proofed galleries of his now badly battered fort. Braving the dangerous iron fragments of navy shells bursting around him, Lamb issued last minute instructions to his men prior to the enemy's impending ground assault. Knowing that the naval bombardment would have to be halted in order to enable the Union forces to advance, the youthful colonel deployed sharpshooters in the gun chambers to eliminate officers in the assaulting columns. He also directed battery commanders to rush their men to the parapet as soon as the terrific shelling ended. Lamb ordered his electricians to detonate the line of torpedoes once the assailants were near the fort, hoping that he could kill or capture the enemy's first line while demoralizing the remaining supporting troops. He was on his way back to headquarters at the Pulpit Battery on the sea face when the bombardment ceased and the steam whistles of the great armada announced the commencement of the attack.

Despite being hunkered down deep inside their sand covered bomb-proofs, Lamb's soldiers also heard the concerted shriek of the fleet's whistles. Although exhausted from the effects of the unrelenting fifty-five hour naval cannonade, the Confederates quickly emerged from the shelters, determined to meet the enemy as their commander had requested. Lamb split his eager garrison into two forces. He placed 250 of his artillerymen—converted into riflemen—at the west end of the land face and issued instructions for Johnson Hagood's 350 South Carolinians, still resting in the commissary bunker after their long and dangerous run from Battery Buchanan, to support the Tarheels. This disposition gave Major Reilly, entrusted with command of the land front's west end, 600 men to impede the advance of the Federal army while Lamb and Whiting personally directed the defense of the northeast bastion against the Union navy's shore party. Lamb deployed 300 men on or near the northeast redan and another 200 reserves in the adjoining batteries.[1]

It is unlikely Lamb and Whiting believed that the naval column constituted the main thrust of the enemy's two-pronged attack. They were well aware that the Union army comprised a much stronger and better organized force than the naval group, which had come ashore just that morning. Yet the Confederate commanders also realized that the sailors and marines had to be prevented from overrunning the northeast bastion, for a breach at that point would doom the fort. "The success [of the naval column] would have been fatal," Lamb asserted, "as it would capture the center of my work." Vastly outnumbered, Lamb had too few defenders to fight on two fronts for a protracted period. At the same time he was confident that if his men could quickly defeat the sailors and marines, he could reinforce Reilly in time to repulse the Union army. The battle plan unfolded precisely as Lamb hoped—at first. The 12-pounder Napoleon mounted in the demilune at the center sally-port, the surviving columbiad at the northeast bastion, and the Mound Battery's guns blasted the surging naval force, "dropping [men] rapidly in every direction." It appeared to many Confederates that artillery alone might suffice to blunt the navy's assault.[2]

As Admiral Porter's warships shifted their fire away from Fort Fisher's land face, K. Randolph Breese launched his naval ground assault. Cheering loudly, the sailors and marines sprang to their feet and stormed down the beach toward the fort's northeast bastion. They did not even wait to see if the army was surging forward, which was their cue to advance.[3]

Ensign Robley D. Evans of the frigate *Powhatan* remembered charging with his shipmates through a storm of projectiles so destructive that the sailors pulled their hats down over their eyes to avoid seeing the deadly blue

Fort Fisher's thirty-two foot high northeast bastion attacked by Federal sailors and marines on January 15, 1865. *U. S. Army Military History Institute*

flashes of the Confederates' guns. "[We advanced] under a perfect hail of lead," Evans exclaimed. "Oh, such a fire as [we] were under," added Lt. John Bartlett of the *Susquehanna's* shore party. "Sailors and officers were dropping all around me." Captain Benjamin F. Sands of the *Fort Jackson* observed that the men fell like ten-pins in a bowling alley. One of the first Union sailors to be shot down was Ordinary Seaman James Flanigan, a comrade of Robley Evans. Flanigan fell almost as soon as the column came under fire. Evans stopped to see if his friend was badly hurt, placing his hand on his wounded comrade's shoulder. Flanigan managed a smile for Evans before rolling over, dead. As Evans pushed on down the beach, he remembered Flanigan's premonition that he would be killed in this battle, and his request that his personal affects be sent to his sister in Philadelphia. Evans promised his friend he would do so—if he survived the onslaught.[4]

Stunned by the withering effect of the Confederates' canister fire, the Union sailors and marines dropped en masse on their stomachs about 500 yards from Fort Fisher. As the Confederate gunners reloaded their cannon, most of the tars and leathernecks jumped up and continued their advance. More artillery blasts compelled the Federals to flop down again about 300 yards shy of the fort. Once again their officers rallied them, and once again some of the sailors and marines responded by going forward. Most of them, however, refused to advance further. Demoralized and terrified by the lead and iron caseshot whizzing about them, the seamen near the front of the column lay flat upon the sand or sought refuge along the shoreline berm and nearby sand dunes. Sailors bunched up in the back of the column wondered why no forward movement was being made. Already the fire had taken such a heavy toll on the shore party that whatever rank formation had existed when the assault began had been completely shattered.[5]

Despite the hot fire, many sailors and some marines continued their rush toward the fort. By most estimates 150 to 200 men (including all of the executive officers) reached Fort Fisher's palisade, but their progress was made at a dreadful cost. Colonel Lamb withheld his small arms fire until this squad approached within point blank range. Lamb had hoped to weaken the naval assault force by detonating the torpedoes, but most of the sailors had unknowingly bypassed the mines by advancing along the shoreline. As the Federals neared the fort's ramparts, Lamb's riflemen unleashed "a murderous fire. . .and swept them down. Volley after volley was poured into their

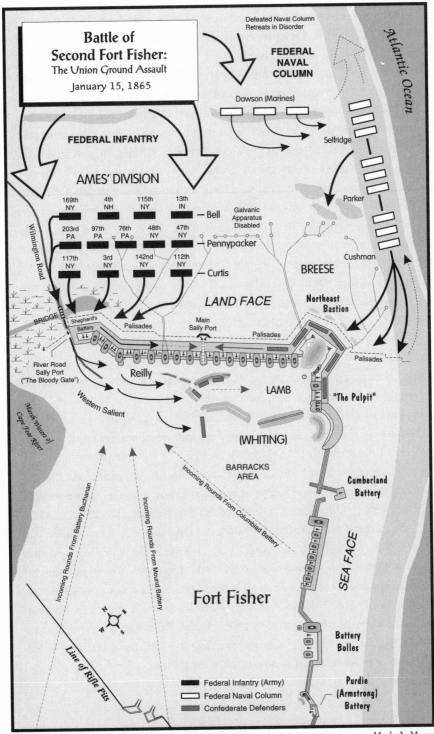

Battle of
Second Fort Fisher:
The Union Ground Assault
January 15, 1865

Mark A. Moore

faltering ranks by cool, determined men," Lamb proudly exclaimed. Ship's Corporal Thomas B. Cosgrove, who was carrying a flag from the *Vanderbilt* in Commander Cushman's lead division, fell dead when two bullets pierced his body as he neared the fort. Cosgrove had told a comrade before the attack that he was determined to enter Fort Fisher or die in the attempt.[6]

Swarming on the battlements like a hive of angry bees, the Confederates—William Lamb and Chase Whiting among them—fired down into the charging Federals as fast as they could shoot. Whiting in particular was animated—barking orders, cursing, and urging his men to kill the enemy. Colonel Lamb likewise encouraged his sharpshooters to gun down the Federals, especially their officers. One Union commander in particular caught Lamb's eye. Wearing a long, gray raincoat, the officer reminded at least one witness of a giant bat when he raised his arms in the air. Although impressed by the courageous Federal, Lamb nonetheless challenged his men to kill him. Try as they might, Confederate marksmen could not hit the "brave and reckless" officer, who turned out to be Cmdr. James Parker, leader of the naval column's second division.[7]

Inspired by their officers' valor, at least five Union sailors reached the earthen fort by sweeping around the end of the palisade at the ocean's edge, or by scrambling through jagged holes in the palisade created by the navy's relentless bombardment. The Southerners above catcalled and hooted, daring the Federals to "come on up." "We were now so close that we could hear the voices of the rebels, and what they said need not be written here," Ensign Robley Evans later recorded. Incensed by these imprecations, some Union sailors accepted the Confederates' audacious invitation. As the tars attempted to clamber the fort's steep ramparts, however, the "dense mass of [Confederate] musketeers" assembled on the parapet shot most of them down. Acting Ensign Joseph M. Simms of the *Minnesota* took a minie ball through his cap and two more in his body as he crawled through the palisade and started up the sloping wall of the fort. "Lie down, Simms, lie down," Cmdr. James Parker yelled out. "There are two bullet holes in you." Acting Master's Mate A. F. Aldrich of the *Tuscarora* forged a few steps ahead of Simms when he sang out, "I'm shot." James Tallentine, a quarter gunner from the *Tacony*, came closest to "boarding the fort" before he was killed. Tallentine reportedly had almost reached the parapet, when he was shot and fell dead.[8]

The courageous Robley Evans was part of this lead group determined to reach the parapet, but a shot that grazed his chest and a bullet that struck his left leg knocked him to the sand. Rising to his feet, Evans attempted to scale the ramparts before a Confederate sharpshooter fired a minie ball into Evans' right knee, stopping him cold in his tracks. As Evans worked feverishly to dress his bleeding wounds, wrenching an ankle in the process, the enemy marksman continued to shoot at him, eventually taking off one of Evans' toes. Severely wounded and fighting mad, Evans rolled over on his stomach and repeatedly fired a pistol at his antagonist, striking him in the neck. The Confederate staggered, dropped his rifle and tumbled down the fort's sandy slope, where he lay dead beside Evans. In the meantime, the few sailors who had managed to breach the palisade and survive the storm of Confederate minie balls quickly shrank back to the north side of the fence. Admiral Porter, who watched the assault from the deck of the *Malvern*, later remarked that "the parapets swarmed with rebels, who poured a destructive fire of musketry. . . .The advance was swept from the parapet like chaff."[9]

Despite the courage of Joseph Simms, Robley Evans, James Tallentine and others who had advanced up to the very walls of the fort, the naval party faltered before the murderous fire from the parapet. Seeing their comrades in the advance checked at the foot of the

Ensign Robley Evans,
USS Powhatan.

Robley Evans, A Sailor's Log

redan, the sailors and marines at the rear of the column halted. Armed with Remington and Whitney revolvers and cutlasses, the small number of Union sailors who reached the fort could muster only a feeble reply to the Confederates' rifle-musket and artillery fusillades. "The sailors might as well have had broomsticks for the good [the pistols and cutlasses] done," lamented Thomas Richardson of the *Yantic*. The marines, who were supposed to use their Sharps rifles to pick off Confederates standing atop the fort, were out of position, many of them having joined the sailors in the fray. After receiving Breese's order to move his command forward to join the sailors along the shoreline, Captain Dawson was unable to reposition his marines in the breastworks on the front line before the attack began. Most of the marines were swept up in the excitement of the charge and found themselves being carried forward by the momentum of the attacking sailors. By the time Dawson reached the front to reorganize his men, the Union naval assault had already broken down.[10]

The fight at Fort Fisher's northeast bastion quickly turned into a madhouse slaughter. Fierce volleys of Confederate musketry clattered from the great sand bastion, riddling the sailors huddled near the palisade or scrambling for cover behind nearby hillocks. The beach was soon covered with dead, dying and wounded Federal seamen. Casualties continued to mount. Lieutenant Commander Charles H. Cushman went down with a gunshot wound to his thigh. William Lemon and Thomas Williams of the *Yantic* were both shot through the head by musket balls. Commander James Parker twice tried to rally the men for a gallant push up the fort's walls, but as Acting Ensign Joseph Simms observed, "It would have been impossible for men made of tougher material than flesh to have withstood that firing."

Under such fire and with only minimal protection from the scattered marines, the naval column wavered and then disintegrated into a frightened mob. Someone in the crowd mumbled something about a retreat and the word swept through the ranks like wildfire. Dazed and confused, most of the sailors and marines—including 100 or more of the gallant band that had reached the palisade—turned and bolted back up the beach. Several determined officers tried to halt them, but it was no use. Panic set in, and the withdrawal quickly became a rout.[11]

The men stopped only if they were shot down by Confederate marksmen or to help a wounded comrade escape the melée. A marine from the

Powhatan named Wasmouth rescued Robley Evans from his exposed position inside the palisade by carrying him to a pit carved out by a navy shell
about fifty yards outside the fort. As Wasmouth lowered Evans into the
shelter a Confederate bullet severed the good samaritan's jugular vein, and
he dropped at the ocean's edge and there bled to death. Fate smiled somewhat more favorably on Ensign Evans. He survived the battle but his leg
wounds left him with a severe limp for the rest of his life. Assistant Surgeon
William Longshaw, Jr. of the *Minnesota* stopped to assist a mortally
wounded sailor when a Confederate bullet shattered his skull. The bodies of
Dr. Longshaw and his patient were found side-by-side after the battle.[12]

Lieutenant Commander Breese chased after his men—"ingloriously flying along the beach away from the fort," was how one Federal sailor described the scene—hoping to reform them for another charge or to provide
cover fire for their helpless comrades pinned down near the northeast bastion. Once it became obvious that the fugitives were ignoring his entreaties
and threats, Breese returned to the front amid a shower of enemy bullets.
"How [Breese] escaped death is a marvel to me," commented Cmdr. James
Parker. At the front, fifty sailors and officers—Breese, Parker, Thomas O.
Selfridge, the wounded Charles H. Cushman and others—together with
Capt. L. L. Dawson and a few of his marines, had taken cover behind the
stockade fence and nearby sand mounds. The Confederate fire was so severe
that the small number of sailors and marines who remained there had to seek
such cover as they could. By Commander Parker's count, twenty to twenty-
five sailors were killed at the foot of the bastion. As Southern bullets splattered around him, Commander Selfridge feigned death while slowly carving
a hole in the sand with his back. Believing he would eventually be hit if he
remained where he was, Selfridge jumped into a nearby shell crater with
Ensign Samuel H. Maunder of the *Huron* and K. Randolph Breese. They
piled sand between them and the fort while Fisher's defenders fired on them.
"Every move on our part brought a shower of bullets," claimed Maunder. "I
think [the Confederates] wanted our uniforms (I had on my best)."[13]

Joseph Simms reflected on the horror of battle as he lay badly wounded
at the foot of the northeast bastion, listening to the din raging around him
while watching an occasional navy shell screech overhead. "The shrieks and
groans, mingling with the fiendish rattling around us, together with the
whistling bullets and the bursting shells over us," Simms exclaimed, "was

enough to cause one to feel that he was in that place General Sherman once described as answering to the name of war."

At least 284 sailors and marines were killed or wounded in the futile twenty-five minute assault. The *Minnesota* alone lost thirty-three men, more than any other ship. Some of the wounded, too weakened by their bloody injuries to move, were sucked into the ocean by the incoming tide and drowned. All told, fifteen officers were wounded and four killed in the action—including Flag Lt. Samuel W. Preston and Lt. Benjamin H. Porter, best friends and fellow classmates at the U. S. Naval Academy.[14]

Though unrelated to the fleet commander, Benjamin Porter was the popular commander of the admiral's flagship. Porter had donned a beautiful blue uniform denoting his rank and proudly carried the *Malvern's* standard when he went ashore that morning to attack Fisher. He boasted to the admiral that his flag would be the first on the fort. But the "bravest of the brave" (as Commander Breese described the lieutenant) was struck down by a Confederate bullet that pierced his breast as he neared the great bastion at the head of his unit. "It was a dreadful blow to me to lose such an officer," mourned Admiral Porter. "Among all the young men who have been on my staff no one had my entire confidence more than [Benjamin Porter]."

Lieutenant Porter's friend, Flag Lt. Samuel W. Preston, was killed just moments after Porter fell. Porter and Preston had graduated together from the Naval Academy and had survived imprisonment after being captured in a daring, ill-fated night attack on Fort Sumter in September 1863. Their long incarceration further strengthened their relationship. Only recently exchanged, Porter and Preston had rejoined their commands in time to participate in the Fort Fisher expeditions. Preston served conspicuously as Cmdr. A. C. Rhind's second-in-command on the *Louisiana* powder boat experiment at First Fort Fisher, and as Commander Breese's aide at Second Fort Fisher. In company with his friends Benjamin Porter and William B. Cushing, Samuel Preston was at the front of the attacking naval column when an enemy bullet severed the femoral artery in his left thigh. Unable to staunch the blood flow, he quickly bled to death. Preston and Porter: midshipmen together at Annapolis, prisoners-of-war together at Charleston, and dead together in the blood-soaked sands at Fort Fisher.[15]

Conspicuous among the survivors of the carnage was Porter's and Preston's good friend, William B. Cushing, the fleet's daring commando. Fate always seemed to smile on Cushing, and this awful battle proved to be no exception. He escaped the carnage unscathed and helped to reform the demoralized sailors and marines who were sent to reinforce General Terry's northern defensive line later that afternoon. But Cushing was not the only fortunate Union sailor that day. After dark the sailors trapped along Fort Fisher's palisade also escaped and joined their comrades near Battery Anderson. Preston Sands of the *Gettysburg* and his brother Hoban of the *Shenandoah* lived to tell the tale of the battle to their father, Capt. Benjamin F. Sands of the *Fort Jackson*. In fact, it was William Cushing who, late on the evening of the battle, encountered Captain Sands on board the admiral's flagship and informed him that his sons "had done good service ashore [and] were both safe." Carlisle P. Porter, Admiral Porter's seventeen-year-old son, also made it through the awful battle.[16]

Although happy that his son had survived the carnage, Admiral Porter was heartbroken over the death of some of his best officers—Porter and Preston in particular—and disappointed by his naval column's unexpected repulse. He blamed the marines for the defeat, claiming that they had failed to provide the support necessary to ensure the assault's success. "I witnessed the whole affair," Porter wrote, "saw how recklessly the rebels exposed themselves, and what an advantage they gave our [marine] sharpshooters, whose guns were scarcely fired, or fired with no precision. . . .At this moment, had the marines performed their duty, every one of the rebels on the parapets would have been killed."[17]

Captain Breese echoed Porter in placing culpability for the failed attack squarely on the marines, who were out of position when the sailors reached the fort. "I can but attribute the failure of the assault to the absence of the marines from their position, as their fire would have enabled our 'boarders' to use their cutlasses and pistols most effectively," Breese reported. All the same, Breese acknowledged that the naval ground assault was a risky venture from the outset. It was unrealistic, he believed, to have expected so much from the shore party, comprised of small squads of men thrown together from the various vessels, wholly unacquainted with one another and poorly armed. "This led to the confusion exhibited," Breese explained, "for it was not due to any want of personal valor on the part of the officers and men." Lieutenant Commander Cushman agreed. "The officers had done their duty well in leading the men," he argued. "The men had followed well so long as they could keep on, but when brought to a standstill under such a fire for the first time, and newly organized, it seems only surprising that they stood at all."[18]

Although Captain L. L. Dawson was commended for personal bravery in Admiral Porter's official report of the battle, the marine corps officer was stunned by the criticism heaped upon his command. After all, K. Randolph Breese had ordered the marines out of their forward breastworks—from where they could have best supported the sailors' assault as planned—to join the disorganized mob of seamen assembled on the beach just prior to the attack. Once he reached the beach with his force, the bewildered Dawson received no additional instructions from Breese "as to what he proposed the marines to do before the order to 'charge' was given, or while [the naval column] was on the move up the beach." The additional weight of their rifle-muskets and forty rounds of ammunition in their cartridge boxes made it virtually impossible for the marines to keep pace with the second division of attacking sailors, much less advance to the front of the column where they were supposed to be. By the time Dawson reached the fort with a few of his brave men, the first division of sailors had already been repulsed, and Dawson saw no reason to advance into the fray with the bulk of his marines. "Admitting, however, that we could have silenced the rebels (an impossibility), it would have amounted to nothing," insisted Captain Dawson, "for the sailors had already broken and were coming back pell-mell, before one volley from my men could have been commanded."

The naval column's defeat notwithstanding, Captain Dawson and the navy officers claimed that their ill-fated attack had not been in vain. If nothing else, they argued, it created a "handsome diversion" for the U. S. Army, enabling the soldiers to gain a foothold on the fort elsewhere. "Regarded as a feint," Dawson maintained, "[the naval column's attack] was a most important part of the action."[19]

The Confederates atop the northeast bastion cheered and whooped and waved their hats and kepis in triumph as the Union sailors and marines fled before them. Their celebration was but short-lived. As he turned and looked to his left, Colonel Lamb was shocked to see Union battle flags planted on

Shepherd's Battery at the far western end of the land face. Federal troops were inside the fort! General Whiting, who saw the enemy flags at the same moment, rushed down the parapet, urging his men to follow him and push back the Union army as they had the naval party. While Whiting was making for the Union lodgment, Lamb dashed through the center sally-port and beyond the fort's walls to gain a better perspective of the battle unfolding on the fort's western end. What he witnessed concerned him greatly.[20]

It was now 3:50 p.m., and Major Reilly had a desperate fight on his hands. The Federal onslaught was so overpowering that the major's small force could not hold it back. When the assault began Reilly commanded only about 350 soldiers—slightly more than half the number Lamb had placed at his disposal—to halt 4,243 surging enemy troops. Most of the South Carolinians had disobeyed Colonel Lamb's order to join Reilly, and were instead cowering in nearby bombproofs. The same was true of some North Carolina soldiers, whose will to fight had been eroded by sleeplessness, hunger and the strain of enduring the continuous massive naval bombardment. They, too, refused to abandon the relative security of the sand-covered bunkers to defend the fort. Perhaps 100 South Carolina infantrymen finally emerged from the shelters to stand bravely beside 250 Tarheels at the western salient. Even so, Reilly's force was outnumbered more than ten to one. To make a bad situation even worse, Reilly deployed his troops imprudently.[21]

General N. Martin Curtis personally led his brigade into battle when General Terry signaled the advance at 3:25 p.m. Curtis extended his tall frame from his crouched position in the sand and, waving his slouch hat, ordered his men to advance: "Forward, First Brigade, forward." Except for a few scattered "hurrahs," the New Yorkers rushed forward in silence, having been instructed by Curtis to save their breath for the run through the deep sand and the climb up the steep slopes of the fort.[22]

The brigade immediately came under fire from Reilly's Confederates inside the fort. The most destructive blasts came from the sally-port area adjacent to Shepherd's Battery, Curtis' main point of attack. There the Southerners had positioned two pieces of light artillery—a 12-pounder Napoleon nestled behind the sandbagged wall blocking the gateway and a

While Union sailors and marines attacked Fort Fisher's northeast bastion near the oceanfront, Brig. Gen. Adelbert Ames' division of 4, 243 men (shown here) assaulted the western end of the fort's land face. *Harper's Weekly*

3.2-inch Parrott rifle posted at the end of the palisade in the river marsh—to command the Wilmington Road approach to the fort. Lead caseshot spewing from these guns tore into Curtis' units on the right of the line—the 117th New York and the 3rd New York infantry regiments—as they approached the salient. A squad of Confederate riflemen added to the mayhem, firing their weapons through loopholes in the timber fence abutting the gateway. "We had to run about 50 rods right under the fire of the rebs sharp shooters & there grape and canister & I tell you it thinned out our men very bad, going to the fort I could see them fall on every side of me," reported one Union soldier. "I considered it more dangerous going up to the fort than it was after we got into it."[23]

For those of Curtis' soldiers who survived the storm of deadly projectiles, additional obstacles blocked their path to the fort: the morass that fronted the fort's western sector, and the skeletal remains of the wagon bridge that traversed the bog. Lamb's Confederates had ripped up the planks of the bridge, which was 100 feet north of the Shepherd's Battery gate, leaving only the stringers for the Federals soldiers to tiptoe across. Facing the destructive enemy gunfire that raked up the Wilmington Road, many of the New Yorkers avoided the bridge and attempted to ford what they thought was a muddy ditch just outside Shepherd's Battery. But like some prehistoric tar pit, the gooey muck trapped some of the troops, making them easy targets for sharpshooters inside the fort. Amid the chaos, Curtis' brigade shifted further eastward to attempt to enter the fort through the splintered stockade fence rather than the gate.

The infantrymen from the 112th New York on the far left of Curtis' line faced a different sort of obstacle, but one that nonetheless caused heavy casualties as the regiment advanced toward the fort. The distance from the 112th's jumping-off point in front of the fort's center sally-port to Shepherd's Battery was about double that of the regiments on the right and much more exposed, the right being somewhat sheltered by a sand ridge within fifty yards of the earthworks. As they advanced the men of the 112th came under a severe enfilade fire from one of the Napoleons emplaced in the ravelin in the middle of the land face, as well as direct small arms fire from Reilly's troops atop the battlements. The regiment's commander, Col. John F. Smith, was one of the first victims of this deadly fire, falling mortally wounded just as the assault began. Some of Smith's men paused long enough to dig a shallow hole in the sand to protect him until they could return. Despite their best efforts, the regimental surgeon's could not save the colonel, and he died three days later.

Private Paul Horvarth of the 112th New York's Company C fell shortly after his colonel was struck. A young Hungarian immigrant, Horvarth had enlisted in the 112th just a month before the regiment participated in the first Fort Fisher expedition. Before the January assault, Horvarth received two commissions as lieutenant in other New York regiments, which exempted him from duty with the 112th. Horvarth, however, chose to join his comrades in the struggle at the Carolina sand bastion, only to be killed as he approached the palisade. "No purer patriotism burned in the bosom of any of those who have toiled and suffered in this great contest than that which expired on the sands of Federal Point, with the life of Paul Horvarth," eulogized one comrade.

Other soldiers of the 112th New York plunged to the ground either because they were shot or to escape the enemy's heavy gunfire that had claimed their beloved colonel. When they renewed their advance, the New Yorkers shifted to the right in an effort to enter the fort at Shepherd's Battery, as General Curtis had instructed. But with Curtis' right obliquing to the left and his left obliquing to the right, the line of battle quickly rushed together and dissolved into a throng of charging blue-uniformed men. "In the crash and uproar of the battle, and the enthusiasm of the advance the men shouldered their way forward with little regard to the regimental formation," observed a Union officer. "The result was a crowd of men pouring through the log obstacles into the ditch, cheering and impetuous, but with no longer any visible military formation."[24]

Among the Federals dashing toward the fort was William Henry Walling, the daredevil hero of the 142nd New York Infantry who had pilfered the Confederate flag from Shepherd's Battery during First Fort Fisher. Recently promoted to captain of the 142nd's Company C, Walling desired nothing more than to lead his new command to glory. He had advanced only a few steps, however, when he was overcome with dizziness and suddenly went as "blind as a bat." Apparently suffering from a severe anxiety attack, Walling groped his way to the fort's exterior slope, where he collapsed in utter exhaustion. After a brief rest, he rose and staggered into the fort at the rear of the brigade, though he later admitted he had not yet "sufficiently recovered to be of any service."[25]

As Curtis' troops reached the palisade, pioneers used axes and battering rams to widen gaps in the log obstacle made by the naval fire, enabling soldiers to slip through and mount the fort's walls. Captain Albert G. Lawrence of General Ames' staff, having received permission from General Curtis to accompany the First Brigade in the assault, was one of the first men through the palisade. (General Ames later reported that Captain Lawrence actually led the attack). He was also one of the first men inside the fort to be shot down when a shell fragment severed his left arm and minie balls pierced his neck and right arm. The young staff officer crumpled against the fence through which he had just passed. Other soldiers quickly swarmed past the wounded Lawrence, cheering and shouting as they clambered through the palisade and up the fort's steep, sandy slopes.[26]

It was at this point that the Federals beneath the fort's walls received an unexpected respite from the heavy Confederate fire. Instead of duplicating Lamb's and Whiting's effective tactics of meeting the enemy assault from the crest of the earthworks, where riflemen could shoot down into their targets, Major Reilly had mistakenly posted his men on the floor of the gun compartments, behind the planked revetments. The immense height of the fort and the extreme width of the parapet restricted the Confederates' firing range and provided the attacking Federal troops a space near the foot of the fort where they were safe from direct fire. Reilly's defenders were unable to see the leading Federals until they emerged from this dead zone, by which time they were already mounting the parapet. The vastly outnumbered Confederate gunners, struggling to reload and fire their weapons, could not stem the tide of swarming enemy soldiers, and they quickly became locked in fierce hand-to-hand combat.

Federal color bearers led the rush of troops to the top of the fort, but a deadly burst of Rebel musketry greeted them as their heads rose above the level of the parapet. One victim of this fusillade was a flag bearer of the 3rd New York Infantry, who tumbled down the sandy walls of the fort he had ascended just moments before. Sergeant Fred Boden of Company E, 117th New York, dodged the rolling body of his fellow Knickerbocker as he scrambled to the fort's summit with a regimental guidon clutched in his hands. Boden was probably the first soldier to plant a Union emblem on the parapet. As he jabbed the flag staff into the sand, however, a shot from inside the fort cut it in two. Boden grabbed the Fourth Oneida pennant and again plunged the flag staff into the sand. When yet another projectile repeated the "unkind act," the determined sergeant planted the standard on the parapet a third time by "making an auger of his posterior," and "boring a hole in the sand deep enough to shield himself from the Confederate fire." There the flag remained, and at day's end Boden reportedly counted sixteen bullet holes in his staff and pennon.[27]

Curtis' eager troops vied with one another to be the first representatives of their units to reach Fort Fisher's summit. Soldiers of both the 117th New York and the 3rd New York Infantry regiments later claimed that proud distinction. The price they paid for their success was heavy. A survivor of the carnage reported that in the first few minutes of the assault "out of every five who gained the slope of the parapet, three went down dead or wounded."[28] Major Egbert Bagg of the 117th New York was severely wounded in the right shoulder as soon as he mounted the fort, and Capt. John T. Thomas of the 117th's Company F was killed shortly thereafter. Thomas—who during First Fort Fisher had taken Maj. John M. Reece of the North Carolina Junior Reserves into custody near Craig's Landing—took a bullet through the heart as he led his men along the parapet. Sergeant Major Edward K. Wightman, a popular and intelligent veteran of Company C, 3rd New York Infantry, was also mortally wounded early in the battle. After the fight, Wightman's father would make a heart-wrenching 1,000-mile-journey into enemy territory in the dead of winter to retrieve his son's body, so that he could bury it in the family cemetery in Cromwell, Connecticut.[29]

Burrowing for a foothold on the fort, Curtis' New Yorkers struggled for possession of Shepherd's Battery. General Curtis himself was one of the first Federals to reach the fort's twenty-three-foot high summit, wrangling with a Confederate artilleryman reportedly in the act of discharging a columbiad in the second gun chamber. When the cannoneer refused to surrender, Curtis dealt him "a sharp blow from [his] sabre on his outstretched hand" and convinced him to reconsider. Curtis was in the thick of the fight, lifting his men onto the parapet and then pushing them forward to the tops of the traverses. Precariously perched on the high ground, the New Yorkers fired their weapons down into Reilly's Tarheels deployed in the adjacent gun chambers, much as Lamb and Whiting had earlier exploited a similar advan-

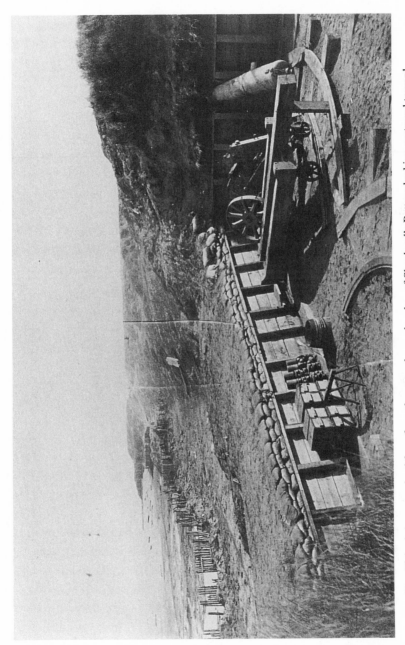

Fort Fisher's immense land face, from the second gun chamber of Shepherd's Battery looking eastward toward the northeast bastion in the distance. *U. S. Army Military History Institute*

tage in repulsing the naval column at the northeast bastion. The fighting quickly devolved into a deadly game of "king of the hill" as the Confederates and Federals struggled for possession of the high sand mounds. "A foothold was barely obtained," confessed a Union soldier, "and [Curtis'] brigade here came to a stand, holding on by the eyelids, as it were, while men fell fast on every side. . .without speedy support its destruction seemed certain."[30]

General Terry watched the action unfolding at Fort Fisher from his field headquarters on the summit of Battery Holland. Observing Curtis' struggle, Terry sent in Pennypacker's brigade as reinforcements. As Galusha Pennypacker passed headquarters at the head of his brigade, Terry went to him, put his arms around the neck of the 20-year-old colonel, and spoke a few words of encouragement. Within ten

Colonel Galusha Pennypacker, 20 years old, was severely wounded while leading his Second Brigade, Ames' division, at Fort Fisher. *Chester County Historical Society, West Chester, PA*

minutes of the First Brigade's advance, the 47th and 48th New York infantry regiments, and the 76th, 97th, and 203rd Pennsylvania infantry regiments of the Second Brigade "came on like an avalanche" to Curtis' support. General Ames and his staff accompanied Pennypacker's advance to the fort. Hot fire still poured from Fort Fisher, severely wounding Lt. Col. William B. Coan as he formed the 48th New York (the second regiment on the left of Pennypacker's battle line), forcing him to leave the field. As Pennypacker's brigade moved forward moments later, the entire color guard of the 47th New York on the far left of the line was killed by a shot from one of the Napoleons in the ravelin at the fort's center sally-port.

"Sure death to stop—almost certain destruction to go on," stated a soldier of the 203rd Pennsylvania. Most of Pennypacker's men followed in the footsteps of Curtis' regiments, charging up the earthworks at Shepherd's Battery, while others overlapped Curtis' right, renewing the attack on the western salient's gate.[31]

The "Bloody Gate" at Shepherd's Battery, where some of the fiercest fighting occurred on January 15, 1865. *U.S. Army Military History Institute*

As Curtis' combatants (now being joined by Pennypacker's support troops), wrestled with Reilly's stubborn Confederates on the ramparts for possession of Shepherd's Battery, another furious struggle ensued for the sally-port and bombproofs below. Some of the day's fiercest fighting took place in the area of the gateway overlooking the wagon bridge on the Wilmington Road. Survivors of the carnage would later refer to it as the "Bloody Gate." The lightly defended sector was held by half of 2nd Company C, 36th North Carolina Regiment (commanded by Capt. Kinchen

Braddy); Co. D, 1st Battalion North Carolina Heavy Artillery, and a detachment of Zachariah T. Adams' Battery (Company D, 13th Battalion North Carolina Light Artillery). Despite their paucity in numbers, their volleys produced telling results which included forcing Curtis' brigade to veer away from the "Bloody Gate." When the Federal troops attacked, Capt. Braddy's soldiers—a mere thirty or thirty-five men of 2nd Company C, 36th North Carolina Regiment—grabbed rifle-muskets to fire at the charging bluecoats. Others manned the 12-pounder Napoleon at the sandbagged gate and the 10-pounder Parrott rifle on the edge of the river, blasting the attacking Federals with caseshot.

The cannon were supposed to be served by Zachariah T. Adams' detachment, but its commander, Lt. Charles H. Latham, and most of his men refused to come out of the bombproofs. Captain Braddy was compelled to work the guns with his meager force, although he was soon joined by a few of Latham's men who dared to emerge from the shelters. For a while the work of Braddy's crew took its toll on the Federals. When some of Curtis' New Yorkers sought refuge from the blizzard of lead by huddling beneath the wooden bridge, the Parrott rifle blew large chunks of the span away. Unfortunately for the Confederates, the Parrott rifle unaccountably fell silent, freeing Union sharpshooters to open fire on the Confederate cannoneers standing at or near the gate. As the sharpshooters' fire began to claim victims, Tarheel gunners stepped forward to replace fallen comrades. Even so, Kinchen Braddy could ill afford to lose any men from his skeleton crew, prompting him to send two couriers dashing off to find reinforcements.[32]

Captain James McCormic, commander of Company D, 1st Battalion North Carolina Heavy Artillery, rushed his forty men out of nearby bunkers to support Braddy. McCormic and his soldiers had been transferred from quiet Fort Caswell on Friday morning, January 13—Friday the 13th—and now found themselves fighting for their lives. "As Adams' men were being shot down one by one, our boys took the places of the dead and disabled," stated Pvt. Zack Fulmore of McCormic's company. "War never witnessed more determined bravery," Colonel Lamb later recorded of his soldiers' stand at the "Bloody Gate." But the raw courage of this small band was no match for two brigades of Union troops, who soon overpowered the Confederates, killing one of their leading officers in the process.[33]

When he had entered Fort Fisher two days earlier, James McCormic carried a five-pound bucket of "fine, golden butter" he had just received by express mail from a girlfriend back home in Robeson County, North Carolina. Butter was a valuable commodity to a Confederate soldier "fighting for his country, and living on coarse corn bread and Nassau bacon." Weary of toting the pail in his hand, McCormic fastened it to his sword belt as the battle ensued at Fort Fisher's "Bloody Gate." But his sword belt was soon cut by a shell fragment, and the bucket fell to the ground. McCormic picked it up, and handed it to one of his soldiers, Pvt. James A. Smith (who was said to have fired the first shot of the battle at the advancing Union army). "Jim, old fellow, your cartridge box is strong," McCormic observed. "Please buckle this bucket of butter to your belt and when the battle is over we will share its contents." Thinking the deal a good one, Smith took the pail and hung it on his belt. Within minutes, however, the private fell slightly wounded. Moments later Captain McCormic was mortally wounded. As James Smith lay on the ground watching his commanding officer and friend die, Pvt. Benjamin F. Seely of Company C, 117th New York Infantry, thrust a bayonet close to Smith's face and declared the Tarheel his prisoner. Smith threw his rifle-musket to the ground and his hands into the air, with James McCormic's now lifeless body stretched on the ground beside him.[34]

While McCormic's fall demoralized the defenders of the "Bloody Gate," it was the sudden appearance of Curtis' blue-uniformed soldiers in their rear that doomed them. After gaining a foothold atop Shepherd's Battery, some of Curtis' infantry turned their guns on the Confederates below them, who were themselves pouring a deadly fire into Pennypacker's charging brigade. As one Union soldier recalled, the 203rd Pennsylvania on the far right of Pennypacker's battle line was being "mowed down in windrows" by Confederate gunners at the gate. With only a small fighting force at his disposal to prevent the Federals from entering the fort through the gate, Capt. Kinchen Braddy had paid scant attention to the escalating combat swirling on the parapet above his head. To the Confederates' surprise, shots began raining down on them from the battlements.

"One of our boys was killed by a shot coming from our rear," exclaimed Pvt. Zack Fulmore. "I looked around and saw the stars and stripes floating from the top of the parapet, with what seemed to me to be a thousand bluecoats around it—some shooting at us." Fulmore attempted to spike the Napoleon gun, but before he could do so soldiers of Curtis' 117th New York descended the ramparts and forced him to surrender. "I saw they had us completely surrounded," Fulmore lamented, "knew we would have to give up the gun, and in that event they would turn it on our men in the fort, hence my determination to spike it if possible." Although a few Confederates escaped the converging Union forces, Zack Fulmore, James Smith (the bucket of butter still attached to his belt), and others taken prisoner at the "Bloody Gate" or pulled out of adjacent bombproofs were hustled out of the fort under guard and taken to the Union rear at Howard's Hill.[35]

Kinchen Braddy eluded capture—at least for the time being. When neither of his two messengers returned with reinforcements, Braddy went looking for Colonel Lamb or General Whiting. Up to that point he did not know that Major Reilly was in command of the western salient, nor had he seen Reilly on the battlefield. Braddy told his men to hold on at the gate and he would soon return with help. Exasperated by the desperate state of affairs in his sector of the fort, things went from bad to worse for Captain Braddy. As he turned the corner of Shepherd's Battery on his way to Lamb's headquarters, the captain was astonished to see a squad of South Carolina soldiers unleash a volley of minie balls in his direction. Hagood's infantrymen either had mistaken the Tarheel captain and his entourage for Yankees, or were firing at Federals near the "Bloody Gate" with little regard for the safety of Braddy and his men. Regardless of whom they were firing at, the South Carolinians succeeded in foiling Braddy's attempt to secure reinforcements. "I don't know how many they killed," Braddy raged, "but two men on either side of me were shot down." Braddy called out to the Palmetto State riflemen to cease firing and come to his command's relief, but they paid no attention to him. Nor was this the only occasion in which Confederates at Fort Fisher fell as a result of friendly fire. Just moments after the South Carolinians fired on Braddy, heavy artillery at Battery Buchanan opened fire on Shepherd's Battery, killing Pvt. John Cooper, whom Braddy described as one of his best men. Braddy's men were now being riddled by fire from both outside and inside the fort, from friend and foe alike. He later discovered that "friendly shots" directed at Shepherd's Battery were aimed at the Federal force that had overrun his small command defending the "Bloody Gate."[36]

The fire from Battery Buchanan, as intended, also took its toll on Union troops at Shepherd's Battery. George G. Spencer, a recent recruit of Company E, 117th New York, was killed instantly when a Confederate projectile shattered his skull. Spencer was celebrating his nineteenth birthday and had earlier remarked to a friend that he thought the impending battle would be a "great birthday excursion." The "birthday excursion" turned out to be Spencer's last. One of his comrades was mortally wounded moments later. As he fell his head became wedged in the spokes of a caisson wheel, and in that gruesome position his friends found him early the next morning. "The fighting at the sally-port was terrific and the carnage the most terrible that I had ever witnessed," exclaimed Lt. George Simpson of the 142nd New York. "Rivulets of blood ran from the gateway."[37]

The first man Lieutenant Walling (who had finally recovered from his anxiety and/or exhaustion attack) recognized when he rejoined his command was Pvt. James Spring of Company G, 142nd New York. Spring was the soldier whom Walling had sent to General Curtis with the captured flag during the first Fort Fisher expedition. The reunion was brief. As Walling looked on in horror, Spring was shot through the head by a Confederate rifleman on the battlements.[38]

As the tide of battle swung in favor of the Federals at the "Bloody Gate," the fight on the fort's battlements was just heating up. The savage hand-to-hand combat proved costly. Colonel Galusha Pennypacker received a severe groin wound while planting the colors of his old regiment, the 97th Pennsylvania, near the land face's third traverse. Rescued by his men, Pennypacker was carried to the rear. Surgeons regarded his wound as mortal and a coffin was ordered for him. But though he suffered through an eleven-month confinement in a hospital recovery ward at Fort Monroe, Pennypacker refused to die. "Colonel Pennypacker's conduct leading his brigade with the colors of his own regiment, placed him second to none for gallantry that day," General Ames later reported.

Pennypacker was not the only casualty among the officers of his brigade. Eight commissioned officers of the 97th Pennsylvania were either killed or wounded on Fort Fisher's parapet, along with leading officers of other regiments. The popular commander of the 203rd Pennsylvania, Col. John W. Moore, was mortally wounded by a minie ball that struck him in the abdomen as he led his men into the fray at Shepherd's Battery. "Colonel

Moore is killed," cried one of his men. "No, boys, I am not killed," Moore gasped, "but I am badly hurt. Never mind me—keep on and give them hell." It was the last time Moore's men would see him alive. Colonel John S. Littell of the 76th Pennsylvania and Lt. Col. Francis X. Meyer of the 117th New York were also wounded. Federal officers and men fell in such great numbers that their bodies

A previously unpublished image of Col. John W. Moore of the 203rd Pennsylvania Infantry, who was mortally wounded at Fort Fisher. *Author's Collection*

impeded troop movements on the parapet.[39]

Despite their mounting casualties, the Federal capture of the gate at Shepherd's Battery enabled soldiers of Pennypacker's brigade, as well as General Ames and his staff, to enter the fort through the sally-port. It also allowed the Third Brigade—comprised of the 13th Indiana, 4th New Hampshire, and the 115th and 169th New York infantry regiments—to enter the fort via the Wilmington Road and advance into the fort's interior behind the land face. About fifteen minutes after Pennypacker's brigade went forward, General Terry sent in Col. Louis Bell's brigade, at General Ames' request. Louis Bell never reached the fort. The strapping colonel presented an easy target for an unknown Confederate rifleman, whose bullet felled him as he crossed the bridge at Shepherd's Battery. With his chest pierced by a minie ball, Colonel Bell was told by his regimental surgeon that the wound was mortal. Although blood-soaked and weak, Bell refused to be carried from the battlefield until he had seen the flag of his old regiment, the 4th New Hampshire, planted atop the fort. Propping himself up on his stretcher, Bell smiled as he saw his dying wish satisfied. The young colonel died early the following morning. Both New Hampshire and Terry's Provisional Corps lost one of their favorite sons in Louis Bell, an intelligent, well-respected lawyer and son of a former New Hampshire governor. Like every battle death, Bell's passing touched others as well. His wife, four-year-old daughter and six-week-old son (whom Bell had never seen), lost a husband

Colonel Louis Bell, commander of Ames' Third Brigade, was mortally wounded in the attack on Fort Fisher. *U.S. Army History Institute*

and a father.[40]

Within thirty minutes after the battle began more than 4,000 Union soldiers had either entered Fort Fisher or were attempting to do so. While the brigades of Curtis and Pennypacker struggled to maintain their precarious foothold on the ramparts, Bell's troops—somewhat disorganized after the fall of their esteemed commander—advanced through the western sally-port and onto the parade ground south of the land face. General Ames deployed Bell's soldiers on the terre plain with orders to fight their way toward the northeast bastion, which Ames believed was the key to the fort. To cover the brigade's movement, Ames ordered the captured Napoleon at the "Bloody Gate" to be turned on the enemy, who maintained a galling fire on his position. Confederates rallied to fend off this new threat, taking up positions behind demolished barracks and piles of lumber and debris to fire on the Federals inside the fort. "The Rebels fought desperately," acknowledged one of Ames' men. "They fought like tigers," agreed another.[41]

Their stubborn resistance notwithstanding, the Confederates could not hold back the overwhelming surge of Union troops on the parapet, and they soon lost possession of the western salient's three traverses and gun chambers. At the fourth traverse, however, the Southerners made a desperate stand, for it was here that General Whiting and reinforcements fresh from the fight at the northeast bastion crashed into the Union army's onslaught. Shouting, slashing and stabbing their way into the fray, Whiting and his soldiers pushed the Federals off the fourth traverse and moved to recapture the third. Little Billy Whiting fought alongside his men, and his presence seemed to inspire them with renewed will to drive the Yankees from the fort. "The struggle for the fourth traverse," General Curtis claimed, "was the hottest and most prolonged single contest of the day." The shift of the initiative threw the Southerners into the role of assailants and forced the Federals onto the defensive. "The Confederates were still undaunted and seemed determined to recover the captured salient and gun chambers," Colonel Lamb recalled.

While Whiting fought on the battlements, Lamb swiveled his 8-inch columbiad at the northeast bastion and his light artillery in the center sally-port ravelin to fire on that part of the Union army advancing toward the fort. He instructed Capt. Zachariah T. Adams to employ both of his Napoleons (which had been so effective against the naval column) against Bell's brigade, which was entering at Shepherd's Battery. Lamb attempted to explode his torpedoes beneath this last Union brigade but the explosives failed to detonate. Lamb correctly presumed that the tremendous fire of the fleet had severed the connecting wires, rendering the mines completely useless. Though disheartened by the foreboding turn of events, Lamb was confident that if his men could hold the Federals in check until dark, he could still drive them from the fort with General Bragg's assistance. Lamb sent yet another message to the commanding general at Sugar Loaf, imploring him to attack Terry's rear: "We still hold the fort, but are sorely pressed. Can't you assist us from the outside?"[42]

Although his telegram eventually reached the general at Sugar Loaf, it was not what the department commander was looking for. Rather, Bragg was awaiting the arrival of General Whiting. Miffed by the insolent tone of Whiting's messages on Saturday, Bragg had summoned Whiting to Sugar

Loaf for a conference, perhaps to reassert his authority by dressing down his wayward subordinate. Given the present situation, however, Whiting's most recent messages appeared strangely calm, and may have unintentionally lulled Bragg into a false sense of security concerning Fort Fisher. Although Whiting continued to request Bragg's aid, he made no strong demands for it as he had during First Fort Fisher. Having been chastised by Bragg for his impudent behavior after the December battle, Whiting perhaps believed he could more readily elicit the department commander's help by altering his manner in requesting it. Shortly after 2:00 p.m., only an hour before the Federal ground forces attacked the fort, Whiting had informed Bragg that the enemy's heavy naval bombardment had so far caused few casualties to the fort's defenders. "Is Fort Fisher to be besieged, or you to attack?" Whiting wanted to know. Later that afternoon another Whiting message reached Bragg's hands at Sugar Loaf. "The enemy are assaulting us by land and sea. Can't you help us?" Whiting inquired with some deference. Though offended by what he apparently considered Whiting's sarcastic tone, the overly-sensitive Bragg misinterpreted Whiting's apparent nonchalance to mean that all was well at the fort. Bragg sent word to Robert E. Lee that he believed the enemy attack would fail, and at a heavy price in Union casualties. "If defended, as I believe it will be, by your veterans and the former garrison," Bragg informed Lee, "it cannot be taken."

True to his word, Bragg was making an effort—albeit a halfhearted one—to send reinforcements to Fort Fisher. He requested steamers sent from Wilmington to Fort Anderson to embark the remainder of Hagood's Brigade for transport to Battery Buchanan. The vessels failed to reach Fort Anderson in time. After learning that Fort Fisher was under attack by enemy ground forces, Bragg ordered Hoke to form his troops for an attack on the Federals' rear.[43]

Colonel John W. Ames of the 6th U. S. Colored Troops was at Battery Holland on business when General Terry launched his assault on Fort Fisher. Enthralled by the unfolding action, Ames dallied at the front to watch "the terrible game." For more than half an hour he observed the battle on the ramparts until the sound of musketry to the north about 4:00 p.m. reminded

Ames that he was supposed to be with his command on General Paine's northern line. General Terry had warned Paine to expect an attack by Hoke's infantry at Sugar Loaf once the battle at Fort Fisher began. "With reluctant haste and anxious foreboding," Ames ran through the ankle-deep sand of the Wilmington Road toward Paine's fortified position. But when the firing abruptly ceased, the colonel slackened his pace, confident that the emergency had passed. Ames soon came upon several groups of black soldiers relaxing in the rear of their breastworks, seeming confirmation that Hoke's Confederates had made no serious attempt to overrun their position.

Nonetheless, Ames hurried to check the picket line in the woods fronting Paine's main works. He soon discovered that three picket stations in front of Abbott's white brigade on the right of the line had been overrun and their sentries captured, but soldiers deployed near the river had seen nothing of the enemy. Confederates may have temporarily occupied a few picket posts, but Paine's men reported seeing no gray-uniformed soldiers within sight of their main defenses.

Ames quickly re-garrisoned the vacant picket stations, thereby restoring Paine's early warning system, but the Federals were satisfied that Hoke's attack—if it could be called an attack—was little more than a weak attempt to "carry the picket line" or a diversion "in favor of the garrison at Fort Fisher." "Its feebleness was so striking that it did us good service in showing how little we had to fear from that quarter," Colonel Ames contended. General Paine was both bewildered and amused by Hoke's impotent display of force. "If [Hoke] had made an attack & if he had carried my line & they held out in the fort, we should have been in a tight place," Paine confessed. At the very least, Paine suggested somewhat tongue-in-cheek, "[the Rebels] ought to have driven in my pickets & opened artillery on my line. Hoke will catch it in Richmond & he deserves to."[44]

Fortunately for Robert Hoke, the high command in Richmond never read Charles J. Paine's version of Hoke's "attack." The War Department received Braxton Bragg's account of Hoke's movement, which painted a far different picture than the Union reports. Bragg claimed that General Hoke had indeed made a "heavy demonstration" upon the enemy with Kirkland's and Clingman's brigades, but found the Federals "in very strong position and force ready to receive them." According to Bragg, Hoke personally advanced with his skirmishers close to the enemy's line and was fired on, taking two minie balls in his tunic. Just as he had concluded after reconnoitering the same enemy defenses on Saturday morning, Hoke deemed a full-scale assault against the strongly held works "impracticable" with his "small command." Bragg concurred, insisting that "[Hoke] could not have succeeded." There was no reason to attack, Bragg contended. Having heard only ten minutes' worth of "feeble musketry" in the direction of Fort Fisher about 3:30 p.m. (in addition to the continual firing of the fleet on the fort) and having received reassuring communiqués from General Whiting, Bragg believed that the Confederates still held the bastion and faced no serious danger. Moreover, Hoke's attack undoubtedly created a diversion for the fort's garrison by preventing a large portion of the Union army from joining in the attack on the fort. Even when reports began coming in later that night that the Federals had captured Fort Fisher, Bragg chose to disregard them.[45]

Reiterating their disdain for Bragg's and Hoke's refusal to attack the Federals as they came ashore on January 13—or for attacking them in their newly-constructed breastworks on January 14—some of Hoke's men ridiculed their commanders' decision not to assault the enemy line as a means of supporting Fort Fisher on the 15th. "We easily drove in the enemy's skirmish line, occupied their rifle pits, and our skirmishers were making their main line keep their heads down behind the intrenchments," claimed Capt. Charles G. Elliott of the 17th North Carolina Infantry, Kirkland's Brigade. "When we all expected the order to charge a courier came to Hoke from Bragg ordering him to withdraw to Sugar Loaf. We confidently expected to run over the troops in our front and drive them in confusion upon Terry's attacking column. . . .I felt that all had not been done to save [Fort Fisher]." General Paine reported capturing a "reb officer" who seemed "extremely disgusted that [Hoke] made no attack." Hoke's soldiers were apparently anxious to attack the Yankee Colored Troops for whom they had no respect. "I believe our charge would have been successful, because the troops in front were blacks," stated a North Carolina soldier. A comrade agreed. "The troops at the time in our front were all negroes," he observed, "and did not number more than 2,500, defending a mile in extent."[46]

Despite their misgivings about Braxton Bragg, Chase Whiting and William Lamb fully expected the department commander to come to their rescue at Fort Fisher. Surely Bragg understood that if the great bastion fell, not only Wilmington, but Richmond, the Army of Northern Virginia and indeed the Confederacy itself were all doomed. Robert E. Lee had said as much, and Jefferson Davis had placed responsibility for safeguarding Wilmington in Bragg's hands. "We are trustfully looking to your operations," the Confederate president had wired Bragg from Richmond just that morning (January 15). If Bragg hoped to save Fort Fisher, however, he would have to hurry. The tide of battle was turning against the Confederates.

Fort Fisher had become a killing ground. Thousands of gray and blue-uniformed soldiers were locked in a fierce struggle on the battlements, stabbing and slashing with their bayonets and swords, firing their rifle-muskets at point-blank range, clubbing with their musket stocks, beating each other with their fists. Thousands more fired their weapons at one another from close range on the parade ground behind the land face and hugged the sand as projectiles buzzed overhead like swarming bees. This brutal close-quarters struggle continued for five-and-a-half hours, with survivors later reporting that it was some of the most savage fighting they had experienced in the war. "The fight was very desperate and bloody," General Whiting exclaimed. One of Little Billy's soldiers, Pvt. James A. Montgomery of 3rd Company B, 36th North Carolina Regiment, described the battle as "a soldier's fight." When one soldier fell, another sprang forward to take his place, with officers loading and firing alongside their men. "Then it became a hand-to-hand fight," Montgomery noted. "We were too close to fire." The pitched brawl was so violent, claimed one horrified Pennsylvania infantry-men, that "it was all too much for even demons."[47]

Much of the desperate fighting raged for control of the huge sand traverses, which were the highest points in the fort. Soldiers on both sides took temporary refuge in the gun compartments below, until they had assembled a sufficient number of troops to launch a sortie against adjoining traverses, then rushed to the crests of the mounds, where they would be met by enemy guns and bayonets. "Our men would make a charge to the summit of a traverse, to be met by the Confederates coming from the other side, where these hand-to-hand struggles occurred," marveled one Union soldier. "Every mound had [to] be taken by hand to hand conflict," recalled another

Federal. "Officers used their sabres and revolvers freely, and every traverse was piled up, some places two deep, with the dead and dying of both parties. Every charge was death, or surrender. . . ."[48]

On the western salient's third traverse Chase Whiting wrestled with a Union standard bearer for possession of the U. S. flag. Easily recognizable in his general officer's tunic, Whiting defied danger to join his men at the front. But on this day fate frowned on the courageous Whiting. Two Yankee minie balls pierced his right leg, crumpling him to his knees. Several of the general's soldiers rushed to lift him up, including Captain Braddy, who had left the melee at the "Bloody Gate" to search for reinforcements. While being tended to General Whiting confided to Braddy that he was seriously wounded. With the battle swirling around them, Braddy informed the fallen general that "everything was confusion" and that the South Carolina troops were killing more Confederates than Federals. "For God's sake," Whiting pleaded, "try and stop it." That was the only advice the critically wounded Whiting could offer before being carried to the hospital at the Pulpit Battery on the sea face—never to return to the battle.[49]

Although Little Billy's fall stunned his soldiers, they continued the furious struggle for possession of the western salient. Under Whiting's inspired leadership, they had already regained control of one traverse. "The Rebels attacked our men like savage dogs," exclaimed E. D. Williams of the 117th New York. "Give and take was the watchword on both sides, face to face and gun to gun." The Confederates would "jump up on the top of a traverse and shoot down upon our men, and if that failed, they would attempt their slaughter with clubbed muskets," explained a New York soldier. "Not in a few instances were found also in which our men and theirs had pinned each other with their bayonets, and died together." Minie balls took an even greater toll than bayonets, and the wounds at close range were often fatal. According to Cpl. Henry Clay McQueen of Company D, 1st Battalion North Carolina Heavy Artillery, "A comrade next to me on the traverse was shot in his brains and killed. His brains splattered in my face."[50]

During a particularly stubborn scrap for a traverse, Lt. Col. Samuel M. Zent of the 13th Indiana attempted to peek over the top of the besieged mound. "All I remember seeing was a flash and feeling a sensation similar to an electric shock," the Hoosier officer later recalled. "The fellow had pulled the trigger a little too soon and the ball passed through my hat just grazing the top of my head." Grudgingly, the vastly outnumbered Confederates yielded to the overwhelming Federal force that advanced slowly eastward from one traverse to the next. "The Rebels fought with a courage and determination worthy of a better cause," confessed a Union soldier. "They flinched not a hairs-breadth, but steel to steel they resisted our advance."[51]

Death and destruction did not confine themselves to the fort's ramparts, but stalked as well the open sand plain behind the land face. Bell's brigade, now commanded by Col. Alonzo Alden of the 169th New York, together with some of Pennypacker's regiments, deployed on the parade ground, attempting to advance eastward toward the northeast bastion, as General Ames had instructed. But the further Ames' force progressed, the stiffer the resistance became.

Observing this growing threat to the rear of his fort, Colonel Lamb determined to turn it back. He reinforced the squads of men already disputing the Union advance from the shelter of old earthworks, the ruins of barracks, out-buildings, piles of lumber and shell craters. Having left the wounded General Whiting's side, Captain Kinchen Braddy approached Lamb and offered his services. Lamb ordered Braddy to "get some men" and help him "drive those Yankees out of the fort." Lamb then dashed down the sea face to search for additional reinforcements and instruct his men serving the remaining big guns in the waterside batteries—two 8-inch columbiads in the Columbiad Battery and the Mound Battery's two guns—to turn their sights on the advancing enemy, which was already being riddled by fire from the guns at Battery Buchanan. Lamb then returned to the land face fight with more than 100 reinforcements and implored the sick and slightly wounded—as well as the recalcitrant South Carolinians—to join him in his desperate struggle. The young colonel ordered Captain Adams to haul his two Napoleons from their position inside the demilune to the fort's interior, where they could be used to fire on the advancing Federals.

As intent as he was on stopping the enemy, Lamb was shocked by the carnage inside his fort. "Great cannon broken in two, their carriages wrecked and among their ruins the mutilated bodies of my dead and dying comrades," Lamb grieved. If these scenes were to be altered, Lamb was beginning to realize he and his men would have to do it on their own. There were still no tidings from Braxton Bragg, although, as one of Lamb's men confessed, "[we] were fighting with one ear listening for Hoke."[52]

Lamb believed that his efforts would turn the tide of battle in the Confederates' favor. For a time it appeared that the Confederates had stalled the Union advance. The Southerners' fire was so destructive that Ames' men either plunged to the sandy floor of the fort's parade ground or took shelter behind nearby traverses along the land face. Lieutenant William H. Walling observed "acres of men lying on their faces crowded together so thickly there was no room to lie down." The fighting was done without regard to unit organization, for it was impossible to do so under those chaotic conditions. It was every man for himself. General Ames' later admitted that brigade and regimental formations were impossible to maintain, and that success was due to "the heroic efforts of small bodies of officers and men." Lieutenant Walling stated that officers occasionally tried to rally their men for a charge, but they often ignored the commands. "Our hands were full, but we held on. . .the men fought on," wrote Lt. Col. Nathan J. Johnson of the 115th "Iron-Hearted" New York. "We kept struggling. . .bleeding. . .dying. . .we kept on." Because of the defenders' severe artillery and small-arms fire, there was little protection for the Federals unless they hugged the ground. Each man loaded his gun by rolling over on his side or back, and fired by resting on an elbow. "I saw one man kill another man 30 or 40 feet in front of him," William Walling noted. "The rear man was aiming at the rebels when the one in front turned on his stomach raised his head to aim, just in time to receive the charge of his comrade in the back of his head."[53]

While the Federals made no progress on the parade ground and very little on the ramparts, Lamb's Confederates were likewise making little headway in pushing the Federals out of the fort. Then, at that critical moment in the battle, Admiral Porter renewed his bombardment of Fort Fisher's land face. For about an hour the warships on the second and third lines had been shelling the sea face batteries exclusively, but at General Terry's request, Porter authorized his ironclad vessels to resume their bombardment of the land front. Their efforts were directed at the gun chambers still occupied by Confederate defenders, although it was impossible at that range for the *New Ironsides* and monitors to pinpoint their targets with anything approaching reasonable accuracy. The result was that several of the projectiles fell wide of the mark, accidentally killing and wounding some of Curtis' New Yorkers on the fort's ramparts. "While contending for the fifth traverse," General Curtis reported, "a shot from the navy landed on the wrong side of the traverse, and killed and disabled all the attacking party but four men and the brigade commander." Even so, most of the navy shells landed with remarkable precision on their intended targets, killing and wounding many of Lamb's men and driving others in confusion toward the northeast bastion. As Lamb's men withdrew, Curtis' New Yorkers surged forward, capturing additional traverses and gun chambers. Knowing he was pressing his luck if he continued, Porter maintained his fierce bombardment of the fort only until dark, when he he halted the firing.

Sensing that the momentum was shifting against him, Lamb determined to lead a counterattack against Ames' troops on the floor of the fort, where they were now beginning to entrench. Lamb passed down the rear of his line, asking his officers and men if they would follow him. "They all responded fearlessly that they would," Lamb recalled proudly. The colonel quickly organized his line of battle, then sprang to the top of a breastwork and yelled: "Charge bayonets, forward, double quick, march!" But at the instant Lamb uttered the command to advance, a minie ball ripped into his left side and sent him sprawling to the sand. One of Lamb's best officers, Lt. Daniel R. Perry of 3rd Company B, 36th North Carolina Regiment, was mortally wounded by the colonel's side. While the Yankee volley that wounded Lamb and killed Perry was fired too high to be effective against Lamb's rank and file, it succeeded in stalling the attack. The Tarheels withdrew behind their defenses. Severely wounded, Lamb turned his command over to Capt. Daniel Munn, telling him to keep the enemy in check and that he would rejoin the fight as soon as his injury was bandaged.

By the time Lamb reached the hospital shortly after 4:30 p.m., he was in excruciating pain and was weakened by loss of blood. Inside he found General Whiting being treated by the fort's head surgeon, complaining that General Bragg had ignored their pleas for help. A dismayed Lamb soon learned that his hip had been broken by the shot from a Yankee rifle, which meant that he would be unable to return to his men. A despondent Lamb sent for the next in command, Maj. James Reilly (Maj. James Martin Stevenson being too ill for duty), and turned the fort's defense over to him. Reilly promised Lamb and Whiting that he would continue the struggle for as long as possible. The major proved to be as good as his word.[54]

The situation that devolved upon Reilly was anything but enviable, yet he shouldered it, as he said, "with all its responsibility and with a small number of brave men." The major even persuaded some of the reluctant South Carolinians to join their Tarheel comrades in the battle. At that point the Palmetto State boys had little choice, realizing that if the fort was over-run it would mean either death or imprisonment to all of the Carolinians, South and North. Even with this additional support it is unlikely that Reilly commanded more than several hundred effectives against the wave of blue-uniformed infantrymen in his front. He managed to deploy a force of about 150 troops in the open space behind the center sally-port and, like Lamb before him, attempted to dislodge the enemy with a frontal assault. The fire Reilly and his men met, however, was most destructive, killing or wounding two-thirds of the attackers and driving the survivors to the rear. "Under such a fire our men began to waiver and fall back," Reilly recalled, "and by the time I reached near the angle of the work I had not sixty men with me." One soldier killed in the attack was the color bearer of a South Carolina regiment that Reilly had coaxed into the fight. Some of Reilly's survivors took refuge behind nearby traverses and inside the sally-port, while most retreated to a sand bank in rear of the postern. Here Reilly reformed his troops and "kept up as heavy and as destructive a fire as [his] small command would allow." Shortly after this ill-fated attack, Federal troops surged forward, capturing additional traverses and precious yards of the fought-over parade ground.[55]

Across the Cape Fear River, a group of ladies watched the terrible battle for Fort Fisher from bluffs on the west bank. Their stake in the struggle was a dear one, for their husbands and sons were among the fort's defenders. With the assistance of field glasses they could make out masses of soldiers fighting inside the fort. But the distance was too great and the smoke of battle too thick for them to recognize individuals, which only heightened their anxiety for the safety of their men. One of the observers was Mrs. T. C.

Davis, whose husband, Sgt. Thaddeus C. Davis of 3rd Company G, 40th North Carolina, was a member of the fort's garrison. Like all of the women in her company, Mrs. Davis feared for her own husband's safety.

> At times my imagination would tell me that my anxious eyes were resting upon him in that little group of heroic defenders. The next instant a monster shell would explode in their midst, enveloping everything in smoke and dust. At such moments I would feel as if my heart would burst. When the smoke would lift, we could see distinctly the lines engaged often in hand-to-hand fighting; but O! we could see so distinctly that the thin, gray line was growing thinner, and that the dark, heavy masses were growing heavier.[56]

Despite Major Reilly's best efforts, the Federals had seized seven land face traverses by 4:45 p.m., and had maintained their inexorable—albeit deliberate—assault on the parapet. Navy shells continued to burst with deadly accuracy amid the stubborn Confederate defenders on the ramparts and on the floor of the fort. Inexorably, the Confederates' will to fight was eroding. Reduced in number to a handful, exhausted by almost two hours of unrelenting combat, low on ammunition and demoralized by the fall of Lamb and Whiting and the failure of Bragg to reinforce them, the defenders found it more and more difficult to raise their rifle-muskets to their shoulders to fire on their vastly superior foe. What determination remained among the Confederates was undermined when a sizable contingent of their comrades raised their hands together in surrender.

During the height of the struggle in rear of the battlements, a white flag suddenly appeared at the entrance to the center sally-port. The musketry abruptly ceased as officers and enlisted men from both sides spotted the flag of truce. Major Reilly requested Capt. Kinchen Braddy to "go and see what it meant." Reilly thought that perhaps some Yankees were surrendering. Taking a white handkerchief loaned to him by Reilly, Captain Braddy attached it to the tip of his sword and advanced toward the postern. As he neared the covered way beneath the land face, Braddy recognized the soldiers as Confederates, and was shocked when they suddenly exited the postern and dashed toward the Union line. Major Reilly also observed this inexplicable surrender and immediately recalled Braddy. The captain snatched the handkerchief from his sword as he dashed to the rear, while

Reilly ordered his loyal troops to open fire on the Federal captors. A volley of rifle-musket fire rattled across the sandy expanse. "My gallant troops [were] greatly incensed at the dastardly conduct of their comrades," fumed James Reilly. "The men fought with more determination than ever."

On the Union side, Capt. R. D. Morehouse and a squad of men from the 142nd New York and 203rd Pennsylvania accepted the surrender of about eighty "sally-port Confederates," reportedly commanded by Capt. John T. Melvin of 2nd Company I, 36th North Carolina Regiment. According to a Keystone State soldier, the Rebels "gave up gracefully," with one exception: a disgusted Southern officer "threw his sword, belt and revolver into a pool of water close by." The prisoners were quickly taken to a bombproof in the rear and placed under heavy guard.[57]

General N. Martin Curtis had been on the front line all afternoon, fighting alongside his men as they filled one traverse and inexorably spilled into the next. As the Confederates obstinately relinquished possession of one traverse after another, Curtis sensed that the enemy's enthusiasm was beginning to wane. The New York officer was convinced that one more determined rush along the land face parapet would win the day. By then his troops had captured seven traverses and were close enough to the northeast bastion to prevent the Confederates from serving the lone 8-inch columbiad, whose fire had wreaked havoc on the naval column and Union infantrymen entering the fort. With his sharpshooters able to keep the Southern cannoneers from manning their heavy gun, Curtis proposed to attack the northeast bastion by marching a force between the land face's exterior slope and the palisade. It was, he believed, the safest line of approach.

Having suffered heavy casualties during the afternoon's fight, however, Curtis lacked the manpower for his proposed advance. He sent a courier to the rear to request reinforcements from General Ames, but to Curtis' dismay, the messenger returned with word from the division commander that no reinforcements would be forthcoming. Ames contended that his troops were too exhausted to make the effort and were making preparations to entrench for the night. Curtis should do the same.

A bewildered Curtis sent his orderly, A. D. Knight, to press for reinforcements, but Knight also reappeared with another order from General Ames to stand down. No further advance would be made that evening, and Curtis' troops should rest on their arms until morning, when they would again resume the fight with fresh troops that would be brought down from the northern line during the night. Absolutely convinced that he could capture the northeast bastion with a bold attack before dark (just as he had been convinced that he could have captured Fort Fisher during the December battle), Curtis sent Knight to the rear again with orders to bring officers and men of the First Brigade forward. If Ames would not provide him with soldiers, Curtis would attack with his own good men.

Instead of returning to the front with New Yorkers, Knight brought back an armful of shovels—courtesy of General Ames. Curtis was livid. Grabbing the tools, he hurled them over the traverse in the direction of the Confederates while screaming, "dig, Johnnies, I shall soon follow the shovels." Curtis then directed Silas W. Kempton of the U. S. Navy (who had earlier reported to the general as a temporary aide-de-camp), to find General Terry at Battery Holland and implore him to send reinforcements into the fort. "I instructed Kempton to state that the enemy were offering slight resistance, and that a bold push would secure a victory already substantially won," Curtis recalled. After sending off Kempton, Curtis instructed Capt. David B. Magill of Company A, 117th New York, to keep pressing the attack on the eighth traverse.

Having made these dispositions, Curtis hustled to the western end of the land face and onto the floor of the fort searching for men of his brigade to send to the front. While he was assembling his force, General Ames approached and verbally accosted Curtis. "I have two or three times sent word to fortify your position and hold until reinforcements can be sent to aid us," yelled Ames, addressing Curtis directly for the first time that day. "The men are exhausted, and I will not order them to go forward." Curtis replied by pointing to two transports on the Cape Fear River, apparently loaded with Confederate troops awaiting nightfall, which was only minutes away, to come ashore. "Should they succeed in landing they may be able to drive us out," Curtis retorted, "therefore, the fort should be captured before fresh troops come to the enemy." Victory was within the Federals' grasp, Curtis maintained, and could be won with one more determined push.

While making his argument, Curtis ascended a small sand dune in order to see the rear of the northeast bastion, the objective of his planned attack, when a shell fragment struck him in the face. The hot fragment of iron gouged out his left eye and blew away part of his frontal bone. The severe injury—at least Curtis' fifth wound of the day—was also his last. Unconscious and believed by his men to be mortally wounded, N. Martin Curtis—the Union hero of Fort Fisher—was unceremoniously dragged off the sandy battlefield at about 5:30 p.m.[58] The moment of crisis had arrived.

General Curtis was being carried from the fort when Alfred Terry sent reinforcements forward. The Provisional Corps commander was able to respond to Curtis' plea for assistance so quickly because he had already prepared for such a contingency. After the repulse of the naval column, Terry had requested Lieutenant Commander Cushing to deploy the sailors and marines on the northern line as replacements for Colonel Abbott's brigade, which Terry planned to send to the fort in support of Ames' division. It took some time to reassemble the scattered seamen, but by 4:30 p.m. they occupied the position vacated by Abbott's troops, who marched southward toward the fort, two miles distant. They reached Terry's headquarters at Battery Holland a little after sundown. Curtis' entreaty for additional men had just arrived, and without hesitation Terry sent Abbott's 1,500-man brigade to the fort with orders to report to Ames. The regiments went forward amid shouts of encouragement from veterans of the battle. "Hurry up, boys, we got 'em," and "Good for you; we've got seven mounds, and there's more [for the taking]." Abbott's spirited troops entered the fort about 6:00 p.m.[59]

For more than an hour Terry waited anxiously for the sudden burst of musketry that would indicate a renewal of the fighting at the fort. By 5:30 p.m. the small arms fire inside Fort Fisher had nearly ceased, as darkness and fatigue enveloped the soldiers on both sides. The dark night was broken only by the fiery flashes of guns and bursting shells. Although the firing had not entirely abated, the Federal advance had clearly ground to a halt. A worried Terry decided to go in person to the fort to assess the situation, while sending word to Charles Paine to dispatch one of the strongest regiments of his division of U.S. Colored Troops to the fort as additional reinforcements. Comstock had urged Terry to send for one of Paine's brigades "to make the greatest possible effort to get the fort now," but Terry did not want to risk sacrificing an entire brigade *and* his northern line in his effort to conquer the fort. As a result, Paine forwarded one regiment: Brig. Gen. Albert M. Blackman's 27th U. S. Colored Troops. As the 27th marched southward, Terry and Comstock entered Fort Fisher about 7:00 p.m.

The situation that confronted Terry inside the fort concerned him greatly. Ames' division was a mass of humanity haphazardly deployed on the fort's parade ground. Shortly after General Curtis' wounding, his resolute followers—Captain Magill, Lt. Col. Samuel Zent, Lt. William H. Walling, along with a squad of enlisted men—captured the eighth traverse on the parapet, but their advance had also since halted in the face of stiff enemy resistance. "The heavy loss of officers had thrown the machinery out of gear," was the analogy Capt. Adrian Terry used in describing the state of affairs inside the fort. Moreover, instead of attacking the demoralized Confederates with Abbott's fresh brigade of infantry (many of whom were armed with Spencer repeating rifles), General Ames had deployed three of the regiments—the 6th and 7th Connecticut and the 3rd New Hampshire—in reserve on the floor of the fort. General Terry found Abbott's fourth regiment, the 7th New Hampshire, posted in rear of Shepherd's Battery awaiting orders.

In conference with General Terry, Adelbert Ames proposed to continue fortifying his position, which he had begun doing about sunset, and wait until morning to resume operations. Alfred Terry flatly rejected Ames' plan. The Rebels, Terry contended, were just as exhausted as Ames' men, and should not be given time to rest, receive reinforcements or escape. Terry had observed steam transports plying the river all afternoon and was certain (as General Curtis had been earlier), that they would dock during the night to either disembark fresh Confederate troops at Fort Fisher or carry the fort's beleaguered garrison to safety. Terry was determined to prevent either possibility from occurring.

The corps commander and his subordinates briefly discussed the feasibility of relieving Ames' division by bringing Charles J. Paine's two brigades into the fort, but decided against it. Such a movement would be both logistically difficult and too time consuming. Cyrus Comstock suggested using Abbott's newly-arrived brigade (as Terry had originally intended), as

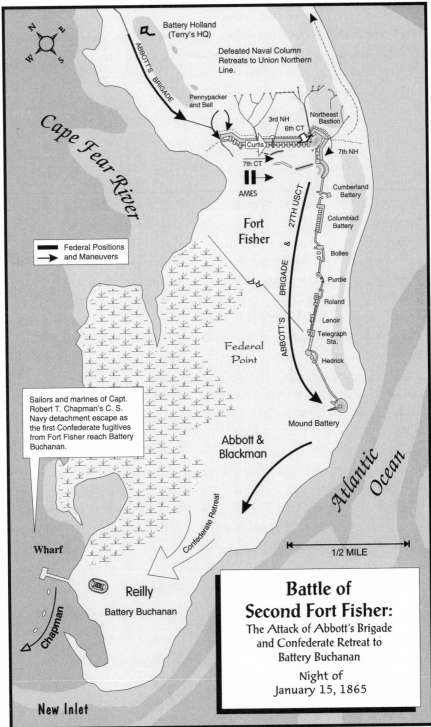

Battle of
Second Fort Fisher:
The Attack of Abbott's Brigade
and Confederate Retreat to
Battery Buchanan

Night of
January 15, 1865

Mark A. Moore

shock troops in a renewed assault on the enemy-held traverses along the land face. Terry agreed, and orders for the movement were immediately dispatched to Colonel Abbott. The darkness hampered Abbott's efforts, and it was almost 9:00 p.m. before the New Englanders were ready to launch their new attack.[60]

While Abbott's Federals were preparing to advance, an aide reported to Colonel Lamb at the Pulpit Battery hospital. The situation appeared hopeless, the soldier lamented. Ammunition was nearly depleted and the men were worn out, while the Yankees—with half the land face and much of the parade ground in their possession—appeared to be gearing up for yet another assault. Under the circumstances, the aide suggested, a continuation of the struggle would be a needless sacrifice of Lamb's remaining soldiers. Lamb adamantly refused to stop the fighting. "When it is remembered that I had promised the noble women of Wilmington who had visited the fort after our Christmas victory that their homes should be protected by my garrison," Lamb noted, "and that General Lee had sent word that if the fort fell he could not maintain his army (and that meant the loss of our cause), is it to be wondered that I felt it my sacred duty, even after I was shot down, to appeal to the officers and men to fight in defence of the last gateway to the South, as long as there was a ray of hope?" William Lamb truly believed that the fate of the Confederacy was in his hands. Whiting agreed with his protégé, assuring him that should Lamb die, he would not surrender either.[61]

The struggle for Fort Fisher had degenerated into a battle of wills between the Confederate and Union commanders. But while Whiting and Lamb had little other than sheer determination upon which to rely, the Federals had access to large numbers of fresh reinforcements—including Colonel Abbott's brigade of Connecticut and New Hampshire boys, which was even now moving into position to renew the attack.

At 9:00 p.m. Capt. William H. Trickey advanced his 3rd New Hampshire along the parapet to the eighth traverse, which was still occupied by

Curtis' band of infantrymen. Armed with rapid-firing Spencer rifles and supported by enfilade fire from their brigade comrades of the 7th Connecticut on the parade ground to their right, twenty of Trickey's hand-picked marksmen charged and quickly overran the obstinate Confederates manning the ninth traverse. While Trickey and his soldiers clambered over the bodies of the dead and wounded to secure the huge sand mound, the 7th New Hampshire—followed soon thereafter by the 6th Connecticut—dashed along the land face between the foot of the fort and the palisade. The New Hampshire men swept around the northeast bastion, scaled the sea face and unleashed a heavy volley from atop the battery's immense thirty-two foot high walls into the fort's surprised defenders. The 6th Connecticut followed with a charge over the north wall of the fort. Their flagging spirits renewed by the success of Abbott's brigade, Ames' troops rushed forward "with a momentum no power could stop," cheering as they advanced.[62]

Confederate soldiers at the northeast bastion scrambled for refuge in nearby bombproofs or attempted to escape by retreating southward along the line of sea face batteries. Despite their best efforts, many fleeing Southerners were captured by the swarming Federal soldiers. Anticipating the fort's fall, Major Reilly had Colonel Lamb and General Whiting carried on stretchers from the Pulpit Battery hospital to Battery Buchanan. As Lamb was being carried away, Capt. Edward B. Dudley, 2nd Company D, 36th North Carolina, took the colonel's saber and sword belt. "No damned Yankee shall ever have this sword!" he exclaimed as he heaved it into the Atlantic Ocean.

Reilly held on long enough to give Lamb's and Whiting's litter bearers a good head start, but when Abbott's brigade overran the northeast bastion, he had no choice but to evacuate the massive sand fort. By then, Reilly's effective force had dwindled to a mere handful of exhausted men. "I formed my brave little command of thirty-two into a column of fours, and with saddened hearts marched away from the fort we had defended with all our might," Reilly recalled.

The major planned to reform his scattered command once it reached Battery Buchanan, where the Confederates expected support from Capt. Robert T. Chapman's naval contingent and the battery's big seacoast guns. Upon their arrival, however, the major and his men were shocked to discover that the sailors and marines had left their posts. About 500 escapees from Fort Fisher milled about the battery, their only route of escape having vanished with Captain Chapman's boats, whose abrupt departure abandoned "[the fort's] garrison to their fate." Hearing rumors during the evening that the fort's fall was imminent, Chapman decided to save himself and his small command by ordering his men to "get away as best they could," using the boats at Battery Buchanan's wharf. The last of Chapman's vessels pulled away from the banks of the Cape Fear River just as the first fugitives from Fort Fisher reached Buchanan.

James Reilly was furious. Abandoned first by Bragg and now by Chapman, his survivors were left stranded on Federal Point. Reilly, who had been depending on Chapman to assist Fort Fisher's defenders, later claimed that he had sent Capt. Zachariah Adams to Buchanan that afternoon with orders for the naval commander to hold the battery and be ready to fight the enemy. Adams had returned to Fort Fisher with Chapman's terse reply: "very well." "I thought [Chapman] too good a soldier to abandon us," Reilly wrote. He was wrong. Left with few options, Reilly and several other officers worked to reorganize their troops to meet the approaching Federal juggernaut. It was a futile exercise. Three-fourths of the men were without weapons and could offer no armed resistance. There was nothing left for the Confederates to do but surrender.[63]

Accompanied by Maj. James H. Hill, General Whiting's chief-of-staff, and Capt. A. C. Van Benthuysen of the C. S. Marine Corps, Major Reilly retraced his steps toward the fort to meet the enemy commander. The Confederate officers halted about three hundred yards from Battery Buchanan. Reilly pulled a handkerchief from his pocket (perhaps the same handkerchief he had loaned to Captain Braddy at the fort earlier that afternoon) and tied it to the tip of his saber. With nothing left to do, he awaited the enemy. "It was a distressing time to me and the brave officers and men under my command," Reilly admitted.[64]

Regiments of Colonel Abbott's brigade—augmented by General Blackman's 27th U. S. Colored Troops of Paine's division, which was brought down for mop-up operations at the fort—cautiously advanced in skirmish formation, securing the fort's lower batteries. When the Federals reached the Mound Battery, Capt. J. Homer Edgerly of Company F, 3rd New Hampshire, left the column temporarily to secure a trophy of the great battle. He scaled the lofty gun emplacement and captured the Confederate flag, which still waved defiantly from the same staff Pvt. Christopher Bland had climbed during the Battle of First Fort Fisher. Now the famous Mound Battery and its coveted banner belonged to the Union. The advance along the sea face had captured several Confederate stragglers, who informed Colonel Abbott that Fort Fisher's garrison had retreated to Battery Buchanan. Abbott deployed his men into a line of battle and slowly pushed them southward, fully expecting "a shower of grape and musketry from the last refuge of rebels." A rising moon brightly illuminated the sandy peninsula and the blue-uniformed troops as they marched uncontested toward Buchanan. The deadly Southern fire never materialized.[65]

The line of Federals continued its cautious advance until Capt. E. Lewis Moore, the adjutant of the 7th Connecticut, encountered Major Reilly and his small entourage of officers clustered near Battery Buchanan. Reilly offered his sword in surrender, and Moore accepted it. Colonel Abbott and General Blackman soon arrived at the scene and were directed by James H. Hill to Battery Buchanan and the stretchers bearing the wounded General Whiting and Colonel Lamb.[66]

Moments before the Federals reached the Confederate commanders, Brig. Gen. Alfred H. Colquitt appeared at Battery Buchanan, having been sent by boat from Sugar Loaf with orders from General Bragg to take command at Fort Fisher. Lamb and Whiting had not heard from Bragg since the bungled attempt early that morning to land reinforcements from Hagood's Brigade. Though painfully wounded, William Lamb implored Colquitt to appeal to Bragg to counterattack, believing that a fresh brigade could retake Fort Fisher from the battle-weary Federals. Lamb also pleaded with Colquitt to take General Whiting with him to Sugar Loaf, arguing that his superior was more gravely wounded than himself, and that he preferred to remain and share the fate of his soldiers. Suddenly, Federal troops appeared out of the darkness, and Colquitt, like Captain Chapman before him, beat a hasty retreat, abandoning Whiting and Lamb—and their men—to their fate.[67]

Abbott's and Blackman's troops surrounded Battery Buchanan about 10:00 p.m. They found the Confederates standing silently in groups, waiting for the end. Having followed close behind the pursuing force, Alfred H. Terry came forward and received the formal surrender of the fort from its commanding officers—Colonel Lamb and General Whiting, who were both lying in agony on stretchers in the sand. Adrian Terry described the imperfect ceremony: "Gen. Whiting inquired for the Comdg. Officer and Alfred walked up to him and stated his name and rank. Gen. Whiting said I surrender, sir, to you the forces under my command, I care not what becomes of myself." General Terry promised Whiting that he and his command would receive kind treatment. The prisoners were rounded up and marched under guard back to Fort Fisher during the early morning hours of January 16. The severely wounded Whiting was borne on a litter by some of his staff. When the time came for the captured officers and enlisted men to be separated, Little Billy bade farewell to his troops. "Goodbye, boys," he said with a wave of his hand. "They have got us but you have done your duty well." It was the last time the soldiers would see their beloved commander.[68]

Soon after Whiting's assisted departure, General Terry mounted a captured Southerner's horse and galloped back to Fort Fisher. Along the way he met Captain Edgerly of the 3rd New Hampshire, who presented the commanding general with the Confederate flag he had pilfered from the Mound Battery. A short time later Terry rode into the main part of the fort with the Mound Battery's standard wrapped around him. Recognizing the flag-draped conqueror of Fort Fisher, the Union soldiers cheered him. Terry acknowledged their applause: "Boys, rather than that you should cheer for me, I ought to cheer for you."[69]

General Terry immediately relayed news of the triumph to Admiral Porter, but the tidings of victory had already reached the navy through the hearty cheers of the Union troops onshore. It was not long before the warships set off a magnificent fireworks display to celebrate the fort's fall. "At once the [eastern] sky was full of rockets and many colored lights," observed one Federal soldier, "and as the showers of red, white, and blue stars fell into the sea, we knew that the navy was proclaiming victory!"[70]

Battery Buchanan, at the tip of Federal Point, where Confederate troops from Fort Fisher surrendered after being abandoned by Buchanan's naval commander. *U.S. Army Military History Institute*

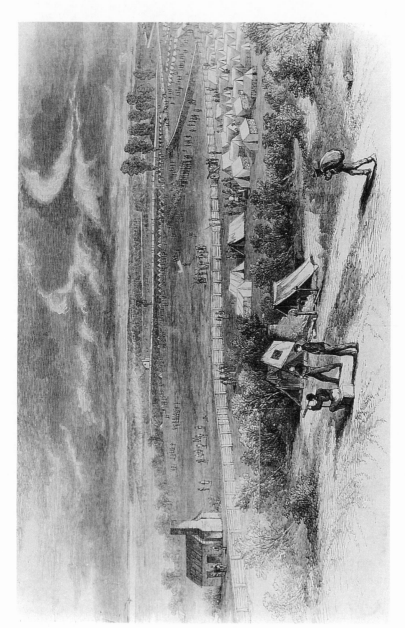

General Alfred Terry's fortified encampment on Federal Point. *Frank Leslie's Illustrated Newspaper*

". . .thus is sealed the door through which this rebellion is fed."
– *Rear Admiral David D. Porter*

VICTORY—AND STALEMATE

James Chapman Stevenson was fortunate to have escaped from Federal Point. As Union soldiers pursued Fort Fisher's garrison withdrawing down the peninsula, Stevenson fled with the sailors and marines from Battery Buchanan, Captain Chapman having ordered them to evacuate and save themselves. Stevenson commandeered a fishing boat that was docked at the battery's wharf and quickly sailed off into the darkness, heading for Battery Lamb on the west side of the Cape Fear River opposite Fort Fisher. He also managed to load several wounded soldiers into his boat and carry them to safety.

Stevenson had begun his wartime service as a teenaged purser's clerk on board the blockade runner *Advance*, and was now an operator in the Confederate Signal Corps. As such, he had been stationed at Battery Buchanan, only a mile from Fort Fisher's lower sea face batteries, which were commanded by his father, Maj. James Martin Stevenson of the 36th North Carolina Regiment. During lulls in the ferocious bombardment, Stevenson had run from Buchanan to the fort to visit his father, who was desperately ill and had also been wounded during the battle. His ailing father was not among the soldiers he was transporting from Federal Point, a fact that deeply concerned the young Stevenson. But, there was still a chance the elder Stevenson might be rescued.

When Stevenson reached Battery Lamb, he was told that a message had been received from Battery Buchanan requesting that a boat be sent to transport wounded officers. Hopeful that his father might be among them,

Stevenson volunteered to return with his craft and immediately started back across the river. He and his crew were impeded by a heavy flood tide, however, and were having difficulty making headway. They had sailed about halfway across the river when the night sky over the ocean was suddenly illuminated by hundreds of color rockets. "The boat's crew knew this meant surrender," Stevenson commented, "and they refused to go further."

As he and his comrades swung their boat around and headed back toward Battery Lamb, a dejected Stevenson thought about the last time he had seen his father and what they had discussed. His father had talked to him as if it would be their last meeting. "He called me to

A previously unpublished portrait of Maj. James Martin Stevenson, 36th North Carolina Regiment (2nd North Carolina Artillery), who died in captivity. *Author's Collection*

him, took my hand in his and told me that the care of the family would devolve on me and he felt satisfied that I would prove equal to the occasion," young Stevenson wrote. "He gave me some good advice which I remember to this day." Not until the war was over did Stevenson learn that his father had died a prisoner-of-war at Fort Columbus on Governor's Island in New York harbor.[1]

Other Confederate soldiers, watching from their posts in the Cape Fear estuary, also realized that the naval fireworks signified a disaster. Stragglers who had escaped the melée at Fort Fisher slowly made their way across the river and reported on the fort's fall. About midnight General Hébert at Smithville telegraphed Bragg: "Last information is that Fort Fisher is surrendered. I await orders." General Colquitt confirmed the reports of the demise of the fort when he returned from his ill-fated trip to Battery Buchanan. There was no doubt: the Federals had conquered Fort Fisher.[2]

Braxton Bragg was stunned by the "unexpected blow," as he described the fort's fall. How could this have happened? Only two hours before Bragg had been confident that the fort would hold. "My mind was easy," he maintained. "The defense of the fort ought to have been successful against this attack." But the commander in whom the Confederate president and the commanding general of the Army of Northern Virginia had placed so much faith in safeguarding the South's last major pipeline of supplies also stated that Fort Fisher's fall was inevitable. "It had to fall eventually," Bragg wrote rather indifferently. In Braxton Bragg's mind, neither he or any other soldier could have prevented the outcome. "Blockade running has cured itself," Bragg argued. "I knew its demoralizing influence, and even before I came here, and urged the President to remove these officers and troops and replacing them by veterans. I was at work on these evils, gradually correcting them, but meeting with the usual denunciation. Time was not allowed." Bragg believed that had he been given more time to "remove these evils" from Wilmington, he might have delayed the inevitable. Under the circumstances, he could hardly be blamed for the loss of Fort Fisher. After all, Union soldiers reported that they had "walked into the fort without resistance, not a shot being fired at them, [Whiting's] men all being in the bombproofs." Small squads of Confederate defenders offered stubborn resistance, but hundreds of Southerners, Bragg believed, milled about in their bunkers without firearms, "many of them drunk, and no one apparently in command," waiting for the Federals to capture them. "The expedition brought against [Fort Fisher] was able to reduce it in spite of all I could do," Bragg lamented.

Bragg had no choice but to inform Richmond of the tragic turn of events. At 1:00 p.m. on January 16 he telegraphed President Davis: "I am mortified to report the unexpected capture of Fort Fisher, with most of its garrison." Copies were also wired to General Lee and Governor Vance. Horrified, Davis quickly responded. "Can you retake the fort?" he wanted to know. "If anything is to be done you will appreciate the necessity of its being attempted without a moment's delay." Bragg refused to consider the idea, fearful that the huge guns of Porter's fleet alone would be sufficient to destroy his assaulting force before it could even reach the fort.[3]

Unlike his hollow response to the Federal attack on Fort Fisher, Bragg was quick to respond to the fort's fall, instructing all of his forces to withdraw to the Sugar Loaf-Fort Anderson line in order to protect Wilmington. Bragg's decision resulted in the evacuation of the fortifications in the estuary south of Fort Fisher, including Forts Caswell and Campbell, Battery Shaw on Oak Island, Fort Holmes on Smith Island, Fort Pender at Smithville, as well as Battery Lamb on Reeves Point. Bragg realized that their abandonment would give the Federals control of both Old and New inlets, but these positions were of little use in protecting Wilmington-bound blockade runners now that Fort Fisher had fallen. Bragg was more concerned now that Porter could steam his gunboats through New Inlet and into the Cape Fear River, isolating Confederate troops below. He immediately ordered General Hébert to destroy the fortifications and their contents and to do so quickly. But many of Bragg's troops believed that the department commander was simply withdrawing because he was frightened. "[Bragg] is too fond of retreating or too fearful of being taken by the enemy," one thoroughly disgusted soldier contended.[4]

While the Confederates were preparing to abandon their positions at Old Inlet and Smithville, Union and Confederate survivors of the horrific battle at Fort Fisher were just beginning to stir. Thoroughly exhausted by the fierce hand-to-hand combat of the day before, many of the soldiers had dropped to the ground and fallen asleep, oblivious to the carnage about them. The men awoke on the morning of January 16 to a grisly scene almost too horrible to describe. "Headless trunks, shattered limbs, and bodies lay thick on the parapets, in the traverses, as well as everywhere all over the fort, which indicated the terribly destructive nature of the fire of our fleet among the Rebels," recalled one New York soldier. Paymaster Henry M. Rogers of the *Gettysburg* claimed that the sights he saw in Fort Fisher would "horrify even the stoutest heart. Devastation, ruin, [and] death in every attitude and every form, these are the things that I have looked upon, and these are the things we lose sight of when the pride, pomp and circumstance of 'Glorious War' are mentioned."[5]

A Union naval officer's description was even more surreal:

Within the fallen Fort were sights sickening and dreadful. Guns dismounted, guns split, guns broken; caps, clothes, bayonets, swords, muskets, rifles, scattered, battered, blood-stained; belts, knapsacks, powder in bags, cartridges, dead horses, broken bottles, shells exploded, bullets, scabbards, bedding. And then the dead! Men in all postures, mangled in the head and body, with brains out, but with perfect features, covered with sand and grimed with powder. Arms, legs, hands, faces distorted, swollen, all in the traverses, in the trenches, in green water pools, in the bombproofs, upon the parapet, down the embankments, here, there, everywhere. Piles of dead men upon which the victorious soldiers were partaking lunch, while, in another place, the same ghastly table was made for the convenience of the euchre players. The carrying past of the wounded, the groans of the dying, and the smell of blood and powder!"[6]

The demons had feasted at Fort Fisher and then had allowed the survivors to slumber. The bombproofs and large sand mounds that dotted the interior of the fort made inviting beds. Sunrise brought a strange discovery. In some cases, men had slumbered side-by-side with the dead or with enemy soldiers whom they had tried so hard to kill only hours before.

Yet for others it had been impossible to sleep, as chaos reigned in the fort following the battle. Weary Union troops of Abbott's brigade had been detailed to escort the Confederate prisoners from Battery Buchanan to bivouac near old Camp Wyatt a mile north of the fort. Other soldiers spent much of the night in search of plunder, ransacking the bodies of friend and foe alike. The greed of one band of looters had tragic consequences for unsuspecting Union and Confederate soldiers within the fort.

Just after sunrise on January 16, a gigantic explosion rocked Fort Fisher. An immense column of sand, debris and bodies shot as high as 600 feet into the air, mushroomed out above the fort, and then descended as quickly as it had risen, burying everything beneath it. The fort's main magazine in rear of the northeast bastion had blown up. The 13,000 pounds of gunpowder stored within the magazine was far less that the 430,000 pounds on board General Butler's powder boat *Louisiana*, (detonated during First Fort Fisher), but it had exploded with far more devastating effect.

By most estimates, about 200 Union and Confederate soldiers were killed by the blast, many buried alive under tons of sand. Among the various units near the blast site, infantrymen from the 4th New Hampshire and the 115th and 169th New York regiments of the Third Brigade suffered the greatest number of casualties. The 169th reportedly lost forty men killed and

The explosion of Fort Fisher's main powder magazine early on January 16, 1865, buried more than 200 Federals and Confederates under tons of sand and debris. *Frank Leslie's Illustrated History*

sixty wounded, including Col. Alonzo Alden, the regiment's commander. Alden suffered a concussion and two broken legs in the explosion. Though he survived, he spent the next six weeks in a coma. Others were crushed or buried alive, including Cpl. Anton Reder of Company A, 169th New York. Although Reder escaped a horrible death by suffocation when his comrades dug him out of the sand and debris, the explosion left him with a crippling back injury. The men of the 115th New York failed to find three of their favorite comrades—a hospital steward, a drummer boy and a Frenchman of Company G—after the explosion. The bodies of ten men of the 203rd Pennsylvania were allegedly found together in one hole. The naval arm also suffered in the ordeal, losing about twelve men in the blast. "Brave men and officers, who yesterday had passed safely through the baptism of death in battle, have now, in a twinkle and entirely unexpected, been blown to atoms by this explosion," lamented one of the survivors.[7]

James A. Mowris, surgeon of the 117th New York, miraculously survived the blast. He had been on the exterior slope of Fort Fisher near the northeast bastion when the explosion occurred. The earth shook violently, knocking Mowris to the

Corporal Anton Reder, Company A, 169th New York Infantry, in a previously unpublished image. Reder suffered a crippling back injury when Fort Fisher's magazine exploded.

Courtesy of
Laurine and Orville Mooberry

ground, and he soon found himself buried beneath a mound of sand. His arm broken, Mowris somehow dug his way out of his "rude grave" before struggling up to the parapet to look inside the fort. "What a sight presented!" he exclaimed. "The great mound of sand which had been the magazine had disappeared. A wide excavation marked the spot where it had stood." The victims of the terrible casualty," Mowris continued, "were seen here and there. [Other soldiers] had been buried in a nameless grave, while the surface of the general graveyard was already dotted with mutilated victims."[8]

Angry Union soldiers suspected sabotage by dastardly Rebels despondent over the loss of their precious fort. Rumor had it that a Confederate officer had been caught sneaking around inside the bunker just a half an hour before the explosion occurred. Lieutenant Colonel Nathan J. Johnson of the 115th New York discovered a "submarine wire" leading from the magazine to the Cape Fear River, suggesting to him that the store of gunpowder had been detonated by saboteurs on the waterway's west bank. Cries of revenge were heard throughout the fort before cooler heads prevailed and order was restored.

General Terry immediately opened an official investigation, interviewing witnesses and key personnel from both armies, including the wounded General Whiting. The Confederate commander assured Terry that his men would never have committed such a cowardly act, and indeed the evidence seemed to support Whiting's contention. Throughout the night and the early morning hours following the battle, blue-uniformed soldiers, sailors and marines roamed the fort at liberty. Many of them were drunk and discharging their firearms in celebration of the victory. To prevent any mishaps, Lt. Col. Samuel M. Zent of the 13th Indiana was ordered to place guards at the entrances to all magazines and bombproofs. The main magazine somehow escaped Zent's notice and he failed to post guards at that point. "Not seeing an entrance to this mound (it was on the side and mostly underground) it did not occur to us that it was a magazine containing some thirteen thousand pounds of powder," explained Zent.

Zent and others observed several marines bearing torches enter the bunker a short time before the explosion. "We noticed a squad of marines—3 or 4 in number—enter a trap door on the side of the mound along side of which the 169th N.Y. was sleeping," Zent testified. Moments later the mound blew up. After considering the testimony of Zent and many other eyewitnesses, the court of inquiry ruled that the explosion was "the result of carelessness on the part of persons unknown," though in all likelihood those persons were Union seamen.

If the "fizzle" of Ben Butler's powder boat experiment opened the first battle of Fort Fisher on a comic note, the explosion of the fort's main powder magazine closed the second battle in the dark hues of tragedy.[9]

And so it was over. The most powerful Confederate seacoast fortification had fallen. In order to capture Fort Fisher, the Union navy had supported the Union army with the two greatest bombardments in the history of modern warfare up to that time. The gunboats fired 39,953 projectiles at the fort—20,271 in the December attack, and another 19,682 in the January fight, or 1,464 tons of metal. The combined Union losses in the second battle totaled between 1,166 and 1,452 killed, wounded and missing. Official reports show 664 casualties in Ames' division alone. This figure does not include losses in Abbott's or Paines' brigades or from the powder magazine tragedy. Unofficial army returns place the corps' casualty figures much higher—an aggregate of 955 battle victims and at least another 104 casualties in the magazine explosion. Of the eighteen Union army regiments engaged in the battle, the 203rd Pennsylvania suffered the greatest number of casualties: forty killed (including its colonel and lieutenant colonel), 146 wounded and one missing. That number comprised almost thirty-six percent of the regiment's 525 soldiers that saw action. Official U.S. Navy casualty reports are higher than most unofficial accounts, with a grand total of 393 sailors and marines listed as either killed or wounded in the battle or the morning after. Confederate casualties are more difficult to calculate due to incomplete records. Southern losses in the second battle totaled about 500 men killed and wounded, with the remainder of the garrison, about 1,400 men, taken prisoner.[10]

Admiral Porter entertained General Terry on board the *Malvern*, through much of January 16. Porter expressed his great admiration for the Connecticut officer. "He is my beau ideal of a soldier and a general," the veteran seaman exclaimed. "Our cooperation has been most cordial; the result is victory, which will always be ours when the Army and Navy go hand in hand." Terry evinced a similar statement of respect for the admiral.

The celebration continued when Secretary of War Edwin M. Stanton arrived at Fort Fisher unexpectedly late that afternoon. Lincoln's cabinet officer was making a six-hour layover during his journey back to Washington, D.C. after a visit with General Sherman in Georgia. The secretary rejoiced over the news of the victory at Fort Fisher by reportedly throwing his hat into the ocean. "Probably no man was ever more overcome with joy than was Secretary Stanton. . .," noted a Union soldier. As befitted the occasion, General Terry presented Stanton with the Confederate flag taken off the Mound Battery. After receiving a full report of the action, Stanton penned an official note of congratulations and thanks in the president's name to both Porter and Terry and their respective forces for their "great achievement against Fort Fisher." The Secretary also immediately promoted the soldiers who had been prominent in the battle. Brevet Major General Terry was appointed major general and later brigadier general in the Regular Army—the only volunteer officer in the army to attain that rank during the war.

In appreciation for his valued assistance to Terry, Lt. Col. Cyrus Comstock was promoted to brevet brigadier general, jumping two grades in the process. Though both were badly wounded, Brevet Brigadier General Curtis was made brigadier general, and Col. Galusha Pennypacker was promoted to brevet brigadier general. When his appointment was approved the following month, twenty-year-old Pennypacker became the youngest general in U.S. military history. Adelbert Ames was pleased to be promoted to brevet major general, but was incensed to learn that Secretary Stanton's official report to President Lincoln noted that the assault on Fort Fisher "was made by. . .the Old Tenth Corps, led by [General] Curtis, under the immediate supervision of General Terry." Ames was convinced that Terry had purposely neglected to give the division commander credit for leading the attack. "Ames is mad," one officer stated, "(and) won't speak to Terry except officially with his sword on."

The bad blood between Terry and Ames did not dampen the North's jubilation over the "great triumph" along the Cape Fear River. Calling it "one of the most important successes of the war" when he received the news on January 17, U.S. Grant ordered a 100-gun salute to be fired by each army. The lieutenant general also instructed his own officers to make sure the Rebels in their front knew of affairs at the Cape Fear, knowing full well that news of the fort's fall would have a demoralizing effect on the Southerners. Gideon Welles also ordered the U.S. Navy to fire honorary salutes. Congress sent resolutions to General Terry and Admiral Porter, the veteran seaman's fourth wartime thank you from the Senate and the House of Representatives. "We had some very important naval victories during the war, but none so important as Fort Fisher" Porter boasted. "Its fall sealed the fate of the Confederacy."

The general and the admiral went ashore the following morning to inspect the prize. Porter was awed by what he saw. "[I] find [Fort Fisher's] strength greatly beyond what I had conceived; an engineer might be excusable in saying they could not be captured except by regular siege. I wonder even now how it was done," Porter marveled. "How it was done" is no mystery. The overwhelming firepower from the largest fleet of gunboats assembled during the war all but assured a Federal victory. Fifty-eight vessels mounting 594 guns maintained a continuous bombardment for three days and two nights, eventually destroying or dismounting almost every Confederate cannon on the land face, splintering the palisade and severing the wires to the torpedoes in front of the fort. This extensive damage made the fort's defenses vulnerable to a ground assault by a numerically superior force. The organization of, and the cooperation between the Union army and navy, the determination of their commanders and the proper execution of their strategy, ensured the Union victory.[11]

Wilmingtonians were stunned and angry when they awoke January 16 to the news that Fort Fisher had been captured. Their seaport was now cut off from the rest of the world. "Another disaster is added to our long list of defeats and croaking has received another impulse," wrote the editor of the *Wilmington Daily North Carolinian*. "[The fall of Fort Fisher] does mean closing up the blockade running port of Wilmington," conceded another journalist. "In that sense of the word it is a severe blow." The fort's fall was also felt in Europe, which had not recognized Confederate sovereignty and now appeared even less likely to do so. "The storm of Fort Fisher killed the Confederacy in Europe and Europe in the Confederacy," was the general, if not quite accurate, consensus.

Many Southerners, however, viewed the defeat as simply another setback that could be overcome with determination, sacrifice and hard fighting. "In the future we shall have no more importations from Europe," announced the *Richmond Whig*. "This will be a great inconvenience certainly, but it by no means decides the questions of independence or subjugation. That question has yet to be decided on the battlefield." The editor of the *Wilmington Daily Journal* echoed that optimistic sentiment. "The cause is not gone up," he wrote. "We must expect difficulties. Now is the time to try our manhood." To many Southerners, the war was as of yet undecided.[12]

The citizens of Wilmington knew, however, that their city was now the Federals' primary objective. But when—and from what point—would the next phase of the campaign commence?

While the Federals celebrated their great triumph at Fort Fisher, the Confederates prepared to abandon their forts to the south. The evacuation of Fort Holmes on Bald Head Island progressed poorly. The 40th North Carolina (3rd North Carolina Artillery), commanded by Col. John J. Hedrick, set fire to everything that would burn, including some provisions that might have been salvaged. Storehouses replete with new gray wool uniforms and imported rifle-muskets were committed to the flames, along with barracks, wagons and gun carriages. The wasteful destruction infuriated one incredulous soldier, who queried sarcastically: "Were the troops on Smith Island allowed to take off new clothing that was there and leave their old clothes? Could not the [British] Enfield rifles have been saved?" Captain William Badham, Jr., commander of Company B, 3rd Battalion North Carolina Light Artillery, rescued his field pieces and horses, but other cannon were needlessly destroyed and the throats of the draft horses slit. Amid the confusion of the evacuation, some soldiers broke into the fort's whiskey supply and drank deeply of the liquid. It was a disgraceful affair, according to some, but others conceded that at least some of the whiskey thereby escaped destruction. Within five hours of receiving orders to withdraw, Hedrick's soldiers abandoned Fort Holmes to the crackling flames.[13]

When Hedrick's evacuees reached Smithville, they found General Hébert and some of his troops drunk. Hébert was generally considered "a faithful and brave officer," but according to one of his soldiers, his conduct during the evacuation was inexcusable, and he failed to execute Bragg's orders. The department commander had instructed Hébert to use the transport steamers *Cape Fear* and *Petteway* to remove troops and supplies at the forts, but with the exception of Fort Holmes, Hébert failed to do so. Instead, he requested that wagons be sent down from Wilmington, and ordered the *Cape Fear* and *Petteway* burned at their Smithville moorings before daylight on January 17. Hébert assumed that Federal gunboats were already in the river, prompting him to destroy his transports to keep them from falling into enemy hands. "The destruction of the vessels was the result of the General's imbecility," rebuked Capt. William Badham. "They could have been easily saved, and brought to [Fort Anderson] more than half of the commissary and quarter stores, which were recklessly destroyed."[14]

Hébert retreated from Smithville at 7:40 a.m. on January 17. The wagons that were supposed to have been sent from Wilmington never arrived, so the supplies that he managed to save were transferred to Fort Anderson in whatever method of conveyance he had on hand—including ambulances. There was some suspicion among the troops that Hébert transported "private property" while leaving behind vital government stores and sick and wounded soldiers. There is some evidence to support these allegations of Hébert's negligence. According to one observer, as soon as the Confederates moved out of Smithville, its residents descended on Fort Pender's commissary storehouse and soldiers' quarters to plunder their contents. They took a "respectable quantity of provisions," including pork, meal, hardtack and canned beef, as well as uniforms, muskets, swords, bayonets and plenty of ammunition. Young boys who were said to resemble "sawed-off militiamen," toted rifle-muskets with fixed bayonets while parading through Smithville's streets, occasionally pausing to "blaze away" with their weapons. When the Federals entered Smithville the next day, they captured fortyfour Confederate invalids and their attendants and confiscated the firearms of the would-be boy soldiers. Within days Hébert was reassigned to the post of chief engineer of the Department of North Carolina. Although his new posting was technically a promotion, some of Hébert's soldiers suspected that his mismanagement of the evacuation had prompted the high command to remove him from field duty.[15]

The abandonment of the works on Oak Island, though also marked by unnecessary loss, was well coordinated and executed. Colonel Charles H. Simonton, a South Carolina officer who was in overall command on the island, received Hébert's order to withdraw shortly before 3:00 a.m. on January 16. Simonton hurriedly assembled the officers of the island's fortifications—Maj. Alexander MacRae from Fort Campbell, Lt. Col. John Douglas Taylor at Fort Caswell, and the commander of Battery Shaw—to plan the retreat to Fort Anderson.[16]

Hébert made no attempt to aid Simonton by loaning him the *Cape Fear* and *Petteway* to remove troops and stores. Instead the garrison troops made a forced march to Fort Anderson, removing their own equipment and what personal affects they could carry. They left the forts at 6:00 a.m. on January 16, and "wound their way with heavy hearts" down the beach and into the woods to await the demolition teams that had been left behind to destroy the forts. "It was with bitter feelings that I turned my back upon the mouth of the Cape Fear," lamented Lt. William Calder, an adjutant in the 1st Battalion North Carolina Heavy Artillery and a native Wilmingtonian. "I left many things I cannot replace, but saved all that was actually necessary. . .life and liberty."[17]

Throughout January 16, Lt. Eugene S. Martin, chief ordnance officer on Oak Island, made preparations to destroy the forts. Guns were spiked, carriages were set on fire (including the beautiful mahogany carriage that mounted Fort Caswell's imported 8-inch 150-pounder Armstrong gun), and powder piled high with fuses laid to explode the ordnance magazines. Hébert's order to blow the works came at 1:20 a.m. on January 17. Within minutes the buildings and gun carriages were torched and the fuses lit. The explosion of Fort Caswell's main magazine—said to have contained 100,000 pounds of gunpowder—was immense. It demolished much of the old fort's northside brick wall, hurled several massive seacoast guns off their carriages and nearly buried others in the sand, unroofed nearby buildings and left behind a deep crater. "As if a mighty volcano had sprung its blazing contents from the sea into the sky, a great light flashed up from Fort Caswell, accompanied by a roar and a jar that smashed

A previously unpublished image of Pvt. James Dallas Croom, Company B, 1st Battalion North Carolina Heavy Artillery. Croom, one of the defenders of Fort Caswell until Braxton Bragg ordered its evacuation, withdrew with his comrades to Fort Anderson.

Courtesy of
James McCallum

the glass in our house like the wave of an earthquake," noted a young boy who watched the explosion from his home in Smithville. Apparently the explosion's loud report led the Federals at New Inlet to believe that another magazine in Fort Fisher had blown up. Detonations of the other fortifications' magazines in the following hour-and-a-half produced several more powerful reports and shock waves that were distinctly felt in Wilmington twenty-seven miles upriver. From on board the *Malvern*, Admiral Porter listened to the explosions and recognized their significance. "The death knell of another fort is booming in the distance. Fort Caswell with its powerful batteries is in flames and being blown up, and thus is sealed the door through which this rebellion is fed."[18]

The following morning, January 18, Porter sent Lieutenant Commander Cushing to reconnoiter Old Inlet. Cushing took possession of the dismantled fortifications on Oak Island and then proceeded across the harbor to occupy Smithville. Cushing's ship, the *Monticello*, drew too much water to cross the bar, so Cushing and a small party of sailors rowed over in a launch. At the sight of the approaching Federals, Smithville's residents raised a white flag over Fort Pender, while a committee of prominent citizens sailed out into the harbor to meet them. A large crowd, "with mingled curiosity and fear," gathered at Fort Pender's wharf, where Cushing landed about 10:00 a.m. and accepted the mayor's surrender of the town.[19]

Most of Smithville's white citizens remained subdued, but blacks openly rejoiced at the appearance of their Union deliverers. They paraded through the streets "frantically waving small U. S. flags and crying 'hallelujah, hallelujah.'" Cushing, who appointed himself military governor of the district, addressed a huge throng of slaves and declared them free. They cheered him, and to show their gratitude, guided the sailors around the town to search for concealed firearms. Sailors and marines from the *Monticello* reinforced "Governor Cushing" that afternoon, and by the following day, January 19, some 150 of them had arrived to garrison Smithville. They occupied the town for about a week before being relieved by army troops.[20]

Most of the Union warships remained close by Federal Point the day after the Fort Fisher battle, awaiting orders for their next deployment and receiving Confederate prisoners-of-war. Admiral Porter dispersed his grand fleet, sending ships to bolster the James River squadron in Virginia and take the captives north. But Porter kept a substantial force of gunboats off the inlets to protect the Union forces on Federal Point and Oak Island, and eventually assembled a flotilla of some thirty river-going vessels to cooperate with the army in its proposed attack on Wilmington. Sailors in launches spent much of January 16 removing torpedoes from New Inlet to enable the gunboats to enter the Cape Fear River. The *Tacony* and *Sassacus* were the first vessels to steam into the waterway early that same afternoon. In the meantime, the navy continued its efforts to secure control of the Cape Fear estuary.[21]

On January 19 two boatloads of sailors from the *Wilderness* (the same ship that had guided the powder boat *Louisiana* to her infamous destruction during First Fort Fisher) and the *Pequot* took possession of Bald Head

Island. Eighteen Confederate stragglers, "the tail end of the lot," noted one Union sailor, surrendered to the Federal tars when they came ashore. Lieutenant Daniel L. Braine of the *Pequot* reported that Fort Holmes remained in good condition, despite the dismounted cannon and burned gun carriages. "Although the enemy had destroyed large amounts of stores," Braine wrote, "much yet remains."[22]

Indeed, the Federals acquired a substantial quantity of artillery and ordnance, quartermaster and commissary stores from the fortifications in the estuary despite Confederate efforts to destroy them and the civilians' subsequent plundering of what had survived. According to military records, the Federals captured 138 seacoast guns, thirty pieces of light artillery (as well as ammunition), firearms, accouterments and provisions. The U. S. Army claimed ownership of Fort Fisher's famed 8-inch 150-pounder Armstrong and shipped it to West Point, where it was mounted at Trophy Point overlooking the Hudson River. Her sister gun that had been run through the blockade at the same time and then mounted in Fort Caswell was confiscated by the U. S. Navy and transferred to the Naval Academy at Annapolis. Also found at Fort Caswell was a considerable quantity of provisions and supplies. Moreover, several hundred rifle-muskets were discovered at Fort Pender in Smithville. The capture of these various works not only provided the Union with control of both inlets and a foothold for future operations, but copious quantities of valuable military arms and supplies as well.[23]

Blockade runners were unaware for some days of Wilmington's closure. Some of these traders were en route to the Carolina port, while others were still loading Wilmington-bound cargoes at Bermuda and Nassau. Several eluded capture, including the *Owl*, which slipped in undetected through Old Inlet during the night of January 16. As she pulled into Smithville's harbor, word reached her captain, the famous John Newland Maffitt, that Fort Fisher had fallen. Maffitt immediately steamed the *Owl* back out to sea and made his escape to Bermuda. Four nights later Captain M. P. Usina of the *Rattlesnake*, also ignorant of affairs at the Cape Fear, prepared to enter New Inlet. But the multitude of campfires visible about Fort Fisher made Usina suspicious enough to call off the attempt. At about the same time the steamer *Chameleon* (the former gunboat *Tallahassee*), captained by John Wilkinson, twice approached New Inlet. After receiving no favorable replies from the signal lights on Mound Battery and spotting two suspicious ships inside the bar, Wilkinson reversed course and headed back out to sea.[24]

Other blockade runners were less fortunate. Admiral Porter ordered the Mound Battery signal lights at Fort Fisher to be "properly trimmed and lighted, as has been the custom with the rebels during the blockade [and] be ready to grab anyone that enters" New Inlet. Porter placed Cushing in charge of efforts to lure blockade runners into Old Inlet. The U. S. Navy's fearless daredevil promptly arrested several blockade runner pilots and threatened to hang them unless they displayed the correct signal lights on Oak Island. Cushing's intimidating threats quickly paid dividends.[25]

The Confederate-owned blockade runner *Stag*, commanded by Lt. Richard H. Gayle of the C.S. Navy, dropped anchor at Smithville about 2:00 a.m. on January 20, having just made the dangerous three-day journey from Bermuda. Union sailors immediately boarded the ship, which was laden with firearms, blankets and shoes destined for Lee's beleaguered army. Half an hour later the British steamer *Charlotte*, also out of Bermuda, stopped at Smithville. An elegant champagne dinner in celebration of the successful run was in full swing when Lieutenant Commander Cushing came aboard to inform the astonished captain, Thomas E. Cocker, that the *Charlotte* had just become the property of the U. S. Navy. Among the Charlotte's passengers were several distinguished British army officers and adventurers who had run the blockade "on a lark." They expressed their "beastly luck" at being captured, but saw no reason for it to spoil their fine meal. Cushing agreed, and joined them as a self-invited guest. Unlike the *Stag*, the *Charlotte's* cargo consisted primarily of "articles for ladies use. . .French bonnets, cloaks, shoes, and other feminine bric-a-brac," prompting Admiral Porter to comment "that ladies will indulge in their little vanities in spite of war and desolation."[26]

During the early morning hours of January 25, Union tars also captured the *Blenheim* on its way in from Nassau. Her captain realized that he had fallen into a trap at New Inlet and was attempting to get his vessel underway when a boarding party from the *Tristram Shandy* seized her. Moments later sailors from the *Gettysburg* boarded the *Blenheim* and also claimed the prize. A sailor who received a share of the bounty when the *Blenheim's* cargo was auctioned off remarked: "This is the kind of blockading that I like, where the prizes come to us, instead of our going out for them."[27]

Captain Maffitt aboard the *Owl* returned to Bermuda on January 21, bearing news that Wilmington was no longer open to commerce. He arrived in time to stop the *Maude Campbell*, *Old Dominion*, *Florence*, *Deer*, and *Virginia*, which were all loaded and ready to sail for the port city. Warehouses at Nassau reportedly had in storage 30,000 British Enfield rifles, four 100-pounder Armstrong cannon, and more than 2,500,000 pounds of bacon awaiting shipment to the Confederacy. With Wilmington closed, those desperately-needed supplies would never reach their destination.[28]

From a military standpoint Wilmington still retained some importance to the Confederacy even after it had ceased to be an entrepôt for supplies. Bragg's presence at the Cape Fear distracted the attention of a sizable Union army, and although Lee could ill-afford to leave Hoke's Division there indefinitely, there was sound reason for doing so. Union deserters and prisoners informed General Bragg that Terry and Porter planned to attack Wilmington in cooperation with Sherman's advance through the Carolinas. Armed with this information, the Confederate high command encouraged Bragg to prevent Terry from reinforcing and resupplying Sherman's army. Lee hoped that scattered forces could be consolidated to strike Sherman a lethal blow once he reached North Carolina, and Bragg would protect the flank of the assault force.[29]

In any event, Wilmington had to be held until the stockpile of government stores there could be removed. In order to accomplish this, Confederate authorities contemplated moving rolling stock and rails from seaboard lines to maintain and repair interior rail lines with connections to Richmond. To help in the defense of Wilmington, chief naval constructor John L. Porter—co-designer of the famous ironclad *Virginia*—traveled to the city to oversee completion of the ironclad *Wilmington* at Beery's Shipyard on Eagles Island. Secretary of the Navy Stephen R. Mallory sought assurances from Bragg that he could hold the port long enough for Porter to complete the ironclad and get it into action. "This place will be held as long as our means enable us," Bragg replied with less than reassuring confidence.[30]

Bragg at first showed signs that he meant to vigorously defend Wilmington. He ordered the city's fortifications strengthened, borrowing or impressing slaves from nearby plantations to aid his soldiers in buttressing earthworks and erecting abatis. Ordnance personnel planted additional torpedoes in the river channel, while engineers sank derelict vessels to block

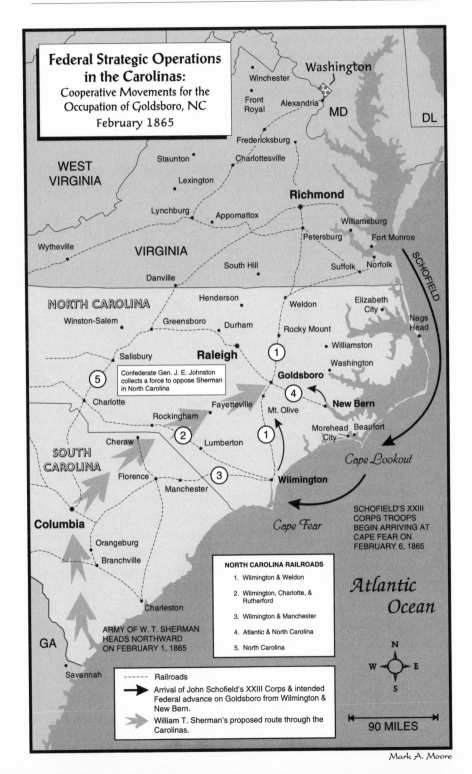

Federal Strategic Operations in the Carolinas:
Cooperative Movements for the Occupation of Goldsboro, NC
February 1865

Confederate Gen. J. E. Johnston collects a force to oppose Sherman in North Carolina

SCHOFIELD'S XXIII CORPS TROOPS BEGIN ARRIVING AT CAPE FEAR ON FEBRUARY 6, 1865

ARMY OF W. T. SHERMAN HEADS NORTHWARD ON FEBRUARY 1, 1865

NORTH CAROLINA RAILROADS

1. Wilmington & Weldon
2. Wilmington, Charlotte, & Rutherford
3. Wilmington & Manchester
4. Atlantic & North Carolina
5. North Carolina

Atlantic Ocean

- - - - - Railroads

➤ Arrival of John Schofield's XXIII Corps & intended Federal advance on Goldsboro from Wilmington & New Bern.

➤ William T. Sherman's proposed route through the Carolinas.

90 MILES

Mark A. Moore

the waterway opposite the river batteries just below the city. Bragg did not consider the fortifications along the river capable of resisting the Federal navy's "heavy metal." Having squandered the chance to save heavy artillery from Forts Caswell, Holmes, and Pender, Bragg requisitioned cannon from armories at Augusta and Columbia for Wilmington's protection. He also called on local home guard units to mobilize, and again urged Governor Vance to send reinforcements to defend the port city. Bragg's effective force—consisting of infantry, light and heavy artillery, cavalry, engineers, sailors, marines, signal corps, coast guard, and senior reserves—numbered about 7,600 men.[31]

General Hoke commanded Bragg's field forces from his headquarters at Sugar Loaf. There, he entrenched three of his division's four brigades, totaling by then about 4,400 troops. Brigadier General Alfred Colquitt's Georgia infantry brigade—the 6th, 19th, 23rd, and 27th regiments—commanded by Col. Charles T. Zachry, manned the right of Hoke's line, which was anchored on the river. Zachry had been put in temporary charge of the unit when General Colquitt was sent to Georgia on a recruiting trip. To the left of Colquitt's Brigade was Capt. Andrew J. Ellis' Northhampton Battery—Company A, 3rd Battalion North Carolina Light Artillery. Brigadier General William W. Kirkland's North Carolina brigade—the 42nd, 66th, and remnants of the 17th North Carolina regiments—and Capt. Andrew B. Paris' Staunton Hill artillery battery, held the center. Colonel William S. Devane of the 61st North Carolina oversaw the defense on the far left of the earthworks, which rested on Myrtle Sound. Devane commanded the North Carolina brigade of Brig. Gen. Thomas L. Clingman—the 8th, 31st, 51st, and 61st North Carolina regiments. Clingman was not on hand, as he was still recovering from wounds suffered in battle the previous summer. Captain Thomas J. Southerland's 2nd Company I (Wilmington Horse Artillery), 10th North Carolina Regiment, overlooked Hoke's defenses from the summit of Sugar Loaf, while a contingent of Col. Thomas J. Lipscomb's 2nd South Carolina Cavalry patrolled the environs. Colonel Lipscomb personally commanded a detachment of his horsemen at Fort Anderson, opposite Sugar Loaf on the other side of the Cape Fear River.[32]

Hoke sent Brig. Gen. Johnson Hagood, who finally returned from his trip home to South Carolina, to command Fort Anderson, where the remnant of his brigade had been holed-up since its ill-fated attempts to reinforce Fort

Fisher. A noted lawyer and successful Palmetto State planter, Hagood had set aside his practice and plow in 1861 to fight the Yankees. He had commanded the 1st South Carolina Infantry at Fort Sumter and in various actions on the sea islands near Charleston before transferring to Virginia, where he fought in numerous battles from Manassas to Petersburg. Hagood, a competent—but arrogant—brigadier, was an indifferent tactician, which might account for his having never risen above the level of brigade commander, in which capacity he had served since 1862. Hagood's contingent of 2,300 troops comprised the remnants of his own brigade of South Carolinians (bolstered to about 1,200 men after Hagood's recruiting trip to South Carolina), the garrison of North Carolinians previously stationed at Fort Anderson, and the soldiers from the Cape Fear's abandoned fortifications under the command of Colonel Hedrick.[33]

General Terry faced Hoke on Federal Point with a command of about 8,500 Federals, less two infantry regiments stationed at Smithville and Fort Caswell. Until reinforcements arrived in early February, Terry's force remained that which had captured Fort Fisher—albeit bloodied and battered. Terry was anxious to push on to Wilmington to take advantage of the hard-won momentum gained from the victory at Fort Fisher. Although he admired the general's audacity, Admiral Porter cautioned against a premature strike. Porter worried that Terry might advance his army too far from its base and get "cut to pieces by Bragg's force of cavalry," of which Terry had none. In reality Porter's fears proved unfounded, for Bragg had only enough cavalry on hand to serve as scouts and orderlies.[34]

Aside from this rather trifling concern, Porter wanted more time to resupply his warships with ammunition and to gain better control of the Cape Fear River before undertaking an advance on Wilmington. The admiral was more concerned with safeguarding Fort Fisher against a counterattack. "A desperate rush would give us much trouble," he maintained. "What has been taken by one party can be retaken by another." But Porter overestimated the Confederate troop strength in the area and Bragg's willingness to commit his men to battle. Nonetheless, he advised Terry to dig in and await reinforcements from Grant or Sherman. While Porter's excessive caution appears uncharacteristic for such an aggressive commander, it may have been the result of a mild breakdown the admiral had suffered following the victory at Fort Fisher, which he attributed to the excitement and hard work of the campaign.[35]

Terry heeded the admiral's advice and ordered that Fort Fisher be restored as a defensive work. The 15th New York Engineers rebuilt the palisade, repaired the earthworks and remounted artillery captured in the work. Terry also scouted enemy dispositions, dispatching reconnaissance parties to determine Hoke's strength at Sugar Loaf. On January 18, Terry ordered Col. John W. Ames to make a reconnaissance with the 4th, 6th, and 30th U. S. Colored Troops from General Paine's division. As Ames' force was preparing to move, however, a Confederate party appeared bearing a flag of truce. Among the members of this group were Colonel Lamb's wife Daisy, who sought information about her husband, and several of General Hoke's staff officers, who inquired as to General Whiting's condition. Requests were made for permission to send personal effects through the lines for the Confederate officers already on their way north to prisoner-of-war camps. By he time the authorized exchange was completed it was too late in the day for Ames' mission to accomplish much.

About 4:00 p.m. his skirmishers encountered Confederate pickets and pushed them back to within sight of the Sugar Loaf defenses. General Terry, who had come forward to view Hoke's earthworks, was fired on by Confederate sharpshooters. The commanding general could see little in the fast fading winter twilight and suspended the movement. Colonel Ames retreated, having lost one man killed and one wounded.[36]

Terry renewed the reconnaissance at first light the next morning. This time Colonel Ames led his entire brigade (the three regiments that had participated in the probe the day before plus the 39th U. S. Colored Troops), as well as the division's sharpshooters. The column advanced up the center and west bank of Federal Point. Newly promoted Bvt. Brig. Gen. Joseph C. Abbott, commanding a detachment from his brigade (250 men of the 7th New Hampshire and 41 soldiers from the 7th Connecticut) marched along the beach in cooperation with Ames. At 2:00 p.m., Ames' brigade drove in the Confederate pickets and engaged Hoke's main line. Sporadic fighting raged for about three hours. Meanwhile, Abbott moved his force to the head of Myrtle Sound, where it halted while the gunboat *Governor Buckingham*

Previously unpublished image of Col. John W. Ames, Second Brigade commander, Paine's division, U.S. Colored Troops. *Author's Collection*

shelled a Confederate outwork blocking the Federal infantry's advance. As soon as Abbott heard Ames' gunfire beyond his left, which was his cue to open the attack, he and his men waded the shallow end of the sound and advanced on the outpost.[37]

Abbott deployed his skirmishers, but they were quickly pinned down by heavy small arms fire from Confederate skirmishers in an outwork about 500 yards in front of Hoke's line. Fearing that Confederates dug in on the main line might counterattack, Abbott knew he had to act swiftly. He instructed Lt. Paul Whipple of the 7th New Hampshire to take a detachment around to the right flank and determine whether he could capture the enemy outpost. Whipple led a force of seventy men from his company and moved stealthily, unseen by the Confederates. The Federals charged and quickly overran the Southerners' earthworks, capturing two surprised officers and about fifty men in the process.[38]

Abbott pushed his force, shielded by cover fire from the *Governor Buckingham* and the *Montgomery*, to within 100 yards of Hoke's field-works. A tangled undergrowth of vines and bushes obscured his view, prompting Abbott to climb to the top of the nearby James Burriss house to get a better look at the enemy's defenses. From this vantage point, Abbott could see that Hoke's earthworks were both sturdy and well manned. Colonel Ames had reached the same conclusion after encountering stubborn Confederate resistance on the west side of the peninsula, where Captain N. J. Hotchkiss of the 6th U. S. Colored Troops was mortally wounded on the skirmish line, and a dozen other men were shot down. Finding themselves caught in a blistering fire, Ames and Abbott were compelled to withdraw. A cold, steady rain fell on the troops as they marched back to their encampment. The lone bright spot of the movement was the relatively small number of casualties incurred (one man killed, four officers and twenty-five men wounded, and five missing). The reconnaissance also convinced Terry that Hoke held a formidable position. One of Terry's subordinates remarked that Hoke's entrenchments were "as strong as any Lee had at Petersburg or Richmond & from water to water." Porter was right in advising Terry to await additional troops before making a serious advance against Wilmington.[39]

In the meantime, Admiral Porter (who was feeling better after a much needed rest) decided to do a little reconnoitering of his own. On January 22 he sent the *Pequot* upriver to test the defenses of Fort Anderson. The *Pequot* steamed within range and fired seven shots at the fort, which replied with several rounds from two light artillery pieces. This brief exchange proved to be the extent of the reconnaissance-based engagement. Commander Braine kept the *Pequot* in range for nearly two hours, just long enough to annoy the enemy and make some careful observations. He counted six cannon pointing downstream, but also discovered that the narrowness of the channel would allow only a few vessels to simultaneously maneuver within range of the fort. Braine's observations further convinced Porter of the wisdom of his advice to General Terry.[40]

And thus January drew to a close, the Union and Confederate forces at Cape Fear settling into a stalemate. Terry and Porter adopted a strategy of intimidation, while Bragg dug in deeper, seemingly content to hold the Federals in check as he awaited instructions from Richmond. The campaign devolved into a routine in which pickets traded pot-shots on a daily basis, while the two sides shelled each other in an attempt to demoralize and disrupt. Porter's gunboats regularly fired on Sugar Loaf and Fort Anderson, while the Confederate gunboat *Chickamauga* steamed downriver to hurl shells at Terry's fortified encampment. Among the victims of these naval barterings was Col. John T. Lofton, commander of the 6th Georgia of Colquitt's Brigade, who was killed by a random shot from one of Porter's gunboats. Although both armies harassed each other for several weeks, neither made a serious effort to attack.[41]

The gathering Federal menace soon unnerved the faint-hearted Bragg, however, who reported at the end of January that "the enemy movements. . . indicate further operations at an early date." Bragg designated a line to fall back upon and plotted an avenue of retreat. He ordered engineers to construct a secondary line of earthworks on the east side of the Cape Fear River, from Fort Campbell south of Wilmington to Hewlitt's Creek near Masonboro Sound. They also erected breastworks on the north bank of Town Creek, a narrow but deep stream that cut the opposite shore of the river about midway between Wilmington and Fort Anderson. Bragg apparently had no intention of manning the defenses beyond the city limits for fear that if he did so, the Federals would lay siege to Wilmington. Consequently, he ordered a survey of, and made necessary repairs to, the Duplin Road heading north, particularly between Wilmington and the northeast Cape Fear River.[42]

Bragg also instructed that all government and private property of military value be moved out of Wilmington. He threatened to destroy all remaining cotton, tobacco, naval stores and other property that could be of use to the enemy. "We are informed that if it becomes necessary to evacuate this town," the *Wilmington Daily Journal* reported, "it is the intention of the Commanding General to exercise the authority vested in him by act of Congress and destroy remaining cotton here." Most of Wilmington's stores were transferred to Raleigh, but a substantial quantity of cotton was hoarded by speculators who planned to sell it to the Federals should they capture Wilmington.[43]

Regardless of military policy, citizens viewed General Bragg's actions as a clear sign that he planned to abandon Wilmington—just as he had Lamb and Whiting at Fort Fisher. "This place is still in the Confederacy," acknowledged a resident, "but from all indications I judge it will pass over to the stars and stripes ere many days, as things point to an early evacuation, and it is generally believed here that the Yankees have only to demand the place to get it." Another Wilmingtonian claimed that the fall of Fort Fisher was a dreadful blow not only to North Carolina, but also portended the Confederacy's doom. "We felt that the Confederacy must go," she lamented, "the end was before us." Since Fort Fisher's capture a pall of apprehension, anxiety and gloom had enveloped Wilmington. As the Federal tempest gathered nearby, citizens lost any remaining trust in Bragg's leadership. "They have no confidence whatever in General Bragg," observed a soldier after visiting Wilmington. "I hope the place can be held, but must say, that if we had some other General in command, confidence would be greater." Only two weeks before Wilmingtonians had been singing Bragg's praises. Now they turned on him with venom, berating and ridiculing him to no end. "Bragg has had bad luck wherever he has been," one citizen was heard to say. "General Bragg's presence, wherever he has controlled" claimed a newspaper editor, "has been felt as a harbinger of disaster, an omen of impending evil—like a dark, cold, dreary cloud. . . ."[44]

The constant criticism distressed Bragg, but his actions merely fanned the flames of discontent. He imposed a blackout of military news, and soon the families, friends and loved ones of soldiers clamored to hear something more than wild rumors on the streets and the constant rumbling of cannon fire downriver. Still, Bragg remained silent. "Is it a military necessity to keep our people ignorant of every occurrence connected with their interests?" a Wilmingtonian asked. "The stereotyped phraseology of 'all quiet below' will have no effect upon us. We place [no] confidence in such reports."[45]

Social and economic conditions deteriorated in Wilmington as confidence in the local Confederate high command eroded. Fearing for their safety, many residents left town. Supplies of food and fuel dried up as local suppliers ceased bringing their products to town, where they could expect to sell them for worthless Confederate currency or fall victim to military confiscation. "We are seeing very scarce and dry times now," observed one soldier. "The scarcity of provisions will soon begin to tell strongly against us." Prices on consumer goods escalated to an all-time high, and for the poor it was "totally out of their power to procure the absolute necessaries of life." Local philanthropists revived the Relief Association and lobbied the state senate for food and money for Wilmington's disadvantaged. Governor Vance visited the city in mid-February, hoping to boost with his renowned oratory the morale which had so diminished under Bragg's control.[46]

Bragg's seeming indifference to Wilmington's fate also eroded the spirit of his troops, and many expressed their displeasure by deserting him. With the war going badly for the Confederacy, soldiers left the ranks in ever-increasing numbers in the winter of 1865, and Hoke's command was no exception. The number of troops in his division dropped from 6,400 to 5,500 in the four weeks following the Second Battle of Fort Fisher—a net loss of 900 effectives. While attrition, illness and wounds account for some of the absence, desertion also took its toll. "I can tell you the soldiers are the worst cut down I ever saw them," exclaimed a Tarheel, "they have all come to the conclusion that we are whiped and they are leaving by the whole sail & retail." One deserter conceded to his Union captors that he believed the war in eastern North Carolina had "gone up," and he attributed the sorry state of affairs to Braxton Bragg. A North Carolina infantryman worried that Bragg's despondent army would not hold together through another campaign. "The men are all very much disheartened," he confessed, "and the people at home are even more so and they write that strain to the soldiers and that makes them more dispirited. . .there would be very few deserters if the soldiers letters [from home] were of a cheerful tone."[47]

There was little for anyone in the Confederacy to be cheerful about. Setbacks on the battlefield, Sherman's March to the Sea and his capture of Savannah, the refusal of either Great Britain or France to recognize Confederate sovereignty, rampant inflation and shortages on the home front all contributed to the decay of Southerners' will to fight on. Perhaps General Sherman best described the effect of his campaign on Confederate morale when he wrote: "The simple fact that a man's home had been visited by an enemy makes a soldier. . .anxious to get home to look after his family and property. . . ."[48]

Yet demoralization struck only a portion of Bragg's command, according to George M. Rose, an adjutant in the 66th North Carolina. Rose claimed that "the spirits of the troops never flagged; they were always willing to do their duty. . . ." The isolated position of Hoke's Division at Sugar Loaf dissuaded the soldiers from running away. Bounded on two sides by water and separated from Wilmington by seemingly endless miles of sand hills, there were few places for soldiers to run other than over to the enemy. If for no other reason, most of Bragg's men preferred remaining in their wind-blown trenches at Sugar Loaf to wasting away in a cold, dank Northern prison.[49]

Union soldiers at the Cape Fear also deserted their ranks, though fewer in number than their Southern counterparts. Federal military records reveal that nine soldiers of the 6th Connecticut—all of whom were substitutes and not veterans—went over to the Confederates at Sugar Loaf. Records of other regiments show a similar rate of troop attrition. Yet, most Union desertions occurred after the U. S. Army had captured Wilmington.[50]

More than desertion, bad weather, homesickness, isolation and deprivation wrought greater harm to the two armies at the Cape Fear. Even so, garrison troops at Wilmington and Smithville were better off than those on Federal Point, living in warm barracks and associating with civilians—especially young ladies—which mitigated the boredom of military duty. Even Porter's sailors lived a relatively comfortable existence on board their ships, though they might have preferred to enjoy the company of Smithville's ladies on a more frequent basis. But the soldiers on Federal Point had to endure much harsher conditions, in which sand, wind and loneliness ruled their everyday lives. One Union soldier claimed that he felt more like Robinson Crusoe on an island, "which as far as [one] could see, was as bare of vegetation and fuel as the watery waste from which [he] had disembarked." In a letter to his father, General Paine described military life on Federal Point as a far cry from his comfortable prewar life in Boston. "I'm in the middle of a range of swamps, thickets, briars, and scrubby oaks," he complained. Another soldier asserted that only the enchanting roar of the Atlantic Ocean's waves as they broke upon the sandy shore could relieve his monotonous existence.[51]

Conditions for the Confederates at Fort Anderson were somewhat better. The soldiers stationed there took advantage of the surrounding pine forest, with its abundance of wild game and the fresh water ponds stocked with fish. Many Southerners lived in barracks constructed of salvaged materials plucked from the ruins of Brunswick Town's old colonial buildings. Most of the soldiers, however, slept along the extensive line of earthworks "in whatever rude shelters they could construct," wrote Lt. William Calder. The felling of trees around the fort for such building projects exposed the troops to cold winds that blew throughout that winter, and they were "sharp enough to cut a man in two," the lieutenant claimed.[52]

Blustery winds, freezing temperatures and frequent rains in January and February 1865 made life almost unbearable for soldiers in the lower Cape Fear region. Although there were intermittent pleasant days, the weather overall was unusually bad. "We have had the most infernally cold weather, the river beach is 6 in. deep of ice, [and] it is too cold to sleep at night," General Paine contended. "I pile in the blankets but it is of no use." Lieutenant Calder, a Wilmington-born officer concurred with his enemy's assessment of the weather. "I think it is as cold weather as I ever felt," he wrote to his mother from Fort Anderson. The gray-clad lieutenant awoke one evening soaked to the skin by a chilly rain and the resulting pools of water that had formed under him. "Tried to lay there & sleep it out but couldn't do it," Calder recorded in his diary. "Got up and built a large fire around which we stood until morning, altogether a miserable night." In a letter to his brother, one Union soldier claimed that "a man of the 112th [New York Infantry] froze to death in their camp" on Federal Point one night.[53]

January and February produced no lack of bad weather, but the Confederates also had to endure a dire shortage of food. The insufficient rations drove some soldiers to plunder farms and houses near their encampments. In an effort to halt the depredations General Bragg ordered an officer from each company to remain on duty all night to prevent their men from roaming about the countryside. He also enforced regular drills and dress parades and closed down camp infirmaries, moving the sick—many of whom were apparently guilty of the infractions—to permanent hospitals in Wilmington. Hoke was reluctant to push his men too hard, believing that their mental state was so fragile that he should guard against providing any reason for complaint. One Georgia soldier in Colquitt's Brigade offered a simple solution: "an increase in rations. . .and more attention paid to the enlisted man."[54]

Altogether it was a hard life for soldiers of both armies at the Cape Fear, but there was little they could do other than make the best of it. Some soldiers professed to looking forward to skirmishing with the enemy as a means to relieve the monotony. Out of boredom soldiers sometimes indulged in unauthorized socializing, including fraternizing with the enemy. They swapped newspapers, coffee, tobacco and braggadocio. "Everything here is dull, no excitement " lamented one Union general, "[thank goodness] my whiskey barrel holds out." Confederate soldiers at Sugar Loaf invented a unique—albeit dangerous—game to pass their off-duty time. During the Union navy's bombardments, the Southerners would recklessly expose themselves to exploding shells in order to claim the brass fuses, which they fashioned into rings and other ornaments. "As soon as a missile burst," explained one player, "you would see men running in every direction toward the place for the purpose of finding the broken parts." Despite the occasional merriment, however, the men passed a tough existence. "In my experience in the field there was always something to keep up a pleasant state of excitement," recorded Lieutenant Calder. "But here, there is neither the march nor the anticipation of a fight to cause our blood to move hurriedly through our veins, while at the same time we are experiencing as rough a time in the field as troops ever do."[55]

Such was the soldier's life on the eve of the second stage of the Wilmington Campaign. Hoke's troops held a strong defensive position at Sugar Loaf and Fort Anderson, but they were profoundly disillusioned by the war's progress. Their morale rose sharply when they heard news of peace talks between a Confederate delegation and President Lincoln at Hampton

Roads in early February. By that point in the war, most soldiers believed that only a miracle—such as European intervention—could rescue the Confederacy from defeat. Nothing could prevent them from praying for peace. "We have been jubilant. . .over the numerous peace rumors affront," proclaimed William Calder. "God grant that our hopes and prayers may be realized and Peace! blessed Peace! soon smile upon our land. . . ." While a treaty would have done much to buoy the sagging spirits of Southern soldiers, their hopes were dashed when the Hampton Roads peace conference ended unfavorably for the gasping Confederacy. "Better a thousand times [that] peace had not been mentioned," argued a soldier. "The relapse will be too much for the army to bear."[56]

Yet the failure of the Virginia peace negotiations was exactly what most Union soldiers desired. With a victory in sight, the Federals at the Cape Fear received the news of the unsuccessful talks with great excitement because, as one of General Terry's infantrymen pointed out, he and his comrades wanted "a soldier's peace, not a politicians peace." When asked by a war correspondent what he meant by a soldier's peace, the musket-bearer replied: "To fight till one side is completely whipped, whipped till they own up, that sir, is a soldier's peace."[57]

Maj. Gen. John M. Schofield, commander of the XXIII Army Corps, whose appointment by U.S. Grant to direct the Wilmington Campaign angered Adm. David D. Porter and hurt Maj. Gen. Alfred H. Terry. *U.S. Army Military History Institute*

Chapter 10

". . .To Forge a Thunderbolt"

– *Philadelphia Inquirer*

ADVANCE

B y late January 1865, U. S. Grant was so intent on capturing Wilmington that he left the main theater of war in Virginia—a rare move for him—to travel to the Cape Fear to confer with Admiral Porter and General Terry. Accompanying him were Assistant Secretary of the Navy Gustavus Fox and Maj. Gen. John McAllister Schofield, commander of the XXIII Corps, Army of the Ohio. For three-and-a-half hours on the night of January 28, the commanders studied maps and charts on board Porter's flagship in the Cape Fear River. The idea, as Grant indicated, was to formulate a strategy to "open communication between the seacoast and Goldsboro by rail, so as to meet Sherman with supplies for his army and to put at his disposal an available force."[1]

As Grant and his officers conversed aboard the *Malvern*, General Sherman was preparing to invade the Carolinas with a strike at Columbia, South Carolina, followed by a move upon Fayetteville, North Carolina. Both of these important logistical centers contained Confederate armories. Sherman's ultimate object in North Carolina, however, was Goldsboro, the capture of which would be advantageous for two reasons: first, it was the junction for two coastal railroads (the Wilmington & Weldon and the Atlantic & North Carolina to New Bern) by which Sherman could be resupplied and reinforced; and second, from Goldsboro Sherman could easily strike Raleigh, where Confederate supplies from Wilmington were being sent and from which point Sherman would be poised to strike the rear of the Army of

Northern Virginia. "If Lee lets us get [Goldsboro], he is gone up," Sherman predicted. "[From there] I can easily take Raleigh, when it seems that Lee must come out of his trenches or allow his army to be absolutely invested." With Fort Fisher now in Union hands, Sherman saw little reason to attack Wilmington, whose fall, he believed, was inevitable.[2]

At their Cape Fear meeting, Grant agreed with the advice of his subordinates that Wilmington was the best point from which to move toward Goldsboro with a supporting force for Sherman. Although New Bern possessed a deeper harbor more favorable for a supply base, the railroad from that point to Goldsboro needed extensive repairs. Grant assumed that the presence of Bragg's army at Wilmington was an indication that the railroads there were still operational. A bold strike might capture the rail lines, locomotives, and cars before the Confederates could destroy or remove them. While the Union possession of Fort Fisher gave Sherman a safe haven on the seaboard, he might need Wilmington as a temporary supply depot and as a place to concentrate troops south of Goldsboro. In this light, Grant deemed "the capture of Wilmington of the greatest importance."[3]

Having studied both the approaches to the city and the defenses protecting it, Admiral Porter and General Terry recommended advancing against Wilmington from the west side of the Cape Fear River. There the army would have more room to maneuver on the mainland than was possible on Federal Point. Porter's and Terry's plan was straightforward: while the navy bombarded Fort Anderson, the army would launch a ground assault against the fort or attempt to outflank it by going around Orton Pond on the fort's right flank. Grant approved the plan, saying "it is the best and only thing to be done."[4]

According to Porter, the operation would require at least 13,000 troops, about 4,500 more than Terry commanded on Federal Point. Grant, however, had already provided for such a contingency by ordering Schofield's 21,000-man XXIII Army Corps from Tennessee to support Terry's efforts to take Fort Fisher and Wilmington—or to reinforce Sherman's advancing army. Grant decided there was a greater need for the XXIII Corps in the move against Wilmington, and he instructed Schofield to transfer his force to the Cape Fear as soon as possible. Upon his return to Virginia early on the morning of January 31, Grant asked the War Department to recreate the Department of North Carolina and assign Schofield as its commander.[5]

Despite Schofield's inexperience with combined operations, Grant considered the appointment a good one. Schofield was a regular army officer, a graduate of West Point (seventh in the Class of 1853), and a reasonably successful and dependable corps commander. Civil War found the New York native teaching physics in St. Louis, and he opted to remain in the western theater of operations as chief of staff for Brig. Gen. Nathaniel Lyon. It was Schofield who counseled Lyon to withdraw the outnumbered Union forces from the field at Wilson's Creek. The advice was not followed and the Federals received a sound drubbing at the hands of Sterling Price's Missourians. After his promotion to brigadier general in October 1862, Schofield went on to command the Army of the Frontier in southwest Missouri, northwest Arkansas and northeast Indian Territory—while politicking for a more important post. A promotion to major general followed in May 1863, as he assumed the reins of command of the Department of Missouri. During Sherman's Atlanta campaign in the summer of 1864 Schofield led the Army of the Ohio (XXIII Corps), the smallest of Sherman's three armies. After the fall of Atlanta in September 1864, Sherman turned east and marched to the sea, leaving Schofield behind with Maj. Gen. George H. Thomas to oppose Gen. John Bell Hood's Army of Tennessee. Schofield's strongly entrenched corps crippled Hood's attacking army at Franklin, Tennessee, on November 30, 1864, a defensive victory that contributed greatly to Thomas' crushing defeat of Hood's remaining force at Nashville two weeks later. Chubby, almost boyish in appearance with a balding head and scraggly red beard, Schofield proved an intensely ambitious man. His burning ambition may have contributed to his pettiness and underhanded dealings with fellow officers. These foibles, however, were offset by his unquestioned ability as an organizer and administrator. Overall, Schofield was a sound choice for departmental command.[6]

But Schofield's appointment did not please everyone. The assignment of Schofield rather than Alfred Terry to command the Department of North Carolina—and hence the army in the Wilmington operation—angered Admiral Porter and hurt Terry's feelings. Grant not only committed a grave error, contended Porter, but performed an "actual injustice" to Terry in light of his "gallant exploit" at Fort Fisher, which had earned for him the signal honor of the thanks of the U. S. Congress. "I am not one of those who consider [Grant] the military genius of the age, and think he makes mistakes," Porter charged. As far as the admiral was concerned, sending Schofield to North Carolina was one of them. Privately, Porter insisted that he and Terry would have already captured Wilmington if Grant had only "kept Schofield away." Porter's resentment may also have been motivated by what he considered a usurpation of his own authority. No longer would he call the shots as he did during Second Fort Fisher. Now, both he and Terry would be under Schofield's charge. Despite the admiral's resentment, Grant's action was not intended as a personal affront against either Porter or Terry. Schofield's rank made him the senior officer present, regardless of Terry's status as the conqueror of Fort Fisher.[7]

While Porter was unhappy with the new command organization, there were some who were pleased to see General Terry superseded. General Charles Paine commented that some of the officers, Adelbert Ames in particular, were "delighted to hear that Schofield was coming, not because any of them like S. for they don't know him," but because Ames was still angry at Terry for not giving him what he considered due credit for his role in the capture of Fort Fisher.[8]

For his part, Grant paid little heed or was oblivious to the controversy Schofield's appointment aroused. The lieutenant general instructed Schofield to capture Wilmington and then to advance rapidly from either there or New Bern (or from both cities) toward Goldsboro. Should Schofield fail to capture Wilmington, he was to secure the west bank of the Cape Fear River and open communications with Sherman in the direction of Florence, South Carolina, via the Wilmington & Manchester Railroad, or toward Lumberton, North Carolina, by way of the Wilmington, Charlotte, & Rutherford Railroad. Regardless of the outcome of the Wilmington Campaign, Schofield was to move on Goldsboro from New Bern.

His objectives for the campaign were clear and concise: lend Sherman supplies and/or manpower, as needed; open a base of supply for his army at or near Goldsboro; and prevent Braxton Bragg from impeding Sherman's advance. The last was of special concern to Grant, who worried about the possibilities of a newly-amalgamated Rebel force operating in the interior of the state. If Bragg's command could combine with the remnants of the Army of Tennessee, Lt. Gen. William J. Hardee's Corps, and various reinforcements from Virginia, it was possible they could strike Sherman before he reached Goldsboro. The commanding general's concern was evident in his order to Schofield to do whatever was necessary to assist Sherman's army.[9]

Grant's anxiety ultimately proved unfounded. The Confederacy was in a far worse state of affairs than he supposed. The Rebel high command wasted precious time debating a strategy to halt the Union juggernaut rolling through the remains of the Southern Confederacy. Perhaps the Federals' habitual failure to follow up their coastal operations with thrusts against strategic interior targets encouraged Confederate authorities to believe the enemy would content themselves with the capture of Fort Fisher and either disperse their forces or remain idle at the Cape Fear. Richmond's vacillations, however, left Southern forces in the Carolinas scattered and poorly-organized. In addition, rampant desertion ruled out the possibility that reinforcements would be forthcoming from Lee's severely weakened Army of Northern Virginia.[10]

While Confederate authorities dithered, Sherman advanced northward from the Savannah River on February 1, 1865, while Schofield prepared to embark on his own campaign. The XXIII Corps was ready to sail from Alexandria, Virginia, on February 1, but severe cold had frozen the Potomac River and delayed the departure of the transports for three days. On February 4, Schofield and the Third Division, Maj. Gen. Jacob Dolson Cox commanding, finally set sail. The remainder of the corps shipped out in the following two weeks as transports became available and weather permitted. At the same time a provisional corps comprised of troops from the Army of the Tennessee transferred to New Bern under the command of Brig. Gen. Thomas F. Meagher, the former commander of the Army of the Potomac's legendary Irish Brigade. Meagher's corps was to advance simultaneously with Schofield on Goldsboro once Wilmington had been captured.[11]

General Terry and Admiral Porter wasted no time awaiting Schofield's arrival, but prepared to move at once on Wilmington. Terry's troops continued to reconnoiter Confederate defenses on Federal Point searching for weak points. Infantry from Terry's command who had been on detached duty in Virginia began arriving at Fort Fisher, boosting the provisional corps' strength to about 9,000 troops. Terry also received a small contingent of cavalry. Admiral Porter managed to overlook his injured pride when he realized that, like the successful Fort Fisher operation, capturing Wilmington would require the hearty cooperation of both the navy and army. He assembled a flotilla of some thirty vessels for the task, including the *Montauk*, a light draft monitor sent from the Charleston blockading force specifically for operations in the shallow Cape Fear River. The navy spent much of its time replacing damaged artillery pieces which had burst or cracked during the Fort Fisher battles. The new ordnance arrived from the North and was mounted in about ten days, despite a lack of proper facilities and the onset of cold, wet weather.

As soon as the ordnance work was completed, Porter employed his new weapons against the Confederates, hoping to contain them in their trenches and prevent them from constructing new works. "I am maneuvering to make them believe we are going to attack them, and keep them on the alert [from] adding to present works and building others," he reported. Porter instructed his gunboats to shell the enemy "whenever they show[ed] themselves or [gave] indications of their presence."[12]

With these orders in mind, on the morning of January 29 the *Montgomery* opened fire on Confederate soldiers occupying a line of rifle pits directly opposite the vessel on the west bank of Myrtle Sound. A few well-directed shots sent the Southerners scrambling for cover in a nearby swamp (probably present-day Cook's Swamp), but the *Montgomery* continued firing for two-and-a-half hours. When the Confederates emerged from the swamp at dusk, the *Montgomery* shelled them again. The next afternoon the *Cherokee* picked up where the *Montgomery* had left off. Her commander, Acting Volunteer Lt. William E. Dennison, reported spotting "small detachments of men moving about through the edge of the woods northward of Half-Moon Battery [Battery Gatlin]." In order to ascertain whether the men were constructing additional fortifications, Dennison quietly eased his ship forward into three fathoms of water. The change of position exposed a large body of troops, 800 by Dennison's estimate, equipped in full marching gear on the shore near the same rifle pits shelled the previous day by the *Montgomery*. The *Cherokee* opened fire "with my rifle and broadside guns, which had the effect of scattering them in all directions," reported the vessel's commander. The shelling once again drove the Confederates into the swamp or woods. The brief encounter convinced Dennison that "the enemy have a large body of men at work in the rear of. . .the battery."[13]

While the navy did not provoke a general engagement, on February 3 it found itself involved in a tough scrap with Fort Anderson. About 4:00 p.m.

the *Tacony* (which had been one of the first ships to enter the harbor after the fall of Fort Fisher) steamed upriver and fired on Fort Anderson. Her second shot tore into a barrack and wounded six men, one mortally and three severely, of Company B, 40th North Carolina Regiment. The Confederates inside the fort swiftly retaliated. Captain Abner Moseley's Battery of light artillery responded with five shots, including several from its Whitworth rifle-cannon. The Whitworth, noted for its deadly accuracy and spiraled projectiles that whistled eerily in flight, proved its value yet again when three iron bolts passed through the *Tacony's* hull. One of the shots entered below the waterline, causing a dangerous leak. The wounded vessel quickly withdrew downstream. The *Shawmut* replaced the *Tacony* on the firing line until dark, but inflicted no further serious damage to the fort or its defenders. Together the double-ended gunboats fired only twenty-six projectiles, yet they struck with "infernal accuracy, nearly every shot falling within the work," one eyewitness attested. The navy increased its bombardment of Confederate targets in order to establish its effective range of fire. The efficacy of the navy's long arm would later prove beneficial in supporting the army's advance on Wilmington.[14]

At 2:00 p.m. on February 6, the *Herman Loring* dropped anchor off Fort Fisher and began disembarking the first of Maj. Gen. John Schofield's troops, the 65th Indiana Infantry and other regiments of the Third Division, XXIII Army Corps. Other transports steamed in after dark, but most of the soldiers did not arrive until the following day, including Schofield and Maj. Gen. Jacob Cox. The ships straggled in, a gale off Cape Hatteras having slowed their voyage down the North Carolina coast. Seasickness afflicted many of the soldiers, most of whom were Westerners who until recently had never seen the ocean, much less sailed on it. One landlubber in the 104th Ohio Infantry was so convinced he was going to die before setting foot on dry ground again that he willed his personal property to his comrades and asked that his body be delivered to the sharks. After many hours of suffering, however, he declared himself too sick to breathe his last and, true to his word, lived on to suffer even more. By the time Schofield's nauseated

soldiers reached the Cape Fear, they were "tired of naval service" and ready to get off the ships.[15]

Fog and high wind kept Cox's troops from going ashore at Fort Fisher until the morning of February 8, and even then the weather remained bad. Delivering 4,500 fully equipped soldiers onto Federal Point through choppy seas in a cold, driving rain storm proved to be a slow and difficult task. In fact, it took two days to land all of them. Of this contingent, Schofield was one of the first men to hit the beach. Wasting no time, the western veteran immediately took command and established his headquarters. General Cox did not land until February 10, establishing his division encampment in rear of General Terry's corps two miles north of Fort Fisher.[16]

As he stepped ashore on Federal Point that crisp February 1865 morning, thirty-six year old Jacob Dolson Cox could point with pride at his service record in the U. S. Army. Although not a soldier by profession, Cox had risen swiftly through the volunteer ranks to become the XXIII Corps' senior division commander and perhaps Schofield's most reliable general officer. In fact, Cox had been a member of the corps since December 1863, five months longer than Schofield. The corps commander thought highly enough of Cox's command to bring it with him personally to the Cape Fear before transferring his other two divisions south from Alexandria.

Though a proud U. S. soldier, Jacob Cox was a Canadian by birth. He was born in Montreal on October 27, 1828, while his father, a New York building contractor, was working on the Church of Notre Dame. Cox was a bright young man with interests in law, mathematics and classical languages. He studied theology at Oberlin College, where he received two degrees and the hand-in marriage of the college president's daughter, Helen Finney. Foregoing a career in the ministry, Cox served as superintendent of schools and then as a lawyer of considerable renown in Warren, Ohio, during the 1850s. A devout antislavery man, Cox helped form the Ohio Republican Party and thus became closely aligned with future general and American president James A. Garfield, and Salmon P. Chase, Lincoln's Secretary of the Treasury.

When the Civil War began Cox helped organize and train Ohio troops at the request of his friend Governor William Dennison. Within a month Cox had been commissioned a brigadier general in the U. S. Army, and went on to serve with distinction under Maj. Gen. George B. McClellan and Brig.

Gen. William S. Rosecrans in the western Virginia Campaign of 1861. Moving east in the summer of 1862, Cox and his Kanawha division fought gallantly as part of the IX Army Corps at South Mountain. He spent the following year commanding Union forces in western Virginia and the District of Ohio and in mid-December 1863, assumed command of the newly-

Maj. Gen. Jacob D. Cox, the able and respected commander of the Third Division, XXIII Army Corps, in the campaign for Wilmington. *U.S. Army Military History Institute*

formed XXIII Army Corps' Third Division. He fought his division with distinction under Schofield in Sherman's Atlanta Campaign and in the battles of Franklin and Nashville. In the midst of the Tennessee battles, Cox was confirmed as major general.

Cox's transfer to the Cape Fear marked his first experience in combined operations, though the Ohio general believed his veteran troops would perform as well on the sandy beaches of southeastern North Carolina as they had on the rolling hills of Tennessee. Cox's division consisted of three brigades, all led by colonels: Oscar W. Sterl, John S. Casement, and Thomas J. Henderson. Once all of Cox's troops were ashore, the transports returned to Alexandria, Virginia, to haul south Schofield's other two divisions.[17]

The massive Union build-up at the Cape Fear and New Bern worried Braxton Bragg, who informed Governor Vance that he believed the concentration of Union troops indicated a movement on Raleigh. Bragg realized that simultaneous enemy advances from the Cape Fear and New Bern would jeopardize the capital city as well as his army, and he recognized the increasing need for consolidating Confederate forces in the state's interior. Yet Bragg continued to urge Vance to organize all the forces he could muster and send them at once to Wilmington. Then, as if turning his back on Wilmington's fate, Bragg relinquished his command to General Hoke on February 10 (the eve of the Union attack on Wilmington) and left for Richmond. From a public relations perspective the eleven day trip was an illtimed disaster that only reinforced Bragg's reputation for "being not a fighting general." Bragg's explanation for his absence at such a critical time was that he had been summoned to Virginia to reorganize his staff.[18]

On the same day Bragg left for Virginia, Admiral Porter, together with Generals Schofield, Terry, and Cox, held a council of war on board the *Malvern* to "forge a thunderbolt," as one reporter described it. Time was of the essence, as Sherman's army had already been on the march northward from Savannah for ten days. Schofield decided to begin active operations without waiting for the remainder of his corps to reach the Cape Fear. He believed he could capture Fort Anderson and Wilmington with the 13,500 troops he had on hand.[19]

Before attacking Fort Anderson, however, Schofield determined to threaten Sugar Loaf. Schofield believed that pushing Terry's corps, with Porter's warships in close support, toward Sugar Loaf "would compel [Hoke] to hold [his works] in force," and prevent him from detaching reinforcements to Fort Anderson. Schofield hoped that a devastating bombardment by Porter's gunboats would enable Terry to overrun Hoke, thus obviating an attack on Fort Anderson. Even if Hoke held his position, the assault would give Schofield more time to bring up the remainder of his corps.[20]

Schofield scheduled the assault for the following day, February 11. He instructed Terry to "make a strong demonstration upon the enemy" and be ready to take Sugar Loaf if practicable. If capturing Hoke's line proved impossible, Terry was to establish a defensive front near enough to threaten the Confederate position. Schofield called on Porter to provide Terry's assaulting force with cover fire by shelling both Sugar Loaf and Fort Anderson. Porter, however, grumbled his disapproval of Schofield's plan. In his opinion, even if the Federals "succeeded in dislodging the [Rebels], they would retreat by roads known only to themselves and leave [Federal troops] in possession of barren sand hills and large numbers of killed and wounded." Despite his misgivings, Porter reluctantly obeyed Schofield's orders.[21]

Misgivings or not, Porter had been preparing for Schofield's operation by dispatching reconnoitering parties toward Fort Anderson to ascertain its strength. On two successive nights he sent Lt. Cmdr. William B. Cushing of the *Monticello* and a hand-picked crew upriver to reconnoiter Fort Anderson's obstructions and search for a torpedo ram rumored to be anchored nearby. On the first night, February 10, Cushing's party scouted to within one mile of Wilmington, examining the heavy obstructions abreast of Fort Anderson as well as the river batteries below the city. While he managed a glimpse of the *Chickamauga* anchored upstream, Cushing failed to find the alleged torpedo ram. On the next evening Cushing and his men conducted a more thorough inspection of the obstructions at Fort Anderson. This time they discovered not only a formidable line of pilings and chains, but torpedoes as well.[22]

While studying the obstructions in the river, Cushing heard loud cheering coming from inside Fort Anderson. The excitement of being so close to

Lt. Cmdr. William B. Cushing, the U.S. Navy's daring and flamboyant commando, in a previously unpublished image. *Courtesy of Charles V. Peery*

the enemy enticed the young daredevil officer to undertake greater risks. He landed his boat in a cove just north of the fort and boldly crept up to the work. None of Cushing's crew was willing to chance capture just to view some Rebel soldiers, so the daring commando went forward alone. Hiding just outside the fort's dirt and sod ramparts, Cushing listened for some time to a brass band, and then to "speeches being made by enthusiastic Confederates." One zealous officer in particular praised the gallantry of the troops, told them that the time had come to strike the final blow for Southern independence, and asked the soldiers to stand steadfast in the great struggle. As if he finally realized the danger he faced, Cushing finally stole back to his gig and crew, who were hidden in the marsh upstream. As Cushing's launch pulled away from shore, Confederate sentinels spotted the vessel. When it refused to acknowledge their challenge, the guards alerted the officer of the day. "Yankee boats in the river," they cried. A drummer beat the long roll and Confederate soldiers rushed to their batteries along the shoreline. As the enemy craft proceeded down river, the Southerners opened fire with rifle-muskets and cannon. Cushing stood defiantly on the prow of his little boat and fired back at the fort with his Colt Navy revolver. Unscathed, he and his cohorts escaped to the warships anchored downstream. Never one to pass up an opportunity for self promotion, Cushing related his exploit to Thomas M. Cook, a *New York Herald* war correspondent accompanying the flotilla, who promptly dispatched the story north for publication. Cushing claimed that the speaker inside Fort Anderson was none other than General Braxton Bragg himself.[23]

As it turned out, Cushing had overheard a rally at Fort Anderson featuring the Eutaw Band of the 25th South Carolina of Johnson Hagood's Brigade, and a stirring speech delivered by Lt. Col. John Douglas Taylor of the 36th North Carolina. Colonel John J. Hedrick of the 40th North Carolina had been called on to speak, but declined, asking Taylor to make an appearance in his stead. The assembly was interrupted by a report of an enemy boat in the river near the fort. Despite the Confederates' best efforts, the enemy vessel managed to escape. Three weeks later some of General Hoke's troops near Kinston captured a Union soldier with a copy of the February 18, 1865, issue of the *New York Herald* containing the story of Cushing's exciting reconnaissance of Fort Anderson. The article reported in detail Lieutenant Colonel Taylor's oration to his men. For the rest of his long life John Douglas Taylor enjoyed telling the story of his impromptu speech at Fort Anderson being published in a wartime Yankee newspaper.[24]

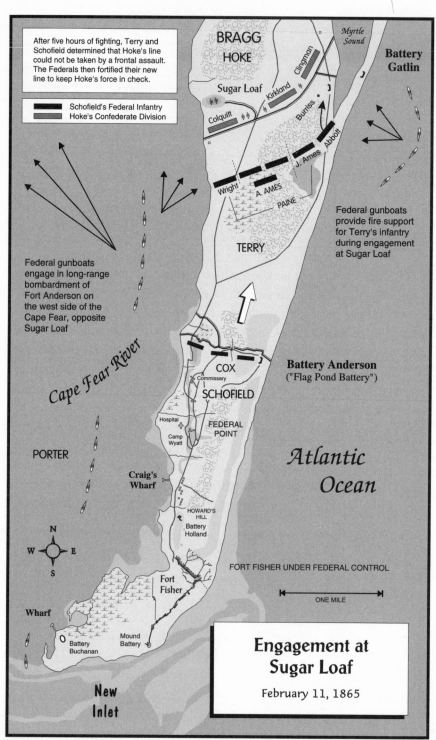

After five hours of fighting, Terry and Schofield determined that Hoke's line could not be taken by a frontal assault. The Federals then fortified their new line to keep Hoke's force in check.

Schofield's Federal Infantry
Hoke's Confederate Division

BRAGG
HOKE
Myrtle Sound
Battery Gatlin
Clingman
Sugar Loaf
Kirkland
Colquitt
Burriss
Abbott
J. Ames
Wright
A. AMES
PAINE
TERRY

Federal gunboats provide fire support for Terry's infantry during engagement at Sugar Loaf

Federal gunboats engage in long-range bombardment of Fort Anderson on the west side of the Cape Fear, opposite Sugar Loaf

Cape Fear River

COX
Battery Anderson ("Flag Pond Battery")
Commissary
SCHOFIELD
Hospital
FEDERAL POINT
Camp Wyatt

PORTER

Atlantic Ocean

Craig's Wharf

HOWARD'S HILL
Battery Holland

N
W — E
S

FORT FISHER UNDER FEDERAL CONTROL

ONE MILE

Fort Fisher

Wharf

Mound Battery
Battery Buchanan

New Inlet

Engagement at Sugar Loaf

February 11, 1865

Mark A. Moore

By February 11, General Terry's soldiers were eager for a fight. It had been a month since they had captured Fort Fisher, and they were anxious for relief from the "monotony of sand, surf, and salt water." While Terry's men advanced toward Sugar Loaf, Porter's warships began their bombardment. Although Terry personally directed the army's movement on that frosty morning, he was ill—from malaria, according to one report—and had to ride in a dilapidated buggy confiscated from a Smithville doctor. The brigade of Joseph C. Abbott formed on the right near the ocean and connected with Col. John W. Ames' Second Brigade of General Paine's division. Brevet Major General Adelbert Ames' division controlled the center, while Brig. Gen. Charles J. Paine's Third Brigade, led by Col. Elias Wright, advanced up the river bank. Fatigued by the long and stormy sea voyage, General Cox's division was held in reserve.[25]

Union gunboats on the Atlantic side of the peninsula opened the day's fighting about 9:00 a.m., with the *Keystone State*, *Aries*, *Emma*, *Howquah*, *Montgomery*, and *Vicksburg* hurling shells over Federal Point at Hoke's works. An hour later the *Lenapee*, *Mackinaw*, and *Unadilla* in the Cape Fear River also commenced firing on both Sugar Loaf and Fort Anderson. Sometime after 11:00 a. m. the monitor *Montauk* joined the Fort Anderson fight. One journalist marveled at the accuracy of the monitor's fire: "Every shot struck with the most remarkable accuracy. One after another they glanced along [the fort's] ramparts or burst on its glacis, sending the sand in clouds to the sky." Although the fort responded about noon, its fire was sporadic and ineffective.[26]

From his vantage point on Federal Point General Cox watched the duel between the *Montauk* and Fort Anderson. He was amused by the sight of some sailors who stood on the monitor's deck to inspect the effect of her fire, but were occasionally forced to take refuge behind her revolving turret when Confederate counter-shots ventured too near for comfort. The ironclad's deck was almost awash in the river, offering Fort Anderson's gunners virtually no target upon which to train their pieces. Still, some of the Southerners' shots ricocheted off the monitor's armored plating or passed perilously close to it.[27]

The U. S. Navy's long-range bombardment of Fort Anderson kept its defenders hugging the earthworks for protection, although most of the shells burst harmlessly on the parade ground among the ruins of Brunswick Town fronting the fort. Casualties were light, with only one soldier wounded in the heel, though the Confederates admitted they did "some tall dodging" to escape the incoming shells. Admiral Porter was satisfied with the results of his bombardment, despite its failure to inflict mortal damage on either the fort or its occupants. While the shower of projectiles had not succeeded in silencing the fort, it did prevent the Confederates from shelling Terry's troops advancing on Federal Point.[28]

About 9:30 a.m., just one-half hour after Porter's ships had opened on Fort Anderson, Terry's skirmishers slipped forward and encountered Hoke's pickets in front of Sugar Loaf. A brisk exchange of gunfire ensued as Paine's U. S. Colored Troops slowly but steadily pushed back the Confederates. For more than an hour the shooting was heavy and continuous, with Paine himself near the front "directing and animating his soldiers." "For a little while it was a lively and interesting fight," commented Maj. John McMurray of the 6th U. S. Colored Troops.[29]

Many of Schofield's western troops had never seen black soldiers before and were anxious to observe their performance on the battlefield. By day's end Paine's men left little doubt as to their courage and fighting ability. General Cox spent much of the day watching them and concluded that "they were disciplined and well led, and went forward with alacrity in capital form, showing that they were good soldiers." Another eyewitness said that "their advance, in deployment as skirmishers under sharp fire, was performed as crack regiments have executed it on their parade grounds, but seldom under

Brig. Gen. Charles J. Paine,
Third Division,
XXV Army Corps

U.S. Army
Military History Institute

Soldiers of Co. E, 4th U.S. Colored Troops and their comrades in Charles' Paine's division bore the brunt of the fighting and casualties on the east side of the Cape Fear River. *U.S. Army Military History Institute*

an enemy's fire. Their marching in line of battle and in column was cool, accurate, and soldierly." Captain Thomas Speed of the 12th Kentucky Infantry was more blunt in his praise of the black troops. "You must not turn up your nose when I say they fight splendidly," he cautioned. "I saw them and our regiment saw it—and they all acknowledge that. . .old nigger will fight."[30]

It should have come as no surprise. Paine's soldiers were veterans of many hard-fought battles in Virginia during the summer and autumn of 1864, including Petersburg, Chaffin's Farm, New Market Heights and Fort Harrison. Nine soldiers whose units were fighting on Federal Point—including Sgt. Maj. Christian A. Fleetwood of Company D, 4th U. S. Colored Troops—had won the Medal of Honor for gallantry during the Battle of New Market Heights on September 29, 1864. They also performed most of the fighting on Federal Point on February 11, 1865, losing sixteen men killed and seventy-six wounded. This was by far the greatest loss suffered by any Federal unit that day and comprised almost half of the Union casualties for the entire post-Fort Fisher– Wilmington Campaign.[31]

The Confederates suffered casualties of their own at the hands of Paine's U. S. Colored Troops. One Southerner was captured by his escaped slave-turned-Union infantryman as General Paine's units advanced toward Sugar Loaf on February 11. The black soldier beamed with delight as he escorted his former master back into Union lines later that afternoon. "I'se got 'im boys—I done got 'im," he exclaimed to some white Illinois soldiers. "Got who?" someone asked. "I'se got my old massa boys. I tuk him in, I did. He's my prisoner, ole massa is." The Confederate admitted that his former slave had the better of him, and his face reflected his despondency as he was taken to a holding pen in the rear.[32]

General Ames' advance met stiff opposition of a different kind—a dense swamp extending across its line of march. Ames' battle line found it difficult to penetrate the thick undergrowth and its advance slowed to a crawl and became disjointed. "We marched through the swamps back and fourth, we tryed every way to git through, but we could not git through" recalled Pvt. Simon Bennage of Company E, 76th Pennsylvania Infantry. When the scattered troops finally emerged on the north side of the swamp, they were greeted by sharp gunfire from masked Confederate positions that pinned them down. "The shells and miny balls would come pouring into us as thick as hail," Private Bennage claimed. "We ware scermishing all day and trying to brake through, but it was of no youse. Some times we got very close up to the rebels they commenced to fire on us before we knowed any thing of them."[33]

Abbott's Brigade found the going much easier. It managed to march about a mile up the beach before meeting resistance near the south end of Myrtle Sound. There the Confederates had repossessed, strengthened and expanded the rifle pits taken from them on January 19, and subsequently abandoned by Abbott's men. At Abbott's command, Capt. William Trickey led his 3rd New Hampshire Infantry to within thirty yards or so of the earthworks. Though these works appeared well-manned the fire from behind them was feeble. Sensing that the enemy line was but weakly garrisoned, Trickey ordered a charge. Within three minutes the New Hampshire troops overran the Confederate works, capturing sixty-four soldiers of the 17th North Carolina Infantry. The men from New England lost only one man in the assault.[34]

The dejected Confederate prisoners were marched to the rear as the remainder of Abbott's brigade advanced. At about 11:00 a. m., Terry's entire corps, shielded by a vigorous naval barrage, surged forward to within rifle-musket range of Hoke's main works. The noisy but generally stationary engagement, described as "a rattling, disconnected fire," that at times grew very heavy along the entire line, continued until 4:00 p.m. General Terry, still confined to his buggy, calmly observed the battle while puffing on a cigar. After five hours of fighting it became apparent to the Connecticut general that neither his infantrymen nor Porter's gunboats were going to dislodge Hoke's Confederates. His troops had been exposed to a steady fire all afternoon and casualties were mounting, particularly in Paine's brigades. Unwilling to spill further blood for little or no gain, Terry entrenched his corps about 900 yards south of Hoke's fortifications.[35]

General Schofield joined Terry at the front late in the afternoon and concurred with his opinion that Hoke's line probably could not be overrun by a frontal assault. "Hoke will desperately dispute our advance towards Wilmington via Federal Point," noted one Union observer. "He is. . .ever vigilant and wakeful against surprises. . .his well constructed earthworks mount artillery, and have a force behind them large enough to hold them." Despite this dire assessment, Schofield and Terry believed the day's fighting

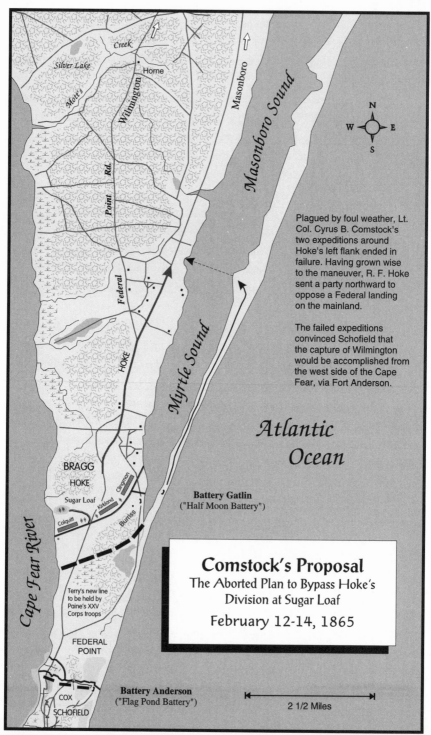

Plagued by foul weather, Lt. Col. Cyrus B. Comstock's two expeditions around Hoke's left flank ended in failure. Having grown wise to the maneuver, R. F. Hoke sent a party northward to oppose a Federal landing on the mainland.

The failed expeditions convinced Schofield that the capture of Wilmington would be accomplished from the west side of the Cape Fear, via Fort Anderson.

Atlantic Ocean

Battery Gatlin ("Half Moon Battery")

Comstock's Proposal
The Aborted Plan to Bypass Hoke's Division at Sugar Loaf

February 12-14, 1865

Battery Anderson ("Flag Pond Battery")

2 1/2 Miles

Mark A. Moore

had been advantageous. A new line had been established close enough to Sugar Loaf to keep Hoke in check. Given the hard-pressed nature of Terry's thrust—and the proximity of his main force—Hoke could not afford to dispatch reinforcements to Fort Anderson, thereby weakening his own division on Federal Point. Ironically, the Federal advantage gained in the face of stubborn Confederate defensive action also made Schofield uneasy about dividing his command to strike Fort Anderson. Should he divide his army in the face of such opposition?[36]

A report from Cyrus Comstock shelved the issue, at least temporarily, after the chief engineer reported that he believed he had found a weakness in Hoke's defenses. As Terry's corps attacked Sugar Loaf, Comstock reconnoitered up the beach, discovering in the process that the Confederates' left flank on Myrtle Sound could be turned. The long, narrow tongue of sand that snaked up the coast separating the sound from the ocean (present-day Masonboro Island), skirted Hoke's left flank. With the shoreline open, Comstock believed that a swift, secret movement could put troops in Hoke's rear.

Comstock proposed to march a force under cover of darkness to Big Hill, a huge sand dune about seven miles up the beach. There the army contingent would rendezvous with navy steamers transporting additional troops and pontoons. The pontoons would be hauled across the beach and used either to construct a makeshift bridge or ferry the soldiers across the narrow sound to the mainland before daylight. Comstock was convinced that a sizable force placed between Fed-

Lt. Col. Cyrus B. Comstock, Chief U.S. Engineer during the Fort Fisher expeditions and Wilmington Campaign.

U.S. Army Military History Institute

eral Point and Wilmington would pry the Confederates away from Sugar Loaf and into more open country, where Schofield would have a better chance of defeating them. To screen the flanking movement, Terry was again to press Hoke's center while Porter renewed his bombardment.[37]

Schofield deemed the plan "quite practicable," and agreed to try it after a more thorough examination of Fort Anderson suggested that capturing it by frontal assault was going to be a difficult task. Fort Anderson probably could not be taken without bypassing Orton Pond, a large millpond some six miles long at the west end of the work. Furthermore, time was less of a concern for Schofield, who received word that Sherman's advance through South Carolina had been hampered by incessant rain and flooded roads. Schofield saw little point in "making a considerable advance along the Wilmington [& Weldon] Railroad before Sherman comes up." With his decision made, Schofield placed Comstock in charge of the flanking operation and designated Cox's division and the Second and Third brigades of Ames' division to comprise the land force. Ames' First Brigade, now commanded by Col. Rufus Daggett, would be carried up the coastline by Porter's ships. General Paine's U. S. Colored Troops would man the trenches in Hoke's front.[38]

The change in plans sowed additional tension within the ranks of the Federal high command. Admiral Porter was infuriated when he received news of Comstock's beach expedition. Privately, he accused Schofield of reversing the agreed-upon plan to attack Fort Anderson as soon as General Grant had left the Cape Fear. Porter considered it "imbecile" to attack by the beach "where all [Schofield's] movements could be seen and he stood the chance of being roughly handled." Moreover, both Porter and Terry felt slighted because Schofield had consulted neither of them before deciding on his plan. Yet the generally outspoken Porter did not challenge Schofield, and instead readied his ships for the operation.[39]

Led by Lieutenant Colonel Comstock, the troop transports carrying Daggett's brigade shoved off from Fort Fisher just after dark on February 12. Porter's gunboats met them as they cleared New Inlet and escorted them up the shore. Schofield personally led the infantry force up the beach as soon as it was dark enough to conceal its movement. To avoid detection by the Confederates, whose camp fires were in view on the west side of Myrtle Sound, Schofield's troops marched as close to the water as the tide would allow. Guided in the darkness by the waves' white caps, the soldiers marched along the beach in silence.[40]

A cold wind had been increasing in strength all afternoon and by nightfall had whipped into a northeast gale. The deteriorating weather slowed Schofield's march and succeeded in finding every opening in the men's clothing, chilling them to the bone. "The sand driving with the wind cuts like a knife," complained a Federal officer, "adding much to the unpleasantness of the night." The column had struggled to within three miles of its destination when Schofield received word from Comstock that naval efforts to bring up the pontoons had failed because of heavy seas. A disappointed Schofield countermanded the order to advance and the troops slogged back to their camps, where they arrived about 11:00 p. m.[41]

Comstock urged Schofield to try the movement again. "If successful," he argued, "it would [give them] half of Hoke's army and Wilmington." Schofield acquiesced since it appeared the Confederates had not detected his first attempt. The foul weather persisted, however, and the seas continued too rough to tow the pontoon boats. Comstock recommended hauling the pontoons up the beach on mule-drawn wagons, and the boats were brought ashore on February 13 and readied for the second movement.[42]

Schofield once again accompanied the expedition but left Comstock in active command of it. Ill omens plagued the operation from the start. The pontoon train was supposed to be ready to move by 4:00 p.m. on February 14, but it was several hours late in reaching Cox's earthworks, the departure point for the expedition. By then the skies had cleared somewhat, but a brisk cold wind whipped up a high surf, impeding the progress of the mule teams in the soft sand. It was nearly midnight before they reached the outer picket station at Battery Gatlin (Half Moon Battery), barely a mile north of Terry's new line. "The high tide and surf proved too great a hindrance," General Cox later reported, "the sand, where not washed by the water, was too deep and soft for the teams, and where the waves broke, the sea was too much for them." Moreover, the winds again made the troops so uncomfortable that whenever the army halted for a brief rest, soldiers quickly dug holes in the sand, crawled in, and covered themselves with gum blankets. "[Then] after a wile we got rounded up and started and marched up along the beach," complained Simon Bennage, one of the long-suffering privates.[43]

The troops and perhaps half of the pontoon-laden wagons pressed on for another two miles, but the remainder of the train became scattered up and down the strand. Schofield began to doubt that the men could make the crossing before sunrise in order to launch a surprise assault. To make matters worse, a bright moon peeped out from behind dissipating clouds, illuminating the convoy on the beach and the gunboats that had moved up to support the attack. Campfires were observed on the mainland at the crossing point, suggesting to Schofield that the Confederates were expecting the Federals. Schofield again canceled the expedition, and again the troops faced about and marched back down the beach. They had gotten about halfway back to camp when it started to rain. The drizzle quickly turned into a torrential downpour. By the time the soldiers reached their camps between 2:00 and 5:00 a.m., high winds and pounding rain had blown down their tents. "It rained heavy, I was very tired, I could lay down and sleep most any place," observed Private Bennage. "We had a terrible night."[44]

It was still raining when the troops emerged from their soggy blanket rolls the next morning. Despite the inclement weather, a disappointed Comstock was convinced the army should have pushed on at least another hour or so the night before. Many soldiers agreed, preferring a fight to all the marching and countermarching. "I was disgusted with the retreat as it was made without firing a shot," exclaimed Lt. Nicholas DeGraff of the 115th New York Infantry. Jacob Cox, on the other hand, wondered why Schofield had not abandoned the movement "as soon as it was evident that the pontoons would be behind time." He suspected that Schofield "thought it best not to stop till it had been well tried," because Comstock was a respected member of Grant's inner circle.[45]

Cox's supposition was true enough. Schofield knew "the plan was a favorite of. . .Comstock's." Regardless of accusations that he was showing favoritism or playing politics, Schofield believed that "had the wind been favorable [the operation] would undoubtedly have been successful." In any event, he did not see that anything had been lost in the attempts. Admiral Porter vehemently disagreed, asserting that they "lost about two weeks by the imbecile maneuvering." All the same, the admiral seemed happy over Schofield's failure. "Terry, myself, and the rebels laughed at it," he scoffed. The opinionated Porter also declared Schofield incompetent, claiming that "although General Grant. . .consider[ed] Schofield a great soldier, he was never more mistaken in his life."[46]

Even under the best circumstances, Comstock's plan would have probably failed. As Union scouts had reported, Hoke suspected something was afoot and had posted a force to oppose the crossing. In the end, however, bad weather rather than Confederate preparedness foiled Comstock's expedition. Although the operation was a frustrating setback for Schofield, Comstock and their rain-soaked troops, it was hardly a catastrophe. Once again Schofield resolved to adopt the original plan of attacking Wilmington by way of Fort Anderson.

"The dying struggle of J. D. [Jefferson Davis] & Co. is coming," a confident Union officer wrote, "though they die hard."[47]

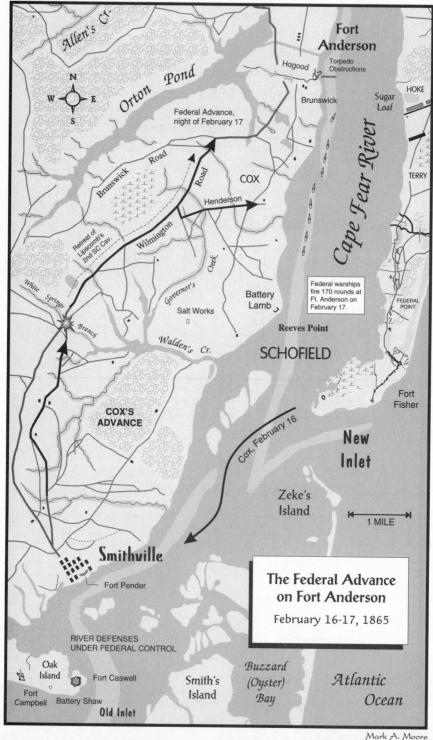

The Federal Advance
on Fort Anderson

February 16-17, 1865

Mark A. Moore

Chapter 11

"The Rebs stand up to their work manfully,
but we are too much for them."

– Cmdr. William G. Temple, USS Pontoosuc

OUTFLANKED

Thomas J. Lipscomb sat astride his horse on a bluff on the Cape Fear River's west bank and peered out across the murky waters. With his field glasses Lipscomb could see the rear of Fort Fisher and Union soldiers moving about inside. As colonel of the 2nd South Carolina Cavalry, it was Lipscomb's responsibility to watch the movements of the enemy, who until this time had remained at or near Fort Fisher. Federal infantry also occupied Smithville, but thus far they were too few to constitute a threat. Union sailors from the gunboat flotilla on the river sometimes came ashore in Brunswick County, but the Confederates kept their distance, content merely to observe.

A movement on the river caught Lipscomb's eye, and he focused his attention on the fuzzy images taking shape in the distance. Emerging from New Inlet were ships carrying a large number of Union troops, heading in the direction of Smithville. Lipscomb turned his mount and galloped to Fort Anderson to report that the Yankees were on the move.

Reinforcements from Maj. Gen. John Schofield's other two divisions, en route from Alexandria, Virginia, finally began to arrive at the Cape Fear on February 14. The first of these were from the Second Division—the 23rd

Michigan Infantry of the Second Brigade, and 100 men of the 26th Kentucky Infantry, temporarily attached to the Second Brigade from the First Brigade. The balance of the Second Brigade was in transport and close behind. The news of the additional troops was welcomed by Schofield, for it eased his apprehension about dividing his army to operate on both sides of the Cape Fear River. He immediately sent the newly arrived regiments to Smithville. Schofield also made further arrangements with Admiral Porter to transfer General Cox's Third Division from Federal Point across the river to attack Fort Anderson, and ordered another reconnaissance of the fort's approaches.[1]

Lieutenant Colonel Albert M. Barney, commanding officer at Smithville, led a scouting party of the 142nd New York Infantry in the direction of Fort Anderson on February 15. Barney marched his men out of Smithville toward the powerful Confederate entrenchments but was prevented from reaching the fort by Col. Thomas Lipscomb's 2nd South Carolina Cavalry. Unable to penetrate the cavalry screen, Barney's New Yorkers spent most of the rainy day examining the broken terrain surrounding the works and the roadways leading to it. Despite hopes to the contrary, the country was not favorable for a full-scale military operation. Instead of accessible terrain the Federals found the ground before Fort Anderson filled with piney lowlands interlaced with creeks, marshy ponds and cypress swamps. While this topography was difficult, the mainland still offered more maneuvering room than Federal Point, an advantage—along with the army's numerical superiority and the navy's firepower—that Schofield meant to exploit in his effort to capture Fort Anderson. Despite the recent rains, however, Barney reported that the roads remained in reasonably good condition.[2]

While the heavy rains had little effect on Brunswick County's roads, they did manage to delay the transfer of Jacob Cox's division from Federal Point to Smithville until February 16. Throughout the day Porter's steamers were busy ferrying soldiers, field artillery and supply wagons across the harbor. The remainder of the Second Brigade, commanded by Col. Orlando Moore, finally arrived from the north and joined Cox's command at Smithville. The only battery of Cox's division that had arrived thus far was Battery D, 1st Ohio Regiment Light Artillery, and Colonel Moore's two units which had disembarked two days earlier. Added to the other units on hand, the Ohio artillerists, together with the 23rd Michigan and the 26th Kentucky, rounded out the force of about 6,000 troops that would assault Fort Anderson. The Federals encamped for the night about half a mile north of Smithville and prepared for battle.[3]

Cox began his advance toward Fort Anderson, about nine miles upriver from Smithville, at 8:00 a.m. the next morning, February 17. Lem Brown and other local blacks familiar with the back roads of Brunswick County served as guides for the advancing Federals. The march on the sandy Wilmington Road, while slow going, was initially uneventful. The few inhabitants who lived along the route gaped from the doors of their cabins as Mr. Lincoln's troops marched past. Most of them had never seen Yankee soldiers before. The slaves "came running out. . .singing and shouting with joy and thanksgiving," glad to see that, contrary to what their white masters had told them, Yankee soldiers did not have horns and tails. Some of the overjoyed slaves rushed forward to embrace the soldiers, while others dropped to their knees in prayer, fully aware that the blue-clad troops heralded their new-found freedom. An Illinois soldier described it as "both an affecting and laughable scene—a prayer meeting and a circus combined."[4]

But the amused Federal troops were soon reminded that the grim business of war was still at hand when Confederate cavalry attacked them about three miles outside of Smithville. For most of the day Lipscomb's ubiquitous horsemen harassed the Union column, staging hit-and-run raids, setting fire to the woods, and felling trees across the road to retard the Federals' advance. Lipscomb's men made a brief stand at White Springs Branch, a tributary of Walden's Creek, but were quickly turned aside by Cox's skirmish line, three companies of the 16th Kentucky Infantry of Col. Oscar W. Sterl's First Brigade.[5]

Near Governor's Creek the road forked, prompting Cox to split his army to cover both avenues of advance. Cox accompanied Col. Thomas Henderson's Third Brigade on a byroad leading in the direction of the river, while Sterl's, Moore's and Col. John Casement's units continued their advance up the Wilmington Road. Late that afternoon Cox and Henderson struck the river about two miles below Fort Anderson and opened communications with Admiral Porter. General Schofield was also on the river, having set up his command post on board the medical steamer *S. R. Spaulding*. From that vantage point Schofield believed he could better coordinate the movements of both Cox's and Terry's forces—now totaling some 15,000 troops—on both sides of the waterway. As soon as Cox established contact, however, Schofield went ashore to join him.[6]

Some of Porter's gunboats had been battling Fort Anderson's batteries all afternoon in an effort to distract the Confederates' attention from Cox's advance. The monitor *Montauk* led the ships upstream shortly after midday where, under a vigorous shelling from Johnson Hagood's Confederates, the ironclad assumed a position about 1,000 yards off the fort and opened fire. Obstructions and torpedoes in the channel prevented the monitor from get-

Union bombardment of Fort Anderson, February 1865. *Harper's Weekly*

ting much closer to the enemy's smoking guns. The *Lenapee*, *Pequot*, *Un-adilla*, *Moratanza*, *Pawtuxet*, *Huron*, and *Tacony* took up their battle stations further away, beyond the range of Confederate artillery, and began bombarding the fort at 3:15 p.m. About two hours later the *Little Ada*, a converted blockade runner, steamed up and joined the battle, which thundered until sunset.[7]

The Confederates subjected the approaching Union ships to a steady cannonade. According to one witness the fort's guns fired "pretty briskly" during the early afternoon, unleashing forty-seven projectiles at the *Montauk* alone. The bolts that struck the monitor, however, could not penetrate the ironclad's thick iron plating, although some of the other vessels sustained minor damage and casualties in the exchange. The *Mackinaw* was hit by two Whitworth bolts—"visitors," a Union sailor called them—which tore through the smoke pipe and damaged the main gaff. Only minutes after the *Pequot* took up her station a whistling Whitworth bolt smashed into one of her stanchions (an upright support beam). Flying splinters struck five sailors, mortally wounding Quartermaster William Brain in the stomach and severely injuring Quartermaster J. Lyons and Ordinary Seaman Carl Poelstrom. Lyons's nasty wound required the amputation of his left arm, while Poelstrom lost a foot to the surgeon's saw. Fortunately for the flotilla, the 12-pounder Whitworth rifle quickly depleted its limited ammunition supply and was withdrawn from the battle.[8]

The rest of the Confederate cannon that were still firing fell silent as the Union ships stopped shelling at dusk and retreated downstream. General Hagood had refrained from firing most of his 32-pounders because the gunboats were well beyond their range and there was no point in wasting scarce ammunition. The Union naval bombardment of Fort Anderson proved to be little more than a wasteful exercise. The Federal warships had fired only 170 projectiles at the fort in about four hours, causing little damage to the works and wounding only one defender. More importantly, the bombardment had failed to disguise Cox's advance: Hagood was well aware of the Federal's approach.[9]

Just as the Union gunboats were ending their fitful exchange with Hagood's defenders, Cox and Henderson reestablished contact with Sterl's, Casement's and Moore's brigades on the Wilmington Road. With his day's advance at an end, Cox ordered his men to throw out a picket line and entrench about one and one-half miles south of Fort Anderson. As the sound of shovels and axes filled the growing darkness the scene in the piney woods took on a slightly macabre air. Earlier in the day Confederate cavalry had set fires in the woods which, fueled by strong winds, continued to sputter and burn well into the night. Cox's soldiers had advanced more than seven miles and had skirmished almost continuously during the day. The Federals slept on their arms that night as various fires crackled and burned around them, knowing that the next day would likely bring a different kind of fire.[10]

As their soldiers rested, Schofield and Cox spent the evening plotting to take Fort Anderson. It appeared the navy would be unable to bring enough heavy ordnance to bear on the fort's elevated batteries to silence them, primarily because the river channel was too narrow and full of obstructions and torpedoes. While the gunboats could provide long range fire, their shelling would have to be delivered beyond the effective range of the warships. No one doubted that it would take longer to knock out the fort's ordnance than it had at Fort Fisher, especially since there were fewer ships to perform the work. It was also possible that, despite its best efforts, the navy would not be able to effectively silence the fort's artillery. The brunt of responsibility for Fort Anderson's capture clearly rested on the army's shoulders.

Schofield instructed Cox to make a reconnaissance-in-force of Fort Anderson the following morning. After a close inspection of the work they would decide how best to proceed. If the naval fire—which Porter would resume at daybreak—had destroyed or dismounted the fort's artillery, then Cox should be able to storm the works. If not, Cox was to entrench two of his brigades before the fort and make a forced march with his two remaining brigades to the west end of Orton Pond. Once beyond that water obstacle, he would be joined by Adelbert Ames' division, which Schofield would bring over from Federal Point. With this combined force Cox could sweep around Orton Pond and attack Fort Anderson from the rear while his two entrenched brigades threatened from in front. Meanwhile, Porter's gunboats would maintain a steady fire on the fort and Terry's force would continue to press General Hoke's Confederates on Federal Point.[11]

February 18 dawned pleasant, promising a third consecutive day of fine weather. General Cox deployed his division in the smoldering woodland and advanced at about 7:00 a.m., with Henderson's brigade moving up the river bank, Casement's unit taking the center, and Sterl's anchoring the left of the line. Moore's brigade followed in echelon in the rear. Within an hour Federal sharpshooters encountered Confederate pickets and the fighting quickly developed across the front. Eleven soldiers of the 65th Indiana Infantry were wounded on the skirmish line during the day. The popping of small arms fire to the south brought Hagood's Confederates inside Fort Anderson to their trenches in expectation of an assault. Within a short time some of their vastly outnumbered comrades on the skirmish line, who had been conducting a stubborn inch-by-inch retreat, withdrew into view south of the fort's walls. Many of the skirmishers took up new positions in a line of rifle pits some 150 yards outside the walls. Those Confederates closest to the river, however, were exposed to heavy fire from both Henderson's skirmishers and Porter's gunboats, which had recently joined in the developing fight. Unable to maintain their position under the thunderous fire, they scurried into the fort for safety. Their retreat created a gap on the firing line that enabled Henderson's leading regiment, the 63rd Indiana Infantry, to advance through some soggy ground within 300 yards of the fort. The Hoosiers did not remain there long. Misdirected shots from the Union gunboats wounded some Indianans and compelled the rest to hustle to the rear.[12]

Fort Anderson, one of only two known wartime views of the Confederate fort west of the Cape Fear River at Brunswick Town. *Frank Leslie's Illustrated Newspaper*

While the skirmishing increased in intensity and giant naval shells arched toward the fort, Cox moved his brigades to within 600 yards of the fort and surveyed the terrain. An impenetrable swamp and creek fed into the river near the fort just south of a strong Confederate battery in front of Cox's right flank, the same area recently evacuated by the Hoosiers who had suffered the friendly fire of their gunboats. That sector was obviously not suited to infantry operations. The ground on Cox's left-center and left, however, was more open—especially along the Wilmington Road, which bisected the fort's sand curtain. About 300 yards of the piney timber, which at

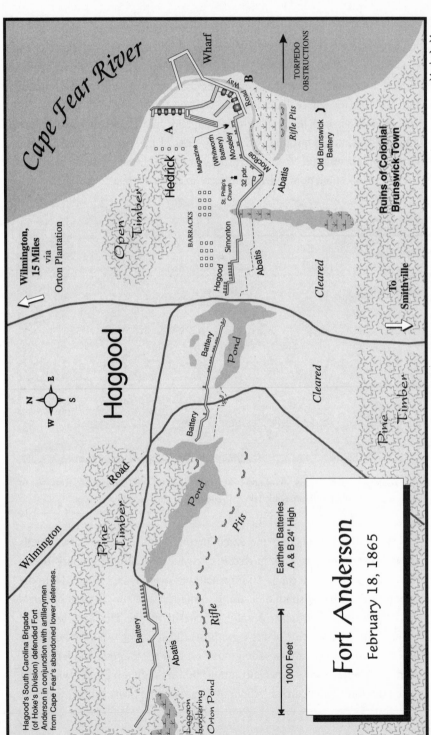

Hagood's South Carolina Brigade
(of Hoke's Division) defended Fort
Anderson in conjunction with artillerymen
from Cape Fear's abandoned lower defenses.

Wilmington, 15 Miles via Orton Plantation

Cape Fear River

Wharf

Open Timber

Hedrick

Magazine

(Whitworth Battery)

Moseley

Road

B

Way

Rifle Pits

32 pdr.

Abatis

Old Brunswick Battery

St. Philip's Church

BARRACKS

Simonton

Hagood

Abatis

Cleared

To Smithville

TORPEDO OBSTRUCTIONS

Ruins of Colonial Brunswick Town

Mark A. Moore

Hagood

N
W E
S

Wilmington

Pine Timber

Road

Battery

Battery

Pond

Pond

Battery

Cleared

Pine Timber

Rifle Pits

Abatis

Battery

Lagoon bordering Orton Pond

Earthen Batteries
A & B 24' High

1000 Feet

Fort Anderson
February 18, 1865

one time had abutted the fort's mammoth walls, had been slashed and burned by the Confederates to provide a clear field of fire. While the abatis would make an infantry attack difficult, the open ground also provided Cox and Schofield with a good view of the fort and its impressive features. And they were impressed.[13]

Fort Anderson, directly opposite Sugar Loaf across the Cape Fear River, was constructed much like Fort Fisher, with imposing earthen ramparts interspersed with artillery chambers and protective traverses. There was a reason for the similarity: many of the engineers who had worked on Fort Fisher, including Colonels William Lamb and John J. Hedrick, had also helped plan and build Fort Anderson. The fort was a mile-long L-shaped sand work, with the short end of the "L" running parallel to the Cape Fear River. Its main strength served as its eastern anchor: two massive earthen batteries overlooking the water approach to Wilmington. Battery A, an imposing 100-yard long, thirty-foot high (to the top of the traverses) fortification with five gun chambers, was constructed facing east about 100 yards north of the main line (at the end of the very short bottom leg of the "L"). A nearly identical in size Battery B—a full bastion also pitted with five large artillery compartments—fronted to the south and east where the two legs of the "L" intersected. Together, the ten chambers contained nine 6.4-inch 32-pounder guns mounted en barbette. Of these nine pieces, only "two. . .were rifled but not banded," observed General Hagood, "and their carriages were old and worn, and bore across and down the river." The positioning of the guns caused Hagood no little worry. "No gun could be brought to bear up the river," he lamented, "and consequently if any portion of the fleet should have passed the fort we would have had no fire upon it, while it would have taken nearly every gun in reverse."

From near Battery B, at St. Philip's Church behind the fort's walls, a thick sandy curtain extended one mile west to Orton Pond. The shank of the "L"—which faced the Federals to the south—was a crooked affair that took advantage of the rough terrain features. Confederate engineers abutted the earthworks on (and partially behind) two fresh water ponds located a few hundred yards apart about midway down the line. This sage engineering feat allowed the defenders to utilize the ponds like giants moats. Portions of the wall were also constructed behind and against a deep cypress swamp near the fort's far western end, which itself fed into Orton Pond. Abatis, epaulements, ditches, tiny ponds, swampy bogs and rifle pits further strengthened the fort's land face, while field artillery—strategically emplaced along the mile-long shank—enjoyed "full play" across the ground in front. The terrain traversed by the defenders behind (north of) the fort's walls was similar to that beyond its front: cleared fields clotted with stands of piney timber, turkey oaks, and interlacing patches of swampy ground. The Confederates had also utilized a small colonial redoubt, Old Brunswick Battery, by placing a 32-pounder gun on a bluff along the river's edge just south of the main fort, but had abandoned it as the Federals approached.[14]

Fort Anderson's Achilles' Heel, as Schofield and Cox (and Hagood) already knew, was identical to the fatal flaw in Fort Fisher: its rear was wide open. The fort could be outflanked by going around the west end of Orton Pond, where the Confederates had neglected to construct adequate defenses. A flanking move around the millpond, which was actually a lake about six miles long, entailed a twelve-mile detour for the Federals.[15]

After surveying Fort Anderson, Schofield concluded that the enveloping maneuver around Orton Pond was the best plan available, and he ordered Cox to undertake it. To disguise his intentions, Cox requested that Porter intensify his shore bombardment as Colonels Moore and Henderson demonstrated with their brigades across Hagood's front. Moore and Henderson entrenched their units inside the tree line 600 yards from the fort before advancing a strong force of skirmishers—the 63rd Indiana Infantry from Henderson's brigade, among other units—into the open fields of sedge broom grass in front. The long-anticipated enemy thrust provoked a sharp reply from the Southern defenders when the Federals stumbled into a line of Confederate rifle pits about 150 yards beyond the fort's walls. The thin line of defenders were supported by two of Hagood's field batteries, which opened "a very vigorous fire with artillery and shelled [the Federals] quite briskly for several hours."[16]

As Moore's and Henderson's troops moved into position and forced Hagood's skirmishers inside the walls, Cox assembled Casement's and Sterl's brigades and the 1st Ohio Artillery battery, commanded by Lt. Cecil Reed, for his flanking force. Guided by a black man, the brigades started out at about 2:00 p.m. on February 18, advancing westward along the Brunswick (or British) Road that skirted the southern edge of Orton Pond. General Hagood was unaware of Cox's movement, though he was fully cognizant of

Fort Anderson's weak right flank. Hagood had posted a small detachment of the 2nd South Carolina Cavalry at the far end of Orton Pond to warn him of any attempt by the enemy to turn that flank.17

With few defensive options, Hagood ordered his gunners and infantry to blast away at the Union troops immediately south of the fort. For most of the day the Confederates kept up this intense fusillade of musketry and field artillery fire. One Union officer commented that the Confederate artillery barrage was "the most accurate shelling [he had] ever witnessed from rebel batteries." The Federals quickly dug in under the deluge of iron and lead. "Officers and men vied with each other in throwing up breastworks with whatever they could bring into requisition," noted a eyewitness. "Tin plates, cups, sticks, and hands were kept very busy until a sufficient temporary protection was formed." Spades and shovels were brought up from Smithville and the men spent most of the afternoon strengthening their breastworks amid all the whizzing projectiles.

During the height of the fighting the brass band of the 104th Ohio Infantry of Sterl's brigade "kept up a constant serenade of patriotic music." Confederates inside the fort could hear the music wafting above the roar of artillery and small arms fire. Not to be outdone, they employed a brass band of their own—probably the Eutaw Band of the 25th South Carolina Infantry—to play Southern melodies. Union soldiers clearly recognized one tune above the din of battle—"Who's Been Here While I've Been Gone." The bands attempted to inspire their comrades in the thick of the fight—or perhaps to dilute its insanity.[18]

As the hours passed and the expected Union infantry attack failed to materialize, Hagood—perhaps suspecting that the enemy effort south of the fort was a feint—ordered his infantry back out onto the skirmish line.[19]

Despite the heavy musketry and exploding projectiles, neither side experienced significant losses. The Federals sustained only about 20 casualties, and most of these were members of the 65th Indiana, which had experienced heavy action on the skirmish line that morning. General Schofield narrowly escaped injury when a Confederate shell exploded near him as he galloped along the line directing the action. Colonel Oliver L. Spaulding, commander of the 23rd Michigan of Orlando Moore's brigade, also had a close call. A projectile struck a sapling under which he was standing, and shook the tree so violently that it knocked Spaulding to the ground.[20]

Naval losses were also very light. A tragic accident and not Confederate iron caused most of Admiral Porter's losses during the day. At nightfall a hawser on the *Lenapee* became fouled and a detail was dispatched in a launch to clear it. As the sailors worked the *Sassacus* inadvertently swung into the small boat, tipping it over and spilling its crew into the cold Cape Fear River. Four of the sailors drowned before rescue boats could reach them.[21]

Confederates losses entailed just twelve casualties. Lieutenant Robert B. Vance of Company A, 40th North Carolina, was killed instantly by concussion, "without a single fragment having struck him," when a navy shell burst above his head. Lieutenant John Z. Davis of the same unit was mortally wounded in the stomach by a shell and died the following day at a hospital in Wilmington. As it transpired, Admiral Porter's terrific naval cannonade inflicted most of the Confederate losses.[22]

Only about one-half of Porter's flotilla engaged Fort Anderson on February 18, with the gunboats coming under fire just after 8:00 a.m. The monitor *Montauk* again led the van upstream. Fourteen vessels—the *Chippewa, Huron, Lenapee, Little Ada, Mackinaw, Malvern, Nyack, Osceola, Pawtuxet, Pontoosuc, Sassacus, Seneca, Shawmut,* and *Unadilla*—followed the ironclad. The Confederate shore batteries fired the opening salvo as the Federal gunboats took up their battle stations. Testing both the river obstructions and the effectiveness of the fort's arsenal, the *Montauk* crept to within 800 yards of the fort—200 yards closer than the previous day. As expected, the narrow channel restricted the movement of the remainder of the wooden ships, forcing them to line up and down the waterway. Nevertheless, by noon they were all in position and opened fire. The river was as smooth as glass, enabling the gunboats to quickly establish their range of fire. "The sight was most magnificent," exclaimed Stephen Bartlett, a surgeon on board the *Lenapee*. "The vessels moved into line splendidly and poured broadsides into the enemy, the enemy replied." For nine hours the warships maintained an intense and accurate bombardment.[23]

Lieutenant William Calder of the 1st Battalion North Carolina Heavy Artillery recalled that the "fire was tremendous and the fall and bursting of shells was almost continuous." By General Hagood's count, the Federal gunboats unleashed 2,723 projectiles on the fort—about one every ten sec-

A previously unpublished portrait of Lt. William Calder, adjutant, 1st Battalion North Carolina Heavy Artillery, an astute observer of conditions and affairs at Fort Anderson. *Courtesy of Robert Calder*

onds—nearly every shell striking the earthworks or landing inside. One Union tar confessed that he found the bombardment both grand and terrible. "The screaming of the shells, loud roar of the artillery, flashing of the guns, bursting of the shells," he recalled, "was well worth remembering." A Confederate soldier confessed to a somewhat different reaction from his vantage point inside the fort. "Our pickets and theirs, and light artillery were firing off and on all day, and with the shelling of the fort from the gunboats, made the place anything but comfortable," he observed.[24]

Under the circumstances it was surprising that the Confederates suffered as few casualties as they did. One Tarheel officer, Lt. Eugene S. Martin, recalled a close brush with death when an 11-inch Dahlgren shell exploded and ricocheted off the brick walls of St. Philip's Church. A large iron chunk of the cannonball flew between him and Colonel Hedrick as they stood on the fort's parapet. The whizzing fragment severed Hedrick's sword from his side, leaving the colonel shaken but unhurt. The fort itself did not pass through the shelling nearly as well, sustaining extensive damage from the bombardment. "The fort was knocked out of all shape," remarked a North Carolinian. Bursting shells pitted the ramparts, knocked down traverses and leveled sections of the parapet. Despite the heavy physical damage inflicted on the works, none of the fort's cannon were dismounted. The presence of the guns provided a strong incentive for the Federals to shy away from attempting a frontal assault.[25]

Confederate artillery answered the flotilla with only occasional shots, firing just fifty-three shot and shell all day. General Hagood admitted that his guns fired "more in defiance than in hopes of injuring the enemy." Fort Anderson's antiquated heavy ordnance was all but useless against the Federal gunboats, which had once again assumed positions beyond the range of the Confederates' smoothbore pieces. Even the two rifled 32-pounders proved ineffective against the enemy gunboats. Unfortunately for the Confederates, their best hope of inflicting damage on Porter's gunboats, the deadly 12-pounder Whitworth, had expended its ammunition during the previous day's fight. The British-made artillery piece remained mute throughout the exchange, unable to fire so much as a single round.

A few of the Confederate projectiles, however, did manage to find their mark. The *Mackinaw* took a port-side hit below the water line, but sustained no serious damage. And as the Southerners quickly learned, even their heaviest ordnance was powerless to injure a monitor. Fort Anderson's guns fired twenty solid iron bolts at the ironclad *Montauk*—almost half of their shots unleashed during the battle. At least seven of them struck the *Montauk's* turret, but each ricocheted harmlessly into the murky waters of the

Cape Fear River. A Confederate artilleryman, Pvt. Thomas Sutton of Company D, 40th North Carolina, left an apt description of Southern efforts to damage the ironclad. The projectiles, he wrote, "would strike and bounce off like cherries from a boy's pop gun against a solid wall of masonry."[26]

Robert Hoke watched and listened to the Fort Anderson fight from his position at Sugar Loaf. In an effort to divert some of the Union naval fire directed at the fort, Hoke ordered a battery of light artillery to shell the enemy gunboats. Stationed atop the summit of Sugar Loaf, Capt. Thomas Southerland's Wilmington Horse Artillery unleashed its shells in the direction of Porter's warships. The firing had little effect other than to distract the *Nyack*, which turned its attention against the pesky field battery for about two hours. By 3:00 p. m. the guns of Fort Anderson and Sugar Loaf had fallen silent. As the sun started to dip behind the pine trees over Fort Anderson, Admiral Porter ordered his warships to slacken their fire as well. The Federal gunners had performed a long and good day's work. Lieutenant Commander William G. Temple of the *Pontoosuc* deemed the battle "a nice little fight. The rebs stand up to their work manfully," he acknowledged, "but we are too much for them, and hope to drive them out of Wilmington before many days."[27]

General Cox had a similar intention in mind as he and his flanking force reached the headwaters of Orton Pond at twilight. Adelbert Ames' division had not yet arrived, but about 100 horsemen of the 2nd South Carolina Cavalry were there to dispute Cox's effort to march around the millpond. The Confederates had dug rifle pits on the north side of Moore's Creek, a shallow stream bordered by a wide marsh that fed into Orton Pond. These pits overlooked a narrow causeway that crossed the creek.[28]

Colonel Lipscomb dutifully sent word to General Hagood of the enemy's movement as soon as the Federals appeared in his front. For some inexplicable reason, Hagood—who had expressed concern about the exposed flank and had sent cavalrymen there to warn of any danger from that direction—now displayed no apparent concern. He dispatched but a single field howitzer and crew to reinforce Lipscomb, Company B (Badham's Battery), 3rd Battalion North Carolina Light Artillery, commanded by Lt. John M. Jones. Perhaps Hagood was misinformed as to the size of Cox's force or foolishly optimistic his fellow South Carolinian's could turn back the Federals. Yet, 100 horse soldiers and a single field piece were hardly

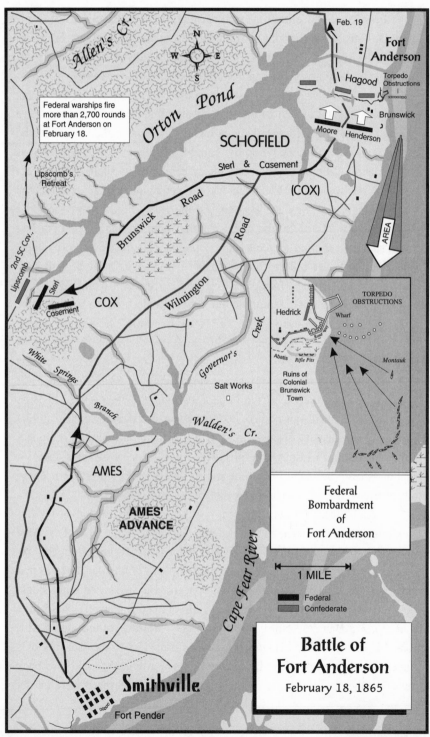

Federal warships fire more than 2,700 rounds at Fort Anderson on February 18.

TORPEDO OBSTRUCTIONS

Federal Bombardment of Fort Anderson

1 MILE

Federal
Confederate

Battle of Fort Anderson

February 18, 1865

Mark A. Moore

sufficient to stop any sizable force, let alone the 3,000 men Cox intended to throw around Hagood's flank. In the end Hagood's Lilliputian-like effort proved moot, for the lone cannon did not reach Lipscomb in time to help him.[29]

Unwilling to let the coming darkness hamper his effort to outflank Fort Anderson, the aggressive Cox pushed his command around Orton Pond. Once in position he deployed four companies (A, D, E and I) from the 104th Ohio Infantry with orders to make their way through the marsh. Lieutenant Horace Reed of Company I advanced his small party along the banks of the causeway under a sharp fire from the dismounted Confederate cavalrymen. Braving the enemy' carbine fire, one by one the Union soldiers reached the far side of the creek. When he felt he had amassed a large enough force, Reed ordered a bayonet charge against the dug-in Southerners. The Ohioans responded with enthusiasm, driving Lipscomb's Southerners out of their works and putting them to flight. Lieutenant Reed, however, who had so brilliantly organized the crossing and attack, collapsed with wounds in both legs while another Ohioan, Pvt. John Hammond of Company E, was killed. Private Adam Weaver survived the attack, but only with the aid of a family member. A bullet had ripped into Weaver's left thigh, knocking him face down into the cold creek. Adam's cousin, Rhody, saw him drop and fearing he would soon drown, dodged zinging minie balls to pull him to safety.[30] The Federals suffered fewer than ten casualties during the half-hour engagement. Confederates losses are unknown, but were probably fairly minimal as well. The Federals chased the Confederate cavalry for a mile or more but managed to capture only a handful of exhausted stragglers.[31]

With the crossing secured Cox advanced Sterl's and Casement's brigades around the pond. The depth of the pursuit seemed to indicate that there was no organized Southern resistance behind the Confederate right flank. The rear of Fort Anderson beckoned.[32]

It had been a long and fatiguing day for General Ames' division. His troops had been awakened before midnight by Schofield's sudden order to move from Federal Point to the west side of the river to reinforce Cox. The transfer across the harbor took all night, and it was not until the early morning hours of February 18 that all of Ames' men had disembarked at Smithville. There Ames' soldiers linked up with Cox's supply wagons for the trip to the headwaters of Orton Pond. But the wagon train, which Ames was supposed to accompany, was not yet prepared to roll, leaving the sleepy and disgruntled troops marking time waiting for the convoy to get started.

The situation appeared more favorable when the wagons and infantry began to advance, but before long the column became lost in the back-woods. Disgusted with their train-sitting chore, Ames' infantrymen trudged on, leaving the wagons to find their own way. With the aid of one of General Cox's staff officers and a black guide, whom Cox had sent to find the missing force, Ames finally reached Orton Pond at 5:45 p.m. The general's woes were not yet at an end. In the encroaching darkness Ames' vanguard, Company D of the 117th New York Infantry, stumbled into Cox's rear guard and a musketry fight threatened to erupt before the two forces discovered they had mistaken each other for the enemy. The frustrating day finally wound down when Ames' troops joined Cox's brigades on the north side of Moore's Creek. Collapsing in the woods, the drained men were soon fast asleep.[33]

As the Union soldiers slept the Confederate garrison at Fort Anderson prepared for an expected Union assault at dawn. Work details repaired damage to the earthworks and placed obstructions at the sally port near the river, in case Federal infantry or a naval landing party tried to attack by way of the shoreline. Meanwhile, Porter's gunboats lobbed shells into Fort Anderson to demoralize its defenders and disrupt any effort at sleep. After 6:00 p.m., the gunboats slackened their fire to one shot every five minutes. An hour before the new day the Federals further reduced their shelling to one shot every half hour, but from 2:00 a.m. until sunrise on February 19, the warships increased their fire to six rounds an hour. Lieutenant William Calder tried to rest alongside his Confederate comrades in their makeshift shanties on the earthen lines, "but it was in fear and trembling lest a shell might penetrate it and blow it to atoms. I don't think I ever passed such a night," Calder lamented, "but I got a little troubled sleep between the shells."[34]

While the gunboats threw missiles into the fort, Admiral Porter unleashed a scheme which, if successful, would enable his flotilla to move closer to the fort in the morning—or even capture it outright. Some days earlier, the resourceful Lt. Cmdr. William B. Cushing had suggested using a fake monitor against Fort Anderson. Cushing hoped the Confederates would mistake it for the *Montauk* and be tricked into detonating their torpedoes in an effort to sink her. With the threat of exploding mines removed, the navy would be able to press its attack with greater vigor from closer range. It is not surprising that Porter found merit in Cushing's idea, since he had employed an imitation gunboat himself during the Vicksburg campaign two years earlier. Using a scow, barrel staves and canvas, carpenters threw together the sham monitor near Smithville. When completed, "it was not possible to distinguish between it and the real one at 200 yards distance," Cushing boasted. The fake warship was promptly dubbed *Old Bogey* and *Albemarle No. 2*, in commemoration of the Confederate ironclad *Albemarle* that Cushing had sabotaged at Plymouth, North Carolina in October 1864.[35]

At 10:00 p.m. on February 18, Cushing had the unmanned mock moni-

William B. Cushing's sham monitor near Wilmington, February 1865. *Harper's Weekly*

tor towed upriver and set adrift. A flood tide carried her through Fort Anderson's obstructions and eventually to the east side of the river north of Sugar Loaf, where she went aground.[36] The "plot worked most successfully," reported a war correspondent on assignment with the U. S. Navy. "The craft sailed past the fort in utter contempt of the guns and the torpedoes which were exploded all about her." Referring to it as "an amusing affair altogether," Porter maintained that "the Rebs blew up all their submarine batteries on her without effect as she drew so little water." One of Porter's subordinates, Lt. Cmdr. William G. Temple of the *Pontoosuc*, confirmed Porter's report, claiming that "Johnny Reb let off his torpedoes."[37] Lieutenant Commander Cushing alleged even more impressive results. He declared that the ruse—for which he could claim much of the credit—prompted the terrified Confederates to retreat from Fort Anderson, and he boasted as much to President Lincoln and Secretary Welles when he met with them in Washington on February 22, less than four days after the incident. (Porter had sent Cushing north to have a torpedo fitted to a boat to combat the Confederate ram *Stonewall*, reportedly en route to Wilmington from France). According to Welles, "the President was cheerful and laughed heartily over Cushing's account of the dumb monitor which he sent past Fort Anderson, causing the Rebels to evacuate without waiting to spike their guns."[38]

Despite Cushing's vainglorious assertion, his ploy did not provoke the evacuation of Fort Anderson. General Hagood did not even mention the affair in his postwar memoirs, which is the best extant Southern account of the battle. It is unlikely the Confederates exploded more than a few torpedoes in an effort to sink the fake monitor. Unknown to Porter and Cushing, Hagood and his garrison had suspected for several days that the Federals were constructing a flotilla of mock ironclads. With amazing foresight Lt. William Calder, 1st Battalion North Carolina Heavy Artillery, wrote: "We imagine they intend floating them by some dark night & make us explode our electric torpedoes under them and then send the real monitor by," or they may, he continued, "send them by all at once, and run the risk of our blowing up the right one. But 'forewarned is forearmed,' you know, and we will try and thwart our cute Yankee friends and render this Yankee trick abortive." The Confederates knew that the sham monitor was but a "cute Yankee" trick and thus paid it little heed. They could not afford to invest much attention to Cushing's ploy because they were much too concerned about the all too real threat approaching their rear.[39]

By 10:00 p.m. on February 18, Johnson Hagood realized he faced a desperate situation. Dispatches from Lipscomb, together with testimony from prisoners and deserters, convinced him that Cox commanded a large force—as many as 6,500 soldiers by one estimate—and was closing in on Fort Anderson's right rear. Hagood's own garrison of 2,280 effectives was far too small to both oppose Cox's flanking force and man the walls against the brigades in front of the fort and warships in the river. Furthermore, the Confederates controlled only two avenues of escape—the Wilmington Road across Orton Pond's milldam bridge, and the Orton plantation causeway. With withdrawal as his only viable option, Hagood dutifully telegraphed General Hoke expressing his concern that his command was on the verge of being surrounded. He was not about to abandon the last major fortification on the west side of the Cape Fear without orders from his division commander.

Hoke immediately sent a staff officer from Sugar Loaf across the river to confer with Hagood. "General Hoke invited [my] expression. . .upon the propriety of withdrawing from the Fort Anderson lines," Hagood wrote after the war. "It was given by telegraph." The report received by Hoke was dismally bleak. In addition to Cox's menacing flanking force, which Hagood carefully detailed for his commander, "I have a very much larger force than my own 600 yards in my front, in full view by daylight, and with the fleet to co-operate." Hagood's conclusion was brief and to the point: "When the force on my right rear moves, I must abandon this position, or sacrifice my command." Although Hagood closed his telegram by informing Hoke that if his right was reinforced "the case presented would be different," both officers knew that there was no sizable Confederate force close enough to accomplish the task.

Despite Hagood's presence at the scene and carefully-detailed situation report, Hoke procrastinated. "What do you think best?" he asked, fully aware that the evacuation of Fort Anderson meant that Sugar Loaf would have to be abandoned as well. The South Carolinian fired back another telegram reiterating his prior conclusion—only in a more urgent tone: "I think this place ought to be evacuated and the movement commenced in half an hour," was Hagood's terse reply. It was 2:05 a.m., February 19th.[40]

Even though Robert Hoke knew a hopeless situation when he saw one, he did not reply to Hagood's telegram for almost three-quarters of an hour. Fort Anderson had been held until the last moment, but there was nothing to be gained by losing both the fort and the garrison. And now, with Hoke dragging his feet, precious minutes were ticking away. Finally, at 2:48 a.m., Hoke wired Hagood his approval to evacuate Anderson along with instructions for him to assume a new line of defense eight miles north at Town Creek. Hagood ordered an immediate withdrawal. "Having but a very small force there to oppose [the enemy], with the fort torn up so badly, and no heavy guns on our left [near the river], and a flanking force on the right with nothing to oppose them," explained a member of the Confederate garrison, "we could do nothing but fall back."

Field artillery, ordnance wagons and ambulances comprised the first wave of withdrawals from the bastion. Quartermaster and commissary wagons, which during the battle had been moved to Allen's Creek, were also sent toward Town Creek. The garrison held on until just before dawn, when it hurriedly evacuated the fort it had defended so well. Hagood's pickets remained at their posts so as not to alert the enemy as to what was transpiring. The pace of the retreat, which began in an organized manner, became so hurried that the dead were left behind, laid out in the ruins of St. Philips Church. The fort's heavy guns and ammunition were also abandoned in the haste to evacuate the position, and the cannon were left unspiked. As Hagood explained it, "No effort was made to blow up the magazine of the fort or to destroy its armament," Hagood noted, "because of the shortness of the time till daylight after the order of evacuation was received." General Hoke, Hagood added, "had requested by telegraph that the magazine should not be exploded before 6:30 a.m." While it is possible that the celerity of the withdrawal prevented the simple spiking of the guns, Hagood's statements can also be read as a not-so-mild rebuke aimed at Hoke for delaying the order to evacuate the fort.

Hagood had sent word to Lipscomb, whose troopers had been keeping an eye on Cox's Federals at Orton Pond, to retire to upper Town Creek bridge. Lipscomb's cavalry was to act as a flanking force for the main column, which was marching to lower Town Creek bridge. It was almost daylight before Hagood directed his pickets to withdraw from their positions in front of the fort.[41]

The Federals attacked Fort Anderson at first light—almost simultaneously with the retreat of Hagood's pickets. Union troops had heard noises coming from inside the work throughout the early morning hours and had suspected an evacuation was underway. Major Frank Wilcox of the 63rd Indiana Infantry led the first attack wave, consisting of skirmishers from Colonel Henderson's brigade.[42] Henderson's men fired a volley in the direction of the battered sand walls and advanced at the double-quick, scaling the fort's parapets without opposition. Fort Anderson was all but deserted. The Hoosiers entered the work in time to capture some fifty soldiers of Hagood's rear guard, but the main Confederate force had escaped to the north.[43] The victorious Federals also took possession of a garrison flag, "which was rolled up and evidently had fallen off a wagon during the hasty withdrawal." A soldier of Company A, 140th Indiana Infantry, discovered the flag on the ground. It was later presented to Governor Oliver P. Morton of Indiana in an elaborate ceremony in Washington. President Lincoln was on hand to witness the presentation of the "captured flag from Fort Anderson." But as one Union soldier scoffed, "it was not captured, it was found."[44]

The Hoosier volley delivered before the storming of the deserted walls caused Col. Orlando Moore to form his brigade into line of battle with fixed bayonets and order it forward against the fort. Moore, oblivious to the Confederate retreat, thought the small arms fire indicated an ensuing battle. The only troops his brigade encountered, however, were some of Maj. Frank Wilcox's Indiana skirmishers spreading word of the fort's abandonment. As soon as he reached the fort, Moore grabbed the colors of the 26th Kentucky Infantry and planted them on the parapet of Battery B as a signal to the navy that Fort Anderson had been captured.[45]

Admiral Porter was unaware of the situation inside the fort when he ordered his warships to renew their bombardment at daylight. There was subsequent speculation that the naval gunners, having spotted the flag of the 26th Kentucky atop Battery B, mistook it for a defiant Confederate standard and opened fire. Fortunately for the fort's new occupants, the Union gunners had fired at most only half a dozen shots when they learned of the fort's fall. Even so, the thunderous reports of the warships' big guns and the bursting shells in and around the fort created panic among the occupying troops. Terrified soldiers dashed to the river, blowing bugles and waving flags, coats and handkerchiefs as a signal to the navy that they occupied the fort. Colonel Moore rode his charger to the river bank and "shook out a square yard of white canvas dog tent and waved toward the fleet as a flag of truce."[46]

Porter's ships got the message, though sailors later admitted their delight at having accepted the fort's surrender from the U. S. Army—perhaps the only such incident of the war. The *Montauk,* lying closest to the fort, hoisted a white flag to halt the bombardment, a display that prompted sailors to climb into the rigging of their ships to cheer the victory. But for Porter, Fort Anderson's fall was not enough. The admiral wanted his fleet to receive due credit for its capture, and would later falsely claim that the navy had occupied the fort for half an hour before the army arrived. An Illinois soldier recalled that he saw Porter come ashore with a marine escort, with the admiral taking "formal possession of the fort in the name of the United States Navy."[47]

While Porter may not have been as excited about Fort Anderson's fall as he had been about Fort Fisher's capitulation, John Schofield was ecstatic. The army commander immediately notified General Terry of the fort's capture, but Terry may already have known. The general and his troops on Federal Point probably heard the celebration across the river, and Terry's pickets had already reported that the Confederates had withdrawn from their entrenchments at Sugar Loaf. Hoke's Southerners had also slipped away during the early morning hours of February 19 and were marching up the east bank of the river toward Wilmington when the Federals discovered their empty earthworks. Terry moved his entire force into the abandoned Sugar Loaf trenches, where it briefly rested before beginning its pursuit.[48]

While Terry's men on Federal Point may have been aware of Fort Anderson's change of ownership, the word had not traveled to the Union left flank. For several hours Jacob Cox and Adelbert Ames were unaware of Hagood's hasty withdrawal. Mid-morning found them still waiting for the supply wagons from Smithville to reach Orton Pond. Cox, whose men were hungry, thought it prudent to wait for the train and feed his troops before pressing an attack on Fort Anderson. After having spent most of the previous day scattered and in utter disarray on the back roads of Brunswick County, the wagon train had turned around and gone back to Smithville to reform and begin its journey anew. The wagons finally reached the front and Cox's famished infantry about 10:00 a.m.[49]

Anxious to make the attack, Cox advanced toward what he believed was Hagood's exposed right flank with Ames' division, the first unit to be resupplied by the late arriving wagons. The Ohioan left behind Sterl's and Casement's brigades to draw rations and follow Ames' brigades. Cox and Ames had advanced about halfway to the fort when they met Capt. William A. Lord of General Schofield's staff, who had been sent to inform them of the fort's capture. Ames proceeded on to the fort with his division while Cox waited for his other two brigades to arrive. Mid-afternoon found the brigades of Colonels Moore and Henderson reunited with Sterl and Casement about three miles north of Fort Anderson. The advance of Henderson and Moore had been delayed until engineers could repair the bridge across Orton canal, which had been damaged by the Confederates during their evacuation. As soon as the brigades had reformed, however, they pushed upriver in pursuit of Hagood's retreating Confederates.[50]

As Cox was advancing his men, Admiral Porter went ashore to meet with Schofield and inspect Fort Anderson. The bastion yielded several handsome prizes, including ten pieces of ordnance, a considerable quantity of ammunition and half a hundred prisoners. The massive earthen fort and its collateral works awed the commanders. "[They] are very strong and rendered almost inaccessible by swamps," Schofield reported. "A small force could have held them until their supplies were exhausted."[51]

Yet Hagood's "small force" had not held Fort Anderson. The fortification's importance to Wilmington's security was evident in Braxton Bragg's message to Hoke on February 8, when he cautioned that "except in an extreme case, involving the safety of the command [it] will not be abandoned." Hagood's retreat was provoked by Cox's flanking column, which would have gained the fort's rear and cut off the garrison had Hagood not evacuated. The South Carolinian committed a fatal error in not adequately supporting his weak right flank, though it should be pointed out that his force was too small to adequately cover the entire mile-long sand wall *and* his extreme right. The loss of the L-shaped sandy fortress, however, had ramifications beyond its own demise. Since Fort Anderson and the defensive position at Sugar Loaf mutually supported one another, the loss of the former meant the latter was no longer tenable. Thus Anderson's evacuation precipitated the abandonment of Sugar Loaf, as Hoke realized that the U. S. Navy would soon control the Cape Fear River above his position, leaving his force exposed to enfilading fire and possible capture.[52]

For the Union, the capture of Fort Anderson—like that of Fort Fisher—attested to the efficiency and cooperation of its army and navy. The strategy behind the operation was well-planned and the tactics executed with determination and solid precision. Now the Federals were ready to move irresistibly on Wilmington. "My information is that the rebels have a line of defense behind Town Creek, where they propose to make a stand," General Schofield reported. "If so, it can probably be only a short one."[53]

(Above) The ruins of St. Philip's Episcopal Church and the sand curtain (background) of Fort Anderson at Brunswick Town. The fort was the Confederates' largest interior defensive work and protected Wilmington's western approaches.

Author's Collection

(Below) A gun chamber and adjoining traverses of Fort Anderson's Battery B, near the Cape Fear River.

Brig. Gen. Johnson Hagood, the South Carolina planter-turned-soldier who was given the unenviable task of halting the Federal juggernaut on the west side of the Cape Fear River. *U.S. Army Military History Institute*

Chapter 12

"These appeared to be the last rays of departing hope"

– Pvt. "Marcus Brutus", 8th North Carolina Infantry

LAST STAND

By sunrise on February 19, the Confederates were in full retreat toward Wilmington. Having abandoned Fort Anderson, Johnson Hagood's command crossed lower Town Creek bridge just before 10:00 a.m. and took up a defensive position on the north bank. The creek represented the final bit of defensible terrain west of the Cape Fear River. Hagood placed Col. John J. Hedrick in command at the bridge, which was defended by Lt. Col. John Douglas Taylor's battalion of North Carolinians and three pieces of artillery, including Capt. Abner A. Moseley's Whitworth, in entrenchments on a bluff overlooking the span. Hagood held the bulk of his force, with his own brigade still under the command of Col. Charles Simonton, near a small clapboard church a half-mile north of the bridge. A mounted party of twenty men, commanded by Lieutenant Jeffords, patrolled the road south of the creek to watch for the approaching Federals.[1]

Soon after Hagood's force reached lower Town Creek, Colonel Lipscomb reported that he and his cavalry, together with Lt. John Jones' howitzer and crew, had reached upper Town Creek bridge seven miles to the northwest. Hagood directed Lipscomb to scout across his front and along the creek between the two bridges. As soon as his troops were deployed Hagood telegraphed General Hoke to let him know he was in position at Town Creek and to ask for instructions. "Future operations will depend on circumstances," Hoke replied. "Will telegraph you in the morning." For the moment, Hagood could only await the Federal advance.[2]

The South Carolinian faced no immediate threat. The burned bridge and cut sluices at the Orton Pond canal had retarded the Union pursuit, and his position at Town Creek was a strong one. Named for an ill-fated English settlement in the 1660s, Town Creek was narrow but deep and unfordable, with wide marshes and vast rice fields and dikes on both sides. An occasional wooded bluff touched the stream, but the two bridges were the only regular crossings. Both spans had been lightly fortified earlier and were now adequately defended. Hagood also controlled two possible avenues of retreat—the Public Road (the main thoroughfare to Wilmington), and the Telegraph Road, an aptly named byway closer to the river along which a telegraph line ran to the city.[3]

As Hagood's men fell back to Town Creek, General Hoke had withdrawn up the east bank of the Cape Fear River and had assumed a position just three miles south of Wilmington, roughly opposite Hagood's new line. Hoke's force occupied newly constructed earthworks that stretched eastward from Battery Meares on the river to the headwaters of Hewlett's Creek near Masonboro Sound. Most of Hoke's troops were deployed near the river batteries and across Forks Road, a junction of the Federal Point Road and a byroad about two miles from the river. Like his subordinate, Robert Hoke had little to do other than position his men and patiently await the enemy he knew would be coming.[4]

John Schofield was not about to let his adversaries get comfortable behind fresh defensive positions. With virtually no opposition on either side of the wide waterway, the Federals staged a three-pronged pursuit of the Confederates. General Cox's brigades chased Johnson Hagood up the west bank of the river toward Town Creek, while General Terry's corps advanced in General Hoke's wake on the east side of the Cape Fear River. While the two prongs of the army moved northward, Admiral Porter's flotilla formed the third prong of the trident-like thrust as it ascended the Cape Fear in support of both Union wings. After capturing Fort Anderson General Schofield returned to his floating headquarters on board the *S. R. Spaulding*.

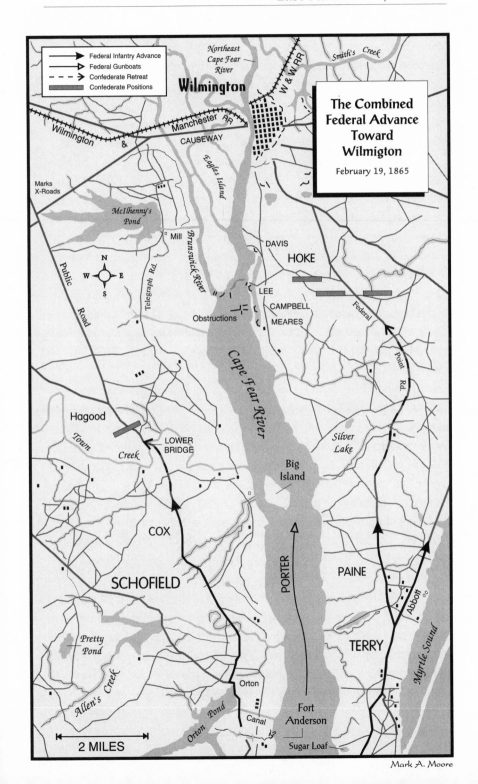

Federal Infantry Advance
Federal Gunboats
Confederate Retreat
Confederate Positions

Northeast
Cape Fear
River

Smith's Creek

W & W RR

Wilmington

**The Combined
Federal Advance
Toward
Wilmigton**

February 19, 1865

Wilmington & Manchester RR

CAUSEWAY

Eagles Island

Marks
X-Roads

McIlhenny's
Pond

Mill

DAVIS

HOKE

Brunswick River

Public Road

N
W E
S

Telegraph Rd.

LEE

Obstructions

CAMPBELL

MEARES

Federal

Point Rd.

Cape Fear River

Hagood

Town Creek

LOWER
BRIDGE

Silver
Lake

Big
Island

COX

SCHOFIELD

Pretty
Pond

PORTER

PAINE

Abbott

TERRY

Myrtle Sound

Allen's Creek

Orton

Orton
Pond

Canal

Fort
Anderson

Sugar Loaf

2 MILES

Mark A. Moore

With the Cape Fear River running through the center of the Confederate defenses, Schofield believed he could best direct the Union advance from the steamer, and be in a position to disembark on one bank or the other as circumstances required.

The serious pursuit of Hoke did not begin until about noon on February 19, when Terry launched his drive northward with Brig. Gen. Charles J. Paine's two brigades and Bvt. Brig. Gen. Joseph C. Abbott's brigade. Terry's skirmishers, the 5th U. S. Colored Troops of Col. Elias Wright's brigade, traded shots with the Confederate rear guard and captured a few weary stragglers, but no serious fighting occurred, in part because Terry did not want to provoke a general engagement. Unsure of Hoke's whereabouts, the cautious Terry was concerned about stumbling into an ambush by being too dogged in his pursuit. Demonstrating a firm grasp of the local geography, Terry divided his force four miles north of Sugar Loaf, sending Abbott's brigade eastward to advance up the Military Road on Myrtle Sound. The move was designed to discover whether Hoke had sequestered a force near Masonboro for a strike against the Union right flank. Terry had no intention of being surprised.[5]

As Paine's brigades marched up the Federal Point Road, the main highway to Wilmington, Terry rode with them in order to keep abreast of developments as they unfolded. As he warily pursued Hoke, Terry decided to await the arrival of Ames' division, which had to be recrossed to the east side of the river from Fort Anderson, before pressing the attack. The deliberate Federal advance carved out about six miles of Southern terrain before halting to dig breastworks and bivouac at dusk, about nine miles from the city. Unwilling to risk a separate attack against either of his wings, Terry made certain that Abbott's brigade, encamped at Gonto's farm on Myrtle Sound, spent the night with its left flank firmly abutted against Terry's fortified encampment.[6]

While Schofield and his generals organized the pursuit of Hagood and Hoke, the U. S. Navy began the more mundane task of clearing the river of torpedoes to allow the warships to advance. Porter dispatched thirty or more launches to drag for the mines and to sound and mark the channel. Led by the steamer *Pontoosuc*, the gunboats followed the mine sweepers methodically upstream throughout the afternoon. While the Union infantry forces were often out of sight of Porter's flotilla, the navy nevertheless kept pace with the the land-based advance during the day.[7]

Late on the afternoon of February 19, fourteen of Porter's launches rowed within sight of the Confederate river batteries—Batteries Meares, Campbell, Lee, and Davis (known collectively as Fort Strong by the Federals)—perched on high sandy bluffs three miles below Wilmington and opposite the southern end of Eagles Island. These four earthen fortifications mounted a total of sixteen pieces of heavy artillery. In front of the batteries Confederate engineers had filled the river channel with pilings, chains and sawyers. They had also recently sunk the Confederate gunboats *Arctic*, *Yadkin* and *North Heath* to further impede the enemy's progress.[8]

Colonel Peter C. Gaillard calmly surveyed the scene as the Federal boats approached his position. The 52-year-old commander of the river batteries was no stranger to defensive warfare. A Charleston native, he had graduated from West Point in 1835 and spent three years in the Regular Army before following civilian pursuits. When the Civil War arrived, Gaillard enlisted with the storied 1st South Carolina Battalion and played an instrumental role in throwing back the Federal attack against Fort Lamar at the Battle of Secessionville, June 16, 1862. The South Carolinian was also a veteran of the gallant defensive victory at Battery Wagner on July 18, 1863, where during the subsequent siege of that place a shell removed one of his hands. Although out of action for some time, Gaillard returned to assist the dying Confederacy during her final months.

When the enemy launches pulled within effective range, Gaillard ordered artillery in Battery Campbell to open fire. A few well-placed shots from a 30-pounder Parrott rifle and a 6.4-inch 32-pounder gun sent the boats scurrying back to the safety of the flotilla. Admiral Porter signaled the *Montauk* to come up and engage the batteries, but she ran aground in shoal water off Campbell Island (also known as Big Island). In place of the powerful *Montauk* came the ersatz monitor *Old Bogey*. According to several accounts she had been retrieved after grounding near Sugar Loaf and brought up to feign an attack on Fort Strong. Porter, however, reported that the *Old Bogey's* timely arrival was purely fortuitous, and that she joined the fleet on her own, propelled by a flood tide and a favorable wind. Whatever the case may have been, darkness quickly followed and ended the "best of the joke." The gunboats cast anchor for the night and prepared for the next day's inevitable engagement.[9]

Like Colonel Gaillerd at the river batteries, Confederate sentinels at Town Creek had also watched Porter's flotilla ascend the river that afternoon. Concerned about the possibility of an amphibious landing beyond his left flank, Hagood dispatched the 11th South Carolina to picket the two-and-a-half mile stretch of ground along the stream from the lower bridge to the Cape Fear River. While Hagood's move was prudent, his fears about a possible naval landing party proved unfounded. The Federal navy was still smarting from the debacle its shore contingent had suffered on the beach in front of Fort Fisher's northeast bastion in January. Even if a force did come ashore, it was a long and difficult trek from the river to Hagood's position across ground unfamiliar to Union sailors and marines.[10]

Jacob Cox's brigades, however, managed to reach lower Town Creek bridge at about 3:30 p.m. on February 19. The approaching vanguard—Col. Thomas J. Henderson's brigade—had been ordered to "move forward cautiously and to advance as near to the enemy as practicable before night." Henderson's men met little opposition until they neared the bridge, where Henderson found what he later described as "a strong rebel picket." This "strong" picket force was Lieutenant Jeffords' mounted troopers, who on Hagood's order retired for the safety of the north side of the stream after a round of light skirmishing. The Confederates pulled up the planks of the bridge as they retreated, but did not have enough time to destroy the span.[11]

Henderson deployed his infantry on a sandy ridge a half-mile south of the creek and set about fortifying his position. A few Confederate artillery shells came crashing down, though most passed harmlessly overhead and exploded in the rear. As ordered, Henderson had driven his brigade "as near to the enemy as practicable," and could go no further. While Confederate sharpshooters tried to pick off Henderson's skirmishers advancing into the bulrush bordering the stream, the colonel surveyed the scene before him. He later described this portion of Hagood's new defensive line as "a very strong position," complete with "heavy works and. . .three pieces of artillery." The creek before him was "not wide, but deep," he related, "and could not be passed by troops without a bridge or boat." Further complicating matters was a large and impassable marsh, which covered the line between Henderson and the creek. There was only one viable route over Town Creek, and that was over the causeway and into the teeth of the Southern defenses. While Henderson pondered his options, the brigades of Colonels Moore, Sterl, and Casement remained out of sight and under cover in his rear.[12]

With light skirmishing in his front, Hagood telegraphed the developing situation to Robert Hoke at 5:35 p.m. "Town Creek is a line [that] can be held whenever occupied," he cautiously stated, making it clear immediately thereafter that he did not have enough men to hold the entire line. "I have examined several miles of it today," he continued. "From my observation it can be crossed almost anywhere that sufficient troops are not stationed. Let me know your views and intentions." Hoke's response later that night was simply "Hold Town Creek till you hear from me." Hagood's new position at Town Creek was uncomfortably similar to the dreadful situation he had just left behind at Fort Anderson. He had a wide front with too few troops to hold it, and an aggressive enemy itching to force a crossing.

While Hagood contemplated his own state of affairs, Jacob Cox sent reconnaissance parties to search for a place to ford Town Creek. As Colonel Henderson was just discovering and Cox's scouts would soon learn, the stream was not fordable. Cox was faced with a dilemma. Confederate guns swept the lower bridge's only approach—a long corduroy causeway through the wide marsh of tall reeds. The only other span, which Cox assumed the Confederates had already destroyed, was seven miles upstream to the west. Moreover, getting pontoons ashore under these conditions appeared impractical. The Cape Fear River was wide where Town Creek emptied into it, and the pontoon-laden ships were in the channel on the east side of Campbell Island. As Cox pondered his course of action, fate intervened on his behalf.

After dark, an elderly black man approached Colonel Henderson to inform him of a rice barge that was docked at a warehouse on the south side of Town Creek about one and a half-miles downstream. The Confederates had overlooked it when they had crossed the creek earlier that morning. Henderson sent word of his discovery to Cox, who immediately ordered that the flatboat be confiscated. Cox in turn notified Schofield on the *S. R. Spaulding*, recommending that the scow be used to outflank the Confederates. Schofield approved Cox's suggestion by telling him to "see what could be done with the flat boat."[13]

Before sunrise the next morning Cox ordered Casement's and Sterl's brigades to attempt the crossing. It was slow going. The flatboat could carry

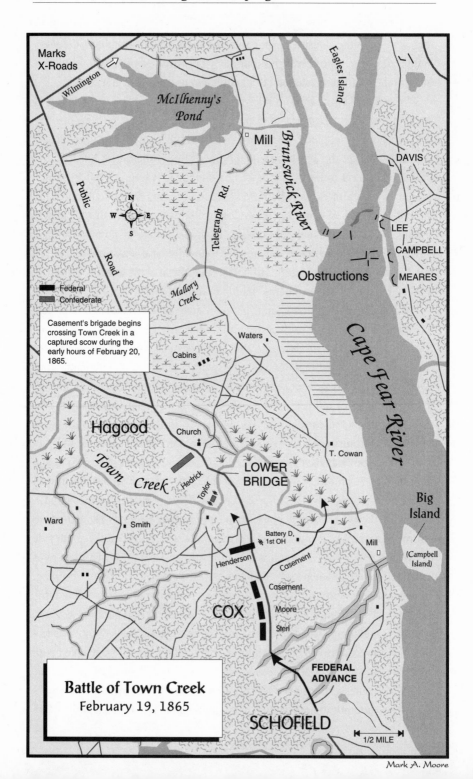

Marks
X-Roads

Wilmington

McIlhenny's Pond

Mill

Brunswick River

Eagles Island

DAVIS

LEE

CAMPBELL

MEARES

Obstructions

Public

Telegraph Rd.

Road

N
W E
S

Federal
Confederate

Casement's brigade begins
crossing Town Creek in a
captured scow during the
early hours of February 20,
1865.

Mallory Creek

Waters

Cabins

Cape Fear River

Hagood

Church

Town

Creek

Hedrick

Taylor

LOWER
BRIDGE

T. Cowan

Big
Island

Ward

Smith

Henderson

Battery D,
1st OH

Casement

Mill

(Campbell
Island)

COX

Casement

Moore

Sterl

FEDERAL
ADVANCE

SCHOFIELD

Battle of Town Creek
February 19, 1865

1/2 MILE

Mark A. Moore

only seventy-five men at a time, and when the soldiers disembarked on the north side of the stream, they had to wade a considerable distance through rice paddies, reeds and sticky marshland before reaching dry ground. By 11:00 a.m., only Casement's brigade had been ferried across. The unsupported soldiers erected crude breastworks as they anxiously waited for their comrades to follow them.[14]

At dawn Colonel Henderson sent out a strong skirmish line toward the bridge to divert Hagood's attention from the Federal flanking movement. Henderson's skirmishers advanced into the low ground along the creek, though the marsh grass offered the Federals little protection against the Confederates' heavy small arms and artillery fire. Even so, one Union officer claimed that the sharpshooters "succeeded in getting so close to the creek as to prevent any of the enemy from showing themselves above the parapet." To cover his skirmishers, Henderson ordered Lieutenant Reed's Battery D, 1st Ohio Artillery, to open on the enemy. Reed deployed his battery of 10-pounder Parrott rifles in the road bed, giving him a clearer shot at the Confederate defenses on the north bank. "Our artillery opened upon them, causing them to scatter," observed a Confederate officer. "In a few moments they returned the fire with rifle guns & it was now our time to scatter." For the remainder of the day the fighting across the stream continued "brisk and animated, enlivened by occasional duels between the Union and Confederate artillery."[15]

From his headquarters at Forks Road, General Hoke could hear the din of battle raging on the opposite side of the river. At some point during the day Hoke telegraphed Hagood, "You must move your command as you think best; at same time recollect the importance of your communication with Wilmington. . .I leave the matter to your judgment." Hoke followed this rather vague directive with more definitive instructions later that day when he ordered Hagood to "dispute their advance at every available point." One of Bragg's staff officers, who had returned from Richmond and resumed command, collaborated Hoke's last order by impressing upon Hagood "the necessity of delaying the enemy's advance." Wilmington had to be held longer than anticipated. The removal of government property and thousands of Union prisoners-of-war sent to Wilmington for exchange had bogged down efforts to evacuate the city. Moreover, Lt. Gen. William J. Hardee had requested Hoke's assistance in transporting his army to Greensboro by way of Wilmington. General Sherman's surge through South Carolina had forced Hardee's evacuation of Charleston three days earlier. "Old Reliable" Hardee was now retreating northward along the Northeastern Railroad and gradually approaching Wilmington. Hoke believed he could pull off Hardee's passage through the port town only so long as Hagood held Town Creek and protected the Wilmington & Manchester rail line, which ran roughly parallel to Hagood's position several miles to his rear. Although Hoke had hoped to battle it out with Schofield, he instead focused his efforts on holding on just long enough to enable Hardee's Corps to withdraw to Greensboro via Wilmington.[16]

The situation looked far more favorable for the Federals. Early on the morning of February 20, as Lieutenant Reed was unleashing his 10-pounder Parrott's in front of the lower Town Creek bridge on the west side of the Cape Fear, General Alfred Terry took up his pursuit of Hoke. Secure in the knowledge that Ames' division had rejoined his corps before sunrise, Terry moved out against his enemy with renewed confidence. Paine's brigades again led Terry's main body in the advance up the Federal Point Road, skirmishing with Hoke's rear guard in a running fight. But the Confederates offered little resistance. "The firing of the Johnnies was. . .desultory and purposeless," remarked one Union rifleman, perhaps with some suspicion, "and our columns moved gaily on to the music of the dropping shots." The march was slow because the troops often had to traverse Carolina bays— pocosins (lowland swamps) of briars, pond pines and evergreen shrubs.[17]

During the march Terry's column halted for a brief rest along the Federal Point Road, halfway between Sugar Loaf and Wilmington. As the soldiers sat down for a few moments to relax along the roadside, a remarkable event transpired, recorded by a war correspondent with the *Philadelphia Inquirer* who witnessed the incident. A corporal requested permission from his commanding officer to leave the line and visit a house on the side of the road. When asked what business he had at the house, the corporal replied that it was his boyhood home. The officer gave his consent and the soldier rushed to the dwelling where, at least according to the newspaperman, he was "soon clasped in the arms of his overjoyed mother. She said, 'your brother was here yesterday; he stopped as the Confederates marched past.'"[18]

The Union soldier was probably Cpl. Jacob Horne, whose brother, Hosea Horne, was a corporal in Capt. Thomas Southerland's Wilmington Horse Artillery, 1st North Carolina Artillery, Hoke's command. According to Horne family tradition, Jacob and Hosea had fought against one another during the Wilmington Campaign. Hosea had enlisted in the Confederate army in New Hanover County in 1862, while his brother Jacob joined a Union army outfit, Company A, 2nd North Carolina U. S. Infantry in late November the following year. One story suggested that Jacob deserted to the Union blockading force off Wilmington, while another claimed that he went over to the enemy at Beaufort. The 2nd North Carolina was not part of the Wilmington expeditionary force, though it is likely that Jacob Horne was temporarily attached to Terry's army at Beaufort as a scout, since he was familiar with New Hanover County.[19]

Hosea, as the family tradition has it, had stopped to say goodbye to his mother, Katherine Lanier Horne, on February 19 as General Hoke's army retreated toward Wilmington. A short time later he was entrenched with his unit at Forks Road, only a short distance north of the Horne homestead on the Federal Point Road. The next day Jacob surprised his mother with a short visit during the Federal army's advance on Wil-

The "Confederate" brother. Corporal Hosea Horne of the Wilmington Horse Artillery. *Courtesy of Horne family descendants.*

Confederate earthworks at Forks Road, where Maj. Gen. Robert F. Hoke made his last stand before evacuating Wilmington. *Author's Collection*

mington. Though it does not mention Corporal Horne by name, the story printed in the *Philadelphia Inquirer* lends substantial credence to the Horne family's story. Just up the road from Jacob was Hosea, his brother—his enemy—waiting to do battle.

Hosea and his comrades were strongly entrenched at Forks Road. Their breastworks—revetted with Carolina heart pine logs—straddled the Federal Point Road. Southerland's battery of five 6-pounder cannon and one 12-pounder gun covered the road, while Brig. Gen. Thomas L. Clingman's 900-man brigade, consisting of the 8th, 31st, 51st, and 61st North Carolina infantry regiments and commanded by Col. William S. Devane, manned the entrenchments. These were Bragg's "bad men," according to one officer of the 6th U. S. Colored Troops. It was at 3:00 p. m. on February 20 when the vanguard of Terry's corps appeared in Hoke's front.[20]

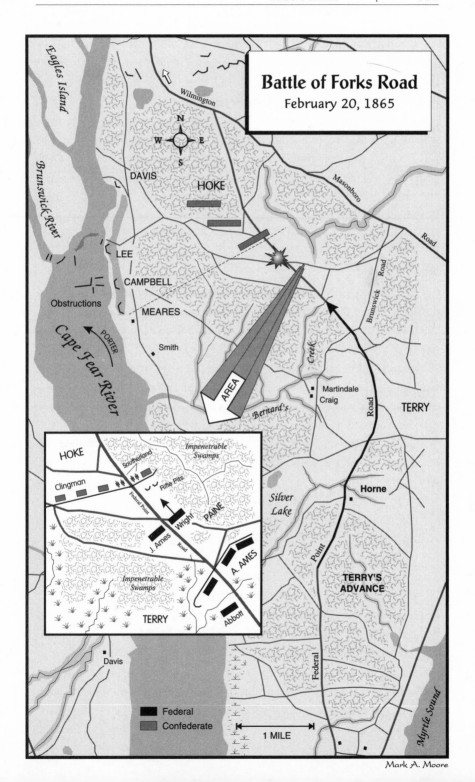

Battle of Forks Road
February 20, 1865

Mark A. Moore

Confederate pickets bolted for their main works as General Paine's skirmishers—the 5th U.S. Colored Troops of Col. Elias Wright's Third Brigade—marched into view. Shells and small arms fire opened on the Federals as they probed Hoke's masked position.

According to General Paine, "The enemy's fire along our whole front was found to be that of a single rank or a little more, and his artillery fire was from six or seven guns." Armed with this important information, General Terry was adamant that the works could be carried by frontal assault and ordered Paine to press the attack. This time Paine sent in Col. Elias Wright's entire brigade, again led by the 5th U.S. Colored Troops. Wright's regiments made a valiant but futile charge against Hoke's defenders, driving to within about 150 yards of the enemy line before being driven back by "strong resistance."[21]

Clingman's fire ravaged Wright's brigade with continuous volleys of musketry, while the Rebel artillery assisted with barrages of iron case shot. "General Terry ordered [us] to charge. . .and we done it," one of Paine's men reported, "but we were unable to take the works." The firing caused fairly substantial Union casualties, especially considering the brief nature of the movement. The 1st, 5th, and 27th U. S. Colored Troops suffering the heaviest losses. General Paine lost one officer and one man killed, and three officers wounded, including Colonel Wright, who was shot in the wrist, and Wright's aide-de-camp, Lieutenant Simms, who lost a leg. Forty-eight enlisted men suffered wounds, six by the explosion of a single 6-pound artillery shell. "I suppose it was fun for [General] Terry but little for us," a soldier in the 5th U. S. Colored Troops sarcastically remarked.[22]

The Confederates' obstinate defense satisfied Terry that Hoke meant to contest any further advance on Wilmington. Entrenching his corps, Terry placed the U. S. Colored Troops on the front line and the white troops about a half-mile to the rear. "[While] the negros were fighting. . .we threw up a line of breastworks: the rebels tried to shell us out but in spite of there shells and miney balls we built our line," recalled Pvt. Simon Bennage of the 76th Pennsylvania. "We worked till late in the evening." Although no further Federal attacks were forthcoming, the sharpshooting, which continued to crackle between Hoke's and Paine's lines, persisted for about thirty-six hours. Joseph C. Abbott's brigade, meanwhile, came up from Myrtle Sound, rejoining the white troops just south of Forks Road.[23]

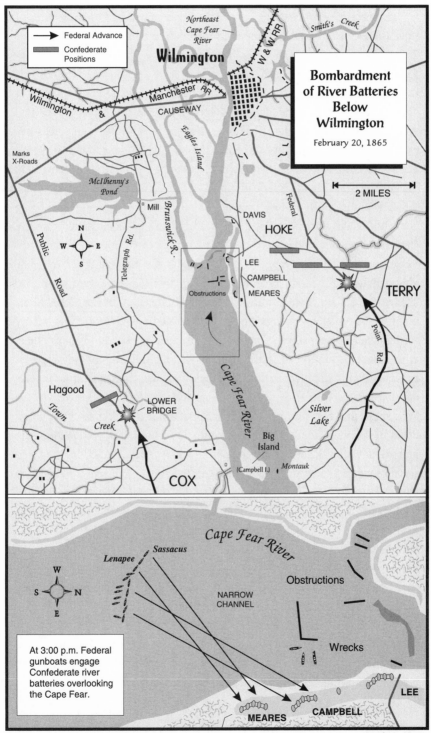

Mark A. Moore

As the Union armies marched, probed and skirmished on both sides of the river, Porter's gunboats supported them. About 10:00 a.m. on February 20, the *Sassacus* and *Lenapee* led the flotilla upstream to engage the Confederate river batteries. Their advance was slow because the channel was narrow and shallow. Some ships struck bottom and the *Montauk* could not get past Campbell Island. Unlike the engagements for Forts Fisher and Anderson, the navy could offer no artillery support to the land forces because they were fighting too far inland, well beyond the range of Porter's gunboats. Unable to assist Schofield's advancing men, Porter concentrated his gunboats' fire on the river batteries.[24]

The battle began at three o'clock that afternoon, with continuous firing from both sides for about three hours. One Union sailor claimed that the ships threw eight to ten projectiles at the batteries every minute. The Federal vessels established their range of fire by means of a buoy that the Confederates had used for target practice. Even so, the warships were unable to silence the defiant Southern artillery perched atop high bluffs. "This afternoon we had a splendid engagement," exclaimed a Union tar. "The enemy made some splendid shots. . .I assure you I dipped my head as well as others who were near me for you have no idea what an ugly scream they give."[25] Peter Gaillard's Confederates handled their guns well, and projectiles repeatedly struck the *Sassacus*, causing her to leak badly. Her damage was so substantial that her gun crews had to cease firing to help bail water in an effort to keep her from sinking. The battle raged until dark with neither side gaining any significant advantage. With Porter's ships stymied on the river, the promising pursuit of the stubborn Confederates ground to a halt. Jacob Cox's divisions were stopped before Hagood's line at Town Creek west of the Cape Fear River, Terry's soldiers were unable to breach Hoke's line east of the stream, and Porter's fleet was powerless to blast his way through the several batteries defending the waterway—and could lend no direct assistance to either wing of the army.[26]

The crafty Jacob D. Cox broke the frustrating stalemate by once again outwitting Johnson Hagood, who seemed unsure how to protect his flanks. By early afternoon on February 20, the brigades of Colonels Sterl and Moore had ferried across and joined Colonel Casement's regiments on the north bank of Town Creek. Cox had decided at the last moment to strike Hagood with three of his brigades rather than two, and he personally took command of the movement. Having missed the chance to spring the trap he had set at Fort Anderson, "this time Genl Cox was determined to catch something."[27]

Fortunately for Cox, Hagood's pickets had not detected the crossing. Apparently the Confederates assumed the deep creek and swampy terrain would prevent the enemy from gaining their flank, and as a result, there were not enough pickets posted along the stream. During the morning of February 20, Capt. Joseph J. Wescoat and Abram W. Clement of the 11th South Carolina Infantry walked down from their picket camp to Town Creek to forage for food. The two soldiers had heard rumors that a load of sweet potatoes and barrels of apple cider, ready for eating and drinking, were at a landing near the videttes' forward position. The sight of Union warships in the river discouraged Wescoat and Clement from raiding nearby Cowan's plantation (which was rich with livestock) because they feared their appearance in the yard might draw the fire of the gunboats. Instead they moved on to the landing, where they found the flatboat, and soon filled their haversacks with potatoes and their canteens with cider. They had just returned to their encampment and were feasting on their plunder when a report came in that the pickets they had left a short time before had been surprised and captured by Union forces. Captain Wescoat retraced his route to the creek, only to discover Union troops assembling en masse. Wescoat turned and dashed off on horseback to alert General Hagood.[28]

About 10:00 a.m. that morning, Col. Charles H. Simonton, the field commander of Hagood's brigade, had dispatched the 21st and 25th South Carolina regiments from their position near the lower bridge to relieve the 11th South Carolina on picket duty near Cowan's plantation. Soon thereafter, Simonton witnessed Captain Wescoat's ride into camp and hasty conversation with General Hagood, and then gallop off again. Sensing that something was amiss, Simonton responded immediately to the general's call for him to come to headquarters at the church. There Simonton learned of Wescoat's report, and was instructed by General Hagood to go at once to Cowan's, taking with him the 27th South Carolina Infantry and two pieces of North Carolina artillery under Lt. John T. Rankin. He was also to retain the two South Carolina units he had sent in that direction earlier, as well as the 11th South Carolina already on patrol. Hagood suggested "that it would be best to attack [the Yankees]."[29]

Two lanes led from the Telegraph Road to the mouth of Town Creek. The southernmost lane, Cowan's Road, intersected the Telegraph Road about a mile north of lower Town Creek bridge. Another road joined the Telegraph Road about a mile further to the north, running roughly parallel to the river and past Cowan's plantation before intersecting with Cowan's Road near the mouth of the creek.[30] Using Cowan's Road, Simonton soon reached the reserve picket station about two miles from Hagood's headquarters, where he discovered that the Federals had already driven Captain Wescoat's skirmishers 300 yards west of Cowan's gate, and were forming for battle. Simonton hurriedly deployed his troops to check the enemy's advance, placing the 27th South Carolina in line of battle on the right side of Cowan's Road, the 11th South Carolina to the left, and Lieutenant Rankin's artillery on the lane. The 21st and 25th South Carolina regiments were sent forward as skirmishers.

Desiring a good look at the enemy, Simonton soon joined the skirmishers and managed to move so close to the Federals that he could distinctly hear officers barking orders to their men. He was astounded by the large number of Union troops, and quickly sent word to Hagood that a "considerable" enemy force was at that moment in his front along the south lane and preparing to advance. Meanwhile, Simonton withdrew his force about thirty yards, placing what he described as a "sort of pond" between him and the enemy. When the Federals failed to immediately launch their attack, Simonton returned to the skirmish line, accompanied by Capt. William E. Stoney, a member of General Hagood's staff who had come down from headquarters to assess the situation. By then, however, most of the Union troops were moving to envelop Simonton's flanks, particularly his left flank, in an effort to gain the north road. When the movement was discovered, Simonton had no choice but to retreat.[31]

Sensing the urgency in Simonton's report when it arrived at headquarters, Hagood decided to go in person to Cowan's to investigate. Simonton was still on the skirmish line when Hagood arrived at the front. Simonton's troops were caught in a sharp skirmish with Cox's force, which Hagood realized was endeavoring to overlap the South Carolinian's flanks. Only the threat of Rankin's artillery, deployed on Cowan's Road, held the Federals at bay up to that point.

A quick reconnaissance convinced Hagood that Cox had managed to outflank him again, just as he had at Fort Anderson. The Federals were now in control of the mouth of Town Creek and, with naval support, could fling their entire force across the stream at any time. Hagood, of course, did not know that the bulk of Cox's division was already on the north side of the creek. He did realize, however, that the enemy force constituted a serious threat to his ability to hold his present position. The Town Creek line must be abandoned at once, Hagood concluded, but he needed time to alert his scattered troops and effect a withdrawal.

Hagood redeployed the 27th South Carolina to the left of Cowan's Road and personally led the 11th South Carolina back to the Telegraph Road, positioning it slightly south of the intersection with Cowan's. After establishing this new line, Hagood returned to Simonton's position, where that officer was trying to keep his small force of some 450 soldiers from disintegrating under the mounting pressure of the oncoming Union tide. Hagood ordered Simonton to delay Cox's advance for as long as possible in order to give the main Confederate force at the bridge time to retreat up the Public Road to Wilmington. The South Carolina brigadier instructed Simonton to deploy his force so as to guard both roads and to fall back slowly, contesting every foot of ground. Simonton was to concentrate his troops and artillery when he reached the Telegraph Road. Hagood would be close by to help support his return to the main army.

Hagood hastened back to his headquarters at the church, taking one piece of Rankin's artillery with him as far as the Telegraph Road to cover Simonton's retreat at that point. Colonel Lipscomb, who had seen no action at all at the upper bridge, was ordered to retire with his force at once to Marks Cross Roads just outside of Wilmington. The general also sent his wagon train, artillery and sick and wounded to Wilmington. Two men were ordered to burn the bridge at McIlhenny's millpond and to cut the sluices to prevent the Federals from using the Telegraph Road to intercept the Confederate retreat to Wilmington via the Public Road. At 3:00 p. m. Hagood directed Colonel Hedrick to start withdrawing his force from the lower bridge. From the sound of heavy rifle musket fire to the east, Hagood knew that Simonton was being hard pressed. "I am now evacuating," Hagood wired General Hoke. "Enemy are turning my flank and are pushing me too strong." Hagood ended his telegram with "Am obliged to do so," as if he felt the need to emphasize that he was giving up the position against his will.[32]

Simonton's small force had put up a good fight, but Cox's division heavily outnumbered the Confederate's over-stretched and worn out force. The Federal general pushed and prodded Simonton all afternoon, concentrating his blue-uniformed troops on the north road in an attempt to gain Hagood's rear. Infantry from the 65th Indiana deployed as skirmishers, supported by the nine other regiments from the brigades of Colonels Casement and Sterl, which were drawn up in a double line of battle on the left side of the road. Colonel Moore's brigade brought up the rear of Cox's force, marching in column on the road. The Federals steadily pushed back Simonton's Carolinians, although their advance was impeded by swamps and thick woods ensnarled with tangled undergrowth.[33]

As Hagood had instructed, Simonton stretched his thin line of troops to cover both lanes and slowly fell back. By 4:00 p.m. the enemy forces had skirmished their way to the Telegraph Road, where Simonton planned to make a more determined stand. Here the terrain changed from thick woods and low ground to a flat sandy plain covered with sedge broom grass and scattered turkey oaks and pine trees—an ideal setting for a battle. Simonton pulled his scattered troops together and advanced the 11th South Carolina from the point where Hagood had placed it south of Cowan's Road. A new line of battle was formed straddling the Telegraph Road and facing north towards Cox's brigades, which were now concentrating their weight on the north road. Simonton pushed the 21st South Carolina into the wooded fields deployed as a strong force of skirmishers. The Carolinians were instructed to form at right angles on the flanks of his line of battle if the Federals overlapped his front.[34]

Colonel Simonton was supported by Lieutenant Rankin's two field pieces, including a bronze 12-pounder howitzer that its crew—members of Company B, 3rd Battalion North Carolina Light Artillery—had nicknamed "St. Paul." The gun and three others like it had been cast at Richmond's Tredegar Iron Works early in the war from bells that had hung in churches, schools, the courthouse and the shipyard in Edenton, North Carolina, which explained the unit's unusual nickname: the Edenton Bell Battery. With "St. Paul" and one other field piece now on the line at Town Creek, Simonton

Colonel Charles Simonton and members of his staff, taken early in the war. *Washington Light Infantry*

and his men hastily erected crude breastworks and awaited the enemy's attack or Hagood's order to retreat—whichever came first.[35]

After reaching the Telegraph Road, General Cox learned from some blacks who lived nearby that Hagood's main body of troops was on the Public Road, further to the west. Armed with that valuable information, Cox ordered Colonel Moore to rush his brigade through the swamp between the two roads and cut off Hagood's retreat. As Moore moved out, both Casement's and Sterl's brigades were sent forward against Simonton's contingent, standing firm between Cox and Town Creek.[36]

As Simonton gallantly stood his ground, General Hagood ordered the remainder of his troops at the lower bridge to retire. A "hurried flight from the trenches followed" under a "storm of shells and minie balls," remembered one Tarheel officer. "The enemy opened on us with infantry & artillery & made the woods pretty hot." Despite the deluge of projectiles not one soldier was wounded or killed in the abandonment of the bridge position. Quick acting Federal skirmishers from the 63rd Indiana Infantry, Henderson's brigade, bolted across the remnants of the bridge, however, and managed to capture about thirty men of the Confederate rear guard. The price was a small one to pay for holding onto the position for so long, and the balance of Hagood's force managed to escape in a hasty retreat up the Public Road. The Southerners were forced to halt two miles from the creek in order to form a line of battle to cover Simonton's withdrawal. Hagood had already abandoned his position north of the bridge at the church when a courier arrived there with a report for him from Colonel Simonton: the Federals were extending around Simonton's left and moving to attack. Simonton added that he could not hold his position on the Telegraph Road much longer. The courier, however, could not find Hagood and was forced to return to Simonton with the distressing news.[37]

Hagood soon had his troops in line to support the rear guard's retreat. The general dispatched Capt. William E. Stoney of his staff, who had earlier been with Simonton on the skirmish line at Cowan's, to tell Simonton to immediately fall back. Stoney, together with a courier, galloped off and located the colonel with his command in two wings on either side of a road, the right wing under imminent threat of attack. As soon as he received the message, Simonton ordered Lieutenant Rankin to limber up his artillery, which had been vigorously responding to the Federals in its front, and

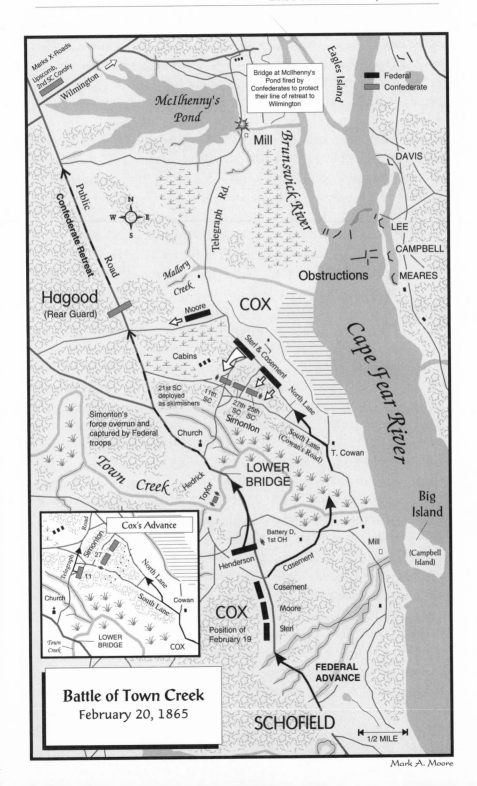

Battle of Town Creek
February 20, 1865

Mark A. Moore

withdraw with the infantry down a path through the swamp in their rear. Just as Simonton issued the command, however, the Federals struck. They came on so suddenly that Simonton had little choice but to stand and fight. Too heavily engaged to withdraw, Simonton sent Stoney back to alert Hagood of his desperate situation.[38]

With fixed bayonets, Casement's and Sterl's brigades attacked Simonton's men "impetuously and with the wildest enthusiasm." The 3,000 troops cheered as they advanced, though it was a long and fatiguing charge across a field dotted with pine trees and scrub oaks. LeVant Dodge of the 177th Ohio Infantry, Casement's brigade, stumbled and fell just as the assault began, losing several large sweet potatoes he had discovered in the same cache foraged by South Carolina soldiers posted at Town Creek earlier that morning. Dodge picked himself up and quickly resumed his position in the battle line, but not without regrets for those lost yams. The initial resistance met by Dodge and his comrades, skirmishers from the 21st South Carolina and a small contingent of Confederate cavalry, were met and dispersed with relative ease.[39] These skirmishers never did rejoin their comrades on the battle line, and were either captured or had simply fled—Simonton suspected the latter. But the remaining Southerners answered Union cheer with Rebel yell and met the bayonet attack with well-timed volleys of small arms fire and artillery canister as the Yankees came into view. "By this time the balls were flying around at a great rate," observed Abram Clement of the 11th South Carolina. "The firing continued to increase until it was a perfect roar." So intense was the gunfire that sparks from discharged weapons ignited the field of sedge broom grass.[40]

The destructive sheet of fire killed three and wounded thirty-one Federals.[41] One lieutenant in the 12th Kentucky Infantry of Sterl's brigade witnessed the terrible result of a discharge by "St. Paul," the 12-pounder howitzer of the Edenton Bell Battery. The Kentuckian managed to fight his way up to the Southern line and demanded the surrender of the gun crew as it was in the act of firing. "If you fire that gun I will kill you," threatened the Federal officer. "Kill and be damned," replied Sgt. Benjamin F. Hunter, commander of the cannon, who turned and ordered a gunner to discharge the weapon. The artilleryman jerked the lanyard and a loud boom erupted. The long burst of barrel flame and cloudy burst of powder smoke was succeeded almost immediately by the thump-thump-thump of lead case balls ripping into flesh and bone. An enormous rolling moan from the victims filled the broken wood lot. The case shot had enfiladed Company H of the 104th Ohio Infantry at point-blank range, killing and wounding twenty soldiers—more than half the Union casualties in the fight. Federal soldiers turned their wrath on the artillery crew, cutting down the gunner and pouncing on Sergeant Hunter. They would have run Hunter through with their bayonets had the lieutenant of the 12th Kentucky not spared him, saying, "He's too brave a man to be killed."[42]

Private William Reese of the 16th Kentucky Infantry of Sterl's brigade was also wounded in the attack, but not by Confederate projectiles. Reese, a 52-year-old enlistee, injured himself with his own rifle-musket. As his unit neared the Confederate line, Reece plummeted into a rifle pit he did not see in the gathering darkness. As he fell, the butt of his gun smashed into his lower abdomen, causing a hernia and severely bruising his testicles. Writhing in pain in the sedge broom grass that burned around him, Reese missed the rest of the battle. It was the only wound Reese had sustained during the war, and would cause him great discomfort for the rest of his life.[43]

Meanwhile, Reese's comrades quickly overwhelmed the Confederates, who were outnumbered about eight to one. Even so, Simonton's men stood their ground until overpowered in hand-to-hand combat with Cox's veterans troops. "There was no running in these rebels," one Union soldier marveled, "they held their ragged works until the guns were snatched out of their hands." It is difficult to determine with any precision the exact casualties in this engagement, primarily because so few reports were filed or have survived from this period of the war. Perhaps twenty Southerners were killed and wounded in Simonton's stout defensive action. Among the casualties was a soldier named "Prince" of Company B, 11th South Carolina, who was shot in the face at point-blank range while fighting with his unit on the left of the line. The Union soldier who shot Prince was so close when he discharged his weapon that cartridge paper from the round protruded from the wound near Prince's mouth. Despite the close quarter fighting, most of the Confederates survived the battle and were taken prisoner. In all, Cox's troops captured 375 officers and men, including Colonel Simonton, who personally surrendered his command to General Cox. Both pieces of Lieutenant Rankin's artillery and three battle flags were also captured.[44]

Among the prisoners were Privates John and James Nixon. Members of the Edenton Bell Battery,

Sgt. William Izlar, Co. G, 25th South Carolina, captured at Town Creek

William Izlar, Edisto Rifles

the Nixon brothers had enlisted together in Bertie County in January 1862. They both had fought and survived the battles of Fredericksburg, White Hall and Goldsboro. For them the war was over. Though captives, the Nixon brothers could take comfort in the notion that they had fought bravely and were together—alive.[45]

Instead of surrendering some Confederates chose to escape—or at least tried to escape—into the surrounding woods and swamps. The Federals pursued them until it was too dark to see and captured many, including Captain Wescoat and Abram Clement. When the Federals had poured over the Southern battle line and encircled the beleaguered defenders, Wescoast and Clement took off on what the latter described as "a race almost of life and death," with four Union soldiers right behind them, firing on the run. The South Carolinians eventually became winded and had to stop, hiding in a clump of bushes. But the Federals, soldiers of the 12th Kentucky Infantry, were close behind and called out for their surrender. "We had nothing to do but give ourselves up," Clement lamented. The Kentuckians confiscated Wescoat's sword, sword belt, and pistol, and almost everything Clement had been carrying except a photograph and a lead pencil. They were then marched back to the battlefield and placed under guard with the rest of the prisoners.[46]

Like Clement and Wescoat, Sgt. William V. Izlar of Company G (Edisto Rifles,) 25th South Carolina, attempted to escape the Federal tidal wave. When the battle ended, Izlar was on the far right of Simonton's line. He and several comrades realized the game was up and fled, hoping to make their way back to Hagood's main force. They struggled through the darkness and a dense swamp to reach the Public Road west of the Telegraph Road. As soon as the South Carolinians stepped onto the thoroughfare, however, they found themselves in the midst of Federals from Henderson's brigade. "Hello, Johnnie," a Union soldier greeted Izlar, "how deep have you been in?" Disgusted with his bad luck, Izlar merely replied, "Just so deep," while holding his hand at the height of his waist. "I felt terribly chagrined," Izlar wrote, "but quiet submission was the only alternative."[47]

An undetermined number of Confederates managed to elude their would-be captors. One of them was General Hagood's staffer, Capt. William E. Stoney. After Stoney had returned with the message that Simonton was too heavily engaged to withdraw, Hagood had sent the staff officer back into the fray with direct orders for Simonton: *"He must come,"* Hagood insisted. Simonton was "to throw away his artillery and make a run for it." Despite thrashing his mount at breakneck speed, Stoney arrived only in time to "see the overwhelming lines of the enemy sweep over Simonton—the artillery firing till the enemy got within a few feet of it, and the infantry standing by the gun and resisting till overpowered hand to hand." The staffer never reached Simonton. As he got sucked into the swirling and confused fighting, Stoney's horse was shot from under him and fell to the ground. Unhurt, Stoney managed to scramble away, though he was unable to rejoin his command for several days.[48]

Johnson Hagood feared the worst. The fighting had long-since ended and yet neither Simonton nor Stoney had reported to him. What little news he received, and all of it was bad, reached his ears from the few stragglers from Simonton's rout able to stumble their way through the boggy terrain and rejoin their commands. Their testimony was proof enough. Hagood ordered a general retreat to Wilmington. He accommodated the stragglers by taking up a temporary position behind Mallory's Creek, keeping a strong skirmish line in his front with a squad of cavalry patrolling the line.

About half of Lipscomb's South Carolina cavalry formed the rear guard for Hagood's haggard column of marchers, while the balance was thrown forward to hold the position at McIlhenny's Mill. Hagood rode ahead of his men and reached the city about half past eight that evening, February 20, his thoughts on that final march into Wilmington unrecorded. Decimated and dejected, the infantry and artillery crossed over the Brunswick River pontoon bridge and by steam ferry over the Cape Fear three hours later. After burning the pontoons the cavalry left a small picket force on Eagles Island. Initially, Hagood's troops were ordered to reinforce Hoke's brigades at the Forks Road entrenchments, but those instructions were soon countermanded and they were sent to bivouac at Hilton, on the northern outskirts of the city.[49]

Hindered by the dense swamp and encroaching darkness, Colonel Moore's brigade failed to intercept Hagood's fleeing soldiers. The evacuation of the enemy compelled the brigade commander to retrace his steps and rejoin Cox, who had bivouacked his troops on the Telegraph Road battlefield. Confederate prisoners from the engagement were rounded up and placed under a heavy guard for the night. One Union soldier remembered that "in a few hours everything was quiet as if no din of battle had ever been there." Federal engineers spent the evening repairing the bridge to enable the Ohio artillery and the bulk of Henderson's brigade, which had fought all day at the lower bridge, to cross and reunite with Cox.[50]

Why had the Confederate defensive position at Town Creek unraveled so quickly? Just as with the Fort Anderson debacle, the blame must fall on Johnson Hagood, who once again blundered by allowing Jacob Cox to outflank him with impunity. Hagood was not about to accept blame for the defeat, however, and fingered Robert Hoke and Charles Simonton as the culprits for the fiasco. The South Carolinian impugned Hoke's generalship in his postwar reminiscences by questioning the exigency for attempting to hold the Town Creek line. "The propriety of making the obstinate stand at Town Creek at all," Hagood wrote, "rests with the direction of affairs." In that deftly-drafted sentence Hagood relieved himself of responsibility, took credit for Simonton's resolute stand—and impaled Hoke. He twisted the blade of his pen once more by adding, "It delayed the evacuation of Wilmington but little and was a hazardous venture."

As disparaging as he was toward Hoke, Hagood saved most of his venom for Charles Simonton. He blamed the colonel, a commander with but limited field experience, for disobeying orders and allowing himself to be coerced into battle. "His fault," censured Hagood," was in allowing his greatly inferior force to become engaged in a line of battle behind obstructions rapidly thrown up, when the occasion required him, and he had been directed [by Hagood], to make an obstinate skirmish fight." In a postscript to this criticism, Hagood added that "For this the country was admirably suited." After heaping additional condemnations upon Simonton, even Hagood was compelled to concede that his troops "behaved with their accustomed gallantry," and that their "obstinate defense of the flank" saved Hagood's entire command. In a final parting discharge that damned Simonton with faint praise, Hagood closed this section of his memoirs by noting that the colonel's "errors certainly leaned to virtue's side." Unfortunately, Hagood's fast and loose rendition of Simonton's supposed field foibles conveniently ignores several critical points. Colonel Simonton had but 400-500 men to throw across a broad front into the face of an aggressive veteran enemy outnumbering him about eight to one. In addition, Hagood requested that Simonton concurrently execute several arguably incompatible tactical feats, including the rapid extension of his line to the left to cover two different roads, and the placement of a "reserve" behind each flank. Given that Simonton himself did not believe his force large enough to adequately guard both points, Hagood's order to spread his men and pull enough soldiers out of line to form two reserves—while in direct contact with Cox's Federals—made little sense. Most significantly, Hagood had *ordered* Simonton to "close his reserves together" to meet the enemy when he reached the Telegraph Road; that is, to consolidate into a battle line. In the end, Hagood's criticism's make him look petty and small.[51]

While Johnson Hagood may have been pleased with his escape from the Town Creek line, the evacuation provided small comfort to General Hoke. The North Carolinian had realized for some time that if Hagood was defeated at Town Creek Wilmington's doom was sealed, for nothing could stop General Cox from marching within range of the city. Yet, Hoke needed additional time to remove government property, the remainder of the Union prisoners—and his own command. Even so, he would not evacuate Wilmington without his superior's approval, and General Bragg was due to return to Wilmington the following day. Hoke decided to let Bragg make the decision. Meanwhile, Hoke continued to hold General Terry in check three miles south of Wilmington at Forks Road while transferring Confederate property and Union captives out of town. He also set in motion a scheme that he hoped would wreak havoc on the Union navy.

On the evening of February 20, the Confederates floated perhaps as many as 100 torpedoes—wooden cylinders filled with 100 pounds of gunpowder—downriver against the Union flotilla anchored off the river batteries. Before the torpedoes reached the warships, however, a slave warned the Federals of their approach. Admiral Porter placed little faith in the informant's story, but ordered the ships' commanders to take precautionary measures nonetheless. Sailors spread fishing nets across the channel to catch any bombs that may float downriver and were deployed in cutters to watch for the floating mines.[52]

Late that evening sailors on board the launches spotted the dreaded torpedoes drifting downstream. They managed to fish some of the mines out of the water and sink others with musketry. Despite their best efforts, however, some of the "infernal" weapons slipped past the dragnet. One floating cylinder exploded underneath a gig from the *Shawmut* when her crew attempted to sink it with a pistol shot at too close range. Seaman James Cobb was killed instantly by the blast, Seaman James Hayes was blown overboard and drowned, and two others were wounded. Another torpedo detonated in the paddle wheel of the *Osceola*, causing extensive damage to the wheelhouse. Nevertheless, the nets intercepted the vast majority of the torpedoes, which were hauled away and destroyed at a safe distance from the warships the next morning. The informant probably saved the Union flotilla from more serious damage. Throughout the campaign slaves and free blacks had assisted the Federals in their effort to capture Wilmington. Though that historic moment was drawing closer, the Confederates were determined to delay it for as long as possible.[53]

Before dawn on February 21, Colonel Lipscomb's cavalry torched the Wilmington & Manchester Railroad trestle and dismantled a pontoon bridge spanning the Brunswick River on the west side of Eagles Island. Some of the troopers crossed into Wilmington, while others remained on the island to watch for the approaching Federals.

Eagles Island separated the Cape Fear and Brunswick rivers opposite Wilmington. The island was large, almost five miles long and two miles across at its widest point, but its marshy interior of rice fields made it habitable only for wildlife. The island's human occupants were confined to the east bank, which was lined with docks, warehouses, a cotton compress, Beery's Shipyard and the Wilmington & Manchester Railroad depot. A corduroy causeway called Eagles Road, together with the Wilmington & Manchester Railroad ran westward across the swampy island into Brunswick County. With Cox's victorious Federals expected on the western shore of the Brunswick River sometime during the day, the Confederates destroyed the bridges leading to Wilmington.[54]

Jacob Cox had hoped to use those bridges to enter Wilmington. Early on the morning of the 21st, he started his brigades moving rapidly toward the city. The route around the west end of McIlhenny's millpond took the Federals some distance from the river, causing Cox to lose contact with Schofield for the first time in the campaign. By noon the Union command had reached Mill Creek, about five miles north of Town Creek, where it was delayed while engineers reconstructed a small bridge destroyed by the retreating Confederate cavalry. After repairs had been made, Cox's troops pushed onto the Brunswick River crossing, arriving about 3:00 p.m. A small Union detachment that had marched up the Telegraph Road had reached the river two hours earlier than the main force. Although the waterway halted their advance, at least temporarily, Cox's men finally got their first glimpse of Wilmington's skyline across Eagles Island.

Cox wanted to continue his advance on Wilmington, but the bridges across the Brunswick River appeared to be useless. The Wilmington & Manchester Railroad trestle was in ruins, its wooden frame still smoldering. The Confederates had also destroyed a pontoon bridge that once spanned the river. The Southerners, however, perhaps in their haste to retreat, had left behind undamaged pontoons. Most of the boats had been scuttled, but others had been simply cut adrift. Several of these were recovered and used to put two infantry regiments, the 16th Kentucky and 65th Illinois, on Eagles Island. At that point the city looked so calm and peaceful, remembered Cox, that he thought the Confederates had already evacuated it. As the Kentuckians and Illinoisans gathered on the island, engineers began repairing other boats and rebuilding the pontoon bridge.[55]

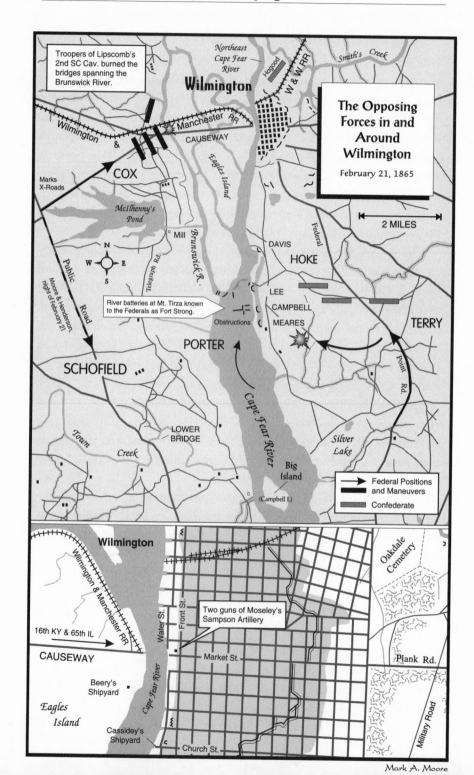

Troopers of Lipscomb's 2nd SC Cav. burned the bridges spanning the Brunswick River.

Northeast Cape Fear River

Wilmington

Smith's Creek

W & W RR

Hogood

Wilmington & Manchester RR

CAUSEWAY

COX

Marks X-Roads

McIlhenny's Pond

Mill

Eagles Island

Brunswick R.

Telegraph Rd.

Public Road

Moore & Henderson, night of February 21

The Opposing Forces in and Around Wilmington

February 21, 1865

2 MILES

Federal

DAVIS

HOKE

LEE

CAMPBELL

MEARES

River batteries at Mt. Tirza known to the Federals as Fort Strong.

Obstructions

PORTER

SCHOFIELD

TERRY

Point Rd.

Cape Fear River

LOWER BRIDGE

Town Creek

Silver Lake

Big Island

(Campbell I.)

Federal Positions and Maneuvers

Confederate

Wilmington

Wilmington & Manchester RR

Water St.

Front St.

Oakdale Cemetery

16th KY & 65th IL

CAUSEWAY

Two guns of Moseley's Sampson Artillery

Market St.

Plank Rd.

Beery's Shipyard

Eagles Island

Cassidey's Shipyard

Cape Fear River

Church St.

Military Road

Mark A. Moore

With flags flying and skirmishers leading the way, the 16th Kentucky and 65th Illinois advanced across Eagles Island on the narrow causeway, the only road across the marshy island. It soon became apparent that the Confederates were still in the vicinity when dismounted horsemen of the 2nd South Carolina Cavalry appeared on the east side of the island. The Confederates fired on the approaching Federals, and a sharp skirmish ensued. The small band of Southerners, who never intended to seriously contest possession of the island, was easily driven back and the Federals moved to within rifle range of the city.

Without warning a masked Confederate battery opened fire on Eagles Island's latest residents from the streets of Wilmington. The first shot ripped down the causeway, showering the Federals with dirt as it bounded past them and exploded in their rear. "This was just not the kind of reception I expected to meet with," exclaimed David C. Bradley of the 65th Illinois. The projectile did not hit anyone, but it scattered the troops, many of whom sought refuge in the soft, spongy ground on either side of the causeway. "In my jump I was fortunate enough to light on top of a soldier who had fallen flat, and to this unfortunate accident I am indebted for not receiving a slimy bath of North Carolina mud," Bradley wryly noted.[56]

Other soldiers dashed for the rear but could not reach a place of safety before a second Confederate shell exploded in their midst. "The blue smoke and flash of fire accompanied by the well known boom, too plainly told us to get out of the way," recalled Sgt. Henry Clay Weaver of the 16th Kentucky. "Scarcely had I slipped off on the left of the pike before the shell struck opposite me on the right of the pike and killing one of my boys, and wounding two others." Weaver believed that the Confederate artillery might have annihilated the 16th Kentucky had its soldiers "not displayed that skill in dodging cannonballs so often practiced on former battlefields." Most of the Federals withdrew to Alligator Creek halfway across the island, and there erected breastworks behind which they took shelter from the incoming shells.[57]

The Confederate fire was from two cannon commanded by Capt. Abner A. Moseley of the Sampson Artillery, an independent North Carolina battery posted on either side of Wilmington's market house on Market Street, between Front and Water. Their discharges caused quite a stir not only among their targets but in town as well, rattling windows in nearby buildings and attracting many onlookers, including women and children. When the Union soldiers only partially withdrew, Colonel Hedrick of the 40th North Carolina took one of the howitzers onto the island itself and opened fire on them.[58] The move, while bold, quickly drew the wrath of Cox's ordnance, which retaliated by sending projectiles into the city, crashing into buildings along the waterfront. "A battery of our rifled guns [Battery D, 1st Ohio Regiment Light Artillery] soon demonstrated that in an artillery duel, the [Confederates] would get more blows than they could give," boasted a Union soldier.[59] The incoming Federal shells created panic among the women and children of Wilmington who ran crying and screaming in the streets. To dissuade the Federals from bombarding the town, General Hagood quickly ordered his cannoneers to cease fire, and the artillery duel quickly gave way to silence.[60]

Confusion reigned in Wilmington as General Bragg stepped off the train at the Wilmington & Weldon Railroad depot on the afternoon of February 21. By then, many Wilmingtonians were fleeing the city with all possible haste. The Wilmington & Weldon line strained to take off the remainder of the weary prisoners-of-war and frightened citizens anxious to leave town before the dreaded Union army moved in. Other residents clogged the avenues with their wagon loads of belongings as they attempted to escape, while merchants labored to close and board up their shops. To make matters worse, some soldiers and civilians broke into stores and warehouses and ransacked them.

Most alarming to Bragg, however, were the numerous enemy troops in plain view on the west bank of the Brunswick River. Moreover, scouts reported seeing Federal soldiers reconnoitering the Cape Fear River north of Wilmington, looking for ways to cross over and cut off Bragg's line of retreat. "This rendered our continued occupation of the town very hazardous to the whole command," Bragg maintained. The commanding general ordered preparations for the army's immediate evacuation. He sent Lt. Gen. William J. Hardee a message calling off the attempt to route his troops through Wilmington, and informed General Hoke to hold his command in readiness to retreat.[61]

February 21 began quietly enough along Hoke's front at Forks Road following General Terry's thwarted Union attack the day before. Although no significant fighting had erupted, skirmishing broke out along the line and occasionally Hoke's artillery opened fire on Union pickets. Two Federal soldiers from Col. Frank Granger's Third Brigade (formerly the command of Col. Louis Bell who was killed at Fort Fisher) of Adelbert Ames' division, were seriously wounded by the bursting of a single cannonball. "We were putting out our picket relief, [and] the officer in charge was foolish enough to march them out in a body," wrote one eyewitness. "The rebs opened with a twelve pounder; one of the shells burst in their midst wounding a man severely in the leg, in Co. A, and tearing another belonging to the 13th Indiana [Infantry] dreadfully; one of his arms was smashed at the elbow, the other at the wrist, and the flesh torn off his thigh some of the pieces flew whizzing over our heads."

The Confederate shells did not discriminate as to rank, and one almost smashed into General Ames as he was making an inspection tour. A small arms battle broke on Hoke's far right flank, adding a punchy staccato counterpoint to the deep-throated artillery blasts.[62]

With the Confederates strongly entrenched at Forks Road, General Terry probed westward seeking a weak spot in their line. At about 10:00 a.m., he sent a portion of Ames' division, Lt. Col. James A. Colvin's Second Brigade—Col. Galusha Pennypacker's old unit—to make a reconnaissance-in-force toward the river. Paine's and Abbott's brigades, together with Ames' two remaining brigades, remained in their trenches to pin Hoke in his Forks Road entrenchments.[63]

A sharp skirmish ensued during Ames' march when his vanguard unexpectedly ran into a Confederate picket post. "Every bush and stump in front of us seemed to be alive with men, who opened a terrible fire at short range immediately upon us," recalled a soldier of the 48th New York Infantry. "[The battle] was a constant series of little flank movements: the men would run ahead and with wonderful ingenuity throw up a few handfuls of dirt in front of them, lying down behind it, firing at the retreating enemy, then advance again and repeat the movement, then they would try flanking them; and the battle continued for hours. Bullets fell thick and fast among us." Major Nere A. Elfwing of the 48th New York caught a minie ball in the knee cap that required the amputation of his leg. When the unit's surgeon informed Elfwing that he would lose his leg, the major replied with stoic humor: "Well, one pair of boots will last me now as long as two pair will you." Although Elfwing was no longer able to lead his troops, his men helped drive the Confederates back into their main works anchored on Battery Meares.[64]

Ames' force encountered even stiffer resistance when it attacked the river batteries themselves. As soon as the Confederates saw Union skirmishers approaching, they opened a heavy small arms fire upon them. "Some time in the afternoon we marched up a road, and marched right up to the rebel works, we was not over a hundred yards from the rebel rifle pits," noted infantry private Simon Bennage of the 76th Pennsylvania Infantry. "They commenced to fire on us before we knowed any thing of them. We returned fire but we could not do much with them for they ware behind there works."[65]

The Confederates increased their fire with field artillery, and the withering barrage wounded at least ten Union soldiers and killed another. Shells also riddled four-legged creatures, including a horse that belonged to a member of General Ames' staff, which absorbed a cannonball through the shoulder that tore through the animal and exited its haunches. Remarkably the rider escaped unhurt. Most of the Confederate projectiles, however, passed harmlessly over the heads of the Union troops taking shelter wherever they could. Those who had knapsacks placed them in front of their heads, and occasionally took pot-shots at the Confederates from behind them. "We had a terrible time of it," exclaimed Private Bennage. "We laid a wile and returned fire, then we got orders to move back." The brigade soon retreated to the safety of a nearby swamp.[66]

Porter's flotilla supported Ames' reconnaissance, the warships renewing their brisk bombardment of the river batteries at about two o'clock on the afternoon of February 21. When Porter spotted Union troops moving against the batteries, he ordered his gunboats to intensify their fire. The Confederates responded indifferently to naval shelling, concentrating on the approaching enemy soldiers instead. "[When the gunboats] commenced to shell the rebels in there works," noted a Union soldier, "that settled them pretty quick." Yet the Confederates' stubborn defense convinced Ames that a full scale assault would prove disastrous, and at midnight he withdrew his men and rejoined Terry near Forks Road.[67]

The firing on Hoke's front only intensified General Bragg's preparations to evacuate Wilmington. To expedite the withdrawal, he confiscated horses, mules and wagons, impressed slaves (about 200 in all), and rounded up able-bodied white males between the ages of seventeen and fifty. Fearful of being conscripted into Bragg's ragtag civilian work force, a number of boys and elderly men fled the city. Sixteen-year-old Joseph Piram King and several of his young friends escaped in a shad boat, rowing up Alligator Creek on Eagles Island and hiding in the bulrush. Army officers complained that the Home Guard was suddenly nowhere to be found. As potential recruits melted away into the confusion, Bragg succeeded in removing the important government property and most of the Union prisoners by rail, while the more healthy captives were marched out of the city.[68]

Two days earlier, before Bragg had returned to the city, General Hoke had offered to turn over thousands of Union prisoners recently sent to Wilmington for exchange as part of a cartel between the C.S. and U.S. governments, but General Schofield declined. He knew that caring for large numbers of captives would interrupt his operations against Wilmington. Better that the Confederates had to deal with them. "We are greatly embarrassed by prisoners," General Bragg later admitted, "the enemy refusing to receive them or entertain any proposition." Some prisoners, perhaps as many as 200, escaped their Confederate captors during the evacuation and waited for the Union troops to occupy Wilmington. Many were hidden about the city by slaves and free blacks, including Cpl. Thomas Entwhistle of Company D, 3rd New Hampshire Infantry and two fellow captives. Together they jumped from train cars and hid under a barn in town, where a black man discovered and fed them.[69]

Unable to evacuate everything of military value, Bragg ordered that all remaining public property and private stores be destroyed to keep them from falling into enemy hands. Cotton, tobacco, and naval stores—and probably the official records of the district's army, navy, and customs office—were all put to the torch or thrown into the river. Some residents hid valuable cotton and tobacco, but the military authorities confiscated and destroyed much of it. James Dawson, brother of Wilmington Mayor John Dawson, rented Andrew J. Yopp's barn on Smith's Creek in order to conceal 100 bales of cotton. The Confederates discovered the contraband and burned it and the building in which it was being stored. Dawson, who had acted with considerable foresight by not putting all of his eggs in one basket, hid other bales in other locations which escaped detection.[70]

Storehouses, foundries, shipyards and vessels were also torched. The Confederates burned Cassidey's shipyard at the foot of Church Street, as well as the industries on Eagles Island. Railroad facilities, government storehouses, cotton compresses, turpentine distilleries and Beery's shipyard were all razed. The ironclad *Wilmington,* which was almost completed, together with several other smaller vessels including a David class submarine, were lost when Beery's went up in smoke. The gunboat *Chickamauga* was steamed up the Cape Fear River and scuttled at Indian Wells.[71]

Wilmington as it appeared on February 21, 1865, presented a stark contrast to its heyday as a bustling and prosperous blockade running port. Gone were the swift, sleek steamers that had lined the docks for years bearing supplies so vital to the Confederacy. Now the waterfront was deserted except for squads of gray-uniformed soldiers igniting buildings containing material that could not be removed, but could not be allowed to be captured by the Yankees. By late afternoon the streets were virtually empty, as those residents who chose to leave town had done so, and those who chose to remain had cloistered themselves in their homes. Lieutenant Zaccheus Ellis, a Confederate soldier from Wilmington, took one last walk through its deserted streets. "You can have no idea, Mother, of my feelings, knowing that our old town was doomed," he penned. "The shops are all closed, Government property being destroyed, huge piles of cotton and rosin being set afire, tobacco being thrown in the river. You can't imagine anything like it." Nor could Zaccheus Ellis have imagined that in just one month he would be killed at the Battle of Bentonville. Despite Ellis' poignant description of the devastation suffered by his hometown, Wilmington was fortunate that the damage was not more extensive. A brisk easterly wind fueled the flames, which nearly raged out of control. Wharves, piers and adjacent warehouses caught fire and were unintentionally destroyed. Had the wind been blowing from the west, the city's entire business district might have been consumed.[72]

Jacob Cox's troops assumed that the Confederates were preparing to abandon Wilmington. From their position on the banks of the Brunswick River the billowing columns of black smoke were clearly seen, the incessant screeching of railroad cars moving in and out of the city easily heard. Bolstering their belief were the numerous disaffected residents, escaped slaves and railroad workers who drifted into Cox's camp reporting Bragg's activities. Cox was therefore understandably surprised when he received orders from Schofield to withdraw.[73]

Schofield had sent instructions for Cox to return with his entire command to Town Creek and cross the Cape Fear River to reinforce Terry's corps. The Confederates' obstinate defense at Forks Road and Fort Strong—as well as deserters' testimony—had persuaded Terry that Hoke had been reinforced by William J. Hardee's force. Terry, who was concerned about his ability to defend against a determined counterattack, had asked Schofield to send him Cox's command.[74]

Although Schofield had initially issued the order at noon on February 21, the courier lost his way and did not reach Cox until six hours later. By then Cox deemed the withdrawal impractical. It was too dark to counter-march 6,000 troops six miles to Town Creek along muddy backroads and then make the river crossing in time to aid Terry. Besides, such a movement might appear to the Confederates to be a retreat, prompting them to alter their plans. Cox did not want to risk that possibility. He was convinced by his observations and reliable reports that Bragg was evacuating Wilmington. "I cannot doubt that [we] will have an open road in the morning, and think from the general indications that I am entirely secure here," Cox reported. He decided to retain the bulk of his force at Brunswick River, but started Orlando Moore's brigade toward Town Creek to appease Schofield. Cox also sent Schofield a message informing him of his intentions. At midnight Cox received Schofield's blessing as to his course of action, but requested another brigade in case Terry needed assistance. Cox sent Thomas Henderson's brigade to join Moore's while concurrently preparing to advance on Wilmington in the morning.[75]

Contrary to Terry's fears, Hardee's corps had not reached Wilmington. In fact, Bragg had turned it away earlier in the day. Wilmington's commander realized that it was time for his army to leave the city, and at 1:00 a.m. on February 22, ordered his army to withdraw. Officers roused their men from their blankets and told them to gather their belongings. The despondent troops were silent as they tramped into the city before dawn and headed northward. "I think this has been one of the saddest days of my life," lamented Lt. William Calder. "I never had such a hard thing to do as leave all my old friends & the home where my childhood days were spent." As the soldiers trudged through the streets a deathlike stillness surrounded them and a thick pall of smoke from the smoldering fires hung above their heads. "[It was] so black and compact as to appear to come from the infernal regions," observed one Confederate. "Lights could be seen from but few windows, and these appeared to be the last rays of departing hope."[76]

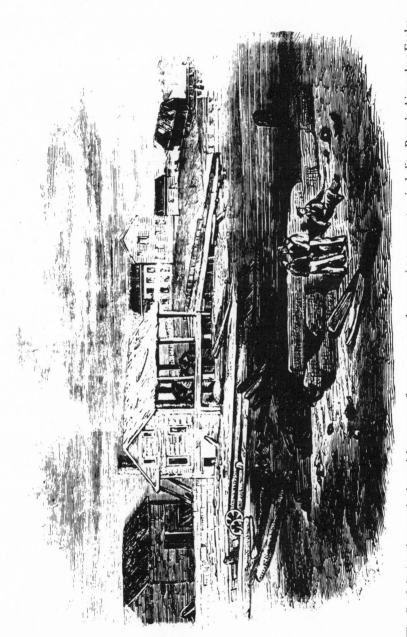

The Confederates destroyed substantial amounts of government and some private property—including Berry's shipyard on Eagles Island—as they prepared to evacuate Wilmington on February 21, 1865. *Frank Leslie's Illustrated Newspaper*

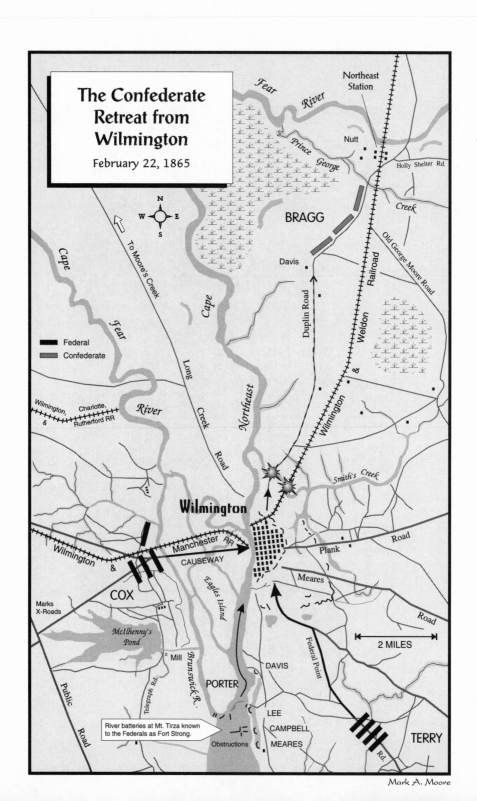

The Confederate
Retreat from
Wilmington

February 22, 1865

Northeast Station

Fear River

Prince George

Nutt

Holly Shelter Rd.

Creek

BRAGG

Davis

Cape Fear

To Moore's Creek

Duplin Road

Old George Moore Road

Cape

Weldon Railroad

N
W   E
S

Federal
Confederate

Long Creek

Wilmington, Charlotte, & Rutherford RR

River

Northeast Creek Road

Smith's Creek

Wilmington

& Wilmington

Manchester RR

CAUSEWAY

Plank

Road

Meares

COX

Eagles Island

Marks X-Roads

McIlhenny's Pond

Mill

Telegraph Rd.

Brunswick R.

PORTER

DAVIS

Federal Point

2 MILES

Public Road

LEE
CAMPBELL
MEARES

River batteries at Mt. Tirza known to the Federals as Fort Strong.

Obstructions

Road

TERRY

Mark A. Moore

Chapter 13

"Wilmington is ours!"

– Maj. Gen. Alfred H. Terry to Maj. Gen. John M. Schofield

SURRENDER

Lieutenant Colonel James F. Randlett had left camp before daybreak on February 22 to scout the Confederate lines at Forks Road. His soldiers of the 3rd New Hampshire Infantry were just beginning to stir, brewing coffee and preparing breakfast. What he saw surprised him and sent him bursting into camp on horseback. "They have gone," he yelled, announcing that the Confederates had abandoned their earthworks. As soon as he heard the news, Gen. Alfred Terry relayed the information to General Schofield (who was still on board the *S. R. Spaulding* on the Cape Fear River), and then started his corps toward Wilmington. General Jacob Cox's pickets on Eagles Island were also reporting that the Confederates had evacuated Wilmington, which prompted Cox to order his men forward as well.[1]

In the city, meanwhile, curious onlookers lined the waterfront to watch Cox's blue-clad troops march across Eagles Island. The band of the 104th Ohio Infantry, which had serenaded the troops during the battle of Fort Anderson, again performed an assortment of martial tunes and national airs, including the "Star Spangled Banner." To let the oncoming Federals know that they would offer no resistance, a group of citizens placed a white flag on top of H. B. Eiler's building at Market and Water Streets, while other civilians met the troops as they reached the Cape Fear River. The Confederates had removed or destroyed all boats on the west side of the river to stave off an enemy pursuit, but residents anxious to discourage the Federals from again shelling the city, crossed over in skiffs to ferry them to the other side. Soldiers of the 16th Kentucky Infantry crossed the river just after 8:00 a.m., earning the distinction of being the first Union troops to enter Wilmington. The remainder of Cox's troops came across in dribblets all morning.[2]

As the Kentuckians entered Wilmington, General Terry's army approached from the south, with the soldiers of General Abbott's brigade in the lead. Their flags unfurled and bayonets at the ready, Abbott's regiments cautiously advanced against the Confederate outer defenses a mile from Wilmington. The Federals charged over the works and found them occupied only by spiked cannon and stacks of ammunition. Moving into the suburbs, the Federals were met by the local police chief, Capt. John Griffith, who bore a white flag in his hand and the mayor's authorization to surrender the city. General Terry rode up and accepted Captain Griffith's offer, then called in Abbott's skirmishers and pushed into town.[3]

At 9:15 a.m. Terry's advance, comprising a small contingent of cavalry, galloped into Wilmington and approached a group of residents at the foot of Market Street. Reverend L. S. Burkhead of the Front Street Methodist Church, who was in the crowd, recalled that a Union officer asked for the mayor. John Dawson stepped forward and replied: "I am the man." The officer stated that "General Terry would meet the Mayor and Commissioners at the city hall in five minutes." The civilian administrators, with Reverend Burkhead in tow, walked the four blocks to city hall at Third and Princess Streets. There they waited for perhaps a half-hour, while the Union troopers dashed up and down the streets capturing Confederate stragglers.[4]

Mounted on a beautiful charger, Terry rode at the head of his army as it entered Wilmington about 9:30 a.m. With tattered flags flapping in the breeze and the drum and bugle corps playing "Yankee Doodle," the victorious troops marched up Front Street. Although the black soldiers had borne the brunt of fighting on the east side of the river, the white soldiers marched into town first amid a surprisingly enthusiastic reception from many residents. General Abbott's brigade, with the 3rd New Hampshire at the head of the column, was the first of Terry's units to enter, with General Ames' division pacing close behind. In the rear paraded General Paine's two brigades of U.S. Colored Troops "with burnished barrels and bayonets gleaming in the bright sunshine. . .and singing with one accord. . .the famous 'John Brown' song."[5]

General Terry left the column at Front and Market Streets to ride to city hall. He dashed up to the building and to the men gathered before it, dismounted and asked, "Is this the mayor?" John Dawson replied, "It is." The two men then took off their hats, shook hands cordially, and together ascended the steps of city hall to discuss the city's surrender. "Wilmington is ours!" Terry notified General Schofield shortly afterward. Later that morning Schofield also met with Dawson and other civic leaders.[6]

Federal forces poured into Wilmington throughout February 22. As it was George Washington's birthday, the soldiers considered their victory a good omen. Terry's corps marched to the north end of town, where it halted for a brief rest. It was late afternoon before Cox got all of his troops across the Cape Fear River. After ceremoniously planting the Stars and Stripes on the abandoned Confederate river batteries, Admiral Porter led his flotilla upriver, arriving at Wilmington about mid-afternoon on the 22nd. To honor the victory, Porter's ships were dressed in full array—colored bunting and flags flying from the yards—and promptly at noon each ship fired a thirty-five gun salute, one for each state. "I shall ever remember this day and I had rather work a year without pay, than miss being here," remarked a Union

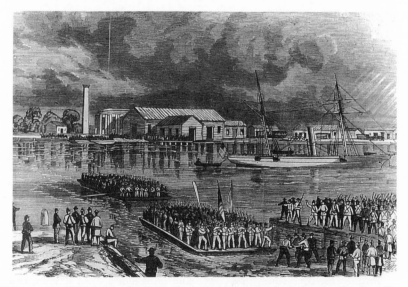

Union troops of Maj. Gen. Jacob D. Cox's division being ferried across the Cape Fear River to Wilmington. *Harper's Weekly*

sailor. "We are having a day of Jubilee today." While the navy celebrated, the army moved after Bragg's army, which remained close by.

About 10:00 a.m. on February 22, Terry's scouts overtook Bragg's rear guard, the 2nd South Carolina Cavalry, at Smith's Creek a half-mile north of Wilmington. Bragg's main force was hastily retreating north on the Duplin Road, heading in the direction of Northeast Station (present-day Castle Hayne) on the northeast Cape Fear River. Hoping to retard Federal pursuit, the Confederates destroyed the Wilmington & Weldon Railroad trestle crossing Smith's Creek and had just set fire to an adjacent wagon bridge. Sharpshooting broke out across the marshy stream for possession of the wooden span. Lucius L. Spencer of the 2nd South Carolina Cavalry, perhaps the last Confederate out of Wilmington, dashed across the bridge just ahead of the Federal advance.[7]

Abbott's brigade, which was resting nearby when its members heard gunfire, was ordered to fall in and march toward the noise. The 3rd New Hampshire was the first regiment to reach the creek, where its men found the remaining bridge aflame and well covered by the enemy's carbine fire. Captain William Trickey, the ranking Union officer on the scene, realized the importance of saving the span and ordered his skirmishers to seize it. Under a hail of bullets, the New Englanders stormed across the burning planks to drive off the Confederate horsemen. Once the bridge was theirs, the Federals jumped into the cold stream to draw water to fight the flames. Using only their canteens, kepis, hats and tin cups, they extinguished the blaze and saved the bridge.[8]

General Terry resumed the pursuit of Bragg's command as soon as repairs to the bridge enabled his corps to cross in force. Although the principal armies did not clash, Terry's advance units and Bragg's rear guard skirmished from Smith's Creek to Northeast Station, nine miles distant. Throughout the afternoon Colonel Lipscomb's cavalry harassed the Union vanguard (regiments of Abbott's brigade), with hit-and-run tactics. After crossing Smith's Creek, Terry relieved the 3rd New Hampshire from skirmish duty, replacing it with the 6th Connecticut and 7th New Hampshire. "[The Confederate troopers] gave us considerable trouble by dashing suddenly down the skirmish line," acknowledged a soldier of the 7th New Hampshire. But the Federals derived some satisfaction from the annoying

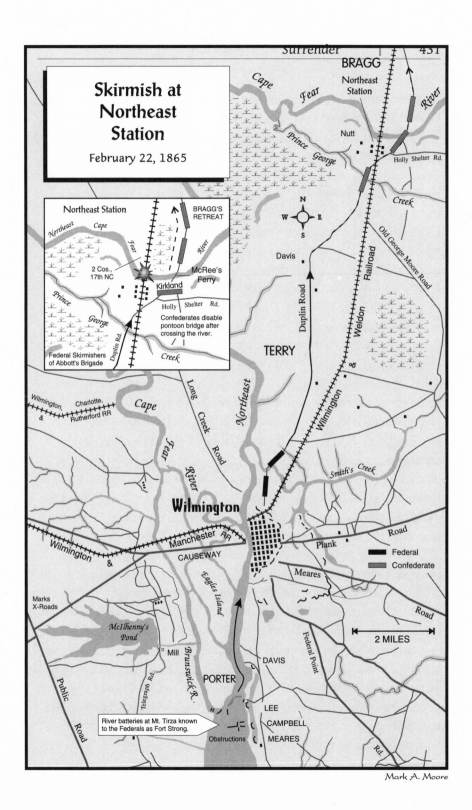

Skirmish at Northeast Station

February 22, 1865

BRAGG

Northeast Station

Nutt

Holly Shelter Rd.

Cape Fear

Prince George

Creek

Inset: Northeast Station

Northeast Cape Fear

BRAGG'S RETREAT

2 Cos., 17th NC

McRee's Ferry

Kirkland

Holly Shelter Rd.

Confederates disable pontoon bridge after crossing the river.

Prince George Creek

Federal Skirmishers of Abbott's Brigade

Duplin Rd.

Davis

TERRY

Duplin Road

Old George Moore Road

Weldon

Railroad

Wilmington &

Wilmington, Charlotte, & Rutherford RR

Cape Fear

Long Creek Road

Northeast

River

Smith's Creek

Wilmington &

Manchester RR

CAUSEWAY

Wilmington

Plank

Road

Meares

Road

Federal
Confederate

Marks X-Roads

McIlhenny's Pond

Mill

Eagles Island

Brunswick R.

Telegraph Rd.

PORTER

DAVIS

Federal Point

2 MILES

Public Road

River batteries at Mt. Tirza known to the Federals as Fort Strong.

Obstructions

LEE

CAMPBELL

MEARES

Rd.

Mark A. Moore

fight by plundering shoes belonging to "rebel cavalrymen who had been killed during the day on the skirmish line."[9]

At dusk Abbott's skirmish line pushed up close to Bragg's main column, its retreat slowed by a deep swamp on the north side of the river. Brig. Gen. William W. Kirkland's Brigade and the 8th North Carolina of Clingman's Brigade (commanded by Col. William S. Devane) were compelled to make a stand to keep the Federals in check and enable the main body to escape. The Confederates' holding action was "a determined one," observed a Union soldier, "and the volleys of musketry were quite heavy."[10]

Bragg's rear guard withdrew slowly toward the crossing point at McRee's Ferry, where the single pontoon bridge bottlenecked the Southern army as it attempted to make good its escape. General Abbott's men, many of whom were armed with Spencer repeating rifles, maintained a blistering fire as they approached the waterway. When they were again met by sharp Confederate rifle-musket fire, General Paine threw forward one of his regiments and a battery of artillery to bolster Abbott's force. A few well-directed cannon shots and the surge of Abbott's and Paine's battle line sent the last of Bragg's men scurrying for safety on the far side of the river.[11]

Kirkland's Brigade had deployed along the river bank to defend the pontoon bridge, while Capt. Charles G. Elliott commanded two companies of the 17th North Carolina overlooking the Wilmington & Weldon Railroad trestle burning several hundred yards to the west. Bragg's main force entrenched on a sand ridge a half-mile north of the waterway. Confederate engineers attempted to demolish the pontoons by knocking out their bottoms. Plunging fire from Federals who soon appeared on the river's south bank, however, gave them only enough time to cut loose the end of the pontoon bridge and let it swing downstream with the current.[12]

Sporadic fighting for possession of the bridges raged across the river, their outlines dimly illuminated in the encroaching darkness by the dying flames that had all but consumed the railroad bridge. Union horsemen tried but failed to save the trestle when Capt. Elliott's Tarheel infantrymen turned them back "in a spirited affair." Union sharpshooters likewise thwarted Confederate efforts to recover or destroy the pontoon bridge. The Southerners finally abandoned the bridge altogether, leaving it to the Federals who retrieved and repaired it the following day.[13]

The fighting died down about 9:00 p.m. when both armies, exhausted from the day's constant marching and skirmishing, collapsed on their arms for the night. Confederate pickets fired one last defiant but ineffective volley into the Union encampment and withdrew from the river bank to rejoin the main body. "During the night they crept down to the bank and opened upon us with small arms, hoping to drive us back so that they could complete the destruction of the bridge," recalled a Connecticut soldier, "but we held our ground and prevented further damage, while we made and drank our coffee in spite of them."[14]

Before sunrise the next morning, February 23, Bragg's army retreated toward Goldsboro, where it planned to unite with other Confederate forces. Bragg's withdrawal from the Cape Fear ignored Robert E. Lee's instructions to "be bold and judicious. . .hang upon [the enemy's] flanks, cripple and retard him." The loss of Wilmington forced the Confederate high command to adopt a last ditch strategy to consolidate its scattered forces in North Carolina for a showdown with Sherman's army. President Davis appointed Joseph E. Johnston to command those forces, including Bragg's command, the Army of Tennessee contingent and General Hardee's corps from South Carolina. If these forces could combine and defeat Sherman before he was reinforced by Schofield and Terry, the Confederacy might gain more favorable peace terms.[15]

U. S. Grant had foreseen such a threat in late January when he dispatched John Schofield's corps to North Carolina to bolster Terry's and Sherman's armies. Grant believed that as long as the armies of the Potomac and James detained Lee in Virginia, it was unlikely that the Confederates could muster even 40,000 troops to oppose Sherman, Schofield and Terry. Grant and Sherman had devised a worthy plan to bring the four-year-long struggle to an end.

The first phase of Grant's strategy proved successful. Schofield, Terry and Porter captured Wilmington—their main objective—giving Sherman a safe base on the seacoast. Although Schofield had not heard from Sherman in some time, paroled prisoners reported him as being near the North Carolina border on February 24. Schofield presumed that Sherman still intended to pass through or near Fayetteville, but deployed scouts to discover his exact whereabouts.[16]

The Confederates' rampant destruction at Wilmington compelled Schofield to alter his plans to support Sherman. The Federals found very little useable rolling stock at Wilmington, and the railroad trestles were virtually destroyed, making the rail lines useless for transporting men and supplies to the front. Determined to meet Sherman at Goldsboro no later than the middle of March, Schofield requested wagons, train cars and material for restoring the Wilmington & Weldon Railroad be sent to Wilmington. When foul weather impeded both their delivery and the repair work, Schofield shifted his base of operations from Wilmington to New Bern, where a handful of locomotives and cars were located.[17]

Schofield reinforced Brig. Gen. Innis N. Palmer's command at New Bern with Brig. Gen. Thomas H. Ruger's First Division, XXIII Corps, and instructed Palmer to move forward with his combined force to guard the workmen repairing the Atlantic & North Carolina Railroad toward Kinston. Major General Darius N. Couch's Second and Third brigades, Second Division, XXIII Corps, arrived at the Cape Fear on February 22-23, and were temporarily retained there. When Schofield learned that Palmer had not advanced as expected, he dispatched General Cox by sea to take command at New Bern and to "push forward as rapidly as possible."[18]

The supply wagons Schofield had requested finally reached Wilmington, enabling General Couch to advance with his and Cox's divisions toward Kinston by way of Richlands on March 6. That route took Couch east from Wilmington on the Plank Road (present-day Market Street) toward Scott's Hill. The same day that Couch marched overland from Wilmington, Schofield sailed to New Bern, where he planned to join Cox's advance on Kinston. Before leaving Wilmington, Schofield directed General Terry to move forward with his Provisional Corps as soon as the Wilmington & Weldon Railroad was in working order. In the meantime, Terry was to continue efforts to contact Sherman.[19]

On March 11, Terry sent the tugboat *Davidson* up the rain swollen Cape Fear River to clear the way to Fayetteville. The tug made contact with Sherman who finally reached Fayetteville on March 12. Although Sherman's army had foraged liberally on its march through South Carolina, it still desperately need supplies—especially food, uniforms and shoes. Refugees, camp followers and hangers-on had consumed much of what the army had obtained.[20]

By then, however, Terry possessed few supplies at Wilmington to send to Sherman. Rations earmarked for his army had been devoured by paroled prisoners and hungry citizens, and additional provisions had been sent to New Bern. As a result, Terry requisitioned goods for Sherman from nearby Beaufort. Within two days Terry sent 3,800 pairs of shoes, 2,400 pairs of boots, 1,500 boxes of hard bread, 158,000 rations of coffee, all the sugar he could get his hands on—and a box of cigars—to General Sherman.[21]

Grateful for the supplies, Sherman replenished his army before moving toward Goldsboro on March 15. With the Wilmington & Weldon Railroad still inoperable, General Terry was compelled to march with his force from Wilmington on March 16, moving north on the Duplin Road toward Burgaw Station and Faison. That same day Sherman's XX Army Corps defeated General Hardee's force at Averasboro, and three days later Johnston launched a vicious counterblow against Sherman at Bentonville (March 19-21). In the largest land battle of the Carolinas Campaign, Sherman and Johnston traded blows for three days. After suffering heavy casualties he could ill afford, Johnston withdrew his embattled army to Smithfield on the night of March 21, while Sherman regrouped and pushed on toward Goldsboro. Schofield and Cox, meanwhile, had engaged Generals Bragg and Hoke at Wise Forks, forcing the Confederate abandonment of Kinston. Schofield marched to Goldsboro, arriving on March 21. Having pushed Johnston's stubborn army aside, Sherman reached Goldsboro two days after Schofield. Terry's corps joined Sherman west of Goldsboro and accompanied him into the city.[22]

Whatever danger Sherman was in evaporated when he united his forces with Schofield, Cox and Terry. Together the armies contained 88,000 soldiers and were positioned near the North Carolina coast, which was now completely controlled by the U. S. Navy. Sherman also had railroads to both Wilmington and New Bern by which he could continually be resupplied and reinforced. Johnston still confronted Sherman, but it was "with an army much inferior to his own," as U. S. Grant pointed out, "both in numbers and morale."[23]

The Union capture of Wilmington had a direct influence on Sherman's operations, providing him with both a safe haven and a base of supply. The troops that reinforced Sherman through Wilmington gave him an army not only capable of contesting any threat inside the state, but strong enough to threaten Robert E. Lee in Virginia. With Grant in his front and Sherman poised to attack his rear, Lee had little choice but to evacuate the Richmond-Petersburg line and move to join forces with Joe Johnston in North Carolina. Grant's hammer blows in early April, which smashed the Confederate lines, dictated the timing of Lee's evacuation. Grant followed closely on Lee's heels, battling the beleaguered Army of Northern Virginia halfway across the Old Dominion to Appomattox Courthouse. There, on April 9, 1865, Lee reluctantly capitulated. Johnston surrendered to Sherman at Durham Station, North Carolina, on April 26. As Lee had predicted, if Wilmington fell "he could not maintain his army." He was feeling the pinch from the loss of his primary line of supply when Grant broke through his lines on April 2. Even if Lee had been able to maintain his position in early April, the lack of supplies would have eventually made it impossible to keep his army in the field, or Sherman would have moved north and sealed off his only viable route of withdrawal. The Wilmington Campaign did not end the Confederacy, but it hastened its downfall.

The Union combined operations against Fort Fisher were the largest of the Civil War. Never before had so much firepower been concentrated on a single target. Second Fort Fisher and the Wilmington Campaign proved to be model amphibious operations. Admiral Porter and General Terry attacked Fort Fisher with a singular determination to capture the earthen stronghold, and they worked hard and harmoniously for victory. Porter proved that a heavy, concentrated naval bombardment could render an earthwork fortification vulnerable to capture, not by destroying the defenses but by neutralizing its artillery.

For the most part, Generals Schofield, Cox and Terry planned their strategy well and executed their tactics with determination in the post Fort Fisher-Wilmington Campaign. This is perhaps most evident in Cox's successful flanking movements against Johnson Hagood at Fort Anderson and Town Creek. The Union army sustained only 200 casualties in the entire (post Fort Fisher) campaign. Admiral Porter's flotilla also placed unwavering pressure on Wilmington's defenders. The Union navy's massed artillery, sufficient mobility and adequate concentration on the Cape Fear River provided the Union army with the necessary support it needed to capture the city. And for the first time in the war, the Federals advanced in large force against a strategic interior target from a captured Atlantic seacoast base. Although that strategy was originally proposed by the Blockade Strategy Board in the summer of 1861, it was not employed until the Wilmington Campaign, almost four years later.

The Federals' task at the Cape Fear was made easier by the Confederates' downward-spiraling morale and Braxton Bragg's indifference to Wilmington's security. His refusal to aid Fort Fisher cost him the support of many of his troops and local residents. If he sacrificed the fort to save Wilmington, he did an equally poor job. In fact, the defense of Wilmington itself devolved onto Robert Hoke's shoulders when Bragg departed for Richmond at an inopportune moment to take care of meaningless bureaucratic business. By the time Bragg returned to Wilmington, the city was lost.[24]

When Union reinforcements arrived at the Cape Fear early in February 1865, Hoke battled insurmountable odds. Although he held tough on Federal Point, General Hagood made several fatal tactical errors on the west bank of the Cape Fear River that enabled the Federals to push rapidly on Wilmington. Hagood's field blunders necessitated Hoke's withdrawal from Sugar Loaf, and eventually Wilmington itself. Wilmington was of comparatively little value to the Confederacy after the fall of Fort Fisher sealed the port to maritime commerce. Nonetheless, Hoke removed vital government stores from Wilmington and protected General Hardee's retreat from South Carolina. His actions, while prolonging the inevitable, allowed Joe Johnston and the Confederacy to fight on in North Carolina.

"God grant us the power to cope with our giant enemy"

– Katherine Douglas DeRosset Meares

OCCUPATION

I n spite of the Confederates' widespread destruction, the Federals still managed to capture valuable material in Wilmington. In addition to some forty pieces of heavy artillery found in the defenses around the city and in the river batteries below, the victors of the campaign seized a Whitworth rifle-cannon, 500 rifle-muskets, accouterments, about $5,000 worth of commissary stores, three wheezy locomotives and a few dilapidated railroad cars. The Confederate stables, some machine shops and the Wilmington & Weldon Railroad facilities also escaped the devastation relatively undamaged and fell into Union hands. Much to the soldiers' delight, the army also seized a warehouse containing tobacco, cigars, and whiskey. Not surprisingly, the soldiers soon emptied it.[1]

With Wilmington occupied Federal authorities turned to the task of restoring the city to the Union. General Schofield assured Mayor Dawson that the army would not interfere with civic affairs so long as residents respected United States rule. Schofield "expected the inhabitants to conduct themselves as becoming citizens of the United States, to respect the representatives and defenders of the National Government, to abide by its laws, and not give aid and comfort to its enemies."[2]

Wilmingtonians expressed mixed feelings about their city's transfer from Confederate to Union control. Many citizens still retained deep feelings for the dying Confederacy while others displayed a strong Union sentiment. For four years Confederate supporters had sacrificed much—including the lives of their loved ones—to the Southern cause. One of these was Katherine Douglas DeRosset Meares, the daughter of a prominent local physician and the widow of a popular Confederate officer, Col. Gaston Meares of the 3rd North Carolina, who was killed at Malvern Hill on July 1, 1862. Widow Meares openly expressed her anguish at being conquered: "God grant us the power to cope with our giant enemy," she prayed. "The sense of captivity, of subjugation. . .is so galling that I cannot see how a manly spirit could submit to it."[3]

Many did not. Ardent Confederates, frightened at the prospect of living under Federal rule, left prior to, or along with General Bragg's retreating army. Southern sympathizers who chose to remain in Wilmington and tolerate the occupation hid behind drawn shades and locked doors when the Union army entered town. Some citizens ventured out to witness the spectacle, but it was mostly out of curiosity and not because they revelled in their city's fall to the Yankees.

All the same, many residents considered Wilmington's capture good cause for celebration, and they turned out with open arms to greet the victorious Northern forces. The streets and sidewalks swarmed with people who cheered, shouted, sang, danced, and waved enthusiastically to Mr. Lincoln's troops as they filed into town. A few residents displayed U. S. flags, hidden since the war began, "which were heartily cheered by the soldiers as they passed." A woman cradling a large tray handed out cooked sweet potatoes and fried ham to the soldiers. Others toted buckets of water, and offered cool drinks to the blue-uniformed soldiers. "The scene was indescribable," exclaimed a surprised Connecticut infantryman. "The people welcomed us. . . with every indication of joy." Such displays of Union sentiment were "a great and pleasing surprise to the officers and [enlisted] men."[4]

Wilmington's slaves and free blacks expressed the greatest excitement over the arrival of the conquering Union forces. A journalist recorded that the "delight of the colored people knew no bounds. They crowded into the streets and followed the troops in throngs." The appearance of General Paine's U. S. Colored Troops stirred their emotions and hopes. "The sight of the colored troops filled the measure of ecstatic joy," declared a witness; "the men danced in jubilation, the women screamed and went into hysterics, then and there on the sidewalks."[5]

A black woman recognized her son whom she had not seen since he had escaped slavery to join the U. S. Army. Now he was returning home a Union soldier and a free man. She ran to embrace him in the ranks, and together they cried. One 93-year-old black man told a Federal soldier he had not been in the streets for seven months. The marching bands' music of Mr. Lincoln's troops revived him, however, and he came out. "There he stood," observed the infantryman "with his white locks and his wrinkled cheeks, saying, 'Welcome, welcome." "It would be a mere attempt for one such as myself to describe the manner in which the colored people of Wilmington welcomed the Union troops," admitted a soldier of the 4th U.S. Colored Troops. "Cheer after cheer they gave us—they had prayed long for their deliverance, and the 22nd of February, 1865, realized their earnest hopes. Free for ever more."[6]

Had the Federals been aware of the city's ante-bellum and early-war politics, they would not have been surprised by the locals' strong display of Unionism. In 1860 and 1861, Wilmington had been almost evenly split over secession. Union rallies often took place just down the street from pro-Southern meetings. George Davis, one of Wilmington's most respected law-yers and civic leaders, had been adamantly opposed to disunion. Davis "steadfastly counseled moderation" as the country plunged toward civil war, and went to Washington in February 1861, as a delegate to the ill-fated Peace Congress. Only when President Lincoln's called for troops on April 15, 1861, did Davis side with the Confederacy, eventually serving as its last attorney general. Moreover, many Wilmington merchants had expressed understandable reluctance to severe their commercial ties to Northern cit-ies.[7]

Observers noted that social class and race tended to distinguish those who welcomed the Federals from those who did not. "There is no showing of themselves by the would be aristocratic portion of the inhabitants," wrote a war correspondent. "The common people receive us gladly." Unionism in Wilmington apparently confined itself to slaves, free blacks, and lower class whites. Blacks knew instinctively that the boys in blue meant freedom from bondage and oppression. "They all seemed to have an intuitive knowledge that their shackles were broken; that henceforth and forever they were free," observed a Union soldier. "No wonder that their pent-up feelings should be beyond restraint. Their cherished dreams of liberty and freedom were at last to be realized. The dawn of a new existence was beginning for them. Born again from slavery to freedom. What a glorious transition."[8]

Poor whites, who suffered disproportionately from skyrocketing inflation created in part by the blockade running trade, often shifted their allegiance to the Union as the war dragged on. More affluent whites generally maintained their devotion to the Confederacy, though some opportunists displayed enthusiasm for whatever cause benefited them most. Some avid Confederates refused to believe that their fellow citizens felt sympathy for the Federals. Katherine Meares claimed that the "raptured greetings existed only in the Yankee imagination." She admitted that some black residents were "loud in their welcome, particularly to the negro troops," but insisted that the George Myers family were the "only demonstrative white people in town."[9]

The Federal occupants found it difficult to gauge the genuine sentiments of Wilmington's population. A newspaper reporter observed a strong affection for the Confederacy in Wilmington, but "not that bitter, unyielding character that [was] generally so conspicuous in southern communities." Most Confederate zealots had left town, and those who remained had little choice but to submit to Yankee rule. "The fire-eaters had vanished, or turned Quaker," a Union soldier asserted. He did not find such behavior so unusual, because he believed that the average Southern citizen was rapidly losing faith in the success of the Confederate cause. "The storm of iron rain from the guns of Admiral Porter's fleet, which had so recently fallen upon their coast; the drum beats of Sherman's 60,000 men approaching from the southward, and the undignified speed with which their army of occupation had gone into the pine woods to the northward," he explained, "was not calculated to inspire the inhabitants of Wilmington with confidence in the future of the Confederacy." A Union sailor had a more cynical view of Wilmingtonians who professed loyalty to the United States. "The people are all for the Union and are glad to see us here for they are almost starved," he scoffed. Undoubtedly, harsh circumstances compelled some citizens to adopt a Unionist stance while harboring a strong Southern partisanship.[10]

Submission to the Federals did not require Southerners to alter their political views, only that they adhere to the policies of the military authorities. Federal commanders contended that it was "not by any means decisive against a man that he was actually engaged in rebellion, if he satisfies us in accordance with [military laws]." Katherine Meares remained a staunch rebel at heart, insisting that if she had strength for anything, it was to stand up for her country and loved ones. She dealt with the Yankees by maintaining her "ladylike deportment with firmness. [That] disarms them quicker than anything else," she maintained. Yet even the defiant widow sometimes found it advantageous to be accommodating to the conquerors. In order to safeguard her home, she and her family were compelled to provide housing for a Federal surgeon, Dr. John Knowlson of the 169th New York Infantry. Much to her amazement, she came to like Dr. Knowles because of his kindness and the "little courtesies" he extended to the DeRosset family. "He is such a perfect gentleman," she wrote. "For myself, I did not suppose so much kindly feeling could have been drawn out for one of our mortal enemies."[11]

Other Wilmingtonians formed similar relationships with Union men. Andrew Yopp's family befriended a soldier named Perkins who stood guard over the neighborhood near their house, and they often invited him in for food and drink. Perkins returned the Yopps' hospitality by obtaining scarce provisions for them. Henry Prater of the 63rd Indiana fell madly in love with and married Miss Virginia Johnson, whose father's barn Prater and a squad of his comrades had been guarding. Prater soon received his discharge from the army and set up residence in Wilmington with his bride. Joseph Becker, an artist employed by *Frank Leslie's Illustrated News*, fell in love, too, while he was on assignment in Wilmington during February and March 1865. The artist fell head-over-heels for "Molly," a fair-faced, soft-spoken Southern belle who showed great interest in him and his art. But when his employer complained that his social life was interfering with his professional responsibilities, Becker was forced to choose between "Molly" and Mr. Leslie. Quite by accident Becker discovered that his beloved "Molly" dipped snuff, and his love sickness was "cured in a flash." The city's change of hands prompted an odd mixture of emotions and relationships—the enthusiasm of the conquerors, the exuberance of the liberated, the indignation of the vanquished and the accommodation between enemies. The Federal occupation of Wilmington was a trying period for citizens and soldiers alike, but most adjusted as well as they could. Fortunately for all concerned, the transition was a smooth one. Even Mrs. Meares, the diehard Rebel widow, admitted that "the Union army entered very orderly."[12]

Union forces may have been orderly when entering Wilmington, but they found the town in grave disorder. The business district had suffered extensive damage during the Confederate evacuation. Wharves, storehouses, foundries, cotton presses and ship yards lay in ashes. Stores and businesses were closed down or broken open by looting civilians and soldiers from both armies. Railroad yards, cars and bridges were ruined. Many houses and plantations were abandoned and boarded up. Garbage and debris littered the streets, yards and vacant lots. Wilmington's appearance was in stark contrast to its heyday as a busy, prosperous blockade running port. "Wilmington was once a beautiful city," one Union soldier observed rather wryly, "but now it is not very attractive." Worse yet, the city swarmed with Confederate deserters and displaced persons from the countryside.[13]

The most distressing problem confronting Wilmington, however, was its shattered economy. The closing of the port to blockade running ravaged its wartime financial base, which depended heavily on the trade. When blockade running stopped, "prosperity disappeared and poverty came in." With the Union blockade still in effect, Wilmington merchants were prohibited from reestablishing outside trade relations. The influx of supplies from the countryside stopped as well. Local farmers and fishermen, harassed by marauders and intimidated by Union soldiers, refused to take their goods to town. With vital supplies no longer being imported by land or sea, the shortage of food, fuel, and other provisions worsened. As a result, scarce consumer goods remained unaffordable to most residents.[14]

To make matters worse, there was not enough currency in Wilmington to satisfy the demand for it. Citizens who had any money at all generally possessed worthless Confederate scrip. Union quartermasters were as yet unable to pay their soldiers, which prevented greenbacks from circulating. And since the Confederates had removed or destroyed most of the cotton, tobacco and naval stores in town, few commodities were available to compensate for the shortage of capital. The early period of Union occupation in Wilmington witnessed an economy in shambles and residents in dire need of basic necessities. "God only knows how all the poor people are to live," wondered a young resident, "no business doing and nothing to be had without money. By poor people I mean everybody—for we all row in the same boat now."[15]

To meet the immediate needs of the inhabitants, the Union military authorities seized all surplus provisions and turned them over to a citizens' committee for distribution. Appeals were also made for private donations of food. Commissary officers alleviated some of the shortage by providing captured produce and rice from abandoned plantations. The Federals also seized abandoned residences and other buildings for use as hospitals, barracks and housing for the destitute. To ensure long-term improvements, General Schofield enacted laws designed to govern the residents, regulate trade and commerce, supply the needy, collect property of use to the department and clean the town.

Union military occupation policy for the lower Cape Fear was outlined in Schofield's Department of North Carolina, General Order Number 8 of February 27, 1865. Persons who came forward voluntarily were administered the oath of allegiance to the United States. Only residents who swore a loyalty oath were allowed to participate in commercial intercourse, as governed by United States laws and supervised by the Treasury Department. The law also entitled them to restoration of property confiscated from them when Wilmington was captured, if they could prove their devotion to the United States during the war. Persons of known disloyalty were to be exiled beyond Union lines or tried by a military board and punished according to the nature of the offense. Foraging was strictly forbidden, but to meet the needs of the citizens and soldiers, loyal farmers were allowed access to town to sell their goods. Destruction of public or private property was prohibited except by permission from military officials.[16]

Schofield appointed Joseph R. Hawley, a North Carolina-born Federal brigadier general and General Alfred Terry's chief of staff, to enforce these laws and supervise the occupation. Hawley took a great interest in his native state and desired "to do much in reconciling it to the new state of affairs. There are many good Union people [in Wilmington]," he observed, "and there are others who will be such with good management." On March 2, 1865, Hawley, a tough, resolute administrator and Radical Republican, assumed command of the District of Wilmington, a zone encompassing all territory in the rear of the Union army in the lower Cape Fear. Three days later Bvt. Brig. Gen. Joseph C. Abbott was assigned commandant of the Post of Wilmington. The regiments of Abbott's infantry brigade—the 3rd New Hampshire, 7th New Hampshire, 6th Connecticut, and 7th Connecti-

Brig. Gen. Joseph R. Hawley, post commandant of Union-occupied Wilmington.

U.S. Army
Military History Institute

cut—served as provost guard during the occupation. The city now had a set of bylaws to regulate its political and economic activities, a military administration to enact them and army units to enforce them. Yet conditions deteriorated before they improved. The necessity of caring for thousands of liberated prisoners-of-war and refugees exhausted local resources, threatened the health of the community and taxed the administrative abilities of Union officials.[17]

Under a February 1865 cartel between the Federal and Confederate governments, Gen. Robert Hoke was instructed to release Union prisoners sent to Wilmington for exchange. The prisoners—coming from Andersonville, Florence, and Salisbury—arrived just as Union forces were approaching the city. General Schofield declined to accept Hoke's offer to turn over the captives, at first because he had not received notice of the trade agreement from General Grant, and then because he feared the prisoners would impede his advance on Wilmington. With his objective now safely secured, Schofield agreed on February 23 to receive the captives. In accordance with the arrangements, they were to be released at the Northeast Cape Fear River.[18]

When Union forces occupied Wilmington they liberated some 200 prisoners sent to the city for exchange. During the chaos of the Confederate evacuation, the prisoners had escaped from train cars and holding pens, and then concealed themselves in and around the city, some with the help of slaves and free blacks. When the Union army marched into Wilmington, the former captives emerged from their hiding places. A number of them were reunited with their old units and comrades, whom in some cases they had not seen in years. Corporal Thomas Entwhistle of Company D, 3rd New Hampshire Infantry and his two fellow captives-turned-escapees, hidden and fed by a slave, waited for the right moment to show themselves. "We remained secreted till our troops came into the city," explained Entwhistle, "and when we saw the Union troops marching up, we came out." In an interesting twist of irony, "the first regiment we met was my own regiment, the 3rd New Hampshire," Entwhistle recalled, "and it seemed as if the boys would eat me."[19]

Preparations to receive the prisoners who had been moved inland by General Hoke began immediately. Schofield appointed General Abbott special agent in charge of the returning captives. Abbott sent commissary stores out to General Terry's encampment at the Northeast Cape Fear River, asking soldiers to cook rations for the prisoners. Vacant houses and buildings in Wilmington were readied to accommodate the former captives. Schofield also sent an urgent appeal for help to the U. S. Sanitary Commission in New York.[20]

Deliveries of the prisoners began at daybreak on a rainy Sunday, February 26, 1865. The men were shipped by train to the intersection of the Duplin Road and the Wilmington & Weldon Railroad about two miles from the river where a Confederate and Union commissioner of exchange checked and counted the men as they disembarked from the cars. A small force of Terry's command was sent out to greet them. The guards stood at present arms as the captives passed into freedom.[21]

There was considerable rejoicing among the parolees who ran about shouting, whooping, crying, laughing, rolling on the ground, and hugging each other. "I felt so happy," one soldier exclaimed, "that I ran and jumped the best I could, and tried to shout, but no sound would come, I was so overjoyed." Items that earlier had held immense intrinsic value—cups, rags, morsels of food—suddenly became worthless articles. The released prisoners gladly discarded them along the side of the road. "So long as there was any doubt in our minds that the exchange might miscarry, we held on to our little worldly possessions," explained a liberated prisoner, "but now, as all doubt had vanished, we reduced our impedimenta unceremoniously."[22]

Most of the freed soldiers marched from the point of exchange to Terry's encampment, where his entire corps turned out to greet them with food, serenading bands and an arched arbor of evergreen, flags and a placard that read "Welcome Brothers!" The former captives responded with hurrahs and tears. Much to the surprise and delight of some of the freed prisoners, their old units had helped capture Wilmington and they were reunited with their former comrades. Major John McMurray of the 6th U.S. Colored Troops was reunited with two old friends from Brookville, Pennsylvania, Capt. Ed Scofield of Company K, 11th Pennsylvania Reserves, and Capt. S. C. Arthurs of the 67th Pennsylvania Infantry. "If we had had a fatted calf we would have killed it," a joyful McMurray said. Arthurs had been a prisoner for more than a year-and-a-half, and Scofield about ten months. While listening to stories and exchanging news, McMurray and another Brookville boy stuffed Scofield and Arthurs full of bread and butter, beefsteak and coffee until they were full. "And then we insisted on them eating more," McMurray commented. After rekindling old friendships, eating a fine meal and taking a brief rest, the men were marched to Wilmington to convalesce. Ambulances and steamers transported those too sick to walk.[23]

The periods of confinement, exposure, starvation and neglect had taken their toll on the paroled prisoners. Many were either sick and dying or dead by the time they reached Wilmington. As unprepared as the Federals were to receive such large numbers of ex-prisoners, they were even less ready for their horrid physical appearance. Witnesses declared that human language failed to describe their condition. Many of them were little more than skeletons with drawn pale skin, matted hair, expressionless faces and ragged clothing. "If spooks or specters could be seen," declared a Union soldier, "I could imagine them to be the truest representatives of many of the returning prisoners. They were human ghosts."[24] A doctor observed that "many of the men were in a state of mind resembling idiocy, unable to tell their names. . .Some of them moved about on their hands and knees. . .looking like hungry dogs. Some. . .hitched along on their hands and buttocks. . .Others giggled and smirked and hobbled like starved idiots."[25] A soldier swore that he would never forget the "feeling of mingled surprise, pity, disgust, and indignation" he experienced on meeting "these wretched creatures. Manhood

Exchanged Federal prisoners-of-war in Wilmington, February 1865. *Frank Leslie's Illustrated Newspaper*

seemed extinguished," he claimed. "In some faces you looked in vain for a single reflection of the human soul." General Hawley expressed his feelings with three words: "Awful, awful, awful." He wrote his wife that reports concerning the condition of the released prisoners were in no way exaggerated. Perhaps not, if Benjamin Booth's story was at all indicative of the physical deterioration many of these men endured. After arriving in Wilmington, Booth, a former infantryman of the 22nd Iowa, weighed himself on a platform scale used for measuring rations. He tipped the beam at eighty-seven-and-a-half pounds, almost 100 pounds below his normal weight.[26]

The released prisoners-of-war came in at an average rate of 1,400 each day for seven consecutive days. When the deliveries ended on March 4, 7,692 enlisted men and 992 commissioned officers had been liberated at the northeast Cape Fear River. Another unexpected 1,050 were taken in at the Brunswick River. People and organizations in Wilmington provided the paroled prisoners with the best relief at hand. Union surgeons attended to their medical needs. Some military sutlers and local residents took pity on the ex-prisoners and sought to mitigate their suffering, and even locals invited the men into their homes. The Wilmington Theater (Thalian Hall) staged benefit performances for the soldiers. On the night of March 4, Miss Elouise Bridges played in "Dead Shot," "Antony and Cleopatra," and "Paddy Miles Boy" and helped raise $1,074 for the former prisoners. On March 19 U. S. Sanitary Commission agents finally arrived in Wilmington and assumed most of the responsibility for their care.[27]

These efforts helped a majority of the ill soldiers recover, but others were not so fortunate. Forty-six released captives died in Wilmington during the first week of March. The Sanitary Commission estimated that on March 20, the fifteen hospitals in town contained 2,500 invalid former prisoners, more than one-fourth of the total number of parolees. Perhaps several hundred of them, many of their names unknown, died by the time the war ended in April. Soldiers of Company A, 18th Indiana Infantry, tendered a resolution of thanks to Mrs. A. V. W. Hewlitt of Wilmington, who cared for their comrade on his death bed. Despite the feeble condition of many of the prisoners, more than 7,000 of them were fit enough or had recovered enough by the end of March to be shipped home.[28]

The appearance of thousands of refugees further hindered efforts to stabilize conditions in Wilmington. Most of the refugees were escaped or liberated slaves and disaffected whites who had attached themselves to the coattails of General Sherman's army as it marched through the Carolinas. Their numbers grew so rapidly that they became a tremendous burden to Sherman's military operations. Consequently, as soon as Sherman reached Fayetteville, he disposed of them by sending them to Wilmington.[29]

The first refugees arrived in Wilmington by the middle of March, followed by a massive column of 6,000 souls that reached the Wilmington area on the 21st of the month. They spent the night on Point Peter at the confluence of the branches of the Cape Fear River. The following morning they began filtering into town. Thousands more arrived within a few days, and soon 8,000 to 10,000 displaced men, women and children thronged the streets of Wilmington.[30]

What to do with the refugees perplexed Union officials, for they quickly became a burden to them as well—especially the Commissary Department.

"They are devouring our stores," General Hawley complained, "and yet we cannot see them die of starvation." Fortunately, 400,000 hard bread rations had just reached the Cape Fear from the North. But with some 15,000 occupation troops, almost 10,000 former prisoners-of-war (many of them quite ill), thousands of needy citizens, and destitute refugees to feed, the food did not last long. There was great need in Wilmington, but little to meet it. It was not that the Federal government lacked the means to meet that need, but provisions were not arriving in Wilmington fast enough for the thousands waiting to be fed. As "generous as the Government is in such matters," General Hawley explained, "there must be embarrassment and suffering. We were utterly unable to furnish many of the necessities of life."[31]

Compassionate residents tried to alleviate the refugees' suffering as they had for the released Union prisoners-of-war. Some Wilmingtonians opened both their hearts and their homes to the displaced persons. Yet the sheer number of the refugees overfilled accommodations and diminished resources. They filled every "nook and corner or vacant room any where to be found" in Wilmington and its suburbs. "I can give you no idea of the utter squalidness of these miserable refugees," exclaimed one shocked Wilmingtonian. "It is heartbreaking to see their sufferings. . . poverty and sickness killing them like sheep."[32]

The issue of caring for the refugees was compounded by an outbreak of infectious fevers. The epidemic actually occurred just prior to the refugees' arrival, but spread rapidly as they swarmed into Wilmington. The simultaneous appearance of damp, warmer weather and the failure of residents to clean their property increased the number of cases. Physicians pinpointed ague, typhoid and typhus as the killers. A medical report of March 19 showed 3,689 sick in Wilmington's hospitals. General Hawley reported near the end of March that eighteen to twenty citizens were dying each day. Stephen C. Bartlett, a doctor on board the *Lenapee*, claimed that the daily fatality rate was fifty. "It is mostly fevers," he diagnosed. Four attending surgeons fell victim to disease. "[The refugees] are pressing us severely, exhausting our resources and threatening pestilence," Hawley asserted.[33]

With the situation rapidly getting out of hand, Hawley was forced to act quickly to regain control of the refugee problem. He appealed to the American Missionary Association for clothing and to the government for food.

While the government donated food to them, the post commandant expected the refugees to earn their keep. As Federal authorities pointed out, it was "not the intention of the government to allow this class of persons to live in luxury and idleness, but merely to sustain life till such time as they [could] help themselves." Consequently, Hawley organized a battalion of refugees and freed slaves to clean Wilmington's streets, wharves and hospitals.[34]

Hawley also asked his superiors to provide transportation to take the refugees out of the Wilmington area. Indeed, General Sherman had intended for the blacks to be sent to South Carolina and the whites to New York. In the meantime, Hawley temporarily relocated them throughout the lower Cape Fear, placing many of them on abandoned or deserted lands and plantations and in captured fortifications. The military established sizable refugee communities on Bald Head Island and at Fort Anderson, and leased them for cultivation to "active and reliable persons, white and colored." Some of the refugees worked the surrounding forests, extracting pine sap for turpentine, tar and other naval stores. By late April, however, most of the refugees had been removed from the lower Cape Fear.[35]

Wilmington's sanitation problem also demanded a forceful response from Hawley, who was concerned that diseases might persist through the hot summer months unless the town was thoroughly sanitized. He directed all citizens to clean their premises and yards of offal and rubbish. Inflammable refuse was to be dumped outside the town limits. Hawley instructed Mayor Dawson "to take such measures as he may deem judicious in relation to the sanitary condition of Wilmington." He authorized Dawson to seize carts and drays for removing garbage and instructed him to impose fines on residents delinquent in cleaning their property. As a result, the health of the community improved rapidly. "The town is being so thoroughly cleansed," commented a citizen, "that I hope we shall be free from the pestilence this summer."[36]

Union authorities also made significant progress in rejuvenating Wilmington's depressed economy. To enable people to earn some income, the Federals employed local labor, allowed businesses to reopen, purchased small amounts of privately owned goods, and finally circulated greenbacks. To ease unemployment, the government tapped Wilmington's vast labor force. The army recruited blacks into the ranks of U. S. Colored Troops. Moreover, the Quartermaster Department hired both skilled and unskilled workers to help operate a foundry, saw mill, carpentry workshop, dry dock and machine shops. The foundry cast parts for ships undergoing repairs on the dry dock. Daily, the sawmill produced thousands of feet of lumber for reconstructing piers, wharves, and warehouses. The government also erected hospitals. Slowly Wilmington was being restored to its former appearance.[37]

The provost marshal allowed businesses to reopen after proprietors had taken the oath of allegiance. Initially merchants were permitted to sell only existing stock to loyal citizens. That mattered little to residents anxious to resume business as usual. They swamped the provost office with requests for swearing the oath and for permits to restore their jobs. On March 11 James Parsons, a boot and shoemaker, was the first businessman authorized to reopen his shop. By the end of the month, seventy-three persons—grocers, dry goods dealers, sutlers, druggists, even a photographer—had sworn the oath and obtained licenses to restart their businesses. To increase the quantity of available consumer goods, General Hawley asked his superiors to increase shipping from the North. They in turn authorized certain commission firms to import supplies through the blockade to help Wilmingtonians better meet their immediate needs. "Wilmington has changed much since we came here," observed a Union surgeon in late March. "The stores are being opened and there is a large amount of shipping here." Soldiers finally received their long-overdue pay which gave them purchasing power. A newspaper reported that $600,000 was circulated into Wilmington's economy.[38]

The Federal government also bought caches of privately owned commodities. Some residents had invested in and hoarded cotton, tobacco and rosin as a hedge against devalued Confederate currency. The Confederates discovered and destroyed much of this stockpile when they evacuated Wilmington, but some of it survived. The occupying Federals considered it Confederate property and seized much that had escaped destruction. Concerned about the effects of poverty in his district of command, General Hawley recommended to his superiors that an agency be allowed to purchase these articles and so "enable many families to supply their daily wants." The government adopted Hawley's suggestion and authorized the Treasury Department to set up a buying program.[39]

The government also returned some captured property only to buy it back. By April, the military had confiscated a large amount of public and private goods, including twenty-seven drums and four boxes of tobacco, eighty barrels of oil, fifteen barrels of turpentine, and approximately 500 bales of cotton. Union provost marshals reviewed ownership claims on these commodities. Owners were required to prove that they had remained loyal to the Union during the war, or that they had sworn an oath of allegiance prior to, or at the time of, their property's seizure.

James Dawson, the mayor's brother, invested heavily in cotton during the war's last days. A substantial quantity had somehow escaped the torch during the evacuation of Wilmington but fell into Union hands upon its capture. After declaring and proving his loyalty, Dawson registered a claim for 109 bales of the once-plentiful staple. Upon approval of his application, he promptly sold the cotton to the Treasury Department for a handsome profit. A newspaper reported that the sale had made Dawson "perhaps the wealthiest individual in Wilmington."[40]

Known Confederate sympathizers who attempted to regain their property, however, received little sympathy from Federal officials. Dr. Armand John DeRosset, a noted physician and wealthy blockade running entrepreneur, succeeded in repossessing his medical office, but the military refused to return his other buildings to him. The Federal government even insisted that the DeRossets pay rent for the privilege of living in their own home at Second and Dock Streets. When they pleaded an inability to make payment, the high command forced them to accept a Union boarder.[41]

Another prominent citizen, Dr. John D. Bellamy, was not even allowed to return to Wilmington, much less repossess his property. Dr. Bellamy, a retired physician and well-to-do planter, had lived with his family at Floral College in Robeson County, far from the deprivations of wartime Wilmington. In late March, with the conflict grinding to a close and Confederate defeat inevitable, Bellamy decided to take his family home. By this time the Federals occupied Wilmington and were using the Bellamy's grand home at Fifth Avenue and Market Street as army headquarters. Bellamy applied for permission to reenter the lines, but General Hawley adamantly refused. He deemed Bellamy a rabid secessionist who should suffer for his Confederate allegiance. "Having for four years been making his bed," Hawley wrote, "he must lie on it for a while. I have no time to take him within the lines." The Bellamys were heartbroken. Mrs. Bellamy was eventually allowed to visit Wilmington, and was granted an interview with Mrs. Hawley at the Bellamy

Mansion. The former owner was furious for having to ask permission to enter her own home, and angry when she saw how the Yankees were treating it. The call did not go well and she left without regaining possession of the house. Not until September 1865, five months after the war, did the Federal government pardon Dr. Bellamy for his Confederate support and allow him to return with his family to the Bellamy Mansion.[42]

Hawley proved a compassionate man when seeing to the needs of the impoverished, but a tough authoritarian when dealing with opponents of the Union. His strictness left no aspect of Wilmington's affairs untouched—even those of the religious community—as the Reverend Alfred A. Watson of St. James Episcopal Church soon discovered. In anticipation of the Federal capture of Wilmington, the Reverend Watson had obtained permission from the diocese bishop to refrain from offering prayers for Confederate leaders. So as not to offend St. James's largely pro-Confederate congregation, the bishop directed Watson (a native of New York) to so modify the liturgy as to avoid expressing allegiance to the United States. Prayers were only to be said for "those in rightful authority," or "those in civil authority." Such temporizing was unacceptable to the local Federal authorities, who considered it openly disloyal. They punished Watson by closing St. James, suspending the reverend's religious privileges, and threatening to banish him from the district. A few weeks later General Hawley seized the church and a squad of U. S. Colored Troops proceeded to tear out the pews, throw them into Third Street, and transform the house of worship into a military hospital.

The Reverend Watson, appalled by the act, appealed to President Lincoln claiming that General Hawley had reacted too harshly against him because his "mental convictions [were] on the side of the Confederacy." Watson maintained that, regardless of a person's political allegiance, the government possessed no right to dictate to the church in matters of religion except insofar as the church assailed the United States in political or secular questions. "Fundamentally," Watson insisted, "to change the Liturgy so as to make it pray for that against which it prayed before—or against that for which it prayed before belongs only to the Church in General Council." President Lincoln was assassinated before Watson's letter reached Washington, but the Andrew Johnson administration agreed with its content. St.

James was returned to its congregation and restored sufficiently to hold Christmas services in 1865.[43]

The squabble with the Reverend Watson was probably only of minor concern to General Hawley. One of his chief concerns, aside from the regular supervision of the district, was Northern speculators who came to Wilmington intending to defraud the government. Deserters and marauders committing outrages against inhabitants in the adjoining counties also worried him because he did not have a sufficient force of cavalry to combat them. He requested but was denied more horsemen to help strengthen his authority in the region, so Hawley encouraged people in the countryside to organize and protect themselves and their homes.[44]

There was, however, comparatively little crime in the city. Some soldiers occasionally misbehaved. After creating a ruckus in a house of ill-repute, a guard was forced to shoot and kill a soldier who resisted arrest. In another instance, a visitor from General Sherman's army was mugged and robbed by two uniformed men late one evening in downtown Wilmington. Racial tension between the blue-uniformed men also manifested itself when white and black Union soldiers clashed on occasion. The two races had been segregated during the campaign, but the day after Wilmington's capture, a white soldier shot a black comrade to death in front of William Goodman's Dry Goods store on Market Street. An infantryman of the 3rd New Hampshire, Samuel Martin of Company I, drowned a black street cleaner who had shot him in the eye during an argument. Because blacks could not testify against whites, Martin was acquitted on the charge of murder. One resident contended that Wilmington was in "constant danger of a serious collision between the races" which only the government and God could avert. For the time being one or both did. The provost marshal and his troops held a tight rein on affairs and Wilmington remained relatively quiet during the initial Union occupation period.[45]

General Hawley's strong-arm policies implemented a Radical Republican approach to Reconstruction in the lower Cape Fear in the late winter and early spring of 1865. Under Hawley's authority the Federal army took control of local plantations, confiscating produce and resettling the estates with freedmen and squatters. Poor whites and disaffected blacks were granted additional rights and were generously supported in their efforts to obtain jobs. Confederate sympathizers, on the other hand, received less support and empathy. In the midst of political change there was much suffering in Wilmington, and the road toward and through Reconstruction would be a long and hard one.

Because of their reduced circumstances, most Wilmingtonians seemed anxious for a "fast returning to a normal way of things." Many residents accepted the fact that the Confederacy was dying and that it could no longer help them. Mayor Dawson called for a "Grand Rally of the People" to discuss the welfare of Wilmington and North Carolina. Civilians were invited regardless of political sentiments. Even Wilmington's occupation newspaper, the *Herald of the Union*, promoted the rally not as "a union meeting or a secessionist meeting; democratic or republican; yankee or abolitionist, etc.," but as a council of the people "to talk their sentiments out freely and express themselves with candor and plainess."[46]

Despite inclement weather, more than 1,000 residents attended the meeting at the Wilmington Theater (Thalian Hall) on the evening of March 14, 1865. A few journalists were allowed to observe the proceedings, but Union soldiers were barred. It quickly became obvious to all who entered the theater that, despite the meeting being touted as an open forum, it was in fact a Union rally. United States flags hung above the stage and bands played "Rally Round the Flag" and the "Star Spangled Banner." Mayor Dawson addressed the crowd of residents—who frequently interrupted his words with applause—speaking words of peace, forgiveness of past differences, and the welfare of the national government. "The arms of the United States have been victorious, and now occupy this city. . .and we hope to enjoy the rights and privileges as citizens," Dawson proclaimed. "My friends," he continued, "let us. . .live for the future resolving that henceforth it shall be our aim and object to secure peace, promote prosperity and add to the glory and grandeur of our common country."[47]

An appointed committee then drew up eight resolutions, which the attendants endorsed unanimously. They determined in part that the citizens of Wilmington should cheerfully submit and pledge obedience and hearty support to the United States. In good faith, the people claimed the rights and privileges of U. S. citizens. They also called upon their fellow North Carolinians to join with them by "protesting against the madness of the authorities of the State in urging the prosecution of this fratricidal war for a cause [they] believed to be hopeless." The signers of the document apparently believed that they were promoting the best interests of Wilmington and North Carolina by advocating the cessation of hostilities and the restoration of the state to the Union. Copies of the resolutions were sent to President Lincoln and Governor Vance.[48]

For weeks afterward national and state newspapers carried stories, editorials and letters concerning the Union rally in Wilmington. Some even published a list of more than one hundred prominent Wilmington men who had attended the meeting. Northern papers hailed the gathering as a powerful influence of opinion to hasten North Carolina's return to the Union. Confederate newspapers, on the other hand, expressed shock and disdain. A Raleigh journalist found it unbelievable "that any highly respectable citizens, could by any possibility, at this stage of the war, convene in public meeting and pass resolutions in favor of [the] enemy. . . ."[49]

After reading about the rally and seeing the list of names of prominent citizens who had attended it, a former resident of Wilmington wrote a letter to the editor of the *Raleigh Daily Confederate*. Having lived for twelve years in the port town, the writer apparently knew all or most of the men and explained their affection for the Union. "In the list of names at the meeting, I find 41 Yankees, 36 Irish and Dutch, 9 strolling play-actors, 20 pluguglies and shoulder-hitters (the same who elected John Dawson mayor), and eight tolerably respectable citizens," he wrote with tongue in cheek.[50]

A Wilmington-born Confederate soldier generally agreed with that assessment. The men, he asserted, fell into three groups: foreigners, transplanted Yankees and Confederate deserters. Mayor Dawson formed a separate class by himself. After all, the soldier claimed, Dawson had obtained his mayoral position through open bribery and corruption. But the soldier was surprised that eight "highly respectable gentlemen" had attended the rally. These men, he noted, had brothers and sons still in the Southern army. Katherine Meares was similarly appalled by the attendance of many at the meeting, especially Reverend A. D. Hepburn of Wilmington's First Presbyterian Church. "[He] has the impudence to proclaim his Yankee self to the world as the representatives of Wilmington's honor and patriotism!" Mrs. Meares fumed. "His people have deserted him in flocks."[51]

The majority of Wilmington's citizens had been devoted to the Confederate cause. Unionists, on the other hand, had remained relatively quiet during the war. With Wilmington occupied, it was no surprise that Northern sympathizers, including Mayor Dawson and Alfred Moore Waddell, former editor of Wilmington's pre-war Unionist newspaper, the *Wilmington Herald*, extolled such a meeting and the return of their community and state to the Union. The meeting undoubtedly attracted a minority of Southern supporters who felt compelled to submit to Federal powers. But Wilmington was not the only occupied Southern community to stage a Union rally. A similar gathering took place in Savannah in January 1865, after that city's capture by General Sherman's army.

Regardless of the reasons that motivated Wilmingtonians to repudiate the Confederacy, large numbers of them did just that. By April 3, Union provost marshals had administered the oath of allegiance to 2,082 persons in the lower Cape Fear. That number included 337 Confederate deserters and 1,336 citizens and refugees in Wilmington. Since the Confederate army had taken a large portion of the male population with it when Wilmington was evacuated, General Hawley believed that the majority of men over twenty-one years of age who had remained had now sworn the oath.[52]

Hawley insisted that his marshals "cheerfully and voluntarily" administered the oath only to residents who desired to restore the national authority. Although Unionists undoubtedly did, evidence suggests that many citizens felt compelled to take the oath. As one resident pointed out, taking the oath was akin to a vaccination. "We 'ums hafter takum boss," he told a soldier. Loyalty meant food for the hungry, clothing for the naked, medicine for the sick and shelter for the homeless. A Confederate journalist recognized the paradox. "A pleasant land this 'land of the free' must be," he wrote, "where men or women are allowed to think as the Provost Marshals think. . .where none but such accommodating thinkers will be permitted to trade. . .and permitted to purchase family supplies." A Raleigh editor berated Wilmingtonians for selling "their honor and liberty for the enjoyment of a day's ease." With the war still raging, most North Carolinians disagreed with Wilmingtonian's response to the Union occupation. That disagreement was evident in the number of pro-Confederate rallies that took place in communities throughout the state in the last days of the war.[53]

Soldiers were still camping, marching and fighting on battlefields far removed from the scene of one of the war's most multifaceted military campaigns, but for residents of Wilmington the war was over. Many of them were no longer willing to endure the privations and tragedy of civil war for a dying cause. Wilmingtonians who believed that it was better to "stand on the last plank and die in the last ditch" than to surrender or submit to the hated Yankees, held onto misplaced hopes. Restoration to the Union was their fate. As Katherine Douglas DeRosset Meares observed: "we [could] only watch, wait, and pray for a brighter day."[54]

Dr. John D. Bellamy and his grand ante-bellum home, the Bellamy Mansion, used as headquarters by Wilmington's Union military authorities in 1865.

Bellamy Mansion Museum

"...[the] grandest event in her historic past"

– William Lamb

TAPS

lthough the battle for Wilmington ended on February 22, 1865, the bickering continued for decades. General W. H. C. Whiting sounded the first clarion call to arms against the man who had been sent to supersede him at the Cape Fear and then abandoned Fort Fisher and Wilmington—Braxton Bragg. "I think that the result might have been avoided, and Fort Fisher still held, if the commanding General had done his duty," Whiting wrote General Lee shortly after the battle. "I charge him with the loss; with neglect of duty [and] I demand, in justice to the country, to the army, and to myself, that the course of this officer be investigated." Had the war not ended in April, Whiting might have received his wish. But it was the wish of a dying man fighting for a dying country. Just two months after the fall of Fort Fisher, Whiting died of dysentery while a prisoner-of-war at Fort Columbus on Governor's Island in New York harbor—the same fort he had played in as a child when his father was stationed there. On his deathbed, Whiting penned a scathing denunciation of Bragg: "That I am here, and that Wilmington and Fisher are gone, is due wholly and solely to the incompetency, the imbecility and the pusillanimity of Braxton Bragg."[1]

William Lamb survived his severe wounding, though he remained on crutches for seven years. At war's end, he returned home to Norfolk with his wife Daisy and their children. Lamb took advantage of the personal relationships he had enjoyed with British blockade runners during the war to establish a successful shipping business. State and local politics also played a big part in Lamb's post-war life, and he served three terms as mayor of Norfolk. He also became an active participant in veterans' reunions, traveling often to Wilmington to speak and reminisce with his old comrades, who dubbed him "the hero of Fort Fisher." The old colonel died in 1909, and is buried beside his beloved Daisy in Elmwood Cemetery in Norfolk. Lamb never forgot his friend and mentor Chase Whiting, or the controversial Braxton Bragg. "No assault [against Fort Fisher] could have succeeded in the presence of Bragg's force, had it been under a competent commander," Lamb maintained. "The fort was treated with utter neglect by the Commanding General."[2]

After the war, Braxton Bragg served as a civil engineer in New Orleans and later as superintendent of harbor improvements in Mobile, Alabama. He eventually moved to Galveston, Texas, where he worked in the railroad business until his sudden death on September 27, 1876. Bragg went to his grave believing that he had acted humanely in not sacrificing Hoke's Division in a futile attempt to save Wilmington.

Bragg's field commander, Robert F. Hoke, returned to private business in North Carolina after he was paroled in April 1865. He developed iron mines, dabbled in real estate, and served a stint as director of the North Carolina Railroad. Although he survived until 1912, Hoke refused to write or speak about his Confederate career—including his command role in the Wilmington Campaign.

David D. Porter was dismayed when Northerners forgot about the Federal navy's role at Fort Fisher and Wilmington so quickly. Public attention focused instead on Sherman's march into the Carolinas, Robert E. Lee's surrender, President Lincoln's assassination—and peace. Only when the Rebels wrote the history of the war, Admiral Porter contended, would the North appreciate the U.S. Navy's contribution to the victory. Porter was promoted vice admiral in 1866, and admiral four years later. He died in 1891 as hot-headed, arrogant and egotistical as ever. And he had a resplendent war record to back up his braggadocio.

Although Alfred Terry was one of the first non-graduates of West Point to hold a generalship in the Regular Army, he is perhaps best known for being George A. Custer's commander at the time of Custer's defeat at the Battle of Little Bighorn in 1876. General Terry died on December 16, 1900, in New Haven, Connecticut.

Adelbert Ames became embroiled in Reconstruction politics in Mississippi, serving first as the state's provisional governor and then as its U.S. senator. His political career ended in disgrace in 1876 (much as the military career of his father-in-law, Benjamin Butler, had ended in disgrace after First Fort Fisher), when Ames resigned from office because of improprieties. His post-war political problems damaged his wartime military notoriety. Ames made a substantial effort to regain his credibility through writings and presentations on the war, Fort Fisher in particular. Ames tried to defend his contentious behavior there, and sought to elevate his standing by downplaying the contributions of Alfred Terry and N. Martin Curtis in the victory.

N. Martin Curtis, who miraculously survived the wound he received at Fort Fisher to become a prominent resident of Ogdensburg, New York, almost came to blows with Ames at a Military Order of the Loyal Legion banquet in 1897, when Ames spoke on his "glorious role" as the real conqueror of Fort Fisher. Curtis lunged toward Ames, calling him a "craven-hearted coward." When calm was finally restored, the Union veterans requested that Curtis offer a rebuttal at their next meeting. The offer prompted him to write a commendable and objective account of both Fort Fisher battles that was based on a plethora of correspondence with his former staff officers and soldiers. Curtis undoubtedly alluded to his own aggressive nature in battle when he wrote: "In pursuit of victory desperate chances were often taken." Curtis and Ames never liked each other after Fort Fisher. Curtis died in 1910, followed by Ames twenty-three years later. Ames outlasted every other Union and Confederate general officer.[3]

U.S. Army troops garrisoned Fort Fisher for at least two years during Reconstruction. Eventually they left, but veterans returned time and time again. William Lamb, James Reilly and Kinchen Braddy were regular visitors to the old fort. A survivor's association tried in vain to obtain Congressional recognition of Fort Fisher as a national battlefield park, although it became a state park in 1962.

The Atlantic Ocean, relentless winds and the passage of the decades has destroyed most of Fort Fisher, accomplishing what Admiral Porter's mighty warships failed to do 132 years ago. Today, only about one-third of the fort's once imposing land face remains, together with a few almost unrecognizable batteries on the sea face's southern end, and a sand hill at the tip of Federal Point once known as Battery Buchanan. The famous Mound Battery washed away more than a century ago. In 1996, North Carolina erected a giant rock revetment in an effort to halt the encroaching sea and preserve the remnants of the fort where occurred, according to William Lamb, the Old North State's "grandest event in her historic past."

The Civil War changed Wilmington forever. Like William Lamb, the "city by the sea," capitalized on the international trade relations it had developed as a blockade running port. After 1875, vast quantities of cotton were again being exported from Wilmington, and it resumed its role as one of the busiest ports on the Atlantic seaboard. Twentieth century improvements in transportation slowly diminished Wilmington's maritime importance, but she remains North Carolina's most active seaport.

Orders of Battle

FIRST FORT FISHER, DECEMBER 24-27, 1864

Confederate States Army, Department of North Carolina, Third Military District (District of the Cape Fear), Maj. Gen. Braxton Bragg, commander.

FORT FISHER

Maj. Gen. William Henry Chase Whiting,
observer, adviser, combatant

Col. William Lamb,
36th Regiment North Carolina Troops (2nd North Carolina Artillery), commander

1st Battalion North Carolina Heavy Artillery (Co. D)
Capt. James L. McCormic

1st Battalion North Carolina Junior Reserves (Cos A, B, C)
Maj. D. T. Millard

3rd Battalion North Carolina Heavy Artillery Co. C (Sutton's Battery)
Capt. John M. Sutton

4th Battalion North Carolina Junior Reserves (Cos. A, B, C, D)
Maj. John M. Reece

7th Battalion North Carolina Junior Reserves (Cos. A, B, C)
Maj. William F. French

8th Battalion North Carolina Junior Reserves (Cos. A, B, C)
Maj. James Ellington
10th North Carolina Troops (1st North Carolina Artillery)
Maj. James Reilly, commander

Co. F   Capt. Edward D. Walsh
Co. K (Shaw's Company)   Capt. William Shaw, Jr.

13th Battalion North Carolina Artillery
Co. D   Capt. Zachariah T. Adams

36th Regiment North Carolina Troops (2nd North Carolina Artillery)
Col. William Lamb, commander
3rd Co. B (Bladen Stars): Capt. Daniel Munn
Co. E (Powell's Artillery): Capt. Oliver Powell
Co. F (Hunter's Company): Capt. Samuel B. Hunter
Co. H (Clarendon Guards): Capt. Daniel Patterson
Co. K (Brunswick Artillery): Capt. William Brooks

40th Regiment North Carolina Troops (3rd North Carolina Artillery)
Co. E (Scotch Greys): Capt. Malcomb McBride
2nd Co. K (Bladen Artillery Guards): Capt. Daniel James Clark

Detachment of C. S. Navy
Lt. Robert T. Chapman

Detachment of C. S. Marines
Capt. A. C. Van Benthuysen

WILMINGTON

Maj. Gen. Theophilus Hunter Holmes, post commandant

6th Battalion North Carolina Troops (Fayetteville Armory Guards)
Cos. A, B, C, D, E, F, G Lt. Col. F. L. Childs

Hahr's Battalion North Carolina Infantry
Maj. Franz J. Hahr

Capt. Henry P. Allen's Company North Carolina Local Defense Troops

Bass' (unattached) Company

Capt. E. D. Sneed's Company North Carolina Local Defense Troops

Detachment of C. S. Engineers and Coast Guard

SUGAR LOAF

Hoke's Division, Maj. Gen. Robert Frederick Hoke

Hagood's Brigade, Brig. Gen. Johnson Hagood
7th Battalion South Carolina Infantry Lt. James H. Rion
11th South Carolina Infantry Col. F. Hay Gantt
21st South Carolina Infantry Col. Robert F. Graham
25th South Carolina Infantry Capt. James Carson
27th South Carolina Infantry

Kirkland's Brigade, Brig. Gen. William W. Kirkland
17th North Carolina Infantry Lt. Col. Thomas Sharp
42nd North Carolina Infantry Col. John E. Brown
66th North Carolina Infantry Col. John H. Nethercutt
10th Regiment North Carolina Troops (1st North Carolina Artillery)
Lt. Col. John P. W. Read, commander

2nd Co. I (Southerland's Battery) Capt. Thomas J. Southerland
Staunton Hill Artillery (Paris' Battery) Capt. Andrew B. Paris

Connally's Brigade of North Carolina Reserves Col. John K. Connally
4th Battalion North Carolina Junior Reserves
Cos. A, B, C, D Maj. John M. Reece
7th Battalion North Carolina Junior Reserves
Cos. A ,B, C Maj. William F. French
8th Battalion North Carolina Junior Reserves
Cos. A, B, C Maj. James Ellington
8th North Carolina Senior Reserves
Cos. B, C, D, E, FCol. Allmond McKoy

FORT ANDERSON

40th Regiment North Carolina Troops (3rd North Carolina Artillery)
Co. A (Lenoir Braves) Capt. Ancram W. Ezzell

FORT PENDER, SMITHVILLE

3rd Battalion North Carolina Light Artillery
Co. A (Northampton Artillery) Capt. Andrew J. Ellis

FORT CASWELL, OAK ISLAND

36th Regiment North Carolina Troops (2nd North Carolina Artillery)

Lt. Col. John Douglas Taylor, commander
1st Battalion North Carolina Heavy Artillery
Co. A (Clark Artillery) Capt. Robert G. Rankin
Co. C (Brown's Battalion) Capt. William H. Brown
Capt. Abner A. Moseley's Company (Sampson Artillery)

FORT CAMPBELL, OAK ISLAND

Col. John J. Hedrick, commander
1st Battalion North Carolina Heavy Artillery
Co. B (River Guards)Capt. John W. Taylor
40th Regiment North Carolina Troops (3rd North Carolina Artillery)
Co. F Capt. John C. Robertson

FEDERAL FORCES

United States Army, Department of Virginia and North Carolina,
Fort Fisher Expeditionary Force, Maj. Gen. Benjamin F. Butler and
Maj. Gen. Godfrey Weitzel, commanders

XXIV Army Corps

Second Division Brig. Gen. Adelbert Ames

First Brigade Bvt. Brig. Gen. N. Martin Curtis
3rd New York Infantry Capt. George W. Warren
112th New York Infantry Lt. Col. John W. Smith
117th New York Infantry Col. Rufus Daggett
142nd New York Infantry Col. Albert M. Barney

Second Brigade   Col. Galusha Pennypacker
47th New York Infantry Capt. Joseph P. McDonald
48th New York Infantry Lt. Col. William B. Coan
76th Pennsylvania Infantry Col. John S. Littell
97th Pennsylvania Infantry Lt. John Wainwright
203rd Pennsylvania Infantry Col. John W. Moore

Third Brigade Col. Louis Bell
13th Indiana InfantryCapt. Samuel M. Zent
4th New Hampshire Infantry Capt. John H. Roberts
115th New York Infantry Maj. Ezra L. Walrath
169th New York Infantry Col. Alonzo Alden
Artillery Brigade Capt. Richard H. Lee

16th New York Independent Battery Light Artillery

XXV Army Corps

Third Division, Brig. Gen. Charles J. Paine

Second Brigade, Col. John W. Ames
4th U. S. Colored Troops Lt. Col. George Rogers
6th U. S. Colored Troops Lt. Col. Clark Royce
30th U. S. Colored Troops Lt. Col. Hiram A. Oakman
39th U. S. Colored Troops Col. Ozora P. Stearns

Third Brigade, Col. Elias Wright
1st U. S. Colored Troops Lt. Col. Giles H. Rich
5th U. S. Colored Troops Col. Giles W. Shurtleff
10th U. S. Colored Troops Lt. Col. Edward H. Powell
37th U. S. Colored Troops Col. Nathan Goff, Jr.
107th U. S. Colored Troops Lt. Col. David M. Sells

Artillery Brigade
3rd U. S., Regular Army, Battery ELt. John Myrick

United States Navy, North Atlantic Blockading Squadron, Fort Fisher Task Force, Rear
Admiral David D. Porter, commanding fleet

Vessel / Guns / Commanding Officer

Line No. 1
Canonicus / 2 guns / Lt. Cmdr. George Balknap
Huron / 5 guns / Lt. Cmdr. Thomas O. Selfridge
Kansas / 8 guns / Lt. Cmdr. Pendleton G. Watmough
Mahopac / 2 guns / Lt. Cmdr. Edward Potter
Monadnock / 4 guns / Cmdr. Enoch G. Parrott
Neurus / 9 guns / Cmdr. John C. Howell
New Ironsides / 20 guns / Cmdr. William Radford
Nyack / 8 guns / Lt. Cmdr. L. Howard Newman
Pequot / 8 guns / Lt. Cmdr. Daniel L. Braine
Pontoosuc / 12 guns / Lt. Cmdr. William G. Temple
Saugus / 2 guns / Cmdr. Edmund R. Calhoun
Unadilla / 6 guns / Lt. Cmdr. Frank M. Ramsay

Line No. 2
Bigonia / 3 guns / Acting Vol. Lt. Warrington D. Roath
Brooklyn / 26 guns / Capt. James Alden

Colorado / 50 guns / Commodore Henry K. Thatcher
Fort Donelson / 1 gun / Capt. Charles W. Pickering
Juanita / 14 guns / Capt. William Rogers Taylor
Mackinaw / 10 guns / Cmdr. John C. Beaumont
Maumee / 8 guns / Lt. Cmdr. Ralph Chandler
Minnesota / 46 guns / Commodore Joseph Lanman
Mohican / 9 guns / Cmdrm Daniel Ammen
Pawtuxet / 10 guns / Cmdr. James H. Spotts
Powhatan / 24 guns / Commodore James F. Schenck
Seneca / 5 guns / Lt. Cmdr. Montgomery Sicard
Shenandoah / 6 guns / Capt. Daniel B. Ridgley
Susquehanna / 18 guns / Commodore Sylvanus W. Godon
Ticonderoga / 14 guns / Capt. Charles Steedman
Tuscarora / 10 guns / Cmdr. James M. Frailey
Vanderbilt / 16 guns / Capt. Charles W. Pickering
Wabash / 44 guns / Capt. Melancton Smith
Yantic / 5 guns / Lt. Cmdr. Thomas Harris

Line No. 3
Chippewa / 6 guns / Lt. Cmdr. Aaron Weaver
Fort Jackson / 11 guns / Capt. Banjamin F. Sands
Iosco / 10 guns / Cmdr. John Guest
Monticello / 6 guns / Acting Vol. Lt. Daniel A. Campbell
Osceola / 10 guns / Cmdr. J. M. B. Clitz
Quaker City / 7 guns / Cmdr. William F. Spicer
Rhode Island / 12 guns / Cmdr. Stephen D. Trenchard
Santiago de Cuba / 11 guns / Capt. Oliver S. Glisson
Sassacus / 12 guns / Lt. Cmdr. John L. Davis
Tacony / 12 guns / Lt. Cmdr. William T. Truxton

Reserves
A. D. Vance / 5 guns / Lt. Cmdr. John H. Upshur
Aires / 7 guns / Acting Vol. Lt. Francis S. Wells
Alabama / 10 guns / Acting Vol. Lt. Frank Smith
Anemone / 4 guns / Acting Ensign William C. Borden
Banshee / 3 guns / Acting Vol. Lt. W. H. Garfield
Britannia / 6 guns / Acting Vol. Lt. Samuel Huse
Cherokee / 6 guns / Acting Vol. Lt. William E. Dennison
Emma / 8 guns / Acting Vol. Lt. Thomas C. Dunn
Eolus / 4 guns / Acting Mstr. Edward S. Keyser
Gettysburg / 7 guns / Lt. R. H. Lamson
Gov. Buckingham / 6 guns / Acting Vol. Lt. J. MacDiarmid
Howquah / 5 guns / Acting Vol. Lt. John W. Balch
Keystone State / 6 guns / Cmdr. Henry Rolando

Lillian / 2 guns / Acting Vol. Lt. T. A. Harris
Little Ada / 2 guns / Acting Mstr. Samuel P. Crafts
Malvern / 12 guns / Lt. Cmdr. Benjamin H. Porter
Maratanza / 6 guns / Lt. Cmdr. George Young
Moccasin / 3 guns / Acting Ensign James Brown
Montgomery / 6 guns / Acting Vol. Lt. Edward H. Faucon
Nansemond / 3 guns / Acting Mstr. James H. Porter
R.R. Cuyler / 12 guns / Cmdr. Charles H. B. Caldwell
Tristram Shandy / 4 guns / Acting Vol. Lt. Edward F. Devens
Wilderness / 4 guns / Acting Mstr. Henry Arey

SECOND FORT FISHER, JANUARY 13-15, 1865

Confederate States Army, Department of North Carolina, Third Military District (District of the Cape Fear), Maj. Gen. Braxton Bragg, commander.

FORT FISHER

Maj. Gen. William Henry Chase Whiting,
adviser, volunteer, combatant

Col. William Lamb,
36th Regiment North Carolina Troops (2nd North Carolina Artillery),
commander

1st Battaltion North Carolina Heavy Artillery
Co. D Capt. James L. McCormic

3rd Battalion, North Carolina Artillery
Co. C (Sutton's Battery) Capt. John M. Sutton

10th Regiment North Carolina Troops (1st North Carolina Artillery)
Maj. James Reilly, commander
Co. F Capt. Edward D. Walsh
Co. K (Shaw's Battery) Capt. William Shaw, Jr.

13th Battalion North Carolina Artillery
Co. D Capt. Zachariah T. Adams

36th North Carolina Troops (2nd North Carolina Artillery)
Col. William Lamb, commander
2nd Co. A (Murphy's Battery) Capt. Robert Murphy
3rd Co. B (Bladen Stars) Capt. Daniel Munn

2nd Co. C (Braddy's Battery)   Capt. Kinchen Braddy
2nd Co. D (Anderson Artillery) Capt. Edward Dudley
Co. E (Powell's Artillery) Capt. Oliver Powell
Co. F (Hunter's Company)   Acting Capt. Exum Lewis Hunter
3rd Co. G (Russell's Battery) Lt. William Swain
Co. H (Clarendon Guards)   Capt. Daniel Patterson
2nd Co. I (Bladen Artillery)   Capt. John T. Melvin
Co. K (Brunswick Artillery)Capt. William Brooks

40th Regiment North Carolina Troops (3rd North Carolina Artillery)
Co. D (Bay River Artillery)Capt. James Lane
Co. E (Scotch Greys)   Capt. Malcomb H. McBryde
3rd Co. G Capt. George Buchan
2nd Co. K (Bladen Artillery Guards) Capt. Daniel James Clark

Detachment of C.S. Navy: Capt. Robert T. Chapman

Detachment of C.S. Marines: Capt. A. C. Van Benthuysen

Johnson Hagood's Brigade
11th South Carolina Infantry (detachment)
21st South Carolina Infantry (detachment) Capt. D. G. DuBose
25th South Carolina Infantry (detachment) Capt. James Carson

SUGAR LOAF

Hoke's Division, Maj. Gen. Robert F. Hoke

Clingman's Brigade Col. Hector McKethan
8th North Carolina Infantry Lt. Col. Rufus A. Barrier
31st North Carolina InfantryLt. Col. Charles Knight
51st North Carolina InfantryCapt. James W. Lippitt
61st North Carolina InfantryCol. William S. Devane

Colquitt's Brigade   Brig. Gen. Alfred H. Colquitt
6th Georgia InfantryCol. John T. Lofton
19th Georgia Infantry Col. James H. Neal
23rd Georgia Infantry Col. Marcus R. Ballenger
27th Georgia Infantry Capt. Elisha D. Graham
28th Georgia Infantry Capt. John A. Johnson

Hagood's BrigadeCol. Robert F. Graham
7th Battalion South Carolina Infantry Lt. Col. James H. Rion
11th South Carolina Infantry   Col. F. Hay Gantt

21st South Carolina Infantry
25th South Carolina Infantry
27th South Carolina Infantry

Kirkland's Brigade Brig. Gen. William W. Kirkland
17th North Carolina Infantry Lt. Col. Thomas H. Sharp
42nd North Carolina Infantry Col. John E. Brown
66th North Carolina Infantry Col. John H. Nethercutt
2nd South Carolina Cavalry Col. Thomas J. Lipscomb

3rd Battalion North Carolina Light Artillery
Co. A (Northampton Artillery) Capt. Andrew J. Ellis

10th Regiment North Carolina Troops (1st North Carolina Artillery)
2nd Co. I (Southerland's Battery) Capt. Thomas Southerland

Staunton Hill Artillery (Paris' Battery) Capt. Andrew B. Paris

FEDERAL FORCES

United States Army, Department of Virginia and North Carolina, Terry's Provisional
Corps, Bvt. Maj. Gen. Alfred H. Terry, commander

XXIV Army Corps
First Division

Second Brigade, Col. Joseph C. Abbott
6th Connecticut Infantry Col. Alfred P. Rockwell
7th Connecticut Infantry Capt. John Thompson
Capt. William S. Marble
3rd New Hampshire Infantry Capt. William H. Trickey
7th New Hampshire Infantry Lt. Col. Augustis W. Rollins

16th New York Heavy Artillery
Cos. A, B, C, F, G, K Maj. Frederick W. Prince

Second Division, Brig. Gen. Adelbert Ames

First Brigade, Bvt. Brig. Gen. N. Martin Curtis
Maj. Ezra L. Walrath
3rd New York InfantryCapt. James H. Reeve
Lt. Edwin A. Behan

112th New York Infantry Col. John F. Smith
117th New York Infantry Lt. Col. Francis X. Meyer
142nd New York Infantry Lt. Col. Albert M. Barney

Second Brigade, Col. Galusha Pennypacker
Maj. Oliver P. Harding
47th New York Infantry Capt. Joseph M. McDonald
48th New York Infantry Lt. Col. William B. Coan
Maj. Nere A. Elfwing
76th Pennsylvania Infantry Col. John S. Littell
97th Pennsylvania Infantry Lt. John Wainwright
203rd Pennsylvania Infantry Col. John W. Moore
Lt. Col. Jonas W. Lyman
Maj. Oliver P. Harding
Capt. Heber B. Essington

Third Brigade, Col. Louis Bell
Col. Alonzo Alden
13th Indiana Infantry Lt. Col. Samuel M. Zent
4th New Hampshire Infantry Capt. John H. Roberts
115th New York Infantry Lt. Col. Nathan J. Johnson
169th New York Infantry Col. Alonzo Alden
Lt. Col. James A. Colvin

Artillery Brigade, Capt. Richard H. Lee
16th New York Independent Battery Light Artillery

XXV Army Corps

Third Division, Brig. Gen. Charles J. Paine

Second Brigade, Col. John W. Ames
4th U. S. Colored Troops Lt. Col. George Rogers
6th U. S. Colored Troops Maj. Augustis S. Boernstein
30th U. S. Colored Troops Lt. Col. Hiram A. Oakman
39th U. S. Colored Troops Col. Ozora P. Stearns

Third Brigade, Col. Elias Wright
1st U. S. Colored Troops Lt. Col. Giles H. Rich
5th U. S. Colored Troops Maj. William R. Brazie
10th U. S. Colored Troops Lt. Col. Edward H. Powell
27th U. S. Colored Troops Col. Albert M. Blackman
37th U. S. Colored Troops Col. Nathan Goff, Jr.

Artillery Brigade
3rd U. S., Regular Army, Battery E   Lt. John Myrick
Artillery Bvt. Brig. Gen. Henry L. Abbot
1st Connecticut Heavy Artillery
Cos. B, G, L   Capt. William G. Pride

Engineers
15th New York
Cos. A, I (or A, B, H)   Lt. K. Samuel O'Keefe

United States Navy, North Atlantic Blockading Squadron, Cape Fear Task Force, Rear
Admiral David D. Porter, commanding fleet

Vessel / Guns / Commanding Officer

Line No. 1
Brooklyn / 26 guns / Capt. James Alden
Canonicus / 2 guns / Lt. Cmdr. George Belknap
Huron / 5 guns / Lt. Cmdr. Thomas O. Selfridge
Kansas / 8 guns / Lt. Cmdr. Pendleton G. Watmough
Mahopac / 2 guns / Lt. Cmdr. Edward Potter
Maumee / 8 guns / Lt. Cmdr. Ralph Chandler
Mohican / 9 guns / Cmdr. Daniel Ammen
Monadnock / 4 guns / Cmdr. Enoch G. Parrott
New Ironsides / 20 guns / Cmdr. William Radford
Pawtuxet / 10 guns / Cmdr. James H. Spotts
Pequot / 8 guns / Lt. Cmdr. Daniel Braine
Pontoosuc / 12 guns / Lt. Cmdr. William G. Temple
Saugus / 2 guns / Cmdr. Edmund R. Colhoun
Seneca / 5 guns / Lt. Cmdr. Montgomery Sicard
Tacony / 12 guns / Lt. Cmdr. William T. Truxton
Unadilla / 6 guns / Lt. Cmdr. Frank M. Ramsay
Yantic / 5 guns / Lt. Cmdr. Thomas C. Harris

Line No. 2
Colorado / 50 guns / Commodore Henry K. Thatcher
Juanita / 14 guns / Capt. William Rogers Taylor
Mackinaw / 10 guns / Cmdr. John C. Beaumont
Minnesota / 46 guns / Commodore Joseph Lanman
Powhatan / 24 guns / Commodore James F. Schenck
Shenandoah / 6 guns / Capt. Daniel B. Ridgley
Susquehanna / 18 guns / Commodore Sylvanus W. Godon
Ticonderoga / 14 guns / Capt. Charles Steedman

Tuscarora / 10 guns / Cmdr. James M. Frailey
Vanderbilt / 16 guns / Capt. Charles W. Pickering
Wabash / 44 guns / Capt. Melancton Smith
Line No. 3
Chippewa / 6 guns / Lt. Cmdr. Aaron Weaver
Fort Jackson / 11 guns / Capt. Benjamin F. Sands
Iosco / 10 guns / Cmdr. John Guest
Maratanza / 6 guns / Lt. Cmdr. George Young
Montgomery / 6 guns / Acting Vol. Lt. Thomas C. Dunn
Monticello / 6 guns / Lt. Cmdr. William B. Cushing
Osceola / 10 guns / Cmdr. J. M. B. Clitz
Quaker City / 7 guns / Cmdr. William F. Spicer
R.R. Cuyler / 12 guns / Cmdr. Charles H. B. Caldwell
Rhode Island / 12 guns / Cmdr. Stephen D. Trenchard
Santiago de Cuba / 11 guns / Capt. Oliver S. Glisson
Sassacus / 12 guns / Lt. Cmdr. John L. Davis

Reserves
A.D. Vance / 5 guns / Lt. Cmdr. John H. Upshur
Alabama / 10 guns / Acting Vol. Lt. Amos R. Langthorne
Aries / 7 guns / Acting Vol. Lt. Francis S. Wells
Britannia / 6 guns / Acting Vol. Lt. William B. Sheldon
Cherokee / 6 guns / Acting Vol. Lt. William E. Dennison
Emma / 8 guns / Acting Vol. Lt. James M. Williams
Eolus / 4 guns / Acting Mstr. Edward S. Keyser
Fort Donelson / 1 gun / Acting Mstr. George W. Frost
Gettysburg / 7 guns / Lt. R. H. Lamsom
Gov Buckingham / 6 guns / Acting Vol. Lt. J. MacDiarmid
Launch No. 6 / 1 gun / Gunner Hubert Peters
Lillian / 2 guns / Acting Vol. Lt. T. A. Harris
Little Ada / 2 guns / Acting Mstr. Samuel P. Crafts
Malvern / 12 guns / Lt. Cmdr. Benjamin H. Porter
Nansemond / 3 guns / Acting Mstr. James H. Porter
Republic / 1 gun / Acting Mstr. John W. Bennett
Tristram Shandy / 4 guns / Acting Vol. Lt. Edward F. Devens
Wilderness / 4 guns / Acting Mstr. Henry Arey

U.S. Army Transports
Atlantic, Blackstone, California, Champion, Charles Leary, Commodore DuPont, De Molay, Euterpe, General Lyon, Governor Chase, Idaho, L. C. Livingston, McClellan, Montauk, North Point, Prometheus, Russia, Thames, Thomas, R. Scott, Tonawanda, Varuna, Weybossett

WILMINGTON CAMPAIGN, FEBRUARY 11-22, 1865

Confederate States Army, Department of North Carolina, Third Military District District of the Cape Fear), Maj. Gen. Braxton Bragg, commander.

SUGAR LOAF

Hoke's Division, Maj. Gen. Robert F. Hoke

Clingman's Brigade, Col. William S. Devane
8th North Carolina Infantry Lt. Col. Rufus A. Barrier
31st North Carolina Infantry Lt. Col. Charles W. Knight
51st North Carolina Infantry Capt. James W. Lippit
61st North Carolina Infantry

Colquitt's Brigade, Col. Charles T. Zachry
6th Georgia Infantry Lt. Col. Sampson W. Harris
19th Georgia Infantry Col. James H. Neal
23rd Georgia Infantry Col. Marcus R. Ballenger
27th Georgia Infantry Capt. Elisha D. Graham ?
28th Georgia Infantry Capt. John A. Johnson ?

Kirkland's Brigade, Brig. Gen. William W. Kirkland
17th North Carolina Infantry Lt. Col. Thomas H. Sharp
42nd North Carolina Infantry Col. John E. Brown
66th North Carolina Infantry Col. John E. Nethercutt

Artillery
3rd Battalion North Carolina Light Artillery
Co. A (Northhampton Artillery) Capt. Andrew J. Ellis
Co. C (detachment) Lt. Alfred M. Darden

10th Regiment North Carolina Troops (1st North Carolina Artillery)
2nd Co. I (Southerland's Battery) Capt. Thomas J. Southerland
Staunton Hill Battery (Paris' Battery) Capt Andrew B. Paris

Cavalry
2nd South Carolina Cavalry (detachment) Col. Thomas J. Lipscomb

FORT ANDERSON

Hagood's Brigade, Brig. Gen. Johnson Hagood
7th Battalion South Carolina Infantry Lt. Col. James H. Rion
11th South Carolina Infantry Col. F. Hay Gantt

21st South Carolina Infantry (remnants) Col. Robert F. Graham
25th South Carolina Infantry (remnants) Col. Charles H. Simonton
27th South Carolina Infantry Capt. Allston

Artillery
3rd Battalion North Carolina Light Artillery
Co. B Capt. William Badham, Jr.
Capt. Abner A. Moseley's Company (Sampson Artillery)

Hedrick's Brigade Col. John J. Hedrick
40th Regiment North Carolina Troops (3rd North Carolina Artillery)
Maj. William Holland, commander
Co. A (Lenoir Braves) Capt. Ancram W. Ezzell
Co. B (McMillan Artillery) Lt. Macon Bonner
Lt. Selby Harden
Co. C (Bridger's Artillery) Capt. John E. Leggett
Co. F Capt. John Robertson
2nd Co. H (Barnes' Battery) Capt. Calvin Barnes
Co. I Capt. Charles C. Whitehurst Taylor's Battery
36th Regiment North Carolina Troops (2nd North Carolina Artillery) (remnants)
Lt. Col. John Douglas Taylor
1st Battalion North Carolina Heavy Artillery
Co. A (Clark Artillery) Capt. Robert G. Rankin
Co. B (River Guards) Capt. John W. Taylor
Co. C (Brown's Battalion) Capt. William H. Brown
Co. D (remnants) Lt. John T. Rankin
71st Regiment North Carolina Troops (2nd North Carolina JuniorReserves), Co. B
Capt. W. J. McDougald's Unattached Company North Carolina Troops
Coast Guard Company (unattached)

Cavalry
2nd South Carolina Cavalry (detachment) Col. Thomas J. Lipscomb

WILMINGTON

Col. George Jackson, post commandant

Armory Guards
Co. B Capt. Armand L. DeRosset
7th Regiment Home Guard Col. James G. Burr (Cos. A, B)
8th North Carolina Senior Reserves Col. Allmand M. McKoy

Engineers
2nd Engineers Co. A Capt. John C. Winder

Signal Corps Lt. George C. Bain

Cape Fear River batteries (Forts Davis, Lee, Campbell, Meares)
Col. Peter C. Gaillard, commander

13th Battalion North Carolina Light/Heavy Artillery
Co. D (Adams' Battery) Lt. Samuel H. Forbes ?
68th North Carolina Troops, Co. C (detachment)
McDougald's Company (detachment) Capt. W. J. McDougald

Naval detachment

FEDERAL FORCES

United States Army, Department of North Carolina, Wilmington Expeditionary Force,
Major General John M. Schofield, commander

XXIII Army Corps

Second Division

Second Brigade, Col. Orlando Moore
107th Illinois Infantry Maj. Thomas J. Milholland
80th Indiana Infantry Lt. Col. Alfred D. Owen
26th Kentucky Infantry (100 men from First Brigade)
23rd Michigan Infantry Col. Oliver L. Spaulding
111th Ohio Infantry Lt. Issac R. Sherwood
118th Ohio Infantry Lt. Col. Edgar Sowers

Third Division Maj. Gen. Jacob D. Cox

First Brigade, Col. Oscar W. Sterl
12th Kentucky Infantry Lt. Col. Laurence Rousseau
16th Kentucky Infantry Lt. Col. John S. White
100th Ohio Infantry Capt. Frank Rundell
104th Ohio Infantry Lt. Col. William J. Jordan
8th Tennessee Infantry Capt. James W. Berry

Second Brigade, Col. John S. Casement
65th Illinois Infantry Maj. George H. Kennedy
Lt. Col. William S. Stewart
65th Indiana Infantry Lt. Col. John W. Hammond
103rd Ohio Infantry Capt. Henry S. Pickands

177th Ohio Infantry Col. Arthur T. Wilcox
5th Tennessee Infantry Lt. Col. Nathaniel Witt

Third Brigade, Col. Thomas J. Henderson
112th Illinois Infantry Lt. Col. Emery S. Bond
63rd Indiana Infantry Lt. Col. Daniel Morris
140th Indiana Infantry Col. Thomas J. Brady

Artillery
1st Ohio Light Artillery
Battery D Lt. Cecil C. Reed
Signal Corps (detachment) Lt. E. H. Russell

Terry's Provisional Corps
Maj. Gen. Alfred H. Terry
XXIV Army Corps

First Division

Second Brigade, Bvt. Brig. Gen. Joseph C. Abbott
6th Connecticut Infantry Lt. Col. Daniel Klein
7th Connecticut Infantry Lt. Col. Seager S. Atwell
3rd New Hampshire Infantry Capt. William H. Trickey
Lt. Col. James F. Randlett
7th New Hampshire Infantry Lt. Col. Augustus W. Rollins
16th New York Heavy Artillery
Cos. A, B, C, F, G, K, Lt. Freeman Huntington

Second Division Bvt. Maj. Gen. Adelbert Ames

First Brigade, Col. Rufus Daggett
3rd New York Infantry Lt. George E. Avent
112th New York Infantry Lt. Col. Ephraim A. Ludwick
117th New York Infantry Capt. Edward Downer
142nd New York Infantry Lt. Col. Albert M. Barney

Second Brigade Lt. Col. James A. Colvin
47th New York Infantry Capt. Joseph M. McDonald
Capt. Frank A. Butts
48th New York Infantry Maj. Nere A. Elfwing
Capt. Van Rensselaer Hilliard
76th Pennsylvania Infantry Maj. Charles Knerr
97th Pennsylvania Infantry Maj. William H. Martin
203rd Pennsylvania Infantry Capt. Heber B. Essington

Lt. Col. Amos W. Bachman

Third Brigade Col. Frank Granger
13th Indiana Infantry Lt. Col. Samuel M. Zent
9th Maine Infantry Lt. Col. Joseph Noble
4th New Hampshire Infantry Capt. John H. Roberts
Lt. Col. Frank Parker
115th New York Infantry Maj. Ezra Walrath
Lt. Col. Nathan J. Johnson
169th New York Infantry Lt. Col. James A. Colvin
Capt. Edwin R. Smith

Artillery
1st Connecticut Heavy Artillery
Cos. B, G, L Capt. William Pride
16th New York Independent Battery Light Artillery
Capt. Richard H. Lee
2nd Pennsylvania Heavy Artillery
Co. A Capt. Benjamin F. Everett

Engineers
15th New York Engineers
Cos. A, I Lt. Keefe S. O'Keefe

XXV Army Corps
Brig. Gen. Charles J. Paine

Third Division

Second Brigade, Col. John W. Ames
4th U. S. Colored Troops Lt. Col. George Rogers
6th U. S. Colored Troops Maj. Augustus S. Boernstein
30th U. S. Colored TroopsLt. Colonel Hiram Oakman
39th U. S. Colored TroopsCol. Ozora P. Stearns

Third Brigade, Col. Elias Wright
1st U. S. Colored Troops Lt. Col. Giles H. Rich
5th U. S. Colored Troops Maj. William R. Brazie
10th U. S. Colored Troops Lt. Col. Edward Powell
27th U. S. Colored Troops Bvt. Brig. Gen. Albert Blackman
Lt. Col. John Donnellan
37th U. S. Colored TroopsCol. Nathan Goff, Jr.

Artillery
3rd U. S., Regular Army, Battery E Lt. John Myrick

Disposition of United States Navy vessels near Wilmington, North Carolina, February 1, 1865, Rear Admiral David D. Porter, commanding

CAPE FEAR RIVER

Vessel / Guns / Commanding Officer

Berberry / 4 guns / Acting Ensign Robert W. Rowntree
Chippewa / 6 guns / Lt. Cmdr. Aaron Weaver
Eolus / 4 guns / Acting Mstr. Edward S. Keyser
Gettysburg / 7 guns / Acting Mstr. Charles B. Dahlgren
Huron / 5 guns / Lt. Cmdr. Thomas O. Selfridge
Iosco / 10 guns / Cmdr. John Guest
Kansas / 8 guns / Lt. Cmdr. Pendleton G. Watmough
Launch # 6 / 1 gun / Gunner Hubert Peters
Lenapee / 10 guns / Lt. Cmdr. Samuel Magaw
Little Ada / 2 guns / Acting Mstr. Samuel P. Crafts
Mackinaw / 10 guns / Cmdr. John C. Beaumont
Malvern / 12 guns / Ensign William C. Wise
Maumee / 3 guns / Lt. Cmdr. Ralph Chandler
Moccasin / 3 guns / Acting Ensign James Brown
Montauk / 2 guns / Lt. Cmdr. Edward Stone
Nansemond / 3 guns / Acting Mstr. James H. Porter
Nyack / 8 guns / Lt. Cmdr. L. Howard Newman
Osceola / 10 guns / Cmdr. J. M. B. Clitz
Pawtuxet / 10 guns / Cmdr. James H. Spotts
Pequot / 3 guns / Lt. Cmdr. Daniel Braine
Pontoosuc / 12 guns / Lt. Cmdr. William Temple
Republic / 1 gun / Acting Ensign John W. Bennett
Sassacus / 12 guns / Lt. Cmdr. John L. Davis
Seneca / 5 guns / Lt. Cmdr. Montgomery Sicard
Shawmut / 8 guns / Lt. Cmdr. John G. Walker
Tacony / 12 guns / Lt. Cmdr. William T. Truxton
Unadilla / 6 guns / Lt. Cmdr. Frank M. Ramsay
Wilderness / 4 guns / Acting Mstr. Henry Arey
Yantic / 5 guns / Lt. Cmdr. Thomas C. Harris

NEW INLET / FORT FISHER

Aries / 7 guns / Acting Vol. Lt. James M. Williams

Emma / 8 guns / Acting Mstr. James Hamilton
Fahkee / 5 guns / Acting Mstr. Francis R. Webb
Fort Donelson / 1 gun / Acting Mstr. George W. Frost
Gov Buckingham / 6 guns / Acting Vol. Lt. J. MacDiarmid
Howquah / 5 guns / Acting Vol. Lt. John W. Balch
Keystone State / 6 guns / Cmdr. Henry Rolando
Montgomery / 6 guns / Acting Vol. Lt. Thomas C. Dunn
Vicksburg / 6 guns / Lt. William U. Grozier

OLD INLET / SMITHVILLE

Bat / 3 guns / Lt. Cmdr. John S. Barnes
Maratanza / 6 guns / Lt. Cmdr. George Young
Monticello / 6 guns / Lt. Cmdr. William B. Cushing
R.R. Cuyler / 12 guns / Cmdr. Charles H. B. Caldwell

Disposition of United States Navy vessels near Wilmington, North Carolina, February 15, 1865, Rear Admiral David D. Porter, commanding

CAPE FEAR RIVER

Vessel / Guns / Commanding Officer

Bat / 3 guns / Lt. Cmdr. John S. Barnes
Berberry / 4 guns / Acting Ensign Robert W. Rowntree
Chippewa / 6 guns / Lt. Cmdr. Aaron Weaver
Emma / 8 guns / Acting Mstr. James Hamilton
Eolus / 4 guns / Acting Mstr. Edward S. Keyser
Huron / 5 guns / Lt. Cmdr. Thomas O. Selfridge
Kansas / 8 guns / Lt. Cmdr. Pendleton G. Watmough
Launch # 1 / 1 gun
Launch # 6 / 1 gun / Acting Ensign C. S. Willcox
Lenapee / 10 guns / Lt. Cmdr. John S. Barnes
Little Ada / 2 guns / Acting Mstr. Samuel P. Crafts
Mackinaw / 10 guns / Cmdr. John C. Beaumont
Malvern / 12 guns / Ensign William C. Wise
Maratanza / 6 guns / Lt. Cmdr. George Young
Maumee / 3 guns / Lt. Cmdr. Ralph Chandler
Moccasin / 3 guns / Acting Ensign James Brown
Montauk / 2 guns / Lt. Cmdr. Edward Stone
Nansemond / 3 guns / Acting Mstr. James H. Porter
Nyack / 8 guns / Lt. Cmdr. L. Howard Newman
Osceola / 10 guns / Cmdr. J. B. M. Clitz
Pawtuxet / 10 guns / Cmdr. James H. Spotts

Pequot / 8 guns / Lt. Cmdr. Daniel Braine
Pontoosuc / 12 guns / Lt. Cmdr. William G. Temple
Republic / 1 gun / Acting Ensign John W. Bennett
Sassacus / 12 guns / Lt. Cmdr. John L. Davis
Seneca / 5 guns / Lt. Cmdr. Montgomery Sicard
Shawmut / 8 guns / Lt. Cmdr. John G. Walker
Unadilla / 6 guns / Lt. Cmdr. Frank M. Ramsay
Wilderness / 4 guns / Acting Mstr Henry Arey
Yantic / 5 guns / Lt. Cmdr. Thomas C. Harris

NEW INLET / FORT FISHER

Aries / 7 guns / Acting Vol. Lt. James M. Williams
Howquah / 5 guns / Acting Vol. Lt. John W. Balch
Keystone State / 6 guns / Cmdr. Henry Rolando
Montgomery / 6 guns / Acting Vol. Lt. Thomas C. Dunn
Monticello / 6 guns / Lt. Cmdr. William B. Cushing
R.R. Cuyler / 12 guns / Cmdr. Charles H. B. Caldwell
Vicksburg / 6 guns / Acting Mstr. William Grozier

Abatis: rows of felled trees or large branches sometimes sharpened to a point and employed for defense.

Barbette: guns are said to be "en barbette" when they are elevated, usually on a high carriage, for firing over a parapet.

Battery: a battery consists of two or more pieces of field artillery. The term battery also implies the emplacement of artillery for offensive or defensive purposes.

Blockade Runner: Confederate vessels and those of neutral nations, mainly British, employed in the profitable though risky violation of trading goods through the Federal blockade of Southern ports. The term also applies to captains, crew, shippers, and agents engaged in blockade running.

Breastwork : hastily constructed earthwork generally for temporary use.

Canister: field artillery canister consisted of a tin cylinder attached to a sabot and filled with small cast-iron or lead shot.

Casemate: vaulted chamber with embrasures for guns.

Curtain: part of a rampart joining batteries, bastions or flanks.

Demilune: a two-face work to cover the curtain and shoulders of a bastion.

Demonstrate: a show of force without an actual attack.

Ditch: excavation around a fortification.

Enfilade: to sweep the whole length of a work or line of troops by artillery or small arms fire.

Entrenchment: ditch or trench with a parapet.

Envelop: to undertake an attack on one or both flanks or rear of the enemy.

Feint: limited attack or movement to mislead the enemy of the real objective.

Fieldworks: earthwork fortifications, generally stronger and more sophisticated than breastworks, built by troops in the field for temporary use (not necessarily garrisoned).

Flotilla: a group of warships smaller than a fleet acting in concert.

Forced march: long march of troops at a fast pace made necessary by an impending battle.

Fortification: consists of a mound of dirt called a *rampart* which encloses the body of the place, a *parapet* surmounting the rampart, and *traverses*, mounds higher than the parapet which cross the breadth of the covered way.

Obstacles: objects strategically placed so as to render access to a fortification more difficult.

Ordnance: artillery, cannon.

Ordnance stores: cannonballs, shot, shells, and artillery equipment.

Outwork: work constructed away from the main fortification.

Parapet: the crest of a rampart (see *Fortification*).

Postern: (see *Sally-port*).

Rampart: a mass of earth which protects a fortified place (see Fortification).

Ravelin: (see *Demilune*).

Reconnaissance in force: tentative or probing attack by a sizeable number of troops.

Redoubt: small work with two faces.

Revetment: the interior slope of a parapet.

Sally-port: opening cut into the face or wall of a fortification to allow access. When not in use, it was usually closed by a strong timber gate.

Traverse: mound of earth higher than the parapet which offer protection to gunners and gun chambers from enfilading fire along the line of a work (see *Fortification*).

Volley: simultaneous firing of their guns by a unit of soldiers.

Notes

1. J. C. Stevenson, "My Personal Experiences," copy in Leora H. McEachern and Isabel M. Williams Collection, Special Collections, Randall Library, University of North Carolina at Wilmington, hereinafter cited as Stevenson, "My Personal Experience," McEachern and Williams Collections, UNCW; Walter Clark, ed., *Histories of the Several Regiments and Battalions From North Carolina in the Great War 1861-'65*, 5 vols. (Wendell, 1982), vol. 5, p. 344, hereinafter cited as Clark, *North Carolina Regiments*.

2. *Wilmington Daily Journal*, September 7, 1863.

3. Daniel Harvey Hill, *Bethel to Sharpsburg*, 2 vols. (Wilmington, 1992), vol. 1, p. 371.

4. By the President of the United States of America—A Proclamation, April 19, 1861, and Proclamation of the President of the United States regarding extension of blockade to the ports of Virginia and North Carolina, April 27, 1861, *Official Records of the Union and Confederate Navies in the War of the Rebellion*, 30 vols. (Washington, D. C., 1900), series 1, vol. 4, pp. 156-157 and 340, hereinafter cited as *ORN*. All references are to series 1 unless otherwise specified. See also: By the President of the United States of America—Proclamations, ibid., 5, pp. 620-621; James R. Soley, *The Navy in the Civil War: The Blockade and the Cruisers* (New York, 1883), p. 27; James M. McPherson, *Battle Cry of Freedom: The Civil War Era* (New York, 1988), pp. 313-314; E. B. Long, *The Civil War Day By Day: An Almanac 1861-1865* (Garden City, 1971), pp. 61-62

5. "By the Queen. A Proclamation. Proclamation By Her Majesty, dated May 13, 1861, enjoining Neutrality in War in America." Broadside in personal collection of Charles V. Peery, Charleston, South Carolina.

6. Robert M. Browning, Jr. *From Cape Charles to Cape Fear: The North Atlantic Blockading Squadron During the Civil War* (Tuscaloosa, 1993), p. 8; Richard E. Beringer, Herman Hattaway, Archer Jones, and William N.. Still, Jr., *Why the South Lost the Civil War* (Athens, 1986), p. 54; Soley, *The Blockade*, pp. 12-14; James Sprunt, *Chron-*

icles of the Cape Fear River 1660-1916 (Spartanburg, 1974), p. 390; *Wilmington Daily Journal*, December 22, 1864; Browning, *The North Atlantic Blockading Squadron During the Civil War*, pp. 1-2.

7. See ibid., chapters 7-10. Browning examines in detail the problems facing the Union blockading squadron.

8. Soley, *The Blockade*, pp. 26-28; See also: Sprunt, *Chronicles of the Cape Fear River*, p. 389; Daniel Ammen, *The Navy in the Civil War: The Atlantic Coast* (New York, 1883), p. 11; Robert W. Daly, ed., *Aboard the USS Florida: 1863-65* (Annapolis, 1968), p. 29.

9. Sprunt, *Chronicles of the Cape Fear River*, pp. 387-388; Alan D. Watson, *Wilmington: Port of North Carolina* (Columbia, 1992), p. 97; John H. Foard, "The Blockade and the Runners," *Wilmington: Magazine of the Cape Fear* (August, 1975), p. 10.

10. Stephen R. Wise, *Lifeline of the Confederacy: Blockade Running During the Civil War* (Columbia, 1988), pp. 110-111; Stevenson, "My Personal Experiences," McEachern and Williams Collection, UNCW.

11. *Wilmington Daily Journal*, July 31, 1861; ibid., November 2, 1864; A Late Confederate Officer, "Wilmington During the Blockade," *Harper's New Monthly Magazine* (September, 1866), p. 498.

12. Watson, *Port of Wilmington*, pp. 95-96; Sprunt, *Chronicles of the Cape Fear River*, p. 283.

13. James R. Randall to Kate Hammond, December 16, 1863, James Ryder Randall Papers, Southern Historical Collection, University of North Carolina, Chapel Hill, hereinafter cited as Randall Papers, SHC; Foard, "The Blockade and the Runners," *Wilmington Magazine*, p. 11.

14. Wise, *Lifeline of the Confederacy*, pp. 200, 286; Naval History Division, Navy Department, *Civil War Naval Chronology* 6 vols. (Washington, D. C., 1971), vol. 6, p. 189.

15. Report of the Secretary of the Navy, 1865 (Washington, D. C., 1865), pp. Xxix-xxx; Frank L. Owsley, *King Cotton Diplomacy: Foreign Relations of the Confederate States of America* (Chicago, 1935), p. 262; Wise, *Lifeline of the Confederacy*, p. 221; Marcus W. Price, "Ships That Tested the Blockade of the Carolina Ports, 1861-1865," *American Neptune*, 8 (July, 1948), pp. 196-241; Wise, *Lifeline of the Confederacy*, pp. 114, 323.

16. Welles to Goldsborough, October 12, 1861, *ORN* 6, p. 313; Navy Department, *Civil War Naval Chronology*, vol. 2, p. 8; Wise, *Lifeline of the Confederacy*, p. 25.

17. Report of the Secretary of the Navy, pp. xxix-xxx.

18. Beringer, et. al., *Why the South Lost*, p. 63.

19. Letter of George A. Trenholm, December 12, 1864, United States War Department, *The War of the Rebellion, A Compilation of the Official Records of the Union and Confederate Armies,* 128 vols. (Washington, D. C., 1880-1901), series IV, pt. 3, p. 955,

hereinafter cited as *OR*. All references are to series 1 unless otherwise specified; Report of Thomas L. Bayne on cargoes received from abroad on Government account, from October 25 to December 6, 1864, *OR* IV, pt. 3, pp. 955-957.

20. Beringer, et. al., *Why the South Lost*, pp. 13, 63.

21. Sprunt, *Chronicles of the Cape Fear River*, p. 145; Watson, *Port of Wilmington*, pp. 68-69.

22. Watson, *Port of Wilmington*, pp. 67-70; Sprunt, *Chronicles of the Cape Fear River*, pp. 156-158; Richard E. Wood, "Port Town at War: Wilmington, North Carolina 1860-1865" (Ph.D. dissertation, Florida State University), p. 1, hereinafter cited as Wood, "Port Town at War"; *Wilmington Daily Journal*, February 15, 1861; George H. Kelley, *Kelley's Wilmington Directory 1860-1861* (Wilmington, 1861); Frank D. Smaw, Jr., *Wilmington Directory 1865* (Wilmington: 1865).

23. Whiting to Smith, November 14, 1862, *OR* 18, pp. 773-774; Whiting to Randolph, November 14, 1862, ibid., pp. 774-776. For the best account of North Carolina's salt making operations at Wilmington, see: Isabel M. Williams and Leora H. McEachern, *Salt—That Necessary Article (Wilmington, 1973)*.

24. John Wilkinson, *The Narrative of a Blockade Runner* (New York, 1877), p. 199; Report of G. J. Pendergrast, July 14, 1861, *ORN* 6, p. 792.

25. William Lamb, "Fort Fisher: Battles Fought There in 1864 and '65," *Southern Historical Society Papers*, 52 vols. (Wilmington, 1990), vol. 21, p. 264. See also, William Lamb, *Colonel Lamb's Story of Fort Fisher* (Carolina Beach, 1966), p. 7, hereinafter cited as Lamb, *Story of Fort Fisher*; Wise, *Lifeline of the Confederacy*, pp. 237-241; B. Lewis Blackford to Mother, October 5, 1863, Blackford Family Papers, University of Virginina, Charlottesville. According to James R. Randall, Secretary to William F. Lynch, commander of the C. S. Navy at Wilmington, the *Alice, Annie, Atalanta, Badger, City of Petersburg, Coquette, Florie, Let Her Be, Lillian, Lucy, Mary Celestia, North Heath, Syren*, and *Will of the Wisp* all ran into Wilmington in the "last fifteen days" prior to June 10, 1864. Another blockade runner, the *Georgiana McCaw*, ran aground on the beach near Old Inlet, the main entrance to the Cape Fear River, on June 2, 1864. Randall noted that Confederate authorities expected her cargo to be saved. James R. Randall to Kate Hammond, June 10, 1864, Randall Papers, SHC.

26. Clement Dowd, *Life of Zebulon B. Vance* (Charlotte, 1897), pp. 489-490; Hill, *Bethel to Sharpsburg*, vol. 1, p. 388; Late Confederate Officer, "Wilmington During the Blockade," *Harper's Magazine*, p. 497. See also: Sprunt, *Chronicles of the Cape Fear River*, p. 483.

27. *Wilmington Weekly Journal*, August 28, 1862; Late Confederate Officer, "Wilmington During the Civil War," *Harper's Magazine*, p. 499.

28. William Henry Tripp to Araminta Guilford Tripp, September 2, 1864, William Henry and Araminta Guilford Tripp Papers, Southern Historical Collection, University of North Carolina, Chapel Hill, hereinafter cited as Tripp Papers, SHC; Wilkinson,

Narrative of a Blockade Runner, p. 199; *Wilmington Daily Journal*, September 11, 1863; John High to Father, April 10, 1863, High Family Papers, Special Collections, Randall Library, University of North Carolina at Wilmington, hereinafter cited as High Family Papers, UNCW; *Wilmington Daily Journal*, October 1 and 10, 1863.

29. Andrew J. Howell, *The Book of Wilmington* (Wilmington, 1930), p. 131; David High to John High, October 1, 1862, High Family Papers, UNCW; William Lamb to Thomas Rowland, November 22, 1863, 6-2-4, file 40, The Museum of the Confederacy, Richmond;

30. *Wilmington Daily Journal*, September 15, 1862; David High to John High, October 1, 1862, High Family Papers, UNCW; Leora H. McEachern and Isabel M. Williams, "The Prevailing Epidemic—1862," *Lower Cape Fear Historical Society Bulletin* (November, 1967), pp. 19-20; Wilkinson, *Narrative of a Blockade Runner*, pp. 199-200; Sprunt, *Chronicles of the Cape Fear River*, pp. 413-414; Lawrence Lee, *New Hanover County: A Brief History* (Raleigh, 1971), p. 68; Leora H. McEachern and Bill Reaves, *History of St. James Parish, 1729-1979* (Wilmington, 1985), p. 58.

31. Late Confederate Officer, "Wilmington During the Blockade," *Harper's Magazine*, p. 497; *Wilmington Daily Journal*, October 29, 1863.

32. John G. Barrett, *The Civil War in North Carolina* (Chapel Hill, 1963), p. 245.

33. Wilkinson, *Narrative of a Blockade Runner*, pp. 130-131; Sprunt, *Chronicles of the Cape Fear River*, pp.411-412; Thomas E. Taylor, *Running the Blockade* (London, 1896), pp. 44-47; Instructions for Blockaders off Wilmington by Samuel Phillips Lee, December 16, 1863, and Memorandum from S. Phillips Lee to David D. Porter, November 23, 1864, David Dixon Porter Papers, Library of Congress, Washington, D.C.

34. Memoir of David D. Porter, David D. Porter Papers, Manuscript Department, Library of Congress, Washington, D. C., hereinafter cited as Porter Memoir, Porter Papers, LOC.

35. Charles L. Price, "North Carolina Railroads During the Civil War," *Civil War History*, 7 (September, 1961), pp. 298-309; Bragg to Gilmer, February 6, 1865, *OR* 47, pt. 2, pp. 1110-1111.

Chapter 2: The Forts

1. *Wilmington Daily Journal*, November 6 & 7, 1863.

2. Fitzgerald Ross, *Cities and Camps of the Confederate States* (Urbana, 1958), p. 187.

3. Wilmington's outer ring of defenses ran south from Smith's Creek atop the ridge along present day Burnt Mill Creek, across Wrightsville Avenue in the area of the old Spofford Mill and Oleander Drive to Cape Fear Country Club. There, the line turned west, extending across 16th and 17th Streets and the sand ridge on the north side of Greenfield Lake toward the Cape Fear River. Remains of the earthworks can be seen in

the rough between the first and ninth fairways on Cape Fear Country Club. The club's seventh and old eighteenth greens were artillery batteries—McRee and Dawson Batteries. Charles S. Powell Papers, Southern Historical Collection, University of North Carolina, Chapel Hill; C. S. Powell, "The Defenses Around Wilmington During the Civil War," *Wilmington Morning Star*, September 9, 1917; "Cape Fear: Civil War and Reconstruction," *Wilmington Star News* supplement, March 7, 1976; J. A. Mowris, *A History of the One Hundred and Seventeenth Regiment N. Y. Volunteers* (Fourth Oneida) (Hartford, 1866), p. 187; *New York Herald*, February 27, 1865.

4. Clark, *North Carolina Regiments*, vol. 4, pp. 417-418.

5. Ross, *Cities and Camps of the Confederate States*, p. 187.

6. Wilmington's river batteries underwent several name changes during the war. Early in the war, Fort Davis was called both Fort Strong and Fort Stokes. Fort French, named for Brig. Gen. Samuel Gibbs French, commander of the District of the Cape Fear in the spring and early summer of 1862, became Fort Lee. On some maps, the battery immediately south of Fort French is plotted as Fort Meares, and on others as Fort Campbell. The weight of evidence uncovered thus far suggests that the third battery was Fort Campbell, remains of which can still be seen on property (old Mt. Tirza) owned by Exxon USA on River Road. The other batteries fell victim to development by the North Carolina Port Authority and oil terminals along River Road, including Fort Meares, the southernmost battery. United States War Department, *Atlas to Accompany the Official Records of the Union and Confederate Armies* (Washington, D. C., 1891-1895), Plates LXVIII, 7 and CXXXII, 1, hereinafter cited as *OR Atlas*; J. F. Gilmer Maps, maps N. C. 312 and N.C. 313, Southern Historical Collection, University of North Carolina, Chapel Hill.

7. *Gleason's Pictorial Drawing Room Companion*, July 16, 1853.

8. Watson, *Port of Wilmington*, pp. 6-7; Sprunt, *Chronicles of the Cape Fear River*, pp. 59-60; William Lord DeRosset, *Pictorial and Historical New Hanover County and Wilmington, North Carolina* (Wilmington, 1938), pp. 8-9.

9. Brigadier General Samuel Gibbs French was assigned command of the District of the Cape Fear by order of the C. S. War Department, March 15, 1862. Special Orders, No. 60, March 15, 1862, *OR* 9, p. 445. French arrived in Wilmington on March 22. General Orders, No. 13, March 22, 1862, ibid., p. 450. He remained in command at Wilmington until mid-July, 1862, when he was promoted major general and the head of the Department of North Carolina, headquartered in Petersburg, Virginia, ibid., 11, pt. 3, p. 643.

Thomas W. Rowland, a Southerner by birth, was in his second year of study at West Point when the Civil War broke out. He returned to the South and joined the Confederate army as a "Cadet of Engineers" with the rank of first lieutenant in the 36th North Carolina Regiment (2nd North Carolina Artillery). Described as an "educated, accomplished soldier of uncommon intelligence," Lieutenant Rowland spent about seven months at Cape Fear overseeing military projects. On July 22, 1862, Rowland joined Brig. Gen. Robert Ransom's staff as captain and assistant adjutant general. Kate Mason Rowland, ed., "Letters of Thomas Rowland, C.S.A.," *William and Mary College Quarterly Historical Magazine*, XXVI (April, 1917), p. 230. See also, Clark, *North Carolina Regiments*, 4, p. 577; Louis Manarin and Weymouth T. Jordan, eds., *North Carolina Troops 1861-1865: A Roster*, 13 vols. (Raleigh, 1973-1993), vol. 1, p. 173; B. F. Travis, *The Story of the Twenty-fifth Michigan* (Kalamazoo, 1897), p. 336.

10. Rowland, "Letters of Thomas Rowland," *William and Mary Historical Magazine*, pp. 230-233. The Confederate garrison apparently had been deliberating for some time on a name for the earthworks under construction, and finally choise Fort St. Philip. An order issued at the fort on May 11, 1862, read: "Headquarters, Old Brunswick Point, Order No.4. Hereafter this post will be called Fort St. Philip after the ancient church of our forefathers at Old Brunswick, which nearly a century ago was a silent witness of our successful struggle of our fathers for liberty and independence, and whose venerable walls, by the grace of God, will witness our successful maintenance of that same liberty and independence. Major [William Lamb] Commanding." *Wilmington Weekly Journal*, May 15, 1862.

11. Patricia L. Faust, ed., *Historical Times Illustrated Encyclopedia of the Civil War* (New York, 1986), p. 13. Ezra Warner, *Generals in Gray* (Baton Rouge, 1959), pp. 5-6. Historians have long (and reasonably) believed that Fort Anderson was named for Brig. Gen. Joseph Reid Anderson. Anderson, superviser of the Tredegar Iron Works in Richmond, the largest supplier of Confederate ordnance products, was also the first commander of the District of the Cape Fear, from September 4, 1861 to March 15, 1862. A marble tablet erected at Fort Anderson in 1919 by the New Hanover Historical Commission cites Joseph R. Anderson as the officer for whom Fort Anderson was named, and historians have since perpetuated that claim. To further cloud the debate, an old Brunswick County story had Fort Anderson named for John William Anderson, a blockade running pilot from Smithville (present-day Southport). An obituary of Anderson's sister, Mrs. Frances Anderson Pate, that appeared in the *Wilmington Morning Star* of April 26, 1870, noted that "early writings pronounce [J. W. Anderson] one of the heroes of the war and Fort Anderson was named for him." But Maj. Gen. W. H. C. Whiting, who named Fort Anderson, denounced blockade running and tolerated it as a necessary evil. It seems unlikely that Whiting would have named a fort after a blockade runner. Cape Fear historian William M. Reaves wrote that in 1863, "John William Anderson, a Smithville pilot, guided the blockade-runner *Mary Celeste* across the bar safely into New Inlet. Anderson died soon after the vessel dropped anchor safely opposite Deep Water Point near Smithville." William M. Reaves, *Southport (Smithville): A Chronology, Volume 1, 1520-1887*, (Wilmington, 1985), p. 45. No records of a blockade runner named *Mary Celeste* have been found. The *Mary Celestia*, however, made eight successful trips through the blockade between May and Septem-

ber, 1864. By then, however, the defenses at Brunswick Town had been called Fort Anderson for about one year.

On July 2, 1863, the *Wilmington Daily Journal* ran a new advertisement for the local Confederate high command: "Head Quarters District Cape Fear, Wilmington, N.C., July 1, 1863, General Orders No. 33. 1. To commemorate some of the many distinguished and gallant dead of North Carolina, who have given their lives for their country, the names of the following of the Forts and Batteries of the Cape Fear, will be changed, viz: Fort St. Philip will be known hereafter as Ft. Anderson. By command of Maj. Gen'l [W. H. C.] Whiting." Thus it seems likely that Whiting named the fort to memorialize Brig. Gen. George Burgwyn Anderson, the only general officer in the Confederate Army from North Carolina with that surname. Joseph Reid Anderson was a Virginian. *Wilmington Daily Journal*, July 2, 1863.

12. *Wilmington Daily Journal*, September 1, 1864; *Wilmington Morning Star*, September 9, 1917.

13. Sprunt, *Chronicles of the Cape Fear River*, pp. 53-54. Fort Johnston was officially renamed Fort Branch on July 2, 1863. *Wilmington Daily Journal*, July 2, 1863. It was later renamed Fort Pender, probably in 1864.

14. Whiting to Randolph, November 14, 1862, *OR* 18, pp. 774-776.

15. Douglas Southall Freeman, *R. E. Lee*, 4 vols. (New York, 1949), vol. 1, p. 184.

16. *Wilmington Daily Journal*, January 10 and 16, 1861; John A. Sloan, *North Carolina in the War Between the States* (Washington, 1883), pp. 82-86; Sprunt, *Chronicles of the Cape Fear River*, pp. 276-280.

17. Sloan, *North Carolina in the War Between the States*, pp. 86-87; Ethel Herring and Carolee Williams, *Fort Caswell in War and Peace* (Wendell, 1983), pp. 9-32; *OR* Atlas, CXXXII, 2.

18. Whiting to Seddon, September 8, 1863, *OR* 29, pt. 2, pp. 704-705; Thomas M. Jones to Assistant-Adjutant General, September 7, 1863, ibid., p. 705; Memorandum for Lieutenant Colonel Frobel from W. H. C. Whiting, September 8, 1863, ibid; David Stick, *Bald Head: A History of Smith Island and Cape Fear* (Wendell, 1985), pp. 43-45; *OR* Atlas, CXXXII, 4; *Wilmington Messenger*, June 26, 1894; *Wilmington Morning Star*, June 26, 1894.

19. William Lamb, "The Defense of Fort Fisher," *Battles and Leaders of the Civil War*, 4 vols. (New York, 1888) vol. 4, p. 642. Battery Anderson was known to Union sailors as "Flag Pond Battery," probably because from their vantage point on board blockading ships they could see a Confederate flag flapping over the battery close to a pond. The "pond," in fact, was a nearby salt marsh or tidal pool near the shoreline. Battery Anderson, situated just north of present-day Kure Beach, was destroyed by the ravages of time and development. Porter to Grant, January 14, 1865, *OR* 46, pt. 3, p. 126. Contrary to some modern-day claims, Battery Gatlin was located on the narrow strip of ocean beach (today's Carolina Beach), and not on the mainland side of Myrtle

Grove sound. *OR* 29, pt. 2, p. 896; Sketch map of Confederate Point in Henry Benton Papers, Division of Archives and History, Raleigh, North Carolina; Diary entry of May 3, 1864, James W. Albright Papers, Southern Historical Collection, University of North Carolina, Chapel Hill.

20. Lamb, *Story of Fort Fisher,* pp. 1-2; Lamb, "Defense of Fort Fisher," *Battles and Leaders,* 4, p. 643.

21. Telegram from James F. M. McRee to Col. Cantwell, April 16, 1861, John L. Cantwell Collection, Division of Archives and History, Raleigh, North Carolina; Extracts of letter from J. Alves Walker to N. Martin Curtis, March, 1901, letter in personal collection of Chris E. Fonvielle, Jr., Wilmington, N. C. See also, *Wilmington Morning Star,* July 2, 1881 and December 21, 1909.

22. Battery Bolles was located about a mile north of New Inlet. Its position was approved by Maj. W. H. C. Whiting, inspector general of North Carolina's defenses in the spring of 1861. Major Whiting may well have suggested the battery's name, since Charles Pattison Bolles was Whiting's brother-in-law. Fort Fisher eventually annexed Battery Bolles as part of its long line of sea face batteries. Its position was about halfway between the northeast bastion, where the land and sea faces intersected, and Battery Lamb (better known as "Mound Battery") that anchored Fort Fisher's ocean-front works. During the battles for Fort Fisher (December 1864 through January 1865), Battery Bolles was armed with two 10-inch rifled columbiads. Letter of Charles Pattison Bolles, March, 1901, personal collection of Chris E. Fonvielle, Jr. See also: *Wilmington Morning Star,* July 22, 1881; Charles Force Deems, *Autobiography of Charles Force Deems* (New York, 1897), p. 175.

23. Sloan, *North Carolina in the War Between the States,* p. 93.

24. William Lord DeRosset left Federal Point when military authorities appointed him major of the 3rd Regiment of North Carolina State Troops on May 18, 1861. Manarin, *North Carolina Troops,* vol. 3, p. 487; *Wilmington Morning Star,* July 22, 1881.

25. *Wilmington Daily Journal,* February 1, 1862; Orders No. 1, August 31, 1861, General Correspondence 1861-1893, Dorothy Fremont Grant Collection, Division of Archives and History, Raleigh, North Carolina; *Wilmington Daily Journal,* August 31, 1861.

26. Clark, *North Carolina Regiments,* vol. 4, pp. 416-417; Charles Pattison Bolles to William Lord DeRosset, October 11, 1906, Charles Pattison Bolles Papers, Division of Archives and History, Raleigh, North Carolina; *Wilmington Morning Star,* July 15 and 22, 1881; *Wilmington Daily Journal,* February 1, 1862.

27. The earliest reference to "Fort Fisher" that I have found is dated September 22, 1861. "Yesterday at Revelee (4 1/2 o'clock a.m.)," wrote Colin Shaw, chaplain of the 8th Regiment of North Carolina Volunteers stationed at Camp Wyatt, "the Scotch Boys [Company F] & the Wilmington Rifle Guards [Company I] struck their tents & were off

by breakfast for Confederate Point to support a new Battery down there dubbed 'Fort Fisher.' The 'Fort' will be ready for business in a week." Colin Shaw to "My Dear," September 22, 1861, Colin Shaw Papers, Division of Archives and History, Raleigh, North Carolina. See also: *Wilmington Morning Star*, July 15, 1881; Jordan, *North Carolina Troops*, vol. 4, p. 267; Barrett, *Civil War in North Carolina*, p. 265; Lee, *New Hanover County*, p. 65; Howell, *Book of Wilmington*, p. 129.

28. X, "Reminiscences of the Lower Cape Fear," *Wilmington Morning Star*, September 26, 1873.

29. John J. Hedrick's company, the Cape Fear Light Artillery, later designated Company C, 36th North Carolina Regiment (1st North Carolina Artillery), was transferred from Zeke's Island to Fort Fisher on December 12, 1861. Manarin, *North Carolina Troops*, vol. 1, p. 218. Hedrick was assisted for a brief time by Capt. Richard K. Meade of the Engineer Corps. Clark, *North Carolina Regiments*, vol. 4, pp. 419, 422.

30. Lamb, "Battles of Fort Fisher," *SHSP*, vol. 21, p. 260; Lamb, *Story of Fort Fisher*, p. 2.

31. Ibid., pp. 259-260; ibid., pp. 1-2.

32. Lamb, "Defense of Fort Fisher," *Battles and Leaders*, vol. 4, p. 643.

33. Clement A. Evans, ed., *Confederate Military History*, 19 vols. (Wilmington, 1987, expanded edition), vol. 4, p. 989.

34. Rowland, "Letters of Thomas Rowland," *William and Mary Historical Magazine*, p. 232.

35. David High to John High, August 22, 1862, High Family Papers, UNCW.

36. William Lamb, "The Heroine of Confederate Point," *SHSP*, vol. 20 (January-December, 1892), pp. 301-302.

37. Daniel Eldredge, *The Third New Hampshire and All About It* (Boston, 1893), p. 575.

38. Lamb, *Story of Fort Fisher*, pp. 3-5; Lamb, "Defense of Fort Fisher," *Battles and Leaders*, vol. 4, p. 643; Barrett, *Civil War in North Carolina*, pp. 265-266; Lee, *New Hanover County*, p. 65. Colonel Lamb recorded that Fort Fisher's land face measured 682 yards in length. Cyrus B. Comstock, Lt. Gen. U. S. Grant's chief engineer of the Fort Fisher expeditionary force, measured Fort Fisher's land face at 480 yards. Lamb's survey probably included the palisade fence in front of the land face, which almost breached the 700 yard wide peninsula. *OR Atlas*, LXXV, 2; Report of Cyrus B. Comstock, January 27, 1865, *OR* 46, pt. 1, p. 407.

39. Colonel Lamb's measurement of the sea face, 1,898 yards, differs considerably from Lieutenant Colonel Comstock's measurement of 1,300 yards. The ocean washed away most of the sea face more than half a century ago, making it impossible to verify either officer's claim. Did Lamb's survey include the line of rifle pits located behind the sea face? Did Comstock discount the first one hundred yards of the sea face, which was built of the same character as the land face and formed the northeast bastion? A

December 1864 report by Lamb clearly states his account of Fort Fisher's size. Report of William Lamb, *OR* 42, pt. 1, p. 1007. Comstock's description of Fort Fisher is contained in his official report dated January 27, 1865, twelve days after the fort's capture. Report of Cyrus B. Comstock, January 27, 1865, *OR* 46, pt. 1, p. 407.

40. Warren Ripley, *Artillery and Ammunition of the Civil War* (New York, 1970), pp. 140-141; Entry of January 20, 1865, Diary of Christian Fleetwood, Manuscript Department, Library of Congress, Washington, D. C.; Letter of John Bartlett, January 18, 1865, *ORN* 11, p. 529.

41. Lamb, "Battles of Fort Fisher," *SHSP*, vol. 21, p. 262; Lamb, *Story of Fort Fisher*, p. 4; Lamb, "Defense of Fort Fisher," *Battles and Leaders*, vol. 4, p. 643; Report of Samuel P. Lee, *ORN* 8, pp. 812-813. Another inconsistency exists between Colonel Lamb's and Cyrus Comstock's measurements, this one dealing with the height of Battery Lamb. Colonel Lamb recorded the Mound Battery towered sixty feet above the beach, while Comstock measured its height at forty-three feet, a fact he noted on an engineer's map made to accompany his battle report of January 27, 1865. See *OR Atlas*, LXXV, 2. It is logical to conclude that Lamb knew the dimensions of his fort and its batteries better than anyone, but photographs taken of the Mound Battery in early February 1865 seem to support Comstock's more modest assessment.

42. Lamb, *Story of Fort Fisher*, pp. 4-5. The plan for Battery Buchanan was drawn and submitted by Reddin Pittman, a young engineer from Halifax County, North Carolina. According to Lamb, Battery Buchanan was "perfect in design." Pittman labeled the earthwork "Augusta Battery" for his girlfriend, but Maj. Gen. Whiting overturned that moniker and directed Lamb to officially name it Battery Buchanan, as a compliment to Admiral Franklin Buchanan of the C. S. Navy. Lamb, "Battles of Fort Fisher," *SHSP*, vol. 21, p. 262.

43. B. Lewis Blackford to Father, October 13, 1863, Blackford Family Papers, University of Virginia, Charlottesville.

44. C. B. Denson, *An Address Delivered in Raleigh, N.C., On Memorial Day (May 10), 1895, Containing a Memoir of the Late Major-General William Henry Chase Whiting of the Confederate Army* (Raleigh, 1895), p. 10; William C. Davis, ed., *The Confederate General*, 6 vols. (1991), vol. 6, p. 132; Evans, *Confederate Military History*, vol. 4, p. 352; *The National Cyclopedia of American Biography* (New York, 1893) vol. 4, p. 488; Richard N. Current, ed., *Encyclopedia of the Confederacy*, 4 vols. (New York, 1993) vol. 4, p. 1171.

45. *American State Papers: Documents, Legislative & Executive of the Congress of the United States, Military Affairs* (Washington, 1861), vol. 6, p. 706.

46. Denson, *Memoir of W. H. C. Whiting*, pp. 10-11.

47. U.S. Military Academy Cadet Application Papers 1805-1866, National Archives Microfilm Publications, Roll 130 (1840), p. 346; Denson, *Memoir of W. H. C. Whiting*,

pp. 10-11; *Official Register of the Officers and Cadets of the U.S. Military Academy, West Point, New York, Class of 1845*, p. 7.

48. *Wilmington Daily North Carolinian*, January 4, 1865; Denson, *Memoir of W. H. C. Whiting*, p. 12; Evans, *Confederate Military History*, vol. 4, p. 352.

49. James R. Randall, "General W. H. C. Whiting: A Chevalier of the Lost Cause," *SHSP*, vol. 24, p. 274; *Wilmington Messenger*, June 26, 1895; James Lowndes to Cousin Harriet, James Lowndes Papers, South Caroliniana Library, University of South Carolina, Columbia.

50. Davis, *Confederate General*, vol. 6, pp. 132-133; *Cyclopedia of American Biography*, vol. 4, p. 488; Current, *Encyclopedia of the Confederacy*, vol. 4, pp. 1711-1712; Jefferson Davis, *The Rise and Fall of the Confederate Government*, 2 vols. (New York, 1881), vol. 2, p. 646; Lee to Davis, February 26, 1863, *OR* 25, pt. 2, p. 643; *Wilmington Messenger*, August 28, 1895.

51. Gustavus W. Smith, *Confederate War Papers* (New York, 1884), p. 328; Denson, *Memoir of W. H. C. Whiting*, p. 26; Benjamin to Johnston, December 27, 1861, *OR* 5, pp. 1011-1012.

52. Denson, *Memoir of W. H. C. Whiting*, pp. 24-25; Clifford Dowdey, *Lee* (Boston, 1965), p. 325; Thomas L. Connelly and Archer Jones, *The Politics of Command* (Baton Rouge, 1973), pp. 89-91.

53. Special Orders, No. 262, November 8, 1862, *OR* 18, p. 770; Late Confederate Officer, "Wilmington During the Blockade," *Harper's Magazine*, p. 497; Denson, *Memoir of W. H. C. Whiting*, p. 54; *Wilmington Daily Journal*, May 27, 1863.

54. Late Confederate Officer, "Wilmington During the Blockade," *Harper's Magazine*, p. 497.

55. Beringer, et. al., *Why the South Lost*, p. 186; Navy Department, *Civil War Naval Chronology*, vol. 1, pp. 23, 31-34; vol. 2, pp. 28, 32-33, 54-56, 62, 100-101, vol. 4, 95-97.

56. Beringer, et. al., *Why the South Lost*, p. 195.

57. Welles to Goldsborough, May 11, 1862, *ORN* 7, p. 341; Goldsborough to Welles, May 12, 1861, *ORN* 7, p. 342.

58. Reports of John G. Foster, December 14, 20, and 27, 1862, *OR* 18, pp. 53-59.

59. Browning, *From Cape Fear to Cape Charles*, p. 277.

60. Porter, Memoir, pp. 879-880, Porter Papers, LOC.

61. Jay Luvaas, "The Fall of Fort Fisher," *Civil War Times Illustrated*, 3 (August, 1964), p. 6; Rowena Reed, *Combined Operations in the Civil War* (Annapolis, 1978); p. 333.

Chapter Three: Preparations

1. Stanton to Grant, September 1, 1864, *OR* 42, pt. 2, p. 624; John Y. Simon, ed., *The Papers of Ulysses S. Grant*, 13 vols. (Carbondale and Edwardsville, 1984), vol. 12, p. 141.

2. Gideon Welles, *Diary of Gideon Welles*, 3 vols. (Boston and New York, 1911), vol. 2, p. 127.

3. Ibid; Lee to Welles, October 18, 1864, *ORN* 10, pp. 572-573.

4. Welles, *Diary of Gideom Welles*, vol. 2, p. 146.

5. Navy Department, *Civil War Naval Chronology*, vol. 6, p. 309; Faust, *Encyclopedia of the Civil War*, p. 741.

6. Long, *Civil War Day By Day*, p. 514.

7. Ibid., p. 563; Stanton to Grant, September 1, 1864, *OR* 42, pt. 2, p. 624; Welles, *Diary of Gideon Welles*, vol. 2, p. 127.

8. Halleck to Grant, September 1, 1864, *OR* 42, pt. 2, p. 624.

9. Welles to Farragut, September 5, 1864, *ORN* 10, p. 430.

10. Long, *Civil War Day By Day*, p. 565; Welles, *Diary of Gideon Welles*, vol. 2, pp. 135-136.

11. Benjamin F. Butler, *Butler's Book* (Boston, 1892), p. 774; Simon, *Papers of U. S. Grant*, vol. 12, pp. 156-157.

12. Gillmore to Halleck, September 6, 1864, *OR* 42, pt. 2, 731; Project for effectually closing the port of Wilmington, N.C., to blockade-runners, September 6, 1864, *OR* 42, pt. 2, pp. 732-734.

13. Report of S. P. Lee, September 8, 1864, *ORN* 10, pp. 441-444.

14. S. P. Lee apparently believed he would command the naval task force at Wilmington, and made preparations to do so. Lee to Welles, September 6, 1864, *ORN* 10, pp. 432-433; Report of S. P. Lee, September 8, 1864, ibid., pp. 441-444; Lee to Welles, September 10, 1864, ibid., p. 450; Benjamin F. Sands, *From Reefer to Rear Admiral* (New York, 1899), p. 256; Welles, *Diary of Gideon Welles*, vol. 2, pp. 146, 161. While Welles relieved Lee of command of the North Atlantic Blockading Squadron on September 17, 1864, Lee retained his position and duties until his successor arrived four weeks later. Initially Welles reassigned Lee to replace the exhausted Admiral Farragut as commander of the West Gulf Blockading Squadron. Farragut, however, decided to stay on and Lee was given command of the Mississippi Squadron on November 1, 1864. Welles to Lee, September 17, 1864, *ORN* 10, p. 467; Welles to Lee, October 7, 1864, ibid., p. 530; Navy Department, *Civil War Naval Chronology*, vol. 4, p. 129.

15. Welles to Farragut, September 5, 1864, *ORN* 10, p. 430; Welles, *Diary of Gideon Welles*, vol. 2, pp. 117, 127-128, and 133.

16. Welles, *Diary of Gideon Welles*, vol. 2, pp. 146-147; Robert Means Thompson and Richard Wainwright, eds., *Confidential Correspondence of Gustavus Vasa Fox*, 2

vols. (New York, 1918-1919), vol. 1, p. 352; Farragut to Welles, September 22, 1864, *ORN* 21, pp. 655, 690-692; Welles to Farragut, September 22, 1864, *ORN* 10, 473; Navy Department, *Civil War Naval Chronology*, vol. 4, pp. 109-110. In truth, Farragut decided to remain on active duty with the West Gulf Blockading Squadron to attempt to capture Mobile. Nevertheless, his failing health finally forced him to leave the navy for a time in December 1864. Welles to Farragut, October 1, 1864, *ORN* 10, pp. 512-513.

17. Welles, *Diary of Gideon Welles*, vol. 2, p. 148.

18. James R. Soley, *Admiral Porter* (New York, 1903), p. 1; Lewis R. Hamersly, *The Records of Living Officers of the U.S. Navy and Marine Corps With a History of Naval Operations During the Rebellion of 1861-5* (Philadelphia, 1870), p. 9.

19. Hamersly, *Records of U. S. Navy Officers*, p. 9; Faust, *Encyclopedia of the Civil War*, p. 594; Joseph T. Glatthar, *Partners in Command: The Relationship Between Leaders in the Civil War* (New York, 1994), p. 181; Navy Department, *Civil War Naval Chronology*, vol. 6, p. 387.

20. Joseph Becker, "Fort Fisher and Wilmington," *Frank Leslie's Popular Monthly*, LXXXVIII, 2 (August, 1894), p. 235.

21. Thompson and Wainwright, *Correspondence of Gustavus Fox*, vol. 1, p. 352; William N. Still, Jr., "Porter Is the Best Man," *Civil War Times Illustrated*, XVI (May, 1977), p. 46; Welles, *Diary of Gideon Welles*, vol. 2, pp. 146-147.

22. Ibid., vol. 2, pp. 150-151; Simon, *Papers of U. S. Grant*, vol. 12, notes, pp. 142 and 177; Faust, *Encyclopedia of the Civil War*, p. 311.

23. Warner, *Generals in Blue*, pp. 548-549; Faust, *Encyclopedia of the Civil War*, p. 812; General Orders, No. 116, September 30, 1864, *OR* 42, pt. 2, 1146.

24. *Report of the Joint Committee on the Conduct of the War, at the Second Session Thirty-Eighth Congress* (Washington, 1865), pp. 67-68, hereinafter cited as *Report on the Conduct of the War: The Fort Fisher Expedition.*

25. Ibid.

26. J. Cutler Andrews, *The North Reports the Civil War* (Pittsburg, 1955), p. 614.

27. Welles to Porter, September 22, 1864, *ORN* 10, p. 473; General Order No. 1, October 12, 1864, ibid., p. 557; General Order No. 6, October 13, 1864, ibid., pp. 560-562; Porter to Welles, October 13, 1864, ibid., p. 563.

28. William Henry Tripp to Araminta Guilford Tripp, November 12, 1864, Tripp Papers, SHC.

29. William Lamb to Thomas Rowland, November 22, 1862, 6-2-4, file 40, The Museum of the Confederacy, Richmond; William Henry Tripp to Araminta Guilford Tripp, January 5, 1863, Tripp Papers, SHC.

30. William Lamb to Thomas Rowland, November 22, 1862, 6-2-4, file 40, The Museum of the Confederacy, Richmond.

31. Robert J. Murphey to Friend Richard, February 15, 1864, Richard Parson Paddison Papers, North Carolina Room, Joyner Library, East Carolina University, Green-

ville, North Carolina; Alex Campbell to Margaret, August 10, 1861, McEachern and Williams Collection, UNCW.

32. B. Lewis Blackford to Mother, October 3, 1863, Blackford Family Papers, University of Virginia, Charlottesville, hereinafter cited as Blackford Family Papers, UVA; David to Miss Kate, February 11, 1864, Catherine McEachey Buie Papers, Perkins Library, Duke University, Durham, North Carolina, hereinafter cited as Kate Buie Papers, Duke; W. H. Best to James High, September 3, 1861, High Family Papers, UNCW; B. Lewis Blackford to Mother, October 5, 1863, Blackford Family Papers, UVA.

33. William A. Burgess to Parents, December 8, 1862, John Haywood Papers, Southern Historical Collection, University of North Carolina, Chapel Hill; John M. Johnston, *Recollections of J. M. Johnston,* copy in personal collection of Chris E. Fonvielle, Jr.; David High to James High, April 30, 1863, High Family Papers, UNCW.

34. Lamb to Vance, June 11, 1863, Zebulon Vance Papers, Division of Archives and History, Raleigh, North Carolina.

35. Whiting to Smith, November 14, 1862, *OR* 18, p. 773; John B. Jones, *A Rebel War Clerk's Diary,* 2 vols. (Philadelphia, 1866), vol. 2, pp. 24, 26.

36. Whiting to Gilmer, September 16, 1864, *OR* 42, pt. 2, p. 1254; Whiting to Seddon, August 24, 1863, *OR* 29, pt. 2, p. 670; Whiting to Beauregard, August 31, 1864, *OR* 42, pt. 2, p. 1212.

37. Seddon to Whiting, September 5, 1864, *OR* 42, pt. 2, pp. 1236-1237.

38. Whiting to Gilmer, September 16, 1864, *OR* 42, pt. 2, p. 1253; Whiting to Beauregard, August 31, 1864, ibid., pt. 2, p. 1212.

39. Whiting to Gilmer, September 16, 1864, ibid., pp. 1253-1254.

40. Ibid., p. 1254. To guard against an attack by way of New Bern, General Whiting ordered the construction of strong fieldworks at Virginia Creek, Holly Shelter Road, and Scott's Hill. Remnants of these works can still be seen.

41. Whiting to Seddon, September 8, 1864, *OR* 42, pt. 2, p. 1240; Whiting to Gilmer, September 16, 1864, ibid., pt. 2, p. 1253.

42. Beauregard to Cooper, September 12, 1864, *OR* 42, pt. 2, p. 1246; Whiting to Vance, September 24, 1864, *OR* 42, pt. 2, pp. 1282-1283.

43. Lee to Smith, January 4, 1863, *OR* 18, pp. 818-819; Whiting to Seddon, September 8, 1864, *OR* 42, pt. 2, p. 1241. See also, Whiting to Beauregard, August 31, 1864, ibid., p. 1212.

44. "Gen. Lee had sent word that if the fort [Fisher] fell he could not maintain his army, (and that meant the loss of our cause). . . ." Lamb, *Story of Fort Fisher,* 35. Admiral Porter reported: "We picked up a telegram from General Lee to his subordinate here [Fort Fisher], saying that if Forts Fisher and Caswell were not held he would have to evacuate Richmond." Report of David D. Porter, January 20, 1865, *ORN* 11, p. 620. See also: Charles Pearce, "The Expeditions Against Fort Fisher," War Papers and

Personal Reminiscences, 1861-1865, Read Before the Commandery of the State of Missouri, Military Order of the Loyal Legion of the United States, 1 (1892), p. 354, hereinafter cited as Pearce, "The Expeditions Against Fort Fisher," *MOLLUS*; Jones, A *Rebel War Clerk's Diary*, vol. 2, p. 467.

45. Lee to Seddon, January 11, 1864, *OR* 29, pt. 2, p. 910; Lee to Vance, August 29, 1864, *OR* 42, pt. 2, p. 1206.

46. Lamb, "The Battles of Fort Fisher," *SHSP*, vol. 21, p. 266. See also: Lamb, *Story of Fort Fisher*, p. 11; Whiting to Mallory, September 27, 1864, *OR* 42, pt. 2, p. 1297; Whiting to Jackson, November 10, 1864, *OR* 42, pt. 3, p. 1208; Whiting to Hébert, November 11, 1864, ibid., pp. 1210-1211; David High to parents, October 23, 1864, High Family Papers, UNCW.

47. Martin D. Peebles, "CSS Raleigh: The History and Archaeology of a Civil War Ironclad in the Cape Fear River," pp. 41-67, MA thesis, East Carolina University, Greenville, North Carolina.

48. *Wilmington Daily Journal*, September 3, 1864; Whiting to Vance, September 26, 1864, *OR* 42, pt. 2, pp. 1293-1294; Whiting to Seddon, October 11, 1864, *OR* 42, pt. 3, p. 1146.

49. Davis to Vance, October 25, 1864, *OR* 42, pt. 3, pp. 1162-1163.

50. John and William Dudgeon of London, England, constructed the *Atalanta* for blockade running in 1863. In July 1864, the C. S. Navy bought and commissioned her the *Tallahassee*. The *Talahassee* (renamed the *Olustee* in October, 1864) operated as a commerce raider out of Wilmington in the late summer and autumn of 1864. In December 1864, the *Olustee* was converted back into a blockade runner and renamed *Chameleon*. Wise, *Lifeline of the Confederacy*, p. 289. "If the naval boats and officers required for the defense of Wilmington can be efficiently used for that purpose I think they had better be so applied. The loss of Wilmington to us would weigh more than the destruction of the enemy's coasters." Lee to Seddon, October 5, 1864, *OR* 42, pt. 2, p. 1295.

51. Late Confederate Officer, "Wilmington During the Blockade," *Harper's Magazine*, p. 497; Catherine Ann Devereux Edmonston, *Journal of a Sesech Lady: The Diary of Catherine Ann Devereux Edmonston* (Raleigh, 1979), p. 682; Vance to Whiting, September 28, 1864, *OR* 42, pt. 2, p. 1299.

52. See, generally, Steven E. Woodworth, "On Smaller Fields: General P. G. T. Beauregard and the Bermuda Hundred Campaign," in Steven E. Woodworth, ed., *Leadership and Command in the American Civil War* (Savas Publishing Co., Campbell, 1995), pp. 197-230, for a good modern study of this action and the Whiting's role therein.

53. Vance to Lee, September 5, 1864, *OR* 42, pt. 2, p. 1235.

54. Ibid., Lee to Vance, October 8, 1864, *OR* 42, pt. 3, p. 1142. "It is uncertain yet whether the enemy will attack Charleston or Wilmington, but it is my desire to give

General Beauregard the defense of whichever place may be attacked." Lee to Vance, September 10, 1864, *OR* 42, pt. 2, p. 1242.

55. Davis, *The Confederate General*, vol. 1, pp. 113-117; Warner, *Generals in Gray*, pp. 30-31; Faust, *Encyclopedia of the Civil War*, p. 75; Jon L. Wakelyn, *Biographical Dictionary of the Confederacy* (Westport, 1977), pp. 105-106; William Tecumseh Sherman, *Memoirs of General W. T. Sherman*, 2 vols. (New York, 1990), p. 181.

56. Jones, *A Rebel War Clerk's Diary*, vol. 2, p. 503.

57. U. S. Grant, *Personal Memoirs of U. S. Grant* (New York, 1885), pp. 449-450.

58. Jack Welsh, *Medical Histories of Confederate Generals* (Kent, 1995), p. 23; *Wilmington Daily Journal*, December 16, 1863. "The condition and threatening aspect of affairs in the District of the Cape Fear River renders it, in my judgment, desirable that you should exercise immediate command of the troops and defenses of Wilmington and its approaches." Davis to Bragg, October 15, 1864, *OR* 42, pt. 3, p. 1149.

59. *Richmond Enquirer*, October 26, 1864; *Wilmington Daily Journal*, October 31, 1864. See also: Lamb, "The Battles of Fort Fisher," *SHSP*, vol. 21, p. 266; Lamb, *Story of Fort Fisher*, pp. 10-11; Denson, *Memoir of W. H. C. Whiting*, p. 40.

60. *Wilmington Daily Journal*, September 29, 1864; Bragg to Lee, October 25, 1864, *OR* 42, pt. 3, p. 1172.

61. Vance to Davis, October 25, 1864, and Lee to Davis, November 8, 1864, *OR* 42, pt. 3, 1163.

62. Denson, *Memoir of W. H. C. Whiting*, p. 49; Whiting to Vance, September 25, 1864, *OR* 42, pt. 2, p. 1289.

63. Edmonston, *Journal of a Sesech Lady*, p. 657; General Orders No. 1, October 22, 1864, *OR* 42, pt. 3, p. 1160; Special Orders, No. 269, November 11, 1864, ibid., pp. 1209-1210; Bragg to Davis, October 25, 1864, ibid., p. 1171.

64. Bragg to Lee, October 25, 1864, ibid., pp. 1171-1172.

65. Ibid., p. 1172; "No matter who is here [Wilmington], were it Napoleon or General Lee, they would have to have troops to be able to save the place." Whiting to Vance, September 25, 1864, ibid., pt. 2, p. 1289.

66. *Wilmington Daily Journal*, October 22, 1864.

Chapter 4: The Experiment

1. Joseph M. Simms, "Personal Experiences in the Volunteer Navy During the Civil War," War Papers Read Before the Commandery of the District of Columbia, Military Order of the Loyal Legion of the United States, vol. 3, 50 (December 2, 1903), p. 22, hereinafter cited as Simms, "Personal Experiences in the Volunteer Navy," *MOLLUS*; James M. Merrill, ed., "The Fort Fisher and Wilmington Campaign: Letters From Rear Admiral David D. Porter," *North Carolina Historical Review*, XXXV, 4 (October,

1958), pp. 462, 466, hereinafter cited as Merrill, "Letters From David D. Porter," *NCHR*.

2. Porter Memoir, Porter Papers, LOC. See also, Porter to Welles, December 15, 1864, *ORN* 11, p. 195.

3. Porter Memoir, Porter Papers, LOC.

4. Merrill, "Letters From David D. Porter," *NCHR*, pp. 464-465.

5. Welles to Lincoln, October 28, 1864, *ORN* 11, p. 3.

6. Porter Memoir, Porter Papers, LOC.

7. Merrill, "Letters From David D. Porter," *NCHR*, p. 466.

8. *Wilmington Daily Journal*, November 5, 1864; "Taking Fort Fisher," *The National Tribune*, May 5, 1892; Faust, *Encyclopedia of the Civil War*, pp. 98-99; Ezra Warner, *Generals in Blue* (Baton Rouge, 1964), pp. 60-61; C. Vann Woodward, ed., *Diary of Mary Chestnut* (New Haven, 1981), p. 411.

9. Porter Memoir, Porter Papers, LOC.

10. Reed, *Combined Operations in the Civil War*, p. 337; Butler, *Butler's Book*, p. 775.

11. Proposals of Fox's Commission, November 23, 1864, *ORN* 11, pp. 215-216.

12. Porter to Watmough, December 8, 1864, ibid., p. 217; Porter to Rhind, December 17, 1864, ibid., p. 222; *Report on the Conduct of the War: The Fort Fisher Expedition*, p. 89.

13. Grant, *Memoirs of U. S. Grant*, p. 663; Horace Porter, *Campaigning With Grant* (New York, 1897), p. 377. "I have no faith in General Butler's scheme," wrote Gideon Welles. Welles, *Diary of Gideon Welles*, vol. 2, pp. 209 and 211; *Report on the Conduct of the War: The Fort Fisher Expedition*, p. 51; Memorandum of Richard Delafield, November 18, 1864, *ORN* 11, pp. 207-214; Merlin E. Sumner, ed., *The Diary of Cyrus B. Comstock* (Dayton, 1987), p. 296.

14. Welles, *Diary of Gideon Welles*, vol. 2, pp. 216-217; Grant, *Memoirs of U. S. Grant*, p. 663; Porter, *Campaigning With Grant*, p. 337.

15. Porter to Fox, November 20, 1864, *ORN* 11, pp. 78; Report of William N. Jefferies, January 16, 1865, ibid., p. 234; Porter to Macomb, November 20 and November 23, 1864,ibid., pp. 79, 83; Paul Silverstone, *Warships of the Civil War Navies* (Annapolis, 1989), p. 92;

16. "Story of the Powder-Boat," *Galaxy Magazine*, IX (January, 1870), pp. 79-80; H. C. Lockwood, "The Capture of Fort Fisher," *Atlantic Monthly Magazine*, XXVII (May, 1871), p. 625; Porter to Fox, December 2, 1864, *ORN* 11, p. 119.

17. Grant to Butler, November 30, 1864, *OR* 42, pt. 3, p. 760; Simon, *Papers of U. S. Grant*, 13, pp. 36-37; Davis to Bragg, November 22, 1864, *OR* 42, pt. 3, p. 1225; Whiting to Lee, November 29, 1864, ibid., p. 1233; Lee to Davis, December 5, 1864, ibid., pp. 1254-1255.

18. Grant to Butler, December 4, 1864, ibid., p. 799; Simon, *Papers of U. S. Grant*, 13, p. 61.

19. *New York World*, December 20, 1864; Butler, *Butler's Book*, p. 780 and Appendix, p. 64.

20. Grant to Butler, December 6, 1864, *OR* 42, pt. 3, p. 835; *Report on the Conduct of the War: The Fort Fisher Expedition*, p. 77.

21. General Weitzel emphatically stated that he never saw U.S. Grant's instructions, and that this affected his command decisions once he reached Federal Point. *Report on the Conduct of the War: The Fort Fisher Expedition*, pp. 69, 79. In his official report of operations against Fort Fisher, December 7-29, 1864, Weitzel referred to General Butler, who accompanied the expedition, as "the major-general commanding." Report of Godfrey Weitzel, December 31, 1864, *OR* 42, pt. 1, pp. 985-986. Admiral Porter claimed that "General Weitzel. . .did not know that he had been selected by General Grant to take supreme command of the troops in the [Wilmington] expedition. . .Genl Grant naturally sent the orders through Genl Butler under whose command Weitzel was and Butler put them quietly in his pocket until such time as he could make use of them. Although Genl Weitzel received some intimation that he was going with the expedition yet he never knew [he was supposed to command] until the attempt was a failure." Porter Memoir, Porter Papers, LOC.

22. Butler to Grant, December 6, 1864, *OR* 42, pt. 1, p. 973; Butler, *Butler's Book*, p. 783. Butler wrote Weitzel: "I am glad I was at [Fort Fisher] to act as a shield to a young officer, in a moment of fearful responsibility." Butler to Weitzel, January 23, 1865, OR 46, pt. 2, p. 211; *Report on the Conduct of the War: The Fort Fisher Expedition*, p. 74.

23. Porter Memoir, Porter Papers, LOC; *Report on the Conduct of the War: The Fort Fisher Expedition*, p. 80; Butler, *Butler's Book*, p. 819.

24. David D. Porter, *Incidents and Anecdotes of the Civil War* (New York, 1886), p. 262; Porter Memoir, Porter Papers, LOC; *Report on the Conduct of the War: The Fort Fisher Expedition*, p. 100; Butler, *Butler's Book*, Appendix 144, p. 89.

25. Edward G. Longacre, "A Union Sergeant in the Fort Fisher Campaign," *American History Illustrated*, XVIII, 5 (September, 1983), p. 14; Edward G. Longacre, ed., *From Antietam to Fort Fisher: The Civil War Letters of Edward K. Wightman 1862-1865* (Cranbury, 1985), p. 219; Sherman, *Memoirs of W. T. Sherman*, pp. 702 and 704.

26. "It was never contemplated that General Butler should accompany the expedition, but that Maj Gen G. Weitzel was specially named as the commander of it." Grant to Stanton, January 7, 1865, *OR* 42, pt. 1, p. 970; *Report on the Conduct of the War: The Fort Fisher Expedition*, p. 74.

27. Butler, *Butler's Book*, Appendix 144, p. 89.

28. *Report on the Conduct of the War: The Fort Fisher Expedition*, p. 73.

Grant to Stanton, January 2, 1865, *OR* 46, pt. 2, pp. 9-10; Simon, *Papers of U. S. Grant*, vol. 13, p. 205; Porter Memoir, Porter Papers, LOC; Welles, *Diary of Gideon*

Welles, vol. 2, p. 214. At one point in time, Admiral Porter claimed he did not know Butler was going to command the Fort Fisher expeditionary force until the fleet reached Cape Fear. "Even up to this time [about December 13] he did not tell me that he, himself, was going along," Porter noted, "but led me to believe Godfrey Weitzel was to be in command." Report of David D. Porter, January 22, 1865, *ORN* 11, p. 268.

29. William L. Hyde, *History of the One Hundred and Twelfth Regiment N. Y. Volunteers* (Fredonia, 1866), p. 113.

30. James Beard to Brother & Sister, December 10, 1864, Civil War Miscellaneous Collection, United States Military History Institute, Carlisle, Pennsylvania, hereinafter cited as Civil War Misc. Collection, USAMHI.

31. Charles J. Paine to Father, December 12, 1864, Charles J. Paine Papers, Virginia Historical Society, Richmond; Longacre, *From Antietam to Fort Fisher*, p. 220.

32. Benjamin J. Lossing, *Annals of the War* (Dayton, 1988), p. 234; Porter to Butler, December 13, 1864, *ORN* 11, p. 191; Report of Benjamin F. Butler, December 20, 1864, *OR* 42, pt. 1, pp. 964, 967; *Report on the Conduct of the War: The Fort Fisher Expedition*, p. 17.

33. Butler to Grant, December 20, 1864, ORA, 42, pt. 2, p. 1049; Butler, *Butler's Book*, p. 785; Entry of December 13, 1864, Scrogg's Diary, *Civil War Times Illustrated* Collection, United States Army Military History Institute, Carlisle, Pennsylvania, hereinafter cited as Scrogg's Diary, *CWTI* Collection, USAMHI; Solon Carter to Emily, December 17, 1864, Solon Carter Papers, United States Army Military History Institute, Carlisle, Pennsylvania, hereinafter cited as Solon Carter Papers, USAMHI; Entry of December 13, 1864, Simon Bennage Diary, Civil War Misc. Collection, USAMH; Isaiah Price, *History of the Ninety-Seventh Regiment Pennsylvania Volunteer Infantry During the War of the Rebellion, 1861-1865* (Philadelphia, 1875), p. 339, hereinafter cited as Price, *History of the 97th Pennsylvania Infantry*.

34. Butler to Grant, December 14, 1864, *OR* 42, pt. 3, p. 1005; *Report on the Conduct of the War: The Fort Fisher Expedition*, p. 16.

35. Entries for December 13-14, 1864, Journal of David Webb Hodgekins, personal collection of Brian E. W. Wood, Secaucus, New Jersey, hereinafter cited as Wood Collection, Secaucus, NJ.

36. Butler, *Butler's Book*, pp. 785-786; Report of Benjamin F. Butler, December 20, 1864, *OR* 42, pt. 1, p. 966; Jerry to Albert, December 11, 1864, Charles W. Smith Papers, Civil War Misc. Collection, USAMHI.

37. Report of David D. Porter, December 26, 1864, *ORN* 11, p. 254. Porter later claimed he suggested that the army and navy vessels rendezvous at Beaufort. *Report on the Conduct of the War: The Fort Fisher Expedition*, p. 90. Earlier correspondence, however, confirms that he instructed Butler to meet him at Cape Fear. "The rest of the fleet will leave here [Hampton Roads] in three hours," Porter informed Butler, "and will proceed to the rendezvous 25 miles east of Cape Fear River." Porter to Butler, Decem-

ber 13, 1864, *ORN* 11, p. 191. Reportedly, the rendezvous point given to the commanders of the ships was latitude 33 deg. 46 min. north, and longitude 27 deg. 20 min. west. *New York World*, December 31, 1864. See also: Butler, *Butler's Book*, p. 786; Report of David D. Porter, January 22, 1865, *OR* 11, pp. 268-269; *Report on the Conduct of the War: The Fort Fisher Expedition*, p. 17; Lanman to Porter, December 16, 1864, *ORN* 11, pp. 196-197; Entries of December 15-16, 1864, Journal of David Webb Hodgekins, Wood Collection, Secaucus, NJ.

38. Entries of December 15-17, 1864, Journal of David Webb Hodgekins, Wood Collection, Secaucus, NJ; *Report on the Conduct of the War: The Fort Fisher Expedition*, p. 17; Butler, *Butler's Book*, p. 787.

39. Entry of December 16, 1864, Simon Bennage Diary, Civil War Times Illustrated Collection, USAMHI; Entries of December 16-17, 1864, Diary of Christian Fleetwood, Manuscript Department, Library of Congress, Washington, D. C; Entires of December 16-17, 1864, Scrogg's Diary, *CWTI* Collection, USAMHI.

40. Porter to Butler, December 16, 1864, *ORN* 11, p. 196; *Report on the Conduct of the War: The Fort Fisher Expedition*, p. 18; Butler, *Butler's Book*, p. 787.

41. *Report on the Conduct of the War: The Fort Fisher Expedition*, p. 18.

42. Butler, *Butler's Book*, pp. 787-788; Sumner, *Diary of Cyrus Comstock*, pp. 297-298.

43. Report of David D. Porter, January 22, 1865, *ORN* 11, p. 269; Butler to Grant, December 20, 1864, *OR* 42, pt. 2, p. 1049; *Report on the Conduct of the War: The Fort Fisher Expedition*, pp. 19, 70; Butler, *Butler's Book*, pp. 788-789; "Story of the Powder-Boat," *Galaxy*, p. 85; Entries of December 18-19, 1864, Journal of David W. Hodgekins, Wood Collection, Secaucus, NJ.

44. *Report on the Conduct of the War: The Fort Fisher Expedition*, p. 19; *New York World*, December 31, 1864.

45. Report of David D. Porter, January 22, 1865, *ORN* 11, p. 268; Butler, *Butler's Book*, p. 789; Report of Cyrus Comstock, January 1, 1865, *ORN* 11, p. 357; David D. Porter, *The Naval History of the Civil War* (New York, 1886), pp. 694-695.

46. Whiting to Vance and Whiting to Hébert, December 18, 1864, *OR* 42, pt. 3, p. 1279; General Orders, No. 12, Hdqrs. Dept. Of North Carolina, ibid.; Lamb, "The Battles of Fort Fisher," *SHSP*, vol. 21, p. 267.

47. Lamb, "Heroine of Confederate Point," *SHSP*, vol. 20, p. 303; Whiting to Seddon, December 19, 1864, *OR* 42, pt. 3, p. 1281.

48. Whiting to Hébert, December 23, 1864, ibid., p. 1298.

49. Whiting to Seddon, December 19, 1864, ibid., p. 1281; Proclamation of Governor Vance, December 20, 1864, ibid., pp. 1284-1285.

50. Lee to Seddon, December 18, 1864, ibid., pp. 1278-1279; Latrobe to Kershaw and Latrobe to Hoke, December 20, 1864, ibid., pp. 1282-1283; Longstreet to Lee, December 19, 1864, ibid., p. 1280.

51. See generally, Daniel W. Barefoot, *General Robert F. Hoke: Lee's Modest Warrior* (Winston-Salem, 1996); Clark, *North Carolina Regiments*, 1, p. 116; Warner, *Generals in Gray*, p. 140; Faust, *Encyclopedia of the Civil War*, p. 365.

52. Lee to Seddon, January 11, 1865, *OR* 46, pt. 2, p. 1035.

53. Charles G. Elliott, "Kirkland's Brigade, Hoke's Division, 1864-'65," *SHSP*, 23, pp. 165-166; Clark, *North Carolina Regiments*, vol. 1, p. 409; vol. 3, pp. 692-693; Hoke to Lee, December 25, 1864, *OR* 46, pt. 2, pp. 1026-1027;

54. *Wilmington Messenger*, November 7, 1894.

55. On December 23, Colonel Lamb was reinforced by Maj. James Reilly and two companies of the 10th North Carolina Regiment (1st North Carolina Artillery), 110 artillerymen, a company of the 13th Battalion North Carolina Artillery, 115 cannoneers, and 140 boys of the 7th Battalion North Carolina Junior Reserves, for a total of 928 men (and boys) inside Fort Fisher. By Christmas day, Lamb's effective force had increased to 1,371 soldiers (921 regulars and 450 Junior Reserves). Report of William Lamb, December 27, 1864, *ORN* 11, p. 369; Lamb, "The Battles of Fort Fisher," *SHSP*, vol. 21, pp. 267, 273; Lamb, *Story of Fort Fisher*, pp. 12, 18.

56. Whiting to James, December 21, 1864, *OR* 42, pt. 3, p. 1288; Whiting to Bragg, December 20, 1864, ibid., p. 1283.

57. Butler, *Butler's Book*, p. 790.

58. General Weitzel claimed that in the opinion of at least one army officer, Admiral Porter wanted to explode the powder boat on his own "because he believed that he could knock the fort all to pieces, and would thus get credit of taking it to himself." *Report on the Conduct of the War: The Fort Fisher Expedition*, p. 81. Weitzel may have been referring to Cyrus B. Comstock, who noted in his diary on December 24, 1864: "I think [Porter] expected to destroy everything & take the work before we [the army] got here." Sumner, *Diary of Cyrus Comstock*, p. 299. Porter accused Grant of denying credit which the admiral believed was due both the navy and himself for achieving Union victories. "I have served with [Grant] before, where I never worked so hard in my life to make a man succeed as I did for him. You will scarcely notice in his reports that the navy did give him any service, when, without the help it has given him all the way through, he would never have been lieutenant-general. When the rebels write the history of this war, then, and only then, will the country be made to feel what the navy has done." Butler, *Butler's Book*, Appendix No. 144, 89. Welles, *Diary of Gideon Welles*, vol. 2, pp. 115 and 228.

59. Porter to Rhind, December 17, 1864, *ORN* 11, p. 222.

60. Ibid; "Story of the Powder-Boat," *Galaxy Magazine*, pp. 80, 88.

61. Report of A. C. Rhind, February 2, 1865, *ORN* 11, pp. 230-232 and 236-240; A. C. Rhind, "The Last of the Fort Fisher Powder-Boat," *United Service Magazine* (February, 1879), pp. 231-233; "Story of the Powder-Boat," *Galaxy Magazine*, pp. 83-84; *New York World*, December 31, 1864; Lossing, *Annals of the War*, pp. 235; Thomas Richardson to Mary Keil, December 28, 1864, personal collection of Agnes Guarrieri,

Philadelphia, Pennsylvania. See also: Report of William N. Jefferies, January 16, 1865, *ORN* 11, pp. 234-236; Reed, *Combined Operations in the Civil War*, p. 341.

62. Report of A. C. Rhind, December 26, 1864, *ORN* 11, pp. 226-227; Ammen, *The Atlantic Coast*, p. 221; *New York World*, December 31, 1864; Edgar Stanton Maclay, *Reminiscences of the Old Navy* (New York, 1898), pp. 304-305; Rhind, "The Last of the Powder-Boat," *United States Service Magazine*, pp. 230-231; "Story of the Powder-Boat," *Galaxy Magazine*, p. 88; Thomas O. Selfridge, Jr., *Memoirs of Thomas O. Selfridge, Jr.* (New York, 1924), p. 122.

63. Report of A. C. Rhind, February 2, 1865, *ORN* 11, pp. 230-232.

64. Lamb, "The Battles of Fort Fisher," *SHSP*, vol. 21, p. 269; Lamb, *Story of Fort Fisher*, pp. 13-14; Answers (numbered) of W. H. C. Whiting to questions propounded by Benjamin F. Butler, *OR* 42, pt. 1, p. 979.

65. Butler, *Butler's Book*, p. 795; Clark, *North Carolina Regiments*, vol. 4, pp. 46-47; G. G. Young to Brother, December 30, 1864, G. G. Young Letters, South Caroliniana Library, University of South Carolina, Columbia.

66. Frank D. Smaw, Jr., *Wilmington Directory, 1867* (Wilmington, 1867), p. 29.

67. Ibid; *New York Herald*, December 31, 1864.

Chapter 5: First Strike

1. Lamb, "The Battles of Fort Fisher," *SHSP*, vol. 21, p. 269; Lamb, *Story of Fort Fisher*, p. 14.

2. Grant to Stanton, July 22, 1865, *ORN* 11, pp. 358-359; Report of David D. Porter, December 26, 1864, ibid., p. 254; Silverstone, *Warships of the Civil War Navies*, p. 15.

3. Stephen Walkley, *History of the Seventh Connecticut Volunteer Infantry, 1861-1865* (Southington, 1905), p. 178.

4. *New York Herald*, December 31, 1864; Report of William Lamb, December 27, 1864, *OR* 42, pt. 1, p. 1003; Lamb, "The Battles of Fort Fisher," *SHSP*, vol. 21, p. 270; Lamb, *Story of Fort Fisher*, p. 15; *Fayetteville (N. C.) Observer Semi-Weekly*, January 2, 1865.

5. Plan of First Attack Upon Fort Fisher, Dec. 24 and 25, 1864, Showing the Position of Vessels and Line of Fire. Map, *ORN* 11, between pp. 244-245; *OR* Atlas, LXVII, 1. Note: although the *ORN* plan of attack displays their battle stations, the *Banshee, Bignonia*, and *Aries* were not present for the first Fort Fisher attack. However, the *Little Ada, Iosco, Quaker City*, and *Alabama* did participate in the battle, though their positions are not marked. See also: Henry Munroe Rogers, *Memories of Ninety Years* (Cambridge, 1928); pp. 92-93.

6. Longacre, *From Antietam to Fort Fisher*, p. 223; *Fayetteville (N.C.) Semi-Weekly Observer*, January 2, 1865; B. F. Blair to Mother, December 27, 1864, Fonvielle Collection, USAMHI.

7. Report of James F. Schenck, January 2, 1865, *ORN* 11, p. 305; Report of H. K. Thatcher, December 31, 1864, ibid., p. 295; Report of Daniel Ammen, December 31, 1864, ibid., p. 311.

8. Simms, "Personal Experiences in the Volunteer Navy," *MOLLUS*, p. 12; Asa Beetham to Emm, December 25, 1864, Asa Beetham Letters, Manuscript Department, Library of Congress, Washington, D.C.

9. B. F. Blair to Mother, December 27, 1864, Fonvielle Collection, USAMHI.

10. Reports of William Lamb, December 24 and 27, 1864, *OR* 42, pt. 1, pp. 1003-1004; Lamb, "The Battles of Fort Fisher," p. 272; Lamb, *Story of Fort Fisher*, p. 17; Report of Daniel Patterson, *OR* 42, pt. 1, p. 1017.

11. Jesse Brake, "A Civil War Memoir of Jesse Brake," personal collection of Mike Brake, Rocky Mount, North Carolina; *Charlotte News*, January 15, 1944.

12. Report of William Lamb, December 27, 1864, *OR* 42, pt. 1, p. 1006; Lamb, "The Battles of Fort Fisher," p. 271; Lamb, *Story of Fort Fisher*, p. 17. Shells from the *Iosco* knocked down the Confederate flag on the Mound Battery during the bombardment of December 24. Report of John Guest, December 27, 1864, *ORN* 11, p. 330; *Pottsville (PA) Miner's Journal*, January 14, 1865. For a rare Union account of Private Bland's feat, see MacLay, *Reminiscences of the Old Navy*, p. 307; *New York World*, December 30, 1864; *New York Herald*, December 31, 1864.

13. Lamb, "The Battles of Fort Fisher," pp. 272-273; Lamb, *Story of Fort Fisher*, pp. 16-17; Report of William Lamb, December 27, 1864, *OR* 42, pt. 1, p. 1004.

14. *Charlotte News*, January 15, 1944.

15. Report of William G. Temple, December 28, 1864, *ORN* 11, p. 286; Report of Jefferson Young, December 24, 1864, ibid., pp. 319-320; Report of J. M. B. Clitz, December 27, 1864, ibid., p. 336; Report of Charles Steedman, December 27, 1864, ibid., pp. 327-329; Report of David D. Porter, December 26, 1864, ibid., p. 256; Report of David D. Porter, December 27, 1864, ibid., p. 261; [Second Endorsement] J. S. Missroon, January 16, 1865, ibid., pp. 359-360; Report of David D. Porter, December 26, 1864, ibid., p. 259; Report of T. C. Harris, January 2, 1865, ibid., p. 312.

16. Report of Charles Steedman, December 30, 1864, ibid., p. 328; Sub-enclosure of casualties on *Ticonderoga*, Report of Charles Steedman, December 27, 1864, ibid., p. 329; Rogers, *Memories of Ninety Years*, pp. 96-97.

17. W. F. Beyer and O. F. Keydel, eds., *Deeds of Valor: How America's Heroes Won the Medal of Honor*, 2 vols (Detroit, 1903), vol. 2, p. 86; Report of Charles Steedman, December 30, 1864, *ORN* 11, p. 328.

18. Porter to Welles, December 24, 1864, ibid., p. 253.

19. Apparently, Porter believed General Butler feared assaulting Fort Fisher after the powder boat experiment had failed. The admiral claimed that he expected the "explosion would be heard on board the transports [at Beaufort, ninety miles away] and bring them all in by [Christmas Eve] morning; but although the water was quite smooth, the

transports seemed to keep as far as possible from Fort Fisher." Porter, *Naval History of the Civil War*, p. 696.

20. Butler to Porter, December 24, 1864, ibid., p. 250; *Report on the Conduct of the War: The Fort Fisher Expedition*, p. 95. Butler noted that Porter said he was too tired to meet that night. Butler, *Butler's Book*, p. 791.

21. Report of W. H. C. Whiting, December 31, 1864, *OR* 42, pt. 1, p. 997; General Orders, No. 14, December 24, 1864, ibid., p. 1303.

22. Report of William W. Kirkland, December 30, 1864, ibid., pp. 1020-1022.

23. Ibid., p. 1021; David High to James High, June 18, 1864, High Family Papers, McEachern and Williams Collection, UNCW; Lamb, "The Battles of Fort Fisher," *SHSP*, vol. 21, p. 268; Lamb, *Story of Fort Fisher,* p. 12.

24. Report of William W. Kirkland, December 30, 1864, *OR* 42, pt. 1, pp. 1020-1022; Elliott, "Kirkland's Brigade, Hoke's Division," *SHSP*, vol. 23, p. 166.

25. Report of William W. Kirkland, December 30, 1864, ibid., pt. 1, p. 1021; Report of John P. W. Read, December 29, 1864, ibid., pt. 1, p. 1023; Report of Thomas J. Southerland, December 29, 1864, ibid., p. 1024; Extract From the Official Diary of William Lamb, *ORN* 11, p. 742.

26. Report of William W. Kirkland, December 30, 1864, *OR* 42, pt. 1, p. 1021; Elliott, "Kirkland's Brigade," p. 166.

27. Entry of December 25, 1864, Journal of David Webb Hodgekins, Wood Collection, Secaucus, NJ.

28. At Admiral Porter's request, Capt. Oliver S. Glisson of the *Santiago De Cuba* superintended the landing of the army. Report of Oliver S. Glisson, December 25, 1864, *ORN* 11, pp. 332-333. See also: Report of Godfrey Weitzel, December 31, 1864, *OR* 42, pt. 1, p. 986.

29. Enclosure: Report of casualties near Sugar Loaf, December 25, 1864, *OR* 42, pt. 1, pp. 1023-1024; Report of Thomas J. Southerland, December 29, 1864, ibid., p. 1024-1025; Elliott, "Kirkland's Brigade, Hoke's Division," *SHSP*, vol. 23, p. 166; Report of John P. W. Read, December 29, 1864, *OR* 42, pt. 1, pp. 1023-1024; Report of Thomas J. Southerland, December 29, 1864, ibid., pp. 1024-1025.

30. Hyde, *History of the 112th N. Y. Volunteers*, p. 116.

31. N. Martin Curtis, *The Capture of Fort Fisher* (n.p., 1897), p. 29; Report of N. Martin Curtis, December 28, 1864, *OR* 42, pt. 1, p. 982; N. Martin Curtis, "Address to Companions," p. 14, N. Martin Curtis Collection, Chicago Historical Society, Chicago, Illinois; Report of Godfrey Weitzel, December 31, 1864, *OR* 42, pt. 1, p. 986; Henry R. Jackson and Thomas F. O'Donnell, eds., *Back Home in Oneida: Hermon Clarke and His Letters* (Syracuse, 1965), p. 182; *New York Herald*, December 30 and 31, 1864; George F. Towle, "Terry's Fort Fisher Expedition," *Old and New*, XI, 3 (March, 1875), p. 290; Warner, *Generals in Blue*, pp. 106-107; Special Orders, No.—, November 11,

1864, *OR* 42, pt. 3, p. 619; St. Lawrence County Historical Association, *St. Lawrence Chronicler*, vol. 8, no. 3 (1993), pp. 1-8.

32. Report of N. Martin Curtis, December 28, 1864, *OR* 42, pt. 1, p. 982; Hyde, *History of the 112th N. Y. Volunteers*, p. 120; Report of Godfrey Weitzel, December 31, 1864, *OR* 42, pt. 1, p. 986.

33. Extract From the Official Diary of William Lamb, *ORN* 11, p. 746. For a listing of the Confederate soldiers captured at Battery Anderson and other casualties of General Kirkland's Brigade, see *Raleigh Daily Confederate*, January 20, 1865. General Kirkland reported that eighty-two of his men were captured at Battery Anderson. Report of William W. Kirkland, December 30, 1864, *OR* 42, pt. 1, pp. 1021, 1023. See also, Report of Godfrey Weitzel, December 31, 1864, ibid., p. 986; Report of Oliver S. Glisson, December 25, 1864, *ORN* 11, pp. 332-333; Report of Samuel Huse, December 31, 1864, ibid., pp. 351-352; James E. Reid, "115th New York Regiment," *Ballston (N. Y.) Journal*, March 4, 1893 and June 6, 1896, Civil War Misc. Collection, USAMHI, Carlisle, Pennsylvania; *New York Herald*, December 31, 1864

34. Report of William W. Kirkland, December 30, 1864, *OR* 42, pt. 1, pp. 1021-1022; Kirkland to Van Der Horst, December 25, 1864, ibid., pt. 3, p. 1309; Clark, *North Carolina Regiments*, vol. 2, p. 9.

35. Rogers, *Memories of Ninety Years*, p. 98; G. G. Young to Brother, December 30, 1864, G. G. Young Letters, South Caroliniana Library, University of South Carolina, Columbia; Journal of Joseph Canning, (n.d.), McEachern and Williams Collection, UNCW.

36. Whiting to Bragg, December 24, 1864, *OR* 42, pt. 3, p. 1302; Whiting to Bragg, January 5, 1865, ibid., pt. 1, 1026; Report of William W. Kirkland, December 30, 1864, ibid., p. 1021; Clark, *North Carolina Regiments*, vol. 4, p. 47.

37. Ibid.; *Wilmington Daily Journal*, December 28, 1864.

38. Alfred Moore Waddell, *Some Memories of My Life* (Raleigh, 1908), pp. 57-58.

39. Report of William Lamb, December 27, 1864, *OR* 42, pt. 1, p. 1004; Chapman to Pinckney, December 29, 1864, *ORN* 11, p. 373; Report of William Truxton, December 27, 1864, ibid., p. 334; Hopkins to Truxton, December 27, 1864, ibid., p. 335; Porter, *Naval History of the Civil War*, p. 698.

40. Reports of Francis M. Roby, December 1864, *ORN* 11, p. 374; Extract From Diary of Clarence Cary, December 25, 1864, ibid., p. 377; Unofficial Letter From Aeneas Armstrong to Francis L. Galt, December 29, 1864, ibid., p. 375.

41. General Weitzel wrote in his official report that he believed he and General Curtis had advanced to within 800 yards of Fort Fisher from where they had "a good view of the work." Later examinations by U.S. Army engineers and by General Curtis, accompanied by Col. William Lamb, determined the distance to be 2,200 yards from Fort Fisher's northeast bastion. N. Martin Curtis, "Speech Before the Army-Navy Club, Washington, February, 1895," pp. 3-4, N. Martin Curtis Civil War Collection, Og-

densburg Public Library, Ogdensburg, New York; N. Martin Curtis, "Notes (Early Draft) of Speech Before the Army-Navy Club, Washington, D.C., February, 1895," pp. 4-5, N. Martin Curtis Civil War Collection, Ogdensburg Public Library, Ogdensburg, New York; Report of Godfrey Weitzel, December 31, 1864, *OR* 42, pt. 1, pp. 985-986; *Report on the Conduct of the War: The Fort Fisher Expedition*, pp. 41-42.

42. Report of Godfrey Weitzel, December 31, 1864, *OR* 42, pt. 1, p. 986; *Report on the Conduct of the War: The Fort Fisher Expedition*, pp. 72-73.

43. Report of N. Martin Curtis, December 28, 1864, *OR* 42, pt. 1, p. 982; Curtis, "Speech Before the Army-Navy Club," p. 4; Curtis, "Draft of Speech Before the Army-Navy Club," N. Martin Curtis Collection, Ogdensburg Public Library.

44. Curtis, *The Capture of Fort Fisher*, p. 30; Report of N. Martin Curtis, December 28, 1864, *OR* 42, pt. 1, pp. 982-983.

45. William H. Walling recalled capturing the Confederate flag sometime before half past three o'clock Christmas afternoon. General Curtis later substantiated that time, probably after conferring with Walling. "How the Flag Was Captured at Fort Fisher," correspondence between W. H. Walling and William Lamb, March, 1888, and W. H. Walling to N. Martin Curtis, April 5, 1897, N. Martin Curtis Collection, Chicago Historical Society, Chicago, Illinois; Beyer and Keydel, *Deeds of Valor*, vol. 1, p. 471. See also: Curtis, *The Capture of Fort Fisher*, p. 30; Report of N. Martin Curtis, December 28, 1865, *OR* 42, pt. 1, p. 983; Testimony of James Spring, Addenda Inclosures, January 17, 1865, *OR* 42, pt. 1, p. 976.

46. Addenda Inclosures, January 17, 1865, *OR* 42, pt. 1, pp. 976-977.

47. Lamb, *Story of Fort Fisher*, p. 18; *Wilmington Daily Journal*, December 30, 1864; E. Hepple Hall, "Reminiscences of the War: The Wilmington Expedition," *United States Service Magazine*, IV (1865), p. 319, hereinafter cited as Hall, "The Wilmington Expedition," *United States Service Magazine*; Entry of December 25, 1864, Journal of David Webb Hodgekins, Wood Collection, Secaucus, NJ.

48. Addenda Inclosures, January 17, 1865, *OR* 42, pt. 1, p. 975; George Simpson, "Capture of Fort Fisher," p. 6, N. Martin Curtis Collection, Chicago Historical Society, Chicago, Illinois, hereinafter cited as Simpson, "Capture of Fort Fisher," Curtis Collection, Chicago Historical Society; Report of N. Martin Curtis, December 28, 1864, *OR* 42, pt. 1, p. 983; Curtis, *The Capture of Fort Fisher*, p. 30; *New York Herald*, December 31, 1864.

49. Simpson, "Capture of Fort Fisher," pp. 6-7, Curtis Collection, Chicago Historical Society.

50. Curtis, "Speech Before the Army-Navy Club," pp. 4-5, Curtis, "Draft of Speech Before the Army-Navy Club," p. 5, Ogdensburg Public Library; Curtis, "Address to Companions," p. 11, Curtis Collection, Chicago Historical Society.

51. Simpson, "Capture of Fort Fisher," p. 7.

52. Ibid; Curtis, "Speech Before the Army-Navy Club," p. 5, Ogdensburg Public Library; Curtis, "Draft of Speech Before the Army-Navy Club," p. 5, Ogdensburg Public Library; Curtis, *The Capture of Fort Fisher*, p. 30.

53. Butler, *Butler's Book*, p. 796.

54. *Report on the Conduct of the War: The Fort Fisher Expedition*, pp. 23-24, 73; Report of Godfrey Weitzel, December 31, 1864, *OR* 42, pt. 1, p. 986.

55. Report of Benjamin Butler, January 3, 1865, *OR* 42, pt. 1, p. 968; *Report on the Conduct of the War: The Fort Fisher Expedition*, pp. 23-24; Reed, *Combined Operations in the Civil War*, pp. 350-351.

56. Curtis, *The Capture of Fort Fisher*, p. 31.

57. Curtis, "Speech Before the Army-Navy Club," p. 5, N. Martin Curtis Collection, Chicago Historical Society.

58. Ibid., p. 6; Curtis, *The Capture of Fort Fisher*, p. 31.

59. Report of N. Martin Curtis, December 28, 1864, *OR* 42, pt. 1, p. 983.

60. Curtis, "Draft of Speech Before the Army-Navy Club," p. 6, Curtis Collection, Ogdensburg, Public Library; Curtis, "Address to Companions," p. 12, Curtis Collection, Chicago Historical Soceity.

61. Report of Adelbert Ames, December 28, 1864, *OR* 42, pt. 1, p. 981; Report of N. Martin Curtis, December 28, 1864, *OR* 42, pt. 1, p. 983; Curtis, "Draft of Speech Before the Army-Navy Club," p. 7, Curtis Collection, Ogdensburg Public Library; Curtis, "Address to Companions," p. 12, Curtis Collection, Chicago Historical Society; Sumner, *Diary of Cyrus Comstock*, p. 299.

62. Brooks Thompson and Frank Lawrence Owsley, Jr., eds., "The War Journal of Midshipman Cary," *Civil War History,* 9 (June, 1963), p. 201. See also: Extract From Diary of Clarence Cary, *ORN* 11, p. 377; Lamb, "The Battles of Fort Fisher," *SHSP*, vol. 21, p. 274; Lamb, *Story of Fort Fisher,* pp. 18-19; Report of W. H. C. Whiting, December 30, 1864, *OR* 42, pt. 1, p. 995.

63. Ibid; Clark, *North Carolina Regiments*, vol. 4, p. 49.

64. Cyrus Comstock testified that he "saw [Fort Fisher] the first time about the same time General Weitzel did, and at about the same distance. . .I thought the work at that time very difficult of assault; I thought then the chances of success were not more than even. . .[Then] I saw General Curtis. . .and he believed he could take it with [a brigade] . . .If I had been in command of the forces at that point, I should have made the trial to take the fort. My opinion as to the practicability of an assault when I first saw the work was changed subsequently by the statement of General Curtis." *Report on the Conduct of the War: The Fort Fisher Expedition*, pp. 84-85.

Adelbert Ames stated that "upon the report of. . .General Curtis that he could take the fort I sent his brigade forward to make the attempt. By the time he reached his position it was dark, and the navy had almost entirely ceased its fire. The [Confederate] troops, which during the day had to seek shelter, now boldly manned their guns. Had the attack been made it would have failed." Report of Adelbert Ames, December 28, 1864, *OR* 42, pt. 1, p. 981. See also: Report of N. Martin Curtis, December 28, 1864, *OR* 42, pt. 1, p. 983; Curtis, "Speech Before the Army-Navy Club," pp. 6-7, Curtis Collection, Ogdensburg Public Library.

65. Report of Adelbert Ames, December 28, 1864, *OR* 42, pt. 1, p. 981; Adelbert Ames, "The Capture of Fort Fisher," *MOLLUS*, (Boston, 1900), vol. 1, p. 276, hereinafter cited as Ames, "The Capture of Fort Fisher," *MOLLUS*; Curtis, *The Capture of Fort Fisher*, p. 31.

66. Pearce, "The Expeditions Against Fort Fisher," *MOLLUS*, p. 386.

67. Curtis, "Address to Companions," p. 13, Curtis Collection, Chicago Historical Soceity; Curtis, "Speech Before the Army-Navy Club," p. 7; Curtis, "Draft of Speech Before the Army-Navy Club," p. 7, Curtis Collection, Ogdensburg Public Library.

68. According to General Butler's testimony to the Congressional Committee on the Conduct of the War, Major Reece surrendered 218 boys and five officers of the 4th and 8th battalions of the North Carolina Junior Reserves. *Report on the Conduct of the War: The Fort Fisher Expedition*, p. 24. See also, Curtis, "Draft of Speech Before the Army-Navy Club," p. 7, Curtis Collection, Ogdensburg Public Library. James A. Mowris, historian of the 117th New York Infantry, claimed that 222 boys and seven officers were taken prisoner. Mowris, *History of the 117th New York Volunteers*, p. 157. Lieutenant F. M. Hamlin of the 4th Battalion North Carolina Junior Reserves listed six officers captured in his report of the incident. Report of F.M. Hamlin, December 28, 1864, *OR* 42, pt. 1, p. 1026.

69. Clark, *North Carolina Regiments*, vol. 4, pp. 47-48.

70. Mowris, *History of the 117th New York Volunteers*, pp. 156-157. See also: Howard Thomas, *Boys In Blue From the Adirondack Foothills* (Prospect, 1960), pp. 248-249.

71. Five officers and four privates of the Junior Reserves refused to surrender and escaped to Sugar Loaf. Report of F. M. Hamlin, December 28, 1864, *OR* 42, pt. 1, pp. 1025-1026; Clark, *North Carolina Regiments*, vol. 4, pp. 48-49. General Whiting reported that Major Reece acted on his own responsibility when he left Fort Fisher with his command during the battle. Whiting to Bragg, January 5, 1865, *OR* 42, pt. 1, p. 1026.

72. Quote is from T. W. Skinner to Dear Friend at Home, January 2, 1865, copy of letter in personal collection of Chris E. Fonvielle, Jr., Wilmington, North Carolina. For a good, anecdotal description of Stevens' capture of Major Reece and his battalion of Junior Reserves, see: Mowris, *History of the 117th New York Volunteers*, pp. 154-157. See also: Simpson, "Capture of Fort Fisher," Curtis Collection, Chicago Historical Society.

73. Curtis, "Speech Before the Army-Navy Club," p. 7, Curtis Collection, Ogdensburg Public Library; *New York World*, December 31, 1864; Longacre, *From Antietam to Fort Fisher*, p. 226.

74. Simpson, "Capture of Fort Fisher," p. 7, Curtis Collection, Chicago Historical Society.

75. Report of William Lamb, December 27, 1864, *OR* 42, pt. 1, p. 1005.

76. Lamb, "The Battles of Fort Fisher," *SHSP*, vol. 21, p. 275; Lamb, *Story of Fort Fisher*, p. 20; Whiting to Bragg, December 25, 1864, *OR* 42, pt. 3, p. 1306; Parker to Whiting, December 25, 1864, ibid., pt. 3, p. 1307; Bragg to Pinckney, December 26, 1864, ibid., pt. 3, p. 1312; Whiting to Bragg, December 26, 1864, ibid., pt. 3, p 1312;

77. Report of William Lamb, December 27, 1864, *OR* 42, pt. 1, p. 1005; Report of W. H. C. Whiting, December 30, 1864, *OR* 42, pt. 1, p. 995; Lamb, *Story of Fort Fisher*, pp. 19-20; Lamb, "The Battles of Fort Fisher," *SHSP*, vol. 21, p. 275.

78. Porter Memoir, Porter Papers, p. 858, LOC. See also: *Report on the Conduct of the War: The Fort Fisher Expedition*, p. 57.

79. Porter to Butler, December 26, 1864, *OR* 51; pt. 1, p. 1291; Porter to Butler, December 26, 1864, *ORN* 11, p. 252.

80. Butler to Porter, December 25, 1864, *OR* 42, pt. 3, pp. 1075-1076; Butler to Porter, December 25, 1864, *ORN* 11, pp. 250-251.

Chapter 6: Recriminations

1. Longacre, *From Antietam to Fort Fisher*, p. 226; Hall, "The Wilmington Expedition," *U. S. Service Magazine*, p. 319.

2. Curtis, "Speech Before the Army-Navy Club," pp. 7-8, Curtis Collection, Ogdensburg Public Library.

3. Correspondence of Chaplain, December 29, 1864, Scrapbook on the 117th New York Volunteers, Rome Historical Society, Rome, New York; *New York Herald*, December 31, 1864.

4. Parker to Whiting, December 26, 1864, *OR* 42, pt. 3, p. 1315; Hoke to Holmes, December 26, 1864, ibid., p. 1318; Arms-bearing men present for duty, Sugar Loaf, December 26, 1864, ibid., p. 1314; Answers (numbered) of W. H. C. Whiting to questions propounded by Benjamin F. Butler, *OR* 42, pt. 1, p. 981; Lamb, *Story of Fort Fisher*, p. 21.

5. Curtis, *The Capture of Fort Fisher*, p. 32; Curtis, "Address to Companions," pp. 14-15, Curtis Collection, Chicago Historical Society; George M. Smith to John C. Howell, December 27, 1864, *ORN* 11, p. 291; *New York Herald*, December 31, 1864.

6. Simpson, "Capture of Fort Fisher," p. 8, Curtis Collection, Chicago Historical Society; Longacre, *From Antietam to Fort Fisher*, p. 221.

7. John M. Johnston, "Recollections of J. M. Johnston," p. 2, copy in personal collection of Chris E. Fonvielle, Jr.

8. Whiting to Seddon, January 1, 1865, *OR* 46, pt. 2, p. 1001; Report of David D. Porter, January 17, 1865, *ORN*, 11, p. 441; Reports of Spyers Singleton, December 30, 1864, *OR* 42, pt. 1, pp. 1007-1009; Report of Louis Hébert, January 3, 1865, ibid., p. 1001.

9. Report of W. H. C. Whiting, December 30, 1864, *OR* 46, pt. 1, p. 996; Extract From the Official Diary of William Lamb, *ORN*, 11, pp. 746-747.

10. Whiting to Seddon, January 1, 1865, *OR* 46, pt. 2, pp. 1000-1001.

11. Report of W. H. C. Whiting, December 30, 1864, *OR* 42, pt. 1, p. 997; Whiting to Anderson, December 30, 1864, *OR* 51, pt. 2, p. 1056; General Orders, No. 17, December 29, 1864, *OR* 42, pt. 1, p. 999.

12. Smaw, *Wilmington Directory*, 1867, p. 30; *Wilmington Daily North Carolinian*, December 29, 1864.

13. Lamb to Vance, January 7, 1865, Zebulon B. Vance Papers, Division of Archives and History, Raleigh, North Carolina; *Wilmington Daily Journal*, January 19, 1865.

14. *Wilmington Daily Journal*, December 31, 1864, January 6, 1865; Extract From the Official Diary of William Lamb, *ORN* 11, p. 747.

15. Whiting to Seddon, January 1, 1865, *OR* 46, pt. 2, p. 1000.

16. *Wilmington Daily Journal*, December 28, 1864; *Wilmington Daily North Carolinian*, January 4, 1865.

17. Bragg to Taylor, January 5, 1865, *OR* 46, pt. 2, p. 1015; Lamb, "The Battles of Fort Fisher," *SHSP*, vol. 21, p. 276; Lamb, The *Story of Fort Fisher*, p. 22; Whiting to Hébert, December 31, 1864, *OR* 42, pt. 3, pp. 1360-1361; Extract From the Official Diary of William Lamb, *ORN* 11, p. 747; George H. Moffett to Wife, January 2, 1865, George Hall Moffett Papers, South Carolina Historical Society, Charleston; Clark, *North Carolina Regiments*, vol. 2, p. 802 and vol. 4, p. 541.

18. Butler to Grant, December 27, 1864, *OR* 42, pt. 1, pp. 965-966; Simon, *Papers of U. S. Grant*, vol. 13, pp. 174-175.

19. Grant to Lincoln, December 28, 1864, *OR* 42, pt. 3, p. 1087.

20. Alonzo Alden to Captain, December 31, Alonzo Alden Letter, Civil War Misc. Collection, United States Army Military History Institute, Carlisle, Pennsylvania; Simpson, "Capture of Fort Fisher," p. 8, Curtis Collection, Chicago Historical Society; Longacre, *From Antietam to Fort Fisher*, pp. 221, 226.

21. Curtis, "Draft of Speech Before the Army-Navy Club," pp. 7-8; Curtis, "Speech Before the Army-Navy Club," pp. 8-9, Curtis Collection, Ogdensburg Public Library; Curtis, *The Capture of Fort Fisher*, p. 32.

22. Addenda Inclosures, January 17, 1865, *OR* 42, pt. 1, pp. 975-976; Curtis, "Draft of Speech Before the Army-Navy Club," pp. 10-11, Curtis Collection, Ogdensburg

Public Library; Simpson, "Capture of Fort Fisher, p. 8, Curtis Collection, Chicago Historical Society.

23. Report of Benjamin F. Butler, January 1, 1865, *OR* 42, pt. 1, pp. 966; Report of Benjamin F. Butler, January 3, 1865, ibid., p. 968; *Report on the Conduct of the War: The Fort Fisher Expedition*, p. 26; Charles J. Paine to Father, January 16, 1865, Charles J. Paine Papers, Virginia Historical Society, Richmond; Curtis, *The Capture of Fort Fisher*, p. 32.

24. Report of David D. Porter, December 27, 1864, *ORN* 11, p. 261.

25. Porter to Sherman, December 29, 1864, *ORN* 11, pp. 388-389.

26. *New York World*, December 30 and 31, 1864; *New York Herald*, January 16, 1865; Charles J. Paine to Charles C. Paine, February 7, 1865, Charles J. Paine Papers, Virginia Historical Society, Richmond; Report of Cyrus B. Comstock, January 1, 1865, *ORN* 11, p. 357; Grant to Stanton, January 1, 1865, *OR* 46, pt. 2, p. 3.

27. Comstock to Rawlins, January 8, 1865, *OR* 46, pt. 2, p. 69; *Report on the Conduct of the War: The Fort Fisher Expedition*, pp. 76, 90.

28. Merrill, "Letters From Rear Admiral David D. Porter," *NCHR*, p. 469; Porter to Sherman, January 3, 1865, *ORN* 11, p. 408; Butler, *Butler's Book*, Appendix 144, pp. 88-91; Porter Memoir, Porter Papers, LOC.

29. Butler, *Butler's Book*, pp. 807, 818-819 and Appendix 138, p. 85; *New York World*, December 31, 1864.

30. *Report on the Conduct of the War: The Fort Fisher Expedition*, pp. 1-56, 67-82.

31. Ibid., p. viii; Grant to Stanton, January 4, 1865, *OR* 46, pt. 2, pp. 29, 60; Simon, *Papers of U. S. Grant*, vol. 13, pp. 223-225.

32. Butler, *Butler's Book*, pp. 888-889; Simon, *Papers of U. S. Grant*, vol. 13, note, p. 224; Ord to Grant, January 11, 1865, *OR* 46, pt. 2, p. 98.

33. Canning Journal, p. 55, McEachern and Williams Collection, UNCW.

34. Welles, *Diary of Gideon Welles*, vol. 2, p. 214.

35. Fox to Grant, January 4, 1865, *OR* 46, pt. 2, p. 29; Welles to Grant, December 29, 1865, *ORN* 11, p. 391.

36. Sherman to Grant, December 24, 1865, *OR* 44, p. 797; Sherman to Halleck, December 24, 1864, *ibid.*, pp. 798-799; Sherman to Porter, December 31, 1864, *ORN* 11, p. 397.

37. Simon, *Papers of U. S. Grant*, vol. 13, pp. 130, 168-169.

38. "The Capture of Fort Fisher," *Harper's Weekly Magazine*, February 4, 1865.

39. Grant to Porter, December 30, 1864, *OR* 42, pt. 3, pp. 1100-1101; Simon, *Papers of U. S. Grant*, vol. 13, p. 190. See also: Grant to Stanton, December 30, 1864, *OR* 42, pt. 3, p. 1099.

40. Porter to Grant, January 1, 1865, *ORN* 11, p. 401; Merrill, "Letters of Rear Admiral David D. Porter," *NCHR*, p. 467.

41. Porter to Grant, January 1, 1865, *ORN* 11, p. 401; Simon, *Papers of U. S. Grant*, vol. 13, pp. 197-199; Grant to Terry, January 3, 1865, *OR* 46, pt. 2, p. 25.

42. Porter, *Campaigning With Grant*, p. 368; Grant to Butler, January 2, 1865, *OR* 46, pt. 2, p. 15.

43. William J. Finan, *Major General Alfred Howe Terry (1827-1890) Hero of Fort Fisher* (Connecticut, 1965), pp. 4-9; *New Haven Register*, January 10, 1965; Warner, *Generals in Blue*, pp. 497-498; Faust, *Encyclopedia of the Civil War*, pp. 748-749; Grant, *Memoirs of U. S. Grant*, p. 772.

44. Special Orders, No. 2, January 2, 1865, *OR* 46, pt. 2, p. 11; Andrews, *The North Reports the Civil War*, pp. 615-619; Longacre, "The Task Before Them," *CWTI*, p. 37.

45. Organization of the U.S. Forces, commanded by Maj. Gen. Alfred H. Terry, at Fort Fisher, N.C., January 13-15, 1865, *OR* 46, pt. 1, pp. 403-404; Frank Welcher, *The Union Army 1861-1865 Organization and Operations, Volume 1: The Eastern Theater* (Bloomington and Indianapolis, 1989), pp. 234-237; Frederick H. Dyer, *A Compendium of the War of the Rebellion*, 2 vols. (Dayton, 1979), vol. 1, pp. 358-359; Henry L. Abbot, *Siege Artillery in the Campaigns Against Richmond* (New York, 1868), p. 174; Abstract from the return of the expeditionary forces, Bvt. Maj. Gen. Alfred H. Terry, U.S. Army, commanding, for January 10, 1865, *OR* 46, pt. 1, p. 403; Report of the Movement and Operations of the 1st Connecticut Heavy Artillery, For the Year Ending March 31, 1865, As Given in the Annual Report of the Adjutant General of Connecticut, April 11, 1865 (Hartford, 1865), p. 61; Sumner, *Diary of Cyrus Comstock*, p. 301.

46. Simon, *Papers of U. S. Grant*, vol. 13, pp. 204-205; Grant to Halleck, January 9, 1865, *OR* 46, pt. 2, p. 74; Reed, *Combined Operations in the Civil War*, pp. 358-359.

47. Carleton to Tilton, January 3, 1865, *OR* 46, pt. 2, p. 26; John W. Ames, "The Victory at Fort Fisher," *Overland Monthly*, IX (1872), pp. 323-324; Francis Minot Weld, *Diaries and Letters of Francis Minot Weld With a Sketch of His Life* (Boston, 1925), p. 180; Walkley, *History of the 7th Connecticut Infantry*, p. 179.

48. Grant to Terry, January 3, 1865, *OR* 46, pt. 2, p. 25; Adrian Terry, "Blockade Running & Its Death Blow at Wilmington, NC., With the Two Expeditions Against Fort Fisher," p. 35, Terry Family Papers, Yale University Library, New Haven, Connecticut, hereinafter cited as Terry, "The Two Expeditions Against Fort Fisher," Yale; Porter, *Campaigning With Grant*, p. 369.

49. Grant to Terry, January 3, 1865, *OR* 46, pt. 2, p. 25.

50. Blanche Ames Ames, *Adelbert Ames* (New York, 1964), pp. 1-4, 23; Faust, *Encyclopedia of the Civil War*, p. 11; Warner, *Generals in Blue*, pp. 5-6.

51. Curtis, "Speech Before the Army-Navy Club," pp. 12-13; Curtis, "Draft of Speech Before the Army-Navy Club," pp. 15-16, Curtis Collection, Ogdensburg Public Library; Walling to Curtis, January 1, 1891, Curtis Collection, Chicago Historical Society; Curtis, *The Capture of Fort Fisher*, p. 33.

52. Eldredge, *Third New Hampshire Infantry*, pp. 575, 831; *New York Tribune*, January 18, 1865.

53. Porter to Grant, January 3, 1865, *OR* 46, pt. 2, p. 20; Merrill, "Letters From Rear Admiral David D. Porter," *NCHR*, p. 467.

54. Porter Memoir, Porter Papers, LOC; Porter, *Naval History of the Civil War*, p. 711.

55. Terry to Rawlins, January 10, 1865, *OR* 46, pt. 2, pp. 89-90; Report of David D. Porter, January 14, 1865, *ORN* 11, p. 432; Francis P. B. Sands, "The Last of the Blockade and the Fall of Fort Fisher," *Military Order of the Loyal Legion of the United States, Commandery of the District of Columbia*, 40 (1902), p. 17; Report of Alfred H. Terry, January 25, 1865, *OR*, 46, pt. 1, p. 396; Longacre, "The Task Before Them," *CWTI*, p. 38; *New York Times*, January 18, 1865.

56. *Charlotte News*, January 15, 1944; Lamb, "The Battles of Fort Fisher," *SHSP*, vol. 21, pp. 276-277; Lamb, "The Defense of Fort Fisher," *Battles and Leaders*, vol. 4, p. 647; Lamb, *Story of Fort Fisher*, p. 22. A contemporary newspaper reported that Dougald MacMillan of Sloop Point near Topsail Sound "discovered. . .the approach of the enemy, and sought to communicate by telegraph to Genl. Bragg the fact; but the operator was not in a condition to send the dispatch, and it became necessary to transmit the news by messenger." The messenger did not reach Wilmington until the next morning, and by then the Battle of Fort Fisher was underway. *Raleigh Daily Confederate*, January 25, 1865; Johnson Hagood, *Memoirs of the War of Secession* (Columbia, 1910), p. 323.

Chapter 7: Reappearance

1. Clark, *North Carolina Regiments*, vol. 1, p. 409, vol. 3, p. 215, 693; Sprunt, *Chronicles of the Cape Fear River*, p. 492.

2. Longstreet to Lee and Longstreet to Taylor, January 8, 1865, *OR* 46, pt. 2, p. 1023; Longstreet to Lee and Latrobe to Ewell, January 8, 1865, ibid., p. 1024.

3. Anderson to Hoke, January 12, 1865, *OR* 46, pt. 2, p. 1044; Report of Efficient and Non Efficient Present in Hoke's Division, January-February, 1865, Robert F. Hoke Papers, Division of Archives and History, Raleigh, North Carolina; Anne King Gregorie, "Diary of Captain Joseph Julius Wescoat, 1863-1865," *South Carolina Historical Magazine*, LIX (1958), p. 89, hereinafter cited as Gregorie, "Diary of J. J. Westcoat," *SCHM*; Elliott, "Kirkland's Brigade, Hoke's Division," *SHSP*, vol. 23, p. 167; Anderson to Grainger, January 13, 1865, *OR* 46, pt. 2, p. 1047; Bragg to Vance, January 14, 1865, ibid., p. 1053.

4. Lamb, "The Battles of Fort Fisher," *SHSP*, vol. 21, pp. 276-277; Lamb, *Story of Fort Fisher*, p. 22; Lamb, "Defense of Fort Fisher," *Battles and Leaders*, vol. 4, p. 647; William Lamb, "Defence of Fort Fisher, North Carolina," *Operations on the Atlantic*

Coast 1861-1865, Virginia 1862, 1864 Vicksburg, IX (Boston, 1912), pp. 370-371, hereinafter cited as Lamb, "Defence of Fort Fisher, NC," *Operations on the Atlantic Coast*; Report of Braxton Bragg, January 20, 1865, *OR* 46, pt. 1, p. 431.

5. Report of Alfred H. Terry, January 28, 1865, *OR* 46, pt. 1, p. 396; Longacre, "The Task Before Them," *CWTI*, p. 38; [Enclosure] Minutes, January 13, 1865, by O. B. McCurdy, *ORN* 11, p. 492; *New York Tribune*, January 18, 1865.

6. *New York Tribune*, January 18, 1865; A. G. Jones, "Fort Fisher: The Part Taken By the 27th U. S. Colored Troops," *National Tribune*, July 17, 1890; *New York Tribune*, January 18, 1865.

7. John W. Ames, "The Victory at Fort Fisher," *Overland Monthly*, p. 325; "A Yankee Account of the Battle of Fort Fisher," *Our Living and Our Dead*, vol. 1, No. 4 (December, 1874), pp. 317-318. See also: Longacre, "The Task Before Them," *CWTI*, p. 38; Edward H. Hall, "Reminiscences of the War: The Wilmington Expedition," *United States Service Magazine*, V (1866), p. 44; Weld, *Diaries and Letters of Francis Weld*, pp. 181-182; *New York Times*, January 18, 1865.

8. Report of Alfred H. Terry, January 25, 1865, *OR* 46, pt. 1, p. 396; *New York Times*, January 18, 1865. Captain Adrian Terry claimed that Abbott's skirmishers crossed Myrtle Sound on a bridge located slightly north of the Federals' beachhead. Adrian Terry, "Capture of Fort Fisher," p. 1, Terry Family Papers, Yale University Library, New Haven, Connecticut; Longacre, "The Task Before Them," *CWTI*, p. 38.

9. Anderson to Whiting, January 13, 1865, *OR* 46, pt. 2, p. 1043; Hoke to Anderson, January 13, 1865, ibid., p. 1048; Elliott, "Kirkland's Brigade, Hoke's Division," *SHSP*, vol. 23, pp. 167-168.

10. Report of Braxton Bragg, January 20, 1865, *OR* 46, pt. 1, p. 432.

11. Asa King Memoir, Confederate Veterans' Talks, Lower Cape Fear Historical Society, Wilmington, North Carolina, hereinafter cited as King Memoir, Lower Cape Fear Historical Society, Wilmington. See also, Rod Gragg, *Confederate Goliath: The Battle of Fort Fisher* (New York, 1991), p. 117.

12. Hoke to Anderson, January 13, 1865, *OR* 46, pt. 2, p. 1048.

13. Lamb to Hill, January 13, 1865, ibid., p. 1047.

14. B. L. Blackmore, "The Fight at Fort Fisher," *Raleigh (NC) News and Observer*, August 30, 1881.

15. Report of David D. Porter, January 17, 1865, *ORN* 11, p. 438; Special Orders, No. 8, North Atlantic Blockading Squadron, January 3, 1865, ibid., p. 427.

16. Report of David D. Porter, January 14, 1865, *ORN* 11, p. 433; Report of E. G. Parrott, n. d., ibid., p. 462.

17. Lieutenant Commander George E. Belknap reported that the *Canonicus'* flag was shot away twice, and was both times replaced by Quartermaster Stevens. Report of George E. Belknap, January 17, 1865, *ORN* 11, p. 464. A postwar account claimed that

Stevens replaced the monitor's flag three times, the third time with the assistance of Acting Master Edward A. Decker. Beyer and Keydel, *Deeds of Valor*, vol. 2, pp. 85-86.

18. Report of David D. Porter, January 17, 1865, *ORN* 11, p. 438; Porter, *Naval History of the Civil War*, pp. 714-715; *Glen Falls (NY) Post-Star*, September 15, 1991; *New York Times*, January 18, 1865; Sands, *From Reefer to Rear Admiral*, p. 263; William Stanley Hoole, *Lawley Covers the Confederacy* (Tuscalossa, 1964), p. 105; John Maxwell to Sister, January 17, 1865, personal collection of Mr. and Mrs. Walter H. Lipke, Santa Barbara, California.

19. R. P. C. to Dearest Cousin, January 24, 1865, Mrs. William M. Lybrook Collection, Division of Archives and History, Raleigh, North Carolina; Memoir of Albert Marion Baldwin, Confederate Veterans' Talks, Lower Cape Fear Historical Society, Wilmington; William N. Still, Jr., "Yankees Were Landing Below Us," *CWTI*, XV, 1 (April, 1976), p. 15.

20. B. L. Blackmore, "The Fight at Fort Fisher," *Raleigh News & Observer*, August 20, 1881; Entry of January 13, 1865, Diary of William Lamb, William Lamb Papers, College of William and Mary, Williamsburg, Virginia; Whiting to Bragg, January 14, 1865, *OR* 46, pt. 2, p. 1055.

21. Lamb, "The Battles of Fort Fisher,' *SHSP*, vol. 21, p. 277; Lamb, *Story of Fort Fisher*, p. 23; Lamb, "Defense of Fort Fisher," *Battles and Leaders*, vol. 4, p. 647; Lamb, "Defence of Fort Fisher, NC," *Operations on the Atlantic Coast*, p. 371.

22. Report of Alfred H. Terry, January 28, 1865, *OR* 46, pt. 1, p. 396; Terry, "The Two Expeditions Against Fort Fisher," note opposite p. 41, Terry Family Papers, Yale; *New York Tribune*, January 18, 1865; Asa King Memoir, Confederate Veteran Talks, Lower Cape Fear Historical Society, Wilmington; Gragg, *Confederate Goliath*, p. 118.

23. Report of Alfred H. Terry, January 28, 1865, *OR* 46, pt. 1, pp. 396-397; Adrian Terry, "The Two Expeditions Against Fort Fisher," p. 40, Terry Family Papers, Yale.

24. Report of Alfred H. Terry, January 28, 1865, *OR* 46, pt. 1, p. 397; Longacre, "The Task Before Them," *CWTI*, pp. 38-39; *New York Tribune*, January 18, 1865.

25. Report of Alfred H. Terry, January 25, 1865, *OR* 46, pt. 1, p. 397; Terry, "The Two Expeditions Against Fort Fisher," p. 40, Terry Family Papers, Yale.

26. Longacre, "The Task Before Them," *CWTI*, p. 40; Leonard R. Thomas, The *Story of Fort Fisher*, January 15, 1865 (Ocean City, 1915), p. 7; Report of Alfred H. Terry, January 25, 1865, *OR* 46, pt. 1, p. 397; Report of Charles J. Paine, January 20, 1865, ibid., pp. 423-424; Sumner, *Comstock Diary*, p. 301; Solon A. Carter, "Fourteen Months' Service With the Colored Troops," Civil War Papers Read Before the Commandery of Massachusetts, *Military Order of the Loyal Legion of the United States*, 2 vols. (Boston, 1900), vol. 1, p. 175; Towle, "Terry's Fort Fisher Expedition," *Old and New*, p. 293; Diary entry of January 13, 1865, Scrogg's Diary, *CWTI* Collection, USAMHI. Remnants of Terry's line can still be seen on the north boundary of Kure

Beach, running from the Atlantic Ocean westward to the Dow Chemical Plant yard adjacent to the Cape Fear River.

27. Whiting to Bragg, January 13, 1865, *OR* 46, pt. 2, p. 1048; Still, "Yankees Were Landing Below Us," *CWTI*, p. 15; *New York Tribune*, January 18, 1865.

28. Report of Braxton Bragg, January 20, 1865, *OR* 46, pt. 1, p. 432.

29. "Letter From General Braxton Bragg," *SHSP*, vol. 10, pp. 346-347.

30. Anderson to Hoke, January 14, 1865, *OR* 46, pt. 2, pp. 1059-1060; "Letter of Braxton Bragg," *SHSP*, vol. 10, p. 347.

31. Report of Braxton Bragg, January 20, 1865, *OR* 46, pt. 1, pp. 432-433; "Letter From General Braxton Bragg," *SHSP*, vol. 10, p. 347; Bragg to Lee, January 14, 1865, *OR* 46, pt. 2, p. 1053.

32. Terry, "The Two Expeditions Against Fort Fisher," p. 42, Terry Family Papers, Yale; Towle, "Terry's Fort Fisher Expedition," *Old and New*, p. 293.

33. Curtis, *The Capture of Fort Fisher*, p. 34; Curtis, "Draft of Speech Before the Army-Navy Club," pp. 13-14, Curtis Collection, Ogdensburg Public Library.

34. Whiting to Bragg, January 14, 1865, *OR* 46, pt. 2, p. 1055; Anderson to Whiting, January 14, 1865, ibid., pp. 1055-1056.

35. Whiting to Bragg, January 14, 1865, ibid., p. 1056.

36. Anderson to Whiting, January 14, 1865, ibid., p. 1057.

37. Report of David D. Porter, January 17, 1865, *ORN* 11, p. 438; Diary entry of January 13, 1865, Scrogg's Diary, *CWTI* Collection, USAMHI; B. L. Blackmore, "The Fight at Fort Fisher," *Raleigh News & Observer*, August 30, 1881.

38. Lamb, "Battles of Fort Fisher," *SHSP*, vol. 21, p. 277; Lamb, *Story of Fort Fisher*, p. 23; Lamb, "Defense of Fort Fisher," *Battles and Leaders*, vol. 4, p. 647; Lamb, "Defence of Fort Fisher, NC," *Operations on the Atlantic Coast*, p. 371.

39. Ibid., p. 278; ibid., p. 24; ibid., p. 648; ibid., p. 372; Extract from the diary of William Lamb, January 14, 1865, *OR* 46, pt. 1, p. 596; Clark, *North Carolina Regiments*, vol. 2, p. 639; Report of Charles J. Paine, January 20, 1865, *OR* 46, pt. 1, p. 424. There is little extant information on the Issac Wells. A Union account of her capture noted that she was a "stern-wheel steamer, laden with ammunition and meal. . . ." Towle, "Terry's Fort Fisher Expedition," *Old and New*, pp. 294, 296.

40. Terry, "The Two Expeditions Against Fort Fisher," p. 42, Terry Family Papers, Yale; Curtis, "Draft of Speech Before the Army-Navy Club," p. 14; Curtis, "Speech Before the Army-Navy Club," p. 11; Curtis Collection, Ogdensburg Public Library; Curtis, "Speech to Companions," Curtis Collection, Chicago Historical Society, p. 17; Return of Casualties in the U.S. Forces Engaged in the Storming of Fort Fisher, N. C. January 15, 1865, *OR* 46, pt. 1, note, p. 405; Mowris, *History of the 117th New York Infantry*, p. 163; Newell B. Richardson to Mother, January 18, 1865, Newell B. Richardson Letter, Civil War Misc. Collection, USAMHI.

41. Terry, "Wilmington and Fort Fisher," pp. 54-55, Terry Family Papers, Yale; Sumner, *Diary of Cyrus Comstock*, pp. 301-302; Curtis, "Draft of Speech Before the Army-Navy Club," p. 14, Curtis Collection, Ogdensburg Public Library.

42. Curtis, *The Capture of Fort Fisher,* p. 35.

43. Terry, "Wilmington and Fort Fisher," pp. 55-56, Terry Family Papers, Yale; *New York Tribune*, January 18, 1865; Report of Henry L. Abbot, March 2, 1865, *OR* 46, pt. 1, p. 167; *Report of the Movement and Operations of the 1st Connecticut Heavy Artillery, For the Year Ending March 31, 1865, As Given in the Annual Report of the Adjutant General of Connecticut, April 11, 1865* (Hartford, 1865), p. 61; Report of Alfred H. Terry, January 25, 1865, *OR* 46, pt. 1, p. 397; Report of Cyrus B. Comstock, January 27, 1865, ibid., p. 407; Sumner, *Diary of Cyrus Comstock*, pp. 301-302; Towle, "Terry's Fort Fisher Expedition," *Old and New*, p. 295; Report of David D. Porter, January 17, 1865, *ORN* 11, p. 438; *History of the First Connecticut Artillery and of the Siege Trains of the Armies Operating Against Richmond 1862-1865* (Hartford, 1893), p. 129; Abbot, *Siege Artillery*, p. 175.

44. Report of Alfred H. Terry, January 25, 1865, *OR* 46, pt. 1, p. 397; Terry, "The Two Expeditions Against Fort Fisher," p. 45; Terry, "Wilmington and Fort Fisher," pp. 53-54, Terry Family Papers, Yale; Report of David D. Porter, January 17, 1865, *ORN* 11, pp. 438-439.

45. General Orders, No. 81, January 4, 1865, *ORN* 11, p. 427; Landing Orders of Rear-Admiral Porter, January 15, 1865, ibid., pp. 429-430; Merrill, "Letters of Rear Admiral David D. Porter," *NCHR*, p. 467.

46. Grant to Terry, January 13, 1865, *OR* 46, pt. 1, p. 43; Grant to Terry, January 3, 1865, *ORN* 11, p. 404; Report of Alfred H. Terry, January 25, 1865, *OR* 46, pt. 1, p. 397. In one report, Admiral Porter noted that he expected a signal from General Terry at 2:00 p.m., January 15, for the vessels to change the direction of their fire to Fort Fisher's sea face batteries so the army and naval column could assault the fort's land face. Report of David D. Porter, January 17, 1865, *ORN* 11, p. 439. Porter's subsequent accounts note, however, that 3:00 p.m. was the agreed upon time to start the land assault. Porter, *Naval History of the Civil War*, p. 715.

47. Towle, "Terry's Fort Fisher Expedition," *Old and New*, p. 296; Curtis, *The Capture of Fort Fisher,* p. 34; Thomas, *Story of Fort Fisher, January 15, 1865*, p. 8; Thomas, *Boys In Blue*, p. 251.

48. Curtis, *The Capture of Fort Fisher,* pp. 35-36; Curtis, "Speech to Companions," pp. 17-18, Curtis Collection, Chicago Historical Society; Curtis, "Speech Before the Army-Navy Club, pp. 11, 14-15," Curtis Collection, Ogdensburg Public Library.

49. Lamb, "Battles of Fort Fisher," *SHSP*, vol. 21, p. 278; Lamb, *Story of Fort Fisher*, p. 24; Lamb, "Defense of Fort Fisher," *Battles and Leaders*, vol. 4, pp. 648-649; Lamb, "Defence of Fort Fisher, NC," *Operations on the Atlantic Coast*, p. 373; Lamb,

"Defence and Fall of Fort Fisher," *SHSP*, 10, p. 356; Clark, *North Carolina Regiments*, vol. 2, p. 639.

50. Denson, *Memoir of W. H. C. Whiting*, pp. 45-46; Lamb, "Battles of Fort Fisher," *SHSP*, vol. 21, p. 279; Lamb, *Story of Fort Fisher*, p. 25; Lamb, "Defense of Fort Fisher," *Battles and Leaders*, vol. 4, p. 649; Lamb, "Defence of Fort Fisher, NC," *Operations on the Atlantic Coast*, p. 373; Clark, *North Carolina Regiments*, vol. 2, pp. 639-640; Report of David D. Porter, January 17, 1865, *ORN* 11, p. 439; Thomas, *Story of Fort Fisher*, January 15, 1865, p. 9.

51. Hagood, *Memoirs of the War of Secession*, pp. 324-325. See also: Diary of James Izlar, Entry of January 15, 1865, South Caroliniana, University of South Carolina, Columbia; Report of George T. Gordon, January 17, 1865 *OR* 46, pt. 1, pp. 435-436. Colonel Lamb claimed that the South Carolinians did not land at Battery Buchanan until "shortly after noon," and did not reach Fort Fisher until almost 3:00 p.m., January 15. Lamb, "Battles of Fort Fisher," *SHSP*, vol. 21, p. 279; Lamb, *Story of Fort Fisher*, p. 26; Lamb, "Defense of Fort Fisher," *Battles and Leaders*, vol. 4, p. 649; Lamb, "Defence of Fort Fisher, NC," *Operations on the Atlantic Coast*, pp. 373-374; Clark, *North Carolina Regiments*, vol. 2, p. 640. Bragg had temporarily assigned the 27th South Carolina to Kirkland's Brigade.

52. Lamb, "Battle of Fort Fisher," *SHSP*, vol. 21, p. 279; Lamb, *Story of Fort Fisher*, p. 26; Lamb, "Defence of Fort Fisher, NC," *Operations on the Atlantic Coast*, p. 374; Clark, *North Carolina Regiments*, vol. 4, p. 640.

53. Thomas O. Selfridge, Jr., "The Navy at Fort Fisher," *Battles and Leaders*, vol. 4, p. 661; Report of K. Randolph Breese, January 16, 1865, *ORN* 11, p. 446; Report of James Parker, January 16, 1865, ibid., p. 497; Report of L. L. Dawson, February 15, 1865, ibid., p. 576.

54. S. H. Maunder, "The Forecastle," *National Tribune*, March 14, 1865; Simms, "Personal Experiences in the Volunteer Navy," *MOLLUS*, p. 33.

55. Report of Louis E. Fagan, January 19, 1865, *ORN* 11, p. 584.

56. Report of *K. Randolph* Breese, January 16, 1865, ibid., p. 446; Report of L. L. Dawson, February 15, 1865, ibid., p. 576.

57. Admiral Porter apparently was to blame for the confusion over the time the attack was to begin. In one of his official reports of the battle—and later in his history of the Union navy during the war—Porter stated that Terry was to signal the navy to change its direction of fire at 2:00 p.m. See: Report of David D. Porter, January 17, 1865, *ORN*, 11, p. 439; Porter, *Naval History of the Civil War*, p. 716. Yet in another account Porter wrote, "It was arranged between the General and Admiral that the ships should all go in early, and fire rapidly until the time for the assault arrived. The hour named was 3:00 p.m." Porter, *Naval History of the Civil War*, p. 715. See also, Report of James Parker, January 16, 1865, *ORN* 11, p. 495; Report of Charles H. Cushman, January 17, 1865, ibid., p. 512; Report of F. B. Blake, January 18, 1865, ibid., p. 525;

Letter of John Bartlett, January 18, 1865, ibid., p. 537; Reed, *Combined Operations in the Civil War*, p. 365.

58. General Curtis claimed that a naval officer (he recalled that it was probably Lt. Benjamin H. Porter, commander of the *Malvern*, but no relation to the admiral) approached him "a short time before advancing" to find out the army's plans for the attack so the naval column could coordinate its movements. It may well have been Captain Breese who interviewed Curtis. Curtis, *Capture of Fort Fisher*, pp. 37-38.

59. Report of L. L. Dawson, February 15, 1865, *ORN* 11, p. 576.

60. Abstract from return of the expeditionary forces, Bvt. Maj. Gen. Alfred H. Terry, U. S. Army, commanding, for January 10, 1865, *OR* 46, pt. 1, p. 403; Sumner, Comstock Diary, p. 302; Lockwood, "History of the Army at Fort Fisher," *United States Service Magazine*, p. 411; Curtis, "Speech Before the Army-Navy Club," p. 12, Curtis Collection, Ogdensburg Public Library.

61. Report of Alfred H. Terry, January 25, 1865, *OR* 46, pt. 1, p. 398; Curtis, *The Capture of Fort Fisher*, p. 35; N. Martin Curtis,*The Capture of Fort Fisher*, Civil War Papers Read Before the Commandery of the State of Massachusetts, *Military Order of the Loyal Legion of the United States*, 2 vols. (Boston, 1900), vol. 1, p. 309, hereinafter cited as Curtis, "Capture of Fort Fisher," *MOLLUS*.

62. George F. Towle to Adrian Terry, July 23, 1898, Terry Family Papers, Yale; Sumner, *Diary of Cyrus Comstock*, p. 302.

63. Curtis, *The Capture of Fort Fisher*, p. 35; Curtis,*The Capture of Fort Fisher*, *MOLLUS*, vol. 1, pp. 308-309; Lockwood, "History of the Army at Fort Fisher," *United States Service Magazine, p. 410.*

64. Report of Alfred H. Terry, January 25, 1865, *OR* 46, pt. 1, p. 398; Curtis, *Capture of Fort Fisher*, p. 36; Curtis,*The Capture of Fort Fisher, MOLLUS*, vol. 1, p. 310; Abraham J. Palmer, *The History of the Forty-Eighth Regiment New York State Volunteers In the War For the Union, 1861-1865* (New York, 1885), pp. 179-180.

65. Newell B. Richardson to Mother, January 18, 1865, Civil War Misc. Collection, USAMHI; Thomas, *Boys In Blue*, p. 251; Mowris, *History of the 117th New York Infantry*, p. 275; Thomas, *Story of Fort Fisher, January 15, 1865*, p. 9.

66. Report of David D. Porter, January 17, 1865, *ORN* 11, note, p. 441; Report of Alfred H. Terry, January 25, 1865, *OR* 46, pt. 1, p. 398; Terry, "Wilmington and Fort Fisher," p. 63, Terry Family Papers, Yale.

Chapter 8: Second Strike

1. Lamb, "The Battles of Fort Fisher," *SHSP*, vol. 21, p. 280; Lamb, "The Defense of Fort Fisher," *Battles and Leaders*, vol. 4, p. 650; Clark, *North Carolina Regiments*, vol. 5, p. 227.

2. Lamb, "Defence and Fall of Fort Fisher," *SHSP*, vol. 10, p. 362; Robley D. Evans, *A Sailor's Log: Recollections of Forty Years of Naval Life* (New York, 1901), p. 89.

3. Report of K. Randolph Breese, January 16, 1865, *ORN* 11, p. 446; Report of James Parker, January 16, 1865, ibid., p. 498; Francis P.B. Sands, "The Last of the Blockade and the Fall of Fort Fisher," *Military Order of the Loyal Legion of the United States, Commandery of the District of Columbia*, 40 (1902), p. 20, hereinafter cited as Sands, "The Last of the Blockade and the Fall of Fort Fisher," *MOLLUS*.

4. Letter of John Bartlett, January 18, 1865, *ORN* 11, p. 527; Sands, "The Last of the Blockade and the Fall of Fort Fisher," *MOLLUS*; Evans, *A Sailor's Log*, pp. 86, 89.

5. Evans, *A Sailor's Log*, pp. 88-89; Report of James Parker, January 16, 1865, *ORN* 11, p. 498; R.H. Lamson to A.C. Rhind, January 16, 1865, ibid., p. 450.

6. Lamb, "The Battles of Fort Fisher," *SHSP*, vol. 21, pp. 280-281; Lamb, *Story of Fort Fisher*, p. 27; Lamb, "Defense of Fort Fisher," *Battles and Leaders*, vol. 4, p. 650; Clark, *North Carolina Regiments*, vol. 2, p. 641; Bloom to Louise, January 18, 1865, John Osborn Papers, Library of Congress, Washington, D. C.

7. Lamb, "Defense of Fort Fisher, NC," *Operations on the Atlantic Coast*, p. 375; Lamb to Parker, January 5, 1879, personal collection of Rod Gragg, Conway, South Carolina; Simms, "Personal Experiences in the Volunteer Navy," *MOLLUS*, p. 21.

8. Report of K. Randolph Breese, January 16, 1865, *ORN* 11, p. 446; Report of David D. Porter, January 17, 1865, ibid., p. 439; Report of James Parker, January 16, 1865, ibid., p. 496, 499; Evans, *A Sailor's Log*, p. 89; Simms, "Personal Experiences in the Volunteer Navy," *MOLLUS*, pp. 21-22; Report of William T. Truxton, January 19, 1865, *ORN* 11, p. 471; Edson J. Harkness, "The Expeditions Against Fort Fisher and Wilmington," Military Essays and Recollections, Papers Read Before the Commandery of the State of Illinois, *Military Order of the Loyal Legion of the United States*, vol. 2 (Chicago, 1894), p. 172, hereinafter cited as Harkness, "The Expeditions Against Fort Fisher and Wilmington," *MOLLUS*.

9. Evans, *A Sailor's Log*, p. 91; Report of David D. Porter, January 17, 1865, *ORN* 11, p. 439.

10. Thomas Richardson to Mary A. Keil, n.d. personal collection of Agnes Guarrieri, Philadelphia, Pennsylvania.

11. Selfridge, "The Navy at Fort Fisher," *Battles and Leaders*, vol. 4, p. 661; Report of H. K. Wheeler, January 16, 1865, *ORN* 11, p. 483;

12. Evans, *A Sailor's Log*, p. 92; Report of James Parker, January 16, 1865, *ORN* 11, p. 496.

13. Report of James Parker, January 16, 1865, *ORN* 11, p. 499; Report of C. H. Cushman, January 17, 1865, ibid., p. 514; Report of K. Randolph Breese, January 16, 1865, ibid., pp. 446-447; Selfridge, *Memoirs of Thomas O. Selfridge*, p. 131; S. H. Maunder, "The Forecastle," *The National Tribune*, March 14, 1865.

14. List of officers killed and wounded during the attack upon Fort Fisher, *ORN* 11, pp. 442-444.

15. John S. C. Abbott, "Heroic Deeds of Heroic Men: True Chivalry, Benjamin H. Porter," *Harper's New Monthly Magazine*, XXXIV (April, 1867), pp. 569-570; Rev. Charles H. Platt, *Lieut. Benj. H. Porter, Sketch of His Life and fall at Fort Fisher in 1865* (Lockport, 1878), p. 24; Letter of John Bartlett, January 18, 1865, *ORN* 11, p. 527; Breese to Porter, January 18, 1865, ibid., p. 449; Lamson to Rhind, January 16, 1865, ibid., p. 450.

16. Sands, "The Last of the Blockade and the Fall of Fort Fisher," *MOLLUS*, p. 22; Sands, *From Reefer to Rear-Admiral*, pp. 265, 267.

17. Report of David D. Porter, *ORN* 11, p. 439.

18. Report of K. Randolph Breese, January 16, 1865, *ORN* 11, p. 447; Report of C. H. Cushman, January 17, 1865, ibid., p. 513.

19. Reports of L. L. Dawson, January 27 and February 15, 1865, *ORN* 11, pp. 576-582.

20. Lamb, "The Battles of Fort Fisher," *SHSP*, vol. 21, p. 281; Lamb, *Story of Fort Fisher*, pp. 27-28; *Wilmington Messenger*, June 27, 1897.

21. Lamb, "The Battles of Fort Fisher," *SHSP*, vol. 21; pp. 281-282, 284; Lamb, *Story of Fort Fisher*, pp. 27-28; Lamb, "Defense of Fort Fisher," *Battles and Leaders*, vol. 4, pp. 650-651; Lamb, "Defence of Fort Fisher, NC," *Operations on the Atlantic Coast*, pp. 375-376; *Wilmington Messenger*, June 27, 1897; Clark, *North Carolina Regiments*, vol. 2, pp. 642-643.

22. Curtis, *Capture of Fort Fisher*, pp. 38-39; Curtis, "Capture of Fort Fisher," *MOLLUS*, vol. 1, p. 313; Thomas, *Story of Fort Fisher, January 15, 1865*, p. 12.

23. Letter of N. M. Robinson, February 27, 1865, Private collection of George M. Slaton, Wilmington, North Carolina.

24. William L. Hyde, *History of the One-Hundred and Twelfth Regiment N.Y. Volunteers* (Fredonia, 1866), p. 122-123; Sumner, *Diary of Cyrus Comstock*, p. 303; Ames, "The Victory at Fort Fisher," *Overland Monthly*, p. 329.

25. Walling to Curtis, April 5, 1897, Curtis Collection, Chicago Historical Society.

26. Lockwood, "A True History of the Army at Fort Fisher," *United States Service Magazine*, pp. 413, 418; H. C. Lockwood, "The Capture of Fort Fisher," *Atlantic Monthly Magazine*, XXVII (June 1871), p. 688; Adelbert Ames, "The Capture of Fort Fisher,"Civil War Papers Read Before the Commandery of the State of Massachusetts, *Military Order of the Loyal Legion of the United States*, 2 vols. (1900), vol. 1, p. 282, hereinafter cited as Ames, "The Capture of Fort Fisher," *MOLLUS*.

27. Report of Rufus Daggett, January 17, 1865, *OR* 46, pt. 1, pp. 418-419; Curtis, *The Capture of Fort Fisher*, 39; Curtis, "Speech Before the Army-Navy Club," p. 15, Ogdensburg Public Library; Thomas, Boys In Blue, p. 251; Mowris, *History of the 117th New York Infantry*, p. 256; J. J. Guernsey, "The Assault at Fort Fisher," *National*

Tribune, September 24, 1914; Towle, "Terry's Fort Fisher Expedition," *Old and New*, p. 297-298.

28. Towle, "Terry's Fort Fisher Expedition," *Old and New*, p. 298.

29. Curtis, *Capture of Fort Fisher*, p. 39; Curtis,*The Capture of Fort Fisher, MOL-LUS*, vol. 1, pp. 313-314; Mowris, *History of the 117th New York Volunteers*, pp. 175, 259; Jackson and O'Donnell, *Back Home in Oneida*, p. 185; Hall, "The Wilmington Expedition," *United States Service Magazine*, p. 47; Longacre, *From Antietam to Fort Fisher*, pp. 10, 228-229; S. K. Wightman, "In Search of My Son," *American Heritage Magazine*, vol. 14, no. 2 (February, 1963), pp. 65-78.

30. Curtis, Capture of Fort Fisher, p. 39; Curtis, "Capture of Fort Fisher," *MOLLUS*, p. 314; Towle, "Terry's Fort Fisher Expedition," *Old and New*, p. 297.

31. Towle, "Terry's Fort Fisher Expedition," *Old and New*, p. 298; Galusha Penny-packer to Adrian Terry, June 1, 1896, Terry Family Papers, Yale; Lockwood, "A True History of the Army at Fort Fisher," *United States Service Magazine*, p. 415; Hermit, *History of the 203rd Pennsylvania Volunteers*, p. 20.

32. *Wilmington Morning Star*, January 30, 1912; Kitchen Braddy to Z. T. Fulmore, March 25, 1901, Civil War Collection, Miscellaneous Records, Division of Archives and History, Raleigh, North Carolina; Clark, *North Carolina Regiments*, vol. 4, pp. 310-311.

33. *Wilmington Messenger*, June 27, 1897; *Philadelphia Weekly Times*, November 12, 1881.

34. *Wilmington Messenger*, June 27, 1897; *Utica (N. Y.) Globe*, October 24, 1908; *Wilmington Morning Star*, November 22, 1908.

35. J. J. Guernsey, "The Assault at Fort Fisher," *National Tribune,* September 24, 1914; *Wilmington Messenger*, June 27, 1897; Clark, *North Carolina Regiments*, vol. 4, pp. 310-311; N. Martin Curtis to Z. T. Fulmore, February 24, 1897, N. Martin Curtis Collection, Chicago Historical Society.

36. Kinchen Braddy to Z. T. Fulmore, March 25, 1901, Misc. Civil War Papers, Division of Archives and History, Raleigh, North Carolina.

37. J. J. Guernsey, "The Assault at Fort Fisher," *National Tribune*, September 24, 1914; Simpson, "Capture of Fort Fisher," p. 12, N. Martin Curtis Collection, Chicago Historical Society.

38. Walling to Curtis, April 5, 1897, N. Martin Curtis Collection, Chicago Historical Society.

39. Report of O. P. Harding, January 17, 1865, *OR* 46, pt. 1, p. 420; Isaiah Price, *History of the Ninety-Seventh Regiment, Pennsylvania Volunteer Infantry, During the War of the Rebellion, 1861-1865* (Philadelphia, 1875), p. 355; *Galusha Pennypacker: America's Youngest General* (Philadelphia, 1917), p. 6; Ames, "The Capture of Fort Fisher," *MOLLUS*, p. 284; Towle "Terry's Fort Fisher Expedition," *Old and New*, p. 299; Hermit, *History of the 203rd Pennsylvania Volunteers*, p. 20-21.

40. John Bell Bouton, *A Memoir of General Louis Bell* (New York, n.p., 1865), pp. 28-30.

41. Ed Vanderbilt to Mc, January 29, 1865, McEachern and Williams Collection, UNCW.

42. Lamb, *Story of Fort Fisher*, pp. 28-29; Lamb, "The Battles of Fort Fisher," *SHSP*, vol. 21, p. 282; *Philadelphia Weekly Times*, November 2, 1881; Curtis,*The Capture of Fort Fisher, MOLLUS*, p. 41; Hill to Anderson, January 15, 1865, *OR* 46, pt. 2, p. 1065.

43. Whiting to Bragg, January 15, 1865, *OR* 46, pt. 2, p. 1064; Bragg to Lee, January 15, 1865, ibid., pp. 1060-1061; Anderson to Cameron, January 15, ibid., p. 1063.

44. Ames, "The Victory at Fort Fisher," *Overland Monthly*, p. 331-332; Report of Charles J. Paine, January 20, 1865, *OR* 46, pt. 1, p. 424; Report of Alfred H. Terry, January 25, 1865, ibid., p. 399; Charles J. Paine to Father, January 16 and 24, 1865, Charles J. Paine Letters, Virginia Historical Society, Richmond.

45. Bragg to Taylor, January 15, 1865, *OR* 46, pt. 2, p. 1062; "Letter From General Braxton Bragg," *SHSP*, vol. 10, p. 348; Clark, *North Carolina Regiments*, vol. 4, p. 542.

46. Clark, *North Carolina Regiments*, vol. 2, p. 10 and vol. 4, p. 342; Charles J. Paine to Father, January 16, 1865, Charles J. Paine Letters, Virginia Historical Society, Richmond.

47. Denson, *Memoir of W. H. C. Whiting*, p. 50; Confederate Veteran Talk of James Alexander Montgomery, Confederate Veteran Talks, Lower Cape Fear Historical Society, Wilmington, North Carolina; Hermit, *History of the 203rd Pennsylvania Volunteers*, p. 22.

48. Harkness, "The Expeditions Against Fort Fisher and Wilmington," *MOLLUS*, p. 174; Hermit, *History of the 203rd Pennsylvania Infantry*, p. 21.

49. Denson, *Memoirs of W. H. C. Whiting*, p. 42; Lockwood, "A True History of the Army at Fort Fisher," *United States Service Magazine*, p. 415; Braddy to Fullmore, March 25, 1901, Misc. Civil War Papers, Division of Archives and History, Raleigh, North Carolina.

50. Alan Conway, "Welshmen in the Union Army," *Civil War History*, 4, no. 2 (June 1958), p. 171; Letter of Chaplain, January 16, 1865, Scrapbook of the 117th New York Volunteers, Rome (N. Y.) Historical Society; Confederate Veteran Experiences of Henry Clay McQueen, Confederate Veteran Talks, Lower Cape Fear Historical Society, Wilmington, North Carolina.

51. Zent to Terry, December 12, 1896, Terry Family Papers, Yale; Ames, "The Capture of Fort Fisher," *MOLLUS*, p. 284; Letter of Chaplain, January 16, 1865, Scrapbook of the 117th New York Volunteers, Rome (N. Y.) Historical Society.

52. Lamb, "The Battles of Fort Fisher," *SHSP*, vol. 21, pp. 285-286, Lamb, *Story of Fort Fisher*, pp. 33-34; Braddy to Fulmore, March 25, 1901, Civil War Misc. Papers, Division of Archives and History, Raleigh, North Carolina.

53. Walling to Curtis, April 5, 1897, N. Martin Curtis Collection, Chicago Historical Society; *Glen Falls (N. Y.) The Post-Star*, September 15, 1991.

54. Lamb, "The Battles of Fort Fisher," *SHSP*, vol. 21, pp. 285-287; Lamb, *Story of Fort Fisher*, pp. 32-34; Lamb, "Defense of Fort Fisher," *Battles and Leaders*, vol. 4, pp. 651-652; Lamb, "Defence of Fort Fisher, NC," *Operations on the Atlantic Coast*, 377-380; Clark, *North Carolina Regiments*, vol. 2, pp. 644-646; Curtis, "Speech Before the Army-Navy Club," p. 16, Ogdensburg Public Library.

55. W. Buck Yearns and John G. Barrett, *North Carolina Civil War Documentary*, p. 87.

56. Mrs. T. C. Davis, "The Fall of Fort Fisher," *Confederate Veteran*, XIII, no. 3 (March, 1905), p. 131. See also: Gragg, *Confederate Goliath*, p. 189.

57. Curtis,*The Capture of Fort Fisher, MOLLUS*, p. 42; Yearns and Barrett, *North Carolina Civil War Documentary*, pp. 87-88; Braddy to Fulmore, March 25, 1901, Civil War Misc. Papers, Division of Archives and History, Raleigh; Hermit, *History of the 203rd Pennsylvania Volunteers*, p. 21.

58. Curtis, *The Capture of Fort Fisher*, p. 44; Curtis,*The Capture of Fort Fisher, MOLLUS*, pp. 42-44; Curtis, "Speech Before the Army-Navy Club," pp. 16-18, Curtis Collection, Ogdensburg Public Library, Curtis, "Speech to Companions," pp. 19-21; D. B. Magill to N. Martin Curtis, December 12, 1893, Curtis Collection, Chicago Historical Society.

59. George F. Towle to Adrian Terry, July 23, 1898, Terry Family Papers, Yale; "Correspondence" of Eugene Atwater, *United States Service Magazine* (New York, 1866), p. 270.

60. Terry, "Wilmington and Fort Fisher," pp. 67-71, Terry Family Papers, Yale; Report of Alfred H. Terry, January 25, 1865, *OR* 46, pt. 1, p. 399; Sumner, *Diary of Cyrus Comstock*, p. 304.

61. Lamb, "The Battles of Fort Fisher," *SHSP*, vol. 21, p. 287; Lamb, *Story of Fort Fisher*, p. 35; Clark, *North Carolina Regiments*, vol. 2, p. 646-647.

62. Report of Joseph C. Abbott, January 17, 1865, *OR* 46, pt. 1, p. 410; Report of William H. Trickey, January 18, 1865, ibid., pp. 413-414; Report of A. W. Rollins, January 16, 1865, ibid., pp. 414-415; Report of Alfred P. Rockwell, January 17, 1865, ibid., pp. 411; Alfred P. Rockwell to Adrian Terry, January 10, 1898, Terry Family Papers, Yale; Walkley, *History of the 7th Connecticut Volunteer Infantry* (Southington, 1905), pp. 191-192; Eldredge, *The Third New Hampshire*, pp. 613-616; Terry, "Wilmington and Fort Fisher," pp. 72-73, Terry Family Papers, Yale; Curtis,*The Capture of Fort Fisher, MOLLUS*, p. 45.

63. Lamb, "The Battles at Fort Fisher," *SHSP*, p. 288; Lamb, *Story of Fort Fisher*, pp. 36-37; Yearns and Barrett, *North Carolina Civil War Documentary*, p. 88-89; Richard P. Pattison to Father, January 17, 1865, Richard Porson Pattison Papers, Joyner Library, East Carolina University, Greenville, North Carolina; *Wilmington Dispatch*, August 13, 1903.

64. Yearns and Barrett, *North Carolina Civil War Documentary*, p. 89; *Wilmington Morning Star*, November 8, 1893.

65. Eldredge, *Third New Hampshire*, p. 717; Terry, "Wilmington and Fort Fisher," pp. 73-75, Terry Family Papers, Yale.

66. *Wilmington Weekly Star*, November 3, 1893; *Wilmington Morning Star*, November 8, 1893.

67. Lamb, "The Battles of Fort Fisher," *SHSP*, vol. 21, pp. 287-289; Lamb, *Story of Fort Fisher*, pp. 35-37; Lamb, "Defense of Fort Fisher," *Battles and Leaders*, vol. 4, pp. 653-654; Clark, *North Carolina Regiments*, vol. 2, pp. 646-648; Report of Alfred H. Colquitt, January 17, 1865, *OR* 46, pt. 1, pp. 442-444; Still, "The Yankees Were Landing Below Us" *CWTI*, p. 16.

68. Report of Joseph C. Abbott, January 17, 1865, *OR* 46, pt. 1, p. 410; Longacre, "The Task Before Them," *CWTI*, p. 43; Sumner, *Diary of Cyrus Comstock*, p. 305; A Survivor, "The Fight at Fort Fisher," *Raleigh (N. C.) News & Observer*, August 30, 1881. In 1979, I fell into a dispute with the descendants of Maj. James Reilly over his role as Fort Fisher's last commander. As the reader will note, I give Major Reilly much credit, as did Colonel Lamb, for "nobly keeping his promise" to do all that was possible to defend Fort Fisher. But as Reilly himself later admitted, his task "was like a mole unto a mountain." To be sure, Reilly made mistakes. Lamb pointed to a flaw in Reilly's disposition of troops on the western end of the land face to contest the charging Union army on January 15, 1865. Captain Kinchen Braddy claimed that "all the commanding officers were out of place," including Reilly, when Ames' division stormed the fort at Shepherd's Battery.

Yet, from the time command of Fort Fisher devolved upon James Reilly about 4:30 p.m., until he surrendered the remnants of his fighting force to Capt. E. Lewis Moore at Battery Buchanan about 10:00 p.m., the major performed as well as could have been expected of any man. He fought his troops with great skill and determination, in keeping with his reputation as a good soldier. As to the "official surrender" of Fort Fisher, I still contend, as I have since 1979 (and for which I have been criticized by Reilly's descendants), that it was tendered by the fort's original commanding officer, Col. William Lamb, and his superior, Maj. Gen. William Henry Chase Whiting, to the commanding officer of the U. S. Army's expeditionary force, Bvt. Maj. Gen. Alfred H. Terry. Documentation supports my contention. Colonel William Lamb, Capt. Adrian Terry, and, indeed, Maj. James Reilly himself, all wrote that the surrender was given by General Whiting. In his own publication of Wilmington's history, James Reilly recalled the surrender of Fort Fisher: "The conflict ceased [and] there being no means of escape to the mainland, Gen. Whiting was compelled to surrender his command as prisoners of war." J. S. Reilly, *Wilmington Past, Present, & Future* (Wilmington, 1884), p. 19.

69. Longacre, "The Task Before Them," *CWTI*, p. 43; Eldredge, *The Third New Hampshire*, p. 616.

70. Ames, "The Victory at Fort Fisher," *Overland Monthly*, p. 332.

Chapter 9: Victory—and Stalemate

1. Stevenson, "My Personal Experiences," M. Box 8, File 7, Item 14, McEachern and Williams Collections, UNCW.

2. Hébert to Bragg, January 15, 1865, *OR* 46, pt. 2, p. 1069.

3. Bragg to Lee, Davis to Bragg, Bragg to Davis, January 16, 1865, *OR* 46, pt. 2, p. 1078.

4. Unidentified Confederate soldier to Kate, January 21, 1865, Brunswick Town State Historic Site Collection, Winnabow, North Carolina.

5. Letter of Chaplain, January 16, 1865, Scrapbook of the 117th New York Volunteers, Rome (N. Y.) Historical Society; Rogers, *Memories of Ninety Years*, pp. 109-110.

6. Joseph Canning Journal, McEachern and Williams Collection, UNCW.

7. Letter of Alonzo Alden, February 28, 1888, Alonzo Alden Collection, Chicago Historical Society, Chicago, Illinois; *Harper's Weekly*, February 4, 1865; Service records of Anton Reder, personal collection of Laurine and Orville Mooberry, Santa Rosa, California; Letter of Chaplain, January 16, 1865, Scrapbook of the 117th New York Volunteers, Rome (N. Y.) Historical Society; Towle, "Terry's Fort Fisher Expedition," *Old and New*, p. 303; *Ballston (N. Y.) Journal*, March 4, 1893, and June 6, 1896, Civil War Misc. Collection, USAMHI

8. Mowris, *History of the 117th New York*, p. 182.

9. J. W. Slate to Parents, January 17, 1865, personal collection of George Slaton, Wilmington, North Carolina; Samuel M. Zent to Adrian Terry, December 12, 1896, Terry Family Papers, Yale. See also, Proceedings of a Court of Inquiry Constituted to Examine into the Cause of the Explosion of the Powder Magazine, January 20, 1865, *OR* 46, pt. 1, pp. 425-431.

Despite the official findings of the cause of the powder magazine explosion at Fort Fisher on the morning of January 16, 1865, there may be another, darker side to the story. J. C. Maxwell of Glendale, California, vividly recalls his grandfather telling him that he had arranged for a timing device to detonate Fort Fisher's main powder magazine in case the fort fell to Union forces. Captain John Maxwell, an independent agent in the Confederate Secret Service (perhaps best known for blowing up the Unon ordnance barge at City Point, Virginia, in August 1864, that almost killed U. S. Grant), claimed responsibility for the explosion at Fort Fisher. According to his grandson,

Maxwell explained that "the U.S. was so embarrassed by their defeat attempting the 'naval boarding' of the fort they could not admit the Rebels had dealt them another disastrous defeat so quickly." According to the grandson:

"Grandfather had a fine grain gunpowder mill on Smith's Creek which feeds into the Northeast Cape Fear River. His manager of this operation steamed downriver each day to deliver primed shells, powder and other supplies. He picked up mail for the fort at Wilmington. Grandfather spent Christmas 1864 in Richmond with Sec. [Judah P] Benjamin and his brother-in-law. After the failed U.S. attempt to land troops and storm the fort [Fisher] late in December, he returned to Wilmington and gave his manager a supply of glass tube 'delayed triggers' primed to go off 48 hours after being activated. The 'triggers' were glass tubes sealed at one end with a measured amount of 'white metal' (the measured amount determined the length of the time delay). To activate the 'trigger' the tube was filled with acid and inserted into the firing cap/fuse of a bomb. His instructions were that if it appeared the fort was going to fall, a 'trigger' was to be activated and placed inside the powder magazine. The 'trigger' was to be removed within 24 hours if the fort did not fall, but replaced with a newly activated 'trigger' on any day it appeared to be in danger of falling within the next 24 hours.

The first 'trigger' was put in place on January 5th, 1865, and was removed and replaced each day until January 15th. Neither the CSA government at Richmond nor Col. Lamb at Fort Fisher were aware of these actions which were a part of the desperate plan to recapture the fort after the explosion.

The manager told grandfather that when he left the fort Saturday, January 14, he expected the fort would fall Sunday before he could return, so he selected and activated a 'trigger' with which he deemed to be the longest delay time. It was placed in the magazine at approximately 6 p.m. Saturday. When he came down river Sunday morning his little steamer (with his supply of triggers aboard) was seized by men from Gen. Bragg's headquarters at Wilmington and placed in messenger service between fortifications along the Cape Fear River south of the city. He did find a horse and headed south overland, but by the time he got near the fort the Yankees had cut the approach. He turned back. He sent a coded telegram to grandfather (who returned to Richmond on January 10) and waited for word that there had been an explosion at the fort. When it hadn't come late Sunday night he concluded the machine had failed. It hadn't. As you know, it went off Monday morning."

J. C. Maxwell to author, July 5, 1995, in personal collection of Chris E. Fonvielle, Jr., Wilmington, NC.

10. Return of Casualties in the U.S. Forces engaged in the storming of Fort Fisher, N.C., January 15, 1865, *OR* 46, pt. 1, p. 405; Samuel Bates, *History of Pennsylvania Volunteers, 1861-5*, 5 vols. (Harrisburg, 1869-1871), vol. 5, p. 579; List of Officers killed and wounded during the attack upon Fort Fisher, January 17, 1865, *ORN* 11, p.

442-444; Selfridge, "The Navy at Fort Fisher," *Battles and Leaders*, vol. 4, pp. 661-662.

11. Porter to Welles, January 15, 1865, *OR* 46, pt. 2, p. 140; Simpson, "Capture of Fort Fisher," p. 14, Curtis Collection, Chicago Historical Society; Stanton to Terry and Stanton to Porter, January 16, 1865, *ORN* 11, p. 458; Terry, "Wilmington and Fort Fisher," p. 76, Terry Family Papers, Yale; Stanton to Lincoln, January 17, 1865, *OR* 46, pt. 2, pp. 155-157; Charles J. Paine to Father, February 7, 1865, Charles J. Paine Letters, Virginia Historical Society, Richmond; Webb to Corps Commander, January 17, 1865, *OR* 46, pt. 2, p. 160; General Orders, No. 97, February 20, 1865, *ORN* 11, pp. 458-459; Porter, Porter Memoir, LOC; Report of David D. Porter, January 17, 1865, *ORN* 11, p. 440; Porter, *Naval History of the Civil War*, p. 717.

12. *Wilmington Daily North Carolinian*, January 22, 1865; *Wilmington Weekly Journal*, January 26, 1865; *Richmond Whig*, January 26, 1865.

13. Unidentified Confederate soldier to Kate, January 21, 1865, Buie Papers, Duke; *Wilmington Daily Journal*, February 17, 1865. As the last transports pulled away from the burning fort, "the dark and lurid smoke as it enveloped the island was gloomy indeed" and "presented a picture not soon to be forgotten" by its garrison. William Badham, Jr. to Wife, February 8 and 20, 1865, William Badham, Jr. Papers, Perkins Library, Duke University, Durham, North Carolina.

14. William Badham, Jr. to wife, February 8, 1865, Badham Papers, Duke; *Wilmington Daily North Carolinian*, January 28, 1865; Hébert to Anderson, January 17, 1865, *OR* 46, pt. 2, p. 1080. "At 4:50 a.m. saw two rebel steamers in the river on fire." Log of the *Monticello*, January 17, 1865, *ORN* 11, p. 627.

15. Overland distance from Wilmington to Smithville was about thirty miles. Hébert wired Confederate headquarters in Wilmington: "Did the wagons you were to send down two nights ago start? I have not been able to find them." Hébert to Anderson, January 18, 1865, *OR* 46, pt. 2, p. 1081. James E. Price, "What a North Carolina Boy Saw of the Civil War," in *Under Both Flags: A Panorama of the Great Civil War* (Boston, 1896), p. 344, hereinafter cited as Price, *Under Both Flags*; *Wilmington Daily Journal*, February 17, 1865; Report of William B. Cushing, January 31, 1865, *ORN* 11, p. 624.

16. William Calder to Mother, January 18 and January 23, 1865, William Calder Papers, Southern Historical Collection, University of North Carolina, Chapel Hill; Eugene S. Martin, *Defence of Fort Anderson* (Wilmington, 1901); John Douglas Taylor, "Personal Reminiscences," personal collection of Allan T. Strange, Wilmington, North Carolina.

17. William Calder to Mother, January 18 and 23, 1865, Calder Papers, SHC.

18. With Martin were Col. Charles Simonton, Lt. Col. John Douglas Taylor, Capt. Booker Jones and a small detachment. Sprunt, *Chronicles of the Cape Fear River*, p. 380. See also: Herring and Williams, *Fort Caswell*, p. 48. William Calder to Mother,

January 18 and January 23, 1865, Calder Papers, SHC; Diary entry of January 17, 1865, William Calder Diary, William Calder Papers, Perkins Library, Duke University, Durham, North Carolina; Log of the *Malvern*, January 17, 1865, *ORN* 11, p. 739. Comstock to Delafield, January 21, 1865, *OR* 46, pt. 2, pp. 197-198; *Philadelphia Inquirer*, February 8, 1865; *Richmond Whig*, February 13, 1865; Price, *Under Both Flags*, p. 343. "At 1:30 a.m. heard a heavy explosion in by Fort Caswell, at 2:05 heard another, between 2 and 3 several more." Log of the *Monticello*, January 16, 1865, *ORN* 11, p. 627. *Wilmington Daily Journal*, January 18, 1865; James Sprunt, *Tales and Traditions of the Lower Cape Fear*, 1661-1896 (Wilmington, 1896), p. 132; Porter to Godon, January 17, 1865, *ORN* 11, p. 609.

19. Report of William B. Cushing, January 31, 1865, *ORN* 11, p. 624; John Grattan, "Under the Blue Pennant," John Grattan Papers, Manuscript Division, Library of Congress, Washington, D. C.; W. G. Curtis, *Reminiscences of Wilmington and Smithville, 1848-1900* (Southport, 1900), p. 34.

20. Curtis, *Reminiscences*, pp. 34-35; Price, *Under Both Flags*, 344; Report of William B. Cushing, January 31, 1865, *ORN* 11, p. 624; Journal of William B. Cushing, Navy Department Records, Record Group 45, National Archives, Washington, D. C., hereinafter cited as Cushing Journal, NA. A U. S. Navy officer commented that when Cushing submitted his official report on Smithville's capture, "Admiral Porter said nothing but went down into his cabin and had a hearty laugh at Cushing's impudence and audacity." Grattan, "Under the Blue Pennant," Grattan Papers, LOC.

21. Report of David D. Porter, January 20, 1865, *ORN* 11, p. 619; Report of William T. Truxton, January 16-18, 1865, ibid., p. 471; Porter, *The Naval History of the Civil War*, p. 727; *New York Tribune*, January 26, 1865.

22. Rogers, *Memories of Ninety Years*, p. 112; Report of Daniel L. Braine, January 20, 1865, *ORN* 11, p. 624.

23. Report of Henry L. Abbot, March 2, 1865, *OR* 46, pt. 1, p. 167; Report of David D. Porter, January 20, 1865, *ORN* 11, pp. 620-621; Report of William B. Cushing, January 31, 1865, ibid., p. 624; Porter to Watmough, January 21, 1865, ibid., pp. 628-629.

24. Wilkinson, *Narrative of a Blockade Runner*, pp. 233-234; Sprunt, *Chronicles of the Cape Fear River*, pp. 470-471; Wise, *Lifeline of the Confederacy*, pp. 208-209.

25. Porter to Clitz, January 17, 1865, *ORN* 11, p. 605; Cushing Journal, NA.

26. Reports of David D. Porter, January 20, 1865, *ORN* 11, pp. 620-623; Log of the *Malvern*, January 20, 1865, ibid., p. 740; Cushing Journal, NA; David D. Porter, *Incidents and Anecdotes of the Civil War* (New York, 1886), p. 274.

27. Report of David D. Porter, January 25, 1865, *ORN* 11, p. 700; Report of Francis M. Green, January 26, 1865, ibid., p. 701. Rogers, *Memories of Ninety Years*, p. 113.

28. *Charleston Mercury*, February 9, 1865.

29. Hoke to Anderson, January 20, 1865, *OR* 46, pt. 2, p. 1115; *New York Herald*, February 25, 1865; *Wilmington Daily North Carolinian*, February 18, 1865.

30. Hagood, *Memoirs of the War of Secession*, pp. 329-332; Mallory to Bragg, February 6, 1865, *OR* 47, pt. 2, p. 1110; Bragg to Mallory, February 8, 1865, ibid., p. 1129.

31. Diary entry of January 22, 1865, Calder Diary, Duke; Anderson to Burr, January 21, 1865, *OR* 46, pt. 2, p. 1121; Sprunt, *Chronicles of the Cape Fear River*, p. 500. Bragg to Pinkney, January 19, 1865, *OR* 46, pt. 2, pp. 1102, 1079. Confederate engineers sank three steamers—the *Arctic*, *Yadkin* and *North Heath*—in the Cape Fear River channel opposite the river batteries (Fort Strong). *OR* Atlas, LXVII, 7. Note is from: Bragg to Taylor, January 27, 1865, *OR* 46, pt. 2, p. 1154. See also: Bragg to Hardee, January 17, 1865, ibid., p. 1089; Lee to Seddon, January 18, 1865, ibid., p. 1091; Hardee to Bragg, January 19, 1865, ibid., p. 1102. Abstract from return of the Department of North Carolina, February 10, 1865, ibid., p. 1154; "Report of Efficient Present in Hoke's Division, January-February, 1865," Order Book of Robert F. Hoke, Robert F. Hoke Papers, North Carolina Division of Archives and History, Raleigh.

32. Unidentified Confederate soldier to Cousin B, January 28, 1865, Southall and Bowan Papers, Southern Historical Collection, University of North Carolina, Chapel Hill.

33. Davis, *The Confederate General*, vol. 3, pp. 48-49; Current, *Encyclopedia of the Confederacy*, vol. 2, p. 780; Warner, *Generals in Gray*, p. 140; Hagood, *Memoirs of the War of Secession*, pp. 334-335.

34. Merrill, "Letters From Rear Admiral David D. Porter," *NCHR*, p. 471.

35. Ibid., pp. 471, 473.

36. Comstock to O'Keefe, January 17, 1865, *OR* 46, pt. 2, p. 167; Terry to Rawlins, January 27, 1865, ibid., p. 275; Report of Charles J. Paine, January 20, 1865, ibid., p. 404; *New York Herald*, January 24, 1865; *Philadelphia Inquirer*, February 16, 1865; Hoke to Anderson, January 18, 1865, *OR* 46, pt. 2, p. 1096; Sumner, *Diary of Cyrus Comstock*, pp. 306-307.

37. Report of Charles J. Paine, January 20, 1865, *OR* 46, pt. 1, p. 424. Abbott's force comprised 250 soldiers of the 7th New Hampshire Infantry and forty-one of the 7th Connecticut Infantry. Report of Joseph C. Abbott, January 20, 1865, ibid., p. 453. Report of John Thompson, January 20, 1865, ibid., p. 454; Little, *History of the 7th New Hampshire Infantry*, pp. 402-403; Abstract log of the *Cherokee*, January 19, 1865, *ORN* 11, pp. 576-578.

38. Report of Joseph C. Abbott, January 20, 1865, *OR* 46, pt. 1, p. 453; Report of John Thompson, January 20, 1865, ibid., p. 454; Little, *History of the 7th New Hampshire Infantry*, p. 403.

39. Report of Joseph C. Abbott, January 20, 1865, *OR* 46, pt. 1, p. 453; Report of John Thompson, January 20, 1865, ibid., p. 454; Report of Charles J. Paine, January 20,

1865, ibid., p. 424; Little, *History of the 7th New Hampshire Infantry*, p. 403; John McMurray, *Recollections of a Colored Troop* (Brookville, 1994), pp. 71-72; Charles J. Paine to Father, January 24, 1865, Charles J. Paine Letters, Virginia Historical Society, Richmond.

40. Report of Daniel L. Braine, January 22, 1865, *ORN* 11, p. 630; Hébert Anderson, January 22, 1865, *OR* 46, pt. 2, p. 1123.

41. Porter to Sherman, January 28, 1865, *OR* 47, pt. 2, p. 142; *Philadelphia Inquirer*, February 14, 1865; Wendell D. Croom, *The War History of Company "C" (Beauregard Volunteers), Sixth Georgia Regiment* (Fort Valley, 1879), p. 27.

42. Bragg to Taylor, January 27, 1865, *OR* 46, pt. 2, p. 1154; Anderson to Hoke, January 19, 1865, ibid., p. 1105; Anderson to James, January 20, 1865, ibid., p. 1113; Anderson to James, January 22, 1865, ibid., p. 1123.

43. Anderson to Jackson, January 19, 1865, *OR* 47, pt. 2, pp. 1119-1120; Seddon to Bragg, January 17, 1865, ibid., 46, pt. 2, p. 1085; Anderson to Seixas, January 17, 1865, ibid., p. 1086; General Order, No. 4, Section 1, Adjutant General's Office, February 8, 1865, copy in possession of the author; *Wilmington Daily Journal*, January 20 and February 16, 1865; *Raleigh Daily Confederate*, February 13, 1865; Jones, *A Rebel War Clerk's Diary*, vol. 2, p. 430.

44. Donald MacRae to Julia, February 7, 1865, Hugh MacRae Papers, Perkins Library, Duke University, Durham, North Carolina; Katherine Douglas DeRosset Meares to Lou, May 18, 1865, DeRosset Family Papers, Southern Historical Society, University of North Carolina, Chapel Hill; Zaccheus Ellis to Sister, February 12, 1865, Ellis Papers, SHC (copy also in Brunswick Town State Historic Site Collection, Winnabow, North Carolina); *Wilmington Daily Journal*, January 17, 19, 20, 24, 25, 1865; Unidentified Confederate soldier to Kate, January 21, 1865, Brunswick Town State Historic Site, Winnabow, North Carolina; *Charleston Mercury*, January 21, 1865.

45. Hoke to Anderson, January 18, 1865, *OR* 46, pt. 2, p. 1096; *Wilmington Daily North Carolinian*, January 26, 1865; Rogers, *Memories of Ninety Years*, p. 118.

46. *Wilmington Daily Journal*, January 23, February 2, 15, 17, 1865; Zaccheus Ellis to Sister, February 7, 1865, SHC (copy also in Brunswick Town State Historic Site Collection, Winnabow, North Carolina).

47. G. B. Cook to sister, February 16, 1865, letter in possession of the author; Rogers, *Memories of Ninety Years*, p. 118; Unidentified Confederate soldier of Clingman's Brigade to Denise, February 1, 1865, Perkins Family Papers, Southern Historical Collection, University of North Carolina, Chapel Hill.

48. Sherman to Gillmore, March 15, 1865, *OR* 47, pt. 2, p. 85.

49. Clark, *North Carolina Regiments*, vol. 3, pp. 694-695.

50. Charles K. Caldwell, *The Old Sixth Regiment, Its War Record, 1861-5* (New Haven, 1875), pp. 127-214.

51. W. S. Thurstin, *History One Hundred and Eleventh Regiment O. V. I.* (Toledo, 1894), p. 112, hereinafter cited as Thurstin, *History of the 111th Ohio Volunteers*; Charles J. Paine to Father, January 16, 1865, Charles J. Paine Letters, Virginia Historical Society, Richmond; B. F. Thompson, *History of the 112th Regiment of Illinois Volunteer Infantry in the Great War of the Rebellion 1862-1865* (Toulan, 1885), pp. 297-298.

52. William Calder to Mother, January 28, 1865, Calder Papers, SHC.

53. Entry of January 20, 1865, Calder Diary, Duke; Jackson and O'Donnell, *Back Home in Oneida*, p. 187.

54. Bragg to Hoke, January 25, 1865, *OR* 46, pt. 2, p. 1138; Circulars for January 26 and February 12, 1865, Hoke Order Book, Hoke Papers, Division of Archives and History, Raleigh; Anderson to Hoke, January 30, 1865, *OR* 46, pt. 2, p. 1164; Hoke to Anderson, February 3, 1865, *OR* 47, pt. 2, p. 1089; *Wilmington Daily Journal*, January 30, 1865.

55. *New York Tribune*, February 18, 1865; Charles J. Paine to Father, January 30, 1865, Charles J. Paine Letters, Virginia Historical Society, Richmond; Clark, *North Carolina Regiments*, vol. 3, p. 695; William Calder to Mother, January 28, 1865, Calder Papers, SHC.

56. William Calder to Mother, January 28, 1865, Calder Papers, SHC; Unidentified soldier to Kate, February 4, 1865, Brunswick Town State Historic Site Collection, Winnabow, North Carolina.

57. *Philadelphia Inquirer*, February 16, 1865.

Chapter 10: Advance

1. Abstract log of *U.S.S. Malvern*, January 28, 1865, *ORN* 12, p. 740; Grant to Sherman, February 1, 1865, *OR* 47, pt. 2, p. 193; Sumner, *Diary of Cyrus Comstock*, p. 308; Navy Department, *Civil War Naval Chronology*, pt. 6, p. 31; Chester G. Hearn, *Admiral David D. Porter* (Annapolis, 1996), p. 305; James L. McDonough, *Schofield: Union General in the Civil War and Reconstruction* (Tallahassee, 1972), p. 150; Grant to Schofield, February 19, 1865, *OR* 47, pt. 2, p. 492.

2. Sherman to Palmer, January 21, 1865, *OR* 47, pt. 2, p. 111; Sherman, *Memoirs of William T. Sherman*, p. 272; Sherman to Foster, January 29, 1865, *OR* 47, pt. 2, p. 163; Jacob D. Cox, *Military Reminiscences of the Civil War*, 2 vols. (New York, 1900), vol. 2, p. 395; Sherman to Grant, January 29, 1865, *OR* 47, pt. 2, pp. 155-156.

3. Cox, *Military Reminiscences*, vol. 2, p. 395; Grant to Schofield, February 19, 1865, *OR* 47, pt. 2, p. 492; Sherman to Grant, January 29, 1865, ibid., pp. 154-156; Schofield to Grant, February 15, 1865, ibid., pp. 436-437; Grant to Sherman, March 16, 1865, ibid., p. 859.

4. Porter, Memoir, pp. 884-885, Porter Papers, LOC; Grant to Sherman, February 1, 1865, *OR* 47, pt. 2, p. 193.

5. Merrill, "Letters From Rear Admiral David D. Porter," *NCHR*, p. 469; Sherman to Foster, January 29, 1865, *OR* 47, pt. 2, p. 163; Issac R. Sherwood, *Memories of the War* (Toledo, 1923), pp. 154-155; Koontz to Stanton, January 25, 1865, *OR* 47, pt. 2, p. 131.

6. Grant to Stanton, January 31, 1865, *OR* 47, pt. 2, p. 179; General Orders No.12, War Department, January 31, 1865, ibid., p. 179; Simon, *Papers of U. S. Grant*, vol. 13, p. 336; Report of U. S. Grant, July 22, 1865, *OR* 47, pt. 1, pp. 44-45; Grant to Stanton, February 4, 1865, *OR* 46, pt. 2, p. 365; Warner, *Generals in Blue*, pp. 425-426; Faust, *Encyclopedia of the Civil War*, p. 661; McDonough, *Schofield*, p. 190.

7. Porter, Memoir, p. 883, Porter Papers, LOC; Merrill, "Letters From Rear Admiral David D. Porter," *NCHR*, p. 478; Thompson and Wainwright, *Correspondence of Gustavus Fox*, vol. 2, p. 200.

8. Charles J. Paine to Charles C. Paine, February 7, 1865, Charles J. Paine Papers, Virginia Historical Society, Richmond.

9. Report of U. S. Grant, July 22, 1865, *OR* 46, pt. 1, p. 45-46; Schofield to Foster, February 16, 1865, *OR* 47, pt. 2, p. 454; Foster to Terry, January 21, 1865, ibid., p. 114; Grant to Stanton, February 4, 1865, *OR*, 46, pt. 2, p. 365; Reed, *Combined Operations in the Civil War*, p. 379.

10. Ibid., pp. 379-381.

11. "Get off at 10 o'clock, General Schofield going with us. . . .The ice is very bad. . .our ship is the *Atlantic.*" Abstract from journal of Jacob D. Cox, February 4, 1865, *OR* 47, pt. 1, p. 927. Cox, *Military Reminiscences*, vol. 2, pp. 399-400; Jacob D. Cox, *The March to the Sea, Franklin and Nashville* (New York, 1900), p. 147, hereinafter cited as Cox, *March to the Sea*; McDonough, *Schofield*, p. 151; Thompson, *History of the 112th Illinois Infantry*, p. 297; Halleck to Grant, February 5, 1865, *OR* 47, pt. 2, pp. 213-214; Meagher to Palmer, February 7, 1865, ibid., pt. 2, p. 371.

12. Porter to Sherman, January 28, 1865, *OR* 47, pt. 2, p. 143; Porter to Rolando, February 4, 1865, *ORN* 12, p. 5.

13. Report of Thomas C. Dunn, January 30, 1865, *ORN* 11, p. 713; Report of William E. Dennison, January 30, 1865, ibid., pp. 713-714.

14. Abstract log of *U.S.S. Shawmut*, Febrary 3, 1865, *ORN* 12, pp. 36-37; Entry of February 3, 1865, Calder Diary, Duke; Hoke to Anderson, February 4, 1865, *OR* 46, pt. 2, p. 1204; *Raleigh Daily Confederate*, February 10, 1865; Unidentified Confederate soldier to Kate McGeachy, February 4, 1865, Buie Papers, Duke; *Wilmington Daily Journal*, February 7, 1865.

15. Diary entries of February 6-7, 1865, Saunders Richard Hornbrook Diary, Smith Library, Indiana Historical Society, Indianapolis; Abstract from journal of Jacob D. Cox, February 7, 1865, *OR* 47, pt. 1, p. 927; Thompson, *History of the 112th Illinois Infantry*, p. 297; Cox, *Military Reminiscences*, vol. 2, p. 404; Thomas P. Adams to

Parents, February 10, 1865, personal collection of Virginia T. Adams, Zimmerman, Ohio; Thomas Speed to Parents, February 8, 1865, Thomas Speed Collection, The Filson Club, Louisville, Kentucky; R. Noble to Dear Friends, February 19, 1865, Federal Soldiers Letters, Southern Historical Collection, University of North Carolina, Chapel Hill; J. W. Gaskill, *Footprints Through Dixie* (Alliance, 1919), p. 169.

16. The 140th Indiana was the first and the 112th Illinois the last of Cox's regiments to land on Federal Point on February 8, 1865. Thompson, *History of the 112th Illinois Infantry*, p. 297; Cox, *Military Reminiscences*, vol. 2, pp. 404-405; Abstract from journal of Jacob D. Cox, February 8-10, 1865, *OR* 47, pt. 1, p. 927; Report of Oscar W. Sterl, April 28, 1865, ibid., p. 965; Schofield to Grant, February 8, 1865, ibid., pt. 2, p. 355; Thurstin, *History of the 111th Ohio Infantry*, p. 112; General Orders No.1, Headquarters Department of North Carolina, Army of the Ohio, February 9, 1865, *OR* 47, pt. 2, p. 370; Navy Department, *Civil War Naval Chronology*, pt. 5, pp. 35-36.

17. Faust, *Encyclopedia of the Civil War*, p. 188; Cox, *March to the Sea*, pp. i-ii; Jacob D. Cox, *Atlanta* (Wilmington, 1989), pp. i-iii; Report of Jacob D. Cox, May 15, 1865, *OR* 47, pt. 1, p. 958.

18. Sale to Bragg, January 26, 1865, *OR* 46, pt. 2, p. 1142; Sale to Bragg, February 2, 1865, ibid., 47, pt. 2, p. 1083; Bragg to Davis, February 3, 1865, ibid., 1088; Bragg to Lee, February 9, 1865, ibid., p. 1138; Don C. Seitz, *Braxton Bragg. General of the Confederacy* (Columbia, 1924), p. 507.

19. *Philadelphia Inquirer*, February 21, 1865; Abstract from journal of Jacob D. Cox, February 10, 1865, *OR* 47, pt. 1, p. 927; Cox, *Military Reminiscences*, vol. 2, pp. 405-406; Schofield to Grant, February 8, 1865, *OR* 47, pt. 2, p. 356.

20. Schofield to Porter, February 9, 1865, *OR* 47, pt. 2, p. 371; Sumner, *Diary of Cyrus Comstock*, p. 309; Barrett, *Civil War in North Carolina*, p. 281; Cox, *Military Reminiscences*, vol. 2, p. 407.

21. Special Orders, No. 1, Department of North Carolina, Army of the Ohio, February 10, 1865, *OR* 47, pt. 2, p. 384; Schofield to Porter, February 9, 1865, ibid., p. 371; Porter, Memoir, pp. 884-885, Porter Papers, LOC.

22. Report of David D. Porter, February 12, 1865, *ORN* 12, p. 16; Grant to Stanton, February 4, 1865, *OR* 46, pt. 2, p. 365; Report of David D. Porter, January 31, 1865, *ORN* 11, p. 721; Porter, *Naval History of the Civil War*, p. 726; Porter to Comstock, February 8, 1865, Porter Papers, LOC.

23. According to the late Cape Fear historian James Sprunt, Cushing's daring reconnaissance occurred on the night of February 17, 1865. See Sprunt, *Tales and Traditions*, pp. 46-48. Admiral Porter, on the other hand, reported that the reconnaissance took place on February 11. "Last night I sent Lieutenant Cushing up again to make a thorough reconnaissance. . . .The boats had barely time to make good observations when they were hailed and then fired upon with grape and cannister from seven or eight guns, which kept up fire until they were out of sight. Fortunately we met with no loss."

Report of David D. Porter, February 12, 1865, *ORN* 12, p. 17. See also: Cushing Journal, NA; Paul Murray and Stephen Russell Bartlett, Jr., eds., "Letters of Stephen C. Bartlett Aboard the *U.S.S. Lenapee*, January to August, 1865," *NCHR*, XXXIII, 1 (January, 1956), p. 74, hereinafter cited as Murray and Bartlett, "Letters of Stephen C. Bartlett," *NCHR*; *New York Herald*, February 18, 1865.

24. Taylor, "Reminiscences," pp. 4-5; *Wilmington Morning Star*, June 4, 1917; *New York Herald*, February 18, 1865.

25. *New York Herald*, February 16, 1865; Report of William H. Trickey, February 11, 1865, *OR* 47, pt. 1, p. 922; Little, *History of the 7th New Hampshire Volunteers*, p. 407; Thompson, *History of the 112th Illinois Infantry*, p. 299; Eldredge, *The Third New Hampshire*, p. 630. A newspaper reported that General Terry was "greatly prostrated by the poisonous malaria in his system." *New York Tribune*, February 18, 1865. Porter, *Incidents and Anecdotes of the Civil War*, pp. 280-281; *Philadelphia Inquirer*, February 18, 1865. See also: Price, *History of the 97th Pennsylvania Infantry*, p. 358; *New York Tribune*, February 17, 1865.

26. Abstract log of *U.S.S. Keystone State*, February 11, 1865, *ORN* 12, p. 38; Abstract log of *U.S.S. Shawmut*, February 11, 1865, ibid., p. 37; *New York Herald*, February 16, 1865.

27. Cox, *Military Reminiscences*, vol. 2, pp. 408-409; Confederate soldier to Kate Buie, Buie Papers, Duke.

28. *Wilmington Daily Journal*, February 13, 1865; Zac to Sister, February 12, 1865, Brunswick Town State Historic Site Collection, Winnabow, North Carolina.

29. *Philadelphia Inquirer*, February 18, 1865; McMurray, *Recollections of a Colored Troop*, p. 72.

30. Cox, *Military Reminiscences*, vol. 2, p. 408; *Philadelphia Inquirer*, February 16, 1865; Thomas Speed to Will, February 12, 1865, Speed Collection, Filson Club.

31. Report of Charles J. Paine, April 24, 1865, *OR* 47, pt. 2, p. 925; John E. Aliyetti, "Gallantry Under Fire," *CWTI*, XXXV, 5 (October, 1996), pp. 50-55. The Sugar Loaf fight of February 11 was the crowning combat experience for U. S. Colored Troops in North Carolina during the Civil War. Locally, the battle is known as the "bullet trench fight" because so many bullets were fired, thousands of which have been found in the sand by relic hunters over the years. Paine's advanced earthworks about 900 yards south of Sugar Loaf were extant until 1981, when the U. S. Corps of Engineers destroyed them for a Carolina Beach renourishment project. Thus, an important historical landmark and witness to a seminal moment in black history was lost forever.

32. Thompson, *History of the 112th Illinois Infantry*, pp. 299-300.

33. *New York Tribune*, February 17, 1865; *Philadelphia Inquirer*, February 18, 1865; Samuel Bates, *History of Pennsylvania Volunteers*, vol. 5, p. 580; Diary entry of February 11, 1865, Simon Bennage Diary, CW Misc. Collection, USAMHI.

34. Report of William H. Trickey, February 12, 1865, *OR* 47, pt. 1, p. 923; Report of Joseph C. Abbott, May 10, 1865, ibid., pt. 1, p. 921; *New York Herald*, February 16, 1865; Eldredge, *The Third New Hampshire Infantry*, p. 630.

35. *Philadelphia Inquirer*, February 18, 1865; *New York Tribune*, February 17, 1865; Price, *History of the 97th Pennsylvania Infantry*, p. 358.

36. *Philadelphia Inquirer*, February 16, 1865; Abstract from journal of Jacob D. Cox, February 11, 1865, *OR* 47, pt. 1, pp. 927-928.

37. Sumner, *Diary of Cyrus Comstock*, p. 309; Report of Jacob D. Cox, May 15, 1865, *OR* 47, pt. 1, p. 959; Cox, *Military Reminiscences*, pp. 409-410; Cyrus B. Comstock Memorandum, February 12, 1865, *OR* 47, pt. 2, pp. 404-405; Report of Jacob D. Cox, May 15, 1865, *OR* 47, pt. 1, p. 959; Special Orders, No.3, Headquarters Department of North Carolina, Army of the Ohio, February 12, 1865, *OR* 47, pt. 2, pp. 403-404.

38. Schofield to Grant, February 15, 1865, *OR* 47, pt. 2, p. 436-437; Special Orders, No.3, Headquarters Department of North Carolina, Army of the Ohio, February 12, 1865, ibid., pp. 403-404; Cyrus B. Comstock Memorandum, February 12, 1865, ibid., p. 404; Navy Department, *Civil War Naval Chronology*, vol. 5, p. 34.

39. Porter, Memoir, pp. 884-885, Porter Papers, LOC.

40. Special Orders, No.3, Headquarters Department of North Carolina, Army of the Ohio, February 12, 1865, *OR* 47, pt. 2, pp. 403-404; Porter to Rolando, February 12, 1865, *ORN* 12, pp. 27-28; Report of Jacob D. Cox, May 15, 1865, *OR* 47, pt. 1, p. 959.

41. Cox, *March to the Sea*, p. 148; Abstract from journal of Jacob D. Cox, February 12, 1865, *OR* 47, pt. 1, p. 928; Schofield to Grant, February 15, 1865, *OR* 47, pt. 2, p. 437; Report of Jacob D. Cox, May 15, 1865, *OR* 47, pt. 1, p. 959; Diary entry February 12, 1865, Nicholas DeGraff Diary, United States Military History Institute, Carlisle, Pennsylvania; Diary entry of February 12, 1865, Hornbrook Diary, Indiana Historical Society.

42. Sumner, *Diary of Cyrus Comstock*, p. 310; Cox, *Military Reminiscences*, vol. 2, p. 410; Porter to Schofield, February 14, 1865, *ORN* 12, p. 29; Special Orders, No.5, Headquarters Department of North Carolina, Army of the Ohio, February 14, 1865, *OR* 47, pt. 2, p. 426.

43. Cox, *March to the Sea*, p. 148; Diary entry of February 14, 1865, Bennage Diary, Civil War Misc. Collection, USAMHI.

44. Sumner, *Diary of Cyrus Comstock*, pp. 309-310; Cox, *March to the Sea*, p. 148; Report of Jacob D. Cox, May 15, 1865, *OR* 47, pt. 1, p. 959; Abstract from journal of Jacob D. Cox, May 15, 1865, ibid., pp. 929-930; Diary entry of February 14, 1865, Hornbrook Diary, Indiana Historical Society; McDonough, *Schofield*, p. 154; Diary entry of February 14, 1865, Bennage Diary, Civil War Misc. Collection, USAMHI.

45. Sumner, *Diary of Cyrus Comstock*, p. 310; Extract of letter from Nicholas DeGraff to Father, February 15, 1865, DeGraff Diary, USAMHI. "My own preference,"

General Cox recorded, "would have been to give up the movement as soon as it was evident that the pontoons would be behind time, so as not to let the enemy have any idea of the movement, which from that time [was] certain to prove a failure." Abstract from journal of Jacob D. Cox, February 15, 1865, *OR* 47, pt. 1, p. 928.

46. Schofield to Grant, February 15, 1865, *OR* 47, pt. 2, p. 437; Porter Memoir, pp. 886-887, Porter Papers, LOC.

47. Hoke to Anderson, January 17, 1865, *ORN* 11, pp. 592-593; Report of Jacob D. Cox, May 15, 1865, *OR* 47, pt. 1, p. 959; Henry Thomas Kennon to Mollie, January 31, 1865, Henry Thomas Kennon Papers, Division of Archives and History, Raleigh, North Carolina; James M. Merrill and James F. Marshall, eds., "The 16th Kentucky and the End of the War—Letters of Henry Clay Weaver," *Filson Club History Quarterly*, vol. 32, No. 4 (October, 1958), p. 342, hereinafter cited as Merrill and Marshall, "Letters of Henry Clay Weaver," *FCHQ*; Charles J. Paine to Charles C. Paine, January 30, 1865, Charles J. Paine Papers, Virginia Historical Society, Richmond.

Chapter 11: Outflanked

1. Diary entry of February 14, 1865, Oliver L. Spaulding Diary, Library of Congress, Washington, D.C., hereinafter cited as Spaulding Diary, LOC; Schofield to Commanding Officer, February 14, 1865, *OR* 47, pt. 2, p. 427.

2. Barney to Assistant Adjutant General, February 15, 1865, *OR* 47, pt. 2, p. 439; Diary entry of February 15, 1865, Calder Diary, Duke.

3. The U.S. Navy tugs *Nansemond*, *Eolus*, *Wilderness* and *Moccasin* transferred Cox's division from Federal Point to Smithville on February 16. Campbell to Dodge, February 15, 1865, *OR* 47, pt. 2, p. 438; Order of David D. Porter, February 13, 1865, *ORN* 12, p. 28; Report of Jacob D. Cox, May 15, 1865, *OR* 47, pt. 1, p. 959; Cox, *March to the Sea*, p. 149; Report of Oscar W. Sterl, April 28, 1865, ibid., p. 965; Thompson, *History of the 112th Illinois Infantry*, p. 301. Official military returns report the strength of Cox's division at 4,458. Report of Jacob D. Cox, May 15, 1865, *OR* 47, pt. 1, p. 958. The author estimates that Colonel Orlando Moore's brigade contained approximately 1,500 troops. Diary entry February 16, 1865, Spaulding Diary, LOC.

4. Report of Jacob D. Cox, May 15, 1865, *OR* 47, pt. 1, p. 960; Barrett, *Civil War in North Carolina*, p. 281; Curtis, *Reminiscences*, p. 33; Thompson, *History of the 112th Illinois Infantry*, pp. 301-302.

5. Report of Jacob D. Cox, May 15, 1865, *OR* 47, pt. 1, p. 960; Cox, *March to the Sea*, p. 149; Report of Thomas J. Henderson, April 6, 1865, *OR* 47, pt. 1, p. 968; Report of Oscar W. Sterl, April 28, 1865, ibid., p. 965; Curtis, *Reminiscences*, p. 33; "Journal of Adam Weaver," *Wilmington Morning Star*, December 27, 1964; *New York Herald*, February 25, 1865.

6. Report of Jacob D. Cox, May 15, 1865, *OR* 47, pt. 1, p. 960; Report of Thomas J. Henderson, April 6, 1865, ibid., pp. 968-969; Cox to Campbell, February 17, 1865, ibid., pt. 2, pp. 471-472; Cox, *March to the Sea*, 149; McDonough, *Schofield*, p. 153.

7. *New York Herald*, February 23, 1865; Murray and Bartlett, "The Letters of Stephen C. Bartlett," *NCHR*, p. 77; Ammen, *The Atlantic Coast*, p. 242; Hagood, *Memoirs of the War of Secession*, pp. 335-336; Diary entry February 17, 1865, George Hern Diary, private collection of Morris L. Yoder, Jr., Philadelphia, Pennsylvania; Abstract log of *U.S.S. Shawmut*, February 17, 1865, *ORN* 12, p. 37; Report of David D. Porter, February 19, 1865, ibid., pp. 33-34.

8. Report of David D. Porter, February 19, 1865, *ORN* 12, p. 33; Extracts From Journal of John C. Beaumont, February 18, 1865, ibid., p. 33; Entry of February 8, unidentified Union sailor's journal, Private collection of Tom Broadfoot, Wilmington, North Carolina; *New York Herald*, February 23, 1865; *Philadelphia Inquirer*, February 24, 1865; Report of Daniel L. Braine, February 17, 1865, *ORN* 12, p. 31; Murray and Bartlett, "Letters of Stephen C. Bartlett," *NCHR*, p. 77; Hagood, *Memoirs of the War of Secession*, p. 336.

9. Hagood, *Memoirs of the War of Secession*, pp. 335-336; *Philadelphia Inquirer*, February 24, 1865; Murray and Bartlett, "Letters of Stephen C. Bartlett," *NCHR*, p. 77.

10. *New York Herald*, February 25, 1865; Report of Thomas J. Henderson, April 6, 1865, *OR* 47, pt. 1, pp. 968-969; Report of Jacob D. Cox, May 15, 1865, ibid., p. 960.

11. Special Orders, No.7, Headquarters Dept. of North Carolina, Army of the Ohio, February 17, 1865, *OR* 47, pt. 2, p. 470.

12. Abstract from journal of Jacob D. Cox, February 18, 1865, *OR* 47, pt. 1, p. 929; Report of John S. Casement, April 9, 1865, ibid., p. 967; *New York Tribune*, February 23, 1865; Hagood, *Memoirs of the War of Secession*, pp. 336-337; Diary entry of February 18, Calder Diary, Duke; Diary entry of February 18, 1865, Hornbrook Diary, Indiana Historical Society; Report of Thomas J. Henderson, April 6, 1865, *OR* 47, pt. 1, p. 969.

13. Report of Jacob D. Cox, May 15, 1865, *OR* 47, pt. 1, p. 960; Murray and Bartlett, "Letters of Stephen C. Bartlett," *NCHR*, p. 76; *New York Tribune*, February 18, 1865.

14. "I inspected the armament of Fort Anderson. . .it consists of nine 32-pounder guns on barbette carriages, front pintle, wooden traverse circles. They are: Two rifled, unbanded; two oldest pattern of the U. S., which kind of guns condemned by U. S. inspectors previous to year 1860; and five pattern 1840. Below the fort is a work [Old Brunswick Battery] armed with one 32-pounder gun of oldest pattern (as described). The projectiles for these guns are 913 shot, 708 shell, 39 grape and 106 cannister shot, with a sufficient supply of projecting charge, making 170 rounds for each gun." Inclosure Report of H. Oladowski, February 5, 1865, *OR* 47, pt. 2, pp. 1116-1117. See also: *OR* Atlas, CXXXV-B, 4; Hagood, *Memoirs of the War of Secession*, p. 333.

15. Report of Jacob D. Cox, May 15, 1865, *OR* 47, pt. 1, p. 960; Cox, *March to the Sea*, p. 149; Barrett, *Civil War in North Carolina*, p. 282; *New York Herald*, February 25, 1865.

16. Report of Jacob D. Cox, May 15, 1865, *OR* 47, pt. 1, pp. 960-961; Thurstin, *History of the 111th Ohio Infantry*, p. 116; Sherwood, *Memories of the War*, p. 161; Report of Thomas J. Henderson, April 6, 1865, *OR* 47, pt. 1, p. 969; Hagood, *Memoirs of the War of Secession*, p. 336; *New York Herald*, February 25, 1865.

17. Report of Jacob D. Cox, May 15, 1865, *OR* 47, pt. 1, p. 960. Cox's flanking force was guided on its march to the west end of Orton Pond by a local black, possibly Lem Brown. Thomas Speed to parents, February 25, 1865, Speed Collection, Filson Club. See also: Curtis, *Reminiscences*. Cox's route of march was along the Brunswick or British Road on the south bank of Orton Pond. *OR* Atlas, CXXXII, 1; Sprunt, *Chronicles of the Cape Fear River*, map between pp. 412-413; Hagood, *Memoirs of the War of Secession*, pp. 335, 337.

18. *New York Tribune*, February 23, 1865; Hagood, *Memoirs of the War of Secession*, p. 336; Thomas Speed to Parents, February 25, 1865, Speed Collection, Filson Club.

19. *New York Tribune*, February 23, 1865.

20. *New York Herald*, February 25, 1865; *New York Tribune*, February 23, 1865.

21. Diary entry of February 18, 1865, George Hern Diary, Morris L. Yoder collection, Philadelphia.

22. Manarin, *North Carolina Troops*, vol. 1, pp. 375-376; *Wilmington Daily Journal*, February 20, 1865. General Hagood claimed that Lieutenant Vance was the only Confederate soldier killed in action at Fort Anderson on February 18. Hagood, *Memoirs of the War of Secession*, p. 337. Thomas H. Sutton of Company D, 40th North Carolina Regiment, recalled nineteen years after the war that Lt. William H. Harrison of Company B, 40th North Carolina, was killed by concussion from an exploded Union shell at Fort Anderson. Thomas H. Sutton, "Fort Fisher: A Soldier's Account of the Defense of the Approaches to Wilmington," *Wilmington Daily Review*, October 21, 1884, hereinafter cited as Sutton, "Defense of Wilmington," *Wilmington Daily Review*, October 21, 1884. Official military returns, however, indicate that Lieutenant Harrison was present or accounted for through February 1865. Manarin, *North Carolina Troops*, vol. 1, p. 386.

23. Report of David D. Porter, February 19, 1865, *ORN* 12, pp. 33-34; Ammen, *The Atlantic Coast*, p. 242; Murray and Bartlett, "Letters of Stephen C. Bartlett," *NCHR*, p. 78.

24. Diary entry of February 18, 1865, Calder Diary, Duke; Hagood, *Memoirs of the War of Secession*, p. 336; Murray and Bartlett, "Letters of Stephen C. Bartlett," *NCHR*, p. 78; Zaccheus Ellis to Mother, March 1, 1865, Zaccheus Ellis Papers, SHC. Copy also in Brunswick Town State Historic Site Collection, Winnabow, North Carolina.

25. Martin, *Fort Anderson*; Diary entry of February 18, 1865, Calder Diary, Duke.

26. Zaccheus Ellis to Mother, March 1, 1865, Zaccheus Ellis Papers, SHC; Hagood, *Memoirs of the War of Secession*, pp. 336-338; Sutton, "Defense of Wilmington," *Wilmington Daily Review*, October 21, 1884.

27. Abstract log of *U.S.S. Nyack*, February 18, 1865, *ORN* 12, p. 35; Temple to Bailey, February 21, 1865, ibid., p. 34.

28. Report of Jacob D. Cox, May 15, 1865, *OR* 47, pt. 1, pp. 960-961; Abstract from journal of Jacob D. Cox, February 18, 1865, ibid., p. 929.

29. Hagood, *Memoirs of the War of Secession*, p. 337; Manarin, *North Carolina Troops*, vol. 1, p. 347.

30. Abstract from journal of Jacob D. Cox, February 18, 1865, *OR* 47, pt. 1, p. 929; Report of Jacob D. Cox, May 15, 1865, ibid., pp. 960-961; Cox, *March to the Sea*, p. 150; Report of Oscar W. Sterl, April 28, 1865, *OR* 47, pt. 1, p. 965; Cox to Campbell, February 18, 1865, ibid., pt. 2, p. 482; Merrill and Marshall "The Letters of Henry Clay Weaver," *FCHQ*; Thomas Speed to parents, February 25, 1865, Speed Collection, Filson Club; Hagood, *Memoirs of the War of Secession*, p. 337; "The Capture of Wilmington," *National Tribune*, January 14, 1915; "Journal of Adam Weaver," *Wilmington Morning Star*, December 27, 1964.

31. Reports vary as to the number of Union casualties at Orton Pond on February 18, 1865. General Cox noted in his journal the day of the fight that he lost seven men wounded and one killed. Abstract from journal of Jacob D. Cox, February 18, 1865, *OR* 47, pt. 1, p. 929. Colonel Oscar W. Sterl reported that "[Lieutenant Reed's] charging party lost 1 man killed and 4 wounded." Report of Oscar W. Sterl, April 28, 1865, ibid., p. 965. These figures are subsequently corroborated by Cox in his official Carolinas Campaign report of May 15, 1865. "After a brisk skirmish of half an hour," he recorded, "a passage was effected with 1 killed and 4 wounded." Report of Jacob D. Cox, May 15, 1865, ibid., p. 961. Confederate casualties are unknown.

32. Cox to Campbell, February 18, 1865, *OR* 47, pt. 2, pp. 482-483; Report of Jacob D. Cox, May 15, 1865, ibid., pt. 1, p. 961.

33. Report of Oscar W. Sterl, April 28, 1865, ibid., pt. 1, p. 965; Jackson and O'Donnell, *Back Home in Oneida*, p. 192; Report of Jacob D. Cox, May 15, 1865, *OR* 47, pt. 1, p. 961; Cox to Schofield, February 18, 1865, ibid., pt. 2, p. 482; Cox to Campbell, February 18, 1865, ibid., pp. 482-483; "The Capture of Wilmington," *National Tribune*, January 14, 1915.

34. Zaccheus Ellis to Mother, March 1, 1865, Zaccheus Ellis Papers, SHC; Barrett, *Civil War in North Carolina*, p. 282; Hagood, *Memoirs of the War of Secession*, p. 337; Abstract log of *U.S.S. Yantic*, February 18-19, 1865, *ORN* 12, p. 36; Diary entry of February 18, 1865, Calder Diary, Duke.

35. Cushing Journal, NA. According to a Union sailor, Cushing supervised the construction of the "Quaker monitor" February 13-14. Diary entry of February 13-14,

1865, Hern Diary, Morris Yoder collection, Philadelphia; *Raleigh Semi-Weekly Standard*, March 24, 1865; Temple to Bailey, February 21, 1865, *ORN* 12, p. 34.

36. Accounts differ as to the night Porter and Cushing deployed the bogus monitor against Fort Anderson. Verification is difficult because no official report of the date has been uncovered. Porter's book of wartime anecdotes published twenty years after the conflict, seems to indicate that he used the sham monitor on the night of February 16. "The night before we attacked that place I had a mock monitor towed up and let go within two hundred yards of the enemy works." Porter, *Incidents and Anecdotes*, p. 275. That date and time may be corroborated by the wartime diary of George Hern, a landsman aboard the *Sassacus*. "16th, clear and moonlight," Hern recorded, "Sent Quaker Monitor up at 11 PM." Diary entry of February 16, 1865, Hern Diary, Morris Yoder collection, Philadelphia. Yet Hern neglected to specify whether the monitor was sent upstream upon its completion or against the fort. Cushing implied in his postwar journal that he cast the ironclad adrift off Fort Anderson on the night of February 18. He recorded a detailed account of the incident and noted: "We took possession [of Fort Anderson] next morning." Cushing Journal, NA. February 18 is supported by at least two contemporary newspaper accounts written by reporters on the scene. E. Smith of the *New York Tribune* reported on February 19: "Admiral Porter played another of his Yankee tricks upon the enemy last night. . .His mock monitor was cautiously towed up close under the guns of the fort about 10 o'clock...." *New York Tribune*, February 23, 1865. A *New York Herald* correspondent, Thomas M. Cook, also wrote on February 19 a good account of the ruse. "The affair was towed up close to the fort at ten o'clock last evening and then cast adrift...." *New York Herald*, February 23, 1865. It is unlikely the fake monitor was used on both February 16 and 18. All but one account reported that she drifted past Fort Anderson and grounded on the east side of the river behind Confederate lines. The weight of existing evidence suggests that the bogus monitor was used on February 18.

37. *New York Tribune*, February 23, 1865; Thompson and Wainright, *Correspondence of Gustavus Fox*, vol. 2, p. 200; Temple to Bailey, February 21, 1865, *ORN* 12, p. 34.

38. "The consequence was," Cushing boasted, "that the commanding Confederate knowing that the army was closing in behind him and thinking a monitor in the river above—evacuated in haste. Confederate officers told me afterwards that this was the true reason for the retreat." Cushing Journal, NA. Gideon Welles recorded in his diary that on February 22, 1865, "young Cushing came in with the intelligence of the capture of Fort Anderson. I went with him to see the President." Welles, *Diary of Gideon Welles*, vol. 2, p. 245. Admiral Porter reported that after the fake monitor floated past Fort Anderson, "the [Confederates] vamoosed as a deserter informed us, 'the damned monitor having cut them off all day'". Thompson and Wainright, *Correspondence of Gustavus Fox*, vol. 2, p. 200. The *New York Herald* perpetuated the myth that the fake

monitor caused the Confederates to evacuate Fort Anderson, reporting that the "Admiral's bogus Monitor, doubtless, was the influential cause of the precipitate abandonment by the rebels of their strong defensive line on the river." *New York Herald*, February 23, 1865.

39. William Calder to Mother, February 15, 1865, Calder Papers, SHC.

40. Hagood, *Memoirs of the War of Secession*, pp. 338-339. Hoke may have been ill during this time. According to Welsh, *Medical Histories of Confederate Generals*, p. 103: "In late January 1865, Hoke was unable to get around much because of a carbuncle on his face. In February he was in the general hospital no. 4 at Wilmington. . ." It is unknown whether Hoke's carbuncle—or any other ailment—affected his ability to command troops in the field during the Fort Anderson debacle.

41. Hagood received Hoke's evacuation orders at 2:48 a.m., February 19. Hagood, *Memoirs of the War of Secession*, p. 339. Zaccheus Ellis to Mother, March 1, 1865, Zaccheus Ellis Papers, SHC. Copy also in Brunswick Town State Historic Site, Winnabow, North Carolina. See also: *New York Tribune*, February 23, 1865; Diary entry of February 18, 1865, Calder Diary, Duke.

42. The Union army disagreed as to which troops were the first to enter Fort Anderson. Evidence suggests that Maj. Frank Wilcox of the 63rd Indiana Infantry led the initial wave of troops—Colonel Henderson's skirmishers—against the fort. In his official report Henderson asserted: "if any credit attaches for the occupation of Fort Anderson, after its evacuation, it is perhaps due to those of my command to say that the skirmishers of my brigade were among the first, if not the first, to enter the fort." Report of Thomas Henderson, April 6, 1865, *OR* 47, pt. 1, p. 970. Henderson apparently wanted to see his brigade receive due recognition for its part in the victory, a desire that may have related from an incident that occurred the previous evening, February 18. After General Cox had left on his flanking movement around Orton Pond, Schofield designated Colonel Henderson to command the troops that remained in front of Fort Anderson. Colonel Orlando Moore protested, stating that he was entitled to the command because his commission predated Henderson's. Upon Schofield's suggestion, Henderson relinquished authority in the interest of harmony. Thompson, *History of the 112th Illinois Infantry*, p. 303.

43. Clark, *North Carolina Regiments*, vol. 2, p. 762; Thompson, *History of the 112th Illinois Infantry*, pp. 303-304; Thurstin, *History of the 111th Ohio Infantry*, p. 116; Hagood, *Memoirs of the War of Secession*, p. 339; Report of Thomas J. Henderson, April 6, 1865, *OR* 47, pt. 1, p. 969; *New York Herald*, February 25, 1865; Sherwood, *Memories of the War*, p. 162.

44. A skirmisher of the 140th Indiana apparently found the Confederate flag at daybreak on February 19, when he entered Fort Anderson with the first wave of Union troops. The regiment's commander, Col. Thomas J. Brady, later gave the "captured flag" to Governor Oliver P. Morton of Indiana. A large crowd gathered on March 17,

1865, to witness the presentation ceremony outside the National Hotel in Washington. President Lincoln was among the honored guests and even made a brief speech. Despite all the hoopla, the Fort Anderson flag was not *captured*. According to an Illinois soldier who helped take the Cape Fear fort, it was *found*. Note is from Thompson, *History of the 112th Illinois Infantry*, p. 304. See also: Report of Thomas J. Henderson, April 6, 1865, *OR* 47, pt. 1, p. 970; *New York Times*, March 18, 1865.

45. Thompson, *History of the 112th Illinois Infantry*, p. 304; *New York Herald*, February 25, 1865.

46. Extract John C. Beaumont journal, February 19, 1865, *ORN* 12, p. 33; *New York Tribune*, February 23 and 25, 1865; *New York Herald*, February 25, 1865; Thurstin, *History of the 111th Ohio Infantry*, p. 116; Sherwood, *Memories of the War*, p. 161.

47. Entry February 19, 1865, Hern Diary, Morris Yoder collection, Philadelphia; Murray and Bartlett, "Letters of Stephen C. Bartlett," *NCHR*, p. 78; Porter, *Naval History of the Civil War*, p. 728; Thompson, *History of the 112th Illinois Infantry*, p. 304.

48. Solon A. Carter to Wife, February 21, 1865, Solon Carter Papers, USAMHI; Little, *History of the 7th New Hampshire*, p. 409; Entry of February 19, 1865, Scrogg's Diary, *CWTI* Collection, USAMHI; Report of Joseph C. Abbott, May 10, 1865, *OR* 47, pt. 1, p. 921.

49. Cox to Campbell, February 19, 1865, *OR* 47, pt. 2, p. 494; Cox to Campbell, February 19, 1865, ibid., p. 495; Abstract from journal of Jacob D. Cox, February 19, 1865, ibid., pt. 1, p. 929.

50. Cox to Campbell, February 19, 1865, *OR* 47, pt. 2, p. 495; Abstract from journal of Jacob D. Cox, February 19, 1865, ibid., pt. 1, p. 929; Report of Jacob D. Cox, May 15, 1865, ibid., p. 961; *New York Herald*, February 25, 1865; Thompson, *History of the 112th Illinois Infantry*, p. 305; Report of Thomas J. Henderson, April 6, 1865, *OR* 47, pt. 1, p. 970.

51. Schofield to Grant, February 19, 1865, *OR* 47, pt. 2, p. 493.

52. Anderson to Hoke, February 8, 1865, ibid., p. 1131.

53. Schofield to Grant, February 19, 1865, ibid., p. 493.

Chapter 12: Last Stand

1. Hagood to Anderson, February 19, 1865, *OR* 47, pt. 2, p. 1228; Hagood, *Memoirs of the War of Secession*, p. 342; Entry of February 19, 1865, Calder Diary, Duke. According to military accounts, the Confederate earthworks at Town Creek contained "a Whitworth rifled cannon and two brass smoothbore twelve pounder field pieces." Cox, *March to the Sea*, p. 150; Report of Jacob D. Cox, May 15, 1865, *OR* 47, pt. 1, p. 961. Hagood's earthworks, since torn down, stood on a bluff on the north bank of Town Creek just west of present-day Highway 133 at Town Creek bridge.

2. Hagood to Anderson, February 19, 1865, *OR* 47, pt. 2, p. 1228; Hagood, *Memoirs of the War of Secession*, p. 342.

3. Report of Jacob D Cox, May 15, 1865, *OR* 47, pt. 1, p. 961; Cox, *March to the Sea*, p. 150; Hagood, *Memoirs of the War of Secession*, pp. 340-341; Sprunt, *Chronicles of the Cape Fear River*, map, p. 412; *OR* Atlas, CV, 8.

4. Parker to Bragg, February 19, 1865, *OR* 47, pt. 2, p. 1227; Clark, *North Carolina Regiments*, vol. 4, p. 427; W. O. Blake, *Pictorial History of the Great Rebellion*, 2 vols. (Columbus, 1866), vol. 2, p. 811; J. R. Hawley to William C. Church, March 9, 1865, William C. Church Papers, Library of Congress, Washington, D. C., hereinafter cited as Church Papers, LOC. Remanants of Hoke's earthworks can still be seen east of River Road. Another section is extant south of Hanover Heights, running east across the intersection of South 17th Street and Independence Blvd. toward Pine Valley. These works are now threatened by development.

5. Entry February 19, 1865, Scrogg's Diary, *CWTI* Collection, USAMHI; Solon A. Carter to wife, February 21, 1865, Solon A. Carter Papers, USAMHI; J. R. Hawley to William C. Church, March 9, 1865, Church Papers, LOC.

6. *Philadelphia Inquirer*, February 27, 1865; Little, *History of the 7th New Hampshire*, p. 409; Solon A. Carter to wife, February 21, 1865, Solon A. Carter Papers, USAMHI; Schofield to Terry and Terry to Schofield, February 19, 1865, *OR* 47, pt. 2, p. 497.

7. Extract from journal of Commander Beaumont, February 19, 1865, *ORN* 12, p. 33; Abstract log of *U.S.S. Yantic*, February 19, 1865, ibid., p. 36; Murray and Bartlett, "Letters of Stephen C. Bartlett," *NCHR*, p. 78; *New York Tribune*, February 23 and 25, 1865; Asa Beetham to Annie, February 20, 1865, Asa Beetham Letters, Library of Congress, Washington, D. C.

8. *OR* Atlas, LXVIII, 7. For armament of the Confederate river batteries see: Hébert to Anderson, February 4, 1865, *OR* 47, pt. 2, pp. 1115-1116; Oladowski to Anderson, February 5, 1865, ibid., pp. 1116-1118. See also: Entry of February 19, 1865, Hern Diary, Morris Yoder collection, Philadelphia; *New York Tribune*, February 25, 1865.

9. Gaillard to Parker, February 19, 1865, *OR* 47, pt. 2, p. 1228; *New York Tribune*, February 25, 1865; Still, "The Yankees Were Landing Below Us," *CWTI*, p. 18; Thompson and Wainwright, *Correspondence of Gustavus Fox*, vol. 2, pp. 200-201.

10. Diary entry of February 19, 1865, Calder Diary, Duke; Campbell to Cox, February 19, 1865, *OR* 47, pt. 2, p. 496.

11. Slann L. C. Simmons, "Diary of Abram W. Clement, 1865," *South Carolina Historical Magazine*, LIX, 2 (April, 1958), p. 79, hereinafter cited as Simmons, "Diary of Abram W. Clement," *SCHM*.

12. Hagood, *Memoirs of the War of Secession*, p. 342; Report of Jacob D. Cox, May 15, 1865, *OR* 47, pt. 2, p. 961; Report of Thomas J. Henderson, April 6, 1865, ibid., pt. 1, p. 969; Cox, *March to the Sea*, p. 150; Thompson, *History of the 112th Illinois*

Infantry, p. 305; Cox to Campbell, February 19, 1865, *OR* 47, pt. 2, p. 495; Report of Oscar W. Sterl, April 28, 1865, ibid., pt. 1, p. 965.

13. Report of Thomas J. Henderson, April 6, 1865, *OR* 47, pt. 1, p. 969; Thompson, *History of the 112th Illinois Infantry*, p. 305; Cox to Campbell, February 19, 1865, *OR* 47, pt. 2, p. 495; Report of Jacob D. Cox, May 15, 1865, ibid., pt. 1, p. 961; Campbell to Cox, February 19, 1865, ibid., pt. 2, p. 496.

14. Report of Jacob D. Cox, May 15, 1865, *OR* 47, pt. 1, p. 961; Report of John S. Casement, April 9, 1865, ibid., p. 968; Report of Oscar W. Sterl, April 28, 1865, ibid., p. 965; Thompson, *History of the 112th Illinois Infantry*, 306; Thurstin, *History of the 111th Ohio Infantry*, p. 118; Cox to Schofield, February 20, 1865, *OR* 47, pt. 2, p. 509; Diary entry of February 20, 1865, Spaulding Diary, LOC; "A Memory," *National Tribune*, February 4, 1915.

15. Cox, *March to the Sea*, 151; Report of Thomas J. Henderson, April 6, 1865, *OR* 47, pt. 1, pp. 969-970; Hagood, *Memoirs of the War of Secession*, p. 342; Entry of February 20, 1865, Calder Diary, Duke.

16. Hagood, *Memoirs of the War of Secession*, pp. 342-343; Hardee to Bragg, February 20, 1865, *OR* 47, pt. 2, p. 1231; Hoke to Hardee, February 20, 1865, ibid., p. 1233; Hoke to Lee, February 20, 1865, ibid., p. 1233.

17. Marching Orders, February 20, 1865, *OR* 47, pt. 2, p. 510; Diary entry of February 20, 1865, Scrogg's Diary, *CWTI* Collection, USAMHI; *Philadelphia Inquirer*, February 27, 1865.

18. *Philadelphia Inquirer*, February 27, 1865.

19. Entry of February 20, 1865, DeGraff Diary, *CWTI* Collection, USAMHI; Report of Joseph C. Abbott, May 10, 1865, *OR* 47, pt. 1, p. 921. I first heard the story of the Horne brothers about 1980 from the late Robert C. Horne, a former employee of Will Rheder Florist on Dawson Street in Wilmington. Mr. Horne also kindly provided me with a photograph of a uniformed Hosea Horne, the Confederate brother. The story was corroborated for me in 1994 by Hosea's grandson, Louis Horne of Wilmington, and then by Bruce Barclay Cameron, also of Wilmington, whose maternal great great grandmother was Katherine Lanier Horne. Mr. Cameron recounts the family story in George W. Willcox and Bruce Barclay Cameron, *The Camerons of Wilmington* (Chapel Hill, 1994), pp. 219-220. The story of Hosea and Jacob Horne illustrates the divisive nature of the Civil War. The Horne home was located on the Federal Point Road, the route both Hoke's and Terry's forces followed to Wilmington. The Horne home, which is no longer standing, stood just northeast of Monkey Junction, the intersection of Carolina Beach Road and South College Road. Manarin, *North Carolina Troops*, vol. 1, p. 153; Chris E. Fonvielle, "The Fall of Wilmington, February, 1865," *Cape Fear Tidewater*, 2 (February, 1985), pp. 9-10.

20. Cross to Parker, February 20, 1865, *OR* 47, pt. 2, p. 1235; Clark, *North Carolina Regiments*, vol. 1, p. 410. Hoke's position at Forks Road was at the west end of

present-day Stonewall Jackson Drive in Pine Valley. Part of Hoke's earthworks can still be seen. They are, however, threatened by development; Edwin S. Redkey, *A Grand Army of Black Men* (Cambridge, 1992), p. 166.

21. Military Order of the Loyal Legion of the United States Insignia Record, Number 9776—Colonel Elias Wright, United States Army Military History Institute, Carlisle Barracks, Pennsylvania, hereinafter cited as *MOLLUS* Insignia Record, Number 9776—Colonel Elias Wright, USAMHI.

22. *MOLLUS* Insignia Record, Number 9776—Colonel Elias Wright, USAMHI; Report of Charles J. Paine, April 24, 1865, *OR* 47, pt. 1, p. 925; Charles J. Paine to Father, February 23 and March 2, 1865, Charles J. Paine Papers, Virginia Historical Society, Richmond; *Philadelphia Inquirer*, February 27, 1865; A. G. Jones, "Colored Troops: March From Fort Fisher to Wilmington," *National Tribune*, October 18, 1888; Solon Carter to "Precious Em," February 21, 1865, Solon A. Carter Collection, USAMHI; Entry of February 20, 1865, Scrogg's Diary, *CWTI* Collection, USAMHI.

23. Ames to Campbell, February 20, 1865, *OR* 47, pt. 2, p. 510; Jackson and O'Donnell, *Back Home In Oneida*, p. 193; Cross to Parker February 20, 1865, *OR* 47, pt. 2, p. 1235. Paine's breastworks were located approximately 500 yards south of Hoke's line at Forks Road, but were destroyed by the construction of Sun Valley subdivision, as was most of the battlefield in the early 1980s. A small section of Terry's line of earthworks is still visible southwest of Pine Valley School; Diary entry of February 20, 1865, Bennage Diary, Civil War Misc. Collection, USAMHI.

24. Still, "The Yankees Were Landing Below Us," *CWTI*, p. 18 Abstract log of *U.S.S. Shawmut*, February 20, 1865, *ORN* 12, p. 37; Report of David D. Porter, February 22, 1865, ibid., p. 45; Murray and Bartlett, "Letters of Stephen C. Bartlett," *NCHR*, p. 79.

25. Still, "The Yankees Were Landing Below Us," *CWTI*, p. 18; Diary entry of February 20, 1865, Hern Diary, Mowris Yoder collection, Philadelphia; Murray and Bartlett, "Letters of Stephen C. Bartlett," *NCHR*, p. 78-79.

26. Diary entry of February 20, 1865, Hern Diary, Mowris Yoder collection, Philadelphia; Report of David D. Porter, February 22, 1865, *ORN* 12, p. 45; Murray and Bartlett, "Letters of Stephen C. Bartlett," *NCHR*, p. 78; Blake, *Pictorial History of the Great Rebellion*, vol. 2, p. 811.

27. Report of Jacob D. Cox, May 15, 1865, *OR* 47, pt. 1, p. 962; Report of John S. Casement, April 9, 1865, ibid., p. 968; Report of Oscar W. Sterl, April 28, 1865, ibid., 965; Thomas Speed to Parents, February 25, 1865, Speed Collection, Filson Club.

28. Simmons, "Diary of Abram W. Clement," *SCHM*, pp. 79-80; The Confederate videttes were probably surprised and captured by soldiers of Cox's division, who were crossing the creek on the morning of February 20. According to one Southern account, however, the pickets were taken captive not by Union infantry but by a shore party of marines from the gunboats in the Cape Fear River. Charles Henry Simonton, "Circum-

stances of the Capture of Hagood's Brigade on 20th Feb'y 1865 at Cowan's Place on Town Creek near Wilmington, N. C.," p. 5, George Hall Moffett Papers, South Carolina Historical Society, Charleston, hereinafter cited as Simonton, "Capture of Hagood's Brigade at Town Creek," Moffett Papers, SCHS.

29. Ibid., p. 1; Hagood, *Memoirs of the War of Secession*, p. 343; William V. Izlar, *A Sketch of the War Record of the Edisto Rifles, 1861-1865* (Columbia, 1914), p. 115, hereinafter cited as Izlar, *Edisto Rifles*.

30. Hagood, *Memoirs of the War of Secession*, map, p. 341.

31. Simonton, "Capture of Hagood's Brigade at Town Creek," pp. 1-2, Moffett Papers, SHC.

32. Hagood, *Memoirs of the War of Secession*, p. 344-345; Simonton, "Capture of Hagood's Brigade at Town Creek," p. 2, Moffett Papers, SHC; Hagood to Parker, February 20, 1865, *OR* 47, pt. 2, p. 1236.

33. Report of Jacob D. Cox, May 15, 1865, *OR* 47, pt. 1, p. 962; Report of John S. Casement, April 9, 1865, ibid., p. 968; Report of Oscar W. Sterl, April 28, 1865, ibid., p. 965.

34. Simonton, "Capture of Hagood's Brigade at Town Creek," p. 3, Moffett Papers, SHC; Hagood, *Memoirs of the War of Secession*, p. 344; Izlar, *Edisto Rifles*, p. 116.

35. Richard Dillard, *The Civil War in Chowan County*, (n. p., 1916), pp. 5-7.

36. Report of Jacob D. Cox, May 15, 1865, *OR*, 47, pt. 1, p. 962; Cox to Schofield, February 20, 1865, ibid., pt. 2, p. 509; *New York Herald*, February 27, 1865.

37. Diary entry of February 20, 1865, Calder Diary, Duke; Zaccheus Ellis to Mother, March 1, 1865, Zaccheus Ellis Papers, SHC; Report of Thomas Henderson, April 6, 1865, *OR* 47, pt. 1, p. 970; Hagood, *Memoirs of the War of Secession*, pp. 345-346; Simonton, "Capture of Hagood's Brigade at Town Creek," p. 3, Moffett Papers, SHC.

38. Hagood, *Memoirs of the War of Secession*, pp. 345-346; "Captain William E. Stoney," *Confederate Veteran*, vol. 4, p. 383.

39. *New York Herald*, February 27, 1865. See also: Thomas Speed to Parents, February 25, 1865, Speed Papers, Filson Club; LeVant Dodge, "A Memory," *National Tribune*, February 4, 1915.

40. Simmons, "Diary of Abram W. Clement," *SCHM*, p. 80.

41. General Cox lost about thirty men (killed and wounded) in the charge at Town Creek. Report of Jacob D. Cox, May 15, 1865, *OR* 47, pt. 1, p. 964. Cox to Schofield, February 20, 1865, ibid., pt. 2, p. 509. Colonel Oscar W. Sterl noted that the Federal loss in the attack was three killed and thirty-one wounded. Report of Oscar W. Sterl, April 28, 1865, ibid., pt. 1, p. 966.

42. According to one of the only four Confederate accounts of the Town Creek battle uncovered to date, Sergeant Hunter ordered Pvt. William H. Hassell to fire "St. Paul" at the attacking Union troops, despite the threat against him by the lieutenant of the 12th Kentucky U. S. Infantry. If Hassell was the gunner who jerked the lanyard, he miracu-

lously escaped capture. According to military records, Private Hassell was paroled with his unit—Company B, 3rd Battalion N. C. Light Artillery—in Greensboro on April 28, 1865. Dillard, *The Civil War in Chowan County*, pp. 6-7; Manarin, *North Carolina Troops*, vol. 1, p. 351. For a Union account of the incident see, James R. Bentley, ed., "The Civil War Memoirs of Captain Thomas Speed," *Filsom Club Historical Quarterly*, 44 (July, 1970), pp. 266-267.

43. Declaration for Original Invalid Pension for William Reese, June 20, 1884, copy in possession of Timothy J. Reese, Burkittsville, Maryland.

44. Thomas Speed to Parents, February 25, 1865, Speed Collection, Filson Club; Simmons, "Diary of Abram W. Clement," *SCHM*, p. 81. General Hagood wrote after the war that Colonel Simonton reported 330 South Carolina soldiers and officers captured by the Federals at Town Creek (perhaps twenty or thirty North Carolina artillerymen were also taken prisoner). Hagood figured that Simonton lost twenty soldiers killed, and 100 escaped, but "coming out of the route and not finding the brigade that night, straggled off to South Carolina, and were no more, with very few exceptions, heard of in the war." Hagood, *Memoirs of the War of Secession*, p. 347. In a 1904 account of the Town Creek battle, Charles H. Simonton noted the the "whole capture" from Hagood's brigade consisted of twenty-seven officers, ninety soldiers of the 11th South Carolina Infantry, forty-five men of the 25th South Carolina Infantry, and 150 of the 27th South Carolina Infantry. Simonton, "Capture of Hagood's Brigade at Town Creek." Simonton's figures do not, however, account for the losses of the 21st South Carolina Infantry. See also, Report of Jacob D. Cox, May 15, 1865, *OR* 47, pt. 1, p. 963; Cox to Schofield, February 20, 1865, ibid., pt. 2, p. 509; Report of Oscar W. Sterl, April 28, 1865, ibid., pt. 1, pp. 965-966; *New York Herald*, February 27, 1865.

45. Manarin, *North Carolina Troops*, vol. 1, p. 354.

46. Simmons, "Diary of Abram W. Clement," *SCHM*, p. 81.

47. Izlar, *Edisto Rifles*, pp. 116-117.

48. Hagood, *Memoirs of the War of Secession*, p. 346; "Captain William E. Stoney," *Confederate Veteran*, vol. 4, p. 383.

49. Hagood to Anderson, February 20, 1865, *OR* 47, pt. 2, p. 1236; Hagood, *Memoirs of the War of Secession*, p. 346; Zaccheus Ellis to Mother, March 1, 1865, Zaccheus Ellis Papers, SHC; Diary entry of February 20, 1865, Calder Diary, Duke.

50. Thomas Speed to Parents, February 25, 1865, Speed Collection, Filson Club.

51. Hagood, *Memoirs of the War of Secession*, pp. 346-348.

52. Murray and Bartlett, "Letters of Stephen C. Bartlett," *NCHR*, p. 79; Ed Vanderbilt to Mac, March 15, 1865, McEachern and Williams Collection, UNCW; Porter, *Naval History of the Civil War*, p. 728; Porter, *Incidents and Anecdotes*, p. 278.

53. Report of David D. Porter, February 22, 1865; *ORN* 12, p. 45; Abstract log of *U.S.S. Shawmut*, February 20, 1865, ibid., p. 37; Porter, *Naval History of the Civil War*, p. 728; Report of David D. Porter, February 21, 1865, *ORN* 12, p. 44; *New York*

Tribune, February 28, 1865; Porter, *Incidents and Anecdotes*, 278; Blake, *Pictorial History*, vol. 2, p. 811.

54. Hagood, *Memoirs of the War of Secession*, p. 346; Parker to Officer Commanding Detachment of Hagood's Command, February 21, 1865, *OR* 47, pt. 2, p. 1244.

55. Report of Jacob Cox, May 15, 1865, *OR* 47, pt. 1, p. 963; Cox, *Military Reminiscences*, vol. 2, p. 411; Thompson, *History of the 112th Illinois Infantry*, pp. 306-307; Thurstin, *History of the 111th Ohio Infantry*, p. 119; Cox to Schofield, February 21, 1865, *OR* 47, pt. 2, p. 521; Cox, *March to the Sea*, p. 153; Report of Thomas J. Henderson, April 6, 1865, *OR* 47, pt. 1, p. 970.

56. Merrill and Marshall, "The Letters of Henry Clay Weaver," *FCHQ*, p. 343; Report of Jacob D. Cox, May 15, 1865, *OR* 47, pt. 1, p. 963; Report of Oscar W. Sterl, April 28, 1865, ibid., p. 966; Cox to Schofield, February 21, 1865, ibid., pt. 2, p. 521; Blake, *Pictorial History*, vol. 2, p. 812; *Wilmington Messenger*, September 8, 1895; David C. Bradley to Mother, February 23, 1865, Civil War Misc. Collection, USAMHI.

57. Merrill and Marshall, "Letters of Henry Clay Weaver," *FCHQ*, p. 343. The remains of a Union soldier—perhaps those of the soldier in the 16th Kentucky U. S. Infantry killed during the Eagles Island fight—were excavated in 1896. "While the men were ditching alongside the [Eagles Island] causeway they unearthed the remains of a soldier," noted a reporter. "They found his brass buttons and other belongings, and again interred them in the same spot. The remains are supposed to have been those of the Federal soldier who was killed by the battery at the foot of Market street, while the Federal army was advancing up the causeway on Wilmington." *Wilmington Messenger*, May 15, 1896. See also: *Philadelphia Inquirer*, March 4, 1865; Report of Oscar W. Sterl, April 28, 1865, *OR* 47, pt. 1, p. 966.

58. William Harris Yopp, a fourteen-year-old boy who witnessed the fall of Wilmington, recalled that Capt. Abner A. Moseley commanded the Confederate battery at Front and Market Streets on February 21, 1865. William Harris Yopp, "The Surrender of Wilmington to the Yankees, February, 1865," *Wilmington Morning Star*, August 16, 1936, hereinafter cited as Yopp, "Surrender of Wilmington," *Wilmington Morning Star*. J. E. Purcell of Company D, 1st Battalion, North Carolina Heavy Artillery, was a sergeant on a gun crew that afternoon in Wilmington and claimed that Lt. Preston Alford commanded the battery. It is likely that Alford commanded one of the cannon, as he was an officer in Captain Moseley's Sampson Artillery. *Wilmington Messenger*, February 11, 1897; Manarin, *North Carolina Troops*, vol. 1, pp. 36, 605. See also: *Wilmington Morning Star*, March 28, 1915; Smaw, *Wilmington Directory*, 1867, p. 36; *Wilmington Messenger*, September 8, 1895 and February 11, 1897; *Raleigh Daily Conservative*, March 21, 1865.

59. Report of Jacob D. Cox, May 15, 1865, *OR* 47, pt. 1, p. 963; Thompson, *History of the 112th Illinois Infantry*, p. 307; Thurstin, *History of the 111th Ohio Infantry*, p. 120; Cox, *March to the Sea*, p. 153.

60. Yopp, "Surrender of Wilmington," *Wilmington Morning Star*, August 16, 1936; Hagood, *Memoirs of the War of Secession*, p. 348.

61. Report of Braxton Bragg, February 25, 1865, *OR* 47, pt. 1, p. 1077. See also: Seitz, *Braxton Bragg*, pp. 508-509; Bragg to Hoke, February 21, 1865, *OR* 47, pt. 2, p. 1244.

62. David Libbey to Mary, February 21, 1865, David Libbey Papers, Perkins Library, Duke University, Durham, North Carolina.

63. Report of Adelbert Ames, April 16, 1865, *OR* 47, pt. 1, p. 924; John B. Foote to Father, February 23, 1865, John B. Foote Papers, Library of Congress, Washington, D. C.; Jackson and O'Donnell, *Back Home in Oneida*, p. 193; *Philadelphia Inquirer*, February 27, 1865.

64. Palmer, *History of the 48th New York Volunteers*, pp. 187-188. See also: James M. Nichols, *Perry's Saints or the Fighting Parson's Regiment* (Boston, 1886), p. 277.

65. Diary entry of February 21, 1865, Bennage Diary, Civil War Misc. Collection, USAMHI.

66. *Philadelphia Inquirer*, February 27, 1865; Mowris, *History of the 117th New York Infantry*, p. 185; Blake, *Pictorial History*, vol. 2, p. 812; Diary entry of February 21, 1865, Bennage Diary, Civil War Misc. Collection, USAMHI.

67. Diary entry of February 21, 1865, Hern Diary, Morris Yoder collection, Philadelphia; Report of David D. Porter, February 22, 1865, *ORN* 12, p. 45; *New York Herald*, February 27, 1865; Jackson and O'Donnell, *Back Home in Oneida*, p. 193; Blake, *Pictorial History*, vol. 2, p. 811; Diary entry of February 21, 1865, Bennage Diary, Civil War Misc. Collection, USAMHI.

68. Report of Braxton Bragg, February 25, 1865, *OR* 47, pt. 1, p. 1077; "Personal Recollections of Joseph Piram King," copy in possession of Larry Walker, Charlotte, North Carolina; Hagood, *Memoirs of the War of Secession*, p. 348; *Raleigh Daily Conservative*, March 1, 1865; *Fayetteville Observer*, February 27, 1865.

69. *Philadelphia Inquirer*, February 27, 1865; Eldredge, *The Third New Hampshire*, p. 637. See also: Sidney Williams, *From Spottsylvania to Wilmington, N.C., By Way of Andersonville and Florence* (Providence, 1899), pp. 13-16.

70. Lee to Bragg, February 21, 1865, *OR* 47, pt. 2, p. 1241; Bragg to Lee, February 21, 1865, ibid., p. 1242; Report of Braxton Bragg, February 25, 1865, ibid., pt. 1, p. 1077; Hagood, *Memoirs of the War of Secession*, p. 348; *Raleigh Daily Conservative*, March 1, 1865; Yopp, "Surrender of Wilmington," *Wilmington Morning Star*, August 23, 1936.

71. *Fayetteville Observer*, February 27, 1865; Sprunt, *Chronicles of the Cape Fear River*, p. 500; *Raleigh Daily Conservative*, March 21, 1865; *New York Herald*, February 27, 1865; Yopp, "Surrender of Wilmington," *Wilmington Morning Star*, September 20, 1936, and November 11-12, 1937; Louis T. Moore, "Warships for Southern Confeder-

acy," Shipbuilding—Civil War File, New Hanover Public Library, Wilmington, North Carolina; Navy Department, *Civil War Naval Chronology*, vol. 5, p. 49, vol. 6, p. 211.

72. Zaccheus Ellis to Mother, March 1, 1865, Zaccheus Ellis Papers, SHC; *Raleigh Daily Conservative*, March 21, 1865.

73. Diary entry February 21, 1865, Spaulding Diary, LOC; Cox to Schofield, February 21, 1865, *OR* 47, pt. 2, p. 522; Schofield to Cox, February 21, 1865, ibid., p. 520; Cox, *March to the Sea*, p. 154; McDonough, *Schofield*, 155.

74. Schofield to Cox, February 21, 1865, *OR* 47, pt. 2, pp. 520, 522; Report of Jacob D. Cox, May 15, 1865, ibid., pt. 1, pp. 963-964; Thompson, *History of the 112th Illinois Infantry*, p. 307; *New York Herald*, February 27, 1865; Blake, *Pictorial History*, p. 812.

75. Cox to Schofield, February 21, 1865, *OR* 47, pt. 2, pp. 521, 523; Report of Jacob D. Cox, May 15, 1865, ibid., pt. 1, p. 964; Schofield to Cox, February 21, 1865, ibid., pt. 2, pp. 522-523; Diary entries of February 21-22, 1865, Spaulding Diary, LOC; Cox to Henderson, February 21, 1865, *OR* 47, pt. 2, p. 524; Report of Thomas Henderson, April 6, 1865, ibid., pt. 1, p. 970; *New York Herald*, February 27, 1865; McDonough, *Schofield*, 155.

76. Still, "The Yankees Were Landing Below Us," *CWTI*, p. 18; Hagood, *Memoirs of the War of Secession*, pp. 348-349; *Fayetteville Observer Semi-Weekly*, March 2, 1865.

Chapter 13: Surrender

1. Eldredge, *The Third New Hampshire*, p. 635; *Philadelphia Inquirer*, February 27, 1865; Walkley, *History of the 7th Connecticut Infantry*, p. 197; Report of Edmund H. Russell, June 20, 1865, *OR* 47, pt. 1, p. 916; Cox, *Military Reminiscences*, vol. 2, p. 417.

2. Memoir of Mrs. Margaret Dixon Davis Philyaw, Lower Cape Fear Historical Society, Wilmington, North Carolina; *Wilmington Herald of the Union*, March 13, 1865; *Philadelphia Inquirer*, February 27, 1865; *New York Tribune*, February 28, 1865; Report of Oscar W. Sterl, April 28, 1865, *OR* 47, pt. 1, p. 966; Cox, *Military Reminiscences*, vol. 2, p. 417; Yopp, "Surrender of Wilmington," *Wilmington Morning Star*, August 23, 1936.

3. *Wilmington Morning Star*, March 6, 1865; Price, *History of the 97th Pennsylvania Infantry*, p. 361.

4. L. S. Burkhead, "History of the Difficulties of the Pastorate of the Front Street Methodist Church, Wilmington, N. C. For the Year 1865," *Historical Society of Trinity College Series*, 8 (1908-1909), pp. 37-38, hereinafter cited as Burkhead, "History of Front Street Methodist Church," *HSTCS*. See also, Yearns and Barrett, *North Carolina Civil War Documentary*, p. 92.

5. Little, *The 7th New Hampshire Infantry*, p. 411; *New York Tribune*, February 28, 1865; *Philadelphia Inquirer*, February 27, 1865; Eldredge, *The Third New Hampshire*, p. 636.

6. Burkhead, "History of the Front Street Methodist Church," *HSTCS*, pp. 37-38; Yearns and Barrett, *North Carolina Civil War Documentary*, p. 92; Wood, "Port Town at War," p. 224; *New York Tribune*, February 28, 1865.

7. Abstract of journal of Jacob D. Cox, February 22, 1865, *OR* 47, pt. 1, p. 930; Mowris, *History of the 117th New York Infantry*, p. 187. The advance of U.S. flotilla was impeded by Confederate obstructions and mines in the Cape Fear River. The first ships, including Porter's flagship *Malvern*, dropped anchor at Wilmington at about 3:00 p.m. on February 22. Entry of February 22, 1865, Hern Diary, Morris Yoder collection, Philadelphia; Grattan, "Under the Blue Pennant," Grattan Papers, LOC; Report of David D. Porter, February 22, 1865, *ORN* 12, p. 45; Navy Department, *Civil War Naval Chronology*, vol. 6, p. 47; *Philadelphia Inquirer*, February 27, 1865; Letter of Joseph Warren Poland, February 22, 1865, *Lower Cape Fear Historical Society Bulletin*, February, 1977.

8. Eldredge, *The Third New Hampshire*, p. 636; Little, *History of the 7th New Hampshire Infantry*, p. 411; Elbridge J. Copp, *Reminiscences of the War of the Rebellion 1861-1865* (Nashau, 1911), pp. 499-500; Report of Joseph C. Abbott, May 10, 1865, *OR* 47, pt. 1, p. 922; *Recollections and Reminiscences 1861-1865* (South Carolina Division, United Daughters of the Confederacy, 1990), p. 445.

9. Bragg's route of retreat was along the Duplin or Goldsboro Road, present day Highway 117, Castle Hayne Road; Little, *History of the 7th New Hampshire Infantry*, pp. 413-414.

10. Report of Joseph C. Abbott, May 10, 1865, *OR* 47, pt. 1, p. 922. Incomplete military records indicate that on February 22, Bragg's rearguard comprised Colonel Lipscomb's 2nd South Carolina Cavalry, General W. W. Kirkland's Brigade (17th, 42nd, and 66th North Carolina Infantry Regiments), and the 8th North Carolina Infantry of Colonel William S. Devane's Brigade. Clark, *North Carolina Regiments*, vol. 2, pp. 10-11, 802, and vol. 3, pp. 695-696; Little, *History of The 7th New Hampshire Infantry*, p. 414.

11. Report of Joseph C. Abbott, May 10, 1865, *OR* 47, pt. 1, p. 922; Eldredge, *The Third New Hampshire*, p. 636. General Paine detached the 4th U. S. Colored Troops and Lt. John Myrick's Battery E, 3rd U. S. Artillery, to reinforce Abbott's brigade. Report of Charles J. Paine, April 24, 1865, *OR* 47, pt. 1, p. 925; Little, *History of the 7th New Hampshire Infantry*, p. 414.

12. Elliott, "Kirkland's Brigade, Hoke's Division," *SHSP*, vol. 23, p. 169; Clark, *North Carolina Regiments*, vol. 3, p. 695; Little, *History of the 7th New Hampshire Infantry*, p. 414; Eldredge, *The Third New Hampshire*, p. 636.

13. Note is from: Elliott, "Kirkland's Brigade, Hoke's Division" *SHSP*, vol. 23, p. 169. See also: Clark, *North Carolina Regiments*, vol. 2, pp. 10-11.

14. Clark, *North Carolina Regiments*, vol. 1, p. 411; Eldredge, *The Third New Hampshire*, p. 637; Little, *History of the 7th New Hampshire Infantry*, p. 412; McMurray, *Recollections of a Colored Troop*, p. 73; Walkley, *History of the 7th Connecticut Infantry*, p. 198.

15. Lee to Bragg, February 22, 1865, *OR* 47, pt. 2, p. 1249; Reed, *Combined Operations in the Civil War*, p. 380.

16. Cox, *March to the Sea*, p. 155; Schofield to Grant, February 28, 1865, *OR* 47, pt. 2, p. 619; Schofield to Cox, March 2, 1865, ibid., p. 654; Schofield to Grant, March 5, 1865, ibid., p. 693.

17. Report of John M. Schofield, April 3, 1865, *OR* 47, pt. 1, p. 911; Wright to McCallum, February 25, 1865, ibid., pt. 2, p. 579; Schofield to Grant, February 28, 1865, ibid., pp. 619-620; Schofield to Grant, March 5, 1865, ibid., p. 694; Grant to Stanton, March 10, 1865, ibid., p. 753; Cox, *March to the Sea*, 155; *New York Tribune*, March 14, 1865.

18. Barrett, *Civil War in North Carolina*, p. 285; Report of John M. Schofield, April 3, 1865, *OR* 47, pt. 1, p. 911; Itinerary of First Division, Twenty-third Army Corps, February, 1865, ibid., p. 155; Schofield to Grant, February 28, 1865, ibid., pt. 2, p. 619; Headquarters Department of North Carolina, Army of the Ohio, February 25, 1865, ibid., pp. 579-580; Note is from: Schofield to Cox, February 25, 1865, *OR* 47, pt. 2, p. 580.

19. Schofield to Couch, March 5, 1865, *OR* 47, pt. 2, p. 694; Schofield to Grant, March 5, 1865, ibid., pp. 693-694; Report of John M. Schofield, April 3, 1865, ibid., pt. 1, pp. 911-912; Schofield to Terry, March 5, 1865, ibid., pt. 2, 695; Terry to Sherman, March 7, 1865, ibid., 725.

20. Sherman to Schofield, March 12, 1865, *OR* 47, pt. 2, pp. 800-801; Sherman to Quartermaster, March 12, 1865, ibid., p. 795; *Wilmington Herald of the Union*, March 14, 1865.

21. Terry to Sherman, March 13, 1865, *OR* 47, pt. 2, p. 818; Terry to Sherman, March 14, 1865, ibid., pp. 840-841; Dodge to Sherman, March 13, 1865, ibid., p. 807.

22. Dodge to Schofield, March 15, 1865, *OR* 47, pt. 2, p. 852; Terry to Sherman, March 13, 1865, ibid., p. 819; Marching Orders, March 15, 1865, ibid., p. 855.

23. Grant, *Memoirs of U. S. Grant*, vol. 2, pp. 418-419.

24. Reed, *Combined Operations in the Civil War*, p. 379.

Postscript: Occupation

1. *New York Herald*, February 27, 1865; *Philadelphia Inquirer*, February 27, 1865; Gaskill, *Footprints Through Dixie*, p. 170; McMurray, *Recollections of a Colored Troop*, p. 72.

2. Price, *History of the 97th Pennsylvania Infantry*, p. 361.

3. Katherine Douglas DeRosset Meares to Mother, March 28, 1865, DeRosset Family Papers, Southern Historical Collection, University of North Carolina, Chapel Hill, hereinafter cited as DeRosset Papers, SHC.

4. Little, *History of the 7th New Hampshire*, p. 411; Walkley, *History of the 7th Connecticut Infantry*, p. 197; *Philadelphia Inquirer*, February 27, 1865.

5. *New York Tribune*, March 9, 1865; *Philadelphia Inquirer*, February 27, 1865.

6. Redkey, *A Grand Army of Black Men*, pp. 165-167.

7. Sprunt, *Chronicles of the Cape Fear River*, pp. 268-271.

8. *New York Tribune*, February 28, 1865; A. G. Jones, "Colored Troops: March From Fort Fisher to Wilmington," *National Tribune*, October 18, 1888.

9. Katherine Douglas DeRosset Meares to Mother, March 28, 1865, DeRosset Papers, SHC.

10. *New York Tribune*, March 13, 1865; Thurstin, *History of the 111th Ohio Infantry*, p. 120; Murray and Bartlett, "Letters of Stephen C. Bartlett," *NCHR*, p. 82.

11. Wood, "Port Town at War," p. 234; Katherine Douglas DeRosset Meares to Mother, March 28, 1865, DeRosset Papers, SHC.

12. Yopp, "Surrender of Wilmington," *Wilmington Morning Star*, September 13, 1865; Jerry Wildenhaus to Chris Fonvielle, December 18, 1995, personal collection of Chris E. Fonvielle, Jr., Wilmington, North Carolina; Becker, "Fort Fisher and Wilmington," *Leslie's Popular Monthly*, p. 238; Katherine Douglas DeRosset Meares to L. H. DeRosset, May 18, 1865, DeRosset Papers, SHC.

13. Murray and Bartlett, "Letters of Stephen C. Bartlett," *NCHR*, p. 84.

14. Becker, "Fort Fisher and Wilmington," *Leslie's Popular Monthly*, p. 237.

15. Hawley to Campbell, March 31, 1865, *OR* 47, pt. 3, p. 93; Becker, "Fort Fisher and Wilmington," *Leslie's Popular Monthly*, p. 237; *Raleigh Daily Conservative*, March 20, 1865; Lassie DeRosset to L. H. DeRosset, June 30, 1865, DeRosset Papers, SHC.

16. *Wilmington Herald of the Union*, February 28, March 9, 1865; Headquarters Department of North Carolina, Army of the Ohio, General Order # 8, February 27, 1865, *OR* 47, pt. 2, pp. 605-606.

17. J. R. Hawley to wife, February 28, 1865, Hawley Papers, LOC; Headquarters Department of North Carolina, Army of the Ohio, Special Orders, No. 18, March 1, 1865, *OR* 47, pt. 2, p. 636; *Wilmington Herald of the Union*, March 4, 5, 1865; Headquarters District of Wilmington, Special Orders, No. 4, March 5, 1865, *OR* 47, pt. 2, p. 696; Moore to Abbott, March 6, 1865, ibid., p. 709.

18. Hatch to Schofield, February 23, 1865, *OR*, series 2, 8, pp. 296-297; Schofield to Hoke, February 23, 1865, ibid., p. 297; Bragg to Lee and Bragg to Holmes, February 24, 1865, ibid., p. 304; Little, *History of the 7th New Hampshire Infantry*, p. 415.

19. Eldredge, *The Third New Hampshire*, p. 637.

20. Headquarters Department of North Carolina, Army of the Ohio, Special Orders No. 12, February 23, 1865, *OR*, series 2, 8, p. 296; Wherry to Terry, February 23, 1865, ibid., p. 297; *New York Tribune*, March 9, 1865; Little, *History of the 7th New Hampshire Infantry*, p. 416.

21. Abbott to Campbell, March 5, 1865, *OR*, series 2, 8, p. 358; A. O. Abbott, *Prison Life in the South* (New York, 1866), p. 189; James M. Ferguson, *Life Struggles In Rebel Prisons* (Philadelphia, 1865), p. 202; Benjamin F. Booth, *Dark Days of the Rebellion or Life In Southern Military Prisons* (Indianola, 1897), p. 319; M. A. Cochran, "Reminiscences of Life in Rebel Prisons," Sketches of War History 1861-1865: Papers Prepared for the Commandery of the State of Ohio, *Military Order of the Loyal Legion of the United States,* V (1903), p. 66, hereinafter cited as Cochran, "Reminiscences of Life in Rebel Prison," *MOLLUS*.

22. Ferguson, *Life Struggles In Rebel Prisons*, p. 202-203; Abbott, *Prison Life in the South*, p. 190; Cochran, "Reminiscences of Life in Rebel Prisons," *MOLLUS*, p. 66; Leon Basile, ed., *The Civil War Diary of Amos E. Stearns* (Associated University Presses, Inc., 1981), p. 114.

23. McMurray, *Recollections of a Colored Troop*, p. 75; Abbott, *Prison Life in the South*, pp. 190-191; Ferguson, *Life Struggles In Rebel Prisons*, pp. 203-204; Booth, *Life In Southern Military Prisons*, pp. 319-323; Cochran, "Reminiscences of Life in Rebel Prisons," *MOLLUS*, p. 67; Walkley, *History of the 7th Connecticut Infantry*, p. 201; *New York Tribune*, February 27, 1865; *Wilmington Herald of the Union*, February 28, 1865.

24. Travis, *The Story of the Twenty-fifth Michigan*, pp. 341, 343.

25. United States Sanitary Commission, *Preliminary Report of the Operations of the U. S. Sanitary Commission in North Carolina, March, 1865, and Upon the Physical Condition of Exchanged Prisoners Lately Received at Wilmington, N. C.* (New York, 1865), Report No. 87, p. 9, hereinafter cited as U. S. Sanitary Commission, *Report of Operations in North Carolina, March, 1865.*

26. Mowris, *History of the 117th New York Infantry*, p. 186; Joseph R. Hawley to Hattie, February 28, 1865, Hawley Papers, LOC; Booth, *Life In Southern Military Prisons*, p. 327.

27. Abbott to Campbell, March 5, 1865, *OR*, series 2, 8, p. 358; Schofield to Townsend, March 9, 1865, ibid., p. 373; Thompson, *History of the 112th Illinois Infantry*, p. 308; *Wilmington Herald of the Union*, March 2, 4-5, 1865; *New York Tribune*, March 15, 1865; George A. Weiser, *Nine Months In Rebel Prisons* (Philadelphia, 1890), pp. 51-52.

28. *Wilmington Herald of the Union*, March 5, 7, 10, 1865; Wood, "Port Town at War," p. 251; U. S. Sanitary Commission, *Report of Operations in North Carolina*, March, 1865, p. 9; Schofield to Grant, March 5, 1865, *OR* 47, pt. 2, p. 694; Schofield to Townsend, March 9, 1865, *OR*, series 2, 8, p. 373; Abbott, *Prison Life in the South*, p. 191.

29. Sherman to Slocum, March 6, 1865, *OR* 47, pt. 2, p. 704; Terry to Schofield, March 11, 1865; ibid., p. 791; Sherman to Grant, March 12, 1865, ibid., p. 791; Hawley to Gillmore, March 23, 1865, ibid., p. 978.

30. J. G. Longley to Reverend M.E. Streely, March 18, 1865, American Missionary Association Records, Microfilm Collection, Joyner Library, East Carolina University, Greenville, North Carolina (hereafter cited as American Missionary Records, ECU); Hawley to Senior Naval Officer, March 21, 1865, *OR* 47, pt. 2, p. 946; Hawley to Terry, March 21, 1865, ibid., p. 946; Hawley to Gillmore, March 23, 1865, ibid., p. 978; *Wilmington Herald of the Union*, March 23, 1865; Becker, "Fort Fisher and Wilmington," *Leslie's Popular Monthly*, p. 237.

31. Hawley to Campbell, March 26, 1865, *OR* 47, pt. 3, p. 30; Wood, "Port Town at War," 252; J. G. Streely to Reverend M. E. Streely, March 18, 1865, American Misssionary Records, ECU; Joseph R. Hawley to Horace James, April 5, 1865, American Missionary Records, ECU.

32. Mrs. Alex Oldham to Mother, March 30, 1865, Pleasant D. Gold Papers, Southern Historical Collection, University of North Carolina, Chapel Hill; Katherine Douglas DeRosset Meares to Cousin, May 18, 1865, DeRosset Papers, SHC.

33. Murray and Bartlett, "Letters of Stephen C. Bartlett," *NCHR*, pp. 82, 84; Mowris, *History of the 117th New York Infantry*, p. 188; Hawley to Campbell, March 20, 1865, *OR* 47, pt. 2, p. 926; Hawley to Terry, March 21, 1865, ibid., p. 946; Hawley to Gillmore, March 23, 1865, ibid., p. 978.

34. Joseph R. Hawley to Horace James, April 5, 1865, American Missionary Records, ECU; *Wilmington Herald of the Union*, March 13, 17, and 28, 1865; Hawley to Campbell, March 20, 1865, *OR* 47, pt. 2, p. 928.

35. Hawley to Gillmore, March 23, 1865, *OR* 47, pt. 2, p. 978; Hawley to Gillmore, March 26, 1865, ibid., pt. 3, p. 30; Headquarters District of Wilmington, Special Orders, No. 21, March 27, 1865, ibid., p. 39; Moore to Abbott, April 1, 1865, ibid., p. 80; *Wilmington Herald of the Union*, March 21, 1865.

36. *Wilmington Herald of the Union*, March 21, 31, 1865; Katherine Douglas DeRosset Meares to Mother, March 28, 1865, DeRosset Papers, SHC.

37. *Wilmington Herald of the Union*, March 13, 1865; Wood, "Port Town at War," p. 236.

38. Register of Letters and Endorsements Received, District of Wilmington, North Carolina, March, 1865, Records of the United States Army Continental Commands 1821-1920, Record Group 393, United States National Archives, Washington, D. C.;

Hawley to Campbell, April 3, 1865, *OR* 47, pt. 3, p. 93; Murray and Bartlett, "Letters of Stephen C. Bartlett," *NCHR*, p. 82; *Wilmington Herald of the Union*, March 7, 1865.

39. Hawley to Campbell, March 31, 1865, *OR* 47, pt. 3, p. 70; Wood, "Port Town at War," p. 237.

40. Wood, "Port Town at War," p. 236; Letters Received and Special Orders Issued, District of Wilmington, North Carolina, Records of the United States Army Continental Commands 1821-1920, Record Group 393, Part 2, Entry 1823, No 179/432 VaNC, April 5, 1865, United States National Archives, Washington, D. C.; *Wilmington Daily Review*, December 27, 1882.

41. Dr. Armand John DeRosset to L. H. DeRosset, July 17, 1865, DeRosset Papers, SHC.

42. John D. Bellamy, *Memoirs of an Octogenarian* (Charlotte, 1942), pp. 22, 29-30; Hawley to Campbel, April 3, 1865, *OR* 47, pt. 3, p. 93; Ellen Douglas Bellamy, *Back With the Tide* (Wilmington, 1941), pp. 4-5; Diane Cobb Cashman, "History of the Bellamy Mansion," pp. 45-46, Bellamy Mansion Museum Collection, Wilmington, North Carolina.

43. Alfred A. Watson to Joseph R. Hawley, March 16, 1865 and Alfred A. Watson to Abraham Lincoln, April 12, 1865, occupation file, McEachern and Williams Collection, UNCW; Katherine Douglas DeRosset Meares to Mrs. Armand John DeRosset, April 11 and May 18, 1865, DeRosset Papers, SHC; McEachern and Reaves, *History of St. James Parish*, pp. 9-10.

44. Hawley to Campbell, March 20, 1865, *OR* 47, pt. 2, p. 928; Hawley to Campbell, April 3, 1865, ibid., pt. 3, p. 93; Hawley to Richardson, March 24, 1865, ibid., p. 14; Hawley to Norcom, March 30, 1865, ibid., p. 64; Hawley to Campbell, April 1, 1865, ibid., p. 79; Campbell to Hawley, April 5, 1865, ibid., p. 80.

45. *Wilmington Herald of the Union*, March 31, 1865; Yopp, "Surrender of Wilmington," *Wilmington Morning Star*, August 23, 1936; Eldredge, *The Third New Hampshire*, p. 1035; Dr. Armand John DeRosset to L. H. DeRosset, July 17, 1865, DeRosset Papers, SHC.

46. *Wilmington Hearld of the Union*, March 11, 31, 1865.

47. *New York Herald*, March 21, 1865. See also: *New York Tribune*, March 24, 1865.

48. Ibid; *Raleigh Daily Conservative*, March 29, 1865.

49. *Raleigh Daily Confederate*, April 5, 1865.

50. Ibid., March 30, 1865.

51. Ibid., April 1, 1865; Letter of Katherine Douglas DeRosset Meares, 1865, DeRosset Papers, SHC.

52. Hawley to Campbell, April 3, 1865, *OR* 47, pt. 3, p. 92.

53. Ibid; Eldredge, *The Third New Hampshire*, p. 774; *Fayetteville Observer*, March 9, 1865; *Raleigh Daily Confederate*, March 29, 1865.

54. Katherine Douglas DeRosset Meares to Mother, March 28, 1865, DeRosset Papers, SHC.

Epilogue: Taps

1. Denson, *Memoir of W. H. C. Whiting*, pp. 47, 50.

2. Lamb, *Story of Fort Fisher*, p. 38; Lamb, "Defense and Fall of Fort Fisher," *SHSP*, vol. 10, p. 367.

3. Curtis, *The Capture of Fort Fisher, MOLLUS*, p. 47.

Bibliography

MANUSCRIPTS

Ralph H. Allen Collection, Maumelle, Arkansas
    William Henry Walling Letters
Bellamy Mansion Museum, Wilmington, North Carolina
    Bellamy Mansion Collection
Mike Brake Collection, Rocky Mount, North Carolina
    Jesse Brake Letter
Brunswick Town State Historic Site, Winnabow, North Carolina
    Miscellaneous Confederate Letters
Chantaugua County Historical Society, Westfield, New York
    William B. Cushing Journal
Chester County Historical Society, West Chester, Pennsylvania
    Norris O. Meyer Letters
Chicago Historical Society, Chicago, Illinois
    Alonzo Alden Collection
    N. Martin Curtis Collection
    William B. Cushing Papers
College of William and Mary
    William Lamb Collection
Duke University, Perkins Library, Durham, North Carolina
    Weld Noble Allen Papers
    William Badham, Jr. Papers
    Asa Biggs Papers
    Joseph Fulton Boyd Papers
    Braxton Bragg Papers
    Eliza Button Letter

Catherine Jane Buie Papers
C. S. A. Archives, Army, Misc. Officers and Soldiers Letters
William Calder Diary
James Cleer Papers
John Clifton Papers
Thomas L. Clingman Papers
John Couch Papers
Arthur Emmerson Papers
Edward Follett Diary
John B. Foote Papers
Thomas W. Higginson Letter
Wade H. Hubbard Papers
John H. Kelley Papers
Horatio King Papers
John H. Kinyon Papers
William Lamb Papers
David Libbey Papers
Hugh MacRae Papers
Hector H. McNeill Papers
Mary Margaret McNeill Papers
James Otis Moore Papers
John Thomas Nichols Papers
Charles S. Powell Papers
William Read, Jr. Papers
Charles Steedman Papers
John J. Taylor Papers
A. J. Turlington Collection
Michael Turrentine Papers
Edward D. Walsh Papers
Joseph J. Wescoat Diary
William Henry Chase Whiting Papers
East Carolina University, Joyner Library, Greenville, North Carolina.
American Missionary Association Papers
William Carl Buchanan Collection
Lucy Cherry Crisp Papers
John C. Fennell Papers
Richard Parson Paddison Papers
Thomas Sparrow Papers
Arthur Whitford Papers
Hunter-Wills Family Papers

Filson Club, Louisville, Kentucky
  Thomas Speed Collection
Chris E. Fonvielle, Jr. Collection, Wilmington, North Carolina
  Charles Pattison Bolles Letters
  G. B. Cook Letters
  N. Martin Curtis Letters
Fort Fisher State Historic Site, Kure Beach, North Carolina
  Confederate Log Book
Tom Greco Collection, Alexandria, Virginia
  Horace Stevens Letters
Agnes Guarrieri Collection, Philadelphia, Pennsylvania
  Thomas Richardson Letters
Indiana Historical Society, W. H. Smith Memorial Library, Indianapolis, Indiana
  Issac Cox Collection
  Thomas Johnson Papers
  Saunders Richard Hornbrook Diary
  Thomas Johnson Papers
  William Ketcham Collection
Library of Congress, Manuscript Department, Washington, D. C.
  Asa Beetham Papers
  Alpheus S. Bloomfield Papers
  Benjamin F. Butler Papers
  Clarence Cary Papers
  William C. Church Papers
  Cyrus B. Comstock Papers
  Christian Fleetwood Papers
  John B. Foote Papers
  John W. Grattan Papers
  Joseph R. Hawley Papers
  Samuel Phillips Lee Papers
  Marshall Miller Papers
  Joseph B. Osborn Family Papers
  David Dixon Porter Papers
  Thomas O. Selfridge Papers
  Montgomery Sicard Letter
  Oliver S. Spaulding Diary
  Gideon Welles Papers
Mr. and Mrs. Walter H. Lipke Collection, Santa Barbara, California
  John S. Maxwell Letters
Lower Cape Fear Historical Society, Wilmington, North Carolina

Confederate Veterans Talks
Margaret Dixon Davis Philyaw Memoir
Museum of the Confederacy, Richmond, Virginia
Miscellaneus Confederate Letters
New Hanover County Public Library
Horace M. and Robert P. Barry Papers
Civil War—Wilmington File
Louis T. Moore Collection
William M. Reaves Collection
North Carolina Division of Archives and History, Raleigh
Moses Bledsoe Papers
Charles Pattison Bolles Papers
Braxton Bragg Papers
Henry Benton Papers
Stephen S. Burrill Papers
John L. Cantwell Papers
Cape Fear Chapter, United Daughters of the Confederacy Papers
John T. Conrad Papers
D. D. Crowell Letter
Claude B. Denson Papers
DeRosset Family Papers
Dorothy Fremont Grant Papers
James H. Hill Papers
Robert F. Hoke Papers
Roy V. Howell Papers
Robert A. Johnson Papers
Henry Thomas Kennon Papers
Wilson G. Lamb Papers
Robert E. Lee Papers
Mrs. William M. Lybrook Collection
Kate McKinnon Papers
Thomas M. Pittman Papers
William S. Powell Papers
Thomas W. Redwine Papers
Colin Shaw Papers
Lyman Sheppard Papers
George C. Tait Papers
John W. Taylor Papers
Zebulon Baird Vance Papers
John D. Whitford Papers

William Henry Chase Whiting Papers
Thomas Fanning Wood Collection
Samuel W. Worthington Collection
Ogdensburg Public Library, Ogdensburg, New York
N. Martin Curtis Collection
Alvin J. Page Collection, Wilmington, North Carolina
Daniel Nelson Letter
Dr. Charles V. Peery Collection, Charleston, South Carolina
Charles Smith Peek Papers
Rome Historical Society, Rome, New York
Scrapbook on the 117th New York Volunteers
George Slaton Collection, Wilmington, North Carolina
N. M. Robinson Letter
South Carolina Historical Society, Charleston
Henry N. Baker Letters
George Hall Moffett Papers
Allan T. Strange Collection, Wilmington, North Carolina
John Douglas Taylor Memoir
Percy P. Turner Collection
United States Army Military History Institute, Carlisle Barracks, Pennsylvania
William Alcorn—Timothy Brookes Collection
Simon Bennage Diary
Amos Brennan Letters
Solon A. Carter Papers
Civil War Miscellaneous Collection
Civil War Times Illustrated Collection
Nicholas DeGraff Diary
Chris E. Fonvielle Collection
Daniel Gingrich Papers
Lewis Leigh Collection
Harrison Nesbitt Letters
W. R. Noble Papers, Bayer Collection
United States National Archives and Records Services, Washington, D. C.
William Barker Cushing Journal, Record Group 45
University of North Carolina, Chapel Hill, Southern Historical Collection
James W. Albright Diary
Stephen C. Bartlett Papers
Herman Biggs Papers
Macon Bonner Papers
Braxton Bragg Papers

Stephen S. Burrill Diary
William Calder Papers
John L. Cantwell Papers
W. G. Curtis Papers
Nicholas DeGraff Diary
DeRosset Family Papers
Zaccheus Ellis Papers
Federal Soldiers Letters
George W. Gift Papers
Jeremy F. Gilmer Maps
Pleasant D. Gold Papers
William Hooper Haigh Papers
John Robert Hawes Papers
John Haywood Papers
Louis Hébert Autobiography
Eugene S. Martin Papers
Henry Nutt Papers
Perkins Family Papers
Charles S. Powell Papers
James Ryder Randall Papers
John McKee Sharpe Papers
Southall and Bowan Papers
John H. Steinmeyer Papers
William Henry and Araminta Guilford Tripp Papers
Lewis Henry Webb Papers
J. J. Wescoat Papers
William Henry Chase Whiting Papers
University of North Carolina at Wilmington, Randall Library, Special Collections
John D. Bellamy Family Papers
High Family Papers
Leora McEachern and Isabel Williams Collection
James R. Womble Letter
University of South Carolina, Columbia, South Caroliniana Collection
Johnson Hagood Papers
James Izlar Diary
James Lowndes Papers
G. G. Young Papers
University of Virginia, Charlottesville
Blackford Family Papers
Virginia Historical Society, Richmond

Charles J. Paine Papers
Larry Walker Collection, Charlotte, North Carolina
   Joseph Piram King Recollections
Richard S. Walling Collection, East Brunswick, New Jersey
   William Henry Walling Letters
Brian E.W. Wood Collection, Secaucus, New Jersey
   David Webb Hodgekins Journal
Yale University, Sterling Memorial Library, New Haven, Connecticut
   Terry Family Papers
Morris L. Yoder, Jr., Collection, Philadelphia, Pennsylvania
   George H. Hern Diary
Steve L. Zerbe Collection, Cherry Hill, New Jersey
   J. Rine Mentzer Letter

OFFICIAL PUBLICATIONS

American State Papers: *Documents, Legislative & Executive of the Congress of the United States, Military Affairs.* Washington: Gales & Seaton, 1861.

Official Register of the Officers and Cadets of the U. S. Military Academy, West Point, New York. West Point, New York: U. S. Military Academy.

Records of United States Army Continental Commands 1821-1920. Record Group 393. United States National Archives and Records Services, Washington, D.C.

Report of the Adjutant General of the State of New Hampshire for the Year Ending June 1, 1866. 2 volumes. Concord: George E. Jenks, State Printer, 1866.

Report of the Joint Committee on the Conduct of the War, at the Second Session Thirty-Eighth Congress. Washington: Government Printing Office, 1865.

Report of the Movement and Operations of the 1st Connecticut Heavy Artillery, For the Year Ending March 31, 1865, As Given in the Annual Report of the Adjutant General of Connecticut, April 11, 1865. Hartford, Connecticut: Case Lockwood and Co., 1865.

Report of the Secretary of the Navy, 1865. Washington: Government Printing Office, 1865.

Supplement to the Official Records of the Union and Confederate Armies. 40 volumes. Wilmington, North Carolina: Broadfoot Publishing Company, 1994-1996.

U. S. Military Academy Cadet Application Papers 1805-1866. Washington, D. C.: National Archives Microfilm Publications.

United States Navy Department. *Official Records of the Union and Confederate Navies in the War of the Rebellion.* 30 volumes. Washington, D. C.: Government Printing Office, 1900-1901.

United States War Department. *Atlas to Accompany the Official Records of the Union and Confederate Armies.* Washington, D. C.: Government Printing Office, 1891-1895.

—. *The War of the Rebellion, A Compilation of the Official Records of the Union and Confederate Armies.* 70 volumes in 128 parts. Washington, D.C.: Government Printing Office, 1880-1901.

NEWSPAPERS

Ballston (NY) *Journal*
Baltimore American
Charleston (SC) *Mercury*
Charlotte (NC) *News*
Fayetteville Observer
Fayetteville Observer Semi-Weekly
Frank Leslie's Illustrated Newspaper
Gleason's Pictorial Drawing Room Companion
Harper's Weekly
Illustrated London News
National Tribune, The
New Haven (CT) *Register*
New York Herald
New York Times
New York Tribune
New York World
Philadelphia Inquirer
Raleigh (NC) *Daily Confederate*
Raleigh Daily Conservative
Raleigh North Carolina Semi-Weekly Standard
Raleigh North Carolina Weekly Standard
Richmond Enquirer
Wilmington (NC) *Daily Journal*
Wilmington Daily North Carolinian
Wilmington Daily Review
Wilmington Herald of the Union
Wilmington Messenger
Wilmington Morning Star
Wilmington Star News
Wilmington Weekly Intelligencer
Wilmington Weekly Journal

PUBLISHED PRIMARY SOURCES

(includes autobiographies, diaries, journals, memoirs, reminiscences and unit histories)

A Late Confederate Officer. "Wilmington During the Blockade." *Harper's New Monthly Magazine,* 196 (September, 1866).

"A Yankee Account of the Battle of Fort Fisher." *Our Living and Our Dead.* Vol. 1, No. 4 (December, 1874).

Abbot, Henry L. *Siege Artillery in the Campaigns Against Richmond.* New York: D. Van Nostrand, 1868.

Abbott, A. O. *Prison Life in the South. New York:* Harper's & Brothers, 1866.

Ames, Adelbert. "Capture of Fort Fisher, North Carolina, Jan. 15, 1865." Commandery of the Loyal Legion of the State of New York (1897).

—. "The Capture of Fort Fisher." Civil War Papers of the Commandery of the State of Massachusetts, Military Order of the Loyal Legion of the United States, I (1900).

Ames, John W. "The Victory at Fort Fisher." *Overland Monthly,* IX (1872).

Ammen, Daniel. "Our Second Bombardment of Fort Fisher." Miltary Order of the Loyal Legion of the United States War Paper, 4 (1887).

Basile, Leon, ed. *The Civil War Diary of Amos E. Stearns, A Prisoner at Andersonville.* East Brunswick, New Jersey: Associated University Pressed, Inc., 1981.

Becker, Joseph. "Fort Fisher and Wilmington." *Frank Leslie's Popular Illustrated Magazine,* XXXVIII (August, 1894).

Bellamy, Ellen Douglas. *Back With the Tide: Memoirs of Ellen Douglas Bellamy.* Wilmington, North Carolina: n. p., 1941.

Bellamy, John D. *Memoirs of an Octogenarian.* Charlotte, North Carolina: Observer Printing House, 1942.

Bennett, A. B. "Closing Up the Last Confederate Port," *The National Tribune* (April 14 and 21, 1927).

Bentley, James R., ed. "The Civil War Memoirs of Captain Thomas Speed." *The Filson Club History Quarterly,* 44 (July, 1970).

Booth, Benjamin F. *Dark Days of the Rebellion or Life in Southern Military Prisons.* Indianola, Iowa: Booth Publishing Co., 1897.

Burkhead, L. S. "History of the Difficulties of the Pastorate of the Front Street Methodist Church, Wilmington, N. C. For the Year 1865." Durham, North Carolina. *Historical Society of Trinity College Series*, 8 (1908-1909).

Butler, Benjamin F. *Butler's Book*. Boston: A. M. Thayer & Co, 1892.

Caldwell, Charles K. *The Old Sixth Regiment, Its War Record, 1861-5*. New Haven, Connecticut: Tuttle, Morehouse & Taylor, 1875.

Carter, Solon A. "Fourteen Months' Service With Colored Troops." Civil War Papers of the Commandery of the State of Massachusetts, Military Order of the Loyal Legion of the United States, I (1900).

Catton, Bruce, ed. "A Civil, and Sometimes Uncivil, War." *American Heritage*, XV (October, 1964).

Chisman, James A, ed. *76th Regiment Pennsylvania Volunteer Infantry, Keystone Zouaves: The Personal Recollections 1861-1865 of Sergeant John A. Porter*. Wilmington, North Carolina: Broadfoot Publishing Company, 1988.

Clark, James. *The Iron Hearted Regiment: Being an Account of the Battles Marches and Gallant Deeds Performed by the 115th Regiment N. Y. Vols*. Albany, New York: J. Munsell, 1865.

Clark, Walter, ed. *Histories of the Several Regiments and Battalions From North Carolina in the Great War 1861-'65*. 5 volumes. Goldsboro, North Carolina: Nash Brothers, 1901.

Cochran, A. W. "Reminiscences of Life in Rebel Prisons." Sketches of War History 1861-1865: Papers Prepared for the Commandery of the State of Ohio, Military Order of the Loyal Legion of the United States, V (1903).

Copp, Elbridge J. *Reminiscences of the War of the Rebellion 1861-1865*. Nashau, New Hampshire: The Telegraph Publishing Company, 1991.

Cox, Jacob Dolson. *Military Reminiscences of the Civil War*. 2 volumes. New York: Charles Scribner's Sons, 1900.

Croom, Wendell D. *The War History of Company "C" (Beauregard Volunteers) Sixth Georgia Regiment*. Fort Valley, Georgia: Advertiser Offices, 1879.

Curtis, N. Martin. *The Capture of Fort Fisher*. n. p., 1897.

——. "The Capture of Fort Fisher." Civil War Papers of the Commandery of the State of Massachusetts, Military Order of the Loyal Legion of the United States, I (1900).

Curtis, W. G. *Reminiscences of Wilmington and Southport, 1848-1900*. Southport, North Carolina: Herald Job Office, 1900.

Daly, Robert W., ed. *Aboard the USS Florida: 1863-65*. Annapolis, Maryland: United States Naval Institute, 1968.

Davis, Jefferson. *The Rise and Fall of the Confederate Government*. D. Appleton and Company, 1881.

Deems, Charles Force. *Autobiography of Charles Force Deems.* New York: Fleming H. Revell Company, 1897.

Derby, W. P. *Bearing Arms in the Twenty-Seventh Massachusetts Regiment of Volunteer Infantry During the Civil War, 1861-1865.* Boston: Wright & Potter Printing Company, 1883.

Dewey, George. *Autobiography of George Dewey, Admiral of the Navy.* New York: Charles Scribner's Sons, 1913.

Dolan, Diane, ed. "A Yankee View of the Fall of Wilmington, 1865." *Lower Cape Fear Historical Society Bulletin,* XX (February, 1977).

Edmondston, Catherine Ann Devereux. *Journal of a Secesh Lady: The Diary of Catherine Ann Devereux Edmondston, 1860-1866.* Raleigh, 1979.

Eldredge, Daniel. *The Third New Hampshire and All About It.* Boston: E. B. Stillings & Company, 1893.

Elliott, Charles G. "Kirkland's Brigade, Hoke's Division, 1865-'65." *Southern Historical Society Papers.* 52 vols. Vol 23 (1895).

Evans, Robley D. *A Sailor's Log: Recollections of Forty Years of Naval Life.* New York: D. Appleton and Company, 1901.

Ferguson, James M. *Life Struggles in Rebel Prisons.* Philadelphia: James Ferguson, 1865.

Fisher, Leonard. *The Story of Fort Fisher.* n. p., 1915.

Gaskill, J. W. *Footprints Through Dixie.* Alliance, Ohio: Bradshaw Publishing Company, 1919.

Grant, U. S. *Personal Memoirs of U. S. Grant.* 2 volumes. New York: Charles L. Webster & Company, 1885.

Gregorie, Anne King, ed. "Diary of Captain Joseph Julius Wescoat." *South Carolina Historical Magazine,* LIX (1958).

Hagood, Johnson. *Memoirs of the War of Secession.* Columbia, South Carolina: The State Company, 1910.

Hall, Edward H. "Reminiscences of the War: The Wilmington Expedition." *The United States Service Magazine,* IV (1866).

—. "Reminiscences of the War: The Wilmington Expedition II." *The United States Service Magazine,* V (1866).

Harkness, Edsen J. "The Expeditions Against Fort Fisher and Wilmington." Military Essays and Recollections: Papers Read Before the Commandery of the State of Illinois, Military Order of the Loyal Legion of the United States, II (1894).

Hayes, Philip C. *Journal History of the One Hundred & Third Ohio Volunteer Infantry.* Toledo, Ohio: Commercial Steam Print, 1872.

Hermit. *Recollections in the Army of Virginia and North Carolina: the 203rd Pennsylvania.* Wilkes-Barre, Pennsylvania: Record of the Times, 1865.

History of the First Connecticut Artillery and of the Siege Trains of the Armies Operating Against Richmond 1862-1865. [n.a.] (Hardtford, Connecticut: Case, Lockwood & Brainard Company, 1893).

Hyde, William L. *History of the One Hundred and Twelfth Regiment N. Y. Volunteers.* Fredonia, New York: W. McKinstry & Co., 1866.

Izlar, William V. *A Sketch of the War Record of the Edisto Rifles, 1861-1865.* Columbia, South Carolina: The State Company, 1914.

Jackson, Henry R. and Thomas F. O'Donnell, eds. *Back Home in Oneida: Hermon Clarke and His Letters.* Syracuse, New York: Syracuse University Press, 1965.

Johnson, Robert A. "The Charge at Fort Fisher." *Wake Forest Student*, XLVI, 3 (January, 1929).

Johnson, Robert U. and Clarence C. Buel, eds. *Battles and Leaders of the Civil War.* 4 volumes. New York: The Century Company, 1887.

Jones, John Beauchamp. *A Rebel War Clerk's Diary.* 2 volumes. Philadelphia: J. B. Lippincott & Co., 1866.

Kelley, George H. *Kelley's Wilmington Directory, 1860-61.* Wilmington, North Carolina: George H. Kelley, 1860.

Kellogg, Robert H. *Life and Death in Rebel Prisons.* Hartford, Connecticut: L. Stebbina, 1865.

Ketchum, Edgar. "Personal Reminiscences of the Capture of Fort Fisher and Wilmington, N. C." *The United Service: A Monthly Review of Military and Naval Affairs*, XVI (1896).

Lamb, William. *Colonel Lamb's Story of Fort Fisher.* Carolina Beach, North Carolina: Blockade Runner Museum, 1966.

—. "Defence of Fort Fisher, North Carolina." *Operations on the Atlantic Coast 1861-1865, Virginia 1862, 1864, Vicksburg: Papers of the Military Historical Society of Massachusetts*, IX (1912).

—. "Defense of Fort Fisher." *Battles and Leaders of the Civil War.* 4 vols. New York: The Century Co., 1888.

—. "Defense and Fall of Fort Fisher." *Southern Historical Society Papers,* 52 vols. Vol. 10 (July, 1882).

—. "Fort Fisher: The Battles Fought There in 1864 and '65." *Southern Historical Society Papers,* 52 vols. Vol. 21 (1893).

—. "The Heroine of Confederate Point." *Southern Historical Society Papers*, 52 vols. Vol. 20 (January-December, 1892).

"Letter of Braxton Bragg, January 20, 1865," *Southern Historical Society Papers*, 52 vols. Vol. 10 (1882).

Little, Henry F. W. *The Seventh New Hampshire Volunteers in the War of the Rebellion.* Concord, New Hampshire: Ira C. Evans, 1896.

Lockwood, Henry Clay "A True History of the Army at Fort Fisher." *The United States Service Magazine*, X (November, 1893).

—. "The Capture of Fort Fisher." *Atlantic Monthly Magazine*, XXVII (May and June, 1871)

Longacre, Edward G. "A Union Sergeant in the Fort Fisher Campaign." *American History Illustrated*, XVIII, 5 (September, 1983).

—. *From Antietam to Fort Fisher: The Civil War Letters of Edward K. Wightman, 1862-1865*. Cranbury, New Jersey: Associated University Presses, 1985.

—. "The Task Before Them: Yanks Attack Fort Fisher." *Civil War Times Illustrated*, XXI (February, 1983).

Lossing, Benson J. "The First Attack on Fort Fisher." *Annals of War*. Dayton, Ohio: Morningside House, Inc., 1988.

Maclay, Edgar Stanton. *Reminiscences of the Old Navy*. New York: The Knickerbocker Press, 1898.

Mann, T. H. "A Yankee in Andersonville." *The Century Magazine*, XL (1890).

Martin, Eugene S. *Defense of Fort Anderson*. Wilmington, North Carolina: North Carolina Society of Colonial Dames, 1901.

McEachern, Leora H. and Isabel M. Williams. "The Prevailing Epidemic—1862." *Lower Cape Historical Society Bulletin*, XI (November, 1967).

McMurray, John. *Recollections of a Colored Troop*. Brookville, Pennsylvania: The McMurray Company reprint, 1994.

Merrill, James M., ed. "The Fort Fisher and Wilmington Campaign: Letters From Rear Admiral David D. Porter." *North Carolina Historical Review*, XXXV (October, 1958).

—, and James F. Marshall, eds. "The 16th Kentucky and the End of the Civil War: The Letters of Henry Clay Weaver." *The Filson Club History Quarterly*, 32 (October, 1958).

Moore, Frank. *The Rebellion Record: A Diary of American Events*. New York: D. Van Nostrand, 1868.

Mowris, J. A. *A History of the One Hundred and Seventeenth Regiment N. Y. Volunteers (Fourth Oneida)*. Hartford, Connecticut: Case Lockwood and Company, 1866.

Murray, Paul and Stephen Russell Bartlett, Jr., eds. "The Letters of Stephen Chaulker Bartlett Aboard the U. S. S. 'Lenapee,' January to August, 1865." *North Carolina Historical Review*, XXXIII (January, 1956).

"Navy, The." *Pottsville Miner's Journal*, January 14, 1865.

Nichols, James M. *Perry's Saints or the Fighting Parson's Regiment*. Boston: D. Lothrop and Company, 1886.

Palmer, Abraham J. *The History of the Forty-Eighth Regiment New York State Volunteers in the War for the Union, 1861-1865.* Brooklyn, New York: Veterans Association of the Regiment, 1885.

Parker, James. "The Navy in the Battles and Capture of Fort Fisher." Personal Recollections of the War of the Rebellion: Addresses Delivered Before the Commandery of the State of New York, Military Order of the Loyal Legion of the United States Second Series (1897).

Pearce, Charles E. "The Expeditions Against Fort Fisher." War Papers and Personal Reminiscences, 1861-1865, Read Before the Commandery of the State of Missouri, Military Order of the Loyal Legion of the United States, I (1892).

Personal Reminiscences and Experiences, By Members of the One Hundred and Third Ohio Volunteer Infantry, Campaigning in the Union Army, From 1862 to 1865. [n.a.] Oberlin, Ohio: News Print Co., 1950.

Pinney, Nelson. *History of the 104th Regiment Ohio Volunteer Infantry During the War of Rebellion.* Akron, Ohio: Werner & Lohmann, 1886.

Porter, David D. *Incidents and Anecdotes of the Civil War.* New York: D. Appleton and Company, 1886.

Porter, Horace. *Campaigning With Grant.* New York: The Century Co., 1897.

Price, Isaiah. *History of the Ninety-Seventh Regiment Pennsylvania Volunteer Infantry During the War of the Rebellion, 1861-1865.* Philadelphia, 1875.

—. "The 97th Regiment Penna. Vols. at Fort Fisher." *Philadelphia Weekly Press* (March 10, 1886).

Price, James E. "What a North Carolina Boy Saw of the Civil War." *Under Both Flags: A Panorama of the Great Civil War.* Boston: J. S. Round & Co., 1896.

Redkey, Edwin S., ed. *A Grand Army of Black Men.* Cambridge: Cambridge University Press, 1992.

Rhind, A. C. "The Last of the Fort Fisher Powder-boat." *The United States Service Magazine* (1879).

Rogers, Henry Munroe. *Memories of Ninety Years.* Cambridge, Massachusetts: Houghton Miflin, 1928.

Ross, Fitzgerald. *Cities and Camps of the Confederate States.* Urbana: University of Illinois Press, 1958.

Rowell, Eliphalet. "Six Months in the Military Department of Virginia and North Carolina." War Papers Read Before the Commandery of the State of Maine, Military Order of the Loyal Legion of the United States, II (1902).

Rowland, Kate Mason, ed. "Letters of Major Thomas Rowland, C. S. A." *William and Mary College Quarterly Historical Magazine,* XXVI (April, 1917).

Sands, Benjaimn F. *From Reefer to Rear-Admiral.* New York: Frederick A. Stokes Company, 1899.

Sands, Francis P. B. "A Volunteer's Reminiscences of Life in the North Atlantic Blockading Squadron, 1861-'5." Military Order of the Loyal Legion of the United States War Paper, 20 (1894).

——. "The Last of the Blockade and the Fall of Fort Fisher." Military Order of the Loyal Legion of the United States War Paper, 40 (1902).

Schofield, John M. *Forty-Six Years in the Army*. New York: The Century Company, 1897.

Selfridge, Thomas O., Jr. *Memoirs of Thomas O. Selfrdige, Jr.* New York: Knickerbocker Press, 1924.

——. "The Navy at Fort Fisher." *Battles and Leaders of the Civil War*. 4 vols. New York: The Century Co., 1888.

Sherman, William Tecumseh. *Memoirs of General W. T. Sherman*. 2 volumes. New York: Literary Classics of the United States, 1990.

Sherwood, Issac R. *Memories of the War*. Toledo, Ohio: H. J. Chittendon Co., 1923.

Simmons, Slann L. C., ed. "Diary of Abram W. Clement, 1865." *South Carolina Historical Magazine,* LIX, 2 (April, 1958).

Simon, John Y., ed. *The Papers of Ulysses S. Grant.* Carbondale and Edwardsville: Southern Illinois University Press, 1984.

Simms, Joseph M. "Personal Experiences in the Volunteer Navy During the Civil War." Military Order of the Loyal Legion of the United States, Commandery of the District of Columbia War Paper, 50 (1903).

Smaw, Frank D., Jr. *Wilmington Directory, 1865.* Wilmington, North Carolina: P. Heinsberger, 1865.

——. *Wilmington Directory, 1867.* Wilmington, North Carolina, 1867.

Smith, Gustavus W. *Confederate War Papers.* New York: Atlantic Publishing & Engraving Co., 1884.

Sprunt, James. *Tales of the Cape Fear Blockade.* Raleigh, North Carolina: Capitol Printing Company, 1902.

Still, William N., Jr., ed. "The Yankees Are Landing Below Us: The Journal of Robert Watson, C. S. N." *Civil War Times Illustrated,* XV (April, 1976).

"Story of the Powder-Boat." *Galaxy Magazine,* IX (January, 1870).

Sumner, Merlin E., ed. *The Diary of Cyrus B. Comstock.* Dayton, Ohio: Morningside House, Inc., 1987.

Sutton, Thomas H. "Fort Fisher: A Soldiers Account of the Defense of the Approaches to Wilmington." *Wilmington* (N. C.) *Daily Review* (October, 21, 1884).

Tanner, Zera. "The Capture of Fort Fisher." Military Order of the Loyal Legion of the United States War Paper, 25 (1897).

Taylor, Thomas E. *Running the Blockade: A Personal Narrative of Adventures, Risks, and Escapes During the American Civil War.* London: John Murray, 1896.

Thomas, Leonard R. "The Capture of Fort Fisher." *The National Tribune* (November 6, 1913).

—. *The Story of Fort Fisher, N. C., January 15, 1865.* Ocean City, New Jersey, 1915.

Thompson, B. F. *History of the 112th Regiment of Illinois Volunteer Infantry in the Great War of the Rebellion 1862-1865.* Toulan, Illinois: Stark County News Office, 1885.

Thompson, Brooks and Frank Lawrence Owsley, Jr. "The War Journal of Midshipman Cary." *Civil War History,* Volume Nine, Number Two (June, 1963).

Thompson, Richard Means and Richard Wainwright, eds. *Confidential Correspondence of Gustavus Vasa Fox.* 2 volumes. New York: Naval Historical Society, 1918-1919.

Thurstin, W. S. *History One Hundred and Eleventh Regiment Ohio Volunteer Infantry.* Toledo, Ohio: Vrooman, Anderson & Bateman, 1894.

Towle, George F. "Terry's Fort Fisher Expedition." *Old and New,* Volume XI, No. III (March, 1875).

Tracie, Theodore. *Annals of the Nineteenth Ohio Battery Volunteer Artillery.* Cleveland, Ohio: J. B. Savage, 1878.

Travis, B. F. *The Story of the Twenty-Fifth Michigan.* Kalamazoo, Michigan: Kalamazoo Publishing Company, 1897.

Turner, Henry M. "Rocked in the Cradle of Consternation," *Civil War Times Illustrated,* 31 (October/November, 1980).

United States Sanitary Commission. *Preliminary Report of the Operations of the U. S. Sanitary Commission in North Carolina, March, 1865, and Upon the Physical Condition of Exchanged Prisoners Lately Received at Wilmington, N. C.* Report number 87. New York: Sanford Harroun & Co., 1865.

Waddell, Alfred Moore. *Some Memories of My Life.* Raleigh, North Carolina: Edwards & Broughton Printing Company, 1908.

Walkley, Stephen. *History of the Seventh Connecticut Volunteer Infantry, 1861-1865.* Southington, Connecticut, 1905.

Weiser, George A. *Nine Months In Rebel Prisons.* Philadelphia: John N. Reeve & Co., 1890.

Weld, Francis Minot. *Diaries and Letters of Francis Minot Weld, With a Sketch of His Life.* Boston: Utetson Press, 1925.

Welles, Gideon. *Diary of Gideon Welles.* 3 volumes. Boston and New York: Houghton Mifflin Company, 1911.

Wightman, S. K. "In Search of My Son," *American Heritage Magazine,* Volume XIV, No. 2 (February, 1963).

Wilkinson, John. *The Narrative of a Blockade Runner.* New York: Sheldon & Company, 1877.

Williams, Sidney. *From Spottsylvania to Wilmington, N. C., By Way of Andersonville and Florence*. Providence: Soldiers and Sailors Historical Society of Rhode Island, 1899.

Woodward, C. Vann, ed. *Mary Chestnut's Civil War*. New Haven, Connecticut: Yale Univesity Press, 1981.

Yearns, W. Buck and John G. Barrett, eds. *North Carolina Civil War Documentary*. Chapel Hill: University of North Carolina Press, 1980.

Yopp, William H. "The Surrender of Wilmington to the Yankees, February, 1865." *Wilmington* (N. C.) *Sunday Star* (August 16, 23, 30, September 13, 20, 1936).

PUBLISHED SECONDARY SOURCES

Abbott, John S.C. "Heroic Deeds of Heroic Men: True Chivalry, Benjamin H. Porter. *Harper's New Monthly Magazine*, XXXIV (April, 1867).

Aliyetti, John E. "Gallantry Under Fire." *Civil War Times Illustrated*, XXXV, 5 (October, 1996).

Angley, Wilson. *A History of Fort Johnston on the Lower Cape Fear*. Southport, North Carolina: Southport Historical Society, 1996.

American Annual Cyclopedia and Register of Important Events of the Year 1865. volume 5. New York: D. Appleton & Company, 1866.

Ames, Blanche Ames. *Adelbert Ames*. New York: Argosy-Antiquarian, Ltd., 1964.

Ammen, Daniel. *The Navy in the Civil War: The Atlantic Coast*. New York: Charles Scribner's Sons, 1883.

Anderson, Bern. *By Sea and By River: The Naval History of The Civil War*. New York: Da Capo Press, 1989.

Andrews, J. Cutler. *The North Reports the Civil War*. Pittsburg, Pennsylvania: University of Pittsburg Press, 1955.

Barefoot, Daniel W. *General Robert F. Hoke: Lee's Modest Warrior*. Winston-Salem, North Carolina: John F. Blair, 1996.

Barrett, John G. *The Civil War in North Carolina*. Chapel Hill: University of North Carolina Press, 1963.

Bates, Samuel. *History of Pennsylvania Volunteers 1861-5*. 5 volumes. Harrisburg, Pennsylvania: B. Singerly, 1869-1871.

Beringer, Richard E., Herman Hattaway, Archer Jones, and William N. Still, Jr. *Why the South Lost the Civil War*. Athens: University of Georgia Press, 1986.

Beyer, W. F. and O. F. Keydel. *Deeds of Valor: How America's Heroes Won the Medal of Honor*. 2 volumes. Detroit, Michigan: The Perrien-Keydel Company, 1903.

Blake, W. O. *Pictorial History of the Great Rebellion*. 2 volumes. Columbus, Ohio: Gilmore and Segner, 1866.

Boaz, Thomas. *Guns For Cotton: England Arms the Confederacy.* Shippensburg, Pennsylvania: Burd Street Press, 1996.

Bouton, John Bell. *A Memoir of General Louis Bell, Late Col. of the Fourth N. H. Regiment, Who Fell at Fort Fisher, N. C., January 15, 1865.* New York: Published By Request, 1865.

Bradlee, Francis. *Blockade Running During the Civil War and the Effect of Land and Water Transportation on the Confederacy.* Salem, Massachusetts: The Essex Institute, 1925.

Browning, Robert M., Jr. *From Cape Charles to Cape Fear: The North Atlantic Blockading Squadron During the Civil War.* Tuscaloosa: University of Alabama Press, 1993.

Buttenbach, Walter J. "Coast Defense in the Civil War: Fort Fisher, North Carolina." *Journal of the United States Artillery,* XLII (1914).

Connelly, Thomas Lawrence and Archer Jones. *The Politics of Command.* Baton Rouge: The University of Louisiana Press, 1982.

Conway, Alan. "Welshmen in the Union Army." *Civil War History,* volume 4, number 2 (June, 1958).

Cox, Jacob Dolson. *Campaigns of the Civil War: The March to the Sea, Franklin and Nashville.* New York: Charles Scribner's Sons, 1900.

Current, Richard N., ed. *Encyclopedia of the Confederacy.* 4 volumes. New York: Simon & Schuster, 1993.

Davis, William C. *The Confederate General.* 6 vols. The National Historical Society, 1991.

Denson, Claude B. *An Address Containing a Memoir of the Late Major-General William Henry Chase Whiting.* Raleigh, North Carolina: Edwards & Broughton, 1895.

—. "William Henry Chase Whiting." *Southern Historical Society Papers.* 52 vols. vol. 26 (1898).

DeRosset, William Lord. *Pictorial and Historical New Hanover County and Wilmington, North Carolina 1723-1938.* Wilmington: DeRosset, 1938.

Dillard, Richard. *The Civil War in Chowan County.* n. p., 1916.

Dowd, Clement. *Life of Zebulon B. Vance.* Charlotte, N. C.: Observer Printing & Publishing House, 1897.

Dowdy, Clifford. *Lee.* Boston, 1965.

Dyer, Frederick H. *A Compendium of the War of the Rebellion.* 2 volumes. Dayton, Ohio: Morningside Bookshop (reprint), 1979.

Edwards. E. M. H. *Commander William Barker Cushing of the United States Navy.* New York: F. Tennyson Neely, 1898.

Evans, Clement A. *Confederate Military History Extended Edition.* Wilmington, North Carolina: Broadfoot Publishing Company, 1987.

Evans, W. McKee. *Ballots and Fence Rails: Reconstruction on the Lower Cape Fear.* New York: W. W. Norton & Company, 1974.

Faust, Patricia L. *Historical Times Illustrated Encyclopedia of the Civil War.* New York: Harper & Row, 1986.

Finan, William J. *Major General Alfred Howe Terry (1827-1890) Hero of Fort Fisher.* Connecticut Civil War Centennial Commission, 1965.

Foard, John H. "The Blockade and the Runners." *Wilmington: Magazine of the Cape Fear* (August, 1975).

Fonvielle, Chris E., Jr., "The Last Rays of Departing Hope: Campaign for Wilmington and Fort Fisher." *Blue & Gray Magazine,* XII (December, 1994).

—. "February, 1865: The Fall of Wilmington." *Cape Fear Tidewater,* II (February, 1985).

Freeman, Douglas Southall. *R. E. Lee.* 4 vols. New York: Charles Scribner's Sons, 1949.

Galusha Pennypacker: America's Youngest General. Philadelphia: Christopher Sower Company, 1917.

Glatthaar, Joseph T. *Partners in Command: The Relationship Between Leaders in the Civil War.* New York: The Free Press, 1994.

Gragg, Rod. *Confederate Goliath: The Battle for Fort Fisher.* New York: Harper-Collins Publishers, 1991.

Hamersly, Lewis R., "A True History of the Army at Fort Fisher." *The United States Service Magazine,* X (1893).

—. *The Records of Living Officers of the U. S. Navy and Marine Corps; With a History of Naval Operations During the Rebellion of 1861-5, and a List of the Ships and Officers Participating in the Great Battles.* Philadelphia: J. B. Lippincott & Co., 1870.

Hattaway, Herman and Archer Jones. *How the North Won: A Military History of the Civil War.* Chicago: University of Chicago Press, 1983.

Hearn, Chester G. *Admiral David Dixon Porter: The Civil War Years.* Annapolis, Maryland: Naval Institute Press, 1996.

Henderson, Edward Prioleau. *Autobiography of Arab.* Columbia, South Carolina: R. L. Bryan Co., 1901.

Herring, Ethel and Carolee Williams. *Fort Caswell in War and Peace.* Wendell, North Carolina: Broadfoot's Bookmark, 1983.

Hill, Daniel Harvey, Jr. *Bethel to Sharpsburg: A History of North Carolina in the War Between the States.* 2 volumes. Wilmington, North Carolina: Broadfoot Publishing Company reprint, 1992.

Hoole, Wm. Stanley. *Lawley Covers the Confederacy.* Tuscaloosa, Alabama: Confederate Publishing Company, Inc., 1964.

Howell, Andrew J. *The Book of Wilmington*. Wilmington, North Carolina: Wilmington Printing Company, 1930.

Kelvin, Kit. "The Naval Battles of Fort Fisher." *N. Y. Evangelist Historical Magazine* (December, 1873).

Lee, Lawrence. *New Hanover County: A Brief History*. Raleigh, North Carolina: State Department of Archives and History, 1971.

—. *The History of Brunswick County, North Carolina*. Charlotte, North Carolina: Heritage Press, 1980.

Long, E. B. *The Civil War Day By Day: An Almanac 1861-1865*. Garden City, New York: Doubleday & Company, Inc., 1971.

Lossing, Benjamin J. *Pictorial History of the Civil War in the United States of America*. Hartford, Connecticut: T. Belknap, 1868.

Luvaas, Jay. "The Fall of Fort Fisher." *Civil War Times Illustrated*, III (August, 1964).

Manarin, Louis H. *A Guide to Military Organizations and Installations, North Carolina 1861-1865*. Raleigh, North Carolina, 1961.

Manarin, Louis H. and Weymouth T. Jordan, eds. *North Carolina Troops 1861-1865: A Roster*. 13 volumes. Raleigh, North Carolina: Division of Archives and History, 1966-1993.

McDonough, James L. *Schofield: Union General in the Civil War and Reconstruction*. Tallahassee: Florida State University Press, 1972.

McEachern, Leora Hiatt and Bill Reaves. *History of St. James Parish, 1729-1979*. Wilmington, North Carolina: n. p., 1985.

McEachern, Leora H. and Isabel M. Williams, "The Prevailing Epidemic—1862." *Lower Cape Fear Historical Society Bulletin* (November, 1964).

McPherson, James M. *Battle Cry of Freedom: The Civil War Era*. New York: Oxford University Press, 1988.

Mitchell, Joseph B. *The Badge of Gallantry: Recollections of Civil War Congressional Medal of Honor Winners*. New York: The Macmillan Company, 1968.

Moore, Louis T. *Stories Old and New of the Cape Fear Region*. Wilmington, North Carolina: Wilmington Printing Company, 1956.

National Cyclopedia of American Biography, The. New York: James T. White & Company, 1893.

Naval History Division, Navy Department. *Civil War Naval Chronology 1861-1865*. Washington, D. C.: Government Printing Office, 1971.

Nichols, James L. *Confederate Engineers*. Tuscaloosa, Alabama: Confederate Publishing Company, Inc, 1957.

Osborne, Arthur D. *The Capture of Fort Fisher By Major General Alfred H. Terry and What It Accomplished*. New Haven, Connecticut: Tuttle, Morehouse & Taylor Press, 1911.

Owsley, Frank. *King Cotton Diplomacy: Foreign Relations of the Confederate States of America*. Chicago: University of Chicago Press, 1935.

Parker, John C. "Admiral David D. Porter." War Papers and Personal Reminiscences 1861-1865, Read Before the Commandery of the State of Missouri, I (1892).

Platt, Rev. Charles H. *Lieut. Benj. H. Porter, Sketch of His Life and Fall at Fort Fisher in 1865*. Lockport, New York: Daily Union Job Print, 1878.

Porter, David D. *The Naval History of the Civil War*. New York: The Sherman Publishing Company, 1886.

Price, Charles L. "North Carolina Railroads During the Civil War." *Civil War History,* 7 (September, 1961).

Price, Marcus. "Ships That Tested the Blockade of the Carolina Ports, 1861-1865." *American Neptune*, 8 (July, 1948).

Randall, James R. "General W. H. C. Whiting: A Chevalier of the Lost Cause." *Southern Historical Society Papers*, 52 vols. Vol. 24 (1896).

Reaves, William M. *Southport (Smithville): A Chronology (1520-1887)*. Southport, North Carolina: Southport Historical Society, 1985.

Reed, Rowena. *Combined Operations in the Civil War*. Annapolis, Maryland: Naval Institute Press, 1978.

Reilly, J. S. *Wilmington Past, Present, & Future Embracing Historical Sketches of Its Growth and Progress From Its Establishment to the Present Time Together With Outlines of North Carolina History.* Wilmington, North Carolina: n. p., 1884.

Ripley, Warren. *Artillery and Ammunition of the Civil War*. New York: Van Nostrand Reinhold Company, 1970.

Scharf, J. Thomas. *History of the Confederate States Navy From Its Organization to the Surrender of Its Last Vessel*. New York: Rogers and Sherwood, 1887.

Scheliha, Von. *A Treatise on Coast-Defence*. Westport, Connecticut: Greenwood Press, 1971.

Scott, Colonel H. L. *Military Dictionary: Comprising Technical Definitions: Information on Raising and Keeping Troops, Actual Service, Including Makeshifts and Improved Materiel; and Law, Government, Regulation, and Administration Relating to Land Forces*. New York: Greenwood Press, 1968.

Seitz, Don C. *Braxton Bragg: General of the Confederacy*. Columbia, South Carolina: The State Company, 1924.

Semmes, Raphael. *Memoirs of Service Afloat During the War Between the States*. Baltimore, Maryland: Baltimore Publishing Company, 1887.

Shomette, Donald G. *Shipwrecks of the Civil War: The Encyclopedia of Union and Confederate Naval Losses.* Washington, D. C.: Donic Ltd, 1973.

Sifakis, Stewart. *The Compendium of The Confederate Armies: North Carolina*. New York: Facts On File, 1992.

Silverstone, Paul H. *Warships of the Civil War Navies*. Annapolis, Maryland: Naval Institute Press, 1989.

Sloan, John. *North Carolina in the War Between the States*. Washington: Rufus H. Darby, Publishers, 1893.

Soley, James R. *Admiral Porter*. New York: D. Appleton and Company, 1903.

—. *The Navy in the Civil War: The Blockade and the Cruisers*. New York: Charles Scribner's Sons, 1883.

Sprunt, James. *Chronicles of the Cape Fear River 1660-1916*. Raleigh, North Carolina: Edwards & Broughton Printing Co., 1916.

—. *Derelicts*. Baltimore, Maryland: The Lord Baltimore Press, 1920.

—. *Tales and Traditions of the Lower Cape Fear, 1661-1896*. Wilmington, North Carolina: LeGwin Brothers, 1896.

—. *Tales of the Cape Fear Blockade*. Raleigh, North Carolina: Capital Printing Company, 1902.

Stick, David. *Bald Head: A History of Smith Island and Cape Fear*. Wendell, North Carolina: Broadfoot's Bookmark, 1985.

Still, William N., Jr., "Porter. . .Is the Best Man." *Civil War Times Illustrated*, XVI (May, 1977).

Thomas, Howard. *Boys in Blue From the Adirondack Foothills*. Prospect, New York: Prospect Books, 1960.

Trotter, William R. *Ironclads and Columbiads, The Civil War in North Carolina Volume III: The Coast*. Greensboro, North Carolina: Signal Research, Inc., 1989.

Waite, Otis F. R. *New Hampshire in the Great Rebellion*. Claremont, New Hampshire: Tracy, Chase & Company, 1870.

Wakelyn, Jon L. *Biographical Dictionary of the Confederacy*. Westport, Connecticut: Greenwood Press, 1977.

Warner, Ezra J. *Generals in Blue*. Baton Rouge: Louisiana State University Press, 1964.

—. *Generals in Gray*. Baton Rouge: Louisiana State University Press, 1959.

Watson, Alan D. *Wilmington: Port of North Carolina*. Columbia: University of South Carolina Press, 1992.

Welch, Jack D. *Medical Histories of Confederate Generals*. Kent, Ohio: Kent State University Press, 1995.

Welcher, Frank J., *The Union Army, 1861-1865 Organization and Operations, Volume 1, The Eastern Theater*. Bloomington and Indianapolis: Indiana University Press, 1989.

Willcox, George W. and Bruce Barclay Cameron. *The Camerons of Wilmington*. Chapel Hill, North Carolina: Professional Press, 1994.

Williams, Isabel M. and Leora H. McEachern. *Salt—That Necessary Article*. Wilmington, North Carolina: Lower Cape Fear Historical Society, 1973.

Wise, Stepehn R. *Lifeline of the Confederacy: Blockade Running During the Civil War*. Columbia: University of South Carolina Press, 1988.

Woodworth, Steven E., ed. *Leadership and Command in the American Civil War.* Campbell, California: Savas Woodbury Publishers, 1995.

Wyatt, Lillian Reeves. *The Reeves, Mercer, Newkirk Families*. Jacksonville, Florida: The Cooper Press, 1956.

THESES AND DISSERTATIONS

Edwin L. Combs, III. "On Duty at Wilmington: The Confederate Navy on the Cape Fear River." Master's thesis, East Carolina University, Greenville, North Carolina, 1996.

Guinn, Gilbert Sumter. "Coastal Defense of the Confederate Atlantic Seaboard States, 1861-1862: A Study in Political and Military Mobilization." Ph.D. dissertation, University of South Carolina, 1973.

Joyner, Clinton, Jr. "Major General Robert Frederick Hoke and the Civil War in North Carolina." Master's thesis, East Carolina University, Greenville, North Carolina, 1974.

McLean, Alexander Torrey, III. "The Fort Fisher and Wilmington Campaign: 1864-1865." Master's thesis, University of North Carolina, Chapel Hill, 1969.

Peebles, Martin D. "CSS Raleigh: The History and Archaeology of a Civil War Ironclad in the Cape Fear River." Master's thesis, East Carolina University, Greenville, North Carolina, 1996.

Wood, Richard Everett. "Port Town at War: Wilmington, North Carolina 1860-1865." Ph.D. dissertation, Florida State University, Tallahassee, 1976.

UNPUBLISHED SPECIAL STUDIES

Cashman, Diane Cobb. "History of the Bellamy Mansion." Research Report, Bellamy Mansion, Inc., 1990.

INDEX

An Interview with Chris E. Fonvielle, Jr.

SPC: Wilmington is not a household word in the Civil War community. Why does the Wilmington Campaign deserve a full-length study?

CEF: Actually, the name "Wilmington" was heard with considerable regularity in most American households in 1865. The city's capture made front page headlines in all of the national newspapers in the war's last winter. The U.S. Navy Department in particular considered it one of the greatest victories of the war. Not only was Wilmington the Confederacy's most important blockade running seaport, but the Union combined operations (army-navy) against Fort Fisher, Wilmington's main protectorate and the South's largest coastal fortification, were the largest of the Civil War.

SPC: Then how did the history of such an important campaign fall away into obscurity?

CEF: Three things, and all occurred in less than sixty days after Wilmington's capture: William T. Sherman's successful and highly publicized march through the Carolinas; Robert E. Lee's surrender at Appomattox, and President Abraham Lincoln's assassination. Those watershed events supplanted the Wilmington story. . .

SPC: . . .and probably upset its participants?

CEF: Absolutely. Admiral David D. Porter, who commanded the U.S. Navy task force that captured Fort Fisher and Wilmington, really resented how quickly the campaign's glow faded from public view.

SPC: Rod Gragg's book, Confederate Goliath: The Battles for Fort Fisher, *told the story of Fisher's struggles very well. Does your study essentially duplicate Gragg's work?*

CEF: Rod's book—Rod and I have been friends for years, by the way—was well researched and exceptionally well written. It's one of my favorite Civil War books. But *Confederate Goliath* deals solely with Fort Fisher. By Rod's own admission he was interested only in what happened on those sand hills along the ocean. And indeed, the battles for Fort Fisher were critically important to Wilmington's ultimate survival—in many ways the crux of the campaign. But they were also only part of a much larger story, one with just as much drama, suspense and as many fascinating characters as the Fort Fisher episodes.

SPC: Is your treatment of the Fort Fisher battles different than Gragg's?

CEF: Actually, yes. I recently discovered a wealth of previously unused manuscript material that dramatically increased my knowledge and understanding of the battles for Fisher. And I have been studying this campaign for as long as I can remember.

SPC: Ok, we are getting ahead of ourselves. If someone asked you to tell them what your book is about, how would you answer them?

CEF: *Last Rays* is the story of Union operations to capture, and Confederate attempts to defend, the South's most important seaport during the last year of the war. The South was largely dependent upon imports from Europe for weapons and supplies to maintain its war effort. In fact, by 1864, Wilmington was the mouth of the Confederacy, and Robert E. Lee's principal supply route. My book chronicles the entire campaign, from the view of both the commanders and the men in the ranks, from both a strategic and tactical point of view. I guess that, in a nutshell, would be how I would answer that question!

SPC: If Wilmington was so important, why didn't the Federal government go after it earlier in the war?

CEF: In retrospect, the government realized its mistake in not doing so. Wilmington might have fallen more easily had Burnside's expedition marched southward after capturing New Bern, North Carolina in 1862, or had the Federal navy devoted its resources in 1863 against Wilmington instead of Charleston. You must keep in mind, however, with limited resources at its disposal, and with little support from the U.S. War Department, the navy had to carefully pick and choose its targets.

SPC: And Charleston was symbolic with Secession...

CEF: Exactly. The city was a favorite target, militarily, politically and publicly, because that is where the war began. In contrast, Wilmington was a comparatively unknown entity to the authorities in Washington, was virtually impossible to blockade, and was not as well known (among Northerners) as other Southern cities. By the time the Lincoln administration gave its blessing to the Navy Department for an attack on Wilmington, vast amounts of important supplies destined for Confederate forces had entered through the Carolina port. And the delay had allowed the defenders to construct a formidable chain of fortifications to protect the city.

SPC: Had it chosen to do so, could the U.S. Navy have taken Wilmington by itself?

CEF: Let me put it this way. Not one major Southern seaport fell to naval efforts alone. At the Cape Fear, which is the southeastern North Carolina region in which Wilmington is located, shoal waters and strong Confederate defenses prevented warships from getting close enough to shore to perform the task alone. So the answer is no, it could not have been done with naval power alone, and the U.S. Navy Department realized this. A powerful land contingent was also needed to conquer Wilmington.

SPC: Eventually the navy received the troops it required to launch the operation?

CEF: Yes, but with no little reluctance from U.S. Grant, the Federal commanding general. He was not at all, at least initially, interested in Wilmington. Like a vicious bulldog, he wanted the teeth of his army to remain chomped onto the Army of Northern Virginia, dug in around Richmond and Petersburg. The pressure was for troops from Virginia—Grant's front—to join the expedition.

SPC: So what changed his mind?

CEF: Two things. First, Grant recognized the political advantage his support of such a mission might offer President Lincoln in the election year of 1864. The appointment of his old friend David D. Porter to command the naval task force also made him more comfortable with the whole idea. After all, Porter had played an instrumental role in Grant's 1863 victory at Vicksburg, and thus was also partially responsible for Grant's rapid rise in the army hierarchy.

SPC: Grant knew what he was getting in Porter. . .

CEF: Yes. But his heart was still not set on Wilmington in the autumn of 1864. He considered the seaport in the backwater of the Confederacy.

SPC: Didn't he grasp the logistical advantage the capture of Wilmington would give the Union?

CEF: It seems surprising, but no he didn't—at least not at first. I don't think he realized how dependent Lee's army was on Wilmington, though Lee himself had sent word to the city's military authorities that the port must be held or else he could not maintain his army and would have to evacuate Richmond. The supposition in the Confederate capital was that if Wilmington fell, Richmond would also fall. Grant's friend, William T. Sherman, was the one who eased Grant's mind about going after Wilmington.

SPC: You make it sound as if the fall of Wilmington was the Confederacy's last gasp.

CEF: Well, you can make a good argument for it. I agree with historian Richard McMurry, who states so eloquently that there were no turning points in the war. It was a continuum, with nails slowly but deliberately being driven in the Confederacy's coffin. In retrospect, historians recognize that the war's outcome had been decided before the Wilmington Campaign, perhaps by the summer of 1864 when Atlanta fell. Perhaps earlier than that. We Southerners take great pride in being the last ones to know when we're licked! [laughter]

SPC: So Wilmington's capture didn't decide the outcome, but it did hasten the Confederacy's downfall?

CEF: Exactly. As Lee had predicted, the loss of Wilmington precipitated his evacuation of Richmond.

SPC: Certainly, though, the strategic ramifications of Sherman's Carolinas Campaign, which are well documented in Mark Bradley's Last Stand in the Carolinas: The Battle of Bentonville *(Savas Publishing, 1996), had something to do with Lee's flight from Richmond's defenses? After all, once Sherman captured Goldsboro, North Carolina, he was poised to strike Lee's rear in Virginia.*

CEF: That's true. And the fall of Wilmington helped make that happen. I argue in *Last Rays* that the Wilmington Campaign helped guarantee the success of Sherman's march through the Carolinas. A Federally-controlled Wilmington was Sherman's insurance policy. After the ill-fated First Battle of Fort Fisher, Grant wholeheartedly supported a renewal of the attack on the "city by the sea." This time, however, he wanted the *city* to be the primary target. The first expedition's design was to capture Fort Fisher and close the Cape Fear River to blockade runners. Any movement against the city would have been considered incidental to that end.

SPC: So Grant realized that seizing Wilmington would benefit Sherman?

CEF: Grant wanted Sherman to have a safe haven on the seacoast between Savannah and Richmond, and a place where reinforcements and supplies could be funneled to his army. That was Wilmington, with its three railroads and a river navigable 100 miles into the state. If Wilmington could serve as a pipeline of supplies for Southern armies, why couldn't the Federals use it for the same thing for their armies? And so the city became the primary objective in the Second Fort Fisher Expedition.

SPC: Ok, I understand that. But then why did the Federals, having failed to capture Fort Fisher late in 1864, lavish so much attention on the fort during the second expedition?

CEF: They considered other alternatives. A move was pondered through Old Inlet, the Cape Fear River's southernmost inlet, as well as an overland attack across Masonboro or Wrightsville east of Wilmington. These plans were eventually scrapped for a variety of reasons, primarily because the navy was so intent on capturing Fort Fisher. What better way for the Navy Department to gain the credit it had been denied in most of the war's combined operations, so argued Secretary Welles and Admiral Porter, than by capturing the Confederacy's most powerful seacoast fortification guarding the South's most important seaport?

SPC: Politics! It has all the makings of an epic!

CEF: Politics played a significant role. And when you consider the number of ships that took part, the incredibly diverse personalities on both sides, the stakes involved, and the way the campaign unfolded, this whole story is indeed an epic that has needed telling for a long while.

SPC: So Fort Fisher was a stepping stone to capturing Wilmington?

CEF: Precisely. Fort Fisher was the biggest stepping stone in the path, but there were other important actions and engagements after the fall of the fort, all of which are documented in detail in *Last Rays*.

SPC: Which is another way your book differs from Gragg's Confederate Goliath?

CEF: Yes. Rod ended his book with the fort's fall. The second half of my book details the second half of the campaign, which few Civil War students know much about.

SPC: What were some of the events after Fort Fisher?

CEF: There is the entire chess match east of the river along the Sugar Loaf Line, where Robert F. Hoke and his veteran division from Lee's Virginia army were dug in. On the west side of the Cape Fear was Fort Anderson, the Confederate's largest interior defensive work protecting the western land approaches to the city. The fight at Anderson pitted Confederate Johnson Hagood against Federal Jacob Cox, a mismatch if there ever was one! It may also have been the only battle of the war in which the U.S. army surrendered to the U.S. Navy! There was also the Battle of Town Creek, a fascinating engagement seven miles below Wilmington. This battle has everything—incredible bravery against hopeless odds, a bayonet charge, hand-to-hand fighting, command mistakes. Town Creek was not Johnson Hagood's finest hour. Neither was Fort Anderson.

SPC: Patrick Brennan, in his recent book Secessionville: Assault on Charleston *(Savas Publishing, 1996), sings Hagood's praises for his handling of troops on James Island. . .*

CEF: Well, that was early in the war, and Hagood may have demonstrated some tactical ability in his home state. But his performance during the Wilmington Campaign was abysmal. There is a reason that man remained a brigadier general for most of the war.

SPC: Who else plays a prominent role in Last Rays?

CEF: On the Southern side, there was the brilliant but broody William Henry Chase Whiting, perhaps the Confederacy's best engineer and the commander of the Cape Fear district. Then there is William Lamb, one of my personal favorites. Lamb was a gifted amateur military engineer and the commander of Fort Fisher. He really rose to the occasion in his role as Fisher's defender. There is also the ubiquitous Braxton Bragg. Controversial and incompetent are the two other adjectives that best describe Bragg.

SPC: He does not come off particularly well in your study!

CEF: There is a reason Bragg was perhaps the most hated man in the Confederacy. His own biographer, Grady McWhiney, grew so sick of him he could not finish the second volume of his study! When he was appointed to command at the Cape Fear, a Richmond newspaper editor wrote: "Bragg has been sent to Wilmington. Goodbye Wilmington." I think I was evenhanded in my treatment of everyone—at least I really tried hard to be objective and let the facts speak for themselves. Bragg's performance at Wilmington, though, ranks pretty low.

SPC: And on the Union side?

CEF: We discussed Porter, who was both very talented and feisty. Benjamin Butler, a rather pompous buffoon, plays a large role in the early chapters of the book.

SPC: You had nice things to say about both Alfred Terry and N. Martin Curtis. . .

CEF: Both of whom did really well in the campaign. Terry led the army forces in the second expedition against Fort Fisher. The unsung Federal hero, though, is Curtis. His writings really changed my thinking about what happened at Fort Fisher.

SPC: Is this the manuscript material you alluded to earlier?

CEF: Yes. A number of people in upstate New York, especially in the Ogdensburg are, where Curtis lived for many years, helped me immensely. Persis Boyesen turned me onto a treasure trove of letters and documents about the battles for Fisher written by or to Curtis after the war. Bruce Allardice, who wrote *More Generals in Gray*, uncovered additional material for me. All of this was indispensable to understanding Fort Fisher—First Fort Fisher in particular, of which there is less written.

SPC: Why is that?

CEF: Because the Federals lost. Chroniclers are usually less inclined to write about a defeat.

SPC: What about Confederate source material?

CEF: There is a lot less of it than there is Union material. That was my greatest source of frustration in researching the book. I was concerned that the study had what I would describe as a "blue lean" to it, but it was perhaps unavoidable. Union soldiers wrote quite a bit about the campaign, especially Second Fort Fisher and the subsequent engagements.

SPC: And the Confederates lost and the war ended, so they left very few accounts.

CEF: With the exception of First Fort Fisher, none of the principal Confederates even wrote an official report of the campaign. Not Bragg, Whiting, Lamb or Robert F. Hoke. . .none of them! As for Lamb and Whiting—and their subordinates—that's understandable. After all, they were all killed, wounded or captured. Most of those who made it out of Fort Fisher alive spent their final days in Northern prisons or hospitals. By the time they were released the war was over and there was no reason to write reports.

SPC: Actually, I was surprised at how much Confederate manuscript material you managed to locate. . .

CEF: I was fortunate in finding a significant amount of primary accounts—letters, diaries, that sort of thing. I am hopeful that more accounts will come to light as more people read this book. In fact, I encourage readers who have material to contact me. The project is now in print, but the research, at least for me, never ends. Maybe in a couple years you would be interested in publishing *Last Rays, Part II, The Saga Continues*? [laughter]